HOLLYWOOD'S AMERICA
United States History
Through Its Films

I Am a Fugitive From a Chain Gang

HOLLYWOOD'S AMERICA

United States History
Through Its Films

THIRD EDITION

Edited with an Introduction by

STEVEN MINTZ
University of Houston

and

RANDY ROBERTS
Purdue University

BRANDYWINE PRESS • St. James, New York

Front Cover: *Casablanca* (1942)
Back Cover: *Dr. Strangelove* (1964)

ISBN: 1-881089-68-1

Copyright © 2001 by Brandywine Press

THIRD EDITION

Telephone Orders: 1-800-345-1776

Printed in the United States of America

TABLE OF CONTENTS

PREFACE

If you want to know about the United States in the twentieth century, go to the movies. Films represent much more than mass entertainment. Movies—even bad ones—are important sociological and cultural documents. Like any other popular commercial art form, movies both reflect and influence public attitudes. From the beginning of this century, films have recorded and even shaped American values, beliefs, and behavior.

The introduction to this book traces the history of American film against a backdrop of broader changes in late nineteenth and twentieth-century popular culture. A series of interpretive essays then examines how classic films treated American political, economic, and social life; primary sources that illuminate film history are also included as is an extensive bibliographic guide to the literature on American movies.

The history of the movies is caught up with broader themes and issues in American cultural history, such as the transition from a Victorian culture, with its emphasis on refinement, self-control, and moralism, to modern mass culture. Popular films offer a valuable way of examining public responses to the social disorder and dislocations of the Great Depression; the fears of domestic subversion of the late 1940s and early 1950s; the cultural and moral upheavals of the 1960s; and the meaning and significance of the Vietnam War.

The anthology will also help students develop the tools to read and interpret visual texts. In a society where visual images have become a dominant mode of entertainment and persuasion—used to promote presidential candidates as well as sell toothpaste and deodorant—visual literacy is an important craft of survival and intellectual growth. Film is a form of communication with its own rules and grammar that demands the same skills of critical thinking and analysis necessary for reading written texts. Analyzing a poem requires understanding patterns of rhyme and rhythm, sound and imagery. Interpreting a film involves a knowledge of the techniques that filmmakers use to construct their texts: camera work, editing devices, lighting, set design, narrative, and so on.

The films examined in this book are feature films—not documentaries or avant-garde or underground films. These are the classic films that engaged the emotions of their American viewers, and made them laugh, weep, cringe with terror, and tremble with excitement. They offered wit, suspense, romance, thrills, highlife and lowlife. Highbrow critics might dismiss most Hollywood films as schlock—but these films gave audiences more pleasure than any other art form and taught fundamental lessons in intimacy, tenderness, initiation, lust, conflict, guilt, and loyalty. As the nation's dream factory manufacturing fantasies and cultural myths, Hollywood has given Americans their most intensive—if highly distorted—picture of their country's past, from the styles of the rich and famous to the underside of American life. It has been instrumental in shaping our deepest presuppositions about race, ethnicity, class, gender, and sexual conduct. Movies have helped form the country's self-image and have provided unifying symbols in a society fragmented along lines of race, class, ethnicity, region, and gender. In certain respects subversive of traditional cultural values, movie culture has helped Americans adapt to an ever-changing society.

The Wizard of Oz

INTRODUCTION

One night a year the country shuts down. All across the United States tens of millions of people press the buttons on their remote controls, sit back in their easy chairs or recline on their couches, and become the world's largest congregation, watching a major event in the country's civic religion—the Oscars. Even though movie attendance has fallen steeply—to just one-fifth of what it was at the time of the first Academy Awards ceremony in 1927—Americans still gawk at the limousines as they pull up to the Dorothy Chandler Pavilion in Los Angeles, gaze at the stars' tuxedoes and gowns, and wait impatiently for a memorable moment—a streaker racing across the stage or perhaps Jack Palance performing one-handed push-ups.

Americans watch the Academy Awards presentations for many reasons: To see briefly a more human side of their favorite movie stars; to pit their judgment against that of the five thousand members of the Academy of Motion Picture Arts and Sciences; to partake in the trashy pleasure of watching the glitziest extravaganza that Hollywood is capable of producing. But the Academy Awards ceremony also gives Americans a chance to recognize the movies that entertained them, engaged their emotions, expressed their deepest hopes and responded to their anxieties and fears. From *All Quiet on the Western Front,* a graphic portrait of the horrors and futility of war that came to embody the pacifism of the late 1920s and early 1930s, to the bleak revisionist western *Unforgiven* that deglamorizes the mythic western frontier and its violent traditions, Oscar winners and nominees have offered a vivid record of shifting American values.

Of all the products of popular culture, none is more sharply etched in our collective imagination than the movies. Many Americans instantly recognize images produced by the movies: Charlie Chaplin, the starving prospector in *The Gold Rush,* eating his shoe, treating the laces like spaghetti; James Cagney, the gun-toting gangster in *Public Enemy,* shoving a grapefruit into Mae Clarke's face; Paul Muni, the jobless World War I veteran in *I Am a Fugitive From a Chain Gang,* who, asked at the end of the bleak, determinist film how he lives, replies, "I steal"; Gloria Swanson, the fading movie goddess in *Sunset Boulevard,* belittling suggestions that she is no longer a big star: "It's the pictures that got small." Even those who have never seen *Citizen Kane* or *Casablanca* or the *Treasure of Sierra Madre* respond to advertisements, parodies, and TV skits that use these films' dialogue, images, and characters.

As cultural artifacts, movies open windows into American cultural and social history. A mixture of art, business, and popular entertainment, they provide a host of insights into Americans' shifting ideals, fantasies, and preoccupations. Like any

1

cultural artifact, the movies can be approached in a variety of ways. Cultural historians have treated movies as sociological documents that record the look and mood of particular historical settings; as ideological constructs that advance particular political or moral values or myths; as psychological texts that speak to individual and social anxieties and tensions; as cultural documents that present particular images of gender, ethnicity, class, romance, and violence; and as visual texts that offer complex levels of meaning and seeing.

This book offers examples of how to interpret classic American films as artifacts of a shifting American culture. Film history is at its clearest against a broader backdrop of American cultural and social history.

THE BIRTH OF MODERN CULTURE

Toward the end of the nineteenth century, a New York neurologist named George M. Beard coined the term "neurasthenia" to describe a psychological ailment that afflicted a growing number of Americans. Neurasthenia's symptoms included "nervous dyspepsia, insomnia, hysteria, hypochondria, asthma, sick-headache, skin rashes, hayfever, premature baldness, inebrity, hot and cold flashes, nervous exhaustion, brain-collapse, or forms of 'elementary insanity.'" Among those who suffered from neurasthenia-like ailments at some point in their lives were Theodore Roosevelt, settlement house founder Jane Addams, psychologist William James, painter Frederic Remington, and novelists Owen Wister and Theodore Dreiser.

According to expert medical opinion, neurasthenia's underlying cause was "over-civilization." The frantic pace of modern life, nervous overstimulation, stress, and emotional repression produced debilitating bouts of depression or attacks of anxiety and nervous prostration. Fears of "over-civilization" pervaded late nineteenth-century American culture. Social critics worried that urban life was producing a generation of pathetic, pampered, physically and morally enfeebled ninety-seven-pound weaklings—a poor successor to the stalwart Americans who had fought the Civil War, battled Indians, and tamed a continent. A sharply falling birth rate sparked fears that the native-born middle class was committing "race suicide." A host of therapies promised to relieve the symptoms of neurasthenia, including such precursors of modern tranquilizers as Dr. Hammond's Nerve and Brain Pills. Sears even sold an electrical contraption called the Heidelberg Electric Belt, designed to reduce anxiety by sending electric shocks to the genitals. Many physicians prescribed physical exercise for men and rest cures for women. But the main forms of release for late nineteenth-century Americans from the pressures, stresses, and restrictions of modern life was by turning to sports, outdoor activities, and popular culture.

Few Americans are unfamiliar with the wrenching economic transformations of the late nineteenth century, the consolidation of industry, the integration of the national economy, and the rise of the corporation. But few Americans realize that this period also brought the birth of our modern culture.

In the last years of the nineteenth century an ethos of self-fulfillment, leisure, and sensual satisfaction began to replace the Victorian spirit of self-denial, self-restraint, and domesticity. Visual images took their place beside words and reading, which had been the essence of Victorian high learning. A new respect for energy, strength, and virility overtook a genteel endorsement of eternal truths and high moral ideals. Above all, a varied culture deeply divided by class, gender, religion, ethnicity, and locality gave way to a vibrant, commercialized mass culture that provided all Americans with standardized entertainment and information.

The Revolt Against Victorianism

The new mood could be seen in a rage for competitive athletics and team sports. It was in the 1890s that boxing began to rival baseball as the nation's most popular sport, basketball was invented, football swept the nation's college campuses, and golf, track, and wrestling became popular pastimes. The celebration of vigor could also be seen in a new enthusiasm for such outdoor activities as hiking, hunting, fishing, mountain climbing, camping, and bicycling.

A new bold, energetic spirit was also apparent in popular music, in a craze for ragtime, jazz, and patriotic military marches. The cult of toughness and virility appeared in the growth of aggressive nationalism (culminating in 1898 in America's "Splendid Little War" against Spain), the condemnation of sissies and stuffed shirts, and the growing popularity of such aggressively masculine western novels as Owen Wister's *The Virginian*. Toward the end of the century, the New Woman—personified by the tall, athletic Gibson Girl—supplanted the frail, submissive Victorian woman as a cultural ideal. The new woman began to work outside the home in rapidly increasing numbers, to attend high schools and college, and increasingly to press for the vote. During the '90s American popular culture was in full-scale revolt against the stifling Victorian code of propriety.

During the mid-nineteenth century, urban reformers responded to the rapid growth of cities by advocating the construction of parks to serve as rural retreats in the midst of urban jungles. Frederick Law Olmsted, the designer of New York City's Central Park, believed that the park's bucolic calm would instill the values of sobriety and self-control in the urban masses. But by the end of the century, it was clear that those masses had grown tired of sobriety and self-control. They craved excitement and self-expression. This was clearly seen at the World's Columbian Exposition of 1893 in Chicago, where the most popular area was the boisterous, rowdy Midway. Here, visitors rode the Ferris Wheel and watched "Little Egypt" perform exotic dances. Entrepreneurs were quick to satisfy the public's desire for fast-paced entertainment. During the 1890s, a series of popular amusement parks opened in Coney Island. Unlike Central Park, Coney Island glorified adventure. It offered exotic, dreamland landscapes and a free, loose social environment. At Coney Island men could remove their coats and ties, and both sexes could enjoy rare personal freedom.

Central Park was supposed to reinforce self-control and delayed gratification; Coney Island was a consumer's world of extravagance, gaity, abandon, revelry, and instant gratification. It attracted working-class Americans who longed for at least a taste of the good life. If a person could never hope to own a mansion in Newport, he could for a few dimes experience the exotic pleasures of Luna Park or Dreamland Park. Even the rides in the amusement parks were designed to create illusions and break down reality. Mirrors distorted people's images and rides threw them off balance. At Luna Park, the "Witching Waves" simulated the bobbing of a ship at high sea, and the "Tickler" featured spinning circular cars that threw riders together.

In part, the desire for intense physical experience would be met through sports, athletics, and out-of-doors activities. But its primary outlet was vicarious—through mass culture. Craving more intense physical and emotional experience, eager to break free of the confining boundaries of genteel culture, Americans turned to new kinds of newspapers and magazines, new forms of commercial entertainment, and, above all, the movies.

The Rise of Mass Communications

The last ten years of the nineteenth century were critical in the emergence of modern American mass culture. In those years emerged the modern instruments of mass communication—the mass-circulation metropolitan newspaper, the best-seller, the mass-market magazine, national advertising campaigns, and the movies. American culture also made a critical shift to commercialized forms of entertainment.

The urban tabloid was the first instrument of modern mass culture to appear. Pioneered by Joseph Pulitzer's New York *World* and William Randolph Hearst's New York *Journal,* these popular newspapers differed dramatically from the staid upper-class and the staunchly partisan political newspapers that had dominated late nineteenth-century journalism: They featured banner headlines; a multitude of photographs and cartoons; an emphasis on local news, crime and scandal, society news, and sports; and large ads, which made up half of a paper's content compared to just thirty percent in earlier newspapers. For easier reading on an omnibus or street railway, page size was cut, stories shortened, and the text heavily illustrated with drawings and photographs.

Entertainment was a stock-in-trade of yellow journalism (named for the "yellow kid" comic strip that appeared in Hearst's *Journal*). Among the innovations introduced by yellow journalists were the first color comic strips, advice columns, women's pages, fashion pages, and sports pages. Using simple words, a lively style, and many illustrations, yellow journalism could reach a mass audience that included many immigrants who understood little English. By 1905, Pulitzer's *World* boasted a circulation of 2 million.

Also during the 1890s, the rise of the country's first mass-circulation national magazines revolutionized the world of magazine publishing, and created a demand for fresh types of news. After the Civil War, the magazine field had been dominated by a small number of sedate magazines—such as *The Atlantic, Harper's,* and *Scribner's*—written for the "gentle" reader of highly intellectual tastes. The poetry, serious fiction, and wood engravings that filled these monthlies' pages rigidly conformed to upper-class Victorian standards of taste. These magazines embodied what the philosopher George Santayana called the "genteel tradition": the idea that art and literature should reinforce morality and refine sensibility, not portray reality. Art and literature, the custodians of culture believed, should transcend the real and uphold the ideal. The poet James Russell Lowell spoke for other genteel writers when he said that no man should describe any activity that would make his wife or daughter blush. The founders of the nation's first mass-circulation magazines considered the older "quality" magazines stale and elitist. In contrast, their magazines featured practical advice, popularized science, gossip, human interest stories, celebrity profiles, interviews, muckraking investigations, pictures, articles on timely topics—and a profusion of ads. Instead of cultivating a select audience, the new magazines aimed to please the urban masses. By running popular articles, editors sought to maximize circulation, which, in turn, attracted advertising that kept the magazine's price low. By 1900 the nation's largest magazine, the *Ladies' Home Journal,* reached 850,000 subscribers—more than eight times the readership of *Scribner's* or *Harper's.*

The end of the nineteenth century also marked a critical turning point in the history of book publishing, as marketing wizards like Frank Doubleday organized the first national book promotional campaigns, created the modern best seller, and transformed popular writers like Jack London into celebrities. The world of the Victorian man of letters, the defender of "Culture" against "Anarchy," had ended.

In 1898, the National Biscuit Company (Nabisco) launched the first million dollar national advertising campaign. It succeeded in making Uneeda biscuits and their waterproof "In-er-Seal" box popular household items. During the 1880s and 1890s, patent medicine manufacturers, department stores, and producers of low-priced, packed consumer goods (such as Campbell Soups, H.J. Heinz, and Quaker Oats), developed modern advertising techniques. Earlier advertisers had made little use of brand names, illustrations, or trademarks; the new ads emblazed snappy slogans and colorful packages. As early as 1900, advertisements began to use psychology to arouse consumer demand by suggesting that a product would contribute to the consumer's social and psychic well-being. To induce purchases, observed a trade journal in 1890, a consumer "must be aroused, excited, terrified." Listerine mouthwash promised to cure "halitosis"; Scott tissue claimed to prevent infections caused by harsh toilet paper.

By stressing instant gratification and personal fulfillment in their ads, modern advertising helped undermine an earlier Victorian ethos of thrift, self-denial, delayed gratification, and hard work. In various ways, it transformed Americans from savers to spenders and told them to give in to their desire for luxury.

The creators of the modern instruments of mass culture arose from similar backgrounds. Most were outsiders—recent immigrants or Southerners, Midwesterners, or Westerners. Joseph Pulitzer was an Austrian Jew; the pioneering new magazine editors, Edward W. Bok and Samuel Sidney McClure, were also first-generation immigrants. Unlike the men and women from Boston's Brahmin culture or upper-class New York who had defined the genteel tradition, the men who created modern mass culture had their initial training in daily newspapers, commerce, and popular entertainment. As a result, they were more in touch with popular tastes. As outsiders, the creators of mass culture betrayed an almost voyeuristic interest in what they called the "romance of real life": high life, low life, power, and status.

The popular culture they created was simple, direct, realistic, and colloquial. A new realistic aesthetic overthrew the florid Victorian style. Writers and artists rebelled against the moralism and sentimentality of Victorian culture and sought to portray life objectively and truthfully, without idealization or avoiding the ugly.

The quest for realism took a variety of guises: in the naturalism of writers like Theodore Dreiser and Stephen Crane, with their nightmarish depictions of urban poverty and exploitation; in the paintings of what was called the "ashcan" school of art, with their vivid portraits of tenements and congested streets; and in the forceful, colorful prose of tabloid reporters and muckraking journalists, who cut through the Victorian veil of reticence surrounding such topics as sex, political corruption, and working conditions in industry. The task of the journalist, novelist, and artist, declared the writer Frank Norris, was to battle "false views of life, false characters, false sentiments, false morality, false history, false philosophy, false emotions, false heroism."

The most influential innovations in mass culture would take place after the turn of the century. Thomas Edison first successfully projected moving pictures on a screen in 1896, but it would not be until 1903 that Edwin S. Porter's *The Great Train Robbery*—the first American movie to tell a story—demonstrated the commercial appeal of motion pictures. And although Guglielmo Marconi showed the possibility of wireless communication in 1895, commercial radio broadcasting did not begin until 1920 and commercial television broadcasts until 1939. These new instruments of mass communications would reach audiences of unprecedented size. As early as 1922, movies sold forty million tickets a week and radios could be found in three million homes.

The emergence of these modern forms of mass communications had far reaching effects upon American society. They broke down the isolation of local neighborhoods and communities and ensured that for the first time all Americans, regardless of their class, ethnicity, or locality, began to share standardized information and entertainment. They also created a truly democratic culture.

Commercialized Leisure

Among the most striking differences between the nineteenth and the twentieth centuries was the rapid growth of commercialized entertainment. For much of the nineteenth century, Americans had regarded commercial amusements as suspect. Drawing on the Puritan criticisms of play and recreation and a republican ideology that was hostile to luxury, hedonism, and extravagance, American Victorians associated theaters, dance halls, circuses, and organized sports with such vices as gambling, swearing, drinking, and immoral sexual behavior. In the late nineteenth century, however, a new outlook challenged Victorian prejudices.

During the first twenty years of the new century, attendance at professional baseball games doubled. Vaudeville, already popular in the 1890s, increased in popularity, featuring singing, dancing, skits, comics, acrobats, and magicians. Amusement parks, penny arcades, dance halls, and other commercial amusements flourished. As early as 1910, when there were 10,000 movie theaters, the movies had become the nation's most popular form of commercial entertainment.

The rise of these commercialized amusements radically reshaped the nature of American leisure activities. Earlier in the nineteenth century, leisure activities had been sharply segregated on the basis of gender, class, and ethnicity. The wealthy attended their own exclusive theaters, concert halls, museums, restaurants, and sporting clubs. For the working class, leisure and amusement was rooted in particular ethnic communities and neighborhoods, each with its own saloons, churches, fraternal organizations, and organized sports. Men and women differed in their leisure activities. Many men (particularly bachelors and immigrants) relaxed in barber shops, billiard halls, and bowling alleys; joined volunteer fire companies or militias; and patronized saloons, gambling halls, and race tracks. Women took part in church activities and socialized with friends and relatives. After 1880, as incomes rose and leisure time expanded, new commercialized forms of cross-class, mixed-sex amusements proliferated. Entertainment became a major industry. Vaudeville theaters attracted women as well as men. The young, in particular, increasingly sought pleasure, escape, and the freedom to experiment in mixed sex relationships in relatively inexpensive amusement parks, dance halls, urban night clubs, and, above all, nickelodeons and movie theaters, free of parental control.

The transformation of Coney Island from a center of male vice—of brothels, saloons, and gambling dens—into the nation's first modern amusement park, complete with ferris wheels, hootchie kootchie girls, restaurants, and concert halls symbolized the emergence of a new leisure culture, emphasizing excitement, glamour, fashion, and romance. Its informality and sheer excitement attracted people of every class.

Coney Island offered an escape from an oppressive urban landscape to an exotic one. The new motion picture industry would offer an even less expensive, more convenient escape. During the early twentieth century, it quickly developed into the country's most popular and influential form of art and entertainment.

THE BIRTH OF THE MOVIES

Beside Macy's Department Store in Herald Square, New York City, a plaque commemorates the first public showing of a motion picture on a screen in the United States. It was here, on April 23, 1896, at Koster and Bial's Music Hall, that Thomas Alva Edison presented a show that included scenes of the surf breaking on a beach, a comic boxing exhibition, and two young women dancing. A review in *The New York Times* described the exhibition as "all wonderfully real and singularly exhilarating."

The Pre-History of Motion Pictures

For centuries, people had wrestled with the problem of realistically reproducing moving images. A discovery by Ptolemy in the second century provided the first step. He noticed that there is a slight imperfection in human perception: The retina retains an image for a fraction of a second after the image has changed or disappeared. Because of this phenomenon, known as the "persistence of vision," a person would merge a rapid succession of individual images into the illusion of continuous motion.

The first successful efforts to project lifelike images on a screen took place in the mid-seventeenth century. By 1659, a Dutch scientist named Christiaen Huygens had invented the magic lantern, the forerunner of the modern slide projector, which he used to project medical drawings before an audience. A magic lantern used sunlight (or another light source) to illuminate a hand-painted glass transparency and project it through a simple lens. In the 1790s, the Belgian Etienne Gaspar Robert terrified audiences with fantasmagoric exhibitions, which used magic lanterns to project images of phantoms and apparitions of the dead. By the mid-nineteenth century, illustrated lectures and dramatic readings had become common. To create the illusion of motion, magic lantern operators used multiple lanterns and mirrors to move the image.

The first true moving images appeared in the 1820s, when the concept of the persistence of vision was used to create children's toys and other simple entertainments. The thaumatrope, which appeared in 1826, was a simple disk with separate images printed on each side (for example, a bird on one side and a cage on another). When rapidly spun, the images appeared to blend together (so that the bird seemed to be inside the cage). In 1834, an Austrian military officer, Baron Franz von Uchatius, developed a more sophisticated device called the "Phenakistoscope." It consisted of a disk, with a series of slots along its edge, which was printed with a series of slightly differing pictures. When the disk was spun in front of a mirror and the viewer looked through the slots, the pictures appeared to move. A simpler way to display movement was the flip book, which became popular by the late 1860s. Each page showed a subject in a subtly different position. When a reader flipped the book's pages, the pictures gave the illusion of movement.

These early devices were not very satisfactory. The slides used in early magic lanterns had to be painted by hand. The pictures displayed by the Phenakistoscope or flip books could not be viewed by more than one person at a time. The solution to these problems lay in photography. In 1826, the French inventor Joseph Nicephore Niepce made the first true photograph. He placed a camera obscura (a box with a tiny opening on one side that admitted light) at his window and for eight hours exposed a metal plate coated with light-sensitive chemicals. During the 1830s, another French inventor, Louis Daguerre, improved Niepce's technique and created the daguerreotype, the first popular form of photography.

The dauguerreotype was not very useful to the inventors who wanted to produce motion pictures. The process used expensive copper plates coated with silver and required a subject to remain motionless for fifteen to thirty seconds. During the mid-nineteenth century, however, two technical advances improved the photographic process. Copper plates were replaced with less expensive glass plates, light-sensitive paper, and, in 1880, flexible film. New film coatings significantly reduced exposure time and gave photographers greater mobility. By the late 1870s, the introduction of "dry-process plates" using gelatin emulsion reduced exposure time to just one twenty-fifth of a second and freed photographers from having to process their prints immediately.

The first successful photographs of motion grew out of a California railroad tycoon's $25,000 wager. In 1872, California Governor Leland Stanford hired a photographer named Eadweard Muybridge to help settle a bet. An avid horse breeder, Stanford had wagered that a galloping horse lifts all four hoofs off the ground simultaneously. In 1878, the English-born photographer lined up twenty-four cameras along the edge of a race track, with strings attached to the shutters. The horse ran by, tripping the shutters, and the twenty-four closely spaced pictures proved Stanford's contention.

Four years later, a French physiologist, Etienne-Jules Marey, became the first person to take pictures of motion with a single camera. Marey built his camera in the shape of a rifle. At the end of the barrel, he placed a circular photographic plate. A small motor rotated the plate after Marey snapped the shutter. With his camera, Marey could take twelve pictures a second.

In 1887, Thomas Edison gave William K.L. Dickson, one of his leading inventors, the task of developing a motion picture apparatus. Edison envisioned a machine "that should do for the eye what the phonograph did for the ear." Dickson initially modelled his device on Edison's phonograph, placing tiny pictures on a revolving drum. A light inside the drum was supposed to illuminate the pictures. Then he decided to use the flexible celluloid film that George Eastman had invented in 1880 and had begun to use in his Kodak camera. Dickson added perforations to the edge of the film strip to help it feed evenly into his camera.

To display their films, Dickson and Edison devised a coin-operated peepshow device called a "kinetoscope." Because the kinetoscope could only hold fifty feet of film, its films lasted from just thirty-five to forty seconds. This was too brief to tell a story; the first kinetoscope films were simply scenes of everyday life, like the first film "Fred Ott's Sneeze," reenactments of historical events, photographed bits of vaudeville routines, and pictures of well-known celebrities. Nevertheless, the kinetoscope was an instant success. By 1894, coin-operated kinetoscopes had begun to appear in hotels, department stores, saloons, and amusement arcades called nickelodeons.

Eager to maximize his profits, Edison showed no interest in building a movie projector. "If we make this screen machine," he argued, ". . . it will spoil everything." As a result, Edison's competitors would take the lead in developing screen projection.

In devising a practical movie projector, inventors faced a serious technical problem: the projector had to be capable of stopping a frame momentarily, so that the image could be clearly fixed in the viewer's retina, and then advance the film quickly between frames. Two French brothers—Auguste and Louis Lumiere—solved this problem. They borrowed the design of their stop-action device from the sewing machine, which holds the material still during stitching before advancing it forward. In 1894, the Lumiere brothers introduced the portable motion picture camera and projector.

Finally recognizing the potential of the motion picture projector, Edison entered into an agreement with a Washington, D.C. realtor, Thomas Armat, who had designed a workable projector. In April, 1896, the two men unveiled the Vitascope and presented the first motion pictures on a public screen in the United States.

Competition in the early movie industry was fierce. Aiming to force their competitors out of the industry, moviemakers turned to the courts, launching over two hundred patent infringement suits. To protect their profits and bring order to the industry, Edison and a number of his competitors decided to cooperate by establishing the Motion Picture Patents Company in 1909, consisting of six American companies and two French firms. Members of the trust agreed that only they had the right to make, print, or distribute cameras, projectors, or films. The trust also negotiated an exclusive agreement with Eastman Kodak for film stock of commercial quality. Led by Carl Laemmle, later the founder of Universal Pictures, independent distributors and exhibitors filed a restraint of trade lawsuit under the

Sherman Anti-Trust Act. A court ruled in the independents' behalf in 1915 and the decision was affirmed by a higher court in 1918. Even before the courts ruled in their favor, the independents had broken the power of the trust in the marketplace. The trust viewed movies, in the famous words of director Erich von Stroheim, as so many sausages to be ground out as quickly as possible and rented at ten cents a foot. The independent moviemakers succeeded in defeating the trust with two potent weapons: the introduction of longer films that told complex stories and the emergence of the star system.

During film's first decade—from 1896 to 1905—movies had been little more than a novelty, often used as a chaser to signal the end of a show in a vaudeville theater. These early films are utterly unlike anything seen today. They lasted just seven to ten minutes—too brief to tell anything more than the simplest story. They used a cast of anonymous actors—for the simple reason that the camera was set back so far that it was impossible clearly to make out the actors' faces. As late as 1908, a movie actor made no more than $8 a day and received no credit on the screen.

In 1905, hundreds of little movie theaters opened, called nickelodeons, since they sold admission nickel by nickel. By 1908, there were an estimated 8,000 to 10,000 nickelodeons. Contrary to popular belief, the nickelodeon's audience was not confined to the poor, the young, or the immigrant. From the start, theaters were situated in rural areas and middle class neighborhoods as well as working-class neighborhoods. Nevertheless, the movies attracted audiences of an unprecedented size. Admission prices were low, seating arrangements "democratic," schedules convenient (films were shown again and again); and lack of spoken dialogue allowed non-English speaking immigrants to enjoy films. Although by 1907, narrative had begun to turn films into an art form, most still emphasized stunts and chases and real life events—like scenes of yacht races or train crashes. They were rented or sold by the foot regardless of subject matter. Exhibitors then assembled scenes together to form a larger show.

While the trust continued much of the practice that was retarding the development of film as a mature art form, it introduced into the movie industry a healthy rationalization. Camera and projecting equipment was standardized; film rental fees were fixed; theaters were upgraded; and the practice of selling films outright ended, which improved the quality of movies by removing damaged prints from circulation. This was also a period of intense artistic and technical innovation. Such pioneering directors as David Wark Griffith created a new language of film and revolutionized screen narrative.

With just six months of film experience, Griffith, a former stage actor, was hired as a director by the Biograph Company and promised $50 a week and one-twentieth of a cent for every foot of film sold to a rental exchange. Each week, Griffith turned out two or three one-reelers. Earlier directors had used such cinematic devices as close ups, slow motion, fade-ins and fade-outs, lighting effects, and editing; Griffith's great contribution to the movie industry was to show how these techniques could be used to create a wholly new style of storytelling, distinct from the theater.

Griffith's approach to movie storytelling has been aptly called "photographic realism." This is not to say that he merely wished to record a story accurately; rather he sought to convey the illusion of realism. He used editing to convey simultaneous events or the passage of time. He demanded that his performers act in a more lifelike manner, avoiding the broad, exaggerated gestures and pantomiming of emotions that had characterized the nineteenth-century stage. He wanted his performers to take on a role rather than directly addressing the camera. Above all, he used close-ups, lighting, editing, and framing and other cinematic techniques to convey suspense and other emotions and to focus the audience's attention on individual performers.

By focusing the camera on particular actors and actresses, Griffith inadvertently encouraged the development of the star system. As early as 1910, newspapers were deluged with requests for actors' names. Most studios refused to divulge their identities, fearing the salary demands of popular performers. But the film trust's leading opponent, Carl Laemmle, was convinced that producing films featuring popular stars would bring financial stability. As one industry observer put it, "In the 'star' your producer gets not only a 'production' value . . . but a 'trademark' value, and an 'insurance' value which are . . . very potent in guaranteeing the sale of this product." In 1910, Laemmle manufactured the first star. Florence Lawrence was already the most popular anonymous star. Laemmle lured her away from Biograph, and launched an unprecedented publicity campaign on her behalf. As the star system emerged, salaries soared. In the course of just two years, the salary of actress Mary Pickford rose from less than $400 a week in 1914—at the time a huge sum in its own right—to $10,000 a week in 1916.

Meanwhile, an influx of feature-length films from Europe, which attracted premium admission prices, led a New York nickelodeon owner named Adolph Zukor to produce four- and five-reel films featuring readily identifiable stars. By 1916, Zukor had taken control of Paramount Pictures, a movie distributor, and had instituted the practice of "block-booking"—requiring theaters to book a number of films rather than just a single film. Within a few years, Zukor's company had achieved vertical integration—not only producing films, but distributing them and owning the theaters that exhibited them.

During the second decade of the twentieth century, immigrants like Laemmle and Zukor came to dominate the movie business. Unlike Edison and the other American-born, Protestant businessmen who had controlled the early film industry, these immigrant entrepreneurs had a strong sense of what the public wanted to see. Virtually all of these new producers were East European and Jewish. Not raised in the Victorian ethos that still held sway in "respectable" Protestant America, they proved better able to exploit ribald humor and sex in their films. Less conservative than the American-born producers, they were more willing to experiment with such innovations as the star system and feature-length productions. Since many had come to the film industry from the garment and fur trades—where fashions change rapidly and success requires staying constantly in touch with the latest styles—they tried to give the public what it wanted. As Samuel Goldwyn, one of the leading moguls, noted, "If the audience don't like a picture, they have a good reason. The public is never wrong. I don't go for all this thing that when I have a failure, it is because the audience doesn't have the taste or education, or isn't sensitive enough. The public pays money. It wants to be entertained. That's all I know." With this philosophy the outsiders wrestled control over the industry away from the American-born producers.

During the 1920s and 1930s, a small group of film companies consolidated their control and formed fully integrated companies. Paramount, Warner Brothers, RKO, 20th Century-Fox, and Lowe's (MGM) were known as the Big Five—and the Little Three consisted of Universal, Columbia, and United Artists. With the exception of United Artists, which was solely a distribution company, the major studios owned their own production facilities, ran their own worldwide distribution networks, and controlled theater chains that were committed to showing the company's products. And at the head of each was a powerful mogul—such giants as Adolph Zukor, Wiliam Fox, Louis B. Mayer, Samuel Goldwyn, Carl Laemmle, Harry Cohn, Joseph Schenck, and the Warner brothers—who determined what the public was going to see. It was their vision—patriotic, sentimental, secular, and generally politically conservative—that millions of Americans shared weekly at local movie theaters. And as expressed by such producers as Irving Thalberg, Darryl F. Zanuck, and Daivd O. Selznick, it was a powerful vision indeed.

American Film in the Silent Era

Some film historians have argued that early silent films revolved around "characteristically working class settings," and expressed the interests of the poor in their struggles with the rich and powerful. Other scholars maintain that early movies drew largely upon conventions, stock characters, and routines derived from vaudeville, popular melodrama, Wild West shows, comic strips, and other forms of late nineteenth century popular entertainment. Since thousands of films were released during the silent era and relatively few have survived, it is dangerous to generalize about movie content. Nevertheless, certain statements about these films do seem warranted.

Kevin Brownlow has demonstrated the preoccupation with the sources of crime, the nature of political corruption, shifting sexual norms, and the changing role of women, themes that were a dark background to the innocent surfaces of well-dressed tramps and childlike waifs. The silent screen offered vivid glimpses of urban tenements and ethnic ghettoes, of gangsters, loan sharks, drug addicts, and panderers. American films were born in an age of reform, and many early silent movies took as their subject matter the major social and moral issues of the Progressive era and beyond: birth control, child labor, divorce, immigration, political corruption, poverty, prisons, prostitution, and women's suffrage. The tone of these films varied widely. Some were realistic and straightforward, others treated their subjects with sentimentality or humor, and many transformed complex social issues into personal melodramas. Yet there can be no doubt that many silent films dealt at least obliquely with the dominant issues of the time.

Many early films mocked authority, poking fun at bumbling cops, corrupt politicians, and intrusive upper-class reformers. Highly physical slapstick comedy offered a particularly potent vehicle of social criticism, spoofing the pretensions of the wealthy and presenting sympathetic portraits of the poor. Mack Sennett, one of the most influential directors of silent comedy, would later recall the themes of his films: "I especially liked the reduction of authority to absurdity, the notion that sex could be funny, and the bold insults hurled at Pretension."

Many films of the early silent era dealt with gender relations. Before 1905, movie screens had played with salacious sexual imagery and risque humor, drawn from burlesque halls and vaudeville theaters. Early films offered glimpses of women disrobing or passionate kisses. As the movies' female audience grew, sexual titilation and voyeurism persisted. But an ever increasing number of films dealt in a more sophisticated manner with the changing work and sexual roles of women. While D.W. Griffith's films presented an idealized picture of the frail Victorian child-woman, and showed an almost obsessive preoccupation with female honor and chastity, other silent movies presented images of femininity ranging from the exotic, sexually aggressive vamp to the athletic, energetic "serial queen"; the street smart urban working gal, who repels the sexual advances of her lascivious boss; and cigarette-smoking, alcohol drinking chorus girls or burlesque queens.

In the late teens and the twenties, the movies began to turn from the remnants of Victorian moralism and sentimentality, as well as reformism, and increasingly featured glamour, sophistication, exoticism, urbanity, and sex appeal. New kinds of movie stars appeared: the mysterious sex goddess, personified by Greta Garbo; the passionate, hotblooded lover, epitomized by Rudolph Valentino; and the flapper, first brought to the screen by Coleen Moore, with her bobbed hair, skimpy skirts, and incandescent vivacity. New genres also appeared: swashbuckling adventures; sophisticated sex comedies revolving around the issue of marital fidelity; romantic dramas examining the manners and morals of the well-bred and well-to-do; and tales of flaming youth and the new sexual freedom.

During the 1920s, a sociologist named Herbert Blumer interviewed students and young workers to assess the impact of movies on their lives, and concluded that the effect was to reorient their lives away from ethnic and working class communities toward a broader consumer culture. Observed one high school student: "The daydreams instigated by the movies consist of clothes, ideas on furnishings and manners." Said an African-American student: "The movies have often made me dissatisfied with my neighborhood because when I see a movie, the beautiful castle, palace, . . . and beautiful house, I wish my home was something like these." Hollywood not only expressed popular values, aspirations, and fantasies, but also promoted cultural change.

The Movies as a Cultural Battleground

Reformers of the Progressive era had taken a highly ambivalent view of the movies. Some praised movies as a benign alternative to the saloon. Others viewed nickelodeons and movie theaters as breeding grounds of crime and sexual promiscuity. In 1907, the *Chicago Tribune* threw its editorial weight against the movies, declaring that they were "without a redeeming feature to warrant their existence . . . ministering to the lowest passions of childhood." That year, Chicago established the nation's first censorship board to protect its population "against the evil influence of obscene and immoral representations." Also in 1907, and again in 1908, New York's mayor, under pressure from various religious and reform groups, temporarily closed down all of the city's nickelodeons and movie theaters. A presidential study concluded that films encouraged "illicit lovemaking and iniquity." A Worcester, Massachusetts, newspaper described the city's movie theaters as centers of delinquent activity, and reported that female gang members "confessed that their early tendencies toward evil came from seeing moving pictures." Several bills were introduced in Congress calling for movie censorship.

The drive to censor films spread from Chicago to other municipalities and states, especially after a 1915 Supreme Court ruling that movies were not protected by the First Amendment since they "were a business pure and simple . . . not to be regarded as part of the press of the country or as organs of public opinion." Eager to combat the trend toward local censorship, movie manufacturers in 1909 began working with moral reformers in New York to establish the voluntary Board of Censorship of Motion Pictures to review the movies' treatment of violence, drugs, prostitution, and, above all, sexual immorality (such as "over-passionate love scenes; stimulating close dancing; unnecessary bedroom scenes in negligee; excessively low-cut gowns; [and] undue or suggestive display of the person").

After World War I, a series of sex scandals raised renewed threats of censorship or boycotts. William Desmond Taylor, a director, was found murdered under suspicious circumstances; actor Wallace Reid committed suicide amid allegations of drug addiction; and comedian Fatty Arbuckle was acquitted of rape and complicity in murder. To clean up Hollywood's image, the industry banned Arbuckle and a number of other people implicated in scandals, and appointed Will Hays, President Warren Harding's Postmaster General, to head their trade organization. Hays introduced a voluntary code of standards.

The Rise of Hollywood and the Arrival of Sound

In cinema's earliest days, the film industry had based itself in the nation's theatrical center, New York, and most films were made in New York or New Jersey. A few were shot in Chicago, Florida, and elsewhere. Beginning in 1908, however, a growing number of filmmakers located in southern California, drawn by cheap land and labor, the ready accessibility of varied scenery, and a climate ideal for year-round outdoor filming. Contrary to popular mythology, moviemakers did not move to Hollywood to escape the film trust; the first studio to move to Hollywood, Selig, was actually a trust member.

By the early 1920s, Hollywood had become the world's film capital. It produced virtually all films shown in the United States and received eighty percent of the revenue from films shown abroad. During the decade, Hollywood bolstered its position of world leader by recruiting many of Europe's most talented actors and actresses, including Greta Garbo and Hedy Lamarr, directors Ernst Lubitsch and Josef von Sternberg, and camera operators, lighting technicians, and set designers. By the end of the decade, Hollywood claimed to be the nation's fifth largest industry, attracting 83 cents out of every dollar Americans spent on amusement.

Hollywood had also come to symbolize the new morality of the 1920s—a mixture of extravagance, glamour, hedonism, and fun. Where else but Hollywood would an actress like Gloria Swanson bathe in a solid gold bathtub or a screen cowboy like Tom Mix have his name raised atop his house in six foot high letters?

During the 1920s, movie attendance soared. By the middle of the decade, weekly attendence was at fifty million—the equivalent of half the nation's population. In Chicago, in 1929, theaters had enough seats for half the city's population to attend a movie each day. And as attendance rose, the movie-going experience underwent a profound change.

During the twentieth century's first two decades, movie going had tended to conform to class and ethnic divisions. Urban workers attended movie houses located in their own working class and ethnic neighborhoods, where admission was extremely inexpensive (averaging just seven cents during the teens), and a movie was often accompanied by an amateur talent show or a performance by a local ethnic troupe. These working class theaters were rowdy, high-spirited centers of neighborhood sociability, where mothers brought their babies and audiences cheered, jeered, shouted, whistled, and stamped their feet. The theaters patronized by the middle class were quite different. By 1910, theaters in downtown or middle class neighborhoods became increasingly luxurious. At first many of these theaters were designed in the same styles as many other public buildings, but by the mid-teens movie houses began to feature French Renaissance, Egyptian, Moorish, and other exotic decors. Worcester, Massachusetts's Strand Theater boasted "red plush seats," "luxurious carpets," "rich velour curtains," "finely appointed toilet rooms," and a $15,000 organ. Unlike the working class movie houses, which showed films continuously, these high class theaters had specific show times and well-groomed, uniformed ushers to enforce standards of decorum.

During the late-twenties, regional and national chains purchased independent neighborhood theaters catering to a distinct working class audience. As a result, the movie-going experience became more uniform, with working class and middle class theaters offering the same programs. Especially after the introduction of the talkies, many working class movie houses shut down, unable to meet the cost of converting to sound.

For decades, engineers had searched for a practical technology to add synchronized recorded sound to the movies. In the 1890s, Thomas Edison tried unsuccessfully to popularize the kinetophone—which combined a kinetoscope with a phonograph. In 1923, Lee De Forest, an American inventor, demonstrated the practicality of placing a soundtrack directly on a film strip, presenting a newsreel interview with President Calvin Coolidge and musical accompaniments to several films. But despite the growing popularity of radio, the film industry showed remarkably little interest in sound. Hollywood feared the high cost of converting its production and exhibition to sound technology.

Warner Brothers, a struggling industry newcomer, turned to sound as a way to compete with its larger rivals. A prerecorded musical sound track eliminated the expense of live entertainment. In 1926, Warner Brothers released the film *Don Juan*—the first film with a synchronized film score—along with a program of talking shorts. The popularity of *The Jazz Singer,* which was released in 1927, erased any doubts about the popular appeal of sound, and within a year, some three hundred theaters were wired for sound.

The arrival of sound made for a sharp upsurge in movie attendance, which jumped from fifty million a week in the mid-twenties to 110 million in 1929. But it also produced a number of fundamental transformations in the movies themselves. As Robert Ray has shown, sound made the movies more American. The words that Al Jolson used in *The Jazz Singer* to herald the arrival of sound in the movies—

"You ain't heard nothing yet"—embodied the new slangy, vernacular tone of the talkies. Distinctive American accents and inflections quickly appeared on the screen. James Cagney's New Yorkese or Gary Cooper's Western drawl became familiar sounds. The introduction of sound also encouraged such new film genres as the musical, the gangster film, and comedies that relied on wit rather than slapstick.

In addition, the talkies dramatically changed the movie-going experience, especially for the working class. Many working class audiences had provided silent films with a spoken dialogue. Movie-goers were now expected to remain quiet. As one film historian has observed: "The talking audience for silent pictures became a silent audience for talking pictures." The stage shows and other forms of live entertainment that had appeared in silent movie houses were disappearing, replaced by newsreels and animated shorts.

The Movies Meet the Great Depression

In 1934, Will Hays, head of the Motion Picture Producers and Distributors Association, said that "No medium has contributed more greatly than the film to the maintenance of the national morale during a period featured by revolution, riot and political turmoil in other countries." During the Great Depression, Hollywood had a valuable psychological and ideological role, providing reassurance and hope to a demoralized nation. Even at the Depression's depths attendance at the movies was from sixty to eighty million each week, and, in the face of doubt and despair, films helped sustain national morale.

Although the movie industry considered itself Depression-proof, Hollywood was no more immune from the Depression's effects than any other industry. To finance the purchase of movie theaters and the conversion to sound, the studios had tripled their debts during the mid- and late-twenties to $410 million. As a result, the industry's very viability seemed in question. By 1933, movie attendance and industry revenues had fallen by forty percent. To survive, the industry trimmed salaries and production costs, and closed the doors of a third of the nation's theaters. To boost attendance, theaters resorted to such gimmicks as lowering admission prices (cut by as much as 25 cents), double bills, give-aways of free dishes, and Bank Night—in which a customer who received a lucky number won a cash prize.

Why did Depression America go to the movies? Escapism is what most people assume. At the movies they could forget their troubles for a couple of hours. Depression films, one left-wing critic maintained, were a modern form of bread and circuses, distracting Americans from their problems, reinforcing older values, and dampening political radicalism. Yet movies were more than mere escapism. Many films of the Depression years were grounded in the social realities of the time. The most realistic films were social problem films—like *I Am a Fugitive From a Chain Gang*—torn from the headlines, usually by Warner Brothers or Columbia Pictures. Yet even the most outrageously extravagant Busby Berkeley musicals—portraying chorus girls as flowers or mechanical windup dolls—were generally set against recognizable depression backdrops.

During the Depression's earliest years, the kinds of movies that Hollywood produced underwent the first of the changes that would reflect shifts in a troubled public's mood. Despair was reflected in the kinds of characters Americans watched on the screen: a succession of Tommy Gun–toting gangsters, haggard prostitutes, sleazy backroom politicians, cynical journalists, and shyster lawyers. The screen comedies released at the Depression's depths expressed an almost anarchistic disdain for traditional institutions and conventions. In the greatest comedies of the early Depression, the Marx Brothers spoofed everything from patriotism (in *Duck Soup*) to universities (in *Horse Feathers*); W.C. Fields ridiculed families and children; and Mae West used sexual innuendo and double entendres to make fun of the middle class code of sexual propriety, with lines like "When a girl goes wrong, men go right after her."

The gangster pictures and sexually suggestive comedies of the early thirties provoked outrage and threats of boycotts from many Protestant and Catholic religious groups. In 1934, Hollywood's producers' association responded by setting up a bureau (later known as the "Breen Office") to review every script that the major studios proposed to shoot and to screen every film before it was released to ensure that the picture did not violate the organization's "Code to Govern the Making of Talking, Synchronized and Silent Motion Pictures." The Production Code, drafted by a Jesuit priest, Father Daniel Lord, had been originally adopted in 1930, but the producers had regarded it as a public relations device, not as a code of censorship. But in 1933, the newly appointed apostolic delegate to the U.S. Catholic Church, the Most Reverend Amleto Giovanni Cicognani, called on Catholics to launch "a united and vigorous campaign for the purification of the cinema, which has become a deadly menace to morals." Many Catholics responded by forming the Legion of Decency, which soon had nine million members pledged to boycott films that the Legion's rating board condemned. Threatened by fear of boycotts, the producers decided to enforce the production code and placed one of their employees, Joseph I. Breen, in charge. The code prohibited nudity, profanity, white slavery, miscegenation, "excessive and lustful kissing," and "scenes of passion" that "stimulate the lower and baser element." It also prohibited Hollywood from glorifying crime or adultery. To enforce the code, the Breen Office was empowered to grant or withhold a seal of approval, and without a seal, a movie could not be played in the major theater chains.

The Breen Office shaped the character of films in the later 1930s. On the positive side, it led Hollywood to cast more actresses in roles as independent career women, instead of as mere sex objects. But it encouraged moviemakers to evade the harsher realities of Depression-era life and to shun controversial political and moral issues. It also contributed to what Maury Klein has called a "stylization of technique" as directors and screenwriters searched for subtle, creative, and often witty ways to treat sexuality and violence while avoiding censorship.

A renewed sense of optimism generated by the New Deal combined with Breen Office censorship to produce new kinds of films in the second half of the Depression decade. G-men, detectives, western heroes and other defenders of law increasingly replaced gangsters. Realistic Warner Brothers exposés rapidly declined in number. Instead audiences enjoyed Frank Capra's comedies and dramas in which a "little man" stands up against corruption and restores America to itself. The complex word-play of the Marx Brothers and Mae West increasingly gave way to a new comic genre—the screwball comedy. Such films as *It Happened One Night* and *My Man Godfrey,* which traced the antics of zany eccentrics, presented, in Pauline

Kael's words, "Americans' idealized view of themselves—breezy, likable, sexy, gallant, and maybe just a little harebrained."

In the face of economic disaster, the fantasy world of the movies kept alive a belief in the possibility of individual success, portrayed a government capable of protecting its citizens from external threats, and sustained a vision of America as a classless society. Again and again, Hollywood repeated the same formulas: A poor boy from the slums uses crime as a perverted ladder of success. A back row chorus girl rises to the lead through luck and pluck. A G-man restores law and order. A poor boy and a rich girl meet, go through wacky adventures, and fall in love. Out of these simple plots, Hollywood restored faith in individual initiative, in the efficacy of government, and in a common American identity transcending social class.

Wartime Hollywood

Beginning in September 1941, a Senate subcommittee launched an investigation into whether Hollywood was campaigning to bring the United States into World War II by inserting pro-British and pro-interventionist messages in its films. Isolationist Senator Gerald Nye charged Hollywood with producing "at least twenty pictures in the last year designed to drug the reason of the American people, set aflame their emotions, turn their hatred into a blaze, fill them with fear that Hitler will come over here and capture them." After reading a list of the names of studio executives—many of whom were Jewish—he condemned Hollywood as "a raging volcano of war fever."

While Hollywood did in fact release a few anti-Nazi films, such as *Confessions of a Nazi Spy,* what is remarkable in retrospect is how slowly Hollywood awoke to the fascist threat. Heavily dependent on the European market for revenue, Hollywood feared offending foreign audiences. Indeed, at the Nazis' request, Hollywood actually fired "non-Aryan" employees in its German business offices. Although between 1939 and 1941 the industry produced such preparedness films as *Sergeant York,* anti-fascist movies as *The Great Dictator,* and pro-British films such as *A Yank in the R.A.F.,* before Pearl Harbor it did not release a single film advocating immediate American intervention in the war on the allies' behalf.

After Pearl Harbor, however, Hollywood quickly enlisted in the war cause. The studios quickly copyrighted topical movie titles like *Sunday in Hawaii, Yellow Peril,* and *V for Victory.* Warner Brothers ordered a hasty rewrite of *Across the Pacific,* which involved a Japanese plot to blow up Pearl Harbor, changing the setting to the Panama Canal. The use of search lights at Hollywood premiers was prohibited, and Jack Warner painted a twenty-foot arrow atop his studio, reading: "Lookheed—Thataway."

Hollywood's greatest contribution to the war effort was morale. Many of the movies produced during the war affirmed a sense of national purpose. Combat films of the war years emphasized patriotism, group effort, and the value of individual sacrifice for a larger cause. They portrayed World War II as a peoples' war, typically featuring a group of men from diverse ethnic backgrounds who are thrown together, tested on the battlefield, and molded into a dedicated fighting unit. Many wartime films featured women characters serving as combat nurses, riveters, welders, and long-suffering mothers who kept the home fires burning. Even cartoons, like Bugs Bunny "Nips the Nips," contributed to morale.

Off the screen, leading actors and actresses led recruitment and bond drives and entertained the troops. Leading directors like Frank Capra, John Ford, and John Huston enlisted and made documentaries to explain "why we fight" and to offer civilians an idea of what actual combat looked like. In less than a year, twelve percent of all film industry employees entered the armed forces, including Clark Gable, Henry Fonda, and Jimmy Stewart. By the war's end, one-quarter of Hollywood's male employees were in uniform.

Hollywood, like other industries, encountered many wartime problems. The government cut the amount of available film stock by twenty-five percent and restricted the money that could be spent on sets to $5,000 for each movie. Nevertheless, the war years proved to be highly profitable for the movie industry. Spurred by shortages of gasoline and tires, as well as the appeal of newsreels, the war boosted movie attendance to near-record levels of ninety million a week.

From the moment America entered the war, Hollywood feared that the industry would be subject to heavy-handed government censorship. But the government itself wanted no repeat of World War I, when the Committee on Public Information had whipped up anti-German hysteria and oversold the war as "a Crusade not merely to re-win the tomb of Christ, but to bring back to earth the rule of right, the peace, goodwill to men and gentleness he taught." Less than two weeks after Pearl Harbor, President Roosevelt declared that the movie industry could make "a very useful contribution" to the war effort. But, he went on, "The motion picture industry must remain free . . . I want no censorship." Convinced that movies could contribute to national morale, but fearing outright censorship, the federal government established two agencies within the Office of War Information (OWI) in 1942 to supervise the film industry: the Bureau of Motion Pictures, which produced educational films and reviewed scripts submitted by the studios, and the Bureau of Censorship, which oversaw film exports.

At the time these agencies were founded, OWI officials were quite unhappy with Hollywood movies, which they considered "escapist and delusive." The movies, these officials believed, failed to convey what the allies were fighting for, grossly exaggerated the extent of Nazi and Japanese espionage and sabotage, portrayed our allies in an offensive manner, and presented a false picture of the United States as a land of gangsters, labor strife, and racial conflict. A study of films issued in 1942 seemed to confirm the OWI concerns. It found that of the films dealing with the war, roughly two-thirds were spy pictures or comedies or musicals about camp life.

To encourage the industry to provide more acceptable films, the Bureau of Motion Pictures issued "The Government Information Manual for the Motion Picture." This manual suggested that before producing a film, moviemakers consider the question: "Will this picture help to win the war?" It also asked the studios to inject images of "people making small sacrifices for victory—making them voluntarily, cheerfully, and because of the people's own sense of responsibility." The Bureau evaluated individual film scripts to assess how they depicted war aims, the American military, the enemy, the allies, and the home front.

After the Bureau of Motion Pictures died out in the spring of 1943, government responsibility for monitoring the film industry shifted to the Office of Censorship. This agency prohibited the export of films that showed racial discrimination, depicted Americans as single-handedly winning the war, or painted our allies as imperialists.

Post-War Hollywood

After experiencing boom years from 1939 to 1946, the film industry began a long, steady period of decline. Within just seven years after 1946, attendance and box receipts fell by half.

Part of the reason was external to the industry. Many veterans returning from World War II got married, started families, attended college on the GI Bill, and bought homes in the suburbs. All these activities took a toll on box office receipts. Families with babies tended to listen to the radio rather than go to the movies; college students placed studying before seeing the latest film; and newlyweds purchasing homes, automobiles, appliances, and other commodities had less money to spend on movies. Then, too, especially after 1950, television challenged and surpassed the movies as America's most popular entertainment form. In 1940, there had been just 3,785 TV sets in the United States. Two decades later, nine homes in every ten had at least one TV set. For pre-war Americans, the movies had shaped clothing styles, speech patterns, and even moral attitudes and political points of view. In postwar days, television largely took the movies' place as a dominant cultural influence. The new medium reached audiences far larger than those attracted by motion pictures, and it projected images right into family living rooms.

Internal troubles also contributed to Hollywood's decline. Hollywood's founding generation—Harry Cohn, Samuel Goldwyn, Louis B. Mayer, Darryl Zanuck—retired or were forced out as new corporate owners, lacking movie experience, took over. The film companies had high profiles, glamour, undervalued stock, strategically located real estate, and film libraries that television networks desperately needed. In short, they were perfect targets for corporate takeovers. The studios reduced production, sold off back lots, and made an increasing number of pictures in Europe, where costs were lower.

Meanwhile, Hollywood's foreign market began to vanish. Hollywood had depended on overseas markets for as much as forty percent of its revenue. But in an effort to nurture their own film industries and prevent an excessive outflow of dollars, Britain, France, and Italy imposed stiff import tariffs and restrictive quotas on imported American movies. The decline in foreign markets made movie making a much riskier business.

Then an antitrust ruling separated the studios from their theater chains. In 1948, the United States Supreme Court handed down its decision in the *Paramount* case, which had been working its ways through the courts for almost a decade. The court's decree called for the major studios to divest themselves of their theater chains. In addition to separating theater and producer-distributor companies, the court also outlawed block booking, a practice whereby the exhibitor is forced to take all of a company's pictures to get any of them, the fixing of admissions prices, unfair runs and clearances, and discriminatory pricing and purchasing arrangements. With this decision, the industry the moguls had built—the vertically integrated studio—died. If the loss of foreign revenues shook the financial foundation of the industry, the end of block booking shattered the weakened buttress.

One result of the *Paramount* decision and the end of the monopoly of film making by the majors was an increase in independent productions. Yet despite a host of innovations and gimmicks—including 3-D, Cinerama, stereophonic sound, and cinemascope—attendance continued to fall.

Hollywood also suffered from Congressional probes of communist influence in the film industry. In the late 1930s, the House of Representatives had established the Un-American Activities Committee (HUAC) to combat subversive right-wing and left-wing movements. Its history was less than distinguished. From the first it tended to see subversive Communists everywhere at work in American society. HUAC even announced that the Boy Scouts were Communist infiltrated. During the late 1940s and early 1950s it picked up the tempo of its investigation, which it conducted in well-publicized sessions. Twice during this period the committee traveled to Hollywood to investigate Communist infiltration of the film industry.

HUAC first went to Hollywood in 1947. Although it did not find the party line preached in the movies, it did call a group of radical screenwriters and producers into its sessions to testify. Asked if they were Communists, the Hollywood Ten refused to answer questions about their political beliefs. As Ring Lardner, Jr., one of the ten, said, "I could answer . . . but if I did, I would hate myself in the morning." The witnesses believed that the First Amendment protected them. In the politically charged late 1940s, however, their rights were not protected. Those who refused to divulge their political affiliations were charged with contempt of Congress, sent to prison for a year, and blacklisted.

HUAC returned to Hollywood in 1951. This time it called hundreds of witnesses from both the political right and the political left. Conservatives told HUAC that Hollywood was littered with "Commies." Walt Disney even recounted attempts to have Mickey Mouse follow the party line. Among the radicals, some talked but most did not. To cooperate with HUAC entailed informing on friends and political acquaintances. Again, those who refused to name names found themselves unemployed and unemployable. All told, about 250 directors, writers, and actors were blacklisted. In 1948, writer Lillian Hellman denounced the industry's moral cowardice in scathing terms: "Naturally, men scared to make pictures about the American Negro, men who only in the last year allowed the word Jew to be spoken in a picture, who took more than ten years to make an anti-fascist picture, these are frightened men and you pick frightened men to frighten first. Judas goats, they'll lead the others to slaughter for you."

The HUAC hearings and blacklistings discouraged Hollywood from producing politically controversial films. Fear that a motion picture dealing with the life of Hiawatha might be regarded as Communist propaganda led Monogram Studio to shelve the project. As *The New York Times* explained: "It was Hiawatha's efforts as a peacemaker among warring Indian tribes that gave Monogram particular concern. These it was decided might cause the picture to be regarded as a message for peace and therefore helpful to present communist designs." The hearings persuaded Hollywood to produce musicals, biblical epics, and other politically neutral films.

The HUAC hearings also persuaded Hollywood producers to make fifty strongly anticommunist films between 1947 and 1954. Most were second-rate movies starring third-rate actors. The films assured Americans that Communists were thoroughly bad people—they didn't have children, they exhaled cigarette smoke too slowly, they murdered their "friends," and they went berserk when arrested. As one film historian has commented, the Communists in these films even looked alike; most were "apt to be exceptionally haggard or disgracefully pudgy," and there was certainly "something terribly wrong with a woman if her slip straps showed through her blouse." These films had an impact. They seemed to confirm HUAC's position that subversives lurked in every shadow.

At the same time that HUAC was conducting its investigations of Communist subversion, moral censorship of the movies began to decline. In 1949, Vittorio de Sica's *The Bicycle Thief* became the first film to be successfully exhibited without a seal of approval. Despite its glimpses of a brothel and a boy urinating, this Italian film's neo-realist portrait of a poor man's search for his stolen bicycle received strong editorial support from newspapers and was shown in many theaters.

In 1952, the Supreme Court reversed a 1915 decision and extended First Amendment protections of free speech to the movies. The landmark case overturned an effort by censors in New York State to ban Roberto Rosselini's film *The Miracle* on grounds of sacrilege. In addition, the court decreed that filmmakers could challenge censors' findings. Otto Preminger's sex comedy *The Moon Is Blue,* appearing the next year, was the first major American film to be released without the code's seal. The Legion of Decency condemned the film for its use of the words "virgin" and "pregnant," but efforts to boycott the film fizzled and the film proved to be a box office success. In 1966, the film industry abandoned the Production Code, replacing it with a film rating system that is still in force.

New Directions in Post-War Film

During the early 1940s, a genre known as film noir had arisen. Though film noir received its name from French film critics and was heavily influenced by German expressionist filmmaking techniques, it stands out as one of the most original and innovative American movie genres. Characterized by sexual insecurity, aberrant psychology, and nightmarish camera work, film noir depicted a world of threatening shadows and ambiguities—a world of obsession, alienation, corruption, deceit, blurred identity, paranoia, dementia, weak men, cold-blooded femme fatales, and inevitably murder. Its style consisted of looming close ups, oblique camera angles, and crowded compositions that produced a sense of entrapment. The film's narratives were rarely straightforward; they contained frequent flashbacks and voice overs. Film noir belonged to a time of indefinable anxieties and apprehensions: the disorientation of returning GIs, fear of nuclear weapons, paranoia generated by the early Cold War, and fears aroused by the changing role of women.

After the war, Hollywood's audience not only shrank but fragmented into distinct subgroups. An audience interested in serious social problem films expanded. Independent filmmakers produced a growing number addressing such problems as ethnic and racial prejudice, antisemitism, the sufferings of maltreated mental patients, and the problems of alcohol and drug addiction.

Although the early postwar period is often regarded as the golden age of the

American family, the popular family melodramas of the 1940s and 1950s reveal a pattern of deeply troubled family relationships. These films depicted sexual frustration; anxious parents; cold, domineering mothers; alienated children; insensitive or fretful fathers; defiant adolescents; and loveless marriages. In part this obsession with the ills of marriage and family life reflected a popularized form of psychoanalytic thought, which offered simplistic formulas to explain human behavior. Films of the early postwar period laboriously repeated the argument that sexual frustration inevitably leads to neurosis and that harsh, neglectful, or uncomprehending parents produce alienated children. It was far from the soothing and funny fare available on TV.

According to many of the popular films of the period, family problems come of a lack of familial love. Love was treated as the answer to problems ranging from juvenile delinquency to schizophrenia. Adolescents in such films as *Splendor in the Grass* are rebellious because their parents "won't listen." Husbands and wives drink too much or stray sexually because they cannot communicate adequately with their spouses. Still, the underlying message is hopeful. Even the most severe family problems can be resolved by love, understanding, and perseverance.

At the same time that it turned out serious social problem films about drugs and family life, Hollywood produced movies that explored disturbing changes in the lives of American youth. Films such as *The Wild One* (1954), *Blackboard Jungle* (1955), and *Rebel Without a Cause* (1955) portrayed adolescents as budding criminals, emerging homosexuals, potential fascists, and pathological misfits—everything but perfectly normal kids. On close inspection, cultural critics concluded that something was indeed wrong with American youth, who like Tony in *I Was a Teenage Werewolf* (1957) seemed closer to uncontrollable beasts than to civilized adults. As Tony tells a psychiatrist, "I say things, I do things—I don't know why." Critics were preoccupied with finding reasons for adolescent moral decline. J. Edgar Hoover, head of the FBI, linked a rise in juvenile delinquency to the decline in the influence of family, home, church, and local community institutions. Frederic Wertham, a psychiatrist, emphasized the pernicious influence of comic books. He believed that crime and horror comic books fostered racism, fascism, and abuse of women.

In fact, these fears were grossly overstated. During the late forties and fifties, juvenile delinquency was not increasing. But changes were taking place, and popular movies suggest some of the responses to these broader social transformations. In retrospect, it appears that the proliferation of juvenile delinquency films reflected adult anxieties and also the growth of a distinct market among adolescents who liked being seen as outlaws. During the 1950s, a new youth culture began to arise, with its distinctive rock-and-roll, dress, and language, as well as a disdain, somewhat affected, for the world of conventional adulthood. Marlon Brando captures the attitude when to the question, "What are you rebelling against?" he responds: "Whadda ya got?"

The growing popularity of science fiction thrillers reflected not only the emergence of the youth market but the spread of a certain paranoid style during the Cold War years. Historian Richard Hofstadter defined the paranoid style:

> The distinguishing thing about the paranoid style is . . . that its exponents see . . . a "vast" or "gigantic" conspiracy as the motive force in historical

events ... The paranoid spokesman sees the fate of this conspiracy in apocalyptic terms—he traffics in the birth and death of whole worlds, whole political orders, whole systems of human values.

As Nora Sayre has shown, science fiction films of the fifties can be viewed as allegories of the Cold War and its byproducts at home: the fear of domestic subversion, the pressures for conformity in a mass society. Unlike the humorous, quasi-religious science fiction of the 1970s and 1980s, the films of the fifties conveyed paranoia and foreboding, the possibility of mind-control, the after-effects of atomic bomb tests.

The "New" Hollywood

As the 1960s began, few would have guessed that the decade would be one of the most socially conscious and stylistically innovative in Hollywood's history. Among the most popular films at the decade's start were Doris Day's romantic comedy *That Touch of Mink* (1962) and the epic blockbusters *The Longest Day* (1962), *Lawrence of Arabia* (1962), and *Cleopatra* (1963). Yet as the decade progressed, Hollywood radically shifted focus and began to produce an increasing number of anti-establishment films, laced with social commentary, directed at the growing youth market.

By the early 1960s, an estimated eighty percent of the filmgoing population was between the ages of sixteen and twenty-five. At first, the major studios largely ignored this audience, leaving it in the hands of smaller studios like American International Pictures, which produced a string of cheaply made horror movies, beach blanket movies—like *Bikini Beach* (1964) and *How to Stuff a Wild Bikini* (1965)—and motorcycle gang pictures like *The Wild Angels* (1966). Two films released in 1967—*Bonnie and Clyde* and *The Graduate*—awoke Hollywood to the size and influence of the youth audience. *Bonnie and Clyde,* the story of two Depression-era bank robbers, was advertised with the slogan: "They're young, they're in love, they kill people." Inspired by such French New Wave pictures as *Breathless* (1960), the film aroused intense controversy for romanticizing gangsters and transforming them into social rebels. A celebration of youthful rebellion also appeared in *The Graduate,* which grossed more money than all but two previously made films. A young college graduate rejects a hypocritical society and the traditional values of his parents—and the promise of a career in plastics—and finds salvation in love.

A number of the most influential films of the late sixties and early seventies revised older film genres—like the war film, the crime film, and the western—and rewrote Hollywood's earlier versions of American history. *Little Big Man* reexamined the nineteenth-century Indian wars, *Patton* presented World War II, and *M*A*S*H* reconsidered the Korean War in light of America's experience in Vietnam. *The Wild Bunch* (1969) and *McCabe and Mrs. Miller* (1971) offered radical reappraisals of the mythology of the American frontier. Francis Ford Coppola's *The Godfather* (1972) revised and enhanced the gangster genre by transforming it into a critical commentary on an immigrant family's pursuit of the American dream.

During the mid- and late-1970s, the mood of American films again shifted sharply. Following the political mood of the country, Hollywood turned right.

Unlike the highly politicized films of the early part of the decade, the most popular films of the late 1970s and early 1980s were escapist blockbusters like *Star Wars* (1977), *Superman* (1978), and *Raiders of the Lost Ark* (1981), featuring spectacular special effects, action, and simplistic conflicts between good and evil; inspirational tales of the indomitable human spirit, like *Rocky* (1976); or nostalgia for a more innocent past, like *Animal House* (1978) and *Grease* (1978). Glamorous outlaws like *Bonnie and Clyde* were replaced by law and order avengers like *Dirty Harry* and *Robocop*. Sports—long regarded as a sure box officer loser—became a major Hollywood obsession, with movies like *Hoosiers, Chariots of Fire, Karate Kid,* and *The Mighty Ducks* celebrating competitiveness and victory. Movies which offered a tragic or subversive perspectives on American society, like *The Godfather* or *Chinatown*, were replaced by more upbeat, undemanding films, and especially by comedies, featuring such actors as Dan Ackroyd, Chevy Chase, Eddie Murphy, Bill Murray, and John Candy.

Critics blamed this trend toward "deliberate anti-realism" on economic changes within the film industry. In 1966, Gulf and Western Industries executed a takeover of Paramount and the conglomerization of the film industry began. In 1967, United Artists merged with Transamerica Corporation; in 1969 Kinney Services acquired Warner Brothers. In one sense the takeovers were logical. Conglomerates wanted to acquire interests in businesses that serviced American leisure needs. The heads of the conglomerates, however, had no idea how to make successful motion pictures. Too often they believed that successful movies could be mass produced, that statisticians could discover a scientific method for making box office hits.

A trend toward the creation of interlocking media companies, encompassing movies, magazines, newspapers, and books accelerated in 1985 when the Department of Justice overturned the 1948 anti-trust decree that had ended vertical integration within the film industry. As a result, many of the major studios were acquired by large media and entertainment corporations, like Sony, which purchased Columbia Pictures, Time-Warner (which owns *Time* magazine, Simon & Schuster publishers, and Warner Brothers), and Rupert Murdoch, whose holdings include HarperCollins publishers, the Fox television network, and Twentieth Century Fox. At the same time that these large entertainment conglomerates arose, many smaller independent producers like Lorimar and De Laurentis disappeared.

Nevertheless, film continued to address important issues. Many movies explored problems of romance, family, gender, and sexuality, aspects of life radically altered by the social transformations of the 1960s and early 1970s. Certainly, some films tried to evade the profound changes that had taken place in gender relations. *An Officer and a Gentleman* featured an old-fashioned screen romance, and *Flashdance* presented an updated version of the Cinderella story. *10* and *Splash* depicted male fantasies about relationships with beautiful, utterly compliant women. But many other popular films addressed such serious questions as the conflict between family responsibilities and personal needs (for example, *Kramer v. Kramer*) or women's need to develop their independence: *An Unmarried Woman, Desperately Seeking Susan,* and *Thelma and Louise*. Movies like *Boyz in the Hood, Grand Canyon, Do the Right Thing, Jungle Fever,* and *Menace II Society* examined social issues politicians and news journalists had abandoned. Film was prepared to portray the racial gulf separating blacks and whites, the conditions in the nation's inner cities, the fate of single parent families, the fact of police brutality and urban violence.

Not until the late 1970s did the Vietnam War begin to be seriously examined on the screen. Although many films of the late sixties and early seventies savored the bitter aftertaste of the war, the conflict itself remained strikingly absent from the screen. Hollywood, like the country as a whole, had difficulty adjusting to the grim legacy of a lost and troubling war. During the conflict, Hollywood produced only a single film dealing with Vietnam—John Wayne's *The Green Berets*. Modelled along the lines of such World War II combat epics as *The Sands of Iwo Jima* and earlier John Wayne westerns like *The Alamo,* the film portrayed decent Americans struggling to defend an embattled outpost along the Laotian border nicknamed Dodge City.

Then, in the 1970s and 1980s, the returning Vietnam War veteran found his way into film. He was first portrayed as a dangerous killer, a deranged ticking time bomb that could explode at any time and in any place. He was Travis Bickle in *Taxi Driver* (1976), a veteran wound tight to the point of snapping. Or he was Colonel Kurtz in *Apocalypse Now* (1979), who adjusts to the madness of war by going mad himself. Not until the end of the '70s did popular culture begin to treat the Vietnam War veteran more seriously than as a madman produced by the war. *Coming Home* (1978) and *The Deer Hunter* (1978) began the popular rehabilitation of the veteran, and such films as *Missing in Action* (1984) and *Rambo: First Blood II* (1985) transformed the veteran into a misunderstood hero. In *First Blood* (1982), the opening film in the Rambo series, John Rambo captures the pain of the returning veterans: "It wasn't my war—you asked me, I didn't ask you . . . and I did what I had to do to win. . . . Then I came back to the world and I see all those maggots at the airport, protesting me, spitting on me, calling me a baby-killer. . . ."

Some films, like the Rambo series, present the exploits of one-man armies or vigilantes armed to the teeth, who had been kept from winning the war because of government cowardice and betrayal. Another group of Vietnam War films, including *Go Tell the Spartans, Platoon, Casualties of War,* and *Born on the Fourth of July,* portray innocent, naive "grunts"—the ground troops who actually fought the war—losing their beliefs, coping with the breakdown of unit cohesion, and struggling to survive and sustain humanity and integrity in the midst of war.

Hollywood Today

In a 1992 bestseller *Hollywood vs. America,* Michael Medved, co-host of public television's *Sneak Previews,* describes Hollywood as a "poison factory," befouling America's moral atmosphere and assaulting the country's "most cherished values." Today's films, he argues, use their enormous capacity to influence opinion by glamorizing violence, maligning marriage, mocking authority, promoting sexual promiscuity, ridiculing religion, and bombarding viewers with an endless stream of profanity, gratuitous sex, and loutish forms of behavior. Once the movies offered sentiment, elegance, and romance. Now, Medved contends, ideologically-motivated producers and directors promote their own divisive agenda: against religion, against the family, against the military.

In fact, the picture is more complicated than Medved suggests. As film critic David Denby has observed, abandonment of the Production Code in 1966 did indeed increase the amount of sex, violence, and profanity on the screen; but particularly in the 1980s and 1990s, Hollywood has also increased the amount of family entertainment it offers, including feature-length cartoons like *Aladdin* and *Beauty and the Beast;* family comedies, among them *Honey, I Shrunk the Kids;* and affirmative portrayals of the teaching profession, such as *Dead Poet's Society* and *Stand and Deliver.* At the same time that Indiana Jones or the *Back to the Future* trilogy merely exploited history as a backdrop for action and adventure, such films as *Glory* and *Malcolm X* seriously examined critical issues in America's past. Independent directors released a growing number of idiosyncratic and sensitive films, such as *The Crying Game.* New voices were also heard. Female movie makers, like Penny Marshall and Susan Seidelman, and African-American film makers, like Spike Lee, have received an unprecedented opportunity to bring fresh viewpoints to the screen.

Nevertheless, as the movie industry enters its second century, Medved is not alone in complaining that quality has declined. A basic problem facing today's Hollywood is the rapidly rising cost of making and marketing a movie: an average of $40 million. The immense cost of producing movies has led the studios to seek guaranteed hits: blockbuster loaded with high-tech special effects, sequels, and remakes of earlier successful movies and even old TV shows. Hollywood has also sought to cope with rising costs by focusing ever more intently on its core audiences. Since the mid-1980s, the moviegoing audience has continued to decrease in size. Ticket sales fell from 1.2 billion in 1983 to 950 million in 1992, the biggest drop occurring among adults. The single largest group of moviegoers now consists of teenage boys, who are particularly attracted to thrills, violence, and crude laughs. And since over half of Hollywood's profits are earned overseas, the industry has concentrated much of its energy on crude action films easily understood by an international audience, featuring stars like Arnold Schwartzenegger and Sylvester Stallone.

For a century, the movie industry has been the nation's most important purveyor of culture and entertainment to the masses, playing a critical role in the shift from Victorian to distinctively modern, consumer values; from a verbal to a visual culture; from a society rooted in islands of localities and ethnic groups to a commercialized mass culture. The movies have taught Americans how to kiss, make love, conceive of gender roles, and understand their place in the world. Whether in the theater or in television and video releases, films will long continue to serve as the nation's preeminent instrument of cultural expression—reflecting and also shaping values and cultural ideals.

PART I

Charlie Chaplin, *The Gold Rush*

THE SILENT ERA

1

INTRODUCTION

Intolerance and the Rise of the Feature Film

Intolerance (1916), the great film director D.W. Griffith's epic attack on bigotry throughout history, was American silent cinema's greatest artistic achievement— and a ruinous box-office failure.

Created in response to charges that Griffith's notorious *Birth of a Nation* (1915) was anti-Negro, as well as to protest efforts to censor that earlier epic, *Intolerance* interweaves four stories that illustrate "how hatred and intolerance, through all the ages, have battled against love and charity": the fall of Babylon, the crucifixion of Christ, the St. Bartholomew's Day Massacre of the French Huguenots in 1572, and the wrenching poverty and exploitation of the modern American urban worker. Initially, the silent epic attracted large crowds; soon, however, increasingly bewildered audiences shrank.

In a masterful display of film editing, director D.W. Griffith cuts among four distinct stories: a mountain girl's struggle to warn the Babylonian king Belshazzar of the imminent arrival of the Persian army; Christ's march toward Calvary; a French Protestant's effort to rescue his fiancée from French mercenaries intent on killing the Huguenots; and, in the modern story, labor strikers battling the state militia, crowded tenements, wretched slums, an unjust legal system, and intrusive social reformers. Linking these four stories is a recurring shot of Lillian Gish rocking a cradle, accompanied by lines from Walt Whitman:

Out of the cradle endlessly rocking.
Today as yesterday, endlessly rocking, ever bringing the same joys and sorrows.

A dramatic illustration of film's artistic possibilities, the picture cost at least $300,000 to make—more than three times the cost of *Birth of a Nation*. Much of this was spent on the grandiose Babylonian set, perhaps the most famous film setting ever built. But in the end the film disappointed as spectacle and went unheard as message. Its plea for peace and tolerance was ignored as the nation crept closer to involvement in World War I.

Intolerance was only the most dramatic example of how rapidly the movies had matured during their first two decades. As early as 1909, primitive films—drawing upon the conventions of vaudeville and featuring sight gags, simple skits, pranks and practical jokes, chases and rescues, and scenes of everyday life—began to give way to the modern feature film. The earliest films had been quite brief, usually involving a single shot, often viewed from a distance. Newer films were longer and more complex in structure. Drawing inspiration from the novel and the dramatic theater rather than vaudeville, these new films emphasized storytelling, and were likely to fix on individual psychology and personality. The new feature films offered a distinctive aesthetic and visual style as well: lighting, camera angles, editing, framing, and camera placement were designed to tell the story as clearly and unobtrusively as possible. To focus the viewers' attention on the film's narrative, directors kept camera angles at eye level and framed shots to keep action in the screen's center. Directors used dissolves and fade outs to convey the passage of time, and cross-cutting to link chains of separate events. Styles of acting changed as well. Exaggerated pantomime increasingly gave way to more restrained forms of expression; emotions more and more were conveyed by facial gestures rather than by elaborate hand gestures.

D.W. Griffith contributed greatly to the creation of the modern narrative film. But in important respects, his epic *Intolerance* departed from the emerging conventions of the classical Hollywood style. Indeed, the film's financial failure may have been due to its radical deviation from audiences' notions of what constituted a feature film. At a time when audiences expected movies to tell an entertaining story, Griffith's goal was to send a clear message. His film consisted of four separate allegories, featuring unnamed characters (like the "Mountain Girl" or "The Friendless One" or "The Dear One") at a time when viewers expected to see a unified narrative focusing on individual characters. This refusal to individualize his characters may have been a large reason for its failure to grip its viewers.

2

SILENT FILM AS SOCIAL CRITICISM

Front Page Movies
Kay Sloan

Many people conceive of silent films as pictures of innocence, filled with gentlemanly tramps and virginal beauties. But many early directors ripped their plots directly from the headlines of newspapers. As film historian Kay Sloan shows in this essay, early cinema directly addressed many of the social problems raised by Progressive Era reformers.

Sheiks, flappers, comic tramps, and vamps: silent film has left a legacy of bizarrely colorful images preserved in the popular mind by nostalgia. Yet in the early days of the primitive film industry, the cinema treated social problems in a way that was, ironically, as fantastic as the glamorous stars and tinsel world of Hollywood's later silver screen. The earliest audiences pushed their coins across box office windows to watch melodramas and comedies that often celebrated characters who literally animated the social and political dilemmas of the Progressive Era. The cinema turned these dilemmas into fairy tales of the day. Greedy corporate tycoons, villainous landlords, corrupt politicians, flamboyant suffragettes, and striking workers flickered across the bedsheets that sometimes sufficed for screens in hastily created moviehouses just after the turn of the century.

This is the story of that early silent cinema, a largely precorporate, inconsistently censored film industry that had its roots not in Hollywood but in the nation's inner cities. It is an important story both for the vision it provides of how entertainment can deliver social problems to the public, and for the historical portrait it paints of America just after the turn of the century. In the era before World War I, moviegoing often involved paying a nickel or a dime to watch a series of short one or two reelers in the cramped quarters of storefront theaters that populated the urban ghettoes. The elaborate movie "palace" was, for the most part, an anomaly; so was the feature film. Film companies were small business operations that might shoot several one-reel films every week in a makeshift studio. This was a time when the traditions of the cinema were in the process of formation, when both the subject matter and the form of film were in flux. Inventions rapidly became conventions that helped shore up a sense of social order, as a new art form began to link human desire with the needs of society.

In New York, Chicago, Boston, and in an obscure community called Hollywood out in California, small film companies often turned to the literary and political milieu of the muckrakers and the Progressives for storylines. The "muckraking" cinema cranked out stories that entertained primarily working-class audiences who could afford the five- or ten-cent price of admission to the nickelodeons. There, seated on wooden folding chairs, moviegoers watched graphic portrayals of America's social problems, some of which were part of their everyday lives.

In 1910, Walter Fitch, a film critic for the *Moving Picture World,* one of the film industry's first trade journals, stepped back from the immediacy of the new medium—it was, indeed, a cinema in search of itself—to take a long look at its potential and its possibilities. Filmmakers, mused Fitch, "may play on every pipe in the great organ of humanity." The early cinema did indeed attempt to compose euphonious sounds from the cacophony of the era. With titles such as *Capital Versus Labor, The Suffragettes' Revenge, A Corner in Wheat, The Usurer's Grip, The Girl Strike Leader,* or *The Reform Candidate,* all released in the first fifteen years of the twentieth century, the cinema championed the cause of labor, lobbied against political "bosses," and often gave dignity to the struggles of the urban poor. Conversely, other films satirized suffragists, ridiculed labor organizers, and celebrated America's corporate leaders in antilabor melodramas that the American Federation of Labor denounced and boycotted.

The period itself encompassed vast contradictions. While socialists such as Eugene Debs and Mother Jones fought for drastic changes in the nation's economic system, the new industrial leaders attempted paternalistic, philanthropic solutions to labor activism. At the same time that radicals pushed for fundamental changes in American life, middle-class reformers lobbied for legislation on labor and women's rights that would offer moderate change within the existing structure. Progressive thinkers such as the economist Richard T. Ely and the sociologists Edward A. Ross and Thorstein Veblen condemned what they saw as the dynamics of inequality in America; their voices became part of the milieu of protest in which the movies were born. Others like Louis D. Brandeis, later a Supreme Court justice, indicted the banking system he analyzed in *Other People's Money,* and successfully challenged corporate America in the courts. Muckraking journalists exposed the horrors of child labor and the corruption of political machinery in the nation's magazines and newspapers. Articles by such investigative journalists decried "the shame of the cities" and their failure to adequately meet the needs of their citizens. Upton Sinclair created a national furor by exposing unsanitary meat-packing conditions in his novel *The Jungle;* Frank Norris took on railroad tycoons in *The Octopus*. Lincoln Steffens's articles for *Everybody's Magazine,* with their prostitutes, gamblers, policemen "on the take," corporate tycoons, and greedy landlords, provided an array of stories that pointed to the need for social change.

It was a volatile, exciting world for the new lively entertainment form of the motion picture to enter. Conflicts that challenged the foundations of society found their way into the cinema as film companies seized on the news in the headlines for rich melodramatic and comic material. They also documented contemporary events in early newsreels. In an era long before the advent of television, motion pictures served as news reportage and propaganda at the same time that they revolutionized entertainment. Savvy political figures quickly learned to use the new medium to advertise themselves. In 1906, William Randolph Hearst made talking films of his campaign speeches to circulate in areas in which his personal travel was difficult. Performing a function similar to that of a modern television reporter, the filmmaker Siegmund Lubin released films in 1908 reporting the campaigns of the political rivals William Jennings Bryan and John W. Kern. But, though the films showing news events or national political campaigns served as important justifications for the existence of the often-criticized new medium of the motion picture, the fictions of those actual conflicts told a richer story about the climate of the period. The fictionalization of conflicts allowed an injection of fantasy and ideology into the stories. Films interpreted the nation's headlines in dramatic visual images that at once persuaded and entertained. The comedies, melodramas, and occasional westerns about labor conflict, tenement poverty, or political corruption reveal through fantasy an America torn with ideological conflict.

Often, special interest groups made their own motion pictures in collaboration with film industrialists. An important part of the process of translating the news involved opening the channels of filmmaking to groups advocating change. The earliest film audiences watched motion pictures made or sponsored by groups like the National Child Labor Committee, the National American Woman Suffrage Association, and even by individuals such as Upton Sinclair and the Progressive New York Govenor, William Sulzer, who produced and starred in his own melodrama in 1914. Other Progressive activists joined them. For instance, the birth control activist Margaret Sanger made a melodrama to promote the basic civil liberties that she was repeatedly denied during the Progressive Era.

Conservatives as well as Progressives seized on the new medium as a way to dramatize their ideas. Organizations such as the National Association of Manufacturers and the Russell Sage Foundation made film melodramas to promote corporate paternalism. Such films circulated through the nation's moviehouses as if they were no different from slapslick comedies, westerns, and historical dramas. Distributors offered such politically oriented films to exhibitors along with material produced solely for entertainment. Often, a film reviewer would suggest to exhibitors that a motion picture with a prolabor message, for instance, or a plea for women's rights would be popular in areas where such ideas were already accepted. Essentially, the early audiences paid their nickels and dimes to see the political tracts of special interest groups on the same program as less controversial material.

Regardless of the ideological message, however, the vision that commercial film could serve as a vehicle for overt political causes seems startling—even revolutionary—today. For instance, Progressive Era woman suffragists made melodramas in collaboration with Hollywood film companies. Certainly it is difficult to imagine a modern day equivalent: the National Organization of Women collaborating with Twentieth Century Fox in the early 1980s to make a melodrama starring Meryl Streep or Jane Fonda promoting the Equal Rights Amendment might be such an event. By contemporary standards, such a film would be an utter aberration from Hollywood practices. Yet in the early twentieth century, such was the notion of what film might—and even should—be. Film became a vehicle for overtly presenting social problems to the public.

The rise of the feature length film during the World War I years contributed to the decline of the numerous early social problem films. Since demand for motion pictures dictated that the companies turn out films rapidly, it was crucial that story ideas be readily found. It was easier for filmmakers to take risks about controversial issues in an era when the companies were releasing, as one Hollywood veteran remembers, at least "one reel a week." When film companies turned out several short films a month, the production of a potentially controversial film was far less of an economic risk than it would be in the later age of the blockbuster. Even without the encouragement and participation of special interest groups, the young film companies made melodramas and comedies that exploited the issues splashed across the nation's headlines.

One of the most notorious of these films bore the innocent title of *Why?*. Released in 1913, *Why?* shocked critics with its tale of corrupt elites and its vision of workers revolting against capitalism in America. The film's hero, a fiery-eyed immigrant with wild hair, dreamed of revenge against the wealthy classes who feasted while enslaved workers starved. The three parts of *Why?* contained episodes of capitalists and workers shooting it out with revolvers over child labor, corporate greed, and class inequality. In a scene that could have been scripted by Marx himself, the capitalists turn into sacks of gold when shot. Released by the American arm of the independent French company Eclair Films, *Why?* culminated with workers burning down Manhattan. The blazes, ironically, had been handpainted red by workers for the capitalist film company. The film ended with the Woolworth building still burning, violating one of the ideological tenets of the bourgeois narrative closure that flames, like western bad guys or melodramatic villains, have to die in the end. Instead of restoring responsibility and order, the film simply left its audience in a liminal world that granted power and legitimacy to unleashed desire. "Socialist doctrine!" cried one outraged reviewer.

Why?'s virtual celebration of anarchy frightened censors as well as critics. Early censors feared the political content of films as much as their occasional sexual content. The potential of the cinema to champion such organized violence disturbed Frederic C. Howe, the chairman of the National Board of Censorship of Motion Pictures. That organization had been formed by the filmmakers themselves in 1909 to discourage "immoral" or "lurid" material that had roused criticism from more traditional sectors of society. Howe feared the mounting success of radical, politically oriented moving pictures. He was a liberal reformer, but hardly a radical. Despite local outcries over the supposed "immorality" of the movies, Howe suggested that the political role of film was potentially as threatening to society as were its challenges to a Victorian moral code.

Particularly since the early films touched the sentiments of masses of people, including the millions of newly arrived immigrants to whom the English printed word was still a mystery, they elicited condemnation from those, like Howe, who feared the power of the motion picture over those in the ghetto. Motion pictures, noted one journalist in 1908, had become "both a clubhouse and an academy for the workingman." The class of people attending motion pictures, stated another observer delicately, "are not of the rich." At their outset, motion pictures found audiences primarily among the many Americans whose lives were dominated by the uncertainties of poverty and the cultural ruptures of immigration.

Thus Frederic Howe worried about the content of films in 1914. The films that "tended to excite class feeling or . . . tend to bring discredit upon the agencies of the government," wrote Howe, could lead to a time "when the movie . . . becomes the daily press of industrial groups, of classes, of Socialism, syndicalism, and radical opinion.

Howe's fears, of course, remained unfounded. The revolutionary content of *Why?* was an anomaly among the early social problem films. The young film companies themselves attempted to make their business more "respectable," and broaden the appeal of motion pictures to the middle classes. They made the social problem films as part of that process, with the notion that such films might be seen as "educational" and "uplifting."

It was a cinematic role encouraged by critics. In 1913, one film journalist suggested that the cinema might be a weapon "in the battle against child labor, white-slavery, labor-conflicts, and vice development." He suggested that film should take up the subjects headlined on the front pages of the nation's newspapers and "expose injustice, cruelty, and suffering in all their naked ugliness." This critic suggested that both the film industry's need for stories and America's pressing social problems might be settled if only the filmmakers would turn their attention to social issues. But the solution to such issues, he emphasized, must be calm, reasoned change, not the revolutionary message of a film like *Why?*.

Such liberal film critics played an important role in channeling film into a vehicle for middle-class reforms. They pointed out causes that might be taken up in melodrama and applauded those films that did crusade. *The Moving Picture World*'s Louis Reeves Harris promoted the role that film could play in pointing out the need for social reform, and he denounced what he called "the desire for power on the part of the ruling classes." Filmmakers, he urged, should pay attention to such inequities in corporate society. The cinema might act as a cultural watchdog, appealing for responsibility from all levels of society. One issue demanding treatment by the moving pictures, suggested Harrison, was child labor—another was what he applauded as women's "broadening knowledge and experience." The expression of those issues could not only strengthen the nation, but the role of film in it.

In 1912, Harrison reminded filmmakers that the often-denigrated cinema might serve as a tool for "uplifting" the masses. He offered a virtual litany of themes for the melodrama that expressed the interests of both the era's reformers and some early filmmakers:

> The social battle for justice to those who do the world's work, the adjustment of compensation to labor, the right of common people to liberty and the pursuit of happiness, the betterment of humanity through the prevention of crime rather than its cure, the prevention of infant mortality, and the prevention of hoggishness wherever theatrical trusts will permit, the self-conflict between material tendency and spiritual clarification, all these furnish subjects of widespread interest which the dramatist may handle with or without gloves.

The film industry increasingly addressed the issues suggested by Harrison. In 1914, one film director boasted that he got the "best points for [his] work from the newspapers," turning the turmoil of the era into comedy and melodrama.

Concerned that the cinema raised subversive questions, Howe neglected the important role it played in laying them to rest. *Why?*'s radical solution to class conflict was, not surprisingly, rare cinema. It represented the starkest challenge to the nation's economic powers—the wheat speculators, tenement owners, loan sharks or captains of industry. More typically, the films dealt with social problems in a way that muted their critiques of economic or social injustice. They called for careful reforms or fatalistic surrenders to uncontrollable "natural" forces that doled out troubles and misfortunes. Such films proved that the radically new entertainment form of the cinema could act as a conservative force in the emerging industrial society.

For instance, the Thomas Edison Company's *The Usurer's Grip* was a modern-day fairy tale set in the tenements. Funded by the Russell Sage Foundation in 1912, the film warned audiences about unscrupulous money lenders who thrived on the poverty stricken, hounding them further and further into financial desperation. The film's hero and heroine found themselves in mounting debt to a usurer, but they were saved at last by an understanding businessman who directed them to the loan division of the Russell Sage Foundation. There they were rescued by the paternalism promoted by Sage's vision of benevolent capitalism. *The Usurer's Grip* was a self-serving advertisement for the Sage Foundation. Such early films precursed modern television advertising by blending entertainment with commercial messages. Through melodrama, the Edison Company and the Russell Sage Foundation advertised direct social reform and suggested that philanthropic measures might remedy urban poverty.

Increasingly, the early films moved from primitive one or two reelers exploiting class conflict to more sophisticated films with complicated plots. At times, they advocated specific reforms. Film began to shift from the sensationalism of muckraking issues into serious calls for reform through "enlightenment"—whether it be better management to assuage striking workers, calls for woman suffrage, the abolition of child labor, poor tenement conditions, or the illegality of birth control. Film industrialists tried to establish the middle-class nature of the cinema by allowing reform groups or special interest groups access to the medium. In 1912, the National Association of Manufacturers (NAM) collaborated with Thomas Edison's Company to make a propagandistic melodrama on factory safety called *The Crime of Carelessness*. It was written by the Progressive writer James Oppenheim, who was quickly earning a reputation as a writer of what the *New York Times* called "social films." His first film for the Edison Company, titled *Hope*, had dealt with the problem of tuberculosis. With *The Crime of Carelessness,* he turned to the more controversial issue of problems in the workplace. The film laid equal blame for hazardous working conditions on workers and negligent owners—but insidiously punished a careless worker for a factory fire. The problems of the workplace, then, might be resolved merely by responsibility on the part of individual employees. It was, wrote the *New York Times* critic, a "long and stirring drama," one of a line of Oppenheim's "social films." NAM's film, of course, did more than link industrial problems with careless workers. It also linked the interests of the film industry with those of the larger corporate interests represented by NAM.

A similar theme emerged in the Vitagraph Company's *Capital Versus Labor,* an exposé of labor problems made in 1910. Punctuated by bloody scenes of rioting workers battling company-hired thugs, the film suggested that the strikers had legitimate grievances to air. But the workers alone were powerless to change their situation. The eventual "happy ending" came not through the organized protests or negotiations of labor unions, but through the intervention of the church. The violence in *Capital Versus Labor* continued until a minister finally calmed the mobs and convinced the greedy capitalist to compromise with his workers. The film thus revealed the futility of rioting in the streets while it still acknowledged the validity of the strikers' complaints. From such plots came a dual statement about workers in America: while the films granted them dignity and self-worth as individuals, it also rendered them and their organizations powerless. *The Crime of Carelessness* and *Capital Versus Labor* serve as examples of how workers might be portrayed as irresponsible individuals who are ultimately dependent on the good graces of their generous bosses.

Such films relied on the "happy ending," which provided audiences with continuity and faith in "the system. . . ."

The headlines were powerful material in a time when muckraking journalists and novelists like Ida Tarbell and Upton Sinclair constantly probed the underside of the "American Dream." Both Sinclair and Tarbell were among the era's crusaders who made their own films. Their cinematic efforts reflected a period in film history when the motion pictures were seen as a medium that might lie open to the public, particularly to those with a cause. Tarbell, who had condemned John L. Rockefeller when she exposed the ruthless practices of the Standard Oil Company in 1902, collaborated with Vitagraph Studios in 1914 as part of their series of photoplays scripted by "famous authors." Interestingly, she chose not a political subject but a historical play to dramatize, as part of a broader effort by the membership of the Authors' League of America to help less recognized writers. In 1913, Upton Sinclair ambitiously put his powerful exposé of the meat-packing industry, *The Jungle,* into five reels of a motion picture. At the same time, however, the issues that Tarbell and Sinclair were publicizing with their news articles and novels found their way into the cinema in ways that were less overtly political than *The Jungle.* Motion pictures took on the preoccupations of muckraking journalists and absorbed them into the ethos of individualism . . . . In that process, they helped establish film as a respectable entertainment form, as they mediated the problems of society.

Many security-minded reformers from the educated middle class saw that new function of film and moved from their early position of unrelenting condemnation of the newly emerged entertainment form to an attempt to "re-form" it. These reformers realized that film had the capacity to solve problems, to suggest solutions that would contain disorder and push forward moderate change. Their motion pictures raised issues among masses of people that the printed word might not reach, as Walter Fitch had commented in 1910. Film critics such as Louis Reeves Harrison and his colleagues at the *Moving Picture World,* W. Stephen Bush and the Reverend E. Boudinot Stockton, all had long stressed the use of film to "uplift." Jane Addams turned from her call for censorship of the moving pictures ("debased" and "primitive" she had called them in 1909) to actually starring in a melodrama in 1913 titled *Votes for Women.* Filmmaking seemed to have become fashionable among liberal reformers. . . .

Those days when the film industry was young reveal that the cinema reverberates through time itself. It goes beyond its specific era to illuminate the ongoing power of the motion picture to dramatize the needs and desires of its viewers through generations of archetypal characters and situations. Like H.G. Wells's heroes, one can travel into the past with the flick of a switch on a projection machine and discover America at the turn of the century. Unfortunately, however, such a cinematic "journey" can be as difficult as a ride on Wells's time machine: many of the films simply no longer exist, and can be known only through reviews or synopses. When silent films lost their commercial viability within several years after release, the film companies, eager for fast production and quick profits, carelessly discarded them. Often the companies themselves were too short-lived to maintain their films. The perishable silver nitrate stock on which the motion pictures were printed further reduced their chance for survival. As early as 1906, one critic recognized the danger of losing such valuable cultural artifacts as the new motion picture. "We often wonder where all the films that are made and used a few times go to," he wrote, "and the questions come up in our minds, again and again: Are the manufacturers aware that they are making history? Do they realize that in fifty or one hundred years the films now being made will he curiosities." Now, some eighty years later, one only wishes that filmmakers had listened to his admonition. The films that exist today are rare cultural documents.

Though the preserved film footage offers valuable insight into the climate of American cultural and political tensions, an understanding of their full impact must, ironically, rely heavily on original printed material. Controversy over the issues of social protest spilled over into the pages of early trade magazines such as the *Moving Picture World, Motography, Variety,* and *Photoplay*. Their reviews testify to the lively arguments over workers' rights, class conflict, political graft, and sexual politics that the films once delivered.

Such themes that the films repeatedly explored illustrate the larger dilemmas of society in dealing with injustices and inequalities. [These include] the class-bound nature of early melodrama and what the sociologist Edward A. Ross called "criminaloids"—those who grew wealthy by exploiting the poor. Such characters made ideal villains in films that ventured into the inner circles of the nation's corrupt elites. . . . [These also include] the "cinema of the submerged," particularly as D.W. Griffith defined it. There, a cinema made heroes and heroines out of those "submerged" in powerlessness. Tenement dwellers attempted to flee the ghetto and escaped prisoners tried to elude their captors in plots that pointed out the plight of the victims of economic or legal injustice. . . .

[Early silent films also showed] working-class heroes [who] fought back against their employers. But the problem of "Capital Versus Labor," as the film of that title designated it, varied from visions of unruly "ferret-eyed workers" to cruel "fat cat" factory owners who exploited children and honest working people. White slavery, was one of the most controversial topics ever sensationalized by the cinema. Taken alone, it was a euphemism for forced prostitution. The central concern of the explosive white slavery films and the melodramas on alcoholism and birth control was the preservation of the private sphere of the family.

The films about the woman suffrage movement . . . brought together a wide spectrum of propaganda for and against the movement. Caricatures of man-hating suffragettes paraded across movie screens as comedies ridiculed the notion of women voting. Suffragists themselves fought back with movie cameras, countering the comic attack with persuasive melodramas starring beautiful suffragist heroines. They elevated film into a significant political tool for their cause. The suffrage films, with their span of satire, newsreels, and melodramas, offer an opportunity to look at the tremendous range of political positions that the cinema took on a single subject.

The early risk-taking silent filmmakers saw their new medium as one that could both entertain and, in due course, instruct. They catered to the masses with a gamut of social commentary that reflected the traditional American belief that once social wrongs were exposed to the people, the people would see to it that they were righted. More importantly, the companies catered to the masses to build their own business empires. Thus they were reformers who also sought a profit; with their sermons on social injustice and their faith in the individual, they became, quite unintentionally, America's newest street preachers, making movies that became indeed "loud silents."

The Birth of a Nation

3

SILENT CINEMA AS HISTORICAL MYTHMAKER

Birth of a Nation—Propaganda as History
John Hope Franklin

The last years of the nineteenth century and the first years of the twentieth may have been the low point in American race relations. The disfranchisement of African Americans proceeded; legal segregation increased; lynchings and other violence against blacks surged. As the eminent historian John Hope Franklin shows in this essay, D.W. Griffith's Birth of a Nation *provided a historical rationalization for the political and economic subordination of African Americans.*

The fact that certain scholars specialize in studying the past does not mean that the past as an area of serious inquiry is beyond the reach of the layman with even the most modest intellectual and professional equipment. One must respect the efforts of anyone who seeks to understand the past; but it does not follow that one must respect or accept the findings of all who inquire into the past. Nor does it follow that the curiosity seekers of one brand or another can speak for those who by training and commitment devote their major attention to a study of the past. The decades and centuries that have receded from contemporary view are too important to all of us to leave their study to those who do not bring to the task all the skills available and present their findings with a clear understanding of what history means to the present and to the future.

The study of the past may mean many things to many people. For some it means that the effort to reconstruct what actually happened in an earlier era demands an honesty and integrity that elevate the study of history to a noble enterprise. For some it means that the search for a usable past provides instruction that may help to avoid the errors of their forefathers. It is not necessary to enumerate each of the many uses of the past, but it is worth noting that not all such quests are characterized by a search for the truth. Some of the most diligent would-be historians have sought out those historical episodes that support some contemporary axe they have to grind. Others look for ways to justify the social and public policy that they and like-minded persons advocate. Others even use the past to hold up to public scorn and ridicule those who are the object of their own prejudices.

The era of Reconstruction after the Civil War is an excellent example of a period that attracts historians—laymen and professionals alike—who seek historical explanations for certain contemporary social and political problems. And Thomas Dixon, Jr. is a peerless example of a historian—in his case a layman—who has mined the era of Reconstruction to seek a historical justification for his own social attitudes and who has exerted as much influence on current opinions of Reconstruction as any historian, lay or professional. Born in 1864 in a farmhouse near Shelby, North Carolina, Dixon was eight years old when he accompanied an uncle to a session of the state legislature in South Carolina where he saw in that body "ninety-four Negroes, seven native scalawags [white South Carolina Republicans] and twenty-three white men [presumably carpetbaggers from the North]." The impression on young Dixon of blacks and unworthy whites sitting in the seats of the mighty was a lasting one and ostensibly had a profound influence on his future career.

Dixon's Reconstruction experience was not unlike that which he had in 1887 when he heard Justin D. Fulton speak in Boston's Tremont Temple on "The Southern Problem." He was so outraged at Fulton's strictures against the South, based on a visit of six months, that he interrupted the distinguished minister midway through his lecture to denounce his assertions as "false and biased." It was on this occasion that Dixon decided to tell the world what he knew about the South first-hand and thus he began seriously to study the Civil War and Reconstruction.

The road that led Dixon to write about the Reconstruction era took him on a long and eventful journey. It led to Wake Forest College, where he was a superior student and leading debater. Then, for a brief sojourn he was at the Johns Hopkins University, where he became friendly with a graduate student, Woodrow Wilson, with whom he would later exchange favors. At the age of twenty young Dixon was a one-term member of the North Carolina legislature, which he quit because he was sickened by the conduct of the politicians whom he called "the prostitutes of the masses."

Incidentally, the number of black members of the Assembly was so small in 1884 that they could not possibly have been the cause of Dixon's disillusionment. Successively, this restless and talented young man became an actor, lawyer, clergyman, essayist, and lecturer. None of these pursuits satisfied Thomas Dixon as long as he was consumed with the desire to "set the record straight," as he would put it, regarding Reconstruction. Consequently, he forsook his other activities and proceeded to write the first volume of his Reconstruction trilogy. He called it *The Leopard's Spots: A Romance of the White Man's Burden*. The title was derived from the Biblical question "Can the Ethiopian change his skin, or the leopard his spots?"

Dixon sent his first novel to his old Raleigh, North Carolina friend, Walter Hines Page, then a partner in the publishing house, Doubleday, Page and Company. Page accepted it immediately and optimistically ordered a first printing of fifteen thousand copies. The success of the work when it appeared in 1903 was instantaneous. Within a few months more than one hundred thousand copies had been sold, and arrangements made for numerous foreign translations. Highly touted as a general history of the racial problem in the South and especially in North Carolina from 1885 to 1900, *The Leopard's Spots* established Dixon as an authority whom many were inclined to take seriously. His "luxuriant imagination" gave him the power to create "human characters that live and love and suffer before your eyes," a critic in the *Chicago Record-Herald* exclaimed. If there were those who were adversely critical—and there were—their voices could scarcely be heard above the din of almost universal praise.

Fame and fortune merely stimulated Dixon to greater accomplishments. He was in constant demand as a lecturer and writer; and soon his tall, commanding figure was on the platform in many parts of the country, constantly pressing his case as if in an adversary relationship with his audience. Within a few years he was ready to begin the second of his works on the Reconstruction, and thirty days after he began the writing he completed *The Clansman: An Historical Romance of the Ku Klux Klan*. Two years later, in July, 1907, he finished the last of the volumes in the Reconstruction trilogy which appeared under the title of *The Traitor: A Story of the Rise and Fall of the Invisible Empire*.

The great success of *The Clansman* as a novel caused Dixon to consider its possibilities as a drama. In a matter of months, in 1905, Dixon had converted his second Reconstruction novel into a dramatic play whose script won the praise of John Hay, the Secretary of State, and Albert Bigelow Paine, who was to become the literary executor of Mark Twain. When the play went on tour, it was acclaimed as "The Greatest Play of the South . . . A Daring Thrilling Romance of the Ku Klux Klan . . ." and it drew enormous crowds even though some critics thought it a bit excessive in its strictures against blacks and the way in which it aroused emotions and animosities that many hoped were abating. But *The Clansman* remained as thrilling on the stage as it had been as a best-selling novel.

On a voyage from Europe in 1912, Dixon, proud of what he had accomplished, began once more to think seriously about his future. By that time he had completed his trilogy on Reconstruction as well as a trilogy on socialism. *The Clansman* had been a success on the stage, and everywhere he was acclaimed as a near-genius. He began to wonder if he should return to acting, but he rejected such a career as being too prosaic. Likewise, he rejected the idea that he should remain a playwright on the thoroughly defensible ground that the endless repetition of plot and scene before relatively small audiences was not a very effective medium for the dissemination of ideas. Books, likewise, were limited in their appeal, and although Dixon would continue to write them, they would never claim all of his attention.

By this time, however, there was a new medium, called motion pictures, just becoming known. This novel method of communication lured Dixon "like the words of a vaguely-heard song," as his biographer put it. If this new medium, still scorned by most actors, most religious groups, and many "respectable" people, could be dignified by some great statement—like a historically vital story—would it not be the means of reaching and influencing millions of people? This could be an exciting, new venture, and this adventuresome man answered his own question in the affirmative.

In the months following his return from Europe, Dixon tried to persuade some producer in the infant motion picture industry to take on his scenario of *The Clansman*, but none would accept the offer. The movies were popular only as low comedies, light farce, and short action sequences with little plot. All the producers whom Dixon approached insisted that *The Clansman* was too long, too serious, and too controversial. Finally, late in 1913, Dixon met Harry E. Aitken, the head of a small company, and through him he met David W. Griffith who had enough daring and imagination to turn from his one-reel productions at least to consider the possibility of producing a large work like *The Clansman*. When Griffith's own company, The Epoch Producing Corporation, was unable to pay Dixon the ten thousand dollars he asked for his work, the author had to content himself by accepting a 25% interest in the picture. Armed with Dixon's blessings and thousands of his suggestions, Griffith set out for Hollywood to find a cast and to proceed with production. The actual filming occupied nine weeks, between July and October, 1914.

Prior to this time the motion picture had been composed of a series of stilted poses taken at random distances and tagged together with little continuity. The motion, not the play, was the thing. Griffith now introduced principles of shooting that were to make the motion picture a new and important art form. "His camera became a living human eye, peering into faces of joy and grief, ranging over great vistas of time and space, and resolving the whole into a meaning flux, which created a sense of dramatic unity and rhythm to the story." It was this living human eye that gave the Reconstruction story a new dimension.

It has been suggested that the film was more Griffith than Dixon. This is patently not the case. To be sure, Griffith was from Kentucky, and he had a certain sympathy for the Southern cause. And in the flush of success, Dixon would say, on opening night between the acts, that none but the son of a Confederate soldier could have directed the film. But Griffith's knowledge of history was scant, and he was much too occupied with the technical aspects of filming the picture to interpose his views regarding its content. Even a casual comparison of the texts of *The Leopard's Spots* and *The Clansman* with the film itself will convince one that "Birth of a Nation" is pure Dixon, all Dixon!

When the twelve-reel drama was completed, Joseph Carl Breil composed a musical score for it that was essentially adaptations from Negro folk songs and passages from Wagner's "Rienzi," and "Die Walkure," and Bellini's "Norma." In February, 1915, there were private showings in Los Angeles and New York. Dixon first saw the film at the New York showing. He sat in the balcony alone, fearing that he would be hooted and jeered by the seventy-odd people on the first floor. There was no such likelihood. Dixon said that his own experience of seeing the film was "uncanny." "When the last scene had faded," he later recounted, "I wondered vaguely if the emotions that had strangled me were purely personal. I hesitated to go down to the little group in the lobby and hear their comments. I descended slowly, cautiously, only to be greeted by the loudest uproar I had ever heard from seventy-five people." It was at that time that Dixon shouted to Griffith across the auditorium and exclaimed that "The Clansman" was too tame a title for such a powerful story. "It should be called 'The Birth of a Nation,' " he exclaimed.

There is a great deal of overlap in the characters and plots of the works in the Dixon Reconstruction trilogy, but "Birth of a Nation" draws more heavily on *The Clansman* than on the others. The first part of the film introduces the Stoneman brothers, Phil and Tod, from Pennsylvania, who are visiting their school friends, the Cameron brothers, in Piedmont, South Carolina. They are the sons of Austin Stoneman, a member of Congress. Phil falls in love with Margaret Cameron, while Ben Cameron falls in love with Elsie Stoneman. When the war erupts, the Stonemans return north to join the Union Army while the Camerons enter the Confederate Army. During the war the two younger Cameron brothers and Tod Stoneman are killed. Ben Cameron is wounded and is nursed by Elsie Stoneman as he lies a prisoner of Phil Stoneman in Washington. Meanwhile, Elsie and Phil's father, Austin Stoneman—in real life Thaddeus Stevens, the North's most unreconcilable radical—is busy urging Southern blacks to rise up against the Southern whites. Dixon does not fail to make the most of the fact that Stoneman has a mulatto housekeeper, and, because of Stoneman's power as leader of Congress and the alleged intimacy of Stoneman and his housekeeper, Dixon in *The Clansman* dubs her "The First Lady of the Land."

As the story of Reconstruction unfolds there is, of course, much corruption, much black presumption and arrogance, much humiliation of whites by black troops, and much looting and lawlessness. In order to avenge the wrongs perpetrated against his people, Ben Cameron becomes the leader of the Ku Klux Klan. It is not in time, however, to save his younger sister from the advances of Gus, a Negro roustabout, from whom she escapes by jumping from a cliff to her death. There are other would-be interracial trysts. When Elsie Stoneman asks Silas Lynch, a leader in the Black League, to save her brother Phil from the Negro militia that had besieged him in a log cabin, Lynch demands that Elsie marry him. The situation is resolved when the clansmen, under the leadership of Ben Cameron, put the black militia to flight, free Elsie from Lynch, and kill Gus. Then, a double wedding takes place between the Stoneman and Cameron families, symbolic of the unification of the North and South. Thus, the long, dark night of Reconstruction ends, and the white people of the South take on an optimistic view of their future as their nation, Phoenix-like, arises from the ashes of war and reconstruction.

The euphoria that Dixon and his friends experienced at the New York theatre in February, 1915, was not sufficient to sustain "The Birth of a Nation" in the face of strong opposition from unexpected quarters. Despite strong criticism of his earlier works on Reconstruction, Dixon had been able to cope with it. When *The Leopard's Spots* appeared, Kelly Miller, the Negro Dean of Howard University, wrote to Dixon, "Your teachings subvert the foundations of law and established order. You are the high priest of lawlessness, the prophet of anarchy." Sutton E. Griggs, the Arkansas black lawyer, asserted that Dixon "said and did all things which he deemed necessary to leave behind him the greatest heritage of hate the world has ever known." Dixon countered by saying, "My books are hard reading for a Negro, and yet the Negroes, in denouncing them, are unwittingly denouncing one of their best friends."

The opposition to "Birth of a Nation" was more formidable. Oswald Garrison Villard, editor of the *New York Evening Post,* and Moorfield Storey, President of the American Bar Association, were both founders and active leaders in the National Association for the Advancement of Colored People. They were representative of a large number of Americans, black and white, who thought that the film was a travesty against truth as well as an insult to an entire race of people. (Villard called it "improper, immoral, and unjust.") They were determined to prevent the showing of the film and began to work assiduously to bring about its doom. But they had not assayed the resourcefulness of Thomas Dixon, Jr., who was equally determined to secure a nationwide showing of his masterpiece. He proved to be a formidable and, indeed, an invincible adversary.

If the President of the United States should give his approval to the film, Dixon thought, perhaps the opposition would be silenced. And so, in February, 1915,

Thomas Dixon decided to visit his old schoolmate, Woodrow Wilson, who now occupied the White House. When Dixon called, Wilson was pleased to see his old friend. The two were soon reminiscing about their days at the Johns Hopkins University and about the manner in which Dixon had been instrumental in securing an honorary degree for Wilson at Wake Forest College. When Dixon told Wilson about his new motion picture, Wilson immediately expressed an interest, but indicated that since he was still mourning the death of his wife he could not attend the theatre. Wilson then suggested that if Dixon could arrange to show the film in the East Room of the White House he, his family, and members of the cabinet and their families could see it. The President said, "I want you to know, Tom, that I am pleased to do this little thing for you, because a long time ago you took a day out of your busy life to do something for me. It came at a crisis in my career, and greatly helped me. I've always cherished the memory of it."

On February 18, 1915, "The Birth of a Nation" was shown at the White House, and at the end of the showing President Wilson is said to have remarked that "It is like writing history with lightning. And my only regret is that it is all so terribly true."

Dixon's next scheme was to show the film to the members of the Supreme Court. With the help of the Secretary of the Navy, Josephus Daniels of North Carolina, Dixon secured an appointment with Chief Justice Edward D. White. The Chief Justice told Dixon that he was not interested in motion pictures, and indicated that the members of the Supreme Court had better ways to spend their time. As Dixon was taking his leave he told the Chief Justice that the motion picture was the true story of Reconstruction and of the redemption of the South by the Ku Klux Klan. Upon learning this, the Chief Justice leaned forward in his chair and said, "I was a member of the Klan, sir," and he agreed to see the picture that evening. Not only were members of the Supreme Court at the ballroom of the Raleigh Hotel to see the picture but many members of the Senate and House of Representatives were also there with their guests.

When opposition to the film persisted, Dixon let it be known that the President, the Supreme Court, and the Congress had seen the film and liked it. When this was confirmed by a call to the White House, the censors in New York withdrew their objection and the film opened there on March 3, 1915, and played for forty-seven weeks at the Liberty Theatre. Although the picture showed to huge audiences in New York and in every city and hamlet across the country, there was always great opposition to it. In New York, Rabbi Stephen Wise, a member of the city's censorship board, called "Birth of a Nation" an "indescribably foul and loathsome libel on a race of human beings. . . . The Board of Censors which allowed this exhibition to go on is stupid or worse. I regret I am a member." In Boston a crowd of 500 persons, including firebrands such as William Monroe Trotter, demonstrated on the grounds of the state capitol, demanding that the governor take steps to ban the film. A bill to that end was rushed through the lower house of the legislature only to be found unconstitutional by the judiciary committee of the upper house.

The President of Harvard University said that the film perverted white ideals. Jane Addams, the founder of Hull House, was greatly disturbed over the picture and wrote vigorously against it. Booker T. Washington denounced the film in the newspapers. Branches of the NAACP protested its showing in cities across the nation. But the film was seldom suppressed anywhere, and the reviews by drama critics were almost universally favorable. Burns Mantle said that there was an "element of excitement that swept a sophisticated audience like a prairie fire in a high wind." Hector Turnbull of the *New York Tribune* called it a "spectacular drama" with "thrills piled upon thrills." But Francis Hackett's review in the *New Republic* conceded that as a spectacle "it is stupendous," but its author was a yellow journalist because he distorted the facts. The film, Hackett insisted, was aggressively vicious and defamatory. "It is spiritual assassination." That may well be, Dixon seemed to think, but to the charges that he had falsified history, Dixon offered a reward of one thousand dollars to anyone who could prove one historical inaccuracy in the story.

I do not know of any person's having proved to Dixon's satisfaction that there were any inaccuracies in the film. I do know that many critics besides Hackett, convinced that it was filled with distortions, half-truths, and outright falsifications, challenged the truth of "Birth of a Nation." Francis J. Grimke, distinguished Negro minister in Washington, published a pamphlet entitled "Fighting a Vicious Film" that was a virtual line-by-line refutation of the Dixon-Griffith work. *Crisis Magazine,* the official organ of the NAACP, ran a series of monthly reports under the heading "Fighting Race Calumny." The film soon became the object of scathing criticism in mass meetings held by Negro religious, educational, and civil groups across the nation. The only concession that Dixon made after the film had been running for several months was to add a reel on the industrial work being done by blacks at Hampton Institute in Virginia. And for cooperating with Dixon in this undertaking, the white President of Hampton was bitterly criticized by the same blacks and whites who had so severely criticized the film.

It is not at all difficult to find inaccuracies and distortions in "Birth of a Nation." Ostensibly a firsthand account of the events that transpired between 1865 and 1877, it could hardly have been firsthand when one recalls that Dixon was one year old when Reconstruction began and was only thirteen when the last federal troops were withdrawn from the South in 1877. That was one reason, though not the principal reason, for Dixon's failure to include anything on Reconstruction in the South between 1865 and 1867, when not one black man had the vote, when all Southern whites except the top Confederate leaders were in charge of all Southern state governments, and when white Southerners enacted laws designed to maintain a social and economic order that was barely distinguishable from the antebellum period. There is not a shred of evidence to support the film's depiction of blacks as impudent, vengeful, or malicious in their conduct toward whites. As pointed out by Francis B. Simkins, a Southern white historian who specialized in Reconstruction in South Carolina where most of "Birth of a Nation" takes place, freedmen manifested virtually no hostility toward former masters. The evidence is overwhelming, although not necessarily commendable, that the vast majority of freedmen worked energetically and peacefully on their former masters' plantations during the entire period of Reconstruction.

The film makes a great deal of the alleged disorderliness, ignorance, and mendacity of the blacks in the South Carolina legislature. It also depicts Silas Lynch, the black lieutenant governor, as an audacious, arrogant, cheap politician whose only interest in life was to marry the blonde daughter of Austin Stoneman, the prototype of Thaddeus Stevens, Pennsylvania's Radical leader in Congress. It did not fit Dixon's scheme of things to acknowledge that the most important black political leader in South Carolina was Francis Cordozo, a graduate of Glasgow University, or that blacks were never in control of the machinery of government in the state. Nor did it matter to Dixon that the two black lieutenant governors of South Carolina during Reconstruction were Richard Gleaves, a Pennsylvania businessman who enjoyed a reputation as an excellent president of the Senate, and Alonzo Ransier, a shipping clerk in antebellum Charleston who was never accused of dishonesty, arrogance, or of harboring any antipathy toward whites. Which of these men, the only two available, did Dixon use as a model for his Silas Lynch? In any case, there was no black lieutenant governor in the closing years of Reconstruction when Dixon gloats over black lieutenant governor Silas Lynch being killed by the Ku Klux Klan for making advances to blonde Elsie Stoneman.

If Southern blacks had a competitor for the most degraded and depraved place in "Birth of a Nation" it was Austin Stoneman, a very thin disguise for Thaddeus Stevens of Pennsylvania. As the member of Congress most deeply committed to racial equality, Stevens was the most hated Northerner in the South. Dixon was so determined to use Thaddeus Stevens for his purposes that he committed every possible violence to the facts of Stevens's life. First, he presented Stoneman (Stevens) as a widower, though Stevens was never married. This was necessary in order to provide Stevens with a son and daughter. That would set the stage for a North-South reconciliation through the double wedding of his son and daughter with two young Southerners. This, in turn, was necessary in order to make Stevens's conversion to Southern principles complete when his black protege sought to marry his daughter.

Secondly, Dixon presented Stevens as being intimate with his black housekeeper, although there is no evidence to support it except that they lived in the same house. For the ultimate proof, Dixon could have had Lydia Brown become pregnant by Stevens, as actually happened in some other instances of intimacies between white leaders and their black "friends." Apparently, this would have interfered with some of the other contrivances. Finally, Dixon was not content until he had Stevens traveling to South Carolina at the climax of Reconstruction in order to experience the ultimate humiliation both from the black lieutenant governor Silas Lynch, who attempted to marry his daughter, and from the Ku Klux Klan, who rescued his daughter from Lynch.

It seems unnecessary to add that Thaddeus Stevens never went to South Carolina and had, indeed, died in 1868, when Dixon was four years old and several years before the high drama of South Carolina Reconstruction actually began. Even so, Thomas Dixon could write as follows: "I drew of old Thaddeus Stevens the first full length portrait of history. I showed him to be, what he was, the greatest and the vilest man who ever trod the halls of the American Congress." This was followed by his customary challenge: "I dare my critic to come out . . . and put his finger on a single word, line, sentence, paragraph, page, or chapter in 'The Clansman' in which I had done Thad Stevens an injustice."

Were it not for other considerations "Birth of a Nation" would be celebrated— and properly so—as the instrument that ushered the world into the era of the modern motion picture, a truly revolutionary medium of communication. Mantle called the pictures "wonderful"; to Charles Darnton, Griffith's work was "big and fine"; while the *New York Times* called it an "impressive new illustration of the scope of the motion picture camera." There were, however, other considerations. By his own admission Dixon's motives were not to discover the truth but to find a means by which to make a case for the South that, regardless of the facts (one is tempted to say, in spite of the facts), would commend itself to the rest of the country. "The real purpose back of my film," Dixon wrote in May, 1915 to Joseph Tumulty, Woodrow Wilson's secretary, "was to revolutionize Northern sentiments by a presentation of history that would transform every man in my audience into a good Democrat! . . . Every man who comes out of one of our theatres is a Southern partisan for life." A few months later he wrote President Wilson, "This play is transforming the entire population of the North and West into sympathetic Southern voters. There will never be an issue of your segregation policy."

Thus, Thomas Woodrow Wilson, twenty-eighth President of the United States and a professionally trained historian, lent the prestige of his high office and the hospitality of the Executive Mansion to promote this unseemly piece of propaganda as history. Dixon was never interested in the truth in history. He was interested in "selling" a particular promotion piece as history. That in itself is not the supreme tragedy, bad as it is. The supreme tragedy is that in *The Clansman* and in "Birth of a Nation," Thomas Dixon succeeded in using a powerful and wonderful new instrument of communication to perpetuate a cruel hoax on the American people that has come distressingly close to being permanent.

In the same year, 1915, that "Birth of a Nation" was showing to millions across the United States, the Ku Klux Klan was reborn. When the film opened in Atlanta that fall, William J. Simmons, who had considered a Klan revival for several years, sprang into action. He gathered together nearly two score men, including two members of the original Klan of 1866 and the speaker of the Georgia legislature. They agreed to found the order, and Simmons picked Thanksgiving eve for the formal ceremonies. As the film opened in Atlanta, a local paper carried Simmons' announcement next to the advertisement of the movie. It was an announcement of the founding of "The World's greatest Secret, Patriotic, Fraternal, Beneficiary Order." With an assist from "Birth of a Nation," the new Ku Klux Klan, a "High Class order of men of Intelligence and Order" was launched. It would spread all across the South and into the North and West in the 1920's and spread terror among Jews and Catholics as well as among blacks.

In the fall and winter of 1915–1916, thousands of Southerners thrilled to the stirring scenes of "Birth of a Nation." "Men who once wore gray uniforms, white sheets and red shirts wept, yelled, whooped, cheered—and on one occasion even shot up the screen in a valiant effort to save Flora Cameron from her black pursuer." They were ripe for enlistment in the new Ku Klux Klan. Thus, "Birth of a Nation" was the midwife in the rebirth of the most vicious terrorist organization in the history of the United States.

When Dixon was writing *The Clansman,* several others were actively competing with him for the title as the most uncompromising racist writer to appear on the American scene. In 1900 Charles Carroll published *The Negro a Beast,* a scurrilous attack on the nature and immorality of blacks which was expanded two years later in his *The Tempter of Eve; or The Criminality of Man's Social, Political and Religious*

Equality with the Negro. In 1902 William P. Calhoun continued the attack in *The Caucasian and the Negro in the United States.* In 1907, two years after Dixon's *The Clansman* appeared, Robert W. Shufeldt published *The Negro, a Menace to American Civilization.*

These, however, were mere books, as *The Clansman* was; and Dixon had already concluded that books were limited in their appeal. The diabolical genius of Dixon lay in his embracing the new medium, the motion picture, and thus using that medium to persuade and even to convince millions of white Americans, even those who could not read books, that his case against Negro Americans was valid and irrefutable. It was not merely that illiterate and unthinking Americans were convinced by Dixon's propaganda. It was also that vast numbers of white Americans, searching for a rationale for their own predilections and prejudices, seized on Dixon's propaganda, by his own admission propaganda designed to win sympathy for the Southern cause, and transformed it into history as the gospel truth.

As one reads *The Tragic Era,* published in 1929 by Claude Bowers, surely one of the country's most respected journalist-historians, one is impressed if not awed by its faithful adherence to the case as argued in "Birth of a Nation." It is all there— the vicious vindictiveness of Thaddeus Stevens, the corruptibility of every black legislator, and the nobility of the Ku Klux Klan in redeeming a white civilization threatened with black rule. It was the scum of Northern society that inflamed "the Negro's egotism," said Bowers, "and soon the lustful assaults began. Rape is the foul daughter of Reconstruction," he exclaimed. And even Dixon must have been forced to concede that an inflammatory book like *The Tragic Era,* selected by the prestigious Literary Guild, was in a position to wield enormous influence. *The Tragic Era* remained the most widely read book on Reconstruction for more than a generation, thus perpetuating the positions taken in "Birth of a Nation."

If one seeks a more recent Dixonesque treatment, he can read *The South During Reconstruction,* published in 1948 by E. Merton Coulter, the Regents Professor of History at the University of Georgia and the first president of the Southern Historical Association. Once again, it is all there—the unwashed, drunken, corrupt black legislators; the innocent disfranchised whites; and the resort to desperate measures by the Klan in order to save the South from complete disaster. There are, moreover, Alistair Cooke's book and television programs that, even in their polish and sophistication, follow, to an incredible degree, the argument set forth in "Birth of a Nation." Pick up almost any elementary or secondary text-book in American history used in our schools and you will discover much about corruption, white oppression by blacks, and the overthrow of Reconstruction by the socially responsible and morally impeccable whites in the South. You will not find there as you will not find in Bowers, Coulter, or Cooke and certainly not in "Birth of a Nation" anything about the oppression of freedmen by Southern whites, the reign of Southern white terror that followed the close of the Civil War, the persistence of white majority rule even during Radical Reconstruction, and the establishment of the first public schools and other social institutions during the period.

Obviously, one cannot place all the blame for the current view of Reconstruction on "Birth of a Nation." There were too many others who shared Dixon's views when he wrote and too many who have held to those views since that time. As an eloquent statement of the position of most white Southerners, using a new and increasingly influential medium of communication, and as an instrument that deliberately and successfully undertook to use propaganda as history, the influence of "Birth of a Nation" on the current view of Reconstruction has been greater than any other single force. There have been many revivals of "Birth of a Nation" and through them the main arguments Dixon set forth have remained alive. The film is shown in many places today as a period piece. It has achieved the status of an antique and its value is supposed to be in what it tells us about the evolution of the technique of film making. But as one sits in a darkened hall viewing the period piece as this writer recently did, one is a bit perplexed by the nervous laughter and scattered applause as the Klan begins its night ride. One can only surmise—and hope—that these reactions are to "Birth of a Nation" as a period piece and not to "Birth of a Nation" as a powerful instrument in promoting propaganda as history.

4

SILENT COMEDY AS CULTURAL COMMENTARY

Work, Ideology and Chaplin's Tramp
Charles Musser

As film historian Charles Musser demonstrates in his essay on Charlie Chaplin, silent comedy was much more than a combination of sight gags, pratfalls, and slapstick. Chaplin's silent comedies were powerful social and cultural commentary, rooted in the economic and social transformations of the early twentieth century. The complete, footnoted version of this essay can be found in Robert Sklar and Charles Musser, eds., Resisting Images: Essays on Cinema and History *(Temple University Press).*

Chaplin's comedy was unique. His wide-ranging jabs at institutions and authority as well as his propensity for crude, even dirty jokes were allowed no other comedian of his time. His humor was so effective that it vanquished its opposition. When audiences were under the spell of his comedy, almost anything became permissible. . . . [T]he screen character he created was a little man buffeted by life. The comedian "worked out a common denominator of fun and feeling that accords with something in every age, class, and race of people the world over. Chaplin is universal and timeless." In a more ironic mode Walter Kerr also focuses on the comedian as Everyman:

> The secret of Chaplin as a character is that he can be anyone. That is his problem. The secret is a devastating one. For the man who can, with a flick of a finger or the blink of an eyelash, instantly transform himself into absolutely anyone is a man who must, in his heart, remains no one.

Such defenses of Chaplin's artistic integrity severed him not only from the very social, economic, and cultural context in which he worked but also from the context in which his films were initially seen. Indeed, they might be regarded as efforts to bowdlerize Chaplin's comedies, to make his humor safe for that universal audience. In contrast, this essay seeks to resituate Chaplin's films within the historical conditions from which they arose. This requires another look at "Charlie," the tramp character that he created for the screen, and the jokes he made about work and "productive" labor.

    Charles Chaplin entered the film industry late in 1913—the year that Henry Ford inaugurated the endless-chain conveyor for final assembly of the Model T.

Treating people as human machines, Ford required workers to execute the same series of actions over and over again at a pace determined by the speed of the line. At the same time, Frederick Taylor and others were proselytizing methods of industrial management that appropriated the knowledge of skilled workers and eliminated their functional autonomy. Through the "rationalization" of work and through time and motion studies, they sought "enforced standardization of methods, enforced adoption of the best implements and working conditions, and enforced cooperation of all the employees under management's detailed direction." . . .

Into this ideologically charged atmosphere came Chaplin. His first employer was the New York Motion Picture Company, although he worked at Mack Sennett's Keystone facility, based at Ince's old Edendale studio. In many respects, the Sennett approach was the opposite of Ince's. Whole films were sometimes improvised by the filmmakers. To the extent that they used scripts, the cast and crew were allowed broad discretion. Yet as Kalton Lahue and Terry Brewer have noted, Keystone had become "a Fun Factory" in which Sennett tried to organize, supervise and discipline a group of anarchic comedians. Management prerogatives, however, were contested at Keystone in ways they never were under Ince. The writers spent almost as much creative energy avoiding work as dreaming up gags. To a considerable extent, Sennett recognized that this resistance was necessary and inevitable, given the kind of pictures he was making. But, as David Robinson has observed, the Keystone style of comedy was well-established and not readily open to other approaches—such as Chaplin's.

The first film in which Chaplin appeared was called, significantly, *Making a Living* (released 2 February, 1914). As one reviewer described it, "the hero [Chaplin] believes in making a living with the least possible amount of work and he is possessed of a nerve which would make a book agent look like a bashful girl at a prize fight." The ethic of hard work and honesty—the entire system of values espoused by society—is lampooned. Chaplin plays an impoverished English fop who cannot even afford to wear a shirt—but conceals this lack with a spiffy morning jacket and cuffs. He bums change from a man, then steals the man's girl. When his rival photographs a sensational auto accident, our "hero" steals the camera, delivers the results to the newspaper and takes credit for the work. He then enthusiastically participates in the production of the newspaper, helping to get his headline article out onto the street. Although the picture was apparently not appreciated on the Keystone lot, it received favorable notices elsewhere; the *New York Telegraph* called it "a screaming piece of farce-comedy of the type that the Keystone Company turns out so successfully."

For the American working class, who flocked to motion picture theaters for amusement, earning a living was tedious, oppressive and often dangerous. This experience was hardly limited to those comparatively small numbers of people working on the line or in businesses that had adopted Frederick Taylor's management techniques. As David Montgomery has shown, most industries simply sought to extract the maximum amount of work at the lowest possible cost through piece work, close and often tyrannical supervision, and detailing of work into minute tasks. Inefficiencies were, in fact, rampant—with their costs usually assumed by the workers. These practices had an intense, far-reaching impact on the many immigrants who found jobs in modern industries, since most had previously worked either in agriculture or traditional crafts for which they could no longer find employment. For many the workplace assumed a life of its own. Thus, the Chaplin character's ability to manipulate and mock the workplace (even via the white collar job of journalist) played off working-class experiences and resonated with the spectators' fantasies.

Although *Making a Living* was directed by Henry Lehrman, the informality of Keystone filmmaking may have enabled Chaplin to shape aspects of this picture. In the end, however, the actor felt that Lehrman had edited out his best comic bits: He experienced a loss of control over his performance foreign to his theatrical experience. In some respects, his anger was displaced and found an appropriate form of retaliation in his next film, *Kid Auto Races at Venice* (2 March, 1914). Although Lehrman directed, the film's basic idea was Chaplin's, and it was improvised on location in such a way that Chaplin's comic sensibility could be given free rein. Here, the emerging commentary on work was further developed as Chaplin assumed the role of a tramp and appeared for the first time in that ill-fitting suit and bowler that defined his subsequent costume. In this simple yet provocative picture, Chaplin's newly established screen persona, "Charlie," makes it impossible for a film crew (headed by Lehrman) to photograph a local news event. Although the tramp appears in almost every shot, the film's apparent intent is proclaimed by its title, intertitles and a few brief glimpses of the soapbox derby. We might say that the film was edited as if the tramp did not exist, but the tramp has disrupted all attempts by the crew to perform its job and to work productively. . . .

In an article published under his name, the increasingly celebrated comedian claimed that "the inspiration for *[The Tramp]* came from an accidental meeting with a hobo in a street in San Francisco":

> He had the usual symptoms of his class, he was suffering a little for lack of food, and intensely from lack of drink. I made a cheerful proposition to him, offering him both and asking him which he would have fust. "Why," he said, "if I get hungry enough, I can eat grass, but what am I to do for this thust of mine. You know what water does to iron? Well, try to think what it will do for your unsides."
>
> We went into a barroom, he got the drink, and we sat right down then and there to have a bite of lunch. The food and the drink warmed him and brought to the surface the unresponsible joy of life possessed by the nomad and the ne'er do well. He told me the story of his life. Of long jaunts through the beautiful country, of longer rides on convenient freights, of misfortunes which attend the unfortunates who are found stealing a ride on a side-door pullman, and of the simplicity of the farmers who lived only a short distance from the city. It was a delight to hear him talk, to gather from it the revelations of his character, to watch his gestures, and his trick of facial expression. All these elements were carefully watched by me, and noted for further reference. He was rather surprised when we parted, at my profuse thanks. He had given me a good deal more than I had given him, but he didn't know it. He had only obtained a little food and drink and a chance talk from me. From him, I had a brand new idea for a picture.

While John McCabe dismisses this account as completely fictional, I am not so sure. Chaplin had played the tramp before; one should not be surprised if he researched his character. He had a production schedule to maintain and was responsible for his own scenarios. The search for new stories would have encouraged such encounters. Yet even if one agrees with McCabe, this account tells us that Chaplin was consciously modeling himself on the American tramp, a figure few people in the United States were able to avoid in the course of their daily lives.

John James McCook, a Connecticut reformer active in the late nineteenth century, made a more systematic study of tramps, interviewing and photographing them for articles and lectures. Of the tramp he wrote, "I know him very well. I have generally found him a pleasant, approachable fellow and I should rather take my chances on reforming him, with purely civil and secular measures, than an ordinary felon." He described society's attitudes toward the tramp in the following terms: "The tramp plays hole and corner with a Public which affects impatience while it really feels tenderness." His attitude suggests that of the well-intentioned farmer in *The Tramp* whose attempts at reforming Charlie are doomed to failure. McCook's survey reveals essential qualities of Chaplin's tramp persona. "Connecticut Fatty" told McCook that "there are just two kinds of people in the world that are really happy—the millionaire and the bum." Chaplin would explore this assertion in *The Idle Class* (25 September, 1921). A McCook questionnaire filled out by tramp William Smith is extraordinary in its parallels to Charlie. Smith listed his occupation as "Gentleman." Asked, "When did you last work at it [the occupation]"? he answered, "Always." Asked, "When are you going to work again" he responded, "Never." Asked, "How do you generally secure food?" he replied, "By my cheek." Asked, "Where do you generally sleep?" he retorted, "The best place I can get." Asked if he was "temperate, intemperate or an abstainer," he concluded, "Take all I get." Charlie might have answered these questions in identical fashion.

McCook's photographs of tramps in the 1890s reveal a style of dress—bowler, vest, and suit—remarkably similar to Charlie's. Charlie's basic costume was created at a particular moment in history and then frozen. Although his costume was not notably out of place in *Kid Auto Races,* in succeeding films it gradually became an anachronism. By the mid-teens, tramps usually dressed more casually (in films as well as in real life). More and more, Charlie was seen as an old-fashioned tramp, a "dying breed" susceptible to romanticization by Chaplin, middle-class commentators and his audience.

As McCook observes, Americans regarded the tramp phenomenon with some ambivalence. Particularly in the 1870s and '80s, the mainstream press condemned these travelers as a menace that needed to be controlled or eradicated by strong doses of law and order. By the turn of the century, there was an increasing tendency to view tramps in more romantic terms. Ten years before Chaplin entered the film industry, the *New York Tribune* described tramps as Rousseauian ideals, 'natural men' unfettered by society's values. . . .

This rejection of proper society, its values and political economy may have implicitly criticized American life but it did not directly threaten society. D.W. Griffith's drama *A Knight of the Road* (released 20 August, 1911) portrays the tramp as this unfettered but nonthreatening "natural man."

> This Biograph subject shows the real nature of the hobo. Being of a senti-
> mental turn, he is impressed by the daughter of a ranch owner and in
> consequence becomes her and her father's protector against the machin-
> ations of several of his type. The owner in gratitude offers him a home
> and a job on the ranch, but work and the hobo never agree, so he steals
> away to remain ever a "Knight of the Road."

Griffith's plot not only closely parallels the one in *The Tramp* but it may well have
been another source for Chaplin.

By the time Chaplin made *The Tramp,* his screen character had become more
complex than at Keystone. Charlie, like William Smith, sees himself as a gentleman
tramp. When a woman (Edna Purviance) is in distress, he protects her and her
money from fellow vagabonds. Charlie behaves like a socially responsible person
even though he is not a member of proper society. "Gentleman" and "tramp"
are opposites. The comic elaboration of this contradiction is central to Chaplin's
developing screen persona. Either under pressure of unfolding events or through
habit, Charlie often reverts to his social role as a hobo. In this basic instability lies
the comedy.

For saving his daughter (and her money), the farmer gives Charlie a meal to
eat and then tells him, "as a reward you can work." For a tramp like Charlie, work
is anything but a reward. Its very naivete burlesques the Protestant work ethic in a
manner that working-class audiences could appreciate. The farmer, of course, does
not work but counts his money and gives orders. When the gentleman tramp is
given a pitchfork, he does not protest. He knows he should appear to comply, for
geniality will prove the path of least (i.e. most successful) resistance. For the rest
of the film, he does not perform a true bit of productive labor. This is a second
comic contradiction in Charlie's character. He often appears as he believes people
want him to be, masking his true self in the process. Yet Charlie knows who he is
and what he wants. He is a tramp living "by his cheek," even if the farmer thinks
he is a potential farmhand.

The "pitchfork sequence" is composed of twenty-four shots filmed in only four
different set-ups. At first, as one might expect of someone who is unaccustomed to
work, Charlie uses the fork ineptly, stabbing the farm hand inadvertently. The
pitchfork is a foreign instrument, the violence funny but seemingly gratuitous. By
the fourth shot, however, Charlie has mastered the tool. He realizes it need not be
an instrument of labor but can be used to prod and direct the farmhand who actually
performs all the work. Chaplin gets more adept with the pitchfork as an instrument
of work avoidance. When the farmer comes to check on them, Charlie jabs the
farmhand with the fork, making the rube drop a sack of flour onto the farmer's
skull, knocking him out. In an earlier Keystone comedy, the farmer might have
bounced up and started a free-for-all. Here the farmer remains unconscious for
some time. While it may have been an "accident," Charlie realizes he doesn't have
to work since the farmer cannot supervise him. He and the farmhand loaf, and
Charlie shows him how to steal eggs from the chicken coop (a little education for
a hand who has all too readily internalized the values of his employer). They return
and drop another sack on the farmer just to make sure he remains unconscious a
little longer. Charlie, preparing for the farmer's revival, resumes work and carries

a bag of flour down the ladder. When the farmer kicks him Charlie drops the bag again it lands on the farmer's head. In the last four shots, Charlie deftly shifts responsibility for the accident onto the rube whom the farmer beats with a stick. Charlie avoids work and deflects punishment, assuming many characteristics of the authoritarian farmer. Only when the farmhand dumps a bucket on his head at the scene's conclusion is Charlie brought back to reality. . . .

Tramping, moreover, encouraged a particular attitude toward work, even among those men anxious to find a job. As John Schneider has remarked, "Tramping may actually have been a way for many men to strike back against the regimen of the industrial workplace. Tramps chided the man who remained chained to one job. . . . They felt he 'ought to leave a job once in a while simply to assert his independence and to learn something else about other jobs.' " In many cases, this was a philosophy (and luxury) of young single working-class men who had few responsibilities and were not yet willing (or able) to accept the regimentation of most workplaces. But this system of beliefs undoubtedly continued to be shared (albeit in modified form) by those who settled down to familial responsibilities and more permanent employment. Tramping was also a way of life that found sympathetic resonance in the theatrical profession. Chaplin's theatrical career had been one of almost constant travel. Nor did he stay with any employer for very long. Leaving Keystone after one year, he remained at Essanay for another (1915) then moved on to the Mutual Film Company for a third (1916).

Charlie's role as new employee in *The Pawnshop* (released 2 October, 1916)— a situation also found in *His New Job, Easy Street* and other films of the Essanay/ Mutual period—is not only compatible with his tramp character but foregrounds the issue of work. The character's job history is unknown to us, but his attitude toward this new opportunity indicates that he never labored anyplace for very long. Although Charlie's relationship to the workplace shifts during the course of *The Pawnshop*, all his actions undermine work as productive labor. Work is often play. Cleaning the balls from the pawnshop symbol, he bounces them off the head of his co-worker; and when he sweeps, he sweeps a piece of string into a straight line and walks on it as if it were a tightrope.

Many of Charlie's actions are destructive: He demolishes a bass fiddle with his head. In another case, through "carelessness" or well concealed intent, he destroys his duster by dusting the fan, letting the blades cut the feathers down to stubble, making it impossible to continue his task. Under such circumstances, Charlie's tenure will be short-lived (he is, in fact, faced with dismissal once during the film). If Charlie stays, it is because of the pawnbroker's daughter. As in *The Tramp,* the rejection of work is made more complicated by Charlie's attraction for someone related to the boss. Here Charlie apparently wins the girl by defeating the crook. Yet Charlie's situation is finally as untenable as it was in *The Tramp.* Allowed to retain his job, he would destroy the business in a manner of months.

The Pawnshop contains one of Chaplin's most famous scenes—the one in which he takes apart a customer's alarm clock. Here work is playful yet aggressive destruction. Charlie assumes the role of doctor, jeweler, housewife, ribbon clerk, and exterminator in the course of demolishing the clock. He seems anxious to grasp its mysterious inner workings, to understand what has given this mechanism such tremendous power over his life. Finally he gives up, admits he does not understand,

and hands the pieces back to the customer. Walter Kerr's unsatisfactory analysis sees this scene as proof that Charlie can and will transform anything, for he finds the clock "an unlikely object" for the tramp's imaginative aggression. In contrast, any analysis of working-class experience finds the clock a singularly appropriate object for Charlie to demolish. The clock is, after all, the instrument that regulates the workplace of modern capitalism. . . .

The anger and violence that Chaplin expresses toward work often catches a modern critic by surprise. His humor is sometimes more frightening than funny. Yet for working-class audiences, films like *Work* (21 June, 1915) and *His New Job* (1 February, 1915) articulated emotions that too often had to be repressed. They provided a release and recognition through laughter. In *Work,* Charlie is ostensibly a paperhanger's helper. In truth he is a beast of burden who drags the paperhanger's wagon up the hill. His large boss sits in the cart and even gives a friend a lift. When they start to paper the house, Charlie seems anxious to perform his task. But is it just accident that Charlie's pastebrush always hits the employer in the face and that the board always boxes the boss' ears? Or is it a barely concealed expression of Charlie's fury?

Chaplin assigned a socially significant role to the family that hires the paperhanger. They are the Fords and their dwelling is compared to the automobile: "A two-passenger, form fitting home. Mr. Ford's first line is "Hurry my breakfast." In a rush, he is plagued by inefficiencies. This bourgeois family is thus associated with Henry Ford, the Model T and the assembly line. Searing moments of social humor abound. As the paperhangers start work, Mrs. Ford runs in and puts the silver in the safe—lest the workmen steal it. Following her example, the two men anxiously take their watches off and hide them deep in their pockets as well. Their suspicion becomes mutual. Because the paperhanging has delayed Mr. Ford's breakfast, Mrs. Ford's lover shows up while her husband is still home. The lover quickly pretends to be a fellow worker, although the ruse is not entirely successful. Over the course of the film, the home/auto, the Ford's domestic relations and the productive relations between family, paperhanger and helper are unmasked and ridiculed.

Similar devastation occurs in *His New Job*. A film company hires Charlie to be a property man's helper. The helper, in fact, does all the work so that when Charlie is needed to act in one of their productions, the property man demands a new assistant "or I'll blow my job." Charlie gets him fired by stabbing the director through a curtain with a sword and then handing the weapon to the property man just before the angry director appears. By the end of the film, the relations of production have been undermined, the studio (the means of production) is in shambles, and the historical drama in which Charlie appears has been turned into a farce. Charlie's ability to destroy the world of work on its multiple levels distinguishes these films from Keystone comedies being made at the same time.

As contemporaneous reviews make clear, Chaplin's films from the mid-teens often offended the polite, refined sensibilities of the leisure class. Sime Silverman, founder of *Variety,* raged against Chaplin's low comedy. *Work* was characterized as

> . . . the usual Chaplin work of late, mussy, messy and dirty Chaplin has found the public will stand for his picture comedy of the worst kind, and

he is giving them the worst kind, although as an excellent pantomimist with a reserve of decent comedy, Chaplin must have decided the time to put his other brand upon the screen is when his present style of "humor" shall have ceased to be in demand. The Censor Board is passing matter in the Chaplin films that could not possibly get by in other pictures. Never anything dirtier was placed upon the screen than Chaplin's "Tramp," and while this may have been objected to by the censors, it merely taught Chaplin what to avoid and how far to go.

Just as Charlie's paintbrush always hits the boss in the face, these films assault the social elite sitting in front of the screen.

For Charlie, class differences are alternately illusions or insurmountable barriers. The contradictions between the illusions of equality and the realities of class difference are sources of comedy and pathos. Take the golf course [in *The Idle Class*]. Charlie indulges in the rich man's game of golf. Of course they begin at the first tee, while Charlie enters later in the course. He is as temperamental as the most finicky amateur. The sand provided by the country club is not good enough for Charlie—he brings his own supply. He lacks a golf ball, however, and must forget his affectations while he steals one. On the course, the rich see little distinction between Charlie and themselves. One golfer chums up to Charlie, offering the tramp his cigarette case. Charlie takes the case, offers his new friend a cigarette and then puts the case in his own pocket. Gradually he acquires the accoutrements of the rich—a fine collection of golf balls and some new clubs pulled out of a golfer's bag by Charlie's independently-minded cane. Superficially he acts like one of them. Yet the tramp's habit of living "by his cheek" operates automatically, audaciously and profoundly.

The only time Charlie is allowed indoors is at the costume ball when he is an imposter. Chased by a policeman, he runs into the ballroom simply to elude his pursuers. Once inside, he is immediately accepted as belonging there. He is, as far as the party-goers are concerned, one of the rich. A man, costumed as a policeman, embraces rather than arrests the nervous tramp. Edna's husband comes later, dressed as a knight in shining armor—with a stuck visor. Charlie is, of course, a knight of the road. In the world of the costume ball, these two knights attain a brief equality. Edna thinks the tramp is her husband. A puzzled Charlie is not prepared to reject her advances. His accommodation to her misidentification, however, is bittersweet because it fullfills his deepest fantasy. Charlie's love appears deeper than the rich husband's. This real difference, when juxtaposed to the illusory equality of confused identities, is amusing and sad. Charlie plays along until the husband shows up and protests his wife's intimacies with the interloper.

Edna and her father (Mack Swain) are not sure which knight is the real husband until Charlie opens the husband's visor with his can opener. Ironically, the gentleman tramp provides the proof that, in their eyes at least, he is only a tramp and not a gentleman. The world of the masquerade ends. Chaplin had played double roles in his *A Night at the Show* (20 November, 1915): Mr. Pest, a rich vaudeville patron in the loge, and Mr. Rowdy, a working-class trouble-maker in the gallery. The two exist in their own separate spaces, maintaining co-equal status. In *The Idle Class,* on the other hand, a moment of truth comes as Charlie opens the visor. No attempt is made to construct, through editing or a split screen, a scene where

Chaplin both opens the armor and is in the armor. In this situation Chaplin plays the tramp while another actor (apparently his half-brother Sid Chaplin!) plays the millionaire. When the masquerade ends, when the tramp stops pretending, Charles Chaplin stops playing the rich idler. The rich man is only a reflection of what the tramp wants to be. In Chaplin's universe, they do not have the same ontological status.

Once the tramp's true identity is established, he is told to leave. Charlie appeals to Edna, but his entreaties are rejected. She has no choice (even if she were so inclined) when asked to violate society's code of proper conduct. But once he leaves, she asks her father to apologize to the man whom they abused so badly. The Mack Swain character does this, offering to shake hands. Charlie shakes but then points to something on the ground. Swain bends over to pick it up. Looking down as he has looked down on Charlie, the father becomes a recipient of the tramp's boot. Thus Charlie shatters the equation of idle rich and outcast that has run throughout the story. The reasons for their idleness, the fact that both are the product of the industrial system but in inverse ways, the differing quality of this idleness: all are finally reaffirmed by Chaplin in this kick. The kick is also Charlie's final assessment of the values exhibited by his "betters." Again Charlie's concluding act paralleled the film's continued vulgarity. Chaplin's popularity was such, however, that even those who were offended would not stay away from the theaters showing his pictures. As *Variety* grudgingly acknowledged, the brilliance of his comedy gave him license—at least for the moment: "Slapstick? Yes, Vulgar? Yes; but it is all done by the inimitable Chaplin, which counteracts all possible adverse criticism."

As the Tramp Phenomenon Declined

With tramping on the wane by the early 1920s, the social basis for Chaplin's tramp character was eroding, perhaps contributing to the comedian's declining output and creative difficulties (as evidenced by *The Circus* [released 6 January, 1928]). In this respect, *The Gold Rush* was a brilliant solution because it is, in effect, a period comedy set at the end of the nineteenth century when tramping was at its height. Charlie goes to Alaska during the 1897–98 gold rush and, through many twists of fate, ends up a millionaire. Suddenly wealthy, the former tramp wins the girl he loves—Georgia (Georgia Hale). Even in this story, where Charlie goes from idle poor to idle rich, a circular structure exists just below the surface. At the end, Charlie leaves Alaska on an ocean liner. He is asked to pose in his old tramp outfit by the press. This he does obligingly. As he backs away from the camera, he falls off the cabin roof and into the arms of a surprised Georgia on the deck below. She is also leaving Alaska but in less favorable circumstances. Previously, a crewman was looking for a stowaway and Georgia, assuming it must be Charlie, tries to hide him in a coil of ropes. Charlie, however, is quickly discovered. For a moment it seems he might be thrown off the ship, separated from his wealth and forced to return to the life of a tramp. Instead the photographers intervene. Charlie is rescued and he rescues Georgia. When the group returns to the upper deck, the camera holds on the coiled rope where Georgia hid Charlie. We are reminded that there still is a stowaway, a tramp who at one time may have been Charlie. We also can imagine that this tramp might be a new "Charlie" since Chaplin could simultaneously play two roles—the rich and the poor. As it is, the old Charlie may have distracted the crew sufficiently for the surrogate tramp to escape detection. At the last moment, *The Gold Rush* tends toward the familiar circular structure.

The Gold Rush returns to a time when the role of the "gentleman" or "millionaire" tramp was being widely articulated. Will Smith, whose exchange with McCook is recounted above, was only one of this character type. In late 1896, Yon Jenkins entered a hotel and introduced himself to a fashionable group of businessmen, he offered them his card: "Yon Jenkins—Tramp." As he told his bemused audience, "I was a gentleman myself once and I never got out of the habit. That's why I'm a tramp now. I couldn't work when I wanted to and afterwards I wouldn't work when I could. You see I wasn't use to it." The complex and potentially fascinating relationship between real tramps of this type and their fictional counterparts perhaps needs more exploring. At least two plays on this theme were popular at the turn of the century. In *The Millionaire Tramp*, "a tramp of the generally impossible kind eats and drinks—mostly drinks—his way through a succession of acts, succoring the needy, helping the virtuous, smashing the wicked and making a general darned fool of himself." *A Thoroughbred Tramp* was in a similar vein. This comedy-drama or comical melodrama "deals with the joys, loves and sorrows of T. Bush Thompson, a tramp, who combines in himself the antagonistic roles of hero of the love interest and low comedian. The sudden changes from patches and slang to Prince Alberts and high class sentiments are dizzying to the ordinary brain." In *The Gold Rush*, Chaplin returned to the source of his comedy, using its populist perspectives, less explicitly and self-consciously than he would later do in *Limelight* (released 23 October, 1952).

At the end of *The Gold Rush*, Charlie is a tramp turned millionaire and thus a millionaire tramp in a very literal fashion. Significantly this wealth is not earned by hard work, but won by luck or, as the intertitles reiterate, by "fate." It was luck that blew Jim McKay (Mack Swain) through the cabin door, changing the balance of power just as Black Larson was about to send Charlie into the snow storm. It was luck that made Jim McKay need Charlie to find the mine, and fate that killed Black Larson, preventing him from registering the mine in his name. Certainly this accounting for Charlie's wealth comically mocks the way fortunes were accumulated. It also suggests that almost anyone, through a series of unlikely events, could become rich.

In *The Gold Rush*, Charlie is an unlikely prospector. His behavior is completely at odds with the other miners. While they struggle up Chinnock pass with heavy baggage, Charlie slides down a steep slope with a small knapsack on his back. As in earlier films, he is a man of few possessions. But here he looks more like a tourist than society's outcast. Again he never works, at least he never pans for gold. As a title indicates, he made more money pawning his pick and pan than prospecting. Class, however, does not play the central role at least until the end, when Charlie is aboard ship, heading for Portland and "civilization." On the frontier, class distinctions break down. The key criteria for social status are masculine qualities—size, physical strength, toughness, burly self-confidence. Charlie, however, is associated with more traditionally feminine qualities. The only work he does is housekeeping. He cooks: a shoe for Jim McKay on Thanksgiving and a roast for Georgia on New Year's. In town, he takes care of a prospector's cabin and mule. He is a domestic. He hovers over Hank Curtis (Henry Bergman) like a wife sending her husband off on a trip.

Georgia is amused by Charlie but does not respect him. She is attracted to a man like Jack Cameron (Malcolm Waite) who is tough, cruel and conventionally masculine. Knowing Jack merely wants to possess her, she has enough sense to make that possession difficult—so it will be worth more. Thus she courts him by treating him with indifference and contempt. Later Cameron humiliates her by redirecting an apology/love note to Charlie. He ridicules both of them, helping to create the bond that unites them at the end. The contradiction between rich and poor is repositioned between masculine and feminine. Charlie transcends traditional conceptions of sexual roles and is truly worthy of Georgia's love. When she finally learns this fact, it is almost—but not quite—too late.

The displacement and muting of class and workplace tensions in *The Gold Rush* are consistent with the prosperity of the 1920s and the increasingly anachronistic qualities of the tramp persona. Yet more generally, Charlie lacks any developed sense of working-class consciousness: his visceral, immediate reactions are frequently opportunistic in the extreme. The violence in Chaplin's comedies is not only directed against the boss and the workplace but against Charlie's fellow workers. In *The Bank* he tramples his counterpart who continues to scrub the floor even as the bank robbery unfolds. The employee, who has become a kind of human machine and a dutiful extension of an employer's will, merits little consideration on Charlie's part. Explicit class solidarity in Chaplin's films is rare and even then only involves short-term alliance. . . .

Connecticut Fatty
ca. 1890

Charlie Chaplin
as *The Tramp*

5

THE REVOLT AGAINST VICTORIANISM

Douglas Fairbanks, Mary Pickford and the New Personality, 1914–1918
Lary May

*The movies played a critical role in promoting the revolution in morals
and manners of the 1910s and 1920s. In this essay, film historian Lary May
describes how films in the teens began to shed their Victorian trappings and to
celebrate glamour and the exotic.*

At the point when Griffith's masterpieces infused Victorianism with moral passion,
there arose from the ranks of his company two offspring who began to match the
promise of the media to something dramatically new: a cultural reorientation. These
disciples went far beyond their master in creating images for the modern era.
Douglas Fairbanks and Mary Pickford became so popular that from 1914 until
America's entry into World War I, they may have been more widely admired than
their political counterparts, Woodrow Wilson and Theodore Roosevelt. "Doug"
and "Mary" had risen to fame by becoming something truly new: movie stars.
Pickford's films gained such acclaim that magazines voted her the "most popular
girl in the world" and "America's Sweetheart." Yet the "Queen of Our People,"
as the *New Republic* called her, gained that love not by radiating pure womanhood,
but by doing what seemed impossible, merging the virgin to the harlot, and moving
beyond the spheres which had divided the sexes in the nineteenth century. At the
same time, her weekly columns in the press and her screen roles depicted her as the
modern working woman who supported suffrage and was emancipated morally as
well. As the perfect parallel male, Fairbanks merged the cowboy to the athletic
urbanite at a time when it appeared that the frontier might be gone. When they
married in 1920, the circled closed. On the screen as in reality, their celebrity
showed that leisure was not an extension of the past, but something dramatically
different.

   Where did this come from? What did it mean for the modern urbanite? In the
beginning of Pickford's and Fairbanks's careers in 1914, it was by no means obvious
that such a reorientation was possible. D. W. Griffith's great film, *The Birth of a
Nation,* had not only given the art a tremendous dynamism, but it infused movie-
going with a sense of energy it would never lose. Nevertheless, Griffith's forward-
looking techniques were fused to a backward-looking ideal. The great director's
work would continue to be popular until the twenties; but in 1914 new producers

arose who realized that resistance to the modern age in the name of Victorianism was no longer viable. These film makers had to appeal to the special needs of an audience gathered after 1914. The "new" middle classes had now joined workers and small property owners, and together they confronted large organizations as a fact of life. Neither these viewers nor the film makers could return to the old ways. Still, as people who had inherited the Anglo-Saxon tradition of ascetic individualism, they were sensitive to the reformers' critique of modern life. The central question in their lives was how to find a morality appropriate to the corporate order, one that solved the difficult issues of work, family, and class status that had infused the politics of the era.

Generally we are accustomed to thinking that the vast cultural and economic changes of the era occurred separately, rather than in some dynamic relation. Yet for the movie audience created after 1914, these forces were vitally connected. Clues to this symbiosis can be gleaned from recent studies which show that the "new middle classes" were undergoing a major political reorientation. In contrast to the pre-1914 audience of workers and small property owners, these groups were not concerned with rolling back the clock to an entrepreneurial world. Rather, as employees and managers of large organizations, they followed the new nationalism of Theodore Roosevelt, believing that well-run corporations and professional organizations might serve the public interest. In this, the code of expertise and efficiency superseded earlier values of local control and individualism. Thus they were not so concerned with moral crusading or attacking large business concerns. In fact, although these people were heir to an Anglo-Saxon tradition, they were shedding the asceticism that demanded control over property, production, and oneself. Describing this change, one participant recalled,

> Our fathers' businesses were run by other men, brought from elsewhere. Our first families became absentee landlords of distant corporations rather than magnates of industry whose gates gaped for us, and if this brought economic evils with it, it at least ended the tyranny of business over the mind of youth.

The result brought a transformation in personal and social behavior. Vice crusaders' worries were not totally unfounded. Recent social historians have documented a measurable change, particularly among the urban middle classes. There was not just a shedding of Victorian norms, but an increase in the pursuit of pleasure. Dress reform, "exotic" dances, and the advent of sports were visible to observers; but there is also hard evidence to show a rise of consumer spending and sexual experimentation during the first two decades of the twentieth century. Contemporaries saw this shift manifested most dramatically in the home. The family seemed less concerned with self-denial and more geared toward self-indulgence. In the Victorian era, youth was something to master and shed, along with play, upon reaching maturity. But now adults seemed eager to bring these elements into their lives as well. As Henry Seidel Canby recalled, "Self expression for youth is supposed to have brought about the change in family life that came with the new generation. It was a cause, but an equally powerful one was self-expression for parents who wanted to stay young and live their own lives, while the boys and girls were sent off to camps and schools. Fathers and mothers in the earlier time put fatherhood and motherhood first.''

The fact that the economic and cultural changes occurred simultaneously opens the possibility that the moral revolution was helping to ease some of the fears people had about the rise of big business. A previous generation of reformers had tried to master the new economy with the values of Victorians and small entrepreneurs. They saw that an organized work world thwarted the sense of freedom and autonomy found in the open marketplace; and the hierarchical order also disrupted the sexual and family roles of the past. People then used affluence to enjoy urban amusements formerly considered degraded. Yet to unleash consumption seemed to threaten the code of asceticism needed for success. Abundance might erode the work ethic which rested on incentive. With so much at stake, how was this task with its dangers of class and sexual chaos accomplished? How could a new urban middle-class ideal be attained, one that might solve the problems of alienating work and social conflict? While few businessmen had solutions to these problems, and reformers tried to master them through state action and Victorian policing, those who had inherited the new order were pioneering new realms of democratic freedom in arenas outside conventional life.

Nowhere was this quest more evident than in the motion picture industry. Before 1908, vice crusaders had seen the movies as a dangerous example of mass culture. The movie theater was a place where people broke from the formalities of work and socializing institutions. In reforming amusements from 1908 to 1914, crusaders hoped that movies could help resist the ill effects of modern life. Paradoxically, *The Birth of a Nation* was both the culmination and collapse of this thrust. It clearly identified motion pictures and mass culture with a reinvigorated sense of individualism against the corrupt powers of the day. It also brought more affluent audiences into the movies. Yet the controversy surrounding the film cracked the consensus of film makers and the censorship board. Then, the expensive failure of Griffith's *Intolerance* signalled that the audiences he helped to generate were not drawn to the themes he cherished: attacking big business and restoring the entrepreneurial economy. Other producers now realized that with the Board in disarray and corporations here to stay, it was time to break away from the old Victorian patterns. In that quest, they would use the liberating aesthetics pioneered by the master, but merge them to new social themes.

One clear indicator of that change was the rise of the movie stars. The use of a featured player to attract audiences had been the custom on the Broadway stage, the nineteenth-century touring companies, vaudeville, melodrama and ethnic theaters catering to the workers. Such players radiated a sense of power and personal magnetism that towered over the story. Yet film makers in the period after reform rarely gave players featured billing. This was partially due to their efforts to cut costs; they did not want to spend money on a "name." More importantly, directors like Griffith saw their art as separate from the entertainment popular with the rich and the immigrants. As agents of a higher destiny, his characters subordinated themselves to the larger message of the plot. Consequently, when movie producers after 1914 began to draw featured players from Broadway, vaudeville, and ethnic theaters, it signaled a crack in a long-standing tradition. Audiences might see characters who did not just serve a higher ideal, but were unique and dynamic personalities. As they came into the movies, they carried with them the aura of upper and lower class styles that the bourgeois had previously avoided. Now marquee favorites might offer models for dealing with the questions of cultural mixing and sexual experimentation.

Running parallel to the rise of the star system was an alteration in the themes of film stories. An examination of the plots listed in the major trade journals from 1907 to 1919 reveals a subtle shift. In the period from 1908 to 1912, the newer photoplays made by the independents had Victorian themes made so popular by Griffith. Shortly thereafter, the Anglo-Saxon tradition began to be questioned. More plots revolved around characters who succumbed to sins that previously had been attributed to foreigners, villains, and aristocrats. Usually the hero or heroine overcame dangers such as drink, overspending, and sexual women, suggesting that the conscience of the old culture still prevailed. Starting around 1913, this began to change, first with the comedy genre. Formerly, the viewers had laughed when characters failed to meet Victorian standards; now they laughed at the Victorian standards themselves. Still none of these films mocking formal roles offered a viable alternative. Eventually, around 1914, the full implications of this questioning yielded a completely modern approach to family life, as well as a reformist style different from Victorians or Progressives of Griffith's ilk. . . .

[T]here was little doubt that both sexes were attracted to something other than Victorianism. Precisely at this point of tension between past and present desires, two players emerged, Douglas Fairbanks and Mary Pickford, who offered a transformation of domestic assumptions. Between 1914 and 1918, they became the first major dramatic stars of the films; only Chaplin's popularity and audience appeal equaled theirs. Coming from Broadway, they brought the prestigious aura of the stage into a formerly immigrant entertainment. Each was also part comic who made fun of restraints, while pointing to the future. In the process, they both shed their original names, a symbolic act of separation from the past which would become typical among stars. For these extremely talented figures, cosmopolitan fun and healthy beauty replaced the spiritual symbolism connected to Hart or Griffith characters. Both on and off the screen, their films, success books, columns, and writings showed their fans how to solve the era's major dilemmas.

This was no small task. In endless interviews, Fairbanks related his own struggle against the ropes binding him to the past. As he told it, he was born in Denver, Colorado, in 1883, and grew up in the heart of a culture that glorified the self-made man. His father was Charles Ulman, the scion of a prominent Pennsylvania family who helped found the American Bar Association and served in the Union Army as a Civil War officer. Shortly thereafter, he went west to become a noted industrialist in Denver, where he wrote speeches for Republican presidential candidate Benjamin Harrison. Yet for some unknown reason he deserted the family, and his wife then changed her two sons' names to Fairbanks. Douglas attended the Colorado School of Mines; but soon he left school for the lure of the Broadway stage. Quickly he became a star, and married Beth Sully, the daughter of a Wall Street banker. Fairbanks then worked in his father-in-law's firm and joined the high society of the New York rich, participating in the European tours and sports of those who had the means to spend lavishly.

In 1915, Fairbanks returned to show business, joining Harry Aitkin's company and working with D. W. Griffith. Yet the great director was soon at odds with the energetic Fairbanks, and the star soon struck a favorable contract with Famous Players-Lasky. So popular would he become that by 1920 he could form his own company with Pickford and Chaplin, United Artists. Throughout this era, "Doug" made over twenty-eight films in which he usually had control over his plots, in order to guarantee that the spirit of the character would reflect his concerns. Typically, the smiling, energetic hero mirrored Fairbanks himself. He has luxury and urban comfort; but within his mind and soul he still wants to be self-made. Even though his cheerful persona suggested to audiences a sense of optimism and a feeling that everything would turn out all right, the typical Fairbanks film would find the hero loaded with the worries of modern middle-class existence.

Fairbanks best dramatized the character in *His Majesty the American* (1919). The story charts the life of a young urbanite who does not know who his father is. Behind the symbolic quest for identity lies the vision of an expanding frontier where the hero might be a cowboy. His New York apartment is filled with snowshoes, saddles, and cowboy hats, suggesting that he is ready to master savages and bandits. But he is trapped in an urban civilization where he is faced with office routine and no challenges. Seeking outlets for his restless energy, he rescues poor girls from vice dens and babies from fires. With no thrills left, he goes west. Next we see him sleeping in a luxury Pullman car. The Indians on the frontier are all tamed, and he is nothing but a tourist. So he goes to Mexico, hoping to find excitement in the Revolution, but it has been quelled. Back in the city, there is nothing left to conquer, for reforms have created order. In desperation, he goes to Europe and finds that his father was not a self-made man, but an aristocrat. Now Fairbanks puts down a rebellion against the nobles at precisely the time when revolutions were spreading across the continent. Here he finds an identity, and marries a princess.

Within this film we see some of the classic dilemmas of the Fairbanks genre. Who am I, what is an American, are questions that reverberate through the film. Usually the hero has a metaphorical name such as Andrew Jackson, Jr., Daniel Boone Brown, or Cassius Lee. He admires the "steel stamina and efficiency" of the symbolic fathers who built and rule the industrial system like Charles Schwab, Andrew Carnegie, and Theodore Roosevelt. Yet at the same time he feels trapped in their creations. Unlike the small producers of a Griffith film, Fairbanks is not outside the corporate system. Rather, he is a manager, clerk, or employee in a large office. His egalitarian spirit is crushed by the capitalists above him whom he admires, but can never equal. These same powerful people have taken his autonomy, and he feels like a helpless cog in the organization. So he dreams nostalgically of a western frontier that is gone. Every now and then a threat to the society erupts, bringing a challenge to the young hero who fears he is not up to the task.

Two central problems face the hero. One is his boredom at work, the other confronts him at leisure. As to the first, through humor, Fairbanks lightened the heaviness of sons trapped in the industrial creations of their fathers. Loyalty to the patriarch, in fact, inhibits rebellion. *Wild and Wooly* (1917) presents a modern urbanite dressed in a suit and tie who dreams of riding a horse across the deserts of Arizona. As the camera pulls backwards from his face, he appears seated in a luxurious New York estate where his father asks the butler to "tell the Comanche Indian we are wanted at the office in ten minutes." At work, Alexis Napoleon

Brown punches a time clock and a caption explains that, "his boundless energy is trapped at a desk in a button factory." *When Clouds Roll By* (1919) amplified the discontent by showing the hero entering an office where "all time and space is economized." As he falls asleep shuffling papers, his uncle, the boss, pronounces that the boy will add up to "nothing." The youth finds this all too true. He leaves work and confronts the overpowering city, where he loiters around Fifth Avenue, hoping to rub elbows with the rich. But at the Plaza Hotel, even the waiters echo his uncle and treat him like a "nobody."

Luxury poses the second problem. Initially, as an heir to the Protestant ethic, the hero fears that pleasure will endanger the frontier spirit. A typical Fairbanks film, *The Mollycoddle* (1920), opens on the dissipation of a sheriff's son. His father had won the West, and he became effete and soft on the inherited wealth, gallivanting around Europe. Similarly, the hero of *When Clouds Roll By* works in an office during the day, but at night his nightmares are filled with monsters who feed him by force. In this film, even the inner life is corrupted, for stuffed with rich pastries he is too fat to master his devilish pursuers. Others show the hero trying to re-charge his boring life through cocaine, amusement parks, boxing matches, or the new women drawn to the bohemian life of New York's Greenwich Village. Often, these threatening activities were personified by non-whites. One dream sequence includes men dressed and masked in black toppling Liberty from her pedestal. And in interviews, Fairbanks talked of his fears of Asians and Negroes, whom he constantly wanted to dominate through physical battle. In other words, the softness of modern life might literally drown the hero and make him "no better than a Negro"....

Today's readers might find it difficult to believe not only that [Mary] Pickford's popularity ran parallel with Doug's, but that she portrayed a heroine who complimented his cultural reorientations. Was she not the sweet little girl of Griffith's films, or the angelic youth of *Pollyanna* (1920) or *Sparrows* (1926)? True, these films show her persona to be little different from nineteenth-century stereotypes. Nevertheless, it is well to note that Pickford did not like her portrayal in Pollyanna, and thereafter deeply regretted conforming to the image of girlhood. One reason why she disdained that association was that in the period from 1914 to 1918, when rising to unprecedented fame and becoming the most popular star in all film history, she did not fit that image at all. In fact, during these key years of her career, "Mary" played a female role which made a fundamental break from the past, and embodied many of the aspirations of women in her generation.

Precisely because Pickford attempted the impossible, she became the most popular star of the day. While Fairbanks questioned the male role, Pickford questioned the female role at work and in the family. Over and over again she portrayed women striving to be economically free and morally emancipated. No doubt because these films took place in real life circumstances and seemed so convincing, publishers asked her to write weekly columns for women on how to deal with their own lives. Mary responded by continually backing women's suffrage and echoing the messages offered on the screen. Above all, she was a self-sufficient woman who hired female writers who were much like herself. Together they created the character of a heroine who pioneered new trails for women into the domains of men. Formerly, for example, the ideal of great wealth and upward mobility was reserved for males; but Pickford made the Horatio Alger aspiration viable for women. The press not only praised her work, but paid a great deal of attention to the star's salary—for it was the first time that such a publicly acclaimed "good girl" made so much money in the degraded, at least for women, marketplace. "Mary Pickford," wrote one typical enthusiast in 1914, "gets more money than the President . . . nine million people would rather see her on the screen than Bryan, Wilson, Roosevelt and Vernon Castle. That is why they will have to pay her $50,000 a year in 1914 and double that in 1915." Indeed, she reached her peak when in 1920 she was the only woman to join Fairbanks, Chaplin, and Griffith to form United Artists, earning the incredible salary of one million dollars a year. Through it all, Pickford realized why she was constantly voted in newspaper polls the "most popular girl in the world":

> I like to see my own sex achieve. My success has been due to the fact that women like the pictures in which I appear. I think I admire most in the world the girls who earn their own living. I am proud to be one of them.

It is no accident that the most noted stars of the era created their unique screen characters largely from their own lives. Like Chaplin, Fairbanks, and others, Pickford made the most of her origins. Pickford loved to tell the press how she was born Gladys Smith of Toronto, Canada, in 1893. On her father's side she was English Methodist, on her mother's she was Irish Catholic. The father ran a small grocery store, and insisted that the women stay dependent at home. Her mother and grandmother on both sides of the family guarded the domestic realm, forbidding drink or any suggestion of impropriety. Mary's grandmother in particular tried to cleanse prostitutes and convert them from sin. Yet when Mr. Smith died, the mother took the first step away from Victorianism by placing her two girls and a son on the stage, allowing them financial independence. Never did Mrs. Smith remarry; she cut her ties with the past by changing the family name to Pickford, a classier name giving status to their still unrespectable occupation. From the age of about ten onwards, Mary toured the country as a stage performer. But always Mrs. Smith trained Mary to stay clear of actresses who smoked, used bad language, or worked in studios which reeked with the scandal surrounding the Stanford White and Evelyn Nesbit affair. Mary's highest aspiration was to join David Belasco's company on Broadway. Yet reluctantly, out of financial desperation, she joined the recently cleansed movies in 1909.

In this realm of "scandal," Pickford was fortunate enough to join D. W. Griffith's company. But the films she made for the master cast her as a traditional Victorian heroine, giving little indication of her future. *Lena and the Geese* (1911), for example, featured her as a poor peasant girl whose love redeems a young man from his wasted life. When she discovers that she is in fact the long-lost child of a noble family, she accepts her true class status. A slight deviation from this melodramatic formula came in *The New York Hat* (1912). In that production she played an orphan whose guardian forbids her using her inheritance to buy a hat. The local minister, charmed by her vivacity, persuades the oppressive guardian to let her have some fun, and buy the bonnet. Following the success of these minor films, Pickford achieved her heart's desire: Belasco brought her to Broadway. There she starred in

The Good Little Devil (1913). As the play became a major hit, Pickford's public persona reflected the high life of New York City.

In the following years, as film makers brought established stars from Broadway, Adolph Zukor hired Pickford to star in a photoplay "completely separate," she recalled, "from what I had been doing. . . . They thought I was just another actress, but when I made *Tess of the Storm Country* that was really the beginning of my career." Now audiences saw a heroine who offered more than old femininity. In contrast to her work with Griffith, where she resisted the director's desire to mold her into genteel patterns, Pickford now took on a personality free of abstract ideals of purity. "Little Mary" was above all a person in her own right. No doubt her projection of a unique personality was because she was one of the premier performers of the day. On the screen her character displayed a whole range of emotions, while mixing drama with humor in an utterly convincing blend. Once audiences came to expect the Pickford image as something special, Pickford left standard roles where she had displayed predictable emotions in equally predictable situations. She then became a model of vitality, and a boundless force that could not be confined to one place or social station. As Pickford recalled of her struggle against the old melodramas that forced one into formalized and educational categories, "I always tried to get laughter into my pictures. Make them laugh and make them cry and back to laughter. What do people go to the theater for? An emotional exercise, and no preachments. I don't believe in taking advantage of someone who comes to the theatre by teaching them a lesson. It's not my prerogative to teach anything."

Nevertheless, the quest for personal freedom had deep social implications. In the film that sparked the Pickford image for the next six years, *Tess of the Storm Country* (1914), the heroine is a rebellious, independent, and energetic Cumberland mountain girl whom we first see dancing a jig. She and her hunter father would live contentedly were it not for Mr. Graves, the sheriff, and the local elite. He takes away her father's livelihood by forbidding "poaching in the forest." At the same time, Graves's daughter has an illegitimate child with a lover who dies. To save herself from paternal "wrath," she gives the baby to the heroine, Tess. As Tess raises the infant, the town assumes it is hers. Graves, as the church elder, refuses to baptize the baby, so Tess marches to the altar and sprinkles sacramental water on the child herself. Continuing this rebellion, she leads the farmers and tradesmen in a successful fight against Graves's game laws. Only when the villain learns whose child Tess protects does he soften, allowing his daughter to raise his grandchild and apologizing to Tess. He now repeals the poaching ordinance, and blesses his son's marriage to Tess.

Pickford's spunky heroine who fought economic and domestic tyranny in the countryside was equally effective in the face of urban problems. *The Eternal Grind* (1916) opens on a rural American girl leaving for the city—an experience relevant to much of her audience. Although she is in quest of freedom, she finds that the only employment available for women is routine and menial. So she takes a job as a sewing machine operator and soon becomes a "slave." Lording over the female workers is the boss. He exploits the laboring women and forbids his sons to mingle with them. Yet the dancing and gaiety of the working girls attracts one son who then has an affair with the heroine's best friend. When the girl becomes pregnant, Mary insists that they marry, reinforced by a gun in her hand. But the lad's father forbids it. Meanwhile, the heroine has fallen in love with the other son, a social worker. Together they convince the father to give up his greedy ways, and he finally allows both marriages. Such love also inspires him to install labor-saving devices to improve the conditions for his workers.

Equally important, Pickford broke from the Victorian mode of purity. Half the star's appeal lay in her ability to confront the major social problems of her day, and resolve them on the personal level. But the other half was her vitality. For she expanded the perimeters of respectable female behavior far beyond their nineteenth-century coordinates. Unlike the serial queens who might look but never touch, Pickford rolled up her sleeves and plunged her hands into previously forbidden realms. Some films showed her as an outsider, fighting against the system. But in others, she was caught in it. These films portray her as a genteel girl stifled in a home with a work-obsessed father and a socialite, charity-worker mother. In response to her restlessness, the heroine looks down the class order for excitement. Reflecting the culture's persistent ambivalence, a common device was the kidnap. *Poor Little Peppina* (1916) and *Less Than the Dust* (1916) show her as an American girl snatched from her Victorian home by foreigners. This gives her an excuse for taking on a different personality without guilt. Growing up with gypsies, Italians, Hindus, or Indians she learns to wear their exotic clothes, assume a swarthy complexion, and participate in public festivals with both men and women. Another formula for breaking down barriers between the sexes was to cast Pickford as a foreigner herself. In *Amarilly of Clothesline Alley* (1918), *Madame Butterfly* (1915), or *Hulda of Holland* (1916), Mary is a real Irish, Japanese, or Dutch girl who mingles in saloons, dances in New York, or embodies exotic qualities of an Asian or European female, complete with bright clothes and a sensual personality. . . .

After the War came the appropriate merging of their careers, when Pickford and Fairbanks divorced their spouses and married each other. As in their films, the modern home was not achieved without a struggle against confining norms of the past. Nevada's district attorney threatened to sue the couple for defying the state's residence laws; the Catholic bishop excommunicated Pickford, using the opportunity to preach against marital infidelity and separation; the Baptist minister who presided over their wedding was nearly censured for marrying a divorced man and woman; Pickford's former husband, Owen Moore, threatened to sue for adultery. Yet the criticism soon gave way to acclaim. Rather than encouraging divorce, their union appeared as the way to perfect wedlock. Neither saw divorce as an admirable thing. Yet they both felt it was the unfortunate price to pay for the domestic ideal. Pickford claimed that her former husband was an abusive drunkard, jealous of her success. Now, with Fairbanks, she had a marriage of equals. As they honeymooned in Europe, the press heralded the golden couple, and the huge crowds seemed to sanction their emancipation. Presumably, their breaks from the past had led to the happiness their films promised to millions.

During the next ten years, their union was constantly in the public eye. Symbolic of the modern marriage they epitomized was their famous Hollywood estate, Pickfair. The home was now expanded far beyond the functional Victorian domicile. Modeled on a European chateau, Pickfair collected and refined elements of upper and lower-class pleasures. It was a consumer's paradise that resembled an innocent doll's house more than a formidable, aristocratic mansion typical of the eastern elites. Swimming pools, gyms, fountains, and cultivated lawns supplied a private "vacation land." Inside, the couple decorated each room in the motif of a foreign country, so that movement from one part of the house to another provided exotic adventure. In this kingdom of eternal youth, Doug and Mary highlighted continual newness by dipping into their vast wardrobes of stylish clothes for each of the day's activities: work, sports, dining, dancing, and parties. It followed that whenever the two sat for photographs, their smiles radiated happiness. A typical reporter described the Pickfair life as "the most successful and famous marriage that the world has ever known," succeeding where "others failed." For neither Pickford nor Fairbanks envisaged the home as "the dumping ground for the cares of the day."

In the attention the press and fan magazines paid to their tastes, likes, and dislikes, the modern imagery of the star was fully born. On and off the screen, they were "Doug and Mary"—ordinary folk like you and me who were blessed by opportunity. Yet as European royalty and the American rich visited Pickfair, and Doug and Mary emulated in small the styles formerly reserved for a Vanderbilt, Astor, or Rockefeller, they showed the aspiring urbanite that upward mobility could be expressed in this new realm of leisure even more than on the job itself. Instead of being resentful of the wealthy, they demonstrated how modern consumption allowed one to emulate the styles of the high and mighty. In real life, "Doug" was the smiling, youthful hero whom Mary described as "always on the jump." Fairbanks himself extolled "sunrises over sunsets, beginnings over endings," and never spoke of failure, death, or depressing things. Pickford recalled that he had an endless habit of writing "success" on scraps of paper—a code that he both lived and preached in self-improvement pamphlets for the boy scouts, as well as fan magazines. In his partner, Mary, he found the new woman with the old values. She participated in charity and orphanage work, yet radiated a modern consumer ideal. Together, their common touch appeared equal to any nobility.

The golden couple eventually divorced, and each went on to a third spouse. Yet in the period from 1914 to 1918, their importance as cultural reformers cannot be overemphasized. Every major player before them suggested that the crisis of the age was not so much status decline or a search for order as it was the dissolution of the family values of the past. Unlike vice crusaders, and early film makers like Griffith, who had tried to hold on to traditional domesticity in the face of the forces that were tearing it apart, Pickford and Fairbanks pointed to the twentieth century. True, they rebelled against the constraints at work and the sexual roles of the past; but they showed how to resolve these potentially explosive issues in private ways. Instead of trying to contain the fruits of the corporate order within a Victorian framework, they tried to make high-level consumption a means for restoring family stability. The idea was not to resist the modern organizations, or to question its rationality with counter-cultural values. Rather, they tried to find freedom in the realm of leisure, which would then offer an uneasy accommodation to the new order. By carrying her moral emancipation into the home, the new woman hoped that an expanded domestic realm might compensate for the inadequacies of public life, and strengthen relations between the sexes. In turn, men would think of success more in terms of the money that would provide the good life. Although there was no conspiracy of big business to foist this formula on the public, the movie industry had synthesized consumption to Progressive ends, which perfectly suited the needs of the emerging corporate era.

6

PRIMARY SOURCES

A. *Edison v. American Mutoscope Company* (1902)

The first two decades of the twentieth century were a time of bitter struggles between the Film Trust, led by Thomas Alva Edison, and independent film producers. In this landmark 1902 decision, the U.S. Circuit Court of Appeals for the Southern District of New York overturned Edison's claim that he held patent rights to the whole of motion picture technology.

The photographic reproduction of moving objects, the production from the negatives of a series of pictures representing the successive stages of motion, and the presentation of them by an exhibiting apparatus to the eye of the spectator in such rapid sequence as to blend them together, and give the effect of a single picture in which the objects are moving, had been accomplished long before Mr. Edison entered the field. The patent in suit pertains mainly to that branch of the art which consists of the production of suitable negatives. The introduction of instantaneous photography, by facilitating the taking of negatives with the necessary rapidity to secure what is termed "persistence of vision," led to the devising of cameras for using sensitized plates and bringing them successively into the fields of the lens, and later for using a continuously moving sensitized band or strip of paper to receive the successive exposures. The invention of the patent in suit was made by Mr. Edison in the summer of 1889. We shall consider only those references to the prior art which show the nearest approximation of it, and are the most valuable of those which have been introduced for the purpose of negativing the novelty of its claims.

The French patent to Du Cos, of 1864, describes a camera apparatus consisting of a battery of lenses placed together in parallel rows, and focused upon a sensitive plate; the lenses being caused to act in rapid succession, by means of a suitable shutter, to depict the successive stages of movement of the object to be photographed. . . .

The camera apparatus of M. Marey, described in the *Scientific American* of June, 1882, and used by him, mounted in a photographic gun, to produce a series of instantaneous photographs, showing the successive phases of motion of birds and animals, describes a single-lens camera and clock mechanism which actuates the several parts. . . .

It is apparent from the references considered that while Mr. Edison was not the first to devise a camera apparatus for taking negatives of objects in motion, and at a rate sufficiently high to result in persistence of vision, the prior art does not disclose the specific type of apparatus which is described in his patent. His apparatus is capable of using a single sensitized and flexible film of great length with a single-lens camera, and of producing an indefinite number of negatives on such a film with a rapidity theretofore unknown. The Du Cos apparatus requires the use of a large number of lenses in succession, and both the lens and the sensitized surface are in continuous motion while the picture is being taken; whereas in the apparatus of the patent but a single lens is employed, which is always at rest, and the film is also at rest at the time when the negative is being taken. Nor is it provided with means for passing the sensitized surface across the camera lenses at the very high rate of speed, which is a feature, though not an essential feature, of the patented apparatus. . . .

The important question is whether the invention was in such sense a primary one as to authorize the claims based upon it. The general statements in the specification imply that Mr. Edison as the creator of the art to which the patent relates, and the descriptive parts are carefully framed to lay the foundation for generic claims which are not to be limited by importing into them any of the operative devices, except those which are indispensable to effect the functional results enumerated. It will be observed that neither the means for moving the film across the lens of the camera, nor for exposing successive portions of it to the operation of the lens, nor for giving it a continuous or intermittent motion, nor for doing these things at a high rate of speed, are specified in the claims otherwise than functionally. Any combination of means that will do these things at a high enough rate of speed to secure the result of persistence of vision, and which includes a stationary single lens and tape-like film, is covered by the claims.

It is obvious that Mr. Edison was not a pioneer, in the large sense of the term, or in the more limited sense in which he would have been if he had also invented the film. He was not the inventor of the film. He was not the first inventor of apparatus capable of producing suitable negatives, taken from practically a single point of view, in a single-line sequence, upon a film like his, and embodying the same general means for rotating drums and shutters for bringing the sensitized surface across the lens, and exposing successive portions of it in rapid succession. Du Cos anticipated him in this, notwithstanding he did not use the film. Neither was he the first inventor of apparatus capable of producing suitable negatives, and embodying means for passing a sensitized surface across a single-lens camera at a high rate of speed, and with an intermittent motion, and for exposing successive portions of the surfaces during the periods of rest. His claim for such an apparatus was rejected by the patent office, and he acquiesced in its rejection. He was anticipated in this by Marey, and Marey also anticipated him in photographing successive positions of the object in motion from the same point of view.

The predecessors of Edison invented apparatus, during a period of transition from plates to flexible paper film, and from paper film to celluloid film, which was capable of producing negatives suitable for reproduction in exhibiting machines. No new principle was to be discovered, or essentially new forms of machine invented, in order to make the improved photographic material available for that purpose. The early inventors had felt the need of such material, but, in the absence of its supply, had either contented themselves with such measure of practical success as was possible, or had allowed their plans to remain upon paper as indications of the forms of mechanical and optical apparatus which might be used when suitable photographic surfaces became available. They had not perfected the details of apparatus especially adapted for the employment of the film of the patent, and to do this required but a moderate amount of mechanical ingenuity. Undoubtedly Mr. Edison, by utilizing this film and perfecting the first apparatus for using it, met all the conditions necessary for commercial success. This, however, did not entitle him, under the patent laws, to a monopoly of all camera apparatus capable of utilizing the film. Nor did it entitle him to a monopoly of all apparatus employing a single camera.

B.   "The Nickel Madness"
Barton W. Currie, *Harper's Weekly*, August 24, 1907

This article provides a vivid first-hand description of early movie theaters at a time when the movies were just beginning to become mass entertainment.

Crusades have been organized against these low-priced moving-picture theatres, and many conservators of the public morals have denounced them as vicious and demoralizing. Yet have they flourished amazingly, and carpenters are busy hammering them up in every big and little community in the country.

The first "nickelodeons," or "nickelet," or whatever it was originally called was merely an experiment, and the first experiment was made more than a year ago. There was nothing singularly novel in the idea, only the individualizing of the motion-picture machine. Before it had served merely as a "turn" in vaudeville. For a very modest sum the outfit could be housed in a narrow store or in a shack in the rear yard of a tenement, provided there was an available hallway and the space for a "front." These shacks and shops are packed with as many chairs as they will hold and the populace welcomed, or rather hailed, by a huge megaphone-horn and lurid placards. The price of admission and entertainment for from fifteen to twenty minutes is a coin of the smallest denomination in circulation west of the Rockies.

In some vaudeville houses you may watch a diversity of performances four hours for so humble a price as ten cents, provided you are willing to sit among the rafters. Yet the roof bleachers were never so profitable as the tiny show-places that have fostered the nickel madness.

Before the dog-days set in, licenses were being granted in Manhattan Borough alone at the rate of one a day for these little hurry-up-and-be-amused booths. They are categorized as "common shows," thanks to the Board of Aldermen. A special ordinance was passed to rate them under this heading. Thereby they were enabled to obtain a license for $25 for the first year, and $12.50 for the second year. The City Fathers did this before Anthony Comstock [the Purity Crusader] and others rose up and proclaimed against them. A full theatrical license costs $500.

An eloquent plea was made for these humble resorts by many "friends of the peepul." They offered harmless diversion for the poor. They were edifying, educational, and amusing. They were broadening. They revealed the universe to the unsophisticated. The variety of the skipping, dancing, flashing, and marching pictures was without limit. For five cents you were admitted to the realms of the prize ring; you might witness the celebration of a Pontifical mass in St. Peter's; Kaiser Wilhelm would prance before you, reviewing his Uhlans. Yes, and even more surprising, you were offered a modern conception of Washington crossing the Delaware "acted out by a trained group of actors." Under the persuasive force of such arguments, was it strange that the Aldermen befriended the nickelodeon man and gave impetus to the craze.

Three hundred licenses were issued within the past year in the Borough of Manhattan alone for common shows. Two hundred of these were for nickelets. They are becoming vastly popular in Brooklyn. They are springing up in the shady places of Queens, and down on Staten Island you will find them in the most unexpected bosky dells, or rising in little rakish shacks on the mosquito flats.

Already statisticians have been estimating how many men, women, and children in the metropolis are being thrilled daily by them. A conservative figure puts it at 200,000, though if I were to accept the total of the showmen the estimate would be nearer half a million. But like all statisticians, who reckon human beings with the same unemotional placidity with which they total beans and potatoes, the statistician I have quoted left out the babies. In a visit to a dozen of these moving-picture hutches I counted an average of ten babies to each theatre-et. Of course they were in their mothers' or the nurse-girls' arms. But they were there and you heard them. They did not disturb the show, as there were no counter-sounds, and many of them seemed profoundly absorbed in the moving pictures.

As a matter of fact, some mothers—and all nurse-girls—will tell you that the cinematograph has a peculiarly hypnotic or narcotic effect upon an infant predisposed to disturb the welkin. You will visit few of these places in Harlem where the doorways are not encumbered with go-carts and perambulators. Likewise they are prodigiously popular with the rising generation in frock and knickerbocker. For this reason they have been condemned by the morality crusaders.

The chief argument against them was that they corrupted the young. Children of any size who could transport a nickel to the cashier's booth were welcomed. Furthermore, undesirables of many kinds haunted them. Pickpockets found them splendidly convenient, for the lights were always cut off when the picture-machine was focussed on the canvas. There is no doubt about the fact that many rogues and miscreants obtained licenses and set up these little show-places merely as snares and traps. There were many who thought they had sufficient pull to defy decency in the choice of their slides. Proprietors were said to work hand in glove with lawbreakers. Some were accused of wanton designs to corrupt young girls. Police-Commissioner Bingham denounced the nickel madness as pernicious, demoralizing, and a direct menace to the young.

But the Commissioner's denunciation was rather too sweeping. His detectives managed to suppress indecencies and immoralities. As for their being a harbor for pickpockets, is it not possible that even they visit these humble places for amusement? . . . .

But if you happen to be an outlaw you may learn many moral lessons from these brief moving-picture performances, for most of the slides offer you a quick flash of melodrama in which the villain and criminal are always getting the worst of it. Pursuits of malefactors are by far the most popular of all nickel deliriums. You may see snatch-purses, burglars, and an infinite variety of criminals hunted by the police and the mob in almost any nickelet you have the curiosity to visit. The scenes of these thrilling chases occur in every quarter of the globe, from Cape Town to Medicine Hat.

The speed with which pursuer and pursued run is marvellous. Never are you cheated by a mere sprint or straightaway flight of a few blocks. The men who "fake" these moving pictures seem impelled by a moral obligation to give their patrons their full nickel's worth. I have seen dozens of these kinetoscope fugitives run at least forty miles before they collided with a fat woman carrying an umbrella, who promptly sat on them and held them for the puffing constabulary. . . .

The popularity of these cheap amusement-places with the new population of New York is not to be wondered at. The newly arrived immigrant from Transylvania can get as much enjoyment out of them as the native. The imagination is appealed to directly and without any circumlocution. The child whose intelligence has just awakened and the doddering old man seem to be on an equal footing in the stuffy little box-like theatres. The passer-by with an idle quarter of an hour on his hands has an opportunity to kill the time swiftly, if he is not above mingling with the hoi polloi. Likewise the student of sociology may get a few points that he could not obtain in a day's journey through the thronged streets of the East Side.

Of course the proprietors of the nickelets and nickelodeons make as much capital out of suggestiveness as possible, but it rarely goes beyond a hint or a lure. For instance, you will come to a little hole in the wall before which there is an ornate sign bearing the legend: FRESH FROM PARIS   Very Naughty.

Should this catch the eye of a Comstock he would immediately enter the place to gather evidence. But he would never apply for a warrant. He would find a "very naughty" boy playing pranks on a Paris street—annoying blind men, tripping up gendarmes, and amusing himself by every antic the ingenuity of the Paris street gamin can conceive.

This fraud on the prurient, as it might be called, is very common, and it has led a great many people, who derive their impressions from a glance at externals, to conclude that these resorts are really a menace to morals. You will hear and see much worse in some high-priced theatres than in these moving- picture show-places.

In some of the crowded quarters of the city the nickelet is cropping up almost as thickly as the saloons, and if the nickel delirium continues to maintain its hold there will be, in a few years, more of these cheap amusement-places than saloons. Even now some of the saloon-keepers are complaining that they injure their trade.

C. Fighting a Vicious Film: Protest against "The Birth of a Nation" Boston Branch of the National Association for the Advancement of Colored People, 1915

Few films ever aroused as much controversy as D.W. Griffith's Birth of a Nation. *Critics denounced it as a gross distortion of American history that promoted racial strife. These two selections offer examples of the kinds of arguments raised against Griffith's epic.*

In its advertisement we are told that *The Birth of a Nation* is founded on Thomas Dixon's novel *The Clansman;* that it is a war play "that worked the audience up into a frenzy"; that "it will make you hate."

In an interview with a Boston editor, Thomas Dixon said, "that one purpose of his play was to create a feeling of abhorrence in people, especially white women, against colored men"; "that he wished to have Negroes removed from the United States and that he hopes to help in the accomplishment of that purpose by *The Birth of a Nation.*"

In furthering these purposes the producers of the film do not hesitate to resort to the meanest vilification of the Negro race, to pervert history, and to use the most subtle form of untruth—a half truth.

Well knowing that such a play would meet strong opposition in Boston, large sums of money were spent in the employment of Pinkerton detectives and policemen to intimidate citizens, and the managers of the theatre refused to sell tickets to colored people. To soften opposition, the impression was given that the president of the United States had endorsed the play and that George Foster Peabody and other distinguished people favored it. One method of working up support was to pass cards among the auditors asking them to endorse the play. These cards were circulated, signed and collected at the end of the first act and before the second act in which appear the foul and loathsome misrepresentations of colored people and the glorification of the hideous and murderous band of the Ku Klux Klan. . . .

Analysis by Francis Hackett

If history bore no relation to life, this motion picture could well be reviewed and applauded as a spectacle. As a spectacle it is stupendous. It lasts three hours, represents a staggering investment of time and money, reproduces entire battle scenes and complex historic events; amazes even when it wearies by its attempt to encompass the Civil War. But since history does bear·on social behavior, *The Birth of a Nation* cannot be reviewed simply as a spectacle. It is more than a spectacle. It is an interpretation, the Rev. Thomas Dixon's interpretation, of the relations of the North and South and their bearing on the Negro. . . .

In *The Birth of a Nation* Mr. Dixon protests sanctimoniously that his drama "is not meant to reflect in any way on any race or people of today." And then he proceeds to give to the Negro a kind of malignity that is really a revelation of his own malignity.

Passing over the initial gibe at the Negro's smell, we early come to a negrophile senator whose mistress is a mulatto. As conceived by Mr. Dixon and as acted in the film, this mulatto is not only a minister to the senator's lust but a woman of inordinate passion, pride and savagery. Gloating as she does over the promise of "Negro equality," she is soon partnered by a male mulatto of similar brute characteristics. Having established this triple alliance between the "uncrowned king," his diabolic colored mistress and his diabolic colored ally, Mr. Dixon shows the revolting processes by which the white South is crushed "under the heel of the black South." "Sowing the wind," he calls it. On the one hand we have "the poor bruised heart" of the white South, on the other "the new citizens inflamed by the growing sense of power." We see Negroes shoving white men off the sidewalk, Negroes quitting work to dance, Negroes beating a crippled old white patriarch, Negroes slinging up "faithful colored servants" and flogging them till they drop, Negro courtesans guzzling champagne with the would-be head of the Black Empire, Negroes "drunk with wine and power," Negroes mocking their white masters in chains, Negroes "crazy with joy" and terrorizing all the whites in South Carolina. We see blacks flaunting placards demanding "equal marriage." We see the black leader demanding a "forced marriage" with an imprisoned and gagged white girl. And we see continually in the background the white Southerner in "agony of soul over the degradation and ruin of his people."

Encouraged by the black leader, we see Gus the renegade hover about another young white girl's home. To hoochy-coochy music we see the long pursuit of the innocent white girl by this lust-maddened Negro, and we see her fling herself to death from a precipice, carrying her honor through "the opal gates of death."

Having painted this insanely apprehensive picture of an unbridled, bestial, horrible race, relieved only by a few touches of low comedy, "the grim reaping begins." We see the operations of the Ku Klux Klan, "the organization that saved the South from the anarchy of black rule." We see Federals and Confederates uniting in a Holy War "in defense of their Aryan birthright," whatever that is. We see the Negroes driven back, beaten, killed. The drama winds up with a suggestion of Lincoln's solution—"back to Liberia"—and then, if you please, with a film representing Jesus Christ in "the halls of brotherly love."

My objection to this drama is based partly on the tendency of the pictures but mainly on the animus of the printed lines I have quoted. The effect of these lines, reinforced by adroit quotations from Woodrow Wilson and repeated assurances of impartiality and goodwill, is to arouse in the audience a strong sense of the evil possibilities of the Negro and the extreme propriety and godliness of the Ku Klux Klan. So strong is this impression that the audience invariably applauds the refusal of the white hero to shake hands with a Negro, and under the circumstances cannot be blamed. Mr. Dixon has identified the Negro with cruelty, superstition, insolence, and lust. . . .

Whatever happened during Reconstruction, this film is aggressively vicious and defamatory. It is spiritual assassination. It degrades the censors that passed it and the white race that endures it.

D.   *Mutual Film Corp.* v. *Industrial Commission of Ohio*
United States Supreme Court, 1915

This landmark Supreme Court decision, which denied motion pictures First Amendment protections of free speech, stood as the law for 37 years, providing legal sanction for public censorship.

In its discussion, counsel have gone into a very elaborate description of moving picture exhibitions and their many useful purposes as graphic expressions of opinion and sentiments, as exponents of policies, as teachers of science and history, as useful, interesting, amusing, educational, and moral. . . . We may concede the praise. It is not questioned by the Ohio statute. . . . Films of a "moral, educational, or amusing and harmless character shall be passed and approved," are the words of the statute. No exhibition, therefore, or "campaign" of complainant will be prevented if its pictures have those qualities. Therefore, however missionary of opinion films are or may become, however educational or entertaining, there is no impediment to their value or effect in the Ohio statute. But they may be used for evil, and against that possibility the statute was enacted. Their power of amusement, and, it may be, education, the audiences they assemble, not of women alone nor of men alone, but together, not of adults only, but of children, make them the more insidious in corruption by a pretense of worthy purpose. Indeed we may go beyond that possibility. They take their attraction from the general interest, eager and wholesome it may be, in their subjects, but a prurient interest may be excited and appealed to. Besides, there are some things that should not have pictorial representation in public places and to all audiences. And not only the state of Ohio, but other states, have considered it to be in the interest of public morals and welfare to supervise moving picture exhibitions. We would have to shut our eyes to the facts of the world to regard the precaution unreasonable or the legislation to effect it mere wanton interference with personal liberty. . . .

It cannot be put out of view that the exhibition of moving pictures is a business, pure and simple, originated and conducted for profit, like other spectacles, not to be regarded by the Ohio Constitution, we think, as part of the press of the country, or as organs of public opinion. They are mere representations of events, of ideas and sentiments published and known; vivid, useful, and entertaining, no doubt, but as we have said, capable of evil, having power for it, the greater because of their attractiveness and manner of exhibition. It is this capability and power, and it may be in experience of them that induced the state of Ohio, in addition to prescribing penalties for immoral exhibition, as it does in its Criminal Code, to require censorship before exhibition, as it does by the act under review. We cannot regard this as beyond the power of government. . . .

The objection to the statute is that it furnishes no standard of what is educational, moral, amusing, or harmless, and hence leaves decision to arbitrary judgment, whim, and caprice; or, aside from those extremes, leaving it to the different views which might be entertained of the effect of the pictures, permitting the "personal equation" to enter, resulting "in unjust discrimination against some propaganda film," while others might be approved without question. But the statute by its provisions guards against such variant judgments, and its terms, like other general terms, get precision from the sense and experience of men, and become certain and useful guides in reasoning and conduct. The exact specification of the instances of their application would be impossible as the attempt would prove futile. Upon such sense and experience, therefore, the law properly relies. . . . If this were not so, the many administrative agencies created by the state and national governments would be denuded of their utility, and government in some of its most important exercises become impossible. . . .

PART II

W.C. Fields

HOLLYWOOD'S GOLDEN AGE

1

INTRODUCTION

Backstage During the Great Depression:
42nd Street, Gold Diggers of 1933, and *Footlight Parade*

Three Warner Brothers musicals that appeared in 1933 occupy a special place in the affections of moviegoers. With the astonishingly intricate examples of Busby Berkeley's choreography (women are arranged in the form of pinwheels and violins), their fast talking chorus girls, smiling ingenues, and tough troubled Broadway directors, and their good natured glimpses of backstage life in the theater, these films have come to represent what the critic Pauline Kael has called "pure thirties."

These films helped form some of our society's most lasting cultural clichés. The basic plot of *42nd Street*—the tale of an untried chorus girl who becomes a star after the leading lady breaks her ankle—remains, even today, a vivid fantasy. The speech that director Warner Baxter uses to urge young Peggy Sawyer on has often been mimicked:

> Miss Sawyer, you listen to me . . . and you listen hard. Two hundred people, 200 jobs, $200,000, five weeks of grind and blood and sweat depend upon you! . . . You've got to go on and you've got to give and give and give! They've got to like you, got to. You understand? You can't fall down, you can't. Because your future's in it, my future and everything all of us have is staked on you. All right now, I'm through. But you keep your feet on the ground and your head on those shoulders of yours, and, Sawyer, you're going out a youngster, but you've got to come back a star!

To the casual viewer today, these backstage musical fantasies may appear to be nothing more than pure escapism. In fact, their appeal to depression-era audiences went far deeper. The tone and message of these films is far more complex than the word "escapism" suggests.

Take, for example, the opening of *Gold Diggers*. Ginger Rogers and sixty chorus girls, wearing costumes made up of oversized silver dollars, sing "We're in the Money." The actresses' costumes and their song's words—"we never read a headline about a breadline"—seem superficially to epitomize the flight into fantasy that characterizes the thirties backstage musical. In actuality, however, the opening sequence is anything but a simple musical escape from depression realities. It concludes when local authorities arrive to shut down the rehearsal and repossess the actresses' costumes because the producer has failed to pay his bills.

On close examination, *42nd Street, Gold Diggers,* and *Footlight Parade* obliquely address broad political and economic issues and anxieties raised by the Great Depression. Their upbeat plots—in which talented newcomers rise to stardom and wealthy bluebloods marry common chorus girls—helped Depression-era Americans sustain a faith that class differences could be overcome and that, despite many obstacles, happiness and success would eventually prevail. Yet alongside this upbeat vision of class healing and success is a more somber vision. The title sequence of *42nd Street* is filled with jarring images of violence and domestic abuse. The musical finale of *Gold Diggers*—"The Forgotten Man"—gained resonance from the 1932 Bonus March of more than 10,000 World War I veterans on Washington, demanding early payment of a bonus for wartime service. Etta Moten, an African American, poignantly reminds viewers of this bitter episode, which concluded when federal troops led by Douglas MacArthur dispersed the veterans and destroyed their encampment with tanks, tear gas, and bayonets:

Remember my forgotten man;
You put a rifle in his hand;
You sent him far away;
You shouted-Hip Hooray!
But look at him today!

2

DEPRESSION AMERICA AND ITS FILMS

Laughing Through Tears:
Hollywood Answers to the Depression
Maury Klein

Hollywood offered Depression America much more than mere escapism. It helped maintain the nation's morale and preserve values. In this selection, the historian Maury Klein surveys Hollywood's response to the Great Depression.

Not even the Great Depression stopped Americans from going to the movies. In 1930 an estimated 110 million people trooped into theaters each week to forget their cares for an hour or two. Three years later, when the economy hit rock bottom, 60 to 80 million citizens still managed to scrounge the price of admission every week. Whatever else they sacrificed, Americans clung to this pleasure with a fervor that went beyond mere escapism. In its short lifetime, the motion picture industry had already assumed the role of dream factory, but hard times gave it a new dimension. Film became the fantasy life of a nation in pain.

On the eve of the stock market crash, movies had just learned to talk and the industry had emerged from an era of upheaval into one dominated by the major studios. The larger studios had evolved into models of vertical integration. Five of them—MGM, Twentieth Century Fox, Paramount, Warner Brothers, and RKO—owned chains of theaters which enabled them to control the process from shooting to showing. Three others, Universal, Columbia, and United Artists produced, sold, and distributed their films but depended on the big five for theaters in which to show them. As a whole the industry churned out upwards of 500 feature films a year, with the major studios each producing fifty or so. Together the eight major film companies accounted for about three-fourths of all feature films released and gathered about eighty five percent of all rental income.

The financial squeeze of the Depression years strengthened the hold of the studio system, which continued to dominate (some said tyrannize) the industry for more than two decades. Movies, like music, sports, and breakfast cereal, had become big business, a product peddled in the vast national marketplace by shrewd entrepreneurs. Intent on reaping large profits, the movie moguls relied heavily on advertising and promotion, which put them in the curious position of using one form of illusion to sell another. Like most businessmen, they tacked wherever the economic winds blew. Pitched and heaved by the gales of depression, they trimmed their sails and steered the safest course possible.

In that sense the moguls followed the lead of the New Deal, which was itself less a revolution than a cautious, minimal response to a cataclysm. Their task was to divine the longings and ambitions of their audience, reduce their findings to a formula, and repeat the formula in film after film. As the mood of the public changed, so did the formulas that embodied it. Those who wonder how network television came to assume its dreary form can find the model from which it sprang in the movie industry of the thirties. Among the 5,000 feature films that rolled off the production line during the decade, there emerged certain distinct genres which—at their worst—meant that each new film was made, as Jeffrey Paine observed, "by the movie immediately preceding it."

The moguls rivaled politicians as barometers of public attitudes. Their films, like the mood of national politics, reflected the abrupt transition from the dark night of Hooverian bleakness to the dawn of Rooseveltian optimism. Prior to 1933, the motion picture industry intensified its attack on traditional middle-class values begun a decade earlier. Studio heads were not social revolutionaries but merely opportunists who found a postwar generation weary of causes, bored with convention, and eager for a taste of the glamorous and the exotic. To these audiences the studios fed a steady diet of titillation; already they had discovered the market value of sex and violence.

The genres that emerged during the early 1930s clearly revealed how severe a blow economic collapse had dealt to traditional values and, paradoxically, how resilient those values were even in the worst of times. A good example was the gangster films, which burst on the scene with such classics as *Little Caesar* (1930), *The Public Enemy* (1931), *City Streets* (1931), and *Scarface* (1932). Sound gave the genre a new dimension of shock with gunfire, screams, wailing sirens, screeching tires, and shattering glass, but the appeal went much deeper. In their own curious way the gangster films offered a twisted version of the Horatio Alger success story. The hero, usually an immigrant from the slums, pulled himself to the top by hard work before suffering his inevitable downfall. He lived and died by the rules: the difference was that the rules lay outside the law.

In these films law and government were impotent, inept, or simply absent. Unemployed viewers warmed to a hero who defied the society that had never given him a break, and who was tough enough to carve his own destiny. The gangster films embodied both the triumph of the individual and the failure of the social system.

Another genre, the shyster films, filled the screen with charming rogues who, their innocence blighted by bitter experience, marched down the avenue of good intentions to a new knowledge of how the whole dirty game was played. The shysters in movies like *The Front Page* (1931), *Scandal Sheet* (1931), *Lawyer Man* (1932), *The Mouthpiece* (1932), and *The Dark Horse* (1932) included not only lawyers but also politicians and journalists—cynics all, who had learned their lessons about corruption in the classroom of the big city.

For the shyster as well as for his client, the gangster, society was a fraud, politics was a sham, and the law was a joke or a vacuum, with the root of all evil somehow connected to that most enduring American theme: corruption. Against these forces, the forces of good seemed helpless. In *The Dark Horse,* a savvy politico was plucked from jail to manage a gubernatorial campaign for an idiot nominee. "He's the dumbest human being I ever saw," said the manager. "We're going to convince the voters that they're getting one of them. That's what voters want in these days of corruption and depression." The candidate won in a landslide after learning to answer all questions first "Yes," then "No."

One common theme bound the gangsters and shysters together. In an age of national paralysis, they were men who knew how to get things done, however deplorable their means. Their appeal lay mainly in the fact that they were both victims and men of action. So too with the comics. While sound rendered the rich genre of silent comedy extinct, it ushered in a new breed who demolished everything from the grandest institutions to the most ordinary of conventions. Borrowing heavily from their native soil, vaudeville, the new comedians mixed sight gags with verbal patter to create routines that were no less definitive trademarks than Charlie Chaplin's walk. Whether it was the Marx Brothers making shambles of every sacred cow from education to the state, or W.C. Fields lacerating the pretensions of the middle class family, the comics embodied the outrage of thousands embittered by a system that was not supposed to fail them, but had.

In *Duck Soup* (1932) the Marx Brothers lambasted politics, patriotism, the state, and war. Historian Robert Sklar has rightly called it "as thorough a satire on politics and patriotism as any film before *Dr. Strangelove.*" A masterpiece of invention, it had the misfortune to be released shortly after Roosevelt took office and, in the new mood of hope, did poorly at the box office. "Even a small town knows when there is a flop," declared the manager of a Nebraska theater, while an Iowa manager was "afraid these boys are washed up." Benito Mussolini got the message; the film was banned in Italy. Afterward the Marx Brothers retreated to safer themes until, like Fields, they were reduced to a form of self-parody by the decade's end.

As usual sex reared its alluring head, but the unique presence of Mae West gave it an unexpected twist toward comedy. Early Depression films like *Susan Lenox* (1931), *Safe in Hell* (1931), *Blonde Venus* (1932), and *Faithless* (1932) cast major stars as women forced to become prostitutes or mistresses of wealthy men. Unable to control their own destinies, they fell back on sex as their only bargaining chip and suffered the inevitable degradation and punishment. It was the old recipe of titillation wrapped in a layer of moralism.

West discarded the image in favor of one that approached the battle of the sexes boldly and frankly. "Neither the sweet ingenue nor the glamour girl fit the depression years," recalled producer-director Adolph Zukor of Paramount Pictures. "Mae did. She was the strong, confident woman, always in command." In her first film *She Done Him Wrong* (1933), West displayed the formula that wilted the flower of American manhood. As Andrew Bergman described it, "Her voice radiated irony, her eyes sized up potential lovers as though they were sides of beef, and her hips mesmerized a nation." The "fallen woman" tradition would never recover from her liberated spirit and unabashed appetite for pleasure. "Haven't you ever met a man who could make you happy?" Cary Grant asked her in the film. "Sure," West replied. "Lots of times."

Such frankness was too much for the watchdogs of morality. Hollywood filmmakers had been skating on thin ice since 1922 when they hired Will Hays, a prominent Republican and Presbyterian elder, to launder their excesses. When observant moralists protested that nothing had changed, the Hays office responded in 1930 with the Production Code, a curious document drafted by a Catholic professor and a prominent Catholic layman. Jack C. Ellis has observed that "Like the Ten Commandments, the Code's language was largely negative." Under twelve headings the code itemized the forbidden fruit of film, and a crazy-quilt garden it was. Nevertheless, complaints arose that it was being ignored. Outraged Catholics formed the Legion of Decency in 1934 and promised to boycott offending films.

The threat of lost revenue was enough to galvanize the moguls into creating their own enforcing mechanism. Joseph I. Breen, a Catholic journalist, was given the task of certifying every film with a code seal. Breen's authority was such that for two decades no major film was released without the seal. For moralists the victory was at best a Pyrrhic one. Ellis noted that "The reasons for the Code and the Seal were financial rather than moral," and that "it sapped creative energy at the source." Sklar agreed that "the code cut the movies off from many of the most important moral and social themes of the contemporary world."

The code's effects were predictable and farreaching. It reinforced the peculiar American tendency to substitute violence for sex. As Robert Warshow observed long ago, two of our most classic genres, the western and the gangster films, featured the gun as their central symbol. Not that sex vanished; it merely changed form. The leer replaced candor, and what could not be shown could be suggested in a dozen ways. Perhaps the most significant legacy of the code was that it nudged directors toward stylization of technique as they realized that serious themes could only be treated obliquely.

The trend toward stylization coincided with the upbeat mood generated by the election of Roosevelt and the onset of the New Deal. Impressed by the rising spirit of hope and the return of national pride, the studios discarded their attack on traditional values with unabashed speed and began pouring old wine into cheerful new bottles. Law and order returned not only to the streets but to the frontier as well. James Cagney signaled the change in *G-Men* (1935) by switching from gangster to federal agent. As an ad proclaimed, "HOLLYWOOD'S MOST FAMOUS BAD MAN JOINS THE G-MEN AND HALTS THE MARCH OF CRIME " Edward G. Robinson followed suit in *Bullets or Ballots* (1936), proving, as Robinson said, that "A good detective should be a tough guy, too." In most cases it was not cops who subdued the mob but the feds, who had the muscle to do what local authorities could not manage.

Early in the decade the popularity of westerns had languished to the point where studios did no more than churn out endless strings of grade B "oaters." With most of the old heroes like Tom Mix and William S. Hart gone, the genre seemed played out until several directors, inspired by the new national mood, discovered history. In such films as *The Plainsman* (1936), *The Texas Rangers* (1936), *Stagecoach* (1939), and *Drums Along the Mohawk* (1939), the western was reborn as the epic of "How the West Was Won." The old elements were still there—the violence, the oversimplification of good and evil, the hero as rugged individual—but now they were fused into larger, mythic themes of taming the frontier, curbing lawlessness, and forging a nation. That they took gross liberties with history did not affect their appeal at the box office.

Three other genres of the new vintage revealed its potency for myth making. The musical, creature of the new technology, was at first content to transfer theater revues to the screen but soon went beyond anything possible on a stage. In 1933 three Warner Brothers' blockbusters, *Gold Diggers of 1933, 42nd Street,* and *Footlight Parade* created the new idiom. If these lavish pastries, with their extravagant staging by Busby Berkeley and others, seemed rampant escapism, they were in part reincarnations of Horatio Alger. All three featured success stories grounded in the Depression. Thanks to faith, hard work, and some luck, the kid(s) came through in each one, with some spectacular singing and dancing along the way. The timing was perfect to enthrall audiences starved for reaffirmation of the old verities. Later musicals lost this core of relevancy and, for all their glitz and glamour, seemed vapid by comparison. An Indiana theater manager thought he knew why, "The ensembles are well done," he said about *Gold Diggers of 1937,* ". . . but why expect musical numbers to hold up a weak, shallow, artificial story."

Another offspring of technical wizardry, the cartoon, came of age thanks to the unique genius of Walt Disney. As Sklar has pointed out, Disney's philosophy was as conservative as his techniques were innovative. The world of fantasy he created might lift one above the cares of ordinary life, but it was a world solidly grounded in the tradition of free enterprise, rugged individualism, and self-help. *Three Little Pigs* released in May 1933 amid Roosevelt's first Hundred Days, became a runaway hit with its timely, upbeat theme song, "Who's Afraid of the Big Bad Wolf?" By the time of his first feature film, *Snow White and the Seven Dwarfs* (1937), Disney had won the nation's heart and formed the moral boundaries of a fantasy world in which those who did not stick to the rules or trust the tried-and-true got burned.

A third genre, the screwball comedy, demonstrated brilliantly that one did not need cartoons to construct myth out of entertainment. The undisputed master of screwball was film director Frank Capra, who enchanted audiences with a string of hits: *Lady for a Day* (1933), *It Happened One Night* (1934), *Mr. Deeds Comes To Town* (1936), *Lost Horizon* (1937), *You Can't Take It With You,* and *Mr. Smith Goes to Washington* (1939). Capra's films were shrewdly topical, yet born of a vision intent on healing the wounds and divisions of a dispirited nation. Andrew Bergman called them "the masterwork of an idealist and door-to-door salesman."

The true screwball comedy featured wealthy eccentrics who stood the world on its ear with antics at once zany and larded with common sense. In *It Happened One Night* Capra reversed the premise: poor boy and bored rich girl met improbably, delighted in their differences and, through a series of wacky adventures, fell in love. The poor boy made good, the rich girl found true happiness, class divisions were healed, and all lived happily ever after. Capra made this formula work with his extraordinary warmth, humor, comic inventiveness, and eye for detail. The message of his films satisfied everyone's fantasies; the endearing charm of his characters made everyone wonder what the fuss had been about.

Capra's instinct for convincing audiences that his world was the way life should be lived was uncanny. To it he added topical relevance that fashioned mythical portraits of an America in which people longed to believe. The poor boy got the beautiful rich girl and climbed the social ladder; Mr. Deeds shrugged off a $20 million inheritance ("Twenty million! That's a lot, isn't it?"), used it to buy farms for the poor, and subdued the swells and slickers with his simplicity and goodness; Mr. Smith fought political corruption on behalf of the people and won. No one did more to build the national image than Capra. When later he harnessed his talent to the war effort, he said of audiences, "For two hours you've got 'em. Hitler can't keep 'em that long."

Capra's films, like the frontier epics, appealed directly to the craving for an earlier, simpler America where life had not yet been scrambled by the baffling complexities of war, industrialization, and depression. No one captured this mood more poignantly than Thorton Wilder in the play *Our Town* (1938). On screen the yearning for nostalgia gave immense popularity to a string of movies starring Will Rogers. An incomparable folk humorist, Rogers had made films since 1918 but did not blossom until the advent of sound, which brought the full warmth and wit of his personality to audiences. Playing himself in such films as *State Fair* (1933), *David Harum* (1934), and *Steamboat 'Round the Bend* (1935), Rogers invoked the mythical harmony of small town America (*David Harum* was set in Homeville), a place where the larger, uglier world never intruded beyond a point where Uncle Will could handle it. Such was Rogers' popularity that two of his films were released after his untimely death in 1935. "He is," wrote one reviewer, "what Americans think other Americans are like."

Homeville was a warm, friendly place that had little to do with the world outside the theater. What almost no one seemed willing or able to do was look the Depression straight in the eye. Except for the bleak realism of Mervyn Leroy's *I Am a Fugitive From a Chain Gang* (1932), the topical films churned out by Warner Brothers failed to capture the searing pain of Depression life. Elsewhere, director King Vidor took an earnest but naive swipe at social statement in *Our Daily Bread* (1934), while John Ford's rendition of *The Grapes of Wrath* (1939) stayed carefully within the norms of traditional American myths and values. Pare Lorentz's two epic documentaries *The Plow That Broke the Plains* (1936) and *The River* (1937), were self-conscious hymns of affirmation.

"No medium has contributed more greatly than the film to the maintenance of the national morale during a period featured by revolution, riot and political turmoil in other countries," crowed Will Hays in 1934. "It has been the mission of the screen, without ignoring the serious social problems of the day, to reflect aspiration, optimism, and kindly humor in its entertainment."

Perhaps Hays was more right than he knew. Whatever else the films of the 1930s accomplished the best of them displayed a brilliance of style and technique that has endured as a living legacy of the craft. Certainly they impressed today's generation of filmmakers, who seem capable of nothing more original than imitating or remaking their work.

3

THE DEPRESSION'S HUMAN TOLL

Gangsters and Fallen Women
Peter Roffman and Jim Purdy

The early Depression mood of despair was reflected on the screen through a succession of gangsters, prostitutes, and prison inmates. But as film historians Peter Roffman and Jim Purdy show, the appeal of these characters came of much more than fondness for outlaws at a time when the social order appeared to be breaking down. These figures also helped to preserve older cultural ideals during a period of upheaval.

The Gangster Cycle

Between the beginning of the Depression in 1930 and the early days of the Roosevelt administration in 1933, when confusion and desperation gripped much of the country, Hollywood momentarily floundered. Not only did the studios have to make the difficult transition to sound, they had to adjust to the rapidly changing tastes of a nation in upheaval. These two variables—sound and the Depression—created a whole new set of aesthetic demands requiring that the old Formula be placed within a new context. The studios at first experimented with extravagant musicals and photographed plays, but dwindling audience interest quickly prompted them to revert to action and melodrama. It didn't take too long to realize that the talkies required a greater surface realism. The romantic, ethereal fantasies of the twenties' films sounded ridiculous when put into words: John Gilbert's passion may have been eloquently mirrored in his face and eyes, but when he attempted to express it verbally the emotions seemed silly and banal. Correspondingly, the hard facts of the Depression demanded a shift in subject matter. Latin lovers and college flappers now seemed rather remote, completely unrelated to the changed mood and the overriding preoccupation with social breakdown. The romantic ideals of the thirties had to be more firmly grounded in a topical context.

The films of the early Depression years reflect much of the desperation of the time, both in their initial groping for new character types and settings and in their eventual preoccupation with an amoral society and the inefficacy of once-sacred values. By late 1933, with the New Deal inspiring confidence, Hollywood had found its bearings. The studios were now secure with the new sound medium and had established the dramatic conventions expressive of new attitudes. New Deal confidence and Hays Office moralism removed much of the hard edge from the early thirties cycles, but the basic groundwork for the remainder of the decade had been laid and Hollywood could now proceed with greater self-assurance.

It was during this period that the social problem film emerged as an important genre. It did not immediately spring into existence with the arrival of a major social crisis but was rather the end product of a gradual evolution. Important stylistic and narrative motifs had to be developed before the talkies could begin self-consciously to analyze the issues of the day. First among these were character prototypes—the gangster, the fallen woman, the convict, and the shyster—and a contemporary setting—the alleyways, slums, and speakeasies of the big city. Shot in a racy but essentially realistic style, these early films are the archetypal Depression movies. Though they do not really constitute problem films in themselves, the gangster, fallen woman, and prison cycles metaphorically comment on the relationship between the individual and society, taking a highly cynical attitude toward social institutions. The hero must be tough and amoral in order to endure in a society crumbling under the weight of its own corruption and ineffectuality. Dramas lingering on images of a hostile urban environment and glorifying criminal heroes seethed with antisocial undertones. Then by 1932–33, with these dramatic conventions firmly entrenched as part of popular culture, they could be readily extended into an overt discussion of modern society. The implied social criticism of these cycles quickly gave way to the exposés, commentaries, and inquiries of the problem film.

The most popular of the prototype cycles was the gangster movie. It reestablished the action movie as Hollywood's staple by grafting a realistic, fast-paced narrative style onto stories out of the headlines. For the first time, films went beyond mere talk and exploited the full possibilities of sound, utilizing the sound track to create a physical impact which increased dramatic tension. The screen exploded with "the terrifying splutter of the machine gun, the screaming of brakes and squealing of automobile tyres." Furthermore, the gangsters were character types more familiar to audiences than the teacup sophisticates of the photographed plays. They spoke like truckdrivers (Bugs Raymond in *Quick Millions,* 1931), slum kids (Tommy Powers in *Public Enemy,* 1931), Italian immigrants (Rico in *Little Caesar,* 1930, and Tony Camonte in *Scarface,* 1932), and stockyard workers ("Slaughterhouse" in *The Secret Six,* 1931). And most important of all, the films adapted the Formula to make the gangster a contemporary hero. Stress was still placed on the individual but his circumstances were made more appropriate to the times. Like the traditional Formula hero, the gangster hungers after personal success, but he is different in that he can no longer fulfill this goal within the bounds of society and must pursue it through crime. The old avenues of fulfillment had been circumvented by the Depression.

Rico (Edward G. Robinson) in *Little Caesar* demonstrates an absolute faith in the American Dream by carefully following Andrew Carnegie's step-by-step formula for success: he starts at the bottom and with a single-minded dedication works his way to the top, the whole time abstaining from such distractions as sex and alcohol and studying hard to learn the operation of his organization. Rico typifies the hardworking Puritan businessman, except that the corporation has been replaced by the gang and murder is Rico's main business tactic. Similarly, Tommy

Powers of *Public Enemy* is a more cynical version of the early Douglas Fairbanks comic hero. Lewis Jacobs' description of the Fairbanks persona perfectly fits Jimmy Cagney's portrayal of Powers: "In all these films Fairbanks was the 'self-made man,' unbeatable and undismayed. Quick intelligence and indefatigable energy always won him success in terms of money and the girl." But the only area that can accommodate Powers' drive and energy is that of the corrupt underworld. So Tommy, the true thirties go-getter, turns to bootlegging to fulfill his potential.

Thus the traditional good guy whose success affirms society had been transformed into the good bad guy whose success questions society. The films demonstrate that in thirties America only crime pays. Tommy's virtuous older brother (Donald Cook) is ambitious but stays within the law and languishes as a frustrated trolley conductor, while Tommy graduates to stylish suits, fast cars, and luxury penthouses. This of course contradicts a basic moral tenet and the films must therefore kill off their heroes to invalidate lawlessness as a route to success. But in trying to uphold society, the endings only reinforce the films' basic pessimism. The success drive either leads to frustration within the system or violent death outside it. The viewer is left with the choice between the bland existence of Tommy's brother and the exciting, doomed career of Tommy.

Public Enemy

The Happy Ending has been temporarily turned topsy-turvy. The audience identifies with the evil gangster's aims and frustrations and is invited to laugh at the representatives of good. Tommy sneers that his brother is just a "ding-dong on the streetcar." The legal establishment is likewise hopelessly inept, something to beat. If the police manage to arrest a gangster, a mouthpiece lawyer is immediately able to secure his release. Newton (Lewis Stone), the lawyer-gangleader in *The Secret Six,* is able to clear Slaughterhouse (Wallace Beery) of murder by manipulating the jury with courtroom tricks and bribery. In *Scarface,* the manipulation becomes a running gag. Every time Tony Camonte (Paul Muni) is arrested, he uses the phrase "habeas corpus" as an open sesame for his automatic release. The gangster's downfall is usually the result of gangland rivalry or a tragic personal flaw, not police efficiency. Rico has already been toppled by his rivals and has turned to alcohol when the police kill him, while Tony Camonte is destroyed by his incestuous love for his sister.

Thus, Good is hardly triumphant, and the audience, which vicariously identifies with the gangster's flaunting of every accepted code of social behavior (e.g., Cagney mashing the grapefruit in Mae Clarke's face), has very mixed feelings about Evil being vanquished. Robert Warshow suggests that the films are emblematic of our deepest fears, that the gangster expresses "that part of the American psyche which rejects the qualities and the demands of modern life, which rejects 'Americanism' itself."

> At bottom, the gangster is doomed because he is under the obligation to succeed, not because the means he employs are unlawful. In the deeper layers of the modern consciousness, all means are unlawful, every attempt to succeed is an act of aggression, leaving one alone and guilty and defenseless among enemies: one is punished for success. This is our intolerable dilemma: that failure is a kind of death and success is evil and dangerous, is—ultimately—impossible. The effect of the gangster film is to embody this dilemma in the person of the gangster and resolve it by his death. The dilemma is resolved because it is his death, not ours. We are safe; for the moment, we can acquiesce in our failure, we can choose to fail.

Warshow's thesis that the success ethic and Evil are one finds its most explicit expression in the films of writer-director Rowland Brown. His *Quick Millions* and *Blood Money* (1933) are the only gangster films to self-consciously connect the corruption of the gangster with that of society, to directly state that organized crime is just another form of business. In *Quick Millions,* Bugs Raymond (Spencer Tracy) succeeds by applying efficient business techniques to the rackets. He is the perfect corporate man, thinking up the plans for a protective organization and having others do the work while he collects the profits. His is less the world of machine guns and booze than of managerial manipulation. Likewise, Bill Bailey (George Bancroft) of *Blood Money* succeeds through his business acumen, making an excellent living by supplying bail money for members of the underworld. Bill's partner, nightclub owner Ruby Darling (Judith Anderson), combines legitimate business with more dubious enterprises, bluntly declaring that crime is a business like any other.

Brown continually emphasizes the many ties between the underworld and straight society, showing that the two are practically indistinguishable. Both Bugs and Bill have considerable contact with officials of law and government who seem no less corrupt than the gangsters. Bugs avoids police harassment through either bribery or blackmail, keeping files on the illicit activities of various officials. Bill backs a conservative mayoralty candidate for the same reason that businessmen support particular politicians—because the candidate's election will be good for business: "The only difference between a liberal and a conservative is that a liberal recognizes the existence of vice and controls it while a conservative turns his back and pretends it doesn't exist." In Brown's chain gang exposé, *Hell's Highway* (1932), the equation is reversed to prove that business is just another form of crime. Legitimate businessmen and government officials prove to be more criminal than the convicts, overworking and underfeeding them in order to build a highway at the smallest cost for the greatest profit.

But except for the intimations of Brown's films, which were never as popular as the others of the series, social commentary in the gangster movies rarely moves beyond metaphor. They may tell us much about the attitudes of the times, but they can hardly be labeled social problem films. Economic breakdown is not an explicit issue within the films but rather an assumed backdrop for the action. Nor do the films make more than token attempts to analyze the social roots of criminality. Despite *Public Enemy*'s claim that its purpose is "to depict an environment rather than glorify the criminal," there is little dramatic or sociological connection between the film's early depiction of Tommy Powers' slum childhood and his later career as a racketeer. Similarly, the prefatory statement that *Scarface* "is an indictment against gang rule in America and the careless indifference of the government. . . . What are you going do about it?" has nothing to do with the actual drama. Rather than indict the criminal, the film glorifies his ingenuity. We laugh with Tony when his lawyer gets him out of jail and he proves himself invulnerable to the law. The only "analysis" of a social problem occurs when a newspaper editor makes a plea for martial law. The scene is completely gratuitous to the rest of the plot—we never see or hear from the editor again—and its reactionary law-and-order viewpoint is out of keeping with the film's mockery of authority. While the police do kill Tony, no connection is made between his death and the editorial. It turns out that the scene was indeed added to the film long after its completion in order to placate censorship pressure. Director Howard Hawks disclaims it, stating that it was not part of the original script and was shot against his wishes by another director.

As the addition to *Scarface* indicates, these elements of overt social analysis are flimsy attempts to mask the films' antisocial implications. The producers' failure to effectively counter the glorification of violence and crime aroused a flurry of censorship activity which eventually killed the cycle. The censors understood that such glorification was central to the audience's experience of the films and the main reason for the gangster film's popularity in the early thirties.

Though the gangster of 1930–1932 disappeared from Hollywood films, his influence remained. The sound film was transformed by the biting dialogue, naturalistic characterizations, and fast-paced continuity of the cycle. Essential to the style and technique of the gangster films is the cynicism and topicality which verges on social criticism. Although the blatant glorification of criminal violence faded from the screen after 1932, the corrosiveness lingered on in other films. The individual's relation to society continued to be viewed with disaffection, but the reasons for such disaffection gradually emerged as central to the drama. Social criticism became a major motivating force behind the films and society was now directly indicted for the plight of the hero.

The Fallen Woman Cycle

Another group of films popular during the pre-FDR Depression years was the "fallen woman" cycle. As with the gangster film, this cycle rarely deals with the Depression in terms of social problems, but nevertheless clearly reflects the situation. The films have three basic subjects, each one demonstrating a moral breakdown within society—the unwed mother, the mistress of a married man, and the prostitute. All the films attempt to shore up morals and reaffirm America's Puritan heritage, but the drastic plot twists necessary for this reaffirmation reveal the strains of the times.

Though the films allow for the fact that crime and sin are justifiable in times of social duress, they display a heavy-handed moralism foreign to the gangster cycle. Apparently a more sensitive issue than gangland racketeering, female sexuality requires a more complicated set of rationalizations and more severe forms of punishment. It is naturally accepted that crime is a positive expression of the energetic male's rugged individualism and there is no real need to explain why a gangster is a gangster. The fallen woman's fall, however, must be thoroughly explicated and is only acceptable as an extreme necessity, a last recourse which is never a positive experience so much as a tragic degradation.

First of all, the heroine loses her chastity only for the purest of motives, usually that of true love. In the early films of the cycle centering on the unwed mother, she and her lover are prevented from marriage through extenuating circumstances. He is either a well meaning, sincere fellow inadvertently separated from the heroine or a wealthy irresponsible playboy who abandons her in her time of need. *Born to Lose* (1931), featuring Constance Bennett, "queen of the confession films," and her most frequent partner, Joel McCrea, is typical of this series. McCrea plays Barry Craig, a World War I aviator on leave, and Bennett, Doris Kendall, an off-duty nurse. With no time or opportunity to get married but still madly in love, they spend the night together. Afterwards, he returns to the front where he is soon reported missing and presumed dead while she finds herself pregnant, husbandless, and living in shame. *Common Clay* (1930), representative of the playboy seducer plot, has the pregnant serving girl (Constance Bennett) deserted by wealthy heir (Lew Ayres) who bows to his family's class prejudice.

In these and similar films, the heroine struggles to legitimize her child. Either her lover relents and marries her or some adoring boob takes his place. *Born to Love*'s nurse weds British stuffed shirt Sir Wilfred Drake (Paul Cavanaugh) for the sake of the baby; the abandoned heroine of *Common Clay* goes to court to sue for support. In both cases, the heroine suffers harsh treatment but valiantly fights on to selflessly provide the baby with a father, financial security, and social approval. And even in those films where she manages to win both true love and the baby's well being, this happens only after the heroine has languished in a trap which seems throughout to be inescapable.

The circumstances which force her to detour around the altar and head straight for bed are rarely economic. At a time when lack of money led to countless wedding postponements and made premarital sex a necessary alternative, when families were torn apart as members scattered over the country searching for work, the early confession films avoided explicitly linking the breakdown of socioeconomic structures with the strains on morality and personal relationships. Still, with their portrait of frustrated love, their stress on sacrifice for children and the struggle for security within a tragic set of circumstances, they reflect the instabilities of the times. The continual emphasis on the need to maintain the family seems a conscious effort to reaffirm traditional mores to reassure a shaky audience that the family unit is still the basis of American life.

This reaffirmation is strongly evident in the mistress films. The mistress character continually sacrifices her own happiness rather than have her lover break up his marriage and leave his children fatherless. In *Rockabye* (1932) the ubiquitous Ms. Bennett sends playwright Jake Pell (Joel McCrea) home to his estranged wife because Mrs. Pell is pregnant. When *Christopher Strong*'s (1933) mistress, aviatrix Cynthia Darlington (Katharine Hepburn) discovers her pregnancy, she crash dives to her death so that honorable Christopher (Colin Clive) will not have to abandon his family for her. In *Back Street* (1932), the most famous of the fallen woman weepies, Ray Schmidt (Irene Dunne) forgoes her desire to have children rather than disrupt her lover's family. She acquiescently lives out her years in their back street hideaway, fantasizing about the children she never had. The mistress is a martyr, valiantly surrendering personal satisfaction to uphold the sanctity of the family.

As the cycle developed and the Depression worsened, the fall of the heroine became ever more severe. By 1932, she was taking to the streets as a prostitute. The prostitute films best illustrate the relationship between moral and economic breakdown and hence provide the cycle's most direct, if still metaphoric, allusions to the Depression. The prostitute, like the gangster, must move outside a system that cannot accommodate her. Just as the gangster turns to crime to fulfill his success drive, so the prostitute takes to the streets to provide food for herself and her family.

Though the standard plot of these films finds the heroine beset by an economic crisis, only rarely is this crisis labeled as the Depression. It is because a husband or boyfriend suddenly becomes ill or abandons her that the heroine must quickly find some alternative means of support. Through various plot circumstances, she is unable to find work and has no choice but to use her one saleable commodity. Stranded and jobless in Panama, awaiting the return of her boyfriend, the heroine (Helen Twelvetrees) of *Panama Flo* (1932) reluctantly becomes involved in a world of crime and sin.

The title character (Greta Garbo) in *Susan Lennox: Her Fall and Rise* (1931) is also led into sin while searching for her missing lover. When she does find him, her ruined reputation prompts his rejection and, still alone, she is forced to take a number of progressively sleazy jobs which trade on her sex. Helen Faraday (Marlene Dietrich) in *Blonde Venus* (1932) becomes the mistress of a corrupt politician to pay for an expensive operation which will save her husband's life. When the cured but outraged husband casts her out, she kidnaps their son and flees across the country. The only way she can feed the boy while evading police is to become a prostitute.

The sole films to indicate any concrete relation between the heroine's prostitution and social circumstances are *The Easiest Way* (1931) and *Faithless* (1932). In the former, department store clerk Laura Murdock (Constance Bennett, again) is the daughter of an unemployed longshoreman. The film depicts a poverty-stricken environment, but the father's joblessness, it is made clear, is the result of his own laziness, not of any unemployment crisis. It is not society but her father's irresponsibility that has created Laura's revulsion for poverty and lust for the security and comfort of wealth. This leads her first to pose as a model for an ad agency (always the sign of a loose woman) and from there to become the mistress of agency president Willard Brockton (Adolphe Menjou). He keeps her in a luxurious apartment complete with lavish wardrobe and chauffeured limousine, all of which she accepts not necessarily because it is the only way (she has been employed in the department store) so much as the easiest way to get by.

In *Faithless*, Carol Morgan (Tallulah Bankhead) is a rich heiress wiped out by the Crash who becomes the mistress of a wealthy boor in order to maintain her lifestyle. Unable to tolerate his sadistic treatment she decides to fend for herself but cannot find a job and slips into poverty. Eventually she marries the penniless William Wade (Robert Montgomery) and when he is brutally beaten while looking for a job, she must return to a life of sin in order to pay for his food and medicine. Carol rushes into the night, declaring "There isn't anything I won't do." For the first time in the series, the sacrifice the woman makes for her man is clearly the result of the Depression.

But even in those films where the Depression backdrop remains amorphous, the implications are clear. Prostitution can be presented only as a last recourse and it can only be a last recourse within a broken-down world where all normal means of survival are cut off. The weakened or missing male figure is clearly representative of a society no longer able to support those it is responsible for.

Like the gangster films, the prostitute pictures must undercut the antisocial implications of the thesis that crime or sin is the only option available for the heroine: The conventional morality must be upheld and the women punished. But whereas the gangster is allowed to wreak havoc and enjoy the good life until the very last shootout, the prostitute continually pays the price for her violation of the Puritan code. Her career is a series of ever more degrading acts and escalating anguish. Susan Lennox has to sleep with a circus owner for the right to work in his sleazy sideshow. Later, stranded in the tropics, she is reduced to entertaining sailors in a cheap cafe-cum-brothel. Helen Faraday is forced to dress in rags and hide with her son in a New Orleans bordello. When the police finally catch up with her and take custody of the boy, she is left alone to languish with other tramps in an over-crowded flophouse. Noting the fact that all these women gradually proceed southward as their fortunes deteriorate, Andrew Bergman remarks "how accurately it demonstrates the really iron-clad moralism of the 'fallen woman' pictures. The heavy symbolism of deflowered women sweating off their sins in fetid tropics gave away Hollywood's assumptions about sin and its price."

Even when the prostitutes find their trade profitable, they remain unhappy and unfulfilled. Susan Lennox, Carol Morgan, and Helen Faraday suffer through periods of affluence as kept women and in the end shamefully submit themselves to their one true love. Though Carol and Helen have saved their husbands' lives, they must still plead for the male's forgiveness and depend on his generosity before they can be happy again. Susan Lennox must repeatedly try to convince her lover that she is not what she really seems despite the fact that his rejection has contributed to her compromised situation.

The films make paradoxical statements: the only way to survive is through sin, thus implying a condemnation of society; but as long as a woman is sinning she must be miserably unhappy, thus upholding the established social morality. Society cannot supply the economic means to support true love and family; prostitution provides the means yet excludes the possibilities of love and family. The paradox is resolved by having the heroine overcome her economic plight through sin and then reject the sin. Both Carol Morgan and Helen Faraday can repentantly return to their healthy and stable husbands only because they have sinned to save them.

This reaffirmation of moral values is obviously rather shaky. The films final and illogical declaration that love is more important than wealth and can, after all, be achieved within society is about as believable as the gangster films' assertion that crime doesn't pay. Carol Morgan's final submission to docile Robert Montgomery completely contradicts the vitality and independence of the Tallulah Bankhead persona.

This paradox is played out on a more sophisticated level in *Blonde Venus,* the one film in the cycle with any lasting artistic merit. Director von Sternberg despised the film, his original story significantly rewritten by Paramount to follow the fallen women conventions. But although the movie in plot outline sounds very much like other anonymous potboilers of the cycle, there is a subversive subtext that points up the dilemma of Helen's and woman's position in society. Helen's descent from family normality to cabaret singer/prostitute represents a quest for identity, so that her final return to the husband she now clearly resents indicates the impossibility of finding any satisfying sense of self. As wife-mother in the opening scenes, Dietrich is desexualized, reduced to knitting in an apron with her hair pinned back and her singing career frustrated. When she does return to the stage, it is her legs that get her the job and her sexual favors the attention and money of politician Nick Townsend (Cary Grant). Her attempts to combine career with motherhood are then thwarted by her husband and officialdom. She finally gives up trying to be a self-fulfilled woman using sex only to manipulate her way to the top of Parisian night life. In her Montmartre night club, she mocks the notion of manhood and even takes on the male role as aggressor by wearing a tuxedo. But her life is empty— "Nothing means much to me now"—and her return to Faraday, on one level a positive assertion of motherly love as self-definition, also implies a return to the tepid domesticity of the beginning, an admission of failure and despair. According to Robin Wood:

> The film . . . can be taken as a classic statement of one of the radical tenets of Feminism: that true femininity cannot yet exist, since all available roles for women in society are determined by male dominance. Every myth

of woman is exposed in the film, not celebrated. It also constitutes an astonishingly comprehensive analysis of the manifold forms of prostitution—from the home to the dollhouse—available to women within our culture.

Though *Blonde Venus* is the only one of these films that could be described as radical, there is nevertheless an inherent tension within the entire cycle indicative of a strained affirmation. The unhappy hookers and unwed mothers find eventual normality through contorted, last minute plot twists, with the heroine's final marriage to her love occurring only after she has endured countless indignities and years of suffering. In the mistress films, the family unit is upheld through tragedy: Cynthia Darlington's suicide and Ray Schmidt's lonely, childless aging. Despite the reassurances of the cycle, the most resonant images are those of suffering and degradation. Woman is a martyr and must endure pain no matter which course of action she takes. The films supplement the image of the individual and society established by the gangster film: the individual is an innocent victim entrapped by a broken-down society with few options open to him or her.

This strained affirmation was soon comically turned on its ear by Mae West. Through sarcastic slander she reveled in what the fallen woman film had to disguise and circumvent, completely reversing their moral deadliness by making sin a sheer delight and woman a strong assertive individual who didn't need any man. She quite frankly boasted, "Goodness had nothing to do with it." And like the gangster, she became a central target for the Hays Office.

4

DEPRESSION ALLEGORIES

Gone With the Wind and The Grapes of Wrath as Hollywood Histories of the Great Depression

Thomas H. Pauly

Two of the most popular films to appear during the Great Depression— Gone With the Wind *and* The Grapes of Wrath—*had particular meaning to Depression-era audiences. Both films tell stories of social dislocation and economic upheaval. As Thomas H. Pauly shows in this essay, both films can be understood as allegories of Depression experience.*

Popular culture of the later Depression years was dominated by *Gone With the Wind* and *The Grapes of Wrath*. As novels these two creations topped the best-seller lists during 1936, 1937, and 1939. Interest in both works was then renewed in early 1940—perhaps even reached its greatest peak—when both opened as movies within weeks of one another (*Gone With the Wind* on December 15, 1939 and *Grapes of Wrath* on January 24, 1940). Though both were tremendous box office successes their critics responded to each quite differently. While the reviews of *Gone With the Wind* strove to top one another with accounts of all the gossip, glitter, and money involved in the making of *Gone With the Wind* those discussing *The Grapes of Wrath* stressed the outstanding quality of the film itself. "No artificial make-up, no false sentiment, no glamour stars mar the authentic documentary form of this provocative film," asserted Philip Hartung in his review of *The Grapes of Wrath* for *Commonweal*. Similarly Otis Ferguson was confident enough of the dissatisfaction *Gone With the Wind* would bring that he postponed going, but he opened his review entitled "Show for the People," "The word that comes in most handily for *The Grapes of Wrath* is magnificent . . . this is the best that has no very near comparison to date." Despite the overwhelming critical preference for Ford's movie, however, it won only one Oscar (Best Director) in the 1940 balloting whereas Selznick's extravaganza swept all the major awards in 1939 except one (Best Actor). Clearly the latter film was the people's choice. At issue here was an intense unacknowledged debate over what the age preferred in its movies. In an era fraught with intense sociological upheaval *Gone With the Wind* seemed consciously intended to project its audience into a realm of sentiment and nostalgia beyond the confines of actual experience. As Lincoln Kirstein complained in the opening paragraph of his scathing review for *Films*:

> ... history has rarely been told with even an approximation of truth in Hollywood because the few men in control there have no interest in the real forces behind historical movements and the new forces that every new epoch sets into motion. *Gone With the Wind* deserves our attention because it is an over-inflated example of the usual false movie approach to history.

Implicit in these remarks is a charge often leveled against the movies produced during this era. Critics and historians of the cinema repeatedly call attention to Hollywood's striking reluctance to address itself to the problems of the Depression. Nothing they point out could have been further from the bread lines and the deprivation photographed by Dorothea Lange than the social comedies of Lubitsch, the slapstick of the Marx Brothers, and the polished dance routines of Fred Astaire and Ginger Rogers. Nonetheless as Andrew Bergman has asserted and then persuasively demonstrated in his book on films of the Depression *We're in the Money,* people do not escape into something they cannot relate to. The movies were meaningful because they depicted things lost or things desired. "What is 'fantastic' in fantasy is an extension of something real." In other words the "dreams" the audience is said to have demanded, those for which they spent the little extra money they had, were not mere illusions or abstractions but exciting imaginative articulations of their greatest hopes and fears their deepest doubts and beliefs. On this score *Gone With the Wind* possesses a significant measure of both historical validity and importance. The fact that it was far and away the most successful film of the decade probably had less to do with the glittering surface that so annoyed the critics than the common ground it shared with *The Grapes of Wrath.* Though it was less daring and less accomplished than Ford's work as an artistic creation, *Gone With the Wind* was similarly preoccupied with the problem of survival in the face of financial deprivation and social upheaval. Both movies also demonstrate a nostalgic longing for the agrarian way of life which is ruthlessly being replaced by the fearful new economic forces of capitalism and industrialization. By way of extension both reflect an intense concern for the devastating consequences of these conditions upon self-reliant individualism and family unity, two of America's most cherished beliefs. In each case however serious concern for these implications is dissipated into indulgent sentimentalism so that the audience's anxieties are alleviated rather than aggravated.

Even if the script had been available *The Grapes of Wrath* dealt with issues that were too familiar and too painful to have been made during the early thirties. Yet in deciding to produce a movie of this controversial novel at the time he did, Darryl Zanuck was sufficiently concerned about the specter of the Depression that he decided to mute and even eliminate some of the more charged aspects of Steinbeck's social criticism. As Mel Gussow has explained, "For Zanuck, *The Grapes of Wrath* and *How Green Was My Valley* were not really social documents but family pictures of a very special kind: movies about families in stress." Thus the movie's emphasis falls upon the sentimental aspect of the conditions controlling the Joads. At the outset this takes the character of the loss of a home which deprives the family of its essential connection with the land. Tom's initial return assumes the character of a search for a place of refuge from the suffering and hostility he has been forced

Gone With the Wind

to endure in prison and on his truck ride. That everything has changed is made clear by his encounter with Casy; but the full impact of this upheaval is registered only when he beholds the vacant crumbling house in which he was raised and hears Muley's distracted tale of how his reverence for the land has been desecrated. "My pa was born here," he insists: "We was all born on it and some of us got killed on it and some died on it. And that's what makes it ourn. . . . ." Equally striking in this regard is the later scene where Grampa asserts: "I ain't a-goin' to California! This here's my country. I b'long here. It ain't no good—but its mine" and then under-lines his points by distractedly gripping his native soil.

In dramatizing the intense suffering these people experience these lines serve the more important function of locating its source. The former agrarian way of life predicated upon man's intimate attachment to the land has given way to an economy of industrialization with its efficiency, practicality, and inhumanity. For Tom and his fellow farmers there is no possibility of retaliation. The fury that drives Muley to take up a gun produces only frustration and helpless dejection because there is no enemy to shoot. The man on the caterpillar turns out to be his neighbor who is trapped by the same problem of survival. The machines that level their homes like the foreclosures which are delivered in dark sinister automobiles cannot be associated with particular individuals; they are the weapons of a system devoid of both personality and humanity.

> The Man: Now don't go blaming me. It ain't my fault.
> Son: Whose fault is it? . . .
> The Man: It ain't nobody. It's a company. He ain't anything but the manager. . . .
> Muley (bewildered): Then who do we shoot?
> The Man: . . . Brother I don't know.

Deprived of the only home he has known Tom Joad joins his family in their quest for a new one. However great may be their need for food and money keeping the family together, Ma Joad makes clear, is the most pressing concern. She sees that nourishment involves the spirit as well and in the face of the increasingly deper-sonalized world confronting her the shared concerns of the family offer the only remaining source of humanity. These become the basic issues by which the audience measures the significance of the ensuing trip to California. As Ford dramatizes them the policemen who harass the Joads, the strawbosses who dictate to them, the thugs who break up the dances and union gatherings, are like the handbills that bring them to California, products of a sinister conspiracy beyond human control. They combine with the inhospitable landscape encountered to create an environment in which the family is unable to survive. Grampa and Gramma die before the destina-tion is reached; Connie cannot stand up to the punishment inflicted upon him and flees; Casy is killed by the growers' hired guns; having avenged Casy's death Tom is forced to flee for his life.

The Grapes of Wrath however is more than a mere drama of defeat. The futility of individualism and the breakdown of the family furnish in the end a distinct source of optimism. Having witnessed the miserable living conditions in which the Joads have futilely struggled to endure—the filthy tent in the clapboard road camp, the concentration of starving people in Hooverville, the gloomy squalor of the cabin at the Keene ranch—the audience is now introduced to a utopia of cooperative socialism which has been as scrupulously sanitized of communism as it is of filth. In contrast to the derogatory view expressed earlier in the movie, working with the government is shown to offer a more valid prospect of salvation than fighting against the prevailing conditions at the Wheat Patch camp, the spirit of Tom's involvement with Casy is realized without the self-defeating violence and killing. Here, as George Bluestone notes, the Joads find "a kind of miniature planned economy efficiently run, boasting modern sanitation, self-government, cooperative living, and moderate prices." Here people work together with the same automatic efficacy as the flush toilets. Cleanliness nourishes kindness, the caretaker explains with the serene wisdom of his kindly confident manner (does he remind you of FDR?).

Even the language has been changed to accord with this new society; one finds here not a shelter, a house, or a home, but a "sanitary unit." Though this community has been conceived to accord with the depersonalized society outside its gates it has also incorporated a basic respect for human dignity. It is a world characterized by its Saturday dance with its democratic acceptance, its well-controlled exclusion of the forces of anarchy, its ritualistic incorporation of the outdated family into a healthy new society—a new society which would actually be realized only two years later in the "comfortable" concentration camps for Japanese-Americans during World War II. Above all, the Wheat Patch camp episode affords a bridge to the "new" ending Zanuck was moved to write for his movie. As Tom and the Joad truck return to the outside world and strike out in different directions they have no idea where they are going but they all have renewed hope that they can find salvation just by being with "the people."

> Rich fellas come up an' they die an' their kids ain't no good an' they die out. But we keep a'coming. We're the people that live. Can't nobody wipe us out. Can't nobody lick us. We'll go on forever Pa. We're the people.

Such conviction, Zanuck concluded, was not to be thwarted by the "No Help Wanted" originally indicated in Nunnally Johnson's screenplay, so he gave them an open road—which appropriately enough leads off to nowhere.

The Grapes of Wrath is a fine movie but it is considerably flawed. Furthermore, for all its "documentary" technique, it is badly distorted history. Its depiction of the plight of the migrant worker contributes considerably less to our understanding of the conditions of the Depression than its suspicion of big business, its manifest agrarianism, and, above all, its sentimental concern for the breakdown of the family. Given the striking commercial success of the movie one cannot help wondering what it was the public went to see—an artistic masterpiece, a direct confrontation with the reality of the Depression, or its handling of the above concerns. Of the three the last was perhaps the most important for this was the one striking point of resemblance between it and the biggest box office movie of the decade. *Gone With the Wind* succeeded as well as it did in large part because it so effectively sublimated the audience's own response to the Depression. For them, the panoramic shot of the Confederate wounded littering the center of Atlanta was not a matter of fact but of feeling. All concern for the scene's historical authenticity simply vanished in the face of its dramatization of the sense of helplessness and devastation they themselves had experienced.

Amidst these circumstances, Scarlett's subsequent return to Tara bears a striking resemblance to Tom's homecoming in her quest for refuge from the adversities she has endured. Yet her expectation is shattered by the same scene of desolation that Tom discovered. For her, also, there is the same decaying ruin in place of the secure home she formerly knew. Tom's encounter with Muley seems almost a rerun of Scarlett's even more painful confrontation with her father, whose demented condition strikingly illustrates the magnitude of change resulting from the war's upheaval. As in *The Grapes of Wrath* this breakdown in the integrity of the family is associated with the destruction of an agrarian way of life which strikes at the very core of Scarlett's emotional being. The burned soil of Tara that Scarlett grips in the concluding scene of Part I is fraught with the same significance which attended Grampa's similar gesture in *The Grapes of Wrath*.

Scarlett's response, however, marks an important point of difference. Unlike Tom Joad, who took to the road and sought to survive by working with his family, Scarlett resolves to be master of her destiny. Her moving declaration, "As God is my witness . . . I'll never be hungry again," pits her will against the prevailing conditions. Her determination is such that she not only antagonizes the remnants of her family but she also exploits them; having slapped Suellen she proceeds to steal her prospective husband Frank Kennedy. Nonetheless her actions are prompted by some of the same motives that carried the Joads to California.

In the characterization of Scarlett is to be found most of the complexity that *Gone With the Wind* possesses. As the reviewer of the *New York Times* observed, "Miss Leigh's Scarlett is the pivot of the picture." Were she merely a bitch or strong-willed feminist the appeal of this movie would have been considerably diminished. In order to appreciate the intense response she elicited from the audience one has to understand the particular way in which Scarlett's return to Tara and her subsequent commitment to rebuilding it qualifies her initial assertion of independence and results in a tragic misunderstanding that brings her downfall. In the opening scenes of the movie Scarlett wins the audience's sympathy for her determined spirit of rebellion. It is she who provides critical perspective on the glittering world of plantation society. Tara and Twelve Oaks with their surrounding profusion of flowers and lush background sweep of countryside are as magnificently attired as the people who congregate there and therefore are perfect settings for the featured scenes of dressing and undressing, posturing and strutting. The main function of women in this world is providing ornamental beauty. The illusion of grace and elegance they sustain is predicated upon a harsh standard of propriety a painfully tight corset. Parties become major moments in their lives in helping them to achieve their ordained goal of marriage but their area of decision is limited to the choice of a dress or hat. Since the threat of a rival is the only war they can be expected to understand they are all herded off to bedrooms to freshen their appearances and restore their frail energies while the men debate the future of the South. Given the stilling confinement of this role Scarlett balks. Like the other women she entertains a vision of marriage and consciously attends to her appearance but unlike them she is determined to act on her wishes. Thus while her rivals retire according to the convention of the submissive female she slips downstairs to confront Ashley in the belief that he will not be able to resist her assault.

The war which preempts Scarlett's fight for Ashley dramatically affirms these and all the other deficiencies of this society but as a "lost cause," it also forces Scarlett to determine her highest priorities. At first she displays only a selfish interest; its tragedy is for her a source of gain in relieving her of an unwanted husband. However, the flames of Atlanta which occasion a nightmare of emotion as they destroy the Old South illuminate a new romantic potential in Scarlett's deepening relationship with Rhett. During their flight, their affair of convenience predicated upon the same spirited but pragmatic individualism which alienates them both from plantation society achieves a new level of interdependency in the intense feelings they exchange and share. Having been stripped of her gentility, her vanity, and finally her self-confidence, Scarlett is reduced to her greatest moment of need. At this point Rhett's selfishness which reveals itself to have been basically an emotional shield also gives way. For the first time both reach out for something greater than themselves. The result however is not a common understanding. Rhett proposes a marriage and a new future only to discover that Scarlett prefers to retreat to the past. Survival, she has come to believe lies in the red earth of Tara. Rejected, Rhett goes off to fight for the cause. Thus the situation which brought Rhett and Scarlett together propels them along separate paths in search of ideals which ironically the war is at that moment destroying. Though they survive to marry one another the decisions forced by the war constitute an insurmountable breach which the conclusion of the movie simply reaffirms as Rhett goes off to Charleston in search of "the calm dignity life can have when it's lived by gentle folks, the genial grace of days that are gone" while Scarlett heeds her father's words calling her back to Tara.

In his concerted effort to reproduce the novel as thoroughly as possible Selznick felt that the increased emphasis he accorded to Tara was one or the few points of departure. "I felt," he explained in one of his memos, "that the one thing that was really open to us was to stress the Tara thought more than Miss Mitchell did." For him, Scarlett's character was grounded in Tara, in agrarianism, and the family just as the identity of the Joads was. Yet, in according it much the same meaning, he dramatized its tragic consequence quite differently. Scarlett's vow never to be hungry again as she grips the burned soil of Tara at the end of Part I moves the audience with its stirring determination but this vow is severely qualified by the scene's logic. Quite simply Tara or "terra" cannot provide the nourishment she requires. The turnip she ravenously devours and then vomits is strikingly emblematic of Tara's true value. In the first place the fact that the earth is red is an obvious signal that the soil sustains crops with great difficulty. Without the slaves and strong-willed owners Tara is not even capable of generating enough capital to pay its taxes. The main reason for Scarlett's determination to return to Tara however transcends all these considerations. Tara is home—its essence is to be found more in the echoing sound of her father's voice and the heart-tugging strains of Max Steiner's music. For her, Tara is the sphere of her father's influence a refuge where matters were firmly under control and she was treated with tolerance and indulgence. Yet this is equally foolish for she discovers that her father has been broken by the war and now relies on her for the consolation she has expected him to provide. Nowhere are the disadvantages of Tara revealed more dramatically than in the buckboard visit of Jonas Wilkerson whose association with the new economic forces supplanting agrarianism recalls the nameless men of *The Grapes of Wrath* in their sinister cars.

Since money has become the only source of power Scarlett must seek beyond Tara for survival. Scarlett appears to marry Frank Kennedy to pay the taxes on Tara but she obviously sees that he is associated with the prospering forces of industrialization. Consequently in becoming his wife she really becomes a business-woman. These conflicting allegiances to Tara and to her lumber mill place Scarlett in the paradoxical position of shunning the role of wife and mother in order to uphold her passionate commitment to family and the home. Her identification with business and its ruthless practices now loses her the audience's sympathy yet because she never understands the character and consequences of what she is doing she proves more tragic than villainous. Her determined quest for the greatest margin of profit is not to be understood as her predominant aim. Much more essential is her desire that Tara be rebuilt. To do so is not only to eliminate the desperate state of poverty to which she had been reduced but also to restore the spiritual strength of her family home. Only the audience, however, comprehends the hidden cost. Frank becomes her lackey and her marriage no more than a working partnership. She herself becomes a social pariah. Most important Scarlett begins to die from emotional starvation as her business absorbs her energies without providing any of the attention and compassion she has always craved. The sorrow she drowns with liquor following Kennedy's death is neither anguish nor a pained sense of confine-ment—it is a strange lack of feeling.

Once again Rhett comes to offer her salvation. Despite his manifest contempt for propriety, Rhett's invasion of her privacy and his cynical proposal of marriage are joyfully welcomed because they offer Scarlett an opportunity to escape her business and enjoy her own home. Unfortunately the seeds of her undoing have already been sown. The self-reliant determination of her struggles has rendered her temperamentally incapable of filling the role of the devoted wife she would like to be. Rhett's gifts—the house and even Bonnie—all simply deprive her of the thing she needs most—a challenge. For this she returns to Ashley whose embodiment of the devoted husband she must destroy in order to win. Her visit with the dying Melanie causes her finally to realize this as well as the fact that Rhett is a much worthier ideal. Sensing her folly she rushes home to find that he has indeed become unreachable. As a mother without a child, a wife without a husband, Scarlett is left by Selznick at the end of the picture turning to a home she can inhabit only in her dreams. The famous concluding line of the novel, "tomorrow is another day," is almost drowned out in the movie by the emotionally charged flashback scene of Tara with Gerald O'Hara's words echoing in the background. Thus Scarlett stands at the end a strong-willed individualist in possession of all the wealth the audience could imagine yet no better off than they because of her inability to realize her impossible dream of a happy home and a loving family.

At the height of the Depression thirteen million workers were unemployed. People who had enjoyed marked prosperity during the twenties suddenly found themselves struggling just to stay alive. Equally troubling was their inability to comprehend the reasons for this devastating reversal. As Leo Gurko has observed "The decade of the thirties was uniquely one in which time outran consciousness

. . . the misery of the country was equalled only by its bewilderment." The absence of checks and balances in the market place which was supposed to provide the ordinary citizen with opportunity seemed only to be making the rich richer and the poor poorer. Everywhere, big business seemed to be prospering. The general lack of knowledge about those who ran it or how it operated simply added to the pervasive belief that these companies were somehow profiting at the expense of the suffering individual. Similarly frustrating was the helplessness and loss of dignity caused by unemployment. No longer was the working man able to fill his expected role as head of the household. Either he could not support his family or he was forced to strike out on his own in order to do so. Consequently his traditional source of consolation now only contributed to his distress. In the cities where these problems were most acute the idea of "getting back to the land" seemed to offer a ready-made solution. As Broadus Mitchell explains:

> In the cities unemployment emphasized crowding squalor and cold; the bread lines were visual reproaches. In the country on the other hand was ample room. Further in the cities workers won bread by an indirect process which for some reason had broken down. But life in the rural setting was held to be synonymous with raising family food. The thing was simple, direct, individually and socially wholesome.

This solution, of course, turned out to be most impractical. Yet it reveals the direction in which the people's anxieties were working. Coming at the end of the Depression as they did, *Gone With the Wind* and *The Grapes of Wrath* appealed to viewers who had lived through this ordeal. Both succeeded in large measure because they so effectively tapped the emotional wellsprings of this urban audience which was their chief patron. Repeatedly, the viewer found himself confronting these same troubling issues; but they were presented in such a way that he was reassured that everything would work out just as he hoped it would. At the same time, neither could have been as compelling had this sentimentality not been treated with a subtlety and understanding notably lacking in similar films like *Our Daily Bread*.

5

AFRICAN AMERICANS ON THE SILVER SCREEN

The Evolution of Black Film
Thomas R. Cripps

*Since the movies' beginning, African Americans have played a critical—
but largely neglected—role in film production and acting. In this essay, historian Thomas R. Cripps chronicles the African American experience in film, from
the 1890s until World War II.*

From the very beginning of American cinema in the 1890s, Afro-Americans
appeared on the screen. One might argue that these early films were not truly black
because their function, more or less, was to tell whites about the black curiosa on
the periphery of their culture. Early topical vignettes in Thomas Edison's films
included watermelon-eating contests, Negroes leading parades, black soldiers in
Cuba, reenactments of campaigns against guerrillas in the Philippines, and fragments of anthropological ephemera such as West Indian women dancing, coaling
ships, or bathing babies. There were occasional bits, such as Biograph's *A Bucket
of Cream Ale* (1904), which was drawn from a vaudeville routine in which a
"Dutchman" is hit in the face with a growler of beer tossed by his blackfaced maid.
In a small way these films attained a range of black imagery that has gone remarkably unnoticed. In their day, the films were black only in the sense that they thrust
a heretofore invisible image upon general American viewers. Their roots emerged
from a faddish popular anthropology that had been a fountainhead of European
exploration in Africa, complete with rival expeditions in search of the sources of
the Nile, voyages to polar icecaps, attempts by the U.S. Department of the Interior
to collect Indian lore, and even whitewater adventures down the Colorado River.
Therefore many early black figures on the screen were no more than the subjects
of a quest for the legendary, the curious, and the bizarre, through darkest Africa and
Carib isle. Along with stray vaudeville routines and gag shots, occasional faithfully
recorded visual records appeared, such as that of Theodore Roosevelt's journey to
Africa and *The Military Drill of the Kikuyu Tribes and Other Native Ceremonies*
(1914). In another vein, cameramen pursued the black heavyweight champion Jack
Johnson, either to record his frequent breaches of racial etiquette or to document
his hoped-for eventual defeat.

But if early films, lacking as they were in black sources, point of view, or
advocacy, whetted black appetites, they hardly could have satisfied them. In fact,

within a dozen years of their beginnings, the early black appearances were snuffed out by a renewed fascination with the Civil War era brought on by the approach of its Golden Anniversary. During these early years, amidst the stereotyped crap-shooters, chicken thieves, and coon shows that the screen inherited from Southern popular literature, movies also offered, in addition to reportorial film of exotic locales, Edwin S. Porter's *Uncle Tom's Cabin* (1903) with its wisp of Abolitionism and a flurry of authentic cakewalking. A genuine bit of "rubberlegs" dancing in Biograph's *The Fights of Nations* (1907) was another example of occasional devia-tions from Southern metaphor. But after 1910 the celebration of the Civil War removed almost all authentic depiction of black Americans from the nation's screens, the semicentennial serving as an inspiration to put aside realism in favor of romantic nostalgia as a model for presenting Negroes on film.

In a movie world populated by Afro-Americans who embraced slavery, loved the Union but not the principle of Abolition, expressed their deepest humanity through loyal service to white masters, and counted the master class, its families, and fortunes above their own, there could not have been a genuinely black film. The movie slaves either served the white cause in such films as *A Slave's Devotion* (1913), *Old Mammy's Charge* (1914), *The Littlest Rebel* (1914), *His Trust* (1911), *His Trust Fulfilled* (1911), and *Old Mammy's Secret Code* (1913), or they at least stood by passively, lending atmosphere to the Southern setting in *The Empty Sleeve* (1914), *Days of War* (ca. 1914), *For the Cause of the South* (1914), *A Fair Rebel* (1914), *The Soldier Brothers of Susannah* (1912), and literally hundreds more.

Coincident with these social forces, the editorial techniques of filmmaking had been growing more sophisticated. In 1915, D.W. Griffith, a sentimental Southerner with a feel for Victorian melodrama and a keen visual sense, synthesized nearly a decade's observation and practice into a film of unprecedented three-hour length— *The Birth of a Nation*—and sold it through the grandest publicity campaign ever given a motion picture. The film was an illiberal racial tract that celebrated Southern slavery, the fortitude of the Ku Klux Klan, and the fealty of "good Negroes."

The national Negro leadership, just beginning to enjoy the fruits of a quarter century of experiment (and tinkering with various Afro-American Leagues, the National Negro Business League, the Niagara Movement, and the like), came together in the National Association for the Advancement of Colored People. Its urbane bourgeois members, including many whites, felt singularly offended by the hoary Southern metaphors signified by Griffith's imagery. Unfortunately for the future of black film, they countered with censorship rather than filmmaking, resulting in a briefly successful campaign that unwittingly had the long-range effect of driving all but the most comic black roles from the screen.

During the year following *The Birth of a Nation,* black genre film began in earnest. Although newspaper stories hinted of a few early attempts in the Middle West—notably those of Bill Foster—the first truly genuinely black film companies were those organized by Emmett J. Scott and the brothers George and Noble Johnson.

Scott's group promised more, but perhaps because it came first, suffered the more resounding failure. Scott, a former Texas newspaperman and Booker T. Washington's secretary at Tuskegee Institute for almost twenty years, looked to filmmaking as a first step to his independence after the death of the authoritarian

Washington in 1915. At first Scott, together with the NAACP, pursued an impossible course, making *Lincoln's Dream,* a film graced with the scholarly credentials of historian Albert Bushnell Hart, written by a veteran scriptwriter, financed by matching funds from the NAACP and Universal Pictures, and showcased in a prestigious premiere. Unfortunately, Carl Laemmle of Universal, the prospective "angel," backed off. When the NAACP was paralyzed by a resulting internal debate, Scott was forced to take up negotiations with a small and greedy Chicago firm.

The resulting *Birth of a Race* (1919) suffered from the absence of a strong black voice in defense of a film concept, scattered and often deferred shooting schedules and locations ranging from Chicago to Tampa, and a theme and plot that shifted its emphasis from a biblical to a pacifist idea conditioned by the coming of World War I. After almost three years of shooting and cutting, most of all the black elements had been pushed aside by presumably more timely and universal themes. Despite a glittering opening in Chicago and a few additional bookings, the film dropped from sight and Scott gave up cultivating prospective black middle-class investors in a film project.

Nevertheless, the project attracted the attention of the Johnsons: George, then a postman in Omaha, and Noble, a Universal contract player. In 1916, together with black investors from Los Angeles and a white cameraman, Harry Gant, they had set out to make motion pictures with a black point of view.

Like most of the black middle class in the 1920s, they embraced the American success myth brought to light by Horatio Alger. Between 1916 and 1922, the Johnsons' Lincoln Motion Picture Company averaged almost one film per year, each filled with individualist heroes, who promised blacks the hope of success and the conquest of despair. *By Right of Birth* (1921) was an anatomy of the genteel black upper class of Los Angeles. It starred Clarence Brooks, who later appeared in John Ford's *Arrowsmith* (1931), and Anita Thompson, a tall, stylish actress from the cast of *Runnin' Wild,* a black revue.

Another Lincoln film, *The Realization of a Negro's Ambition* (ca. 1917) recast the Horatio Alger legend in black terms. *The Trooper of Troop K* (ca. 1920) recounted the yarn of the rough western loner, played by Noble Johnson, who, carrying a pure heart under his saddle dust and army blues, proves his goodness and wins the girl after fighting in a reenactment of a famous cavalry battle with Mexican marauders in the Southwest.

The marketing efforts of both the Birth of a Race Company and the Lincoln Motion Picture Company revealed the hazards of distributing movies outside established Hollywood channels. Hollywood had become an oligopoly that controlled almost all aspects of American filmmaking. All Independent companies, whether "B" producers on Hollywood's "poverty row," Yiddish moviemakers in Manhattan, or race movie makers, suffered from both a lack of capital and outlets for sufficient distribution. Their finished films generally ran only in small second-run "grind" houses which owed no scheduling obligations to the large theater chains that were the backbone of Hollywood profits. At both ends of the production line, the economic structure threatened independent filmmakers with either loss of control or actual extinction. The Johnsons' inventive but eventually unsuccessful solution employed a string of black newspapermen, who both plugged their movies and acted as bookers.

Rather than holding out the promise of another stride toward a black genre, the next stage of black filmmaking revealed a negative aspect of making race movies. The Ebony Motion Picture of Chicago, like a number of other small white companies, produced films for black audiences behind a facade of black managers. But apparently their white "angels" and Southern white writer, Leslie T. Peacock, insisted on films like *A Black Sherlock Holmes* (ca. 1918) that were mirror images of white movies. Ebony's *Spying the Spy* (1919), for example, employed a talented black comedian in the role of an American spy in pursuit of a stereotyped German agent, the film's climax was an orgy of editorial effects which played upon the old-fashioned notion of the Afro-American fear of ghosts. While many blacks had migrated to cities, surprisingly, little of urban black life appeared on the screen. Furthermore, interest in foreign exotica had declined into a cycle of Edgar Rice Burroughs's Tarzan with its African supernumeraries. Revived by the coming of sound, blackface roles persisted.

Before 1925, strong black roles were brought to the screen by corps of black Hollywood regulars in a handful of films that touched some unconscious truth about American racial life. Madame Sul-te-Wan, Onest Conley, Carolynne Snowden, Nathan Curry, Zach Williams, Raymond Turner, and boxers Sam Baker and George Godfrey brought conviction to these few roles. Noble Johnson typified their accomplishment and captivity by white Hollywood. His career spanned from World War I with Lubin, to a job as the Indian hothead, Red Shirt, in John Ford's *She Wore a Yellow Ribbon* (1949). Because his work with the Lincoln Motion Picture Company competed with the movies produced by his white employer, Universal Pictures, Johnson was asked to give up his work at Lincoln. Thereafter, through World War I, not only did he continue as a stock heavy in Universal's various "B" western series, *Red Feather, Red Ace,* and *Bull's Eye,* but went on to appear as scores of Indians, Latins, Asians, and primitive tribesmen in such movies as *Robinson Crusoe* (1917), *Leopard Woman* (1920), *Kismet* (1920), *The Four Horsemen of the Apocalypse* (1921) (in which he was one of the mounted plagues), *The Ten Commandments* (1923), *Flaming Frontier* (1926), *Aloma of the South Seas* (1926), *Ben Hur* (1927), and *Lady of the Harem* (1926). In some years he appeared in a half dozen or more pictures, ranging from major "epics" to routine "programmers."

The other source of strong black characterizations appeared in white movies in an indirect, muted way that barely hinted at the fact that American society had begun to deal with a new Negro who had migrated to Northern cities. In 1916 Bert Williams, the distinguished black comedian of the Ziegfeld Follies, appeared in *Fish* and *A Natural Born Gambler,* two movies that used blackface routines in a fresh way. In the former Williams was a gangling country boy, who tries to sell a fish as it grows stale. In *A Natural Born Gambler* he presides over the card table at his fraternal lodge while contriving to elude the white police. In the same period, Vitagraph made two parodies of white boxers whose fear of Jack Johnson formed the basis of comedy—*Some White Hope* (1915) and *The Night I Fought Jack Johnson* (1913). A black confidante far shrewder and more knowing than the Civil War cycle maids appeared in *Hoodoo Ann* (1916). Aggressive and even derisive black women appeared in Cecil B. DeMille's *Manslaughter* (1922). Several children's series that set the mood for the debut of Hal Roach's egalitarian *Our Gang* began in the late 1920s. The variety of black roles expanded to include French and American soldiers, wise old boxing trainers, horse trainers, and a number of servants who resembled Tonto, the Lone Ranger's sidekick, more than they did Rastus, the ante-bellum butler.

Despite their contribution to the wearing away of old icons that had symbolized the former inferior status of Afro-Americans, these deviations from ancient norms spoke little of the "new Negro" who was already celebrated in Northeastern literary circles. If white moviemakers understandably failed to take into account the changed circumstances of urban blacks, their black counterparts also failed to fill the existing void. Nor did a growing number of black critics suggest new images to replace the outdated ones, except for a vague plea for presenting "positive"—meaning middle-class—characters on the screen.

But the condition of the "new Negro" was not that clearcut. As Afro-Americans moved from Southern farms to Northern cities, they fell prey to oppressive forces from outside the group. Their plight may be likened to that of the Germans, described in an essay by Erich Kahler (1974). In the Middle Ages, Germans, like blacks, spoke a language built upon linguistic traditions from outside the group; lived in rural regions and disdained the city or found it alien; embraced millennial ideals rather than small victories; and chose in-group stratification as a means of preserving the group, despite anarchic forces pressing from the outside. Moreover, in the face of these external forces, whether Frankish kings in Paris, Italian condottieri in the pay of the Pope, or Magyar invaders, the Germans often responded with in-group aggression.

The wide gulf between white movies and black aspirations may be seen in a fragmentary glance at some of D.W. Griffith's 192 films. After the release of *The Birth of a Nation*, Griffith went on to make several masterpieces such as *Intolerance* (1916), *Broken Blossoms* (1919), *Way Down East* (1920), and *Orphans of the Storm* (1921). Like most of his works, these films commented on social issues from the safe vantage point of the past or foreign locales. In the mid-1920s, however, Griffith addressed himself to modern times.

Here Griffith's racial vision, like that of most of his white countrymen, was unable to distinguish rural blacks from the new urban Negro. The black characters in *One Exciting Night* (1922) were strikingly off the mark. The central character, an improbable detective, was a "Kaffir, the dark terror of the bootleg gang." The remaining black roles were played by blackfaced whites as traditional servile flunkies, who trailed through the plot. A year later in *The White Rose* (1923), Griffith attempted to return to Southern ground, but his critics leapt upon him for his "mawkish sickening sentimentality" and his "jumbled and pointless plot." According to them, he seemed a "genius out of touch with the world." Next he began *His Darker Self* (1924), another blackface picture starring Al Jolson, who eventually deserted the project. Still later Griffith made an unsatisfying and fruitless appearance on the set of Universal's *Topsy and Eva* (1927), an exploitation spinoff from that studio's successful *Uncle Tom's Cabin*. In every case these were "white" movies, retailing Negroes almost as an in-group joke.

At last in the mid-1920s black critics on black newspapers, among them Lester Walton of the *New York Age,* Romeo Daugherty of the *Amsterdam News,* J. A. Rogers, and D. Ireland Thomas, began to develop a common vision. A few white papers also developed a racial sensitivity, in particular, *Variety* crowed in glee when the Ku Klux Klan muddled a filmmaking project. When promoters gave a preview for a racist tract called *Free and Equal* (1925), *Variety* howled: "it is not only old fashioned but so crudely done that the Sunday night audience laughed it practically out of the theater."

But neither Griffith nor the press provided the fairest gauge of Hollywood's inability to deal with black themes. Rather, it was the mixed response that blacks gave to the best and most well-meaning Hollywood movie, Universal's *Uncle Tom's Cabin.* In 1926 Carl Laemmle started the project by signing Charles Gilpin, the most distinguished black actor of his day, to play Tom. However, Gilpin was soon replaced by James Lowe, who gave one of the finest black cinema performances in a faithful rendering of the spirit of Harriet Beecher Stowe's novel.

Unfortunately for Laemmle, black critics and audiences alike split in their judgment of the film that had been aimed at a "crossover" audience of blacks and whites, who would like either its abolitionism or its nostalgia. But no amount of mere preaching on the subject of race satisfied those blacks who looked to film as a medium for communicating to a black audience.

Nevertheless, in comparison with the films of the early 1920s, blacks saw in *Uncle Tom's Cabin* a new Hollywood that seemed to promise a fair representation of black characters, liberal progress, and cause for hope. One producer promised a movie of the new Broadway hit, *Porgy* (1927); John M. Stahl put a serious black love scene in *In Old Kentucky* (1927); William Wellman's hopeful *Beggars of Life* featured a fine role by Edgar "Blue" Washington; DeMille's *Old Ironsides* (1926) carried a crew that included strong black roles, as did Alan Crosland's *The Sea Beast* (1926); and Monta Bell's *Man, Woman, and Sin* (1927) established its urban milieu with neat vignettes of black city life.

In the absence of movies that spoke directly to black concerns, a kind of black underground grew outside the major studios. Although largely white-owned, it nonetheless attempted to reach the black audience that was untouched by Hollywood. Strapped by poor distribution channels, paltry budgets, amateurish actors, technical failings, and untrained crews, these production companies were somehow able to release films for black audiences throughout the silent era. Their films reached beyond mere representation of Negroes on the screen to depict Afro-Americans as a presence in American life.

Most of these race movie makers felt an obligation to present blacks as icons of virtue and honor. One case in point, the Douglass Company of New Jersey, used war film heroism "to show the better side of 'Negro life'" and to "inspire in the Negro a desire to climb higher." They also adapted films from the works of popular Negro authors such as Paul Laurence Dunbar's *The Scapegoat* (1917). Another Douglass project, *The Colored American Winning His Suit* (1916), followed the career of the Negro hero who was "getting ahead." Other companies turned War Department films into *From Harlem to the Rhine* (ca. 1918), *Our Hell Fighters Return* (1919), and other compilations showing black troops in combat.

By the early 1920s the *New York Age* headlined that COLORED MOTION

PICTURES ARE IN GREAT DEMAND. The filmmakers were undaunted by any topic; the whole black world was their stage, and their regional roots gave a varied flavor to the black experience they recorded on film. This excitement stirred still other prospective producers to grind out glossy prospectuses that promised great black films which would never be made. Their known films included the Norman Company's all-black westerns shot in the famous all-black town of Boley, Oklahoma, starring the New York actress Anita Bush. The Cotton Blossom Company and the Lone Star Company made similar pictures in San Antonio. Dr. A. Porter Davis made *The Lure of a Woman* (1921), the first film produced in Kansas City.

After 1922, the Renaissance Company made black newsreels. White producers like Ben Strasser and Robert Levy (whose Reol Company made a movie from Dunbar's *Sport of the Gods* [1921]) joined the ranks of race movie makers. War movies persisted as a genre. Among these, Sidney P. Dones's *Injustice* (1920) was a wartime tale of Negroes and the Red Cross; two others, *Democracy, Or a Fight for Right* (1919) and *Loyal Hearts* (1919), "a smashing Virile Story of Our Race Heroes," were released by the Democracy Photoplay Corporation.

The most dogged of the race movie makers was Oscar Micheaux. Micheaux, a young black who had been a homesteader on the Dakota prairie, survived nearly twenty-five years in a desperately cutthroat business, turning out approximately two dozen movies in Chicago, New York, and New Jersey. As early as 1919, Micheaux tried unsuccessfully to link up with the Lincoln Company, a union that failed because the Johnsons considered him an upstart, a mountebank, and an untrustworthy hustler ironically all traits that would help him achieve success.

Micheaux's production style gave texture to black genre films even if his work was not noted for its excellence of cinematic technique. To make up for a lack of technical expertise his black and white casts and crews exhibited a fellowship that blended the ideals of African tribal communities with the like values of a typical John Ford stock company of the 1940s. Ford's people shared the dust, cursed the heat, and passed the whiskey bottle together, thereby giving an unmistakable Ford quality to their films. Micheaux never shot a film in the desert, but his companies, by sharing poverty, late paychecks, and shabby working conditions, somehow managed to give a generic texture to their films.

In like manner, Micheaux's shooting in idle and antique studios in Chicago, Fort Lee, and the Bronx; the jarring effect of the uneven talents of his actors; his use of unsung, under-employed white cameramen abandoned by the drift of filmmaking to Hollywood; and his shoestring operation which reflected the cast's own lives, all lent the enterprise an aura of outlawry. By merely finishing a film, Micheaux's company was like the legendary tricksters of black folklore, who win the game against the system. Thus the low pay, borrowed equipment, and nagging debtors helped define the character of the completed movie.

The difference between Micheaux and the other producers of the black genre can be compared to the difference between Orson Welles and Irving Thalberg. Welles was the outsider, flippant and contemptuous of established custom; Thalberg was the middle-class company man, loyal to MGM until his dying day, who succeeded by not offending either boss or audience. Micheaux, like Welles, had the gall to be opinionated in the presence of more experienced filmmakers. Welles once described his studio facilities as the finest Erector set a boy could ever hope for. Like Welles from his vantage point outside the system, Micheaux may have experienced a similar feeling of raw, fey power over the conventional filmmaking regime.

Motion pictures gave Micheaux the power to say, however amateurishly, what no other Negro filmmakers even thought of saying. He filmed the unnameable, arcane, disturbing things that set black against black. When others sought only uplifting and positive images, Micheaux searched for ironies.

A recurring theme appeared in his work from his very first film in 1919. The autobiographical *The Homesteader* recounted the story of a farm boy torn between rural values and urban glitter, a vehicle later used by Richard Wright in *Native Son* and Ralph Ellison in *The Invisible Man*. In this film, the conflict between the values of Southern black migrants to the city and the urbane sensibility that had scant room for enthusiastic religion, filiopietism, and the pride of land ownership, was examined.

Save for his densely packed polemic against jackleg preachers, *Body and Soul,* Oscar Micheaux's silent films are lost. But surviving reviews indicate that Micheaux was capable of an arrogant variety of themes, each one bringing some corner of Negro life to the screen. Indeed, he explored even white life as it impinged upon blacks—a rarity in race movies. His movies formed an anatomy of black filmmaking by the breadth of their topicality. In *Within Our Gates* (1920), Micheaux reconstructed an anti-Semitic lynching he had witnessed in Atlanta. *The Brute* (1925) starred black boxer Sam Langford. *The Symbol of the Unconquered* (1921) indicted the Ku Klux Klan at the height of its Middle Western revival.

Birthright (1924) adapted T. S. Stribling's novel about the racism that blighted the life of a black Harvard graduate. *The Spider's Web* (1927) dramatized the ghetto's love-hate affair with the infamous gambling system, the numbers game. With the release of *The Conjure Woman* (1926) and *The House Behind the Cedars* (1927), Micheaux revealed his most unabashed nerve by persuading the distinguished black novelist, Charles Waddell Chesnutt, not only to sell the movie rights to two of his books for a few dollars, but also to tolerate Micheaux's heavy-handed rewriting.

Sadly, only *Body and Soul,* the lone survivor of Micheaux's early films, reveals the quality of his silent work. Although flawed by censors' efforts, *Body and Soul* made use of the young and marginally employed football player, singer, budding actor, and preacher's son, Paul Robeson, to make a strong case against venal preachers. This film helped make Micheaux a central figure in black genre film, if for no other reason than he willingly, even sensationally, assaulted black problems. In addition, he brought black fiction to the screen, criticized American racial custom, and made his own migratory life an allegory for the black experience in the twentieth century.

Parallel to Micheaux's career in the 1920s, another variant of black genre film producers emerged: the company rich in white capital, technical capacity, and leadership, with a self-conscious ambition to present films that reflected the lives of its Negro audiences. Unlike their competitors who ground out shabby black mimics of white life, this enterprising group of easterners kept a keen ear tuned to black circles and a sharp eye on box office trends as sensors of black taste. In the early 1920s, the best of them, theater owner Robert Levy, a backer of the Lafayette Players black theatre group, founded Reol as a studio that intended to produce such films as Chesnutt's *The Marrow of Tradition.*

Still another white force was the owner whose theater gradually had turned "colored" and who subsequently made films for the new audiences. On the eve of sound film, such a group led by David Starkman and a white studio crew united behind Sherman "Uncle Dud" Dudley, a black vaudevillian and impresario from Washington. The resulting Colored Players Company produced its first film by July 1926, *A Prince of His Race,* a melodrama on the theme of the black bourgeois fear of lost status. By the end of the year they released a black version of the old temperance tract, *Ten Nights in a Bar Room,* starring Charles Gilpin. Far from a rehash, the brief film used its all-black cast to achieve a certain poignancy, as though the actors themselves were making a special plea to urban blacks, warning them against urban vices in a manner reminiscent of Micheaux.

In 1928 the Colored Players Company achieved its finest hour with *The Scar of Shame,* which, in the wrong hands, might have become no more than a sentimental "women's picture." In style, mood, and theme, however, the Colored Players' film brought a sophisticated close to the silent film era. Scriptwriter David Starkman, two Italian collaborators, director Frank Perugini and cameraman Al Ligouri, and black stars Lucia Lynn Moses, Harry Henderson, Lawrence Chenault, and Pearl McCormick, combined efforts to produce a wistful satire on the color caste system that stratified urban black society. The completed film went beyond its premise by adding a commentary on the American success myth. Perhaps because authors can most successfully romanticize or satirize what they know from a distance, as in Samuel Taylor Coleridge's *Xanadu,* J.M.W. Turner's painting of a shimmering man-o-war in the tow of a steam tug, or J.R.R. Tolkien's *Middle Earth,* the largely white Colored Players sympathetically exposed an anomaly in black life—Negroes, the victims of racial discrimination, sometimes stratified into fraternities, professions, marriages, and even churches along lines denoted by skin color.

The boom of the 1920s ended sadly for Afro-Americans. The Great Depression proved a shattering experience, hitting blacks sooner and more severely than it did whites. Even the Republican party cast them aside in Herbert Hoover's so-called "lily white" convention of 1928.

And yet, the sound film era began at the same time, holding out the promise of revolutionary change for blacks in Hollywood. MGM and Fox stumbled over each other trying to exploit sound film through the use of Negro themes and motifs. These studios were so successful that their work instigated the gradual turning away of black film audiences from race movies, toward Hollywood.

Although Christie Comedies had once used Spencer Williams as a writer, for the first time Hollywood producers really made use of black consultants. MGM's *Hallelujah!* benefitted from the counsel of Harold Garrison, the studio bootblack, and James Weldon Johnson of the NAACP. Fox's *Hearts in Dixie,* like the MGM film, brought black religion, tragedy, music, and emotion to the screen with the help of Clarence Muse and other blacks on the set.

Immediately a rash of musical shorts emerged from the studios. The worst of them, such as Christie's comedies, were based on Octavus Roy Cohen's old *Saturday Evening Post* dialect stories. The best of them used black performers in ways that allowed them to influence the ambience of the films. Aubrey Lyles and Flournoy Miller, the comedy team from the original Shuffle Along revue of 1921, the dancing Covans, the Hall Johnson Choir, baritone Jules Bledsoe, Duke Ellington, and many others were signed by Hollywood studios.

The best of these appeared early in the decade. Louis Armstrong and Cab Calloway infused a strong jazz beat into *I'll Be Glad When You're Dead, You Rascal You* (1932), *Minnie the Moocher* (1932), *Rhapsody in Black and Blue* (1932), and *Jitterbug Party* (1935). Eubie Blake and Noble Sissle enlivened *Pie Pie Blackbird* (ca. 1932). The Nicholas Brothers brought their jazz acrobatics to *Barbershop Blues* (1933) and *The Black Network* (1936). Jimmy Mordecai, one of the greatest jazz dancers, did a stylized, moody rendering of Southern folk life in *Yamacraw* (1930). These films continued until World War II when Lena Horne, Teddy Wilson, Albert Ammons, and Pete Johnson did a musical fantasy of the disinherited, *Boogie Woogie Dream* (1944).

The most balanced combinations of mood, lighting, music, black social themes, and theatrical elements were offered in Duke Ellington's *Symphony in Black* (1935) and *Black and Tan* (1929). *Symphony* was scored in four movements with stylized bits of black history cut to match the beat of work songs, chants, and fervent religious moods. The film's ending featured Billie Holiday and Earl "Snakehips" Tucker in an urban scene that symbolized Negro migration from Africa, to the South, to Harlem, to modern times. Almost ritual in form, the film demonstrated the possibilities of black art emerging from a Hollywood factory. In like manner *Black and Tan* recreated a similar ambience but stressed plot more than music by focusing on Ellington's woman, who, despite poor health, dances so that he might finish his composition; but she dies on the dance floor, a martyr to black music. Both films were effectively heightened by chiaroscuro lighting of a quality that seldom graced feature movies.

A few musical films made outside Hollywood provided still more promising avenues of black expression within the context of a medium dominated by whites. The best single case is Dudley Murphy's *The St. Louis Blues* (1928). Its gritty black mood emanated from the musical contributions of W.C. Handy, Jimmy Mordecai, J. Rosamond Johnson, and Bessie Smith. It was as though Murphy served only as a neutral vehicle which carried the black imagery to the screen.

Five years later, another combination of cinematically inexperienced blacks joined Murphy to produce a unique film version of Eugene O'Neill's *The Emperor Jones* (1933). O'Neill's play mixed psychological depth with racial grotesques through the treatment of a black hero, who aimed beyond traditionally accepted black channels of endeavor. Murphy's film became an instrument through which white writers, and black musicians and performers combined to construct a black film. Paul Robeson, Fredi Washington, and Frank Wilson starred in the black roles and Rosamond Johnson scored the music, using traditional black themes, motifs, and styles.

Many Hollywood movies that followed treated Negroes with awareness if not sensibility, with politesse if not equality, and affection if not understanding. Nevertheless, these films of the depression years amounted to a quantum jump from the old-fashioned racial metaphors of the previous decade. These gestures toward a liberalized cinema promised enough to attract larger black audiences into 1930s movie palaces. As a result, during the Great Depression, producers of race movies lost ground to their Hollywood adversaries. The black press, motivated by increased studio and theater advertising and loyalty to black actors, cheered the trend. In contrast to the Hollywood product, race movie makers appeared more than ever as inept, erratic mavericks.

The trendy black images ranged broadly, if not deeply. Lewis Milestone's *Hallelujah, I'm a Bum* (1933) featured a black hobo among its down-and-outers. A cycle of exposés of horrible prison conditions featured black prisoners. Etta Moten and Ivie Anderson sang important songs in *Gold Diggers of 1933, Flying Down to Rio* (1933), and *A Day at the Races* (1937). Louis Armstrong and Martha Raye's raucous interracial number in *Artists and Models* (1937) shocked southern censors. Stepin Fetchit, the archfoe of the black bourgeoisie, worked steadily, though with ever narrowing range. Following a trend set by MGM's *Trader Horn* (1931), the worst painted-savage stereotypes faded from major movies, although they continued to survive in the "B" pictures shot on the backlots of "poverty row." A few movies depicted the South in unflattering terms and its Negroes às less than happy with their lot. Among these were *Cabin in the Cotton* (1932), *I Am a Fugitive From a Chain Gang* (1932), *Slave Ship, Jezebel* (1938), and *The Little Foxes* (1941). Black boon companions grew more humane in *Dirigible* (1931), *Broadway Bill* (1934), *O'Shaughnessy's Boy* (1937), *Prestige* (1932), *The Count of Monte Cristo* (1934), and especially *Massacre* (1934). A few genuinely fine roles appeared: Clarence Brooks's Haitian-doctor in John Ford's *Arrowsmith*, Fredi Washington's wistful mulattoes in *Imitation of Life* (1934) and *One Mile from Heaven* (1937), Muse's angry rebel and Daniel Haynes's big-house butler in *So Red the Rose,* Hattie McDaniel's prickly servants in *Alice Adams* (1935), *The Mad Miss Manton* (1938), and *Gone with the Wind* (1939), and Clinton Rosamond's outraged father in *Golden Boy* (1939).

A sample taken from twenty months at mid-decade reveals the broad sweep of change in Hollywood Negro roles during the New Deal. Despite the changing times, some traditional roles persisted. Old Southern legends were faithfully served by Bill Robinson's dancing servants in *The Little Colonel* (1935) and *The Littlest Rebel,* along with nostalgic relics such as Edward Sutherland's *Mississippi* (1935). Stepin Fetchit's career reached high gear in a string of Fox's celebrations of rural folk life such as *Steam Boat Round the Bend* (1935), *David Harum* (1934), *Judge Priest* (1934), and *The County Chairman* (1934). *Bullets or Ballots* (1936) and *Hooray for Love* (1935) brought Negroes into urban contexts through Louise Beavers's "numbers' queen" and Bill Robinson's street-dandy. John Ford's *The Prisoner of Shark Island* (1936) depicted black soldiers as well as slaves. A few Broadway successes brought strong black roles to Hollywood intact, among them Edward Thompson's "Slim" in *The Petrified Forest* (1936), Leigh Whipper's "Crooks" in John Steinbeck's *Of Mice and Men* (1939), and Rex Ingram's "De Lawd" and "Hezdrel" roles in Marc Connelly's fable of black folk religion, *The Green Pastures* (a less than total success among black critics). Universal's remake of *Showboat* (1936) brought "Joe" to the screen in the person of Paul Robeson. And Fritz Lang and Mervyn LeRoy made indictments of lynching, *Fury* (1936) and *They Won't Forget* (1937), although each was weakened by placing blacks on the periphery rather than depicting them as victims of mobs.

Black critics and audiences waffled. On the one hand they were happy to see more blacks on the screen, but on the other, they fretted over Hollywood's superficiality and its ignorance of black life.

David O. Selznick's *Gone With the Wind* grew into the media event most symptomatic of black division over the merits of a Hollywood movie. Nominally a film version of Margaret Mitchell's overweight novel of the South during Reconstruction, the movie quickly developed a split personality. Selznick was torn between the conflicting goals of wishing to accommodate to liberal political trends by having (according to a memorandum) "the Negroes come out decidedly on the right side of the ledger," at the same time that he was striving for historicity and genuine Southern ambience.

To achieve this all but impossible ambition, Selznick hired experts—Atlanta architect, artist, and antiquarian Wilbur G. Kurtz and Susan Myrick of the *Macon Telegraph* to authenticate details of regional atmosphere and racial etiquette. They saved the film from countless errors of manners, accents, and clichés, such as warning the company against having the slaves rise in song; in the latter episode, they worked in cooperation with Hall Johnson, the black choirmaster. From the North, writers Sidney Howard, Ben Hecht, O.H.P. Garrett, and F. Scott Fitzgerald, in deference to modern tastes, elided references to the Ku Klux Klan and depictions of the Yankee army as marauders and looters. The hoped-for result, Selznick felt, would be that authentic black maids, mammies, and field hands were considerably more humanized than those appearing in earlier Southern genre films.

Despite its brilliance as a work of popular art, *Gone With the Wind* inspired both black praise and calumny, revealing a still unsatisfied hunger for a black genre cinema. On one side many urban blacks agreed with a *Pittsburgh Courier* critic who found that "much of it was distasteful to the Negro race." On the other, Bill Chase of the *Amsterdam News* responded with exaggerated disbelief. "Ye gads, what's happening to Hollywood?" he wrote. Several writers focused on the black acting, especially that of Hattie McDaniel, who made mammy "more than a servant" and won an Oscar. She tipped still more black opinion in favor of the movie.

This is not to say *Gone With the Wind* revolutionized Hollywood into a center of black genre filmmaking. Yet, the film stood astride two epochs. In the period between the wars, black roles had slowly moved away from tradition. With the coming of World War II, the liberal drift became part of the rhetoric of Allied war aims.

Gone With the Wind admirably expressed the tension between the two poles of racial ideals—tradition and change—with the result that on the eve of World War II, Afro-Americans responded to cinema in two distinct ways, both of them new departures from convention. They tempered their customary cynical view of Hollywood with a renewed faith in their own ability to change Hollywood through social and political pressure. . . .

Citizen Kane

6

ORSON WELLES AS POET AND HISTORIAN

The Magnificent Ambersons
Charles Higham

He was called (partly sincerely, partly sarcastically) the "boy genius." Orson Welles was just 25 years old when he directed and starred in Citizen Kane, *which is generally considered the greatest American film of the sound period. Based on the life of publisher William Randolph Hearst,* Citizen Kane *was much more than a muckraking exposé of a media baron. It was also a modernist film which told Kane's biography life through a kaleidoscope of conflicting perspectives and traced the evolution of mass communications from the gentlemanly dailies of the late nineteenth century through turn-of-the-century yellow journalism through the corporate journalism of Henry Luce and his "March of Time."* The Magnificent Ambersons *is, as the critic Pauline Kael has noted, a work of even greater depth, which traces the breakup of the nineteenth century world, the impact of the automobile, and a broad transformation of values.*

Like *Citizen Kane,* the *Magnificent Ambersons* is a valedictory to the American past, filled with regret for the coming of the industrial age. Welles had always had a passion for Booth Tarkington's novel [of that name]; he had brilliantly presented it in an hour-long version on the Mercury Theater of the Air, on October 29, 1939, and there is in existence a silent film version he may well have seen as a child of ten—which was entitled *Pampered Youth,* directed by David Smith at Vitaphone in 1925. The earlier film, with its perfect evocation of Tarkington's midland town and Amberson house and addition, its titles drawn from the text, and its finely observed playing by Alice Calhoun, Emmett King, and Ben Alexander among others, in many ways foreshadows Welles's work.

The subject also attracted Welles because it echoed his own earliest childhood in a town that had moved reluctantly from sleighs to Sears Roebuck motor buggies. He decided to incorporate his radio method of narrating the story, although on radio the tale was told, not by an impersonal disembodied presence—a more lyrical version of the "News on the March" commentator—but by Welles as George himself. He recorded the whole of the script on discs, and the actors were able to study it minutely for tiny vocal flaws. . . .

About halfway through shooting Pearl Harbor was bombed by the Japanese, and the United States entered the war. Just after that Welles received an invitation to make a Pan-American film. He had to rush *Ambersons* to its conclusion, and he had to finished a third picture, *Journey into Fear,* at night in a three-picture deal with the studio. He also had to record his Lady Esther Radio Program, begun, crazily, just before shooting Ambersons, and broadcast each Monday evening. . . .

What happened to *Ambersons* is now a black legend, climaxed by the humiliation of its final release on the lower half of a double bill with a Lupe Velez comedy, *Mexican Spitfire Sees a Ghost.* The studio, involved in a power battle ending in the dismissal of George Schaefer, was unhappy with Welles's Rio carnival footage and with his reportedly wild behavior in Brazil (the most extravagant rumor had him urinating on a crowd from his hotel balcony). Exasperated by audiences' bored reactions to *Ambersons* in out of town previews (often in hick towns on the second half of lengthy double bills), the studio refused to let Robert Wise fly to Rio and work with Welles on bringing the film down from its 148 minutes to a double-bill length of some 88 minutes. He got as far as Miami, then had to come back. Welles did his best to edit the film by telephone and telegram from Rio, running off his own rough cut in synchronization with Wise's copy, but, as Wise says, "it was hopeless". . . .

In June Charles Koerner, head of production in Hollywood, told Jack Moss, Welles's manager, to supervise massive cuts. First, all the important documentary sequences of the growth of the midland city were eliminated, thus accounting for about two reels. Then the final long sequence in which Joseph Cotten visits Agnes Moorehead in the boardinghouse that was once the Amberson mansion was also cut out. In this scene Eugene speaks to Fanny about the past, and as he does so, a record plays in the background. This record is a vaudeville duet, played in weirdly distorted voices by Cotten and by Norman Foster—who wrote it together. It is a new version of the vaudeville sketch, once made popular by the Two Black Crows, in which a master returns after a journey, and is met by his servant. He asks if there is any news (the title is "No News, or, What Killed the Dog?"). He is told that the dog has died. But when he hears the cause of death he learns by degrees that a whole city has been destroyed; the theme is based on the "for want of a nail" premise. The duologue comically underscores the tragedy of the Ambersons and the loss of the old city. At the end, as the record scratchily concludes and Fanny sadly says good-bye, Eugene goes out and the last shot shows him looking up at the skyline of a great industrial town beyond the old house's eaves.

Another scene, of Eugene O'Neill-like length and tone, was removed. This had the family sitting on the veranda in darkness, talking about their crumbling fortunes. Nothing whatever could be seen, only their voices heard plaintively under the trees. Worst of all was the excision of the great silent sequence when the camera, strapped to the operator's chest, explores the stairs and the empty sheeted rooms in a repeat of the great take with which it earlier explored the same setting filled with dancing and carousing figures. . . .

What we see today is a fragment only, but a dazzling one. If *Kane* is a vigorous journalistic work, then *Ambersons* is a poetic one, carried forward in a slow, somber movement in contrast with the razzle-dazzle energy and pace of its predecessor. Like the figures in the Waldteufel-like waltz with which Bernard Herrmann embellished the ballroom scene, it is a doomed, beautiful thing. Its darkness, its nostalgia, fill one still, like the knowledge of its partial destruction, with an unbearable sadness.

Booth Tarkington's novel, published in 1918, was part of a trilogy *(Growth)* which dealt with life in a midland town, an anonymous version of Tarkington's native and beloved Indianapolis. The novel won the Pulitzer Prize and remains, with Tarkington's beautiful story of small-town boyhood, *Penrod* (1914), as a touching and sadly underrated record of a vanished world. One of the central themes was that of the obstreperous youth who, through making a fool of himself, learns humility; George Minafer, the spoiled young villain who dominates the record of the Ambersons, had a literary precursor in Tarkington's Hoosier boy in *His Own People,* who was given his come-uppance and purification by the realities of Europe.

Tarkington's deep love of Indiana and of its youth and beauty endeared him strongly to the American public, if not always to more sophisticated critics. He had the commercial knack of ending his chronicles on a note of strong American optimism, despite all his nostalgia for a vanished carriage age, his hints of doom in his description of the approach of the machines. Even the whipper-snapper heir George Minafer, drawn without a trace of pity, ends up discovering the power to ask the forgiveness of his arch-rival and representative of the machine age, Eugene Morgan.

The Magnificent Ambersons is a film that shows the radical changing of an order, and the conflict of materialism with the romanticism of those still enmeshed in the past. It represents, too, a central conflict in Welles himself: between nostalgia and thrusting ambition, between mild inertia and a desire for action, between a love of the past and a hunger for the excitements of the future. On the one hand he is drawn to the youth and beauty and vigor of the young people in the story, yet on the other he is attracted to the fading older figures pushed aside by the thrust of commerce. Yet the conflict is not dialectically iron-cast: the situation contains an irony. The Amberson house is not really beautiful despite Welles's affectionate treatment of it. The tragedy of the Ambersons was not merely that they were blind to "progress," but that what they clung to was the product of an earlier materialism, as insubstantial as a dream.

What prevents the film from working quite satisfactorily as a work of social comment is Welles's ambiguous response to the material. Tarkington suggested the irony of the Ambersons' predicament more firmly; the local people's regard for the magnificence of the Amberson household was meant to be a trifle absurd, since its grandeur was an expression of vulgarity. Welles, by falling in love with the house, makes the story more tragic, but he removes an important element from it. He mirrors the novel's surface, though, with extraordinary fidelity, capturing to perfection its elegiac tone, mirroring its sober North American poetry in a style less baroque than Kane's. The camerawork of Stanley Cortez shimmers with a beautiful nostalgic glow, moving as effortlessly as a waltzing figure through the tall and genteel Amberson house, catching the shine of lace, the gleam of stained-glass windows, the polish of expensive wooden balustrades.

The technical execution of the images is simple and functional, for all its sumptuous richness of texture. Even a virtuoso effect, when the camera (running on streetcar tracks) leisurely traces a journey by George and his inamorata by carriage in one take, has its meaning; it shows us the ugly telephone poles that are beginning to sprout in the growing city—ironical black figures of doom beyond the old-fashioned ride itself. Elaborate compositions are few, and the more effective for that: George looking into the mirror when his Uncle Jack takes a bath, with George to the left and Jack to the right, framed between bathroom knickknacks; George watching Jack leave the house after George's mother's death, a repetition of the same shot in reverse, with George's face and the reflected figure below as it gets into the carriage beautifully counterpointed. The staircase conversations are all elaborately composed; for the most part, though, this is a film of deliberately subdued, plain photographic character based on the methods of the photographers of 1905.

The groupings throughout are symmetrical, with a preponderance of three-shots, often with a man framed between two women. The heads form very frequently the points of an equilateral triangle, another gesture towards period formalism. In the ballroom scene the figures form into twos, threes, and fours; the scene itself is carefully choreographed. A conversation between gossips at a dressmaker's shows one woman framed in a sewing machine. In a discussion on the first floor corridor of the Amberson house, and in the farewell to the guests after the ball, deep focus effectively shows us two knots of people at different levels, each of equal interest to each other, in perfect counterpoint. Here, ceilinged sets serve a more valid and functional purpose than in *Kane* (and the ceilings look more genuinely solid) because they convey the oppressive nature of the house.

The camera's movements are more fluent and graceful than [Gregory] Toland's in *Kane*. The marvelous dolly shot that accompanies George and his aunt Fanny as they move out of a boiler room into the shrouded living room of the Amberson mansion shows [Stanley] Cortez's virtuousity at its height, since Fanny's hysteria is followed in an unbroken progression through four rooms. Editing here would have destroyed the emotional balance of the scene. The visual narration is frequently taken wholesale from the text, as in the farewell of George's Uncle Jack at a railroad station. The sleigh-ride scene mirrors Tarkington's prose to a fault. "The sleighbells tinkled but intermittently. Gleaming wanly through the whitish vapor that kept rising from the trotter's body and flanks, they were like tiny fog-bells, and made the only sounds in a great winter silence." Though we may perhaps regret that the fashion in Hollywood at the time was not to use locations, the realism of the recreated ride is masterfully achieved.

The film renders an American past, creating with affection a world as formally nostalgic as a cameo brooch. A tram stalled by a house, its horses champing; snow on eaves and heavy on winter's bare trees; the shine of a window where a woman stands listening tenderly to the tripping melody of a serenade; a hat fixed in a cheval glass; faces shining with the glow of cold, and voices raised high as a horseless carriage jigs away on its first journey under a shaking tasseled canopy, while a sleigh forms more delicate swooping parabolas in the snowbanks nearby; the early part of the film has an autumnal lyricism, the mood of a Frost poem. But the second half is even richer, in its deep shadows, its wintry colors, as the swarming darkness of the Amberson mansion presages death for Isabel Amberson Minafer, for her husband, for the General who is the house's most formidable living ghost. As each door closes, whether it bears a glistening black wreath or not, it seems to close forever on all possibility of escape from fate. As each white face fades away in the night, it is like watching the internment of corpses, and we are listening to their last requiem.

The film is composed in scenes which are given theatrically visible exits, but these are not "merely" theatrical. They serve a purpose: they shows that the figures in the film's formal dance are forever retreating into shadows, into death. It is a film of vanishings; as when the figures at the end of the Amberson ball, two knots of people, one in the foreground, the other "rhubarbing" in the background, move out into the windy night, leaving the polished hall silhouetted behind as the musicians pack up their instruments. The Morgan Motor, too, vanishes over a hill past a giant wintry tree, and an iris-out blots its image forever, to be followed by a black wreath, fixed to the door of the Amberson house.

All through the film people are leaving, drifting away like leaves before the wind. In the ballroom scene, the dancing figures seem to recede into infinity, an effect partly achieved by the judicious use of mirrors. Upright struts and pillars constantly create frames within the frame, so that the people seem to be fixed like moths on plates, fluttering and trapped. A variant on this method occurs in Isabel's deathbed scene, when the shadows of the bedstead and the lace curtain traps her in a spider's web of doom, and a sudden, shocking change of light into near darkness as someone draws the curtains, more firmly involves her in death.

The sound track, too, has the effect of isolating the people in the film, of withdrawing them from us. Voices are constantly heard "off"—not quite an innovation, since Wyler had used the method in *These Three*—but here more extensively employed than ever before. Just as we constantly see people not only framed in uprights but half glimpsed through doorways, reflected in mirrors or windows, so we hear their voices almost muffled through doorways or in the far distance of rooms, floating down a remote stairway or mingled with the measures of a dance, the hiss and clang of a factory. It is part of the film's evocation of a deathly atmosphere that, apart from Aunt Fanny's whine, everyone should speak in subdued, sad, falling tones, words with a dying fall in this film of dying falls, of an endless dying. . . .

The performances in *Ambersons* have a complexity and power rare in the cinema: and of them the most famous is Agnes Moorehead's definitive portrait of Aunt Fanny. Although she is not quite the Fanny described in the book, "who, rouged a little, was like fruit which in some climates dries with the bloom on. Her features had remained prettily childlike. . . ." And although the screenplay does not allow her Fanny's violent changes of mood, or her ability to look twenty at one minute and sixty the next, Agnes Moorehead moves deeply inside the frustration and misery of the character, conveying in high-pitched whines, in querulous outbursts of rage, and in her whole taut, cramped, tightly corseted body and pinched hawk-like face, in every movement of her hands, in every fit of hysterical tears, a life wrecked on the rocks of repression.

George Minafer is stiffly but accurately played by Tim Holt; the black, curled hair, the spoiled pretty face, the suggestion of plumpness and impending fatness, the ramrod back, head held haughtily high in defiance of progress. Here is an aggressive masculinity barely concealing a vulnerable feminine streak, the cruelty and vanity conveyed in the strutting gestures. It is a portrait that precisely embodies the Booth Tarkington character, despite Holt's lack of experience (he had previously been seen mainly in Westerns).

Dolores Costello as Isabel, wan, with the vestiges of a great beauty, is a trifle too old for the part (in the novel, she is in her late thirties at first), but she conveys the correct degree of delicacy, the frailty and the melting sadness, her face at all times lit with exquisite softness by Stanley Cortez. Ray Collins is brilliantly apt as Uncle Jack, the epitome of Midwestern behavior: fat, tough, but sentimental, with a shrewd, exact calculation of how much and how little George Minafer is worth. His harsh voice and gross physique—unpleasantly discovered in a bath at one stage—are unfalteringly conveyed.

Joseph Cotten, not as indulged as usual, is perfect as Eugene Morgan, a representation of the ideal husband imagined by Fanny, rejected but still loved by Isabel; but, genial and gentlemanly, he seems to belong more to the old generation than to the one that produced the horseless carriage. As a manufacturer of robust tastes and simple toughness, we cannot wholeheartedly accept him.

For the most part, the cast plays with impeccable period sense, guided by a director at the height of his powers. The art direction of the late Mark Lee Kirk is beautifully apt: the great Amberson ball, with its "flowers and plants and roped vines brought from afar" is perfectly conveyed, admirably restored; and the house is achieved without a flaw: "a house of arches and turrets and girdling stone porches," boasting "the first porte-cochere" (in Indianapolis). It is on the black walnut stairway, against the stained-glass windows and heavy drapes, that the main action of the film often takes place; a doomed, opulent setting for a drama of threatened splendor.

Welles's narration begins with an expert adaptation and condensation of the long nostalgic passage that opens Tarkington's novel:

> In those days, all the women who wore silk or velvet knew all the other women who wore silk or velvet. And everybody knew everybody else's family horse and carriage. The only public conveyance was the streetcar. A lady could whistle to it from an upstairs window, and the car would halt at once, and wait for her, as she shut the window, put on her hat and coat, went downstairs, found an umbrella, told the girl what to have for dinner, and came forth from the house. Too slow for us nowadays, because the faster we're carried, the less time we have to spare.
>
> During the early years of this period, while bangs and bustles were having their way with women, there were seen men of all ages to whom a hat meant only that rigid, tall silk thing known to impudence as a stovepipe. But the long contagion of the derby had arrived; one season the crown of this hat would be a bucket, next it would be a spoon. Every house still kept its bootjack. But hightop boots gave way to shoes and congress gaiters, and these were shaped through fashions that shaped them now with toes like box ends and now with toes like the prows of racing shells.
>
> Trousers with a crease were considered plebian; the crease proved that the garment had lain upon a shelf, and hence was ready-made . . . with evening dress a gentleman wore a tan overcoat, so short that his black coat tails hung visible five inches below the overcoat; but after a season or

two, he lengthened his overcoat till it touched his heels, and he passed out of his tight trousers into trousers like great bags.

In those days, they had time for everything. Time for sleigh rides, and balls, and assemblies, and cotillions, and open house on New Years, and all-day picnics in the woods. And even that prettiest of all banished customs, the serenade. On that summer night, young men would bring an orchestra under a pretty girl's window, and flute, harp, cello, cornet, and bass viol would presently release their melodies to the dulcet stars. Against so homespun a background, the magnificence of the Ambersons was as conspicuous as a brass band at a funeral.

Over this tenderly and nostalgically read passage, a period, a way of life are beautifully evoked. The opening shot shows the Amberson's house, miraculously correct, a streetcar traverses from left to right, stops, and the passengers gather with leisurely movement around it as it waits for Mrs. Amberson to descend the stairs, give instructions to her daughter, and take her place in a seat. The camera remains at a precisely calculated distance, as though framing a mezzotint: the whole scene—like every subsequent one—edged in soft focus, in a haze of memory.

We see hatted men in a saloon drink heartily as the narration turns to hats, the saloon door swinging to and from; a young man in a stovepipe hat sits in a boat with a girl twirling a parasol; Eugene Morgan stands in a mirror trying on hats, using a bootjack. The mood becomes increasingly comic, almost Disneyesque, as, like Goofy in an RKO cartoon comedy, Eugene struggles into successively more absurd trousers and overcoats at the mirror.

Then the mood becomes more tender and elegiac, the music more slow and stately. As Welles speaks the words, "In those days they had time for everything," we see the Amberson house covered in snow, richest of Welles's symbols of vanished purity, and as the serendade is mentioned, the house on a summer night, strung with pretty lanterns, a moon hanging behind the eaves. Then the image darkens, the moon is gone, and only a lamp glows on the left of the frame, big as a harvest moon.

As the serenade is played, Eugene Morgan runs forward with the men carrying the instruments to play in honor of Isabel Amberson, trips, and falls over. Isabel, through the lace curtains, is amused and withdrawn, cut off in the splendid darkness of the house from the comic little scene outside.

As the narrative ends the mood progresses to an *allegro vivace,* various towns-folk describing the splendors of the mansion: "Hot and cold running water, stationary washstands in every last bedroom of the place." A Negro butler opens the front door to Eugene, announcing that Isabel Amberson is not at home to him; his next call is equally fruitless. Outside the house another group of people—including Fanny Minafer—is talking about Eugene's awkward courtship. ("Stepped clean through the bass fiddle.") Finally, we see Eugene luring Isabel at last out of the house; he in driving gear, she in big floppy hat, ringlets, and rings. But, ironi-cally, even as this happens, the bystanders, acting like a Greek chorus, disclose that Isabel is not going to marry Eugene, the up-and-coming young horseless-carriage manufacturer, but Wilbur Minafer, a solid young businessman.

A woman neighbor describes to a group, as in a chorus, the splendors of the

Amberson-Minafer nuptials: "Raw oysters floating in scooped out blocks of ice . . . and she'll be a good wife to him . . . but they'll have the worst-spoiled lot of children this town will ever see."

As she utters these words, a living illustration of her prophesy—George Minafer, in velveteen and ringlets—is seen making a thorough nuisance of himself. In his tiny carriage, he upsets a gardener with hoe, the horse trotting vigorously along, all observed in a brilliant succession of stylized, heavily angled shots which emphasize the nervous obstreperousness of Georgie's career, while the commentary indicates that everyone in town lived in expectation of the boy's ultimate "come-uppance."

A boy Tom Sawyerishly hoots at George a derisive reference to his curly locks, and the pair grapple, rolling over and over on the lawn while a lawyer parent (Erskine Sanford) is seen in his typically Wellesian pose of infuriated gentility and exasperation, at first rapping peremptorily on the window, then descending to the law to drag the two boys apart. George punches him in the stomach, just as Charles Kane rammed Walter Parks Thatcher.

A postmortem on the fight takes place in the garden of the Amberson mansion in a long-held shot as posed and formal as a Landseer: George in kilt and tam-o'-shanter, Isabel in white by a tree, Major Amberson crusty and wound tightly in a cocoon of age. George promises not to use bad language again (the phrase "Unless I get mad at somebody" immediately cancels out the validity of the promise), and a tripping woodwind passage in Bernard Herrmann's score indicates that George has no intention of improving at all.

The transition to George's adulthood is handled with a magical long dolly shot through the front door of the Amberson house, the wind sweeping with us as we move forward into a world of lost elegance and beauty, a wind that moves the chandeliers in a swaying sad dance, that ruffles and tinkles the Christmas tree's bells and baubles with a sweet, sad melody. Here everything is solid, rich, cluttered with the collections of generations, yet shining with an effulgence that already gives a hint of decay.

In the body of the hall the vines are festooned, the couples moving to and from. "It was the last of the great, long-remembered dances that everybody talked about." George looks ideal, "white-gloved, with a carnation in his buttonhole," his young unlined face with "nothing to offer except . . . condescension."

Hearty greetings and robust exchanges accompany a subtle series of group shots often formed into triangles, while all the time we are aware of the couples moving, moving, in graceful procession, an endless parade through the house, accompanied by a minuet playing softly in the background.

A fine, long, gliding movement accompanies the Morgans—Eugene and his daughter—and the Minafers and Ambersons; the camera retreats before them, taking the richly flowered wallpapers, chandeliers, the shimmer of brasswork. We move up the stairs, past the orchestra playing the minuet, past stained-glass windows to an upper landing, in an awestruck exploration of American materialism, "of solid black walnut, every inch of it, balustrades and all. Sixty thousand dollars' worth o' carved woodwork in the house!"

And the ascent continues, in a long dreamlike take, "among the gleaming young heads, white shoulders, jewels, and chiffon," Eugene dancing with Aunt

Fanny, George expressing his contempt of automobiles to Eugene's daughter, Lucy, while unconscious of her identity.

Lucy and her father, George and his mother: they form into intricate patterns, a formal dance of long gliding takes and a shot of a punch bowl, the figures grouped symmetrically around it, and a discussion of relationships, of leisured days and ways. And in the mirror, as Eugene moves into a dance with Isabel, we see reflected the passing of time, as we recall the way they must have danced when he was courting her, long ago. And by contrast, as the sequence ends in a flurry of two- and four-shots, the obstreperousness of George Minafer, who condemns the uselessness of the rich businessmen surrounding him; asked by Lucy what he wants to become, he says, fatuously, "A yachtsman!" as he dances with her into the throng of figures on the dance floor, already blended with them, bringing the sequence of the Amberson ball to a brilliant close.

Now it is night, and the ball is over, the orchestra playing a plaintive air, and Eugene and Isabel still gliding in the shimmering light of the last lamps and the glow of the moon through the stain-glass window. The sequence ends upon an evocation of frost and snow, a window thickly rimmed with white faces in shadowy profile against it, presaging the beautiful journey through the snow that follows in a later scene.

An argument follows between George and Fanny on the various landings of the house's great central staircase: George is suggesting that Eugene Morgan is using the Ambersons to obtain financing for the horseless carriage that George hates; Fanny, who has always been infatuated with Eugene, tells George peremptorily that Eugene is perfectly capable of looking after his own affairs. In the deep shadows the figures wrangle. George whines plaintively: "What makes you and everybody so excited over this man Morgan?" and in the playing and direction what could have been merely an empty grumble about a family rivalry becomes symbolic of a way of thinking that clings to a motorless past. And an opportunity, too, for Aunt Fanny's hysterical attachment to Eugene to be expressed in parrotlike screeches of rage, expostulations of shrill disapproval at George's failure of appreciation: "You're trying to insinuate that I get your mother to invite Eugene Morgan here on my behalf!" Here is a woman whose whole life has been wrapped up in the noble image of one man, and who is doomed to know only loneliness, never to be sexually fulfilled by him.

By contrast with this tense dark scene—staged in the swarming shadows of the house, the arguing figures perched above each other on balconies as though on clifftops—the next has a wonderful sense of release, of dazzling frost, sunlight, and dashing movement; reflected in a frozen pool, with giggling on the sound track and the pretty tinkling of Herrmann's instruments, a sleigh whirls round a bend in a road. The festively beautiful, poetic, motorless movement is set in exquisite contrast with the foundering of the horseless carriage—a vintage 1905 motor buggy hopelessly bogged down as Eugene, Fanny, and Isabel struggle to set it free. At last Eugene gets the Morgan Motor going, but George calls out from the sleigh he is riding in with Lucy, "Get a horse! Get a horse!"—a play on the old cliché, and also a perfect summary of an attitude to life. But the sleigh tilts over, and the couple roll down a mound of snow.

The camera delicately moves through the branches of winter trees as George and Lucy are taken by Eugene to the horseless carriage to continue their journey, George's first sampling of travel in the New Age. The rattling monster stops again, quivering under its tasseled canopy, but progress cannot be stilled, and soon it is bearing its laughing cargo through the wind on an odyssey at eight miles an hour. They sing—even Fanny sings—"The Man Who Broke the Bank at Monte Carlo." And the screen, as at the ball, is continually broken into patterns of heads, each face beautifully contrasted and compared, the sequence closed on an exquisite iris-out as the car vanishes over the horizon, and an era is over.

After the spontaneous excitement and gaiety of this scene comes the shock of reality: a black wreath on the door of the Amberson house indicates that Wilbur Minafer, the colorless man we have glimpsed only briefly, and whom Isabel threw over Eugene to marry, is prematurely dead. Sinister chords; as the Negro butler who once refused entrance to him opens the door to Eugene, we see as from Wilbur Minafer's coffin, the family looming above us, paying its last somber respects. . . . As George walks home, now by his very choice of occupation committing himself to the machine age he had despised so long, we see images of the growing city, and the commentary emphasizes the grim strangeness of the new landscape. Machinery is seen leaping up with the steel fury of a new kind of animal. Telegraph poles deface a once gracious road. Dissolves throw metal struts against a bleak gray sky as the commentary speaks a valedictory, predicting that by tomorrow an era of serenades will be over forever. The screen goes completely dark, and gradually we see George kneeling beside the bed where his mother once died, saying a last prayer, a last farewell: he has got his come-uppance at last. ("He got it three times filled, and running over.")

The next we hear of George he has been run over by an automobile, crushed finally by the New Age. In the newspaper *The Indianapolis Inquirer* a headline announces: "Auto Casualties Mount." (Here is an "in" joke: the paper is a Kane paper, and on the left of the front page is a theatrical column written by Jedediah Leland.) On the right we read: "Serious accident, Geo. Minafer, Akers' Chemical Co., both legs broken." In the final hospital scene Eugene talks to Fanny outside George's room, and Eugene says that George has asked for forgiveness. Eugene says "I never noticed before how much like Isabel Georgie looks." Tears sparkle on Fanny's cheeks, and, in a sentimental glow, she moves out of frame as Eugene talks about being finally "true at last to my true love."

This scene, directed by Robert Wise, has been much maligned, but it echoes, to the tune of a sad, final Herrmann waltz, the precise words of the ending of Tarkington's book: "For Eugene another radiance filled the [hospital] room. He knew that he had been true at last to his true love, and that through him she had brought her boy under shelter again. Her eyes would look wistful no more."

7

PRIMARY SOURCES

A. The Introduction of Sound

The introduction of sound into the film industry is a tale filled with myths. According to the traditional Hollywood legend, the financially-strapped Warner Brothers turned to sound in a desperate gamble to save the company. More recently, film historian Douglas Gomery has shown that the coming of sound in fact reflected calculated corporate decisions about the potential profits to be reaped from introducing the new technology. These primary sources give some sense of the public reaction to the arrival of the talkies.

1. "Pictures That Talk"

Photoplay, 1924

And now the motion pictures really talk. It has been almost twenty years since Thomas A. Edison first tried to accomplish this, but it has remained for Dr. Lee De Forest to bring the "talkies" to their present stage of advancement.

Mr. Edison's first attempt was made by the simple process of playing stock cylinder records on a phonograph and having the actors sing, or pretend to sing, with the record, while the camera photographed the lip movement. By this method synchronization was impossible. Sometimes the singer would be so far ahead or behind the record that the result would be laughable.

Edison knew this would never do, so he finally invented the "kinetophone." Again, he used the phonograph, but he obtained better results by making the phonograph record at the same time as the motion picture negative. This gave perfect synchronization in the taking of the pictures, but two operators were needed for the projection—one for the film in the booth and the other, back stage, to run the phonograph.

Sometimes the results were good. More often they were not. But, nevertheless, these pictures had quite a vogue and drew great audiences all over the country. Edison was not satisfied, but he never was able to get perfect synchronization, nor were any of the dozen others who tried.

About this time Lee De Forest, then a young electrical engineer in the West, was experimenting with wireless, or radio, as it is now called. Out of this came the "audion," which is now a part of every radio set and which makes broadcasting and receiving possible. Three years ago De Forest became interested in motion pictures and began his experiments to make them talk. He realized that synchronization and audibility were essential. After three years he has worked out his "Phonofilm." He has synchronized the picture and the voice by photographing the sound on the same strip of film with the action and at the same time. Instead of the voice being phonographed, it is radioed from the speaker's lips, by sound waves, to the camera. There these sound waves are converted into light waves and photographed on the left side of the film.

All of this is accomplished with any standard motion picture camera, to which has been added an attachment for photographing sound. The negative thus produced is developed in the usual manner and prints made exactly similar to the prints of any other motion picture.

In projecting the De Forest Phonofilms, an inexpensive attachment is necessary, which fits on any stand projection machine. In this attachment is a tiny incandescent lamp. As the film passes this light, the lines made by the voice become "flickers" or light waves. These light waves are picked up by the infinitesimal wires and converted into sound waves again. Other larger wires take the sound waves into the amplifier, from which they are carried from the projection room by ordinary wires back-stage, amplified again, and thrown on the screen in precise synchronization with the action of the scene. . . .

2.   Review of *Don Juan*

Mordaunt Hall, *The New York Times*, 1926

A marvelous new device known as the vitaphone, which synchronizes sound with motion pictures, stirred a distinguished audience in Warners' Theatre to unusual enthusiasm at his initial presentation last Thursday evening. The natural reproduction of voices, the tonal qualities of musical instruments and the timing of the sound to the movements of the lips of singers and the actions of musicians was almost uncanny. . . .

The future of this new contrivance is boundless, for inhabitants of small and remote places will have the opportunity of listening to and seeing grand opera as it is given in New York, and through the picturing of the vocalists and small grounds and small groups of musicians, or instrumental choirs of orchestras, the vitaphone will give its patrons an excellent idea of a singer's acting and an intelligent conception of the efforts of musicians and their instruments. . . .

3. "Silence is Golden"

Aldous Huxley, *Golden Book Magazine*, 1930

I have just been, for the first time, to see and hear a picture talk. "A little late in the day," my up-to-date readers will remark, with a patronizing and contemptuous smile. "This is 1930; there isn't much news in talkies now. But better late than never."

Better late than never? Ah, no! There, my friends, you're wrong. This is one of those cases where it is most decidedly better never than late, better never than early, better never than on the stroke of time. . . .

The explanation of my firm resolve never, if I can help it, to be reintroduced will be found in the following simple narrative of what I saw and heard in that fetid hall on the Boulevard des Italiens, where the latest and most frightful creation-saving device for the production of standardized amusement had been installed.

We entered the hall halfway through the performance of a series of music-hall turns—not substantial ones, of course, but the two-dimensional images of turns with artificial voices. There were no travel films, nothing in the Natural History line, none of those fascinating Events of the Week—lady mayoresses launching battleships, Japanese earthquakes, hundred-to-one outsiders winning races, revolutionaries on the march in Nicaragua—which are always the greatest and often the sole attractions in the programs of our cinema. Nothing but disembodied entertainers, gesticulating flatly on the screen and making gramophonelike noises as they did so. Some sort of comedian was performing as we entered. But he soon vanished to give place to somebody's celebrated jazz band—not merely audible in all its loud vulgarity of brassy guffaw and caterwauling sentiment, but also visible in a series of apocalyptic closeups of the individual performers. A beneficent Providence has dimmed my powers of sight so that at a distance of more than four or five yards I am blissfully unaware of the full horror of the average human countenance. At the cinema, however, there is no escape. Magnified up to Brobdingnagian proportions, the human countenance smiles its six-foot smiles, opens and shuts its thirty-two-inch eyes, registers soulfulness or grief, libido or whimsicality, with every square centimeter of its several roods of pallid mooniness. Nothing short of total blindness can preserve one from the spectacle. The jazz players were forced upon me; I regarded them with a fascinated horror. It was the first time, I suddenly realized, that I had ever clearly seen a jazz band. The spectacle was positively terrifying.

The performers belonged to two contrasted races. There were the dark and polished young Hebrews, whose souls were in those mournfully sagging, seasick-ishly undulating melodies of mother love and nostalgia and yammering amorousness and clotted sensuality which have been the characteristically Jewish contributions to modern popular music. And there were the chubby young Nordics, with Aryan faces transformed by the strange plastic forces of the North American environment into the likeness of very large uncooked muffins or the unveiled posteriors of babes. (The more sympathetic Red Indian type of Nordic-American face was completely absent from this particular assemblage of jazz players.) Gigantically enlarged, these personages appeared one after another on the screen, each singing or playing his instrument and at the same time registering the emotions appropriate to the musical circumstances. The spectacle, I repeat, was really terrifying. For the first time, I felt grateful for the defect of vision which had preserved me from an earlier acquaintance with such aspects of modern life. And at the same time I wished that I could become, for the occasion, a little hard of hearing. For if good music has charms to soothe the savage breast, bad music has no less powerful spells for filling the mildest breast with rage, the happiest with horror and disgust. Oh, those mammy songs, those love longings, those loud hilarities; How was it possible that human emotions intrinsically decent could be so ignobly parodied? I felt like a man who, having asked for wine, is offered a brimming bowl of hogwash. And not even fresh hogwash. Rancid hogwash, decaying hogwash. For there was a horrible tang of putrefaction in all that music. Those yearnings for "Mammy of Mine" and "My Baby," for "Dixie" and the "Land Where Skies Are Blue" and "Dreams Come True," for "Granny" and "Tennessee and You"—they were all a necrophily. The Mammy after whom the black young Hebrews and the blond young muffin-faces so retchingly yearned was an ancient Gorgonzola cheese; the Baby of their tremulously gargled desire was a leg of mutton after a month in warm storage; Granny had been dead for weeks; and as for Dixie and Tennessee and Dream Land—they were odoriferous with the least artificial of manures.

When, after what seemed hours, the jazz band concluded its dreadful performances, I sighed in thankfulness. But the thankfulness was premature. For the film which followed was hardly less distressing. It was the story of the child of a cantor in a synagogue, afflicted, to his father's justifiable fury, with an itch for jazz. This itch, assisted by the cantor's boot, sends him out into the world, where, in due course and thanks to My Baby, his dreams come tree-ue, and he is employed as a jazz singer on the music-hall stage. Promoted from the provinces to Broadway, the jazz singer takes the opportunity to revisit the home of his childhood. But the cantor will have nothing to do with him, absolutely nothing, in spite of his success, in spite, too, of his moving eloquence. "You yourself always taught me," says the son pathetically, "that the voice of music was the voice of God." Vox jazz vox Dei— the truth is new and beautiful. But stern old Poppa's heart refuses to be melted. Even Mammy of Mine is unable to patch up a reconciliation. The singer is reduced to going out once more into the night—and from the night back to his music hall.

The crisis of the drama arrives when, the cantor being mortally sick and unable to fulfil his functions at the synagogue, Mammy of Mine and the Friends of his Childhood implore the young man to come and sing the atonement service in his father's place. Unhappily, this religious function is booked to take place at the same hour as that other act of worship vulgarly known as the First Night. There ensues a terrific struggle, worthy of the pen of a Racine or a Dryden, between love and honor. Love for Mammy of Mine draws the jazz singer toward the synagogue; but love for My Baby draws the cantor's son toward the theater, where she, as principal Star, is serving the deity no less acceptably with her legs and smile than he with his voice. Honor also calls from either side; for honor demands that he should serve the God of his fathers at the synagogue, but it also demands that he should serve the jazz-voiced god of his adoption at the theater. Some very eloquent captions appear at this point. With the air of a Seventeenth Century hero, the jazz singer protests that he must put his career before even his love. The nature of the dilemma has changed, it will be seen, since Dryden's day. In the old dramas it was love that had to be sacrificed to painful duty. In the modern instance the sacrifice is at the shrine of what William James called "the Bitch Goddess Success." Love is to be abandoned for the stern pursuit of any sort of newspaper notoriety and dollars.

In the end the singer makes the best of both worlds—satisfies Mammy of Mine and even Poor Poppa by singing at the synagogue and, on the following evening, scores a terrific success at the postponed first night of My Baby's revue. The film concludes with a scene in the theater, with Mammy of Mine in the stalls (Poor Poppa is by this time safely under ground), and the son, with My Baby in the background, warbling down at her the most nauseatingly luscious, the most pene-tratingly vulgar mammy song that it has ever been my lot to hear. My flesh crept as the loud speaker poured out those sodden words, that greasy, sagging melody. I felt ashamed of myself for listening to such things, for even being a member of the species to which such things are addressed. But I derived a little comfort from the reflection that a species which has allowed all its instincts and emotions to degen-erate and putrefy in such a way must be pretty near either its violent conclusion or else its radical transformation and reform.

B.   Film Censorship

During the 1920s, pressure to censor the movies grew. In 1922 alone, 22 state legislatures considered bills to impose state and local censorship. Holly-wood responded by establishing a trade organization in 1922 known as the Motion Picture Producers and Distributors of America, with Will H. Hays (Post-master General under President Warren Harding) as president. Hays's call for "self-regulation" to forestall outside censorship, and The Don'ts and Be Care-fuls, *adopted in 1927 along with* The Production Code of 1930 *represented important steps toward industry self-censorship. Nevertheless, criticism of the industry mounted, and by 1932 some 40 religious and educational groups had called for censorship. Unlike Protestant religious groups, which were frag-mented, the Catholic church was unified in its demand that the industry recog-nize its moral responsibilities to the public. The threat of movie boycotts by the Catholic Legion of Decency led the industry's trade association in 1934 to establish the Production Code Administration Office, headed by Joseph Breen, to regulate films.*

1. *The Sins of Hollywood*, 1922

To the Public:
The sins of Hollywood are facts—Not Fiction!

The stories in this volume are true stories—the people are real people—

Most of those involved in the events reported herein are today occupying high places in motion pictures—popular idols—applauded, lauded and showered with gold by millions of men, women and children—especially the women and children!

To the boys and girls of this land these mock heroes and heroines have been pictured and painted, for box office purposes, as the living symbols of all the virtues—

An avalanche of propaganda by screen and press has imbued them with every ennobling trait.

Privately they have lived, and are still living, lives of wild debauchery.

In more than one case licentiousness and incest have been the only rungs in the ladders on which they have climbed to fame and fortune!

Unfaithfully and cruelly indifferent to the worship of the youth of the land, they have led or are leading such lives as may, any day, precipitate yet another nation-wide scandal and again shatter the ideals, the dreams, the castles, the faith of our boys and girls!

It is for these reasons that the Sins of Hollywood are given to the public—

That a great medium of national expression may be purified—taken from the hands of those who have misused it—that the childish faith of our boys and girls may again be made sacred!

Fully eighty percent of those engaged in motion pictures are high-grade citizens—self-respecting and respected.

In foolish fear of injuring the industry, Hollywood has permitted less than one per cent of its population to stain its name.

The facts reported in these stories have long been an open book to the organized producers—No need to tell them—they knew!

They knew of the horde of creatures of easy morals who have hovered about the industry and set the standard of price—decided what good, clean women would have to pay—have to give—in order to succeed—

They knew of the macqueraux—of the scum that constituted the camp followers of their great stars. They knew of the wantonness of their leading women—

They knew about the yachting parties—the wild orgies at road houses and private homes—

They knew about Vernon and its wild life—Tia Juana and its mad, drunken revels—

They knew about the "kept" women—and the "kept" men—

They knew about the prominent people among them who were living in illicit relationship—

There was a time at one studio when every star, male and female, was carrying on an open liason—The producer could not help knowing it.

Eight months before the crash that culminated in the Arbuckle cataclysm they knew the kind of parties Roscoe was giving—and some of them were glad to participate in them—

They knew conditions—knew about the "hop" and the "dope"—but they took the stand that it was "none of our business"—

Their business was piling up advance deposits from theater owners and manipulating the motion picture stock market.

They frowned on all attempts to speak the truth—

Any publication that attempted to reveal the real conditions—to cleanse the festering sores—was quickly pounced upon as an "enemy of the industry"—A subsidized trade press helped in this work!

Any attempt to bring about reform was called "hurting the industry."

It was the lapses and laxities of the producer that precipitated the censorship agitation—that led a nauseated nation, determined to cleanse the Augean stables of the screen, into the dangerous notion of censorship—almost fatally imperilling two sacred principles of democracy—freedom of speech and freedom of the press!

They have made "box office" capital of everything—Nothing has been to vile to exploit—

They created the male vamp—

Nothing was sacred—nothing was personal—if it had publicity possibilities. . . .

If the screen is to be "cleaned-up," the sores must be cut open—the pus and corruption removed—This always hurts! But it is the only known way!

2. "The Don'ts and Be Carefuls"

Motion Picture Producers and Distributors of America, 1927

Resolved, That those things which are included in the following list shall not appear in pictures produced by the members of this Association, irrespective of the manner in which they are treated.

1. Pointed profanity—by either title or lip—this includes the words "God," "Lord," "Jesus," "Christ" (unless they be used reverently in connection with proper religious ceremonies), "hell," "damn," "Gawd," and every other profane and vulgar expression however it may be spelled;

2. Any licentious or suggestive nudity—in fact or in silhouette; and any lecherous or licentious notice thereof by other characters in the picture;

3. The illegal traffic in drugs;

4. Any inference of sex perversion;

5. White slavery;

6. Miscegenation (sex relationships between the white and black races);

7. Sex hygiene and venereal diseases;

8. Scenes of actual childbirth—in fact or in silhouette;

9. Children's sex organs;

10. Ridicule of the clergy;

11. Willful offense to any nation, race or creed;

And be it further resolved, That special care be exercised in the manner in which the following subjects are treated, to the end that vulgarity and suggestiveness be eliminated and that good taste may be emphasized:

1. The use of the flag;
2. International relations (avoiding picturizing in an unfavorable light another country's religion, history, institutions, prominent people, and citizenry);
3. Arson;
4. The use of firearms;
5. Theft, robbery, safe-cracking, and dynamiting of trains, mines, buildings, etc. (having in mind the effect which a too-detailed description of these may have upon the moron);
6. Brutality and possible gruesomeness;
7. Techniques of committing murder by whatever method;
8. Methods of smuggling;
9. Third-degree methods;
10. Actual hangings or electrocutions as legal punishment for crime;
11. Sympathy for criminals;
12. Attitude toward public characters and institutions;
13. Sedition;
14. Apparent cruelty to children and animals;
15. Branding of people or animals;
16. The sale of women, or of a woman selling her virtue;
17. Rape or attempted rape;
18. First-night scenes;
19. Man and woman in bed together;
20. Deliberate seduction of girls;
21. The institution of marriage;
22. Surgical operations;
23. The use of drugs;
24. Titles or scenes having to do with law enforcement or law-enforcing officers;
25. Excessive or lustful kissing, particularly when one character or the other is a "heavy."

3. The Motion Picture Production Code of 1930

FIRST SECTION

GENERAL PRINCIPLES

I.   Theatrical motion pictures, that is, pictures intended for the theatre as distinct from pictures intended for churches, schools, lecture halls, educational movements, social reform movements, etc., are primarily to be regarded as *Entertainment*. Mankind has always recognized the importance of entertainment and its value in rebuilding the bodies and souls of human beings.

But it has always recognized that entertainment can be of a character *harmful* to the human race, and, in consequence, has clearly distinguished between:

Entertainment which tends to improve the race, or, at least, to recreate and rebuild human beings exhausted with the realities of life; and

Entertainment which tends to degrade human beings, or to lower their standards of life and living.

Hence the *moral importance* of entertainment is something which has been universally recognized. It enters intimately into the lives of men and women and affects them closely; it occupies their minds and affections during leisure hours, and ultimately touches the whole of their lives. A man may be judged by his standard of entertainment as easily as by the standard of his work.

So *correct entertainment raises* the whole standard of a nation.

Wrong entertainment lowers the whole living condition and moral ideals of a race.

NOTE, for example, the healthy reactions to healthful moral sports like baseball, golf; the unhealthy reactions to sports like cockfighting, bullfighting, bearbaiting, etc. Note, too, the effect on a nation of gladiatorial combats, the obscene plays of Roman times, etc.

II.   Motion pictures are very important as *Art*.
Though a new art, possibly a combination art, it has the same object as the other arts, the presentation of human thoughts, emotions and experiences, in terms of an appeal to the soul thru the senses.
Here, as in entertainment:

Art *enters intimately* into the lives of human beings.

Art can be *morally good,* lifting men to higher levels. This has been done thru good music, great painting, authentic fiction, poetry, drama.

Art can be morally evil in its effects. This is the case clearly enough with unclean art, indecent books, suggestive drama. The effect on the lives of men and women is obvious.

NOTE: It has often been argued that art in itself is unmoral, neither good nor bad. This is perhaps true of the *thing* which is music, painting, poetry, etc. But the thing is the *product* of some person's mind, and that mind was either good or bad morally when it produced the thing. And the thing has its *effect* upon those who come into contact with it. In both these ways, as a product and the cause of definite effects, it has a deep moral significance and an unmistakable moral quality.

HENCE: The motion pictures which are the most popular of modern arts for the masses, have their moral quality from the minds which produce them and from their effects on the moral lives and reactions of their audiences. This gives them a most important morality.

1) They *reproduce* the morality of the men who use the pictures as a medium for the expression of their ideas and ideals;

2) They *affect* the moral standards of those who thru the screen take in these ideas and ideals. In the case of the motion pictures, this effect may be particularly emphasized because no art has so quick and so widespread an appeal to the masses. It has become in an incredibly short period, *the art of the multitudes*.

III.   The motion picture has special *Moral obligations*:

A) Most arts appeal to the mature. This art appeals at once to every class—mature, immature, developed, undeveloped, law-abiding, criminal. Music has its grades for different classes; so has literature and drama. This art of the motion picture, combining as it does the two fundamental appeals of looking at a picture and listening to a story, at once reaches every class of society.

B) Because of the mobility of a film and the ease of picture distribution, and because of the possibility of duplicating positives in large quantities, this art *reaches places* unpenetrated by other forms of art.

C) Because of these two facts, it is difficult to produce films intended for only *certain classes of people*. The exhibitor's theatres are for the masses, for the cultivated and the rude, mature and immature, self restrained and inflammatory, young and old, law respecting and criminal. Films, unlike books and music, can with difficulty be confined to certain selected groups.

D) The latitude given to film material cannot, in consequence, be as wide as the latitude given to *book material*. In addition:

(a) A book describes; a film vividly presents.

(b) A book reaches the mind thru words merely; a film reaches the eyes and ears thru the reproduction of actual events.

(c) The reaction of a reader to a book depends largely on the keenness of the reader; the reaction to a film depends on the vividness of presentation.

E) This is also true when comparing the film with the newspapers. Newspapers present by description, films by actual presentation. Newspapers are after the fact and present things that have taken place; the film gives the events in the process of enactment and with apparent reality of life.

F) Everything possible in a *play is* not possible in a film.

(a) Because of the larger audience of the film, and its consequently mixed character. Psychologically, the larger the audience, the lower the moral mass resistance to suggestion.

(b) Because thru light, enlargement of character presentation, scenic emphasis, etc., the screen story is brought closer to the audience than the play.

(c) The enthusiasm for and interest in the film *actors* and *actresses,* developed beyond anything of the sort in history, makes the audience largely sympathetic toward the characters they portray and the stories in which they figure. Hence they are more ready to confuse the actor and character, and they are most receptive of the emotions and ideals portrayed and presented by their favorite stars.

G) Small communities, remote from sophistication and from the hardening process which often takes place in the ethical and moral standards of larger cities, are easily and readily reached by any sort of film.

H) The grandeur of mass meetings, large action, spectacular features, etc., affects and arouses more intensely the emotional side of the audience.

IN GENERAL: The mobility, popularity, accessibility, emotional appeal, vividness, straight-forward presentation of fact in the films makes for intimate contact on a larger audience and greater emotional appeal. Hence the larger moral responsibilities of the motion pictures.

SECOND SECTION

WORKING PRINCIPLES

I.   No picture should lower the moral standards of those who see it. This is done:

(a) When evil is made to appear *attractive,* and good is made to appear *unattractive.*

(b) When the *sympathy* of the audience is thrown on the side of crime, wrongdoing, evil, sin. The same thing is true of a film that would throw sympathy against goodness, honor, innocence, purity, honesty.

NOTE: *Sympathy with a person who sins, is* not the same as sympathy with the sin or crime of which he is guilty. We may feel sorry for the plight of the murderer or even understand the circumstances which led him to his crime; we may not feel sympathy with the wrong which he has done.

The presentation of evil is often essential for art, or fiction, or drama. This in itself is not wrong, provided:

(a) That evil is *not presented alluringly,* even if later on the evil is condemned or punished, it must not be allowed to appear so attractive that the emotions are drawn to desire or approve so strongly that later they forget the condemnation and remember only the apparent joy of the sin.

(b) That thruout the presentation, *evil and good are not confused* and that evil is always recognized clearly as evil.

(c) That in the end the audience feels that *evil is wrong* and *good is right.*

II.   Law, natural or divine, must not be belittled, ridiculed, nor must a sentiment be created against it.

A) The *presentation of crimes* against the law, human or divine, is often necessary for the carrying out of the plot. But the presentation must not throw sympathy with the criminal as against the law, nor with the crime as against those who punish it.

B) The *courts* of the land should not be presented as unjust.

III.   As far as possible, life should not be misrepresented, at least not in such a way as to place in the mind of youth false values on life.

NOTE: This subject is touched just in passing. The attention of the producers is called, however, to the magnificent possibilities of the screen for character development, the building of right ideals, the inculcation in story-form of right principles. If motion pictures consistently held up high types of character, presented stories that would affect lives for the better, they could become the greatest natural force for the improvement of mankind.

PRINCIPLES OF PLOT

In accordance with the general principles laid down:

1) No plot or theme should definitely side *with evil and against good*.

2) Comedies and farces *should not make fun* of good, innocence, morality or justice.

3) No plot should be constructed as to leave the question of right or *wrong in doubt or fogged*.

4) No plot should by its treatment *throw the sympathy* of the audience with sin, crime, wrong-doing or evil.

5) No plot should present evil *alluringly*.

Serious Film Drama

I.   As stated in the general principles, *sin and evil* enter into the story of human beings, and hence in themselves are dramatic material.

II.   In the use of this material, it must be distinguished between *sin* which by its very nature *repels* and *sin* which by its very nature *attracts*.

(a) In the first class comes murder, most theft, most legal crimes, lying, hypocrisy, cruelty, etc.

(b) In the second class come sex sins, sins and crimes of apparent heroism, such as banditry, daring thefts, leadership in evil, organized crime, revenge, etc.

A) The first class needs little care in handling, as sins and crimes of this class naturally are unattractive. The audience instinctively condemns and is repelled. Hence the one objective must be to avoid the *hardening* of the audiences, especially of those who are young and impressionable, to the thought and the fact of crime. People can become accustomed even to murder, cruelty, brutality and repellent crimes.

B) The second class needs real care in handling, as the response of human natures to their appeal is obvious. This is treated more fully below.

III.   A careful distinction can be made between films intended for *general distribution* and films intended for use in theatres restricted to a *limited audience*. Themes and plots quite appropriate for the latter would be altogether out of place and dangerous in the former.

NOTE: In general, the practice of using a general theatre and limiting the patronage during the showing of a certain film to "adults only" is not completely satisfactory and is only partially effective. However, maturer minds may easily understand and accept without harm subject matter in plots which does younger people positive harm.

HENCE: If there should be created a special type of theatre, catering exclusively to an adult audience, for plays of this character (plays with problem themes, difficult discussions and maturer treatment) it would seem to afford an outlet, which does not now exist, for pictures unsuitable for general distribution but permissible for exhibitions to a restricted audience.

PLOT MATERIAL

1) *The triangle* that is, the love of a third party by one already married, needs careful handling, if marriage, the sanctity of the home, and sex morality are not to be imperilled.

2) *Adultery* as a subject should be avoided:

(a) It is *never a* fit subject for *comedy.* Thru comedy of this sort, ridicule is thrown on the essential relationships of home and family and marriage, and illicit relationships are made to seem permissible, and either delightful or daring.

(b) Sometimes adultery must be counted on as material occurring in serious drama.

In this case:

(1) It should not appear to be justified;

(2) It should not be used to weaken respect for marriage;

(3) It should not be presented as attractive or alluring.

3) *Seduction and rape* are difficult subjects and bad material from the viewpoint of the general audience in the theatre.

(a) They should never be introduced as subject matter *unless* absolutely essential to the plot.

(b) They should *never* be treated as comedy.

(c) Where essential to the plot, they must not be more than *suggested.*

(d) Even the struggles preceding rape should not be shown.

(e) The *methods* by which seduction, essential to the plot, is attained should not be explicit or represented in detail where there is likelihood of arousing wrongful emotions on the part of the audience.

4) *Scenes of passion* are sometimes necessary for the plot. However:

(a) They should appear only where necessary and *not* as an added stimulus to the emotions of the audience.

(b) *When not essential to the plot* they should not occur.

(c) They must *not* be *explicit* in action nor vivid in method, e.g. by handling of the body, by lustful and prolonged kissing, by evidently lustful embraces, by positions which strongly arouse passions.

(d) In general, where essential to the plot, scenes of passion should *not* be presented in such a way as to *arouse or excite the passions of the ordinary spectator.*

5) *Sexual immorality* is sometimes necessary for the plot. It is subject to the following:

GENERAL PRINCIPLES—regarding plots dealing with sex, passion, and incidents relating to them: All legislators have recognized clearly that there are in normal human beings emotions which react naturally and spontaneously to the presentation of certain definite manifestations of sex and passion.

(a) The presentation of scenes, episodes, plots, etc., which are deliberately meant to excite these manifestations on the part of the audience is always wrong, is subversive to the interest of society, and a peril to the human race.

(b) Sex and passion exist and consequently must *sometimes enter* into the stories which deal with human beings.

(1) *Pure love,* the love of a man for a woman permitted by the law of God and man, is the rightful subject of plots. The passion arising from this love is not the subject for plots.

(2) *Impure love* the love of man and woman forbidden by human and divine law, must be presented in such a way that:

a) It is clearly known by the audience to be wrong;

b) Its presentation does not excite sexual reactions, mental or physical, in an ordinary audience;

c) It is not treated as matter for comedy.

HENCE: *Even within the limits of pure love* certain facts have been universally regarded by lawmakers as outside the limits of safe presentation. These are the manifestations of passion and the sacred intimacies of private life:

(1) Either before marriage in the courtship of decent people;

(2) Or after marriage, as is perfectly clear.

In the case of pure love, the difficulty is not so much about what details are permitted for presentation. This is perfectly clear in most cases. The difficulty concerns itself with the tact, delicacy, and general regard for propriety manifested in their presentation.

But in the case of impure love the love which society has always regarded as wrong and which has been banned by divine law, the following are important:

(1) It must not be the subject of comedy or farce or treated as the material for laughter;

(2) It must not be presented as attractive and beautiful;

(3) It must not be presented in such a way as to arouse passion or morbid curiosity on the part of the audience;

(4) It must not be made to seem right and permissible;

(5) In general, it must not be detailed in method or manner.

6) *The presentation of murder* is often necessary for the carrying out of the plot. However:

(a) Frequent presentation of *murder* tends to lessen regard for the sacredness of life.

(b) *Brutal killings* should not be presented in detail.

(c) *Killings for revenge* should not be justified, i.e., the hero should not take justice into his own hands in such a way as to make his killing seem justified. This does not refer to killings in self-defense.

(d) *Dueling* should not be presented as right or just.

7) *Crimes against the law* naturally occur in the course of film stories. However:

    (a) *Criminals* should not be made heroes, even if they are historical criminals.

    (b) *Law and justice* must not by the treatment they receive from criminals be made to seem wrong or ridiculous.

    (c) *Methods of committing crime* e.g., burglary, should not be so explicit as to teach the audience how crime can be committed; that is, the film should not serve as a possible school in crime methods for those who seeing the methods might use them.

    (d) Crime need *not always be punished* as long as the audience is made to know that it is wrong.

DETAILS OF PLOT, EPISODE, AND TREATMENT

Vulgarity

Vulgarity may be carefully distinguished from obscenity. Vulgarity is the treatment of low, disgusting, unpleasant subjects which decent society considers outlawed from normal conversation.

    Vulgarity in the motion pictures is limited in precisely the same way as in decent groups of men and women by the dictates of good taste and civilized usage, and by the effect of shock, scandal, and harm on those coming in contact with this vulgarity.

    (1) *Oaths* should never be used as a comedy element. Where required by the plot, the less offensive oaths may be permitted.

    (2) *Vulgar expressions* come under the same treatment as vulgarity in general. Where women and children are to see the film, vulgar expressions (and oaths) should be cut to the absolute essentials required by the situation.

    (3) The name of *Jesus Christ* should never be used except in reverence.

Obscenity

Obscenity is concerned with immorality, but has the additional connotation of being common, vulgar and coarse.

    (1) *Obscenity in fact,* that is, in spoken word, gesture, episode, plot, is against divine and human law, and hence altogether outside the range of subject matter or treatment.

    (2) Obscenity should *not be suggested* by gesture, manner, etc.

    (3) An obscene reference, even if it is expected to be understandable to only the more sophisticated part of the audience, should not be introduced.

    (4) *Obscene language* is treated as all obscenity.

Costume

GENERAL PRINCIPLES:

(1) The effect of nudity or semi-nudity upon the normal man or woman, and much more upon the young person, has been honestly recognized by all lawmakers and moralists.

(2) Hence the fact that the nude or semi-nude body may be *beautiful* does not make its use in the films moral. For in addition to its beauty, the effects of the nude or semi-nude body on the normal individual must be taken into consideration.

(3) Nudity or semi-nudity used simply to put a "punch" into a picture comes under

the head of immoral actions as treated above. It is immoral in its effect upon the average audience.

(4) Nudity or semi-nudity is sometimes apparently necessary for the plot. *Nudity is never permitted*. Seminudity may be permitted under conditions.

PARTICULAR PRINCIPLES:

(1) *The more intimate parts of the human body* are male and female organs and the breasts of a woman.

    (a) They should *never be uncovered*.

    (b) They should not *be covered with* transparent or translucent material.

    (c) They should not be clearly and unmistakably *outlined* by the garment.

(2) *The less intimate parts of the body* the legs, arms, shoulders and back, are less certain of causing reactions on the part of the audience.

    Hence:

    (a) Exposure necessary *for the plot* or action is permitted.

    (b) Exposure *for the sake of exposure* or the "punch" is wrong.

    (c) *Scenes of undressing should* be avoided. When necessary for the plot, they should be kept within the limits of decency. When not necessary for the plot, they are to be avoided, as their effect on the ordinary spectator is harmful.

    (d) *The manner or treatment of exposure* should not be suggestive or indecent.

    (e) The following is important in connection with *dancing costumes*:

1. Dancing costumes cut to permit *grace* or freedom of movement, provided they remain within the limits of decency indicated are permissible.

2. Dancing costumes cut to *permit indecent actions* or movements or to make possible during the dance indecent exposure, are wrong, especially when permitting:

    a) Movements of the breasts;

    b) Movements or sexual suggestions of the intimate parts of the body;

    c) Suggestion of nudity.

Dancing

(1) Dancing in general is recognized as an *art* and a *beautiful* form of expressing human emotion.

(2) Obscene dances are those:

    (a) Which suggest or represent sexual actions, whether performed solo or with two or more;

    (b) Which are designed to excite an audience, to arouse passions, or to cause physical excitement.

HENCE: Dances of the type known as "Kooch," or "CanCan," since they violate decency in these two ways, are wrong. Dances with movements of the breasts, excessive body movement while the feet remain stationary, the so-called "belly dances"—these dances are immoral, obscene, and hence altogether wrong.

Locations

Certain places are so closely and thoroly associated with sexual life or with sexual sin that their use must be carefully limited.

(1) *Brothels and houses of ill-fame* no matter of what country, are *not* proper loca-

tions for drama. They suggest to the average person at once sex sin, or they excite an unwholesome and morbid curiosity in the minds of youth.

IN GENERAL: They are dangerous and bad dramatic locations.

(2) *Bedrooms.* In themselves they are perfectly innocent. Their suggestion may be kept innocent. However, under certain situations they are bad dramatic locations.
    (a) Their use in a comedy or farce (on the principle of the so-called bedroom farce) is wrong, because they suggest sex laxity and obscenity.
    (b) In serious drama, their use should, where sex is suggested, be confined to absolute essentials, in accordance with the principles laid down above.

Religion
(1) No film or episode in a film should be allowed to *throw ridicule on* any religious faith honestly maintained.
(2) *Ministers of religion* in their characters of ministers should not be used in comedy, as villains, or as unpleasant persons.

NOTE: The reason for this is not that there are not such ministers of religion, but because the attitude toward them tends to be an attitude toward religion in general. Religion is lowered in the minds of the audience because it lowers their respect for the ministers.

(3) *Ceremonies* of any definite religion should be supervised by someone thoroly conversant with that religion.

PARTICULAR APPLICATIONS

I. *Crimes against the law*:
These shall never be presented in such a way as to throw sympathy with the crime as against law and justice or to inspire others with a desire for imitation:
    The treatment of crimes against the law must not:
    a. Teach methods of crime.
    b. Inspire potential criminals with a desire for imitation.
    c. Make criminals seem heroic and justified.
1. MURDER
    a. *The technique of murder must* be presented in a way that will *not* inspire imitation.
    b. *Brutal killings* are not to be presented in detail.
    c. *Revenge* in modern times shall not be justified. In lands and ages of less developed civilization and moral principles, revenge may sometimes be presented. This would be the case especially in places where no law exists to cover the crime because of which revenge is committed.
2. METHODS OF CRIME shall not be explicitly presented.
    a. *Theft, robbery, safecracking* and *dynamiting* of trains, mines, buildings, etc., should not be detailed in method.
    b. *Arson* must be subject to the same safeguards.

    c. *The use of firearms* should be restricted to essentials.

    d. *Methods of smuggling* should not be presented.

3. ILLEGAL DRUG TRAFFIC must never be presented.

    Because of its evil consequences, the drug traffic should never be presented in any form. The existence of the trade should not be brought to the attention of audiences.

4. THE USE OF LIQUOR in American life, when not required by the plot or for proper characterization, should not be shown.

    The use of liquor should never be *excessively* presented even in picturing countries where its use is legal. In scenes from American life, the necessities of plot and proper characterization alone justify its use. And in this case, it should be shown with moderation.

II. *Sex*

The sanctity of the institution of marriage and the home shall be upheld. Pictures shall not infer that low forms of sex relationship are the accepted or common thing.

1. ADULTERY, sometimes necessary plot material, must not be explicitly treated, or justified, or presented attractively. Out of regard for the sanctity of marriage and the home, the *triangle* that is, the love of a third party for one already married, needs careful handling. The treatment should not throw sympathy against marriage as an institution.

2. SCENES OF PASSION must be treated with an honest acknowledgment of human nature and its normal reactions. Many scenes cannot be presented without arousing dangerous emotions on the part of the immature, the young or the criminal classes.

    a. They should not be introduced when not essential to the plot.

    b. Excessive and lustful kissing, lustful embraces, suggestive postures and gestures, are not to be shown.

    c. In general, passion should be so treated that these scenes do not stimulate the lower and baser element.

3. SEDUCTION OR RAPE

    a. They should never be more than suggested, and only when essential for the plot, and even then never shown by explicit method.

    b. They are never the proper subject for comedy.

4. SEX PERVERSION or any inference to it is forbidden.

5. WHITE SLAVERY shall not be treated.

6. MISCEGENATION (sex relationship between the white and black races) is forbidden.

7. SEX HYGIENE AND VENEREAL DISEASES are not subjects for motion pictures.

8. SCENES OF ACTUAL CHILDBIRTH, in fact or in silhouette, are never to be presented.

9. CHILDREN'S SEX ORGANS are never to be exposed. . . .

PART III

Casablanca

WARTIME HOLLYWOOD

1

INTRODUCTION

Hollywood's World War II Combat Films

Ninety million Americans went to the movies every week during World War II. The shows began with a newsreel. The audience might see Hitler dancing a jig. Or a battleship engulfed in flames. Or Roosevelt meeting with Winston Churchill, Joseph Stalin, or some other national leader. A cartoon followed, perhaps Bugs Bunny "Nipping the Nips." Then came the main attraction, with Errol Flynn spitting grenade pins out of his mouth or John Wayne using a bulldozer to push an enemy tank off a cliff.

Many of our deepest images of war's glory and ugliness come from World War II combat films. They helped shape our very conceptions of courage, patriotism, and teamwork. Their images remain firmly etched in our imagination: Axis troops torturing and mutilating prisoners; heavily outnumbered American GIs fending off enemy forces; a corporal telling a young marine, "Nothing wrong with praying. There are no atheists in foxholes."

In comparison to Hollywood's efforts to promote public support for the war effort during World War I, the movies of World War II were relatively subtle and restrained. Many films made during the First World War had imagined enemy atrocities—depicting wicked German soldiers ravishing innocent Belgium women. Hollywood's World War II produced a more diverse response, ranging from films like *Mission to Moscow,* presenting our Soviet allies in a positive light, to *Casablanca,* with its portrait of a Rick Blaine's gradual shift from self-centered detachment to active involvement in the Allied cause.

Of the many kinds of films that Hollywood produced during World War II to rally the public behind the war effort, perhaps the most distinctive was the combat film. Such films as *Air Force, Destination Tokyo, Flying Tigers, Guadalcanal Diary, Objective, Burma!, Thirty Seconds Over Tokyo,* and *Wake Island* gave viewers on the home front a vicarious sense of participating in the war. Employing an almost documentary style, these films helped bring the war home. But these war films did much more: they helped educate viewers in the reasons why we fought by depicting "democracy in action." Apart from offering a sense of wartime crisis, these films are allegories of a democratic nation at war.

Typically, these films focus on a small group of men involved in a life-or-death mission: struggling valiantly to hold an island or to attack a target deep behind enemy lines. Thus, the film *Air Force* tells the story of a single B-17 Flying Fortress; *Wake Island,* the tale of the small group of marines and civilians who struggle to hold off a much larger force of attacking Japanese; and *Destination Tokyo,* a single submarine's efforts to enter Tokyo Bay in preparation for Jimmy Doolittle's raid on Tokyo in 1942. By centering on a single isolated group, Hollywood was able to reveal the human meaning of war to individuals with whom the audience could identify.

Invariably, this small group is a microcosm of the American melting pot, made up of Catholics, Protestants, and Jews, men from diverse ethnic groups, and distinct personality types. *Objective, Burma!* has, for example, a Hennessy, a Miggleori, a Neguesco. The group's very composition signifies that this was a democratic war— a peoples' war—drawing upon every segment of society.

Although these groups are usually commanded by a strong leader, success ultimately depends on the men's ability to operate as a team, balancing individual acts of heroism with professionalism and mutual cooperation. In *Thirty Seconds Over Tokyo,* the story of Jimmy Doolittle's bombing raid, each man has a critically important role, whether he is a mechanic, a navigator, a bombardier, a pilot. Individualism and cooperation—both were necessary, according to these films, to preserve American freedoms.

The key crises in these films' plot tend to come not from the threats posed by enemy forces—which the men face with remarkable stoicism—but rather, as Robert B. Ray has noted, from the arrival of an outsider—a coward, a malcontent, a reckless loner—who threatens group cohesion and the men's ability to concentrate on the task at hand. The plot ultimately turns on whether this outsider can be successfully integrated into the group and become a contributing member of the team. In one of the most famous examples, in the film *Wake Island,* a selfish civilian contractor, who initially refuses to obey air raid warnings, ultimately joins a marine commander in a foxhole in a desperate attack to stave off a Japanese attack.

Much more than mere entertainment, the combat films of World War II were veritable civic lessons that taught Americans that winning the war required the country to live up to its democratic values.

2

WARTIME FILMS AS INSTRUMENTS OF PROPAGANDA

What to Show the World:
The Office of War Information and Hollywood, 1942–1945
Clayton R. Koppes and Gregory D. Black

During World War II, the federal government recognized that movies could play an important part in mobilizing American public opinion. In this essay, Clayton R. Koppes and Gregory D. Black examine the government's efforts to shape wartime films while avoiding outright censorship.

The uneasy relationship between propaganda and democracy proved especially troublesome during World War II. Interpreting the war as a worldwide crusade, liberals in the Office of War Information (OWI) won unprecedented control over the content of American motion pictures. An understanding of the interaction between OWI and Hollywood sheds light on both the objectives and methods of the nation's propaganda campaign and the content of wartime entertainment films. This episode, all but ignored by historians, offers insights into America's war ideology and the intersection of politics and mass culture in wartime. Moreover, it raises the question of whether Roosevelt administration's propaganda strategy helped undermine some of its avowed war aims.

OWI, the chief government propaganda agency during World War II, was formed by an executive order on June 13, 1942, that consolidated several prewar information agencies. OWI's domestic branch handled the home front; its overseas branch supervised all United States foreign propaganda activities, except in Latin America, which remained the preserve of the coordinator of inter-American affairs, Nelson Rockefeller. Franklin D. Roosevelt instructed OWI to implement a program through the press, radio, and motion pictures to enhance public understanding of the war; to coordinate the war-information activities of all federal agencies; and to act as the intermediary between federal agencies and the radio and motion picture industries. OWI director Elmer Davis, a liberal radio commentator, insisted that the agency's policy was to tell the truth. But information could not be separated from interpretation, and OWI told the truth by degrees and with particular bias. In all important respects OWI met the criterion of a propaganda agency. It was an organization designed not only to disseminate information and to clarify issues but also to arouse support for particular symbols and ideas. "The easiest way to inject

157

a propaganda idea into most people's minds," said Davis, "is to let it go in through the medium of an entertainment picture when they do not realize that they are being propagandized."

Around Davis clustered a liberal staff that gave OWI one of the highest percentages of interventionist New Dealers of any wartime agency. Two assistant directors, Pulitzer prize writers, Archibald MacLeish and Robert Sherwood, were enthusiastic New Dealers; another assistant director, Milton S. Eisenhower, though fiscally more cautious, was a New Deal veteran. The only assistant director who held the New Deal at some distance was Gardner Cowles, Jr., a moderate Republican publisher who had been recruited to give OWI an air of bipartisanship. Liberals of various hues permeated the second and third levels of the agency and included such figures as historians Arthur M. Schlesinger, Jr., and Henry Pringle, former Henry A. Wallace speech writer Jack Fleming, novelist Leo Rosten, journalists Joseph Barnes and Alan Cranston, financier James Warburg, and "China hand" Owen Lattimore.

The Bureau of Motion Pictures (BMP) in OWI was a New Deal stronghold. Its chief, Lowell Mellett, a former Scripps Howard newspaper editor who had been a Roosevelt aide since 1939, had headed the first prewar information agency, the Office of Government Reports (OGR). "OGRE" and "Mellett's Madhouse" to conservative critics, OGR supervised the government film program. In response to the movie industry's offer of support in December 1941, Roosevelt told Mellett to advise Hollywood how it could further the war effort. Mellett established a liaison office in Hollywood and appointed as its head Nelson Poynter, a Scripps Howard colleague. Poynter did not follow movies, but he shared Mellett's enthusiasms. Assisting Poynter was a staunchly liberal reviewing staff headed by Dorothy Jones, a former research assistant for Harold Lasswell and a pioneer in film content analysis.

The Hollywood office became part of OWI domestic operations in June 1942 and began one of the agency's more important and controversial activities. The motion picture, said Davis, could be "the most powerful instrument of propaganda in the world, whether it tries to be or not." Roosevelt believed movies were among the most effective means of reaching the American public. The motion-picture industry experienced far fewer wartime restrictions on output than most industries. Hollywood turned out nearly 500 pictures annually during the war and drew eighty million paid admissions per week, well above the prewar peak. Hollywood's international influence far exceeded that of American radio and the press; foreign audiences, which also reached eighty million per week, often determined whether a film made a profit. BMP believed that every film enhanced or diminished America's reputation abroad and hence affected the nation's power.

The movie industry shared OWI's perhaps exaggerated idea of its products' power, but how effectively it would cooperate remained unclear. From the mid-1930s to the eve of World War II the industry was isolated from national intellectual, artistic, and political life. When Benito Mussolini's army invaded Ethiopia in 1935, an agitated friend asked a producer, "Have you heard any late news?" The excited mogul replied: "Italy just banned Marie Antoinette!" Conservative businessmen and their bankers ran the studios. Louis B. Mayer of Metro-Goldwyn-Mayer, the single most influential man in Hollywood, decorated his desk with portraits of Herbert Hoover, Francis Cardinal Spellman, and Douglas MacArthur. The artistic, more liberal side of the industry—the directors and particularly the writers—felt squelched. The industry avoided "message films" in favor of romances, musicals, murder mysteries, and westerns—"pure entertainment" in Hollywood parlance. Stereotypes flourished; accuracy was incidental. Since 1934 the Hays Office had censored sex and profanity and taught that sin was always punished: the movies' ideal world was an adolescent perception of middle class America. Although international themes increased between 1939 and 1941, social awareness remained dim. "Most movies are made in the evident assumption that the audience is passive and wants to remain passive," noted the film critic James Agee: "every effort is made to do all the work; the seeing, the explaining, the understanding, even the feeling."

Hollywood preferred to avoid issues: OWI demanded affirmation of New Deal liberalism for America and the world. When Poynter arrived in the movie capital he found the industry doing little to promote the larger issues of the war. In the summer of 1942 Hollywood had under consideration or in production 213 films that dealt with the war in some manner. Forty percent of those focused on the armed forces, usually in combat. Less than 20 percent dealt with the enemy, and most of those portrayed spies and saboteurs. Other categories—the war issues, the United Nations, and the home front—received minimal attention. Even more disturbing to OWI, Hollywood had simply grafted the war to conventional mystery and action plots or appropriated it as a backdrop for frothy musicals and flippant comedies. Interpretation of the war remained at a rudimentary level: the United States was fighting because it had been attacked, and it would win.

To help the industry "raise its sights," Poynter and his staff wrote a "Manual for the Motion-Picture Industry" in June 1942 that they intended as a guide for movie makers in future projects. The manual ranks as probably the most comprehensive statement of OWI's interpretation of the war. OWI believed the war was not merely a struggle for survival but a "people's war" between fascism and democracy, the crusade of Vice President Henry A. Wallace's "Century of the Common Man." The United States fought for a new democratic world based on the Four Freedoms—freedom of speech and religion and freedom from want and fear. The war was a people's struggle, BMP emphasized, "not a national, class or race war." Every person in the world had a concrete stake in the outcome: an Allied victory promised to all a decent standard of living, including a job, good housing, recreation and health, unemployment, and old age insurance—a world New Deal. The average man would also enjoy the right to participate in government, which suggested OWI's anti-imperialist stance. American minorities had not entered utopia, the bureau conceded, but progress was possible only under democracy, and the wartime gains of blacks, women, and other minorities would be preserved. A nation of united average citizens, who believed deeply in the cause of freedom and sacrificed willingly to promote victory, was the hallmark of BMP's democracy.

The enemy was fascism. The enemy was not the Axis leadership nor all of the Axis-led peoples but fascist supporters anywhere, at home as well as abroad. "Any form of racial discrimination or religious intolerance, special privileges of any citizen are manifestations of Fascism, and should be exposed as such," the manual advised. A fascist victory would entail racial discrimination, destruction of political rights, eradication of the rights of labor, and "complete regimentation of the personal life" of the common man. "There can be no peace until militarism and fascism are completely wiped out," BMP warned. When victory came, the United Nations, eschewing national interest and balance of power politics, would build a new world expressive of the collective will. The manual enjoyed wide distribution in Hollywood: some studios reproduced the entire contents for their personnel, and many writers welcomed the bureau's interpretation.

The manual reflected the intellectual ferment of the 1930s. Many intellectuals had put a premium on some large ideal or movement; a predetermined response, not an examination of experience in its many facets, was all important. The quest for commitment converged in the late 1930s with the search for America; the war seemed to offer that unifying commitment and it reduced intellectual content to an uncritical adulation of America and Allies. Thus, BMP reviewers in 1942 objected to the depiction of Spanish Loyalist violence in Paramount's *For Whom the Bell Tolls*, "particularly at this time when we must believe in the rightness of our cause." The bureau continued:

> Now it is necessary that we see the democratic fascist battle as a whole and recognize that what the Loyalists were fighting for is essentially the same thing that we are. To focus too much attention on the chinks in our allies' armor is just what our enemies might wish. Perhaps it is realist; but it is also going to be confusing to American audiences.

To OWI the reality of experience threatened response.

Before the manual could have much effect, however, the bureau faced some immediate problems. Metro-Goldwyn-Mayer wanted to re-release the 1939 film *The Real Glory,* which dealt with the United States army's suppression of the turn-of-the-century Moro rebellion, but now billed as war between American and Japanese troops. Philippine President Manuel Quezon protested vigorously, and Mellett convinced producer Sam Goldwyn to withdraw the picture. The bureau's patriotic appeals also staved off rerelease of two glorifications of British imperialism, RKO's *Gunga Din* and MGM's *Kim*. When Columbia sought BMP advice on its proposed "Trans-Sahara," Mellett cautioned that American policy in Africa was not yet clear, and the studio dropped the project.

But suggestions and patriotic persuasion had limits, OWI discovered in July 1942 when it screened Twentieth Century-Fox's *Little Tokyo, U.S.A.* The film grafted a fifth-column theme to a conventional murder mystery and portrayed the Japanese-Americans—"this Oriental bund"—as bent on sabotage and trying to take over California. The hero-detective bullied his way into a home without a search warrant, and the police beat up Japanese "spies" they had arrested and disarmed. These "Gestapo methods" dismayed the reviewers, who asked, "Did somebody mention that we are presumably fighting for the preservation of the Bill of Rights?" By the end of the film, the Japanese-Americans were marched off to detention camps; and the detective's sweetheart, converted from isolationism, appeasement, and tolerance for Japanese-Americans, implored patriots to save America. "Invitation to the Witch Hunt," cried BMP.

Poynter appealed to the producer, Colonel Jason Joy, to make enough changes to "take most of the curse off." But Joy accused Poynter of going soft on the Japanese and gave OWI an ultimatum: *Little Tokyo, U.S.A.* would go out as it stood or it could be killed if it contradicted government policy. Poynter capitulated.

Twentieth Century-Fox had received army approval for the film and had rushed camera crews to "Little Tokyo" in Los Angeles to shoot footage of the actual evacuation.

OWI now recognized that to inject its propaganda ideas into feature films, the Hollywood bureau had to influence the studios while films were being produced; moreover, since the army was interested mainly in security not ideology, the bureau had to be the sole point of contact between the government and the industry. Accordingly, Poynter asked the studios to submit their scripts to his office for review. While he had no direct power to demand scripts, Poynter achieved some limited cooperation. He had taken an unprecedented step. The Committee on Public Information (Creel Committee) of World War I had allowed films to go abroad only if the committee's shorts went with them, but George Creel apparently had not attempted to influence the content of entertainment films directly.

As studios hesitantly began submitting scripts, OWI encountered problems. Particularly sensitive was the depiction of home-front race relations. MGM's "Man on America's Conscience" refurbished Andrew Johnson as the hero of Reconstruction; vulture-like Thaddeus Stevens fulfilled the need for a heavy. OWI passed the script to Walter White, executive secretary of the National Association for the Advancement of Colored People, who, with the black press, the *Daily Worker,* and a group of Hollywood luminaries, raised a chorus of protest. Mayer dismissed the outcry as the work of what he called "the communist cell" at MGM. When Mellett appealed to national unity, the studio at last agreed to delete the inflammatory references to slavery and to change Stevens into a sincere, if still misguided, figure. The film, released in December 1942 as *Tennessee Johnson,* did not entirely please OWI, but it demonstrated nonetheless the influence the bureau could wield by reading scripts.

Poynter seized that opportunity with one of the few scripts Paramount submitted, *So Proudly We Hail,* a $2 million epic of the siege of Bataan. He suggested that one of the army nurses headed for martyrdom might say: "Why are we dying? Why are we suffering? We thought we . . . could not be affected by all the pestiferous, political spots elsewhere in the world. We have learned a lot about epidemics and disease. . . . When a political plague broke out there [in Manchuria] by invasion, we would not have been willing to do something about it. We had to wait until this plague spread out further and further until it hit Pearl Harbor." He also outlined a Christmas sermon that traced the cause of democracy from Jesus Christ through the "Century of the Common Man." The studio wrote in some of Poynter's ideas, though not in his exact words, and OWI ranked it among the best of the war films.

Combat films reflected OWI's influence probably as much as any type. In the bureau's ideal combat movie an ethnically and geographically diverse group of Americans would articulate what they were fighting for, pay due regard to the role of the Allies, and battle an enemy who was formidable but not a superman. In RKO's *Bombardiers* a pacifist influenced bombardier worried about bombing innocent civilians. At OWI's suggestion the revised script introduced the concept of a just war and explained that the enemy's targets were everywhere while the Americans', although admittedly not surgically precise, were limited to military targets. Occasionally the studios became too bold for the bureau. "War is horrible," BMP acknowledged, but it nevertheless asked the studio to "minimize the more bloody aspects" in Corregidor. OWI liked reality but not too much of it, which reinforced Hollywood's inclination toward avoidance. This, even more than OWI's sermonettes, vitiated the impact of many combat pictures. *So Proudly We Hail* remained chiefly a cheesecake-studded story of love on the troop carriers and in the foxholes. And "the most sincere thing Paramount's young women did," said Agee, "was to alter their make-up to favor exhaustion (and not too much of it) over prettiness (and not too little of that). . . ." Few feature films approached the impact of combat documentaries, such as John Huston's *Battle of San Pietro* and especially the British *Desert Victory*.

By the fall of 1942 films in all categories were showing OWI's imprint, whether through script review or application of the manual for the industry. The motion picture bureau praised two films released in 1942 for filling in gaps on the home front. MGM's *Keeper of the Flame* dramatized native fascism. A wealthy American wanted to institute antilabor, anti-Negro, anti-Semitic, and anti-Catholic campaigns and to exploit the people of the United States for members of his class. Universal Pictures made *Pittsburgh* to show the home front geared for war. A tempestuous love triangle composed of John Wayne, Randolph Scott, and Marlene Dietrich was resolved when labor and management united behind something greater than themselves, the war effort. Some of the speeches had been "culled directly" from the OWI manual, the bureau observed, "and might have been improved by translation into terms more directly and simply relating to the characters . . . in this particular film." But OWI Hollywood reviewers urged Mellett not to miss *Pittsburgh* or *Keeper of the Flame*.

If the studios chose to ignore OWI, however, they could turn out what Poynter termed "ill-conceived atrocities." Preston Sturges' giddy Paramount comedy *Palm Beach Story* carried on the Hollywood tradition of satirizing the idle rich. But the BMP feared that this "libel on America at war," with its blithe disregard of wartime hardships, would offend the American allies. Another Hollywood staple that disturbed OWI was the gangster film, of which Paramount's *Lucky Jordan* was representative. The hero tried to dodge the draft and swindle the army; but when the Nazi agents beat up a gin-swilling, panhandling grandmother who had befriended him, he converted to the American cause, helped round up the Axis spy ring, and meekly returned to the army. His turnabout dramatized in specific, human terms the reality of fascism. Yet his individualistic commitment suggested to OWI reviewers that the United States had nothing ideological against Adolf Hitler; as the hero put it, Americans just did not like the way Nazis pushed people around. OWI wanted the hero to undergo a more profound intellectual awakening and to announce it explicitly. BMP feared, moreover, that gangster films' cynicism and lawlessness, while not particularly harmful at home, tended to support Axis propaganda abroad. The bureau asked the Office of Censorship to bar *Palm Beach Story, Lucky Jordan,* and other films it disliked from export. The censorship code was limited mainly to security information, however, and since these films hardly contained military secrets, the censor granted them export licenses. The censor, ironically, was more lenient than the advocates of free speech.

Hearing increasingly bad reports on the effect of American films abroad, Davis looked for a way to keep Hollywood from putting across "day in and day out, the most outrageous caricature of the American character." Mellett proposed that a representative of OWI's overseas branch join BMP's Hollywood office; this official could more credibly object that certain films harmed foreign relations and could carry OWI's case to the censor. "It would hurt like hell" if a picture were withheld from foreign distribution, Mellett pointed out. Davis agreed and appointed one of Sherwood's chief aides, Ulric Bell, as the overseas arm's representative to Hollywood. A former Washington bureau chief for the *Louisville Courier-Journal,* Bell possessed impeccable New Deal credentials and had been one of the key figures in the prewar interventionist movement. Arriving in Hollywood in November 1942, he shared Poynter's reviewing staff. Bell's influence soon exceeded what Mellett and Poynter had dreamed of or, indeed, thought proper.

OWI then tried to cut in on the chummy relationship between Hollywood and the more glamorous armed forces in early December 1942. The war and navy departments furnished men, equipment, and advice to the compliant industry. The military branches scrutinized scripts and films mainly for security and seldom cooperated with OWI. Davis asked the war and navy departments to channel all of their contacts with the movie industry through OWI's Hollywood office. The military flatly declined.

At the same time Mellett dispatched a hotly controversial letter to the studios. He advised the industry to submit routinely treatments and synopses of projected films, as well as finished scripts, to Poynter's office. Mellett also asked the producers to submit all films to his Hollywood outpost in the long cut, the last stage before final prints were made. While little new material could be added then, OWI could still recommend that harmful scenes be snipped out. Moreover, all contacts between the studios and federal agencies, including the military services, should be channeled through BMP. "Censors Sharpen Axes," bannered *Variety*. Mellett wanted "complete censorship over the policy and content of our pictures," said Bill Goetz, vice president of Twentieth Century, reflecting the attitude of nearly all studio heads. The magnates wanted an in-house censor, such as Mayer or Y. Frank Freeman, the conservative head of Paramount.

Shocked by the industry's furious reaction, Mellett and Davis tried to soothe the executives. Studios remained free to make any picture they wanted without consulting anybody, and, short of violating treason statutes, they could distribute any picture in the United States. The main purpose of the letter, Mellett and Davis insisted, had been to clarify the relationship between OWI and the armed forces for the industry. Privately Mellett told Poynter to pull back. Suggesting dialogue for *So Proudly We Hail* had been a mistake, Mellett said; Poynter agreed. The Hollywood-office pride in *Pittsburgh* and *Keeper of the Flame* could "only result from the appearance of your own stuff in those two pictures," BMP's chief continued. "The propaganda sticks out disturbingly." "Great things" had already been accomplished, but Mellett warned Poynter to modify his operation in whatever ways necessary until the storm subsided.

In fact, BMP reviewers acknowledged decided improvement in the treatment of OWI themes in late 1942 and early 1943. Hollywood tried to redeem its prewar condescension toward foreigners by stressing the Resistance. BMP liked the 1942 Academy Award winner *Casablanca* for its depiction of the valiant underground, the United States as the haven of the oppressed, and the subordination of personal desires to the greater cause of the war—although they would have preferred that the hero had verbalized the reasons for his conversion. As OWI suggested Fritz Lang's story of Lidice, *Hangmen Also Die,* showed a united Czechoslovakia resisting German barbarism. *This Land Is Mine,* the work of Jean Renoir and Dudley Nichols, seemed to OWI a "superb" picture of the French resistance, capped by the "vital" oration of the once cowardly schoolmaster defying occupation authorities. Yet, as critics such as Leo Braudy noted, the teacher, for all his passion, remained "a man orating in a locked room." Even in the talented hands of Renoir and Nichols, the message overwhelmed the creation of believable characters and real situations.

Such problems, among others, counteracted OWI-approved efforts to reverse Hollywood's negative prewar image of the Soviet Union. The idea of filming Ambassador Joseph E. Davies' *Mission to Moscow* apparently did not originate with OWI, but BMP reviewers made some relatively minor suggestions when they read the script, which followed the book all too faithfully. Beneath a giant world map, the prescient Davies chatted amiably with an avuncular Joseph Stalin, illustrating how Americans and Russians were all brothers under the skin in the global struggle. Bell termed the picture "a socko job on the isolationists and appeasers— the boldest thing yet done by Hollywood." Bold perhaps, but its cosmetic treatment of the occupation of Finland, whitewash of the Moscow purge trials, and abnormally simplistic formula evidently convinced few viewers. *Mission to Moscow* was "mishmash," said Manny Farber of *New Republic.* "A great glad two million-dollar bowl of canned borscht. . . ." sighed Agee.

Brotherhood usually meant Americanization. Lillian Hellman's script for Goldwyn's *North Star* had good possibilities, particularly in its semi-documentary approach to ordinary Russians. But director Lewis Milestone turned the Bessarabian cooperative into an American prairie town, and the handsome peasants sang and danced as if they had strayed from a Broadway musical. "War has put Hollywood's traditional conception of the Muscovites through the wringer," observed *Variety,* "and they have come out shaved, washed, sober, good to their families, Rotarians, brother Elks, and 33rd Degree Masons."

The motion-picture bureau also recorded success in reorienting the portrayal of the home front. *One Destiny* told how Pearl Harbor changed the lives and affections of various persons in an Iowa farm community. The bureau persuaded Twentieth Century-Fox to change the original script's emphasis on ill feeling between an enlisted man and a man who stayed on the farm to an understanding of how the war effort needed various talents in many places. King Vidor's *An American Romance* originally recounted the rags-to-riches saga of a Slavic immigrant who became a great automobile manufacturer, sold out, and then returned to manufacture aircraft for the war effort. The individualistic, Henry Ford-inspired hero troubled OWI, but bureau induced changes softened the picture sufficiently for OWI approval. Blacks, who in the first script had been nice but definitely to be kept in their place, were eliminated. The depiction of labor unions as radical violent conspiracies— "a fascist tactic pure and simple," said OWI—was altered. For OWI and outside reviewers alike, the strength of *An American Romance* lay in its documentary-style celebration of United States geography that conveyed "the greatness of America."

Despite BMP's influence on movie content, Bell began campaigning to curb pictures he felt were still undesirable. The Office of Censorship issued a new code on December 11, 1942, that helped Bell immensely. The new index banned from export films that showed rationing or other economic preparations for a long war, scenes of lawlessness in which order was not restored and the offenders punished (this aimed primarily at gangster films), and portrayals of labor or class conflict in the United States since 1917. Bell wanted the code tightened even more. Poynter vehemently disagreed, especially with the restrictions on post-1917 America. If OWI's strategy was to tell the truth, he argued, it should "make a sacrifice hit now and then." Films should admit the United States had problems, as foreigners knew, but should show how democracy solved them. "Fascist methods need not be used to defeat the common enemy of Fascism," he told Bell. Poynter predicted that the new code would make studios shy away from significant war themes.

Bell nevertheless pressed the censor, particularly as a means of trapping "B" movies that were often shot without scripts and of thwarting studios that tried to parlay military or FBI approval into an export license. *They Came to Blow Up America,* which dealt with the seven saboteurs who landed on Long Island in 1942, was a case in point. The Federal Bureau of Investigation saw nothing wrong with the script, but Bell thought the sabotage was exaggerated and FBI was shown as inefficient. "Even the FBI's approval does not make it suitable for overseas presentation," he said. The censor passed it anyway. Bell enlisted Davis' help in February 1943 for a test case, Republic's quickie "B" feature, *London Blackout Murders.* This picture implied the British government would accept a negotiated peace, took some mild swipes at Lend Lease, and showed an overworked doctor accidentally cutting off a woman's head during a blackout instead of amputating her leg. Censorship director Byron Price could not agree that "suppression should go the lengths Bell has suggested." America's allies could "take it," Price said, "and the enemy would find ways to distort developments anyway." RKO hid its low-budget picture *I Walked With a Zombie from Hell* until the censor granted an export license. In similar fashion other films, including the Bob Hope-Dorothy Lamour picaresque *Road to Morocco,* which Eisenhower had said "simply must not reach North Africa," were spirited out of the country.

In mid-summer 1943, however, Bell triumphed. Congress' anti-New Deal axe chopped OWI's domestic branch to a fraction of its former size. Mellett and Poynter left BMP, Paramount executive Stanton Griffis took charge of what little remained of BMP's own productions, and Bell inherited the Hollywood review staff. Freed of Poynter's restraints Bell convinced West Coast censor Watterson Rothacker to adopt his approach. In quick succession Rothacker denied foreign audiences *Fugitive from a Prison Camp, The Great Swindle, The Batman, Hillbilly Blitzkrieg, Sleepy Lagoon,* and *Secret Service in Darkest Africa.* By fall 1943 the censor followed OWI's recommendations in almost all cases. Films such as *Lucky Jordan,* Bell said, almost certainly would be barred from export now. The major remaining difference between OWI and the censor concerned westerns, such as *Buffalo Bill,* which dramatized whites' mistreatment of Indians. The film had a factual basis, Rothacker observed, and since it was set before 1917 he could not touch it. OWI had become the censor's advance guard. Hollywood could still make any film it chose, but as the *Motion Picture Herald* pointed out, no one would produce a picture "known in advance to be doomed to domestic exhibition exclusively."

BMP's increasing influence over a Hollywood willing to cooperate was apparent in movies about the home front, especially juvenile delinquency. *Where Are Your Children?* appalled BMP reviewers with its "sensational portrayal of a young girl's downfall, youthful drunkenness, orgiastic dancing and necking, a seduction resulting in pregnancy, a stolen car, a joy ride, a murder, an attempted suicide and the repentant older generation." While the film promised something for everyone, OWI told Monogram Pictures to tone it down if it wanted foreign release. The studio's cuts did not satisfy OWI. Following BMP recommendations closely, Rothacker ordered 508 feet cut from the film before he approved it for export. RKO's contribution to delinquency was a film whose progression of titles suggested its modification under OWI pressure: *Youth Runs Wild* became *Are These Our Children?* then *The Dangerous Ape,* which was released as *Look to Your Children,* whose conclusion assembled a series of "stock shots showing how the Boy Scouts, 4-H Clubs, city playgrounds and similar institutions are combatting juvenile problems." Like sin punished in the end, democracy solving its problems was ruled suitable for export.

Almost all the major OWI themes converged in the most expensive picture made up to that time, Darryl Zanuck's hagiographic *Wilson,* released in August 1944. BMP persuaded screenwriter Lamar Trotti to balance machine politicians by emphasizing the people's power The studio excised a line to which BMP objected: "With Wilson now firmly in the saddle and riding herd on a docile Congress. . . ." While the original script had dwelled on the failure of the League of Nations, the revised version stressed hope. A few obstructive men could not kill the League, Woodrow Wilson said; "the dream of a world united against the awful wastes of war is too deeply imbedded in the hearts of men everywhere." OWI recommended *Wilson* for special distribution in liberated areas, not merely because its theme was "so vital to the psychological warfare of the United Nations," but because of the picture's "rare entertainment value." Despite good intentions and a $5.2 million budget, however, Hollywood and OWI reduced a character worthy of William Shakespeare to a cardboard prig and his ideas to primer simplicity. As history it was a travesty; as entertainment, a bore; as box office, a bust.

Wilson was one of the last major films to deal significantly with OWI themes. Combat pictures such as *Thirty Seconds Over Tokyo,* held steady; and pictures about the home front, such as *Pride of the Marines,* which fulfilled OWI's desire for films about returning veterans, showed a slight increase. But the other OWI categories showed sharp declines. The 1944 Academy Award winner, Bing Crosby's *Going My Way,* reflected the shift to non-ideological, frequently religious, entertainment pictures in which war and rumors of war seldom intruded. Several reasons contributed to this shift, among them increasing war weariness and a sense that the war would end soon. But another important cause of the decline was what Poynter had predicted: the alliance between OWI and the censor made the studios shy away from significant themes.

By the fall of 1943 Bell had convinced every studio except Paramount to let OWI read all their scripts instead of certain selected ones, and even Paramount agreed to discuss its scripts with OWI in general terms. In 1943 OWI read 466 scripts, in 1944, 744. The 1,210 scripts reviewed in those two years represented almost three fourths of the 1,652 scripts the Hollywood office read between May

1942 and its demise in August 1945. From September 1943 through August 1944 BMP analyzed eighty-four scripts with American lawlessness or corruption as a main theme, forty-seven were corrected to its satisfaction. Racial problems were corrected or eliminated in twenty of twenty four instances, distortions of military or political facts in forty-four of fifty-nine cases. Fifty-nine of the eighty scripts that portrayed Americans oblivious to the war were improved. During this period OWI managed to have 277 of the 390 cases of objectionable material corrected, a success ratio of 71 percent. Yet these statistics understate OWI's influence. Many scripts already showed the influence of the "Manual for the Motion Picture Industry" when they reached OWI readers, making alterations unnecessary. Complete statistics are not available, but from January through August 1943—before Bell's agreement with the censors had much effect—BMP induced the industry to drop twenty nine scheduled productions and particularly noteworthy, to rework parts of five films already approved by the censor. Bell closed the remaining gaps in the line established by Mellett and Poynter. From mid-1943 until the end of the war, OWI exerted an influence over an American mass medium never equaled before or since by a government agency. The content of World War II motion pictures is inexplicable without reference to the bureau.

Hollywood had proved to be remarkably compliant. The industry found that its sincere desire to help the war effort need not interfere with business that was better than usual. Freedom of the screen had never been Hollywood's long suit: an industry that had feared being "enslaved" by Mellett was already in thrall to Will Hays. As the studios learned that OWI wanted "only to be helpful, their attitudes change[d] miraculously," observed Robert Riskin, a Sherwood aide who had been one of Hollywood's highest-paid writers. In "brutal honesty," Riskin continued, the industry's "unprecedented profits" had encouraged cooperation that surprised even the "movie moguls." The studios let BMP know what stories they were considering for production—some of the hottest secrets in movieland—so that the bureau could steer them into less crowded areas and thus smooth out the picture cycle. OWI's international role was especially important. Hollywood films hit the beaches right behind the American troops, provided they had OWI approval; the agency charged admission and held the money in trust for the studios. United States film makers were planning a large scale invasion of the foreign market after the war, and OWI established indispensable beachheads. Indeed, Riskin lamented in mid-1944: "An unsavory opinion seems to prevail within OWI that the Motion Picture Bureau is unduly concerned with considerations for commercial interests."

Although OWI and Hollywood first seemed to conflict, they eventually developed excellent rapport, for their aims and approaches were essentially compatible. The "chief function of mass culture," Robert Warshow has observed, "is to relieve one of the necessity of experiencing one's life directly." Hollywood, conceiving of its audience as passive, emphasized entertainment and avoidance of issues. OWI encouraged Hollywood to treat more social issues and to move beyond national and racial stereotypes. However, since OWI was interested mainly in response, it stressed ideology and affirmation; it raised social issues only to have democracy wash them away. Here the seemingly divergent paths of Hollywood and OWI joined: avoidance and affirmation both led to evasion of experience. Instead of opening realms of understanding and confronting experience, OWI, the propaganda agency, and Hollywood, the dream factory, joined hands to deny realities. However laudable the goals of propaganda, Jaques Ellul has suggested that it creates a person "who is not at ease except when integrated in the mass, who rejects critical judgments, choices, and differentiations because he clings to clear certainties." Through their influence over motion pictures, the OWI's liberals undermined the liberation for which they said they fought.

Casablanca

3

CASABLANCA AS PROPAGANDA

You Must Remember This:
The Case of Hal Wallis' *Casablanca*
Randy Roberts

Casablanca, *the most famous romantic melodrama in Hollywood history, was also a potent piece of political propaganda. In this essay, historian Randy Roberts traces the genesis of the film, and examines the political messages that it conveys.*

Casablanca haunts the imagination. Fifty years after it was made it still seems fresh. Unlike so many other World War II films that had one eye on the box office and the other on the need to boost wartime morale, *Casablanca* has not gone stale with age. If a scene or two seems a touch campy to us today, the film as a whole can still call forth deep emotions. Watching it, we are apt to laugh at the same jokes, be aroused by the same appeals for patriotism, and sense the same demands for sacrifice that moved audiences a half century ago. How can one not smile when Captain Louis Renault (Claude Rains) questions Richard Blaine (Humphrey Bogart) about why he left America and came to Casablanca:

Renault:	I have often speculated on why you don't return to America. Did you abscond with the church funds? Did you run off with a senator's wife? I like to think you killed a man. It's the romantic in me.
Rick:	It was a combination of the three.
Renault:	And what in heaven's name brought you to Casablanca?
Rick:	My health. I came to Casablanca for the waters.
Renault:	Waters? What waters? We're in the desert.
Rick:	I was misinformed.

The producers of *Casablanca,* however, hoped that their film would educate as well as entertain its viewers. From the first day of production, *Casablanca* was consciously designed to aid America's war effort. To be sure, Warner Bros., the studio that made *Casablanca,* planned to make money from the film, but it also wanted the film dramatically to show the battle between good and evil that had so recently engulfed the world. In short, the movie mixed propaganda with entertainment, patriotism with laughter and romance, and became a document for America at a particular time. Today, a viewer can passively watch *Casablanca* and be thoroughly entertained, but the same viewer can also subject the film to a more critical analysis and as a result be entertained and learn something about Hollywood, America, and the world in the early months of World War II.

The history of the making of *Casablanca* is almost as interesting as the film itself. It started when Murray Burnett, a New York high school vocational teacher, took a trip to Europe in 1938. Although Burnett visited Europe a full year before the outbreak of the European phase of World War II, he saw everywhere signs of an impending conflict. The German dictator Adolph Hitler was on the move, and had been for several years. Since 1936, his armies had reoccupied the Rhineland, forced an anschluss (union) with Austria, and overrun Czechoslovakia. Frightened by Hitler's anti-Semitic and fascist doctrines, many German, Austrian, and Czech Jews, as well as liberal and radical Catholics and Protestants, fled their homelands. Burnett witnessed the sad exodus of the refugees. At one point on his trip, Burnett sat in a cafe on France's Mediterranean coast listening to a black American piano player entertain the cafe's patrons and to refugees discuss the best route out of Europe. Many of the refugees, Burnett noted, were en route to Casablanca in French Morocco, from where they hoped to board a plane to Lisbon and then another to the United States.

It was a dramatic story, and Burnett dabbled in drama. In 1940 he teamed with Joan Allison and the two wrote a play about an American who runs a cafe in Casablanca. Entitled *Everyone Comes to Rick's,* the play centers on Richard Blaine, the disillusioned cafe owner, and a woman torn between loyalty for her heroic husband and her love for Rick. Although the play generated modest interest among several New York producers, it had problems that kept it from being produced. Failing in New York, Burnett and Allison turned to Hollywood. On December 8, 1941, the day after the Japanese attack on Pearl Harbor and the United States' entry into World War II, *Everyone Comes to Rick's* reached the desk of Warner Bros. story analyst Steven Karnot. He thought the story had possibilities and sent it to Hal Wallis, Warner Bros.' leading producer. Wallis was intrigued by the story's mixture of romance and sacrifice, cynicism and idealism. In addition, the story was set in Casablanca, an exotic setting that reminded him of *Algiers,* the successful 1938 film which featured Charles Boyer and Hedy Lamarr. Although Wallis recognized that Burnett and Allison's story had serious problems, he was confident that he could correct the troubled areas and turn the story into a profitable movie. Within a few months, Wallis had purchased the rights to *Everyone Comes to Rick's* and renamed the story *Casablanca* to underscore its exotic setting and identify it in the public mind with *Algiers*.

During the next eight months, a team of Hollywood screenwriters labored to solve the play's problems and turn it into a patriotic romance. To be sure, improvements were made: the central characters and issues were more clearly defined and the dialogue was polished until almost every line and scene became memorable. But the story remained essentially unchanged.

Summary of *Casablanca*

Casablanca is set in early December 1941. As the film opens, a narrator informs the viewers that with the start of World War II many Europeans "turned hopefully, or desperately, toward the freedom of the Americas. Lisbon became the great embarkation point. But not everyone could get to Lisbon directly; and so, a tortuous, roundabout refugee trail sprang up: Paris to Marseilles, across the Mediterranean to Oran, then by train, or auto, or foot, across the rim of Africa to Casablanca in French Morocco. Here, the fortunate ones through money, or influence, or luck, might obtain exit visas and scurry to Lisbon, and from Lisbon to the New World. But the others had to wait in Casablanca, and wait, and wait, and wait."

Into this world of waiting and intrigue comes Victor Laszlo (Paul Henreid), the leader of the Czech underground and symbol of the resistance to Nazi domination of Europe, and his beautiful wife Ilsa (Ingrid Bergman). They too are struggling to obtain passage to Lisbon. In fact, they are scheduled to meet the black marketeer Ugarte (Peter Lorre) who had killed two Nazi couriers and secured two letters of transit signed by General de Gaulle. Unfortunately for Laszlo and Ilsa, Ugarte is killed before he can sell the letters of transit to them but not before he gave them to American Rick Blaine (Humphrey Bogart) for safekeeping.

Rick is a man of mystery. Little is known of his past. Apparently he was once something of an idealist and an anti-fascist. In 1935 he had been involved in supplying guns to Ethiopia, and in 1936 he had fought in Spain on the Loyalists' side. But now he is committed only to his own neutrality. As he says several times in the film, "I stick my neck out for nobody." Rick is a man without a country. Some unknown reason prevents him from returning to the United States, and when asked his nationality, he replies, "I'm a drunkard." To which Captain Louis Renault (Claude Rains), the prefect of the police in Casablanca, adds, "That makes Rick a citizen of the world." Rick, then, is a cold cynic, jealous of his own neutrality and interested only in the affairs of his own cafe. The mystery is what changed Rick from an active idealist to a drunken cynic.

Ilsa provides the answer. Before the war she and Rick had been lovers in Paris, but when Rick had been forced to flee that city, Ilsa had not joined him at the railroad station. When Ilsa and Laszlo show up at Rick's Cafe Americain, the pain of those memories sweeps over Rick, making him bitter and angry. He vows never to give the letters of transit to Laszlo and Ilsa. But slowly Rick's anger and cynicism melt away. He and Ilsa meet, she explains why she couldn't leave Paris with him, and the two profess their love for each other. Rick also hatches a plan to get Laszlo out of Casablanca while they remain behind.

All goes according to plan until they reach the airport. This time Rick forces Ilsa to leave without him. Similar to Ilsa's motives in Paris, Rick's is motivated by idealism and sacrifice. Always a citizen of the world, he has joined the world's fight against fascism. "Where I'm going," he tells Ilsa, "you can't follow. What I've got to do, you can't be any part of. Ilsa, I'm no good at being noble, but it doesn't take much to see that the problems of three little people don't amount to a hill of beans in this crazy world." The film ends with Rick and Renault, another cynic who has suddenly been converted to idealism, striking off for a Free French garrison in Brazaville.

A Critical Examination of *Casablanca*

Casablanca is a wonderful film, but it is also propaganda. The film premiered on Thanksgiving Day, November 26, 1942, only nineteen days after the United

States had landed forces at Casablanca in Morocco and, along with Great Britain, in Algeria. It was the first direct American blow against the Nazis and it thrilled Americans. Casablanca dominated the headlines. The day after the nationwide release of *Casablanca*, the city was once again in the news. On January 24, 1943, American President Franklin Roosevelt, British Prime Minister Winston Churchill, and Soviet Premier Joseph Stalin had met secretly earlier in the month to formulate a joint war plan to fight Germany. The American public learned that Roosevelt's headquarters had been code named "Rick's Place." Certainly, the publicity surrounding the Allied invasion of North Africa and the *Casablanca* Conference generated interest in the film *Casablanca*. But the military and political activity did more than simply guarantee financial success; it gave the film an almost mythic quality. Rick became the symbol of America, and his transition from isolationism to involvement underscored America's similar transition.

Critical thinking involves asking questions. If we consider *Casablanca* as a war time document, what can it tell us about Hollywood, America, and the world during the early months of World War II?

1. What biases or underlying assumptions animate the film?

A movie is a collaborative product. Before considering the message of any film, it is important to recognize that a motion picture is the result of the labor of many people, from the producer, director, writers, and actors to the photographers, gaffers, and grips to the editor, music coordinator, and publicists. At no time was this more true than during the Studio Era, a period in the history of Hollywood that started toward the end of World War I, reached its full maturity during the 1930s, and achieved its high point during World War II.

Casablanca was made at Warner Bros., a studio known for a certain style. "Warners' pictures," said one film historian, "were blunt and tough and fast. Their mise-en-scène was flat and cold; their individual cadences were clipped." Warners' leading actors and actresses—James Cagney, Humphrey Bogart, Edward G. Robinson, George Raft, Paul Muni, John Garfield, Bette Davis, Joan Blondell— were also noted for their tough, raw style. They were urban types, often cynical, sometimes mean, and never stupid. They might die at the end of the film, but they were not rubes or suckers. Warners Bros. did not shy away from making pictures with social messages. *Little Caesar, I Am a Fugitive From a Chain Gang, Dr. Ehrlich's Magic Bullet* and *Angels with Dirty Faces* explored some of the social problems that plagued America during the Depression. And Warner Bros. was the first major studio to make films that emphasized the threat of Adolph Hitler. *Confessions of a Nazi Spy* and *Sergeant York* attempted to warn America of the threat posed by Hitler and German militarism. America, the films suggested, did have a stake in European affairs, and wars were often the result of a real clash between good and evil.

The head of production for Warner Bros. was Jack Warner, an outspoken and irreverent mogul who rubbed almost everyone the wrong way. He told vulgar jokes, dressed in flashy clothes, and seemed to delight in embarrassing people. His nephew once called him "an endearing personality—treacherous, hedonistic, and a tyrant." But as a Roosevelt Democrat, Jack Warner was also perhaps the most liberal of the studio heads, and he was certainly patriotic. He was commissioned as a lieutenant colonel during World War II. From the first, Warner and the other people who worked on *Casablanca* intended that the film would have a pro-war message.

The original play was anti-Nazi but not really pro-war. To tighten the political theme of the picture, Hal Wallis, the film's producer, hired screenwriter Howard Koch to work on the script. Just as anyone who wants to understand fully the biases woven into *Casablanca* has to understand Warner Bros. and Jack Warner, that person should also ask questions about the background and political beliefs of Howard Koch. Like many other screenwriters, Koch came to Hollywood after writing for Broadway and radio. He gained national attention as the man who adapted H. G. Wells's *The War of the World* for Orson Welles' famous 1938 broadcast. But his best work was done in message films. Although he never joined the Communist party, Koch was a political radical who was active in several liberal causes. (During the politically repressive period that followed World War II, Koch was blacklisted in Hollywood.)

Koch gave Rick his political conscience. In the play *Everybody Comes to Rick's,* Rick lacks a defined political philosophy. In *Casablanca* his anti-fascist credentials are impeccable. He had fought against fascism in Ethiopia and Spain and, although he professes his neutrality, it is clear that he will eventually resume the struggle against fascism. Most importantly, Rick sees the folly of America's prewar isolationism. In one exchange with his friend and employee Sam, the black piano player, Rick asks, "Sam, if it's December 1941 in Casablanca, what time is it in New York? I bet they're asleep in New York. I'll bet they're asleep all over America." The point of the exchange could not have been lost on American audiences in 1942 and 1943. Trapped in its isolationism, America was asleep in early December 1941. Pearl Harbor provided an unpleasant wake-up call.

Questioning the biases of the people who made *Casablanca* provides several clues of the nature of the film. Even if you had not seen the film, you could predict that it would be patriotic, politically liberal, and interventionist. You could predict that it would follow fairly closely President Roosevelt's own view of the conflict.

2. How was the film received when it premiered in 1942?

One of the pitfalls of historical—or critical—thinking is presentism. We have a tendency to read our present values into past events. What we think of *Casablanca* or internationalism or even World War II is partially conditioned by our feelings toward the international events—from the Cold War to the Vietnam War to the remarkable international changes of the recent years—that have shaped our own lives. To avoid presentism, historians try to reconstruct how an event was received and interpreted at the time that it occurred. To fully understand the impact and importance of *Casablanca* we have to examine what was written and said about the film in late-1942 and early-1943.

Reviews provide an important clue to how audiences reacted to *Casablanca*. The *New York Times'* reviewer commented that the film "makes the spine tingle and the heart take a leap." Other reviewers agreed that *Casablanca* was a remarkably good film: "a crackling, timely melodrama" *(New York Morning Telegraph);* "today's headlines translated into arresting drama" *(New York Mirror);* "smashing . . . moving . . . superior" *(New York Herald Tribune)*. The Hollywood trade journals echoed the dailies' opinions, emphasizing the film's timeliness as well as its suspense, drama, and entertainment qualities. The review in the *Hollywood Reporter* epitomized the favorable reception of *Casablanca*: "Here is a drama that lifts you right out of your seats. . . . The picture has exceptional merits as absorbing entertainment, reflecting the fine craftsmanship of all who had hands in its making."

A technically near perfect film, to be sure, but how was *Casablanca* judged as an example of propaganda? To answer this question we have to leave the published reviews in newspapers and trade journals and look elsewhere. As you might expect, the United States government was quite interested in the content of movies. The average ticket sales in America each week during World War II ranged between eighty and ninety million, or two-thirds of the country's population. Movies were the nation's leading entertainment outlet, and as such, they exerted an awesome power to influence and mold public opinion. In fact, two months before the Japanese attack on Pearl Harbor, Senator Gerald P. Nye, the isolationist from North Dakota, had charged that Hollywood was making films designed to pull the United States into the European war. A special subcommittee of the Committee on Interstate Commerce looked into Nye's charges. Although the subcommittee issued no report when it adjourned on September 26, 1941, it did suggest that Hollywood was at least partially guilty of the charge.

After Pearl Harbor, the Roosevelt administration quickly enlisted Hollywood in America's war effort. The Office of War Information (OWI), which coordinated the country's wartime information and propaganda activities, established the Bureau of Motion Pictures (BMP) to watch over the film industry. Although the BMP did not have direct control over the film industry, it did exert a powerful influence in Hollywood. In its "Government Informational Manual for the Motion Picture Industry," the BMP asked every producer to consider one central question: "Will this picture help win the war?" The BMP reviewed every film made during the war. Its reports evaluate the contribution—or lack of contribution—that each film made to the war effort.

The BMP report on *Casablanca* assesses the movie's effectiveness as propaganda. "From the standpoint of the war information program," noted the BMP report, "*Casablanca* is a very good picture about the enemy, those whose lives the enemy has wrecked and those underground agents who fight him unremittingly on his own ground." More specifically, the report detailed how *Casablanca* aided America's fight against Germany: the film portrays evil, arrogant Nazis who disregard "human life and dignity" and who create "chaos and misery" throughout Europe; the film demonstrates "the spirit of the underground movement" and suggests that not all of the French people are cooperating with the Nazis; the film presents the United States as "the haven of the oppressed and homeless" and as the defender of democracy and freedom; and the film shows the need to sacrifice "personal desire" to defeat fascism. In short, *Casablanca* presents the BMP's slant on the United States, its enemy, and its allies as well as underscoring the reasons America is in the war (see the BMP report, which follows).

The reviews of *Casablanca* and the BMP report on the film illustrate the need for the critical historian to return to the primary sources to understand how an event—in this case a movie—was greeted. Critical thinkers are aware that their reactions to an older film or event from history may be different from how the film or event was originally perceived. The critical thinker, therefore, attempts to overcome this natural presentism by examining primary sources.

3. Could Ilsa have stayed with Rick?

Legends swirl around *Casablanca*. The most famous legends involve the script, which was still not finished when filming started at the end of May, 1942. One Hollywood legend holds that problems with the script forced director Michael Curtiz to shoot the film, from first scene to last, in the same order as the scenes appeared in the finished movie. This legend is utterly fantastic. No movie is filmed in such a fashion. To do so would involve tying up several sound stages—the most precious commodity at any studio—as well as paying all the actors and actresses and renting all the needed props and equipment for the duration of the filming. No studio could afford that wasteful luxury.

Script problems gave rise to an even more intriguing legend, that until nearly the end of the shooting it had yet to be decided whether Ilsa would leave Casablanca with her husband Victor Laszlo or stay behind with her true love Rick. One variation of the legend holds that the screenwriters wrote two different endings; another claims that both endings were actually shot. Indeed, Ingrid Bergman has said that for most of the production period she had no idea who she would end up with in the film's final scene. At one point, she told the writers, "You must tell me because after all there is a little bit of difference in acting toward a man that you love and another man for whom you may just feel pity or affection." "Well," the writers replied, "don't give too much of anything. Play it in between. . . ."

Clearly *Casablanca* suggests that Ilsa loves Rick but only respects Laszlo. Several times in the film Laszlo professes his love for Ilsa, and each time she deflects his comments. In one scene Laszlo says, "I love you very much, Ilsa." She replies, "Your secret will be safe with me." Later in the film, when Laszlo realizes that Ilsa had been in love with Rick in Paris, he tells her again, "I love you very much, my dear." "Yes, yes I know," she responds. In contrast to her guarded responses with her husband, she freely confesses her love for Rick. Toward the end of the film, Ilsa tells Rick, "The day you left Paris, if you knew what I went through! If you knew how much I loved you, how much I still love you! . . . . I know I'll never have the strength to leave you again. . . . I can't fight it anymore. I ran away once. I can't do it again. . . . I wish I didn't love you so much."

But in the end, Ilsa does leave Rick. Could the film have ended otherwise? Could the scriptwriters have discovered a way to have Laszlo leave without his wife? The question may at first seem trivial and not of any critical significance. But it is not, for its answer illuminates an important aspect of Hollywood and the movies during the 1930s and 1940s. The answer also demonstrates that Hollywood legends, like so many other good stories, should not be taken at face value.

To begin with, although the film differed in many details from the play, *Casablanca* was faithful to the intent of *Everybody Comes to Rick's*. In the play, Rick moves from moody isolationist to passionate patriot. For a higher ideal, he convinces Ilsa to leave Casablanca with Laszlo. He sacrifices his personal desire for the good of a more important cause, the battle against fascism. In none of the drafts of *Casablanca* is there any hint that Ilsa would not leave with Laszlo. Legends are nice, but at no time did the screenwriters consider altering the core of the play's ending.

Even if the screenwriters wanted to change the story and invent a pat Hollywood ending, they would have faced powerful opposition. Throughout the 1930s and 1940s, one of the most influential voices in movie industry was that of Joseph Ignatius Breen, head of the Motion Picture Producers and Distributors Association (MPPDA). Breen's job was to make sure that every Hollywood release was good, clean, wholesome, family entertainment. The mop Breen used to keep movies clean was the Motion Picture Production Code which clearly stated the do's and don'ts of movie making. Almost everything about *Casablanca* attracted Breen's attention. Raised in a devout Catholic family and a former student at the Jesuit St. Joseph's College, Breen was not likely to approve any script or give the Code's blessing to any movie where the hero and heroine had an adulterous love affair. It just couldn't happen, not as long as Breen exerted any power in Hollywood.

The Code was quite specific on such matters. Article II of the Code states, "The sanctity of the institution of marriage and the home shall be upheld. Pictures shall not infer that low forms of sex relationship are the accepted or common thing." And in Article II (1), the Code further notes, "Adultery, sometimes necessary plot material, must not be explicitly treated, or justified, or presented attractively." In short, the producers of *Casablanca* had better dance delicately around the relationship between Ilsa and Rick. One slip, one overly suggestive comment or scene, could doom the film.

Breen poured over the script of *Casablanca,* searching for anything that might offend American tastes—or what he judged to be American tastes. (Remember, in *Gone With the Wind,* Breen objected to the use of the word "damn" in the film's last scene.) He demanded that Renault's character—or at least, dialogue—be cleaned up. Captain Renault, the prefect of police who exchanges visas for sexual favors, upset Breen. Early in the script submitted to Breen, an aide informs Renault that several "visa difficulties" have come up. When Renault discovers that two beautiful women are having "problems," he muses, "Which one?" Then with a sigh, he says to the aide, "Ten years ago there would have been no problem. Oh, well, tell the dark one to wait in my private office and we'll go into her visa matter thoroughly . . . And it wouldn't hurt to have the other one leave her address and phone number." Such suggestive comments were far too direct, Breen decided. They had to be toned down considerably. Hal Wallis, the film's producer, argued that Renault's exploitative nature was important to the film because in the end when Renault joins the anti-fascist cause it proved that even the self-admitted "poor corrupt official" was not beyond political redemption. Using the rule of "compensating moral values," Breen allowed Renault to keep a few of his less blatantly suggestive lines.

As for Ilsa and Rick, Breen was less tolerant. Not only could Ilsa not remain with Rick, the film could not suggest, even obliquely, that the two had a sexual reunion in Casablanca. Ilsa and Rick's affair in Paris could be explained: Ilsa thought Laszlo was dead and that she was therefore single. But in Casablanca, Laszlo is quite alive and Ilsa is indisputably married. Breen insisted that when Ilsa and Rick meet alone in Rick's private quarters and she reaffirms her love that the set contain no bed or couch, "or anything whatever suggestive of a sex affair." In addition, Breen insisted that the scene be shot differently. As originally written, there was a time shift in the middle of the scene. "The action ends," commented one authority on the film, "with her declaration of love and resumes as she is telling Rick why she originally left him." After reading the script, Breen commented, "The present material seems to contain a suggestion of a sex affair which would be unacceptable if it came through in the finished picture. We believe this could possibly be corrected by replacing the fade out on page 135, with a dissolve. . . ." This solution, used in the film, prohibited the audience from imagining that Rick and Ilsa resumed their Paris affair. In *Casablanca,* their love was pure and idealized, not physical.

The question of why Ilsa didn't remain with Rick thus leads into a larger discussion of the morals and politics of the motion picture industry. It involves Joseph Breen, MPPDA, and the regulation of movies, and it touches on censorship in American arts and society. Only by critically thinking about what you read and see, will you be able to move beyond passive consumption to active engagement with the subject and the issues it raises.

BUREAU OF MOTION PICTURES REPORT

Feature Review

Casablanca   95 minutes

Warner Bros.   WB   Feb., 1943 (Sched.)

Screenplay by Julius and Philip Epstein and Howard Koch, from play by Murray Burnett and Joan Alison

Hal Wallis   (A)

    Major: III B (United Nations—Conquered Nations) Drama

    Minor: II C 3 (Enemy—Military) Drama

Nelson Poynter	Warner Bros.	October 26, 1942
Dorothy Jones	"	"
Marjorie Thorsch	"	"
Lillian Bergquist	"	"
Lillian Bergquist	"	October 28, 1942

From the standpoint of the war information program, CASABLANCA is a very good picture about the enemy, those whose lives the enemy has wrecked and those underground agents who fight him unremittingly on his own ground. The war content is dramatically effective. Many excellent points are scored:

(1) The film presents an excellent picture of the spirit of the underground movement. Victor Laszlo, a Czech patriot, has fought fascism by printing the truth about it in illegal newspapers in Prague and Paris. He has suffered in a concentration camp, from which he finally escaped. Unintimidated by his experiences he plans to continue his work. In *Casablanca,* a Norwegian anti-Nazi says: "The underground is well organized here as everywhere." We learn that people of all nationalities meet secretly everywhere, despite the danger, planning the destruction of the oppressor. Their courage, determination and self-sacrifice should make Americans proud of these underground allies.

(2) Some of the chaos and misery which fascism and the war has brought are graphically illustrated. Refugees of all nationalities are crowded into Casablanca. A few have money, but it goes quickly. They attempt to sell their jewels, but the market

is flooded. Some refugees are reduced to stealing; women sell themselves; others bribe corrupt officials who in turn double-cross them. There are pickpockets, murderers, Black Markets in visas. Personal honor and dignity have departed; degradation and treachery have taken their place. This is part of what fascism has brought in its wake. Another facet of Nazi aggression is shown in scenes which depict the Nazi march into Paris. A sense of the honor and confusion of the French population is very well projected.

(3) It is shown that personal desire must be subordinated to the task of defeating fascism. To Laszlo and the other underground workers, the defeat of fascism is of paramount importance. The heroine and the man she loves sacrifice their personal happiness in order that each may carry on the fight in the most effective manner. They realize that they cannot steal happiness with the rest of the world enslaved.

(4) It is brought out that many French are by no means cooperating wholeheartedly with the Nazis. Renault, the French Prefect of Police, tells Rick that he "goes the way the wind blows." He is cynical and not above taking bribes. Yet, when Rick, the American hero murders Strasser, Renault not only allows him to escape, but goes with him to the nearest Free French garrison. Then again, the French people in Rick's cafe, led by Laszlo, the Czech patriot, courageously sing the Marseillaise to drown out the song of their conquerors. Here is illustrated the love and pride of the French in their country, conquered though it is. We feel that it will rise again.

(5) America is shown as the haven of the oppressed and homeless. Refugees want to come to the United States because here they are assured of freedom, democratic privileges and immunity from fear. The love and esteem with which this country is regarded by oppressed peoples should make audiences aware of their responsibilities as Americans to uphold this reputation and fight fascism with all that is in them.

(6) Some of the scope of our present conflict is brought out. It is established that Rick, the American cafe owner, fought for the loyalists in the Spanish Civil War, and for democracy as far back as 1935 and 1936, when he smuggled guns for the Ethiopians. Points like these aid audiences in understanding that our war did not commence with Pearl Harbor, but that the roots of aggression reach far back.

(7) The film presents a good portrayal of the typical Nazi. In the arrogant Major Strasser, with his contempt for anything not German, his disregard for human life and dignity, his determination that all peoples shall bow to the Third Reich, we get a picture of the Nazi outlook. These are the kind of men who would enslave the world.

Mildred Pierce

5

HOW WORLD WAR II AFFECTED WOMEN

Mildred Pierce and Women in Film
June Sochen

World War II brought dramatic changes to the lives of American women. The removal of 16 million men to the armed forces led to a vast increase in the number of working women. Easily the most visible change involved the sudden appearance of large numbers of women in uniform. By 1945, over 140,000 women had joined the Women's Army Corps (WAC); 60,000 the Army Nurses Corps; and 100,000 the Women Accepted for Voluntary Emergency Service (WAVES). But in much larger numbers women also substituted for men on the home front. For the first time in history, married working women outnumbered single working women. The sharp increase in working women gave rise to widespread public anxiety. Many feared that the employment of wives would undermine husbands' self-images and lead to child neglect. Public disapproval of women's ability to cope with the family in the absence of a father focused not only on maternal neglect, but on its mirror image, maternal oversolicitousness. A military psychiatric consultant accused "America's traditional sweet, doting, self-sacrificing mom" of having "failed in the elementary mother function of weaning offspring emotionally as well as physically." A number of films produced during the mid-1940s—most notably Mildred Pierce—*gave expression to the public's deep anxieties over mothering and women's changing roles.*

During the 1930s, the opening of any Joan Crawford movie thrilled thousands of fans and assured MGM box office success. But Crawford, frustrated by the predictability of roles offered to her, left Louis B. Mayer's studio early in the forties. For over two years she rejected all screen roles shown to her and then in 1944 read and accepted a part in the script that marked her return to the screen and gave Crawford her only Academy Award. The screenplay was *Mildred Pierce,* a dark, suspenseful movie based upon a James Cain novel. Crawford fans, ever loyal, flocked to New York's Strand Theater on September 28, 1945, when *Mildred Pierce* opened, and continued to attend in record numbers. Warner Brothers, the producers of the film, reported a gross of five million dollars.

Mildred Pierce was both a familiar and novel character for Crawford to play. A drab California divorcee with two daughters to support, Mildred seemed similar to Sadie McKee and other Crawford heroines of the thirties. As Mildred, Crawford began the movie in Sears, Roebuck specials and then succeeded to the fashionable Adrian outfits that had become her trademark. She was after all no stranger to roles that required her to begin a movie as poor but beautiful. Both she and her fans knew that the poverty would be overcome precisely because of her beauty. *Mildred Pierce,* however, departed from the formula in that the poor but lovely woman not only reached the peaks of success but also experienced the depths of failure; in the end, nothing remained but a flicker of hope. It is the tragedies that befell Mildred and the bleak ending that distinguished *Mildred Pierce* from its innumerable predecessors.

It took six screenwriters to make the Cain novel an acceptable screenplay. Though only Ronald MacDougall received screen credit, the other contributors to the script included novelist William Faulkner and veteran screen writer Catherine Turney. The cast of characters assembled for this production by Jerry Wald for Warner Brothers was impressive: Joan Crawford as Mildred, Zachary Scott as Monte Berragon, III, Jack Carson as Wally Fay, Eve Arden as Ida, Ann Blyth as Veda Pierce, Butterfly McQueen as Letty, and Bruce Bennett as Bert Pierce.

Mildred Pierce is a rich, multi-layered movie. On one level, it is an effective murder mystery. On another, it gives us a stunning portrayal of a woman trying to live by the cultural rules under difficult circumstances. On still another, it is an indictment of the American family and its values. The movie skillfully interweaves all three themes with Mildred at its center. Her life and thought provide the substance for every essential action in the movie. Director Michael Curtiz, a master of Americana, used the flashback technique to heighten tension and to unravel the parts of the mystery. As critic John Davis has said, the flashback was the favorite fatalistic method of the forties film. The murder, shown first, was the inevitable conclusion to everything that had preceded it.

The movie begins with gunshots and a man falling to the floor muttering "Mildred." The next scene shows the back of a well-dressed woman walking along the wharf. It is nighttime and the streets are rain-drenched. The woman stops by the railing of the wharf and looks pensively into the water. She leans over the railing only to be ordered to stop by a policeman. She walks away, stops outside a nightclub, and goes inside when the owner, Wally Fay (Jack Carson) invites her in. The woman, of course, is Mildred Pierce. Wally is surprised to see her slumming; she invites him to have a drink with her at her beachhouse. Delighted by Mildred's invitation (since Wally has been pursuing her for years), he goes with her to the house. As soon as they enter, the viewer recognizes the murder scene. A light from outside illuminates the body of the dead man, though neither Wally nor Mildred see it.

While Mildred excuses herself to get into something more comfortable, arrogant Wally regales her with small talk. Moments go by and Wally discovers he is alone in the house. He runs furtively from room to room looking for Mildred; when he discovers the dead body, his running becomes more intense. The doors are all locked. Wally smashes an upstairs window and jumps out, only to be discovered by two patrolling policemen and taken in for questioning. Mildred is also brought to headquarters and told that her husband, Monte Berragon, III (Zachary Scott), was found dead at the beachhouse. The police think her first husband, Bert Pierce

(Bruce Bennett) was the murderer. Seated in the sergeant's office, Mildred tells her life story to the officer:

> We lived on Corvalis Street where all the houses looked alike. I was always in the kitchen. I felt as though I'd been born in a kitchen and lived there all my life, except for the few hours it took to get married. I married Bert when I was seventeen. I never knew any other kind of life . . . just cooking, washing, and having children.

When Bert loses his job, their mutual frustration leads to frequent quarreling. Their two daughters, Kay and Veda, often become the subject of their arguments. Mildred insists during one argument that the children come first in her life and "I will do their crying for them too." Bert counters that "you are trying to buy love from those kids." Mildred retorts that they were going to have a better life than she had. Bert ends the argument by saying he is going to visit his friend Mrs. Biederhof. Mildred warns him that if he goes to his girlfriend's house, he should never come back. Bert agrees.

Mildred's daughters, the subject of her continuous bickering with Bert, offer a study in contrasts. Kay, the younger girl, is a sweet tomboy; Veda (played by Ann Blyth) is a selfish, deceitful, snobbish teenager. She is ashamed of their modest home, contemptuous of her mother's housewife image, and disgusted with her ineffectual father. Instead of disciplining her, Mildred spoils her. She scrimps and saves to buy Veda a new dress that Veda tells Kay is common. When her mother tries to kiss her good night the first night after Bert leaves, Veda resists saying, "Let's not be sticky about it."

Mildred accepts the crumbs of love given her by Veda, neglects the sweet-natured Kay, and grimly goes looking for a job. She quickly discovers how hard it is to get a job in Depression America when one is female and unskilled. Finally, she finds work as a waitress in a restaurant. Ida, the hostess (played by Eve Arden), teaches her the ropes, and within a few months Mildred is an excellent waitress. At night, she bakes cakes for neighbors' special occasions and is able to employ a maid, Letty (played by Butterfly McQueen) to help her with the baking and housework. Mildred does not tell her children where she works, fearing Veda's contempt for the proletariat. One day Mildred comes home to discover Letty wearing one of her waitress uniforms. When questioned, Letty says Miss Veda asked her to wear it.

Mildred confronts Veda. "Where did you find the uniform?" Veda cooly says she assumed it was bought for Letty. Mildred gets angry at Veda and slaps her face, immediately regretting the action. "I'd rather have cut off my hand," she says. Mildred quickly explains that she is working as a waitress to learn the restaurant business. Ambitious Veda likes this idea, declaring that then they will become rich and she can have the beautiful clothes and beautiful surroundings she so wants. Mildred goes to see Wally Fay, Bert's former real estate partner, and seeks his help in purchasing a piece of property—an old mansion, now in disrepair and owned by the Berragon family.

The next series of sequences seems inevitable. Mildred meets Berragon, a playboy who makes an art out of doing nothing but whose family money is slowly dwindling away. He sells Mildred the house, begins a love affair with her, and stays around to watch Mildred become a female Horatio Alger. Meanwhile, Bert takes his daughters off to Arrowhead one weekend and returns with sweet Kay suffering from pneumonia. Mildred cannot be reached because she is having a tryst with Monte at his Malibu beachhouse. She returns in time to see her daughter whisper "Mommy" and then expire.

After Kay's death, Mildred concentrates on her restaurant and in a short time turns it into a successful enterprise; within a year, there are other "Mildred's" around town. As she becomes a wealthy businesswoman, her daughter Veda becomes an insatiable devourer of more and more things. Monte escorts Veda around town and educates her into the dissipated life, a life financed by Mildred, as Monte is without funds. Mildred disapproves of Monte's influence upon her daughter and finally writes him a last check, telling him to stop seeing Veda. He complies and Veda proceeds to marry a rich young man whom she then promptly sues for divorce. She insists upon a large settlement claiming that she is pregnant. Mildred is stunned by this turn of events; upon confronting Veda, she realizes that Veda faked the pregnancy claim in order to get the money. Mother and daughter exchange bitter words, and Mildred tears up Veda's check only to have her daughter slap her in the face. "Get out before I kill you," are Mildred's parting words to her daughter.

In a state of desperation, Mildred leaves Ida in charge of her business and travels around the country. She returns many months later, weary, shaky, and grimly aware of the fact that "Veda is a part of me. She is still my daughter and I cannot forget that." Ever the cynical friend, Ida reminds Mildred that alligators had the right idea; they ate their young. Mildred laughs bitterly and discovers that her daughter is singing in Wally Fay's dive on the wharf. In order to win Veda back, Mildred decides to achieve the status desired by Veda by purchasing Berragon's in-town mansion and marrying him in order to acquire his prestigious name. A one-third ownership in her business persuades Monte. "Sold one Berragon," Mildred notes as Monte tries to kiss her to consummate the deal. Whatever feeling Mildred had for Monte has disappeared.

Veda returns and the social whirl and spending sprees resume. A business meeting on the evening of Veda's birthday party reveals the fact that Monte has sold his interest in Mildred's and has gotten Wally, who also has a one-third interest, to sell too. Mildred is wiped out. The lavish expenses of Veda and Monte have broken her. That very night Veda and Monte go to the beachhouse; they quarrel when Veda insists that Monte divorce her mother and marry her; Monte laughs and an enraged, jealous Veda shoots him. It is this scene that Mildred walks in upon; she discovers her second husband on the floor and her daughter pleading with her to save her once again. "It's your fault I am the way I am," Veda shouts at Mildred. Mildred agrees to help Veda, walks to the wharf, contemplates suicide, and after being shooed away by the policeman, sees Wally Fay and invites him to the beachhouse.

The sergeant figures it all out as well and the movie ends with Veda being taken away to jail while Mildred walks out of the police headquarters as dawn breaks. Bert Pierce, her first husband, waits on the steps of the building for her, and together they walk away into the sunrise. So ends *Mildred Pierce*.

While women viewers wiped the tears away from their eyes and thought about ungrateful daughters and self-sacrificing mothers, a few discerning critics noted the movie's absolutely bleak portrait of American family life and its corrupting materialistic values. James Agee commented that *Mildred Pierce* was a "nasty, gratifying version of the James Cain novel about suburban grass, widowhood, and the power of the native passion for money and all that money can buy." But most critics agreed with Thomas Pryor of the *New York Times* who found it unrealistic. Pryor wondered, how ". . . a level headed person like Mildred Pierce, who builds a fabulously successful chain of restaurants on practically nothing, could be so completely dominated by a selfish and grasping daughter, who spells trouble in capital letters." Some critics like John McManus of *PM* complained that the movie would be bad propaganda for the United States abroad. None bothered to probe the connection between *Mildred Pierce* and the rich quantity of women's movies that had preceded it from 1930 to 1945. *Mildred Pierce* was the culmination of a long series of screen heroines, a subject to which we will return.

More energetic and entrepreneurial than most, Mildred exhibited the all-American (usually male) traits of hard work, self-reliance, and perseverance. Her efforts paid off in the best Horatio Alger tradition. But, and this is a major but, she was also a mother and this role required primary attention. While businessmen may or may not be fathers, businesswomen-mothers must attend to their mothering first. Thus, Mildred Pierce was blamed implicitly (and blamed herself) for her children's behavior. Though Bert was caring for Kay when she took sick, the implication was that Mildred should have been on call, always ready to care for her children. Making love to Monte, rather than sitting home awaiting the return of her children, was an abdication of maternal responsibility. Similarly, Mildred's indulgence of Veda and her unwillingness to discipline her resulted in Veda's behavior. When Mildred slapped Veda's face for her insolence, she regretted her action. After Veda shot Monte, she declared to Mildred: "It's your fault I am the way I am."

What worse series of events could occur to a mother than to have one daughter die while the other one murdered her second husband? Mildred Pierce, a successful businesswoman, failed miserably in her maternal role. Who was to blame? Individualistic American values, reflected in this movie suggested that the blame belonged upon Mildred's shoulders. Because justice prevailed in Hollywood movies, Mildred lost her business as well as her children. Defeat became her fate: ambitious women beware.

Ineffectual Bert (the inevitable husband to a strong woman?) cannot be blamed for the course of actions. After all, he warned Mildred when they divorced that she was spoiling Veda. Strength is an unwomanly trait, always to be punished. How was Mildred to support herself and her daughters after her unemployed husband left? *Mildred Pierce* raised many more questions than it answered, one of its most intriguing features. It was a tragedy, one experienced by women who, understandably, invested a great deal in their children. Joan Crawford received the empathy of many fans who knew that a woman's lot has always been a hard one and that patience and endurance have been her only course of action.

Mildred's strength was both a blessing and a curse. Surely women viewers admired her ability to care for her daughters, earn a living, and survive psychically intact. But her strength was impotent in the face of a rebellious daughter. While Veda was unimpressed and unaffected by her mother's strength, Bert appeared to be intimidated by the steely Mildred, and corrupt Monte paraded his ineffectuality in public. Was Mildred responsible for the men's inability to cope with life? The

implicit message of *Mildred Pierce* was yes: strong women threatened the development of whole men. There has been a long history of women's films that preach
female submissiveness and warn strong, independent women that they will be
without a man in the last reel unless they learn to submit.

Mildred Pierce acted as a piece of social control for women. Women of America
know your place. Erase any ideas you may have to divorce your husband and/or
enter the big, bad business world. (Mildred, remember, was betrayed by men and
lost her restaurants as a result.) Women, remain within the domestic sphere, an
arena you naturally know and belong to. Attend to the raising of your children,
every hour of the day and night; only then can you be assured of their continued
obedience and loyalty. Don't spoil your children. Be totally devoted but not
possessive.

American women were not revolted by *Mildred Pierce;* neither did they revolt.
They did not question a culture that restricted their adult life to mothering, though
circumstance and inclination may have led them to other pursuits. Neither did they
question the overwhelming burden of motherhood. The message for American
women was clear: stay in the preordained domain.

6

PRIMARY SOURCE

U.S. Senate Subcommittee Hearings on
Motion Picture and Radio Propaganda, 1941

In 1941, a U.S. Senate subcommittee held hearings to investigate charges that the motion-picture industry was manipulating movies in an effort to drag America into war in Europe. The investigation came to an abrupt end with the Japanese attack on Pearl Harbor.

[Senator Gerald Nye]

At the outset, I should like to point out that no contention can validly be raised that any investigation of propaganda in the movies, amounts to censorship of freedom of speech or freedom of the press. The fact is, and the law is, that the movies are not part of the press of this country, and are not protected by the first amendment to our Constitution. . . .

I entertain no desire for moving-picture censorship. . . . I do hope, however, that the industry will largely recognize the obligation it owes our country and its people. . . .

Mr. Chairman, I am sure that you and members of your committee are quite aware of the determined effort that has been put forth to convey to the public that the investigation asked is the result of a desire to serve the un-American, narrow cause of anti-Semitism. . . .

I bitterly resist, Mr. Chairman, this effort to misrepresent our purpose and to prejudice the public mind and your mind by dragging this racial issue to the front. I will not consent to its being used to cover the tracks of those who have been pushing our country on the way to war with their propaganda intended to inflame the American mind with hatred for one foreign cause and magnified respect and glorification for another foreign cause, until we shall come to feel that wars elsewhere in the world are really after all our wars. . . .

Those primarily responsible for the propaganda pictures are born abroad. They came to our land and took citizenship here entertaining violent animosities toward certain causes abroad. Quite natural is their feeling and desire to aid those who are at war against the causes which so naturally antagonize them. If they lose sight of what some Americans might call the first interests of America in times like these, I can excuse them. But their prejudices by no means necessitate our closing our eyes to these interests and refraining from any undertaking to correct their error. . . .

If the anti-Semitic issue is now raised for the moment, it is raised by those of the Jewish faith . . . not by me, not by this committee. . . .

[Senator D. Worth Clark]

[The motion picture studios] declare that this [investigation] is an attempt to restrain the right of the motion-picture screen to present the problems of contemporary life without restraint from the Government. . . .

I am willing and eager to meet these gentlemen on that ground. There are a great many naive souls who think that speech is free so long as political authority, particularly the Government, does not shackle it. They overlook the fact that there can be such a thing, particularly in our day, as the denial of speech when one individual or small collection of individuals can band together and get control of the instruments of speech and deny them to everybody but themselves. . . .

Today a hitherto unknown politician or newspaper columnist can go on the radio and in one night talk to four, five, or ten million people. . . .

It comes down to this: That the man who owns that machine now exercises over the freedom of discussion a power which no government could ever exercise. To interfere with a man's speech the Government has to pass oppressive laws, organize a ruthless constabulary, must hound men and prosecute them and put them in jail and incur the difficulties of opposition and the freedom of revolution. But the man who owns the radio machine can cut off from discussion those who disagree with him by the simple expedient of saying "No." And who is this man? He is not a public official; he is not elected to office; he is not an authorized public censor; he is not chosen by the people. He is just a businessman who by virtue of his acquisitive talents has gotten possession of this little microphone.

Now, the same thing is true of the moving-picture machine, save that the moving-picture machine is even more powerful than the microphone. Any man or any group of men who can get control of the screen can reach every week in this country an audience of 80,000,000 people. If there is a great debate before the Nation involving its economic life or even its liberties, no man can get a syllable in the sound pictures save by the grace of the men who control the sound pictures. And I here formally and deliberately charge that a handful of men have gotten possession of both the radio microphone and the moving-picture screen, beside which all other forms of discussion are antique and feeble, and that men and women in America discussing the great problems of America can use these machines or not only by the grace of this small oligarchy. . . .

There are 17,000 moving-picture theaters in the United States. They do not belong to a handful of men, of course, but the pictures that appear on the screens of those theaters are produced by a handful of men and that handful of men can open or close those 17,000 theaters to ideas at their sweet will. They hold the power of life and death over those motion pictures houses because by their block-booking system, blind-selling system, and other devices they can close almost any house that they please on any day and at any time.

At the present time they have opened those 17,000 theaters to the idea of war, to the glorification of war, to the glorification of England's imperialism, to the hatred of the people of Germany and now of France, to the hatred of those in America who disagree with them. Does anyone see a pictorial representation of life in Russia under "Bloody Joe" Stalin? They do not. In other words, they are turning these 17,000 theaters into 17,000 daily and nightly mass meetings for war. . . .

Dozens of pictures, great features costing—some of them hundreds of thousands of dollars, some of them millions of dollars—are used to infect the minds of their audiences with hatred, to inflame them, to arouse their emotions, and make them clamor for war. And not one word on the side of the argument against war is heard. . . . Unless they are restrained, unless the people of this country are warned about them, they will plunge the country into war. . . .

[Harry M. Warner, President of Warner Bros. Pictures, Inc.]
The charges against my company and myself are untrue. . . .

I am opposed to nazi-ism. I abhor and detest every principle and practice of the Nazi movement. To me, nazi-ism typifies the very opposite of the kind of life every decent man, woman, and child wants to live. I believe nazi-ism is a world revolution whose ultimate objective is to destroy our democracy, wipe out all religion, and enslave our people—just as Germany has destroyed and enslaved Poland, Belgium, Holland, France, and all the other countries. I am ready to give myself and all my personal resources to aid in the defeat of the Nazi menace to the American people. . . .

Shortly after Hitler came to power in Germany I became convinced that Hitlerism was an evil force designed to destroy free people, whether they were Catholics, Protestants, or Jews. I claim no credit as a prophet. Many appraised the Nazis in their true role, from the very day of Hitler's rise to power.

I have always been in accord with President Roosevelt's foreign policy. In September 1939, when the Second World War began, I believed, and I believe today, that the world struggle for freedom was in its final stage. I said publicly then, and I say today, that the freedom which this country fought England to obtain, we may have to fight with England to retain.

I am unequivocally in favor of giving England and her allies all supplies which our country can spare. I also support the President's doctrine of freedom of the seas, as recently explained to the public by him.

Frankly, I am not certain whether or not this country should enter the war in its own defense at the present time. The President knows the world situation and our country's problems better than any other man. I would follow his recommendation concerning a declaration of war.

If Hitler should be the victor abroad, the United States would be faced with a Nazi-dominated world. I believe—and I am sure that the subcommittee shares my feeling—that this would be a catastrophe for our country. I want to avoid such a catastrophe, as I know you do.

I have given my views to you frankly and honestly. They reduce themselves to my previous statement: I am opposed to nazi-ism. I abhor and detest every principle and practice of the Nazi movement. I am not alone in feeling this. I am sure that the overwhelming majority of our people and our Congress share the same views.

While I am opposed to nazi-ism, I deny that the pictures produced by my company are "propaganda," as has been alleged. Senator Nye has said that our picture *Sergeant York* is designed to create war hysteria. Senator Clark has added *Confessions of a Nazi Spy* to the isolationist blacklist. John T. Flynn, in turn, has added *Underground*. These witnesses have not seen these pictures, so I cannot imagine how they can judge them. On the other hand, millions of average citizens have paid to see these pictures. They have enjoyed wide popularity and have been profitable to our company. In short, these pictures have been judged by the public and the judgment has been favorable.

Sergeant York is a factual portrait of the life of one of the great heroes of the last war. If that is propaganda, we plead guilty. *Confessions of a Nazi Spy* is a factual portrayal of a Nazi spy ring that actually operated in New York City. If that is propaganda, we plead guilty.

So it is with each of our pictures dealing with the world situation or with the national defense. These pictures are prepared on the basis of factual happenings and they were not twisted to serve any ulterior purpose.

In truth, the only sin of which Warner Bros. is guilty is that of accurately recording on the screen the world as it is or as it has been. Unfortunately, we cannot change the facts in the world today. . . .

I have no apology to make to the committee for the fact that for many years Warner Bros. has been attempting to record history in the making. We discovered early in our career that our patrons wanted to see accurate stories of the world in which they lived. I know that I have shown to the satisfaction of the impartial observer that War Bros., long before there was a Nazi Germany, had been making pictures on topical subjects. It was only natural, therefore, with the new political movement, however horrible it may be, that we should make some pictures concerning the Nazis. It was equally logical that we should produce motion pictures concerning national defense. . . .

If Warner Bros. had produced no pictures concerning the Nazi movement, our public would have had good reason to criticize. We would have been living in a dream world. Today 70 percent of the nonfiction books published deal with the Nazi menace. Today 10 percent of the fiction novels are anti-Nazi in theme. Today 10 percent of all material submitted to us for consideration is anti-Nazi in character. Today the newspapers and radio devote a good portion of their facilities to describing nazi-ism. Today there is a war involving all hemispheres except our own and touching the lives of all of us. . . .

PART IV

James Dean in *Rebel Without a Cause*

POSTWAR HOLLYWOOD

1

INTRODUCTION

Double Indemnity and Film Noir

During the early 1940s, a new film genre appeared that would exert enormous influence on the shape of post-war American movies. Called "film noir" by French critics, this genre depicted a disturbing world—a world of treachery, entrapment, mistaken identity, psychopathology, greed, lust, betrayal, and finally murder. Dimly lit, set in nightmarish locations, these films featured a cast of amoral or corrupt characters: drifters, patsies, cold-blooded femme fatales, and sinister widows. Film noir drew upon the characters and plots of the gangster movies and hard-boiled detective fiction of the 1930s. But in style and tone, these films were unlike anything Hollywood had ever produced before. They were much more cynical and pessimistic than classical Hollywood films, their characters were more corrupt, their tone much more fatalistic. It was no wonder that French critics used the term "noir" to describe their tone.

Nor was it an accident that many of these films were directed by European emigres who had fled Hitler's Germany, among them Fritz Lang, Otto Preminger, and Billy Wilder. Well versed in the traditions of German expressionist filmmaking, these directors brought a new visual style to the American screen, characterized by looming shadows, oblique camera angles, and stark contrasts of darkness and light. This style also reflected wartime necessity, which limited availability of bright set lighting. Along with their keen visual sense, these directors brought a host of stylistic innovations such as voice-over narration, interior monologues, and flashbacks. The profound sense of alienation, pessimism, and paranoia in their films clearly gave tangible expression to their awareness of the horrors of European fascism.

The appeal of film noir to the mass audience indicates that these directors were also able to tap into broader cultural concerns. Film noir was much more realistic than the films of the Depression era. The public had grown increasingly weary of movies that sought to raise morale and reinforce traditional values. It craved a more gritty view of American society. Film noir offered such realism. Set in everyday locations, it offered an honest, if harsh, view of American life, a view that captured the seedy, sleazy underside of life. Film noir also gave symbolic expression to a deep current of anxiety and apprehensions that pervaded American society during World War II and the early postwar era. Outwardly optimistic, American society was in fact beset by profound fears. Film noir belonged to a time of public confusion in an unsettled world: the disorientation of returning G.I.s, insecurity about the future, radical redefinitions in women's roles, cold war paranoia, and fears of nuclear annihilation.

Billy Wilder's 1944 classic *Double Indemnity* epitomizes what is meant by film noir. The film tells the story of Phyllis Dietrichson (Barbara Stanwyck), a scheming, seductive platinum blond, who lures a weak willed insurance salesman, Walter Neff (Fred MacMurray), into a scheme to murder her husband and collect on the double indemnity clause in his life insurance policy. Based on James M. Cain's tawdry novella, the story is set along the southern California coast, a restless, rootless, unstable society. It was, in film critic Richard Schickel's words, a land of "gas stations and roadside restaurants . . . small hopes and pinched dreams, which modest as they were, often enough ended in foreclosure." This was a world of strangers, where old customs had been disrupted and traditional values subverted, and egos set free from traditional moorings. Despite the bright California sun, it is a place of hopelessness and death.

2

THE RED SCARE IN HOLLYWOOD

HUAC and the End of an Era
Peter Roffman and Jim Purdy

The atmosphere in Hollywood in the late 1940s and early 1950s was charged with fear, anxiety, paranoia, and hatred. In this essay, film historians Peter Roffman and Jim Purdy examine the impact of the House Un-American Activities Committee investigations of Communist infiltration of the film industry.

The Black List

Conservative elements have always attacked liberalism by associating it with the extreme left, seeing in many progressive social welfare programs the dangerous seeds of communism. Throughout the thirties, enemies of New Deal liberalism conducted a campaign to so discredit Roosevelt, but the overall viability of the New Deal's programs and the immense personal appeal of the President overrode such attacks. Then, with Roosevelt's death and the advent of the Cold War, this right-wing thesis found a sympathetic audience. Given a veneer of credibility by international events (the imperialist postures of Stalin, the rise of Red China) and a series of domestic spy scandals (especially the case involving New Dealer Alger Hiss), the "Red scare" snowballed into a major political movement. First the House Un-American Activities Committee in the late forties and then Senator Joseph McCarthy in the early fifties aroused the public to the "danger" in its midst. Any form of social protest became suspect—to have signed an antifascist petition or merely to have been in the presence of a "known" radical was enough to have many people fired from their jobs, slandered and ostracized by the community. All major institutions, from the federal government to the universities, the Army, and the mass media, came under severe scrutiny. In many industries there existed illegal blacklists of supposed Communists who were considered unemployable. That the Red-hunters could never find proof of a substantial Communist threat to the United States and that the American Communist Party was a completely legal political organization until the Communist Control Act of 1954 were irrelevant.

Among the earliest targets of HUAC was the movie industry, an industry with a high public profile and therefore a source of maximum publicity for the Committee and its work. The Hollywood blacklist is now almost as big a legend as the stars and movies of the period. It is a sorry tale of political repression, of individuals unfairly tormented and careers often ruined, of an industry which far too readily surrendered any semblance of its political independence. The initial hearings were called for October 1947 as an "investigation of Communism in motion pictures," but the tone of the proceedings quickly established that the Committee was not so much interested in the subversive content of movies as in the political affiliations and activities of the people who made the movies.

At first, the industry protested. Nineteen of the forty-one witnesses subpoenaed declared their intention to be "unfriendly" and refused to answer questions concerning their political beliefs. A group of Hollywood liberals, including Bogart, Bacall, Danny Kaye, John Huston, Gene Kelly, and William Wyler formed the Committee for the First Amendment, while Eric Johnston, prestigious president of the Motion Picture Association of America, defended the movies' right to freedom of speech.

The hearings quickly dashed liberal hopes. Friendly witnesses such as Jack Warner, L. B. Mayer, Walt Disney, Leo McCarey, Sam Wood, Robert Taylor, Adolphe Menjou, Ronald Reagan, George Murphy, and Gary Cooper were allowed, as *Daily Variety* reported, to "read prepared statements, use notes and ramble widely in offering testimony of strong nature without supporting evidence." The "unfriendlies," on the other hand, were prohibited in all but two cases from making statements so that their protests had to be shouted out over Chairman Parnell Thomas's rulings. The spectacle of the "unfriendly" witnesses vociferously challenging the Committee's legal authority and their refusal to answer any questions boomeranged, creating much adverse publicity. After calling only eleven of the unfriendlies, the Committee abruptly called off the hearings and charged ten of the eleven—the Hollywood Ten—with contempt of Congress. Parnell Thomas ended the hearings by warning the industry to "set about immediately to clean its own house and not wait for public opinion to do so."

Protest quickly gave way to expediency as industry personnel began to worry about their careers. The Committee for the First Amendment disintegrated, with such luminaries as Bogart and Bacall referring to their participation as a "mistake." Within a month, industry heads held the infamous summit meeting at the Waldorf Astoria and issued the "Waldorf Statement," a tacit agreement to form a blacklist: the industry would not reemploy the Ten or any other members of a party advocating the overthrow of the United States government. Eric Johnston declared:

> We are frank to recognize that such a policy involves dangers and risks. There is the danger of hurting innocent people. There is the risk of creating an atmosphere of fear. Creative work at its best cannot be carried on in an atmosphere of fear. We will guard against this danger, this risk, this fear.

But of course, just such an atmosphere was created. In 1950, the Supreme Court upheld the contempt charges against the Hollywood Ten, sending them to prison for a year and paving the way for a new set of HUAC hearings in 1951. This time there was no pretense of investigating Communist propaganda in the movies. Nor was there any protest.

The victim of the blacklist was caught, no matter what course of action he took, in an impossible dilemma. Merely being named at the hearings set off a relentless chain of events even though membership in the Party or signing an antifascist petition represented no transgression of the law.

Once named, the individual was automatically labeled as suspect and found himself on the blacklist. Since the individual had done nothing illegal his accusers required no documented evidence of his transgression and he had no legal recourse to defend himself. When actually called before HUAC, the accused had but two choices, neither of them particularly palatable. First, he could cooperate, confessing to left-wing political affiliations and naming any people engaged in similar activities. By so doing, the individual generally cleared himself and saved his career, but he also lent validity to the Committee and helped perpetuate the investigation by supplying more names and forcing more individuals to face the same predicament. The other alternative was to defy the Committee and thus destroy one's career. The witness could refuse to testify under the First Amendment and face a jail sentence for contempt or he could invoke the Fifth Amendment, refusing to testify on the grounds of self-incrimination. The latter tactic failed to save the witness from blacklisting since, in Representative Morgan M. Moulder's words, any "refusal to testify so consistently leaves a strong inference that you are still an ardent follower of the Communist Party and its purpose." Either way, then, whether confessing to a "crime" that was no crime or refusing to confess on the basis of constitutional rights, the individual was "guilty" and yet without legal recourse.

Over two hundred individuals within the movie industry were named by HUAC, and countless others were judged by the studios and pressure groups as "guilty" by association. Many submitted to the Committee's demands and to other clearance procedures (such as studio loyalty tests) in order to salvage their careers, while many others refused to yield and paid the price. Virtually everyone else within the industry proceeded with extreme caution lest they grant the Committee or any right-wing zealot the slightest grounds for criticism. The very last thing those still employed dared do was stand up for their former coworkers, since such action would only blacklist them to the same limbo.

Movies and Communism: From *Mission to Moscow* to *Big Jim McLain*

Not surprisingly, the 1947 Committee and its successors failed to establish that Communist propaganda had ever been injected into the Hollywood film. A thorough study undertaken by Dorothy Jones failed to uncover any fragments of Marxism in the movies and even Robert Vaughn, himself an anti-Communist, concedes in his book *Only Victims:*

> At no time during the Thomas, Wood, or subsequent investigations of Hollywood film content was the Committee ever able to establish conclusively that Communist Party dogma managed to find its way to the American people via the American screen.

As we have discussed, Hollywood throughout the thirties had taken a strong anti-Communist line, viciously caricaturing leftists as villainous agitators or lazy, cowardly bums. About the only examples of Marxist propaganda the Committee members or witnesses were able to unearth were preposterous: single lines of dialogue as innocuous as "Share and share alike—that's democracy"—spoken by down-and-out college roommates who decide to pool their resources in *Tender Comrade* (1943, written by Dalton Trumbo). Clifford Odets' *None but the Lonely Heart* (1944) was damned by Mrs. Lela Rogers (Ginger's mother) because among other reasons, the *Hollywood Reporter* had said that it was "moody and somber throughout in the Russian manner."

The main basis for HUAC's claims was the series of wartime propaganda films that glorified America's Russian allies. And even here the Committee failed to unearth any real threat: Ayn Rand felt MGM's *Song of Russia* was propagandistic because it presented Russia in a positive light by showing Soviet children laughing and playing. That these films were the expression of the official foreign policy of the time was no defense, since that policy, the product of Roosevelt's "Communist-influenced" New Deal, was itself suspect. In fact, when Jack Warner took the stand, the Committee members were less interested in the film *Mission to Moscow* than in getting Warner to incriminate FDR by admitting that the President personally requested the movie be made.

Mission to Moscow was the only film that could really be said to conform to the official Communist line. While the other wartime films about Russia set out to improve the Russian image in America, *Mission* also took a direct look at the internal policies of the Soviet Union. Based on Ambassador Joseph Davies' book, the film dramatizes Davies' experiences in Russia during the late thirties, where FDR had sent him to assess the Soviets' willingness to fight. In the film, Davies (Walter Huston) first learns that we're all alike, that Soviets are no different from Americans. A factory foreman explains that he has worked hard and studied to get ahead and that the factory operates on a capitalist-like profit motive system to ensure "the most good for the most people." Davies replies, "It's the same in our country." Also, Mrs. Davies upon visiting a cosmetic factory, inquires, "Isn't this against Soviet principles?" to which she is answered, "Women all over the world like to look feminine. Beauty is no luxury." Then, the ambassador comes to his most important discovery—that the purge trials and secret police repression are necessities in a country threatened by sabotage. He does not even mind his own embassy being bugged since he has nothing to hide: "Perhaps counterespionage is a matter of self-preservation."

The film's main thrust is to demonstrate how truly antifascist the Soviets are, and how those aligned against them are pro-Nazi. The Nazi-Soviet pact is justified as a stalling tactic, a means of buying time to prepare for a war Stalin knew was inevitable all along. Internal sabotage is pinned on the Nazis. At the purge trials, Davies learns that Trotsky, along with Bukharin and Radek, was involved with the Germans and Japanese in a plot to overthrow the government. The film naively accepts the Stalinist version of the trials as gospel, something that even the real Davies had trouble believing. Stalin (Mannart Kippen) himself is portrayed as a wise, affable grandfather figure, who along with Roosevelt and Churchill is the only world leader to foresee the dangers of Nazi Germany. Yet, when Davies returns to America and tries to arouse support for Russia, he is confronted with the wrath of isolationists who see no danger in Hitler ("We got a coupla' oceans, ain't we?") but are violently opposed to Stalin. The film thus attacks anti-Communists and isolationists as profascists. Though the Warners could hardly be accused of Bolshevism and *Mission* would never have been made if not for the war cause, any film which supported Stalin was wide open for attack. To paraphrase Alistair Cooke, the film was judged in one era for what it represented in another.

As ever, hypersensitive to such controversy and "advised" by Chairman Thomas to produce films which attack communism, the studio readily complied with an entire cycle of anti-Red pictures. Just as the wartime propaganda films had been a complete reversal in attitude from the thirties anti-Communist movies, so the postwar cycle performed political flip-flop from the war pictures. Within weeks of the 1947 hearings, MGM released its 1939 anti-Communist satire, *Ninotchka,* in which cold commissar Greta Garbo is seduced by captivating capitalist Melvyn Douglas. Then, in May 1948, Twentieth Century-Fox released *Iron Curtain.* The other studios soon followed suit. Except for the modest success of *Iron Curtain* (it was number two at the New York box office for the month of May), none of these films were particularly popular. Yet despite cool public response, Hollywood relentlessly pursued the anti-Communist theme and when it appeared to be waning throughout 1950–51, the second HUAC hearings produced another even greater, flurry of movie Red-baiting. Dorothy Jones estimates that there were between thirty-five and forty films released between 1948 and 1954 attacking communism and the Soviet Union. This perseverance with a political issue in the face of poor box office is unprecedented in Hollywood history and indicates the degree of paranoia felt by the studios during the period.

The cycle itself followed the tradition of the World War II features, translating the ideological conflict between capitalism and communism into the most simplistic form of morality play. As Pauline Kael, among others, has pointed out, if we were not told that the villains were Communists, we could easily mistake them for Nazis:

> the filmgoer who saw the anti-Nazi films of ten years ago will have no trouble recognizing the characters, just as ten years ago he could have detected (under the Nazi black shirts) psychopathic killers, trigger-happy cattle rustlers, and the screen villain of earliest vintage—the man who will foreclose the mortgage if he doesn't get the girl. The Soviet creatures of the night are direct descendants of the early film archetype, the bad man.

Again, the films closely conform to genre conventions, the majority of them indistinguishable from *Confessions of a Nazi Spy.* Films such as *Iron Curtain, Walk a Crooked Mile* (1948), *I Was a Communist for the FBI* (1951), *Walk East on Beacon* (1952), and *Big Jim McLain* (1952) are generally shot in the same documentary style, with the same authoritative narrator who tells us that this is based on a real case, and the familiar plot of the investigator-hero uncovering a scheme by nefarious foreigners to overthrow the country. The other most common story line, seen in *Sofia* (1948), *The Red Danube* (1949), *Never Let Me Go* (1953), *Man on a Tightrope* (1953), and *Night People* (1954), is borrowed from *Escape* (1940) and dramatizes the attempts of the protagonists to flee from repressive Iron Curtain countries to the freedom of America. One genre which the World War II propagandists had failed to use was science fiction. In *Red Planet Mars* (1952), both the Martians and God help destroy the atheistic Soviet regime.

Like the Nazis, the Communists are condemned on character traits more than ideology. Party members are almost always severely disturbed—some are bloodhungry killers (Arnold in *I Married a Communist* [also known as *The Woman on*

Pier 13], 1949); others are mad scientists (*Whip Hand,* 1951); the women, if not nymphomaniacs (Mollie in *The Red Menace,* 1949, and Christine in *I Married a Communist*), are frigid and repressed *(Walk East on Beacon)*. One of the most dramatically deranged Communists is Yvonne (Betty Lou Gerson) in *The Red Menace,* who bursts forth in a demented tirade about the revolution when questioned by authorities. The leaders are either hysterical fanatics like Vanning in *I Married a Communist* or shysters. Generally the Party elite live, as Karel Reisz points out, "in large, luxurious flats with suspect modernistic furniture (but the larder is always a photographic darkroom) and large libraries, eat off silver plates and openly look forward to the age of caviar for the commissar." As one character in *Walk East on Beacon* enthuses, "Someday we won't have to worry about dough. A commissar gets everything for free—everything!"

Just as Hollywood never dealt with the fascist ideology, so the political and economic principles of communism are never really explicated. They receive token expression in crudely distilled comments and speeches. "Man is state—state is man. Someone upstairs says something and that's that," intones a Party intellectual in *I Married a Communist.*

The Communist Party doesn't seem to stand for anything, only against sacred American principles such as God, motherhood, and true love. It is continually in conflict with members of the Catholic Church, including a priest in *I Was a Communist,* a cardinal in *Guilty of Treason* (1949), and a Mother Superior in *The Red Danube.* In *My Son John* (1952), John Jefferson (Robert Walker) betrays both God and his mother when he swears on the Bible that he is not a Communist, while Mollie, an amoral floozie in *The Red Menace,* turns her back on Father O'Leary for the truth "as laid down by Marx, Engels, Lenin, and Stalin." In other films, the Party boss is continually warning romantically inclined members: "Love! Why don't you call it what it is—emotion!" *(I Married a Communist).* According to Karel Reisz, the following lines of dialogue occur with minor variations in four of the films:

> Party Girl: (In love and therefore deviating) Don't worry about my private life.
> Party Boss: You have no private life.

Nor is human life very sacred to the Communists. Party members are expendable, expected to give themselves up to the police in order to protect more important compatriots. In *Iron Curtain,* one imprisoned unfortunate is consoled: "Don't be too unhappy, Keith. We'll name city after you when we take over." The faithful are even expected to kill those close to them when the leaders so demand: a brother is ordered to murder his sister in *Whip Hand* and a husband his wife in *Conspirator* (1950). Whole sections of the population are equally dispensable. In *Whip Hand,* the "Commies" talk of germ warfare, and in *Big Jim McLain,* they plan to poison the waterfront as a strike tactic. In the latter film, John Wayne, with his customary political insight explains to a spy the difference between Americans and Communists:

> I wanted to hit you one punch, just one full-thrown right hand. But now I can't do it. Because you're too small. That's the difference between you

and us, I guess. We don't hit the little guy. We believe in fair play and all that sort of thing.

If the Soviet Union represents the evils of totalitarianism, of course America is the land of freedom and goodness. But though our society is basically sound, the films warn that it is still vulnerable and locates the source of that vulnerability in America's innocence. The country is so free and open that people have become too trusting, taking everyone including the Communists, at their word. Idealistic dupes are seduced into the Party ranks by phony front organizations such as the antifascist group in *I Was a Communist for the FBI* which really raises funds for Party activities. Blacks, Jews, and other minorities are lured into the Party through its platform of racial equality only to discover that the leaders are in fact vicious racists seeking new members to manipulate in their quest for world power. A student who has won a trip to Russia returns home brainwashed in *Big Jim McLain* while to John Jefferson, communism is like a contagious disease: he begins attending meetings for intellectual stimulation and before he knows it he's being enticed into spying for the Party.

When the innocents discover the truth (the cabbie in *Walk East on Beacon* describes it as "like waking up married to a woman you hate") they soon realize that the Communists are much more ruthless than expected and will kill anyone who tries to desert. Such a fate befalls the protagonists in *I Married a Communist* and *My Son John,* as well as minor characters in *The Red Menace. I Was a Communist for the FBI* even implies that this is what happened to such important figures as Trotsky and Masaryk. Many other innocents choose suicide either to avoid corruption (the ballerina in *The Red Danube*) or to free themselves from the living death of Party membership (the Jewish poet in *The Red Menace* and the army officer in *Conspirator*). So great is their sin that the only way the Communists can redeem themselves is through martyrdom. These films echo the common sentiment of "innocence betrayed" propounded by such writers as Leslie Fiedler, who saw the liberals of the New Deal as culpable because they had allowed themselves to be used by the Communists. Just as the liberals have been betrayed, so they have betrayed their countrymen. FDR, under the influence of New Deal "Reds" like Alger Hiss, "sold us out" at Yalta.

To combat any further chance of betrayal, the films offer a vigilant antiintellectualism. In films such as *My Son John* and *Big Jim McLain,* the parents of the fallen youths argue for a return to the old values. John's father (Dean Jagger) is meant to represent the ideal American: a Legionnaire, staunch churchgoer, and small-town schoolteacher who gives lessons in "simple down-to-earth" morality and Americanism. He scorns his son's university education, his important Washington job, and his relations with intellectuals and professors. Mr. Jefferson relies on the Bible and patriotic platitudes for enlightenment and mistrusts any open debate which deviates from these narrow principles. In short, the heroic American patriarch is a right-wing bigot who frequently bursts into song: "If you don't like your Uncle Sammy / Then go back to your home o'er the sea." Mr. Lester, the father in *Big Jim McLain,* reveres the values of hard work and religious faith which have allowed him to "retire on my pension and live free in the sun." He too sees his son's communism as a repudiation of America and God.

Like HUAC, these films rely on their own internal logic which betrays a tendency toward the very totalitarianism that they are supposedly combatting. Any of the beliefs and freedoms which fail to conform precisely to the values of the American right are held up as suspect, as the means by which the Communists infiltrate and poison the country. So, although America is glorified as the land of freedom where everyone can speak and think for himself, the threat of communism is simultaneously located in that very exercise of free thought. This logic is succinctly captured in *Big Jim McLain*. After he breaks up the Communist spy ring, Big Jim does not take the criminals to court where they would be tried as spies under normal procedures, but subpoenas them to appear before HUAC. By thus misrepresenting HUAC's role, the film is able to attack Constitutional freedom. The Communists are guilty of espionage, but by invoking the Fifth Amendment, they elude the Committee's investigations and go free to continue their evil work. By conforming to the principles of the Constitution, HUAC cannot do justice to the traitors and the country remains unprotected. According to *McLain*, America's freedom is both glorious and dangerous: "There are lot of wonderful things written into our Constitution that were meant for honest, decent citizens. I resent the fact that it can be used an abused by the very people who want to destroy it." In short, to preserve our freedom we must relinquish it. Loyalty to motherhood and HUAC must be as absolute as loyalty to the Party.

3

A PERVERSE TRIBUTE TO HOLLYWOOD'S PAST

Sunset Boulevard
Lois Banner

It is, without a doubt, one of the creepiest films ever made. It takes place in an archetypal Gothic setting: a decaying mansion. It is filled with bizarre Gothic images: rats scurry across an empty swimming pool, a chimpanzee is buried at midnight. Its roles are played by some of Hollywood's greatest legends—Gloria Swanson, Cecil B. DeMille, Erich von Stroheim, Buster Keaton, Hedda Hopper—but all are aged and long past their glory days. The film is a remarkably perverse commentary on Hollywood's past.

Norma Desmond slowly descends the grand staircase of her Sunset Boulevard mansion. Floodlights bathe her in light. Cameras roll, clutched by newsreel cameramen on the stairs and in the vestibule below. This scene constitutes one of the most famous moments in film. Norma Desmond, the aging film star, with a career long past, has shot and killed Joe Gillis, an impoverished younger screenwriter, mired in debt and with only "a couple of B pictures to his credit." The news of the slaying once again has brought her into the spotlight. The press has swarmed to her house to immortalize what they can of the aftermath of the lurid deed. Now they catch her on celluloid as she moves slowly down the stairs among them. The film, an extended flashback, details the events that led up to the slaying.

Some months before Norma's fatal action, Joe had stumbled into Norma's mansion while eluding bill collectors attempting to repossess his car. He had wound up living with her. Desperate for money and fascinated by the charisma of her past fame, for months he had worked with her rewriting the screenplay based on the story of Salome and John the Baptist that she herself had previously written for a hoped-for screen comeback. A sometime romance had developed between Norma and Joe. But when he decided to leave her, she reacted with murderous rage and a seeming retreat into madness. Coming down the staircase, she thinks she is on her old movie set, descending the stairs of a great palace as the pagan princess Salome, the incarnation of the heroine of her hoped-for film.

From one point of view *Sunset Boulevard* seems to take a disapproving stance toward Norma Desmond. Because of Norma's age, there may be no way that her relationship with Joe can succeed, just as there may be no way she can regain either her acting career or her youthful beauty. For her Joe may be only a gigolo, a representative of that sort of young man who, for money, services older women sexually. Even Norma seems to acknowledge that that may be the case when she telephones Betty Schaefer, her putative younger rival, in a futile attempt to end Betty's interest in Joe. She alludes to Joe as nothing but a manipulator of older women. Love between Joe and Norma may be problematic; he seems angry with her throughout the film. A voice-over narrative by Joe provides a running commentary on the film's action. Throughout this narrative, Joe is critical of Norma. Most telling is his name: Joe Gillis. For this name, Joe Gillis, almost sounds out the word "gigolo."

In many ways Desmond is presented unsympathetically. The makeup that she wears underscores her theatrical, larger-than-life behavior. For the makeup is heavy, with oversized lips and eyes giving Norma the look of an overaged Kewpie doll. Or, alternatively, with her harsh face and dark, outlined eyes, she looks like the vamp character of her heyday in the 1920s gone to seed. With long, dark fingernails on hands clutching Joe or enfolding him in an embrace, she seems a vampire, feeding off Joe's youth to make it her own.

Even Norma's house, a reflection of her persona (as houses often are for women) seems of negative value. In his dialogue Joe describes Norma's house. It is huge, with eight master bedrooms. There is a sunken tub in every bathroom, a bowling alley in the basement, a swimming pool, and a tennis court. A large living room contains a pipe organ, which Max, Norma's mysterious butler, plays. A large screen is hidden behind a painting in that room, and Norma uncovers it in the evenings to show her twenties films to Joe.

Joe calls the house a "white elephant." It is a curiosity, a relic past its time of usefulness. It seems especially out of date in the post-World War II world which looked to the suburbs and the tract home as the new family nirvana. Norma's house is the sort of place that film stars built in the 1920s, when, in Joe's words, they were "making eighteen thousand dollars a week and [paying] no taxes." When Joe leaves the house, he goes to the milieu of his younger friends. They live in crowded, noisy apartments, sharing their space as they share their dreams. They group together with the balm of youth and its hope for the future around them. "There is nothing like being twenty-two," Joe says to Betty.

Desmond's overblown setting mirrors her curious personal relationships. Desmond has neither children nor family, the standard supports of aging women. She is an appropriate age to be a grandmother, but one could hardly visualize her in that role. What she has is a chimpanzee and her mysterious butler, Max. In addition, she has a group of elderly friends from her film days with whom she plays bridge. Joe calls them the "waxworks" in his voice-over narrative, and that is indeed what they resemble. They are pale; they project a waxen image. Deadpan Buster Keaton is among them, but he is not comic here.

For a moment there seems a different reality for Norma when Max turns out to have been her first husband, the director who discovered her. But this is no pleasant domestic menage formed by two individuals who, having bonded for life, are happily growing old together. This is not Darby and Joan, those eighteenth-century ballad characters whose domestic felicity became a watchword for long, contented marriage. This is not Robert Browning wooing Elizabeth Barrett Browning with: "Grow old along with me!/The best is yet to be." Rather, Max is a combination of Norma's nurse, her flunky, and an impresario who supports her fantasies. For he writes her anonymous fan letters so that she can sustain the illusion that she is still a star, beloved by a public which has not forsaken her.

Then there is her monkey, perhaps the most graphic symbol of her barren life. When the movie begins, the animal has already died, and Desmond is preparing for the internment. On the monkey, Desmond has lavished her maternal drives. Watching the chimp burial from afar, Joe notes that it looks as though "she were laying to rest an only child." With sarcasm, he makes reference to King Kong, the massive monkey of the 1933 movie *King Kong,* whom entrepreneurs captured in his island Eden to exhibit to the American public. King Kong was an epic animal, symbolizing nature destroyed by civilization; he was not an aging woman's pet. Here Desmond becomes one of those lonely, middle-aged women who bestow their attention on pet poodles and parakeets and who have long been a butt of jokes and of the comedian's caustic wit.

More than this, Joe tells us that Norma is fifty years old. Thus we can presume that she is menopausal. The point is important. For by common belief menopausal women are difficult, hysterical, even crazy. Thus Desmond may be a product of her hormones, a middle-aged woman out of whack. Any child born to a menopausal woman runs a high risk of being deformed, a "monster" in shape. To seventeenth-century Puritans, the stillborn, misshapen child born to menopausal Anne Hutchinson soon after her conviction for heresy was ample proof that she was a witch. Thus a monkey (especially a chimpanzee, closest to humans in genetic makeup) is an appropriate offspring for Norma.

The dilemma of this middle-aged woman is further underscored by the confrontation between Norma Desmond and another character, director Cecil B. DeMille. DeMille plays himself in the film, and it is to DeMille that Desmond goes with an appeal to produce the screenplay of Salome and John the Baptist that Gillis is rewriting for her. Desmond interrupts DeMille on the studio set of a movie he is directing. She mistakenly believes that he has phoned her with an offer to back her projected Salome film.

It is a doubly tragic scene, with fantasy and reality thoroughly intermixed. For the real Gloria Swanson's major triumphs three decades before had been in a series of upper-class melodramas directed by DeMille; many contended that he had made her a star. Now twenty years later, DeMille remains a director, vigorous and commanding, still directing films starring seductive women. But younger women star in these films. Among them is Hedy Lamarr, a dark-haired Gloria Swanson descendant. Lamarr plays the siren of *Samson and Delilah,* the film onto the set of which Desmond/Swanson descends in *Sunset Boulevard.* The scene, filmographers tell us, was actually shot on the *Samson and Delilah* set in the midst of work in progress.

The tragic comparison between DeMille the director and his former star is deepened when we realize that DeMille is old enough to be Desmond's father. He is seventy; she is fifty. She calls him "the chief," her title for him in the twenties. She defers to him on the set, as in the old days. There is a rapport between them, but it is like a father with a daughter. With honeyed words he soothes her, but he tells her nothing.

Sunset Boulevard belongs to that genre of cinema known as Hollywood films.

In these films a critique of the movie industry is a central purpose. And what *Sunset Boulevard* as an example of this genre shows us is not only the clash between the old Hollywood and the new Hollywood, between the first generation of Hollywood filmmakers and those who followed them, but also the ways in which both Hollywoods, with their false commercial values, could warp individual lives. "The men in the front office," declaims Norma, "they took the idols and smashed them."

Hollywood created Norma Desmond, and it may have made her monstrous. "You cannot imagine how she was at seventeen," DeMille tells an assistant. "A dozen press agents working overtime can do terrible things to the human spirit." Through their efforts, Norma became a new person. Redrawn to their specifications, steeped in the narcissism of celebrity status, she did not know who she was. With her illusions shattered, Norma retreats into murderous rage.

The story of Salome, the role she wants to play, revolves around Salome's demand for the head of John the Baptist, the biblical prophet who scorned her love. Lacking power, Salome gained revenge through an execution which seems a symbolic castration. For if Joe is angry, Norma is also angry. The Hollywood patriarchy made her; the Hollywood patriarchy cast her aside. They "shot" her all those years with their cameras; now she must shoot them. Perhaps unfortunately, the victim of her murderous rage is only a minor screenwriter. Indeed, Joe had once told her that what she needed was someone of her own status, a "big shot." His words may have been only too true. Norma may have vented her rage at the wrong target, confusing love and power, sexuality and hierarchy.

But it is characteristic of women that they personalize their targets. Norma defers to DeMille, but he does not enter her house. Joe is in her house; he will do for the whole of Hollywood. That Joe's relationship with Norma will end disastrously is foreshadowed early in the film. When Joe stumbles into Norma's mansion after hiding his car in her garage, both Norma and Max mistake Joe for the undertaker come to bury her beloved monkey. There is a burial scene emblematic of what will happen to Joe. He will be the "chump" to replace her "chimp." He will also become the undertaker of her dreams: the person who will bury them. On the gold cigarette case which Norma gives Joe she has had inscribed: "Mad About the Boy." Thus is indicated her infatuation and her need to possess. But eventually Joe will make her mad enough to kill him. Joe cannot be her child; he will not be her lover. Despite the lushness of her locale and the primitive chimp as pet, this is no Edenic paradise, no primeval Adamic retreat. From this perspective Desmond is no Eve, no original earth mother, but only a go-between, a conduit to power. The studio heads, the controlling patriarchs, are the real stars. Norma is a dragon whose powers of seduction are only temporary but the impact of whose actions is eternal.

Following one version of ancient myth, the young god must die when his yearly cycle of regeneration has ended. And so Norma kills Joe, propelling him by the force of her bullets into the swimming pool. As the movie opens—and as it closes— we see him lying in the pool. There he lies peacefully, floating in a state beyond consciousness, buoyed up by water, ever a symbol of women's maternal nature. There he lies peacefully, surrounded by that life-giving amniotic fluid which Norma's body has never produced. There he lies, asleep in a womb which in Norma is desiccated and dry.

After Norma has shot Joe and he lies in the pool, she looks to the sky and triumphantly declaims: "Stars are ageless. . . ." The look in her eyes, the shadings on her face, replicate a figure in an earlier frame of the film. This figure is from a clip of a film in her triumphant years which she has showed Joe in one of her living-room screenings. The figure is actually the young Gloria Swanson in her starring role in *Queen Kelly,* the last important film Swanson made before her career as a star in silent films went into decline.

The message is manifold. The aging Gloria Swanson becomes the young Gloria Swanson; in our eyes the two figures merge into the eternal star, radiant. Metaphorically, and for a moment, Norma Desmond joins the goddesses of myth and legend in several guises, both old and young. But stars, of course, only shine at night; in the light of day they seem to disappear. And so does Norma, advancing and retreating; sometimes powerful through her past fame and her own persona; often powerless, an aging woman yearning after a fame and a love she perhaps no longer can have.

Fantasy and reality are intertwined in *Sunset Boulevard.* And so are age-disparate relationships. The one between Norma Desmond and Joe Gillis forms the central drama of the film. But these sorts of relationships are also intermixed in the history of the film's production and in the real lives of the people involved in that production.

Thus, for example, Wilder had difficulty casting the roles of Norma and Joe. Few actors seemed willing to expose themselves before the public in this dark romance between age and youth. Mae West, Wilder's initial choice for Norma, adamantly refused the role. She thought that playing the part would tarnish her image as a mocking femme fatale. She had created this image during the 1930s, and she maintained it in the 1940s in a successful nightclub act. In this act choruses of young men accompanied her singing and dancing as foils to her vamping. She wanted nothing to do with the role of an aging woman who could not control the young man in her life. Wilder also approached Pola Negri and Mary Pickford to play the role of Norma, but both turned him down.

With regard to the role of Joe, Montgomery Clift initially accepted it and then backed out only a few weeks before production began. He contended that his fans would not like seeing him involved with an older woman. Yet this public reason for his refusal masked a private reality. For some time Clift had been involved with Libby Holman, a popular singer from the 1920s who was thirty years older than he. Many years before, Holman had shot and killed her wealthy husband. Although she had been acquitted of the crime, she did not want to relive the experience.

The pattern of male actors refusing the role of Joe continued. Fred MacMurray was the next to demur. He argued that he did not want to endanger his public image as a wholesome hero by playing the somewhat tarnished Joe. Yet he had previously portrayed the murderous insurance agent in Wilder's *Double Indemnity.* Even though William Holden's career at that point was in the doldrums, he was so reluctant to play the lover of an older woman that the head of Paramount studios, to which he was bound by contract, had to order him to take the part.

Gloria Swanson herself initially hesitated accepting the role of Norma Desmond. Swanson's career had been in eclipse for over a decade, but she did not want to begin the difficult task of trying to regain it with an unimportant role. She wanted a role that would have a striking impact, that would be a "bigger than life part." She had, after all, been a major star of the 1920s, and the decline of her

Hollywood career seemed a caprice of the fate that had brought sound to the movies. There had been no problem with her voice, with her looks, with her movement. Perhaps the issue was her involvement with Joseph Kennedy, their estrangement, and the difficulties of filming *Queen Kelly* (never released in a full version). Perhaps she was deemed simply too old for the new medium of sound. But, in contrast to Norma, Swanson had not become a recluse. She had moved to New York and worked successfully in radio. Still, she had never forgotten Hollywood.

In the end, Swanson was allowed liberty in delineating the character of Norma Desmond. In the original conception of the film, the character of Desmond was secondary in importance to that of Gillis. But the manic brilliance of Swanson's portrayal showed through in her screen test, and Wilder acceded to Swanson's demand that the Desmond role be expanded. Swanson's portrayal is compelling. For it seems driven by some core of rage in her being. The end to her film career may have engendered the rage. Or it may have proceeded from her reaction to the American fixation with youth, a fixation which rendered Swanson obsolete while her sense of a vigorous self was still strong.

To play the role of Norma's butler, Max, Wilder turned to Erich von Stroheim, with whom he had previously worked in Europe. In real life, von Stroheim's involvements with Gloria Swanson were considerable. Von Stroheim had had a career as conflicted as Swanson's. He had been a famed actor and director in the 1920s (second only to D.W. Griffith in reputation). But in the 1930s he could find work only as an actor. The last major Hollywood film he had directed had been *Queen Kelly,* which starred Swanson. For von Stroheim, as for Gloria Swanson, *Sunset Boulevard* was a case of art mirroring life. But the fit may have been too close for him: he called the role of Max "that lousy butler part."

Billy Wilder's own life was also interwoven with the film. A middle-aged man at the time of its making, he was involved with a younger woman. Some said that the character of Betty, the young woman in the film, was based on this woman. Yet, as I shall presently discuss, Betty's negative aspects might indicate a failing relationship. It is also possible that Wilder wrote aspects of himself into *Sunset Boulevard,* that Norma Desmond was partly Billy Wilder, a Wilder experiencing his own discomforts associated with aging and with the difficulty of operating as an artist in commercial Hollywood. Thus art may have mirrored life for Wilder as well as for his actors. In the figure of Norma, Wilder perhaps worked out his own feelings about his European past and his American present and the crass world of Hollywood. Perhaps he, too, wanted to shoot the big shots.

The movie had interesting impacts on the careers of all the individuals involved with it. Erich von Stroheim went back to Europe; he played no more roles in Hollywood. Billy Wilder went on to make more movies. But only *Some Like It Hot,* I would submit, matched the brilliance of *Sunset Boulevard.* For William Holden, *Sunset Boulevard* launched a distinguished career, a career accelerated by his success in a different role that same year. In *Born Yesterday,* he portrayed a journalist hired to instruct showgirl Judy Holliday in proper manners and speech.

Gloria Swanson was not so fortunate as Holden. She had hoped *Sunset Boulevard* would reinvigorate her career. In fact, after this success she was mostly offered similar roles involving aging, fading actresses. Nor did she win the Oscar for best actress at the 1951 Academy Awards. Bette Davis had also been nominated, for her role as another aging actress in *All About Eve,* and most analysts think that academy members' votes were split between Swanson and Davis, leaving Judy Holliday the prize for best actress in *Born Yesterday*.

Again it was youth triumphing over age: the young showgirl seemingly more important than Davis and Swanson, two aging actresses playing aging actresses. For the roles that Swanson and Davis played in *Sunset Boulevard* and *All About Eve* were similar: both were involved with men who seemed to prefer younger women. In *All About Eve,* Davis played a famous actress still vigorous in her career who decided to renounce her profession to keep her husband. Swanson as Desmond killed the younger man she loved who had rejected her. In 1960 Swanson told a writer for *Harper's* magazine: "All they care about here is the ghastly American worship of youth and that's why there is no mature actress on the screen today."

Marlon Brando in *On the Waterfront*

4

THE MORALITY OF INFORMING

Ambivalence in *On the Waterfront*
Kenneth R. Hey

Few films of the Cold War era are more powerful than On the Waterfront. *Ostensibly the story of racketeering within a longshoreman's union, the film metaphorically addresses one of the central issues of the McCarthy era: the morality of informing. The film also features one of the screen's greatest performances: the young Marlon Brando's stirring portrayal of Terry Malloy, the inarticulate, alienated tough and former prize fighter, who "could have been a contender."*

The study of film in American culture poses some interesting challenges to the person using an interdisciplinary method. First, as an historical document, film has contextual connections with the contemporary world. The people who make a film bring to the project their own interests and attitudes, and these various perspectives, when added to the collaborative process, forge a product which resonates in some way with society. Second, as a work of art, film requires textual analysis similar to drama, photography, painting, and music. But as an aesthetic object which combines different artistic media into a single experience, film requires an analytical method which considers all contributing disciplines. Finally, as an art historical object, film stands at the intersection of ongoing traditions in the medium's own history and of theoretical interests alive at the time the film is made. To single out one feature of the film (e.g., its historical context or a self-contained meaning in the text) is to sacrifice the film for something less. To avoid examining the relative contributions of all the major participants is to miss the unique feature of this collaborative art form.

As an example of the collaborative film process and as an object of cultural significance, *On the Waterfront* (1954) has few competitors. Bringing together some of the best and most innovative artists in their respective media, the film was an attempt to weave together the threads of two contemporary events with the strands of aesthetic themes derived from several different artistic media. Unlike many intriguing films which lose their appeal as society changes, this twenty-five-year-old film continues to evince the intended moral outrage from viewers ignorant of its historical background and to receive harsh criticism from detractors aware of the film's origins.

On the Waterfront tells of Terry Malloy (played by Marlon Brando) who begins

211

as an ignorant and complacent member of a corrupt gang that controls the long-shoreman's union. Terry previously boxed professionally for the mob and obedi-ently took "a dive" so the mobsters could win big on the opponent. He now contents himself with a "cushy" dock job and a "little extra change on the side." The mob, headed by Johnny Friendly (played by Lee J. Cobb) with the assistance of Terry's brother, Charley "the Gent" (played by Rod Steiger), applies "muscle" discipline where necessary: when a dissident member breaks the "D and D" rule ("Deaf and Dumb") and talks to the Crime Commission, the mobsters have him killed. Edie Doyle (played by Eva Marie Saint), the sister of the film's first murder victim Joey Doyle, tries to unravel the mystery of union corruption, hoping to uncover the identity of her brother's murderer. Joined by Father Barry (played by Karl Malden). she soon concentrates her attentions on Terry, whose basic philosophy ("Do it to him before he does it to you") clashes with the Christian morality ("Aren't we all part of each other") she has absorbed at a convent school. Terry's indifference to Edie's pleas eventually leads to the murder of "Kayo" Dugan (played by Pat Henning) whose violent death extracts an emotional eulogy from Father Barry. After the mob kills Charley for protecting his brother, the younger Malloy seeks revenge. Father Barry convinces Terry to vent his anger in open testimony before the State Waterfront Crime Commission. But the impersonality of formal testimony fails to appease Terry's desire for vengeance, and he confronts Johnny Friendly directly. Although he loses the ensuing fist fight, he seems to win a "battle" by circumventing Friendly's authority and personally leading the men back to work.

The following study will seek to explain how and why *On the Waterfront* came to be. As a method of explaining the film's origins and meaning, each collaborator's career, point of view and major interests will be discussed briefly and fitted into the evolving product. When all of the artists' efforts are considered as part of the whole, a single theme predominates: ambivalence. The film argues openly that injustice can be remedied through existing political institutions: but it grafts onto this basic liberal position the suggestion that individuals are frequently casualties of the conflict between right and wrong in society and that the individual's response to the clash of absolute moral standards is ambivalent. In the film, the "thesis" of evil (Johnny Friendly) is confronted by its "antithesis" of good (Father Barry and Chris-tian morality): the new "synthesis" (Terry Malloy) miraculously fuses selfishness and selflessness, but as an individual staggering beneath the burden of moral deci-sions he remains unconvinced of the rightness of either extreme.

The idea for a waterfront drama came from a person who had nothing to do with the final product. In 1949 Arthur Miller flushed with the success of two Broadway plays (*All My Sons*, 1947; *Death of a Salesman*, 1949) directed his consid-erable talent toward the social struggle then being waged on the Brooklyn docks. His play *The Bottom of the River* (also titled *The Hook*) told of the misadventures of Peter Panto who in the late 1930s tried to organize dissident longshoremen in Brooklyn's Red Hook district. According to the longshoremen with whom Miller talked, mobsters feared Panto's rapid rise to popularity and had him killed dumping his body in the East River. In 1951 when the first script was finished Miller contacted colleague Elia Kazan, suggesting that they work jointly on the film.

Kazan after completing his studies at the Yale School of Drama in 1932 had joined both the innovative Group Theatre and the energetic Communist Party but his radical fervor soon waned and he severed Party affiliations because of a conflict over artists' prerogatives and freedoms. From his 1930s experiences in dramatic art and radical politics Kazan developed an aesthetic theory which favored optimistic realism and assumed a political posture "left of center and to the right of the Communist Party." A deft creator of dramatic tension on stage Kazan usually directed Broadway plays that projected his liberal ideas. From his work on the Group Theatre's *Golden Boy* to his direction of Tennessee Williams' *A Streetcar Named Desire* (play 1947: film 1951) and of Arthur Miller's *All My Sons* and *Death of a Salesman,* Kazan had helped shape studies of inhuman exploitation bestial degradation and aimless materialism, as well as statements concerning moral responsibility. But the pessimism which often infused these social dramas was not wholly suited to the optimism of a scrapping and successful immigrant like Kazan. In *On the Waterfront* he would resurrect Clifford Odets' "golden boy" and make his own original golden warrior, Terry Malloy, rise from his beating and depose momentarily his corrupt adversary. Kazan would also revive Tennessee Williams' characters from *A Streetcar Named Desire*. In the play Kazan had directed Vivien Leigh to play Blanche DuBois as "an ambivalent figure who is attracted to the harshness and vulgarity" surrounding her at the same time she fears and rejects it. For the waterfront drama, Kazan would transfer the character ambivalence to Terry Malloy converting Blanche DuBois into an effective Edie Doyle and the befuddled Mitch into a forceful Father Barry (both played by Karl Malden). Stanley Kowalski and Terry Malloy (both played by Marlon Brando) would share several characteristics—an inability to express themselves clearly, an incapacity to control or even comprehend their situations and actions, and a vulnerability which belies a certain sensitivity. But unlike Kowalski, Terry Malloy would be permitted to grow and change. Kowalski's bestial drives mixed with brute strength would give way under persistent moral preachings to Malloy's survival instincts tempered with human indecisiveness.

Kazan's successful Group Theatre experiences, his fleeting glance at radical politics, his personal rise from immigrant boy to Broadway's "gray-haired" wonder and his early Hollywood popularity (*A Tree Grows in Brooklyn,* 1945; *Boomerang* and *Gentleman's Agreement,* both 1947) led him to believe in the value of his own work and in the real possibility of reform. But Kazan stopped short of naive idealism. When confronted with large, historical forces, the individual becomes a victim who may, despite a heroic character, flinch and recoil as did Emiliano Zapata when offered the reins of the Mexican government (*Viva Zapata!,* 1952). Thus by the time Arthur Miller contacted Kazan about a waterfront film the two Broadway collaborators had shared several artistic experiences but Miller's clearly defined goods and evils so evident in *All My Sons* did not blend well with Kazan's admixture of optimism and moral ambivalence.

Despite this difference in perspective the two authors collected Miller's completed script and headed west to seek financial backing. After feelers to Kazan's studio, Twentieth Century-Fox, proved unsuccessful, the two appealed to Harry Cohn, president of Columbia Pictures. Cohn, who showed interest in the project, contacted Roy Brewer, whose advice on labor affairs Cohn considered essential. Brewer headed several Hollywood unions and served on the Motion Picture Alliance for the Preservation of American Ideals, an organization of conservative filmmakers who fought communism in Hollywood by aiding the House Committee on Un-American Activities (HUAC). He supplied union workers and projectionists for films he considered politically acceptable and made it impossible for filmmakers disdainful of HUAC to secure a crew in Hollywood. Cohn and Brewer suggested that the authors convert the waterfront mobsters into communists. When Miller and Kazan refused Brewer retorted that the creators were dishonest, immoral, and un-American. The power behind this hardline position must have seemed ominous to Kazan in 1952 when he received a subpoena from the House Committee on Un-American Activities to testify concerning his knowledge of communist activities in the 1930s.

According to Kazan *On the Waterfront* was "partly affected" by his two appearances before the celebrated House Committee on January 14 and April 9, 1952. "I went through that thing," he later admitted, "and it was painful and difficult and not the thing I'm proudest of in my life but it's also not something I'm ashamed of." No doubt Kazan confronted his unfortunate role as friendly witness with the perspective that he was trapped between two opposing and irreconcilable forces of evil, neither of which deserved his allegiance. However, he also must have seen that the federal government and the strong pro-HUAC sentiment lodged in Hollywood could destroy his career. The general "good" he perceived in the exposure and criticism of the American Communist Party's activities could be easily fused with the individual "good" of his personal success. "It is my obligation as a citizen," he told the committee, "to tell everything." Like "golden boy" Joe Bonaparte, Willy Loman, and even Blanche DuBois, Kazan saw himself as another victim of social and political forces which corrupt even the most honorable intentions.

With the committee as audience Kazan read a carefully prepared statement which contained three clearly framed sections. First, he admitted and repudiated membership in the Communist Party. "I was a member of the Communist Party from some time in the summer of 1934 until the late winter or early spring of 1936 when I severed all connection with it permanently. . . . I had had enough anyway. I had had a taste of police state living and I did not like it." Second, he explained the depth of his complicity by describing his mission and by listing people with whom he had worked.

> For the approximately nineteen months of my membership, I was assigned to a "unit" composed of those party members who were like myself members of the Group Theatre acting company. . . . What we were asked to do was four-fold: 1) to educate ourselves in Marxist and party doctrine; 2) to help the party get a foothold in the Actors Equity Association; 3) to support various "front organizations" of the party; 4) to try to capture the Group Theatre and make it a communist mouthpiece.

All the people Kazan named had previously been named and thus he did not actually lengthen the HUAC list. But he gave legitimacy to the Committee's witch hunt, and—not insignificantly—insured his future employment in Hollywood.

In the third section of his dramatic presentation, Kazan defended his career since leaving the party and tried to show that his artistic activities were in no way un-American. "After I left the party in 1936 except for making a two-reel documentary film mentioned above in 1937 *[The People of the Cumberlands]*, I was never active in any organization since listed as subversive." In characterizing his artistic efforts since 1936 Kazan described *Death of a Salesman* as a story which "shows the frustrations of the life of a salesman and contains implicit criticism of his material-istic standards": he called *Viva Zapata!* "an anti-communist picture." He labored to show how even the most critical works were essentially American in intent, purpose, and effect. Depicting himself as a staunch defender of democracy. Kazan asserted that concern for the social problems of the 1930s had drawn him to the Communist Party, but that the Party's preoccupation with political subversion had actually harmed real social reform.

Prior to his second appearance before the House committee Kazan wrote a lengthy letter to the editor of *The Saturday Review,* defending the anti-communist message of *Viva Zapata!* In explicating the democratic theory behind the film's action Kazan described Zapata (played by Marlon Brando) as "no communist; he was that opposite phenomenon, a man of individual conscience." The true reformer was an individualist who fought for the same ends as did the Communist Party but consulted his conscience rather than ideology when making political decisions. Kazan submitted his entire letter to the House committee as part of his formal statement. In the same issue of *The Saturday Review,* Norman Cousins delineated the essential differences between a communist and a liberal. "A Communist, although he pretends to be independent, always takes his order from above; a liberal makes up his own mind. A Communist because he takes orders from above is sometimes trapped by an overnight change in Party policy; a liberal can change his mind but he does so slowly, painfully, and by his own volition." Three days after testifying Kazan purchased advertising space in the amusement section of *The New York Times.* In the two-column, page-long "Statement," Kazan defended his actions before the committee and called upon other liberals to come forward. "Secrecy," he wrote, "serves the communists." In May 1952, Clifford Odets, whom Kazan had named as a former member of the Communist Party, appeared before the Committee and reiterated the emerging liberal theme. "One must pick one's way very carefully through the images of liberalism or leftism today," he told the subcommittee, "or one must remain silent." Odets, Kazan, and others like them had evidently changed their minds "slowly, painfully, and by [their] own volition" because they chose, as Terry Malloy would choose, not to remain silent.

Yielding to political hysteria on the right did not appeal to all liberals. Kazan's performance before the committee incensed his associate, Arthur Miller, and the two embarked on an artistic duel which lasted into the 1960s. Miller fired the first round with *The Crucible* (1953), an apparent study of witchcraft in Puritan Salem. According to Miller, "the witchhunt was a perverse manifestation of the panic which set in among all classes when the balance began to turn away from communal unity and toward greater individual freedom." Miller tried to link the Salem witch-hunts with Washington red-baiting. While hoping to avoid spurious connections between witchcraft and communism he did seek to explore hysterical and oppressive responses to individual acts of conscience. Kazan's return volley in the artistic duel, *On the Waterfront,* made mobster control over the waterfront analogous to Commu-nist Party control over the individual. But the film did not confuse communism *per se* with gangster racketeering; it sought to explore two forms of oppression. Miller and Kazan, the liberal duellists, were firing at each other by firing in opposite directions. Standing back to back Kazan fired at the political left while Miller fired at the right.

Kazan's role as a friendly witness before the House Committee on Un-American Activities and Miller's efforts to capture the "witch-hunt" in dramatic form left undeveloped their ideas for a film on waterfront crime. After testifying Kazan contacted author Budd Schulberg. Son of a famous Hollywood producer B.P. Schulberg, the young writer had grown up surrounded by famous people and great wealth. After graduating from Dartmouth College, he returned to his hometown, wrote extra dialogue for various studios and released his first novel, *What Makes Sammy Run?* (1941). This searing critique of money-hungry executives in the film industry not only singed the coats of all capitalists, it also avenged his father's premature ouster from Paramount Studios. His second novel, *The Harder They Fall* (1947) updated and expanded Odets' *Golden Boy,* detailing the moral failings of comfortable and dependent employees of a corrupt boxing syndicate. Schulberg followed this cynical blast at complacent self-interest with *The Disenchanted* (1950), a partially autobiographical novel which simultaneously traced the demise of Manley Halliday (known to be F. Scott Fitzgerald) during the filming of *Love in Ice* (Walter Wanger's *Winter Carnival*) and the slow disenchantment of a fresh young screenwriter (Shep/Schulberg) with 1930s socialist thought.

In each of these novels Schulberg created a powerful character whose success depended upon pitiable humans who cowered before the very force that exploited them. While exploring the curious dynamics of social structure which propelled the most vicious hoodlums to the top, the three works recorded the slow and agonizing incapacitation of a lone victim struggling to maintain dignity in a hostile environment. From his first novel, which condemned ambitious Hollywood capitalists, to his third, which followed the demise of an "artist" in Hollywood's film factory, Schulberg sketched a debased and graceless society which protected and rewarded the powerful for trouncing upon the weak.

Shortly after his third novel appeared on the market Schulberg's attention was diverted to the New York waterfront. In 1949 Joseph Curtis, an aspiring film producer with Hollywood connections, had founded Monticello Film Corporation for the sole purpose of converting to celluloid Malcolm Johnson's *New York Sun* articles on union corruption. In 1950, the articles which won Johnson a Pulitzer Prize appeared in book form. With this popular momentum Curtis convinced Robert Siodmak to direct the film and asked Schulberg to write the script. Despite his original hesitancy to return to an industry he had lacerated mercilessly in his fiction, Schulberg agreed. Measuring the distance between successful people and social rebels, Schulberg explained his fascination with the film's subject matter. "The epic scale of the corruption and violence intrigued me. Only a few blocks from Sardi's and Shor's and other places where itinerant social philosophers assemble to discuss the problems of the day, guys who said 'no' to industrial-feudalism were getting clobbered and killed." Invigorated by the importance and scale of the project, Schulberg investigated, planned, and finished *Crime on the Waterfront* by the spring of 1951, but due to grievous errors in the financial planning, the script was languishing in production limbo when the House Committee on Un-American Activities summoned the author to Washington.

As a disillusioned ex-member of the Communist Party, Schulberg chose to obey the subpoena. Testifying on May 23, 1951, he admitted Party membership, explained Party methods of controlling dissident writer-members, and named former associates. He argued that the limited choices available to the 1930s reformer matched with the urgent need to do something made Party membership seem reasonable. "I joined," he told the committee, "because at the time I felt that the political issues that they seemed to be in favor of, mostly I recall the opposition to the Nazi and Mussolini and a feeling that something should be done about it, those things attracted me, and there were some others too." He separated offenders into those who joined the Party to advance basically humanitarian causes and those who wished to manipulate the humanists to advance totalitarian ends. Ideological fanatics within the Party exploited socially credible writers who sought to study society's ills. Irritated over the Party's attempts to regulate his own writing, Schulberg left the organization. In his testimony, he contended there were communists and innocent communist dupes, and the "innocent" were really solid democrats fighting for legitimate causes.

In 1952, with the Curtis project still in financial trouble, the rights to *Crime on the Waterfront* reverted to Schulberg. Shortly thereafter, Kazan, who was interested in making a film on corrupt judicial processes in an eastern city, contacted Schulberg. Because they had both been involved in aborted film projects concerned with waterfront crime, they quickly agreed to develop a realistic story based on mobster control of longshore unions. Drawing upon personal investigations, two previously completed scripts, and Johnson's *Crime on the Waterfront,* the two collaborators familiarized themselves with the details of waterfront conditions.

From 1946 to 1951, the docks in New York and New Jersey were rampant with illegal activities. Attempts at reform, as demonstrated by the ill-fated effort of Peter Panto, proved fruitless. After a wildcat strike in 1945 focused national attention on the waterfront William F. Warren, the workers' popular leader, reportedly fell and hurt himself on the job, and before reappearing on the docks, made a public "confession" that he had been "a dupe" of the Communist Party. In 1948 a second major strike reached its peak soon after the New York Anti-Crime Commission subpoenaed mobster John M. Dunn who while awaiting execution in prison promised to name the man known as "Mr. Big"—called "Mr. Upstairs" in the film. While most workers assumed "Mr. Big" to be financier millionaire William "Big Bill" McCormick, dockworker speculation thought New York City's Mayor William O'Dwyer better suited the description. But Dunn reneged on his threat, the strike was settled with force, the Anti-Crime Commission recessed, and Mayor O'Dwyer ran for reelection.

By November 1952, when Kazan and Schulberg started writing their story, the New Jersey harbor, the specific location for the film, was the setting of frequent assaults, firebombings, beatings, and mobster activities. With the year coming to a close, the New York State Crime Commission (the Commission in the film) made known its findings. With a sweep of media sensationalism, the Commission charged the obvious: the docks were battlefields for entrenched corruption. Workers were forced to take extortionary loans for guaranteed work and illegal strikes were called to extract larger fees from shippers. Union leaders abused elections bookkeeping practices and pension systems; and shippers to insure against loss remained silent. Drawing upon this vast cityscape of corruption Kazan and Schulberg ran through eight different scripts, each of which exposed illegal activities on the New York waterfront while providing the authors an opportunity to explain their position on analogous contemporary events of seemingly greater national significance.

The themes which emanated from Kazan's and Schulberg's HUAC testimonies—the beguiled innocent manipulated for unwholesome purposes; individual responsibility to the democratic whole; preference for individual morality over ideological fanaticism—were literary in nature and religious in tone and they helped the authors shape the raw material of waterfront crime. Likewise the testimonial ceremony, which included confessing anti-social activities, identifying associates and theories responsible for those misguided endeavors, and recommending more desirable ways of expressing social concern, suggested dramatic form. The three stages of their testimony became the three major steps of Terry Malloy's conversion. The first segment of the film exposes Malloy's associations with the corrupt gang; a second segment depicts his discovery of corruption as well as the depths of his own guilt; the final segment shows him battling for his own "rights."

Each segment has a ritualized scene which summarizes the action. The "shape-up" scene discloses the dehumanizing conditions fostered by union corruption. A union leader throws "brass checks" on the ground where longshoremen wrestle to retrieve their guarantee of one day's work. Terry, shown separated from the central scramble is given a "cushy" job as a reward for setting up Joey Doyle for "the knock-off." A "martyrdom" scene in the middle of the film includes Father Barry's oration over the dead body of "Kayo" Dugan. The "waterfront priest" pleads with the men to come forward and speak because silence only serves the mobsters. A "testimonial" scene at the Crime Commission hearings completes the trilogy. The legal institutions receive reinforcement and Terry confesses to society his complicity. The state's principal investigator thanks Terry profusely, explaining that his actions "have made it possible for decent people to work the docks again." This speech echoes the one Representative Francis E. Walter addressed to Kazan after his HUAC appearance: "Mr. Kazan, we appreciate your cooperation with our committee. It is only through the assistance of people such as you that we have been able to make the progress that has been made in bringing the attention of the American people to the machinations of this Communist conspiracy for world domination." In the film, confession and reassurance release Terry from his past transgression and enable him to reclaim his "rights."

The first two ritual scenes—the shape-up and the martyrdom—were borrowed from Johnson's *Crime on the Waterfront*. The prize-winning reporter for the *New York Sun* characterized the longshore working conditions "as not befitting the dignity of a human being," a theme consistent with the testimonies and previous creations of both Schulberg and Kazan. The city's district attorney claimed that the abject conditions on the docks were "a direct result of the shape-up system." Johnson's description of the typical dockside call for workers—the morning shape-up—was to fit neatly into the Kazan-Schulberg script:

> The scene is any pier along New York's waterfront. At a designated hour, the longshoremen gather in a semicircle at the entrance to the pier. They are the men who load and unload the ships. They are looking for jobs and

as they stand there in a semicircle their eyes are fastened on one man. He is the hiring stevedore and he stands alone, surveying the waiting men. At this crucial moment he possesses the power of economic life or death over them and the men know it. Their faces betray that knowledge in tense anxiety, eagerness, and fear. They know that the hiring boss, a union man like themselves can accept them or reject them at will. . . . Now the hiring boss moves among them, choosing the man he wants passing over others. He nods or points to the favored ones or calls out their names, indicating that they are hired. For those accepted, relief and joy. The pinched faces of the others reflect bleak disappointment, despair. Still they linger. Others will wander off inconsolately to wait another chance.

The potency of this scene in the film results from camera positioning. When Big Mac (played by James Westerfield) blows his whistle to call the workers the camera stands behind him permitting his large figure to obscure the huddled longshoremen. During the scramble for tags the camera is low to the ground capturing facial expressions; character movement is downward and the camera seems to press the viewer against the dirty dockside surface. When Edie, who has come to the "shape-up" to study the causes of union corruption, tries to retrieve a tag for her father, she comes in contact with Terry Malloy. He overpowers her and recovers the contested tag for his friend suggesting that muscle prevails on the docks. But when Terry learns that his female adversary is the sister of the kid whom he "set-up for the knock-off," his "conscience" convinces him to surrender the tag to her. Thus the conflict between muscle and morality is established. During this encounter, the camera first frames Edie and Terry's contest in the foreground with the longshoremen's struggle in the background. When the scramble gives way to moral considerations the camera changes position isolating their conversation and making a special case within the generally demeaning environment. The moral "conscience" which Edie embodies alters the situation. For the scene as a whole the camera presents the viewer with the facts of the story (a sense of viewing a "real" event in the workers' daily lives), the filmmakers' opinion about the story (Mac and his associates have the power; the workers are oppressed and unorganized), and Terry's special relationship to the depicted waterfront conditions. Through camera positioning the scene establishes conflicts to be explored as the film progresses.

To Kazan and Schulberg the discipline within the communist "unit" of the 1930s depended upon similar insults to personal dignity. "The typical Communist scene of crawling and apologizing and admitting the error of my ways," as Kazan described the practice degraded human intelligence, and the film's "shape-up" scene was intended to capture such dehumanization. After Mac throws the last tags on the ground exasperation leads to pushing which eventually leads to chaos. In the film, this central expository scene attempts to highlight the hopelessness and futility of longshoremen in a place "which ain't part of America."

Johnson's portrait of waterfront conditions also contained a model for the film's moral catalyst, Father Barry. As associate director of the St. Xavier School (Manhattan), Rev. John M. Corridan, the "waterfront priest," delivered sermons, held meetings, contributed advice to troubled longshoremen, and exhorted the dock workers to strike and rebel. On the violent New Jersey docks where the film was actually shot. Corridan delivered a virulent attack on union corruption. His sermon, "A Catholic Looks at the Waterfront" was reproduced in Johnson's book:

> You want to know what's wrong with the waterfront? It's love of a buck. . . . Christ also said "If you do it to the least of mine, you do it to me." Christ is in the shape-up. . . . He stands in the shape-up knowing that all won't get work and maybe He won't. . . . Some people think the Crucifixion took place only on Calvary. . . . What does Christ think of the man who picks up a longshoreman's brass check and takes 20 per cent interest at the end of the week? Christ goes to a union meeting . . . [and] sees a few with $150 suits and diamond rings on their fingers.

As his words make clear, Corridan applied the moral teachings of Christ to waterfront unionism, and this unadorned social gospel reinforced the dualism between brutality and innocence which had figured prominently in previous works by Kazan and Schulberg. Because of the familiar set of visual symbols attached to Christian mythology as well as the moral authority and political safety of such a conservative institution, the filmmakers expanded and made essential Father Barry's role in convincing Terry Malloy to testify.

The filmmakers, both former members of the Communist Party, used Father Barry's funeral oration to air their rejuvenated ideology and to challenge silent liberals to speak out against past totalitarian activities. The emotional speech introduces the idea of shared guilt and encourages action to combat and defeat the mobsters. As the shrill accusations resound through the ship's hold, the forces of chaos (the "mugs" who throw cans and tomatoes) are silenced (Malloy punches Tillio on the chin). With the camera searching high overhead to find Friendly and Charley, it is obvious that the power relationships have not changed. But the men begin to realize that their silence only serves their oppressors.

While Father Barry speaks, the shadow of a cross-like form rises on the wall behind him. After the speech Dugan's body ascends from the worker's hell (the lower depths of the ship) accompanied by Father Barry and Pops, two saintly escorts for the workingman's martyr. The men stand with their hats off, unified at least momentarily by this ritual. Whereas the shape-up belittled the workers, this affirmative scene "resurrects" their self-image. The action of the men at the shape-up was downward to the ground; here it is upward toward the sources of oppression.

A "testimonial" session with the Crime Commission, the third ritual scene in the film, completes the film's structural argument. Corruption and human indignity exposed in the shape-up and then condemned over a martyr's body are finally made public before a tribunal which seeks to punish those responsible. In the Commission hearing room mobsters, newspapermen, commissioners, and interested citizens have a designated place in a physically ordered environment where legal processes are conducted in the open for all to see. Unlike the dreary alleys and dingy asylums of waterfront criminals, the brightly lighted and crowded room encourages photographers and reporters to publish what they hear. Investigators doggedly pursue the illegality hidden behind unions without accounting books and without elections. The degraded competition between workers in the shape-up has become a fair and open contest between equal adversaries made possible by a legal system which insures individual rights. Totalitarian irreverence is supplanted by democratic dignity.

5

SCIENCE FICTION AS SOCIAL COMMENTARY

The Age of Conspiracy and Conformity:
Invasion of the Body Snatchers (1956)
Stuart Samuels

The Cold War left its imprint on American culture during the late 1940s and early 1950s. In this essay, Stuart Samuels examines the "paranoid style" that permeated the early Cold War years and found vivid expression in science fiction films.

"If art reflects life, it does so with special mirrors."

Bertolt Brecht

In what way can a seemingly absurd science fiction/horror film, *Invasion of the Body Snatchers,* give us insight into the history and culture of America in the mid-1950s? How is a film about people being taken over by giant seed pods "reflective" of this critical period in our history?

Films relate to ideological positions in two ways. First, they reflect, embody, reveal, mirror, symbolize existing ideologies by reproducing (consciously or unconsciously) the myths, ideas, concepts, beliefs, images of an historical period in both the film content and film form (technique). Secondly, films produce their own ideology, their own unique expression of reality. Films can do this by reinforcing a specific ideology or undercutting it.

All films are therefore ideological and political insomuch as they are determined by the ideology which produces them. Fictional characters are only prototypes of social roles and social attitudes; every film speaks to some norm. Some behaviors are deemed appropriate, others not. Some acts are condemned, others applauded. Certain characters are depicted as heroic, others as cowardly. Film is one of the products, one of the languages, through which the world communicates itself to itself. Films embody beliefs, not by a mystic communion with the national soul, but because they contain the values, fears, myths, assumptions, point of view of the culture in which they are produced.

While films relate to ideology, they also relate to specific historical and social events, most obviously when the content of a film deals directly with a subject that is identifiable in its own period. In the 1950s, for example, such films as *I Was a Communist for the FBI* (1951) and *My Son John* (1952) spoke to a society increasingly concerned with the nature of the internal communist threat. Similarly, in the previous decade such films as *The Best Years of Our Lives* (1946) attempted to analyze some of the problems and confusions of the immediate post-World War II period and *The Snake Pit* (1948) addressed a society trying to deal with the tremendous increase in the hospital treatment of the mentally ill. As far back as Griffith's *Intolerance* (1916), which relayed a pacifist message to a nation struggling to stay out of war, films have reflected society's attempts to come to grips with contemporary problems.

Film "reflects" an agreed-upon perception of social reality, acceptable and appropriate to the society in question. Thus, in the 1950s when a conspiracy theory of politics was a widely accepted way of explaining behavior (being duped), action (being subversive), and effect (conspiracy), one would expect the films of the period to "reflect" this preoccupation with conspiracy. But *Invasion of the Body Snatchers* is not about McCarthyism. It is about giant seed pods taking over people's bodies. Indirectly, however, it is a statement about the collective paranoia and the issue of conformity widely discussed in the period.

The idea for the film came from Walter Wanger, the producer, who had read Jack Finney's novel of the same name in serial form in *Collier's Magazine* in 1955. Wanger suggested the project to his friend Don Siegel, who in turn assigned Daniel Manwaring to produce a screenplay from Finney's book.

The story of the film is contained within a "framing" device—a seemingly insane man, Miles Bennell (Kevin McCarthy), telling a bizarre story to a doctor and a policeman. In flashback we see Bennell's tale—of giant seed pods taking over the minds and bodies of the people of Santa Mira, a small town in California, where Bennell was the local doctor. Returning home after a medical convention, Miles finds the pretty little town and its peaceful inhabitants in the grip of a "mass hysteria." People seem obsessed by the conviction that relatives and friends are not really themselves, that they have been changed. Despite the outward calm of Santa Mira, there is a creeping contagion of fear and paranoia, of wives not knowing their husbands, children fleeing from parents.

Miles's friend Becky (Dana Wynter) struggles against this delusion, tends to dismiss it as improbable, but nevertheless finds her own Uncle Ira slightly changed: "There's no emotion in him. None. Just the pretense of it." The improbable becomes real when Miles's friend Jack calls him to report something fantastic: a semihuman body, without features, has been found on Jack's billiard table. From this point on events move rapidly. The unformed body is clearly growing into an exact duplicate of Jack, and in the greenhouse Miles stumbles upon giant seed pods, each containing a half-formed body. In Becky's basement Miles finds still another embryonic shape—this time a model of Becky herself. Now Miles believes the fantastic stories, and determines to escape and warn the world of this danger.

But escape is not simple. The town of Santa Mira has nearly been taken over by the pods, who while the inhabitants sleep form themselves into precise replicas of human beings—even-tempered, peaceful, but soulless automatons. Miles is terrified and drags Becky from her bedroom, to flee in his auto. But the town has now mobilized against them; the pod-people cannot allow the story to be told, and the "people" of Santa Mira organize to catch Miles and Becky. In a desperate escape attempt, they flee over the mountains, pursued by those who had once been their friends and neighbors.

The horror mounts when, in a tunnel, Becky succumbs to the pods. She falls asleep and soon her mind and body are taken over, cell by cell. In a moment of utmost panic, Miles looks into her eyes and realizes the awful truth. Continuing on alone, he comes to a highway where he makes wild attempts to flag down motorists who are terrified by his insane behavior. Eventually, he is picked up by the police, who naturally consider him mad, and is taken to a hospital for medical examination. The doctors agree that he is psychotic, but then fate intervenes. An intern reports an accident to a truck from Santa Mira, and in a casual aside, he tells how the driver of the wreck had to be dug out from under a pile of strange giant seed pods. The truth dawns on the police inspector, who orders the roads to Santa Mira closed, and in the final shot tells his assistant to "call the FBI."

The political, social, and intellectual atmosphere of the era that created *Invasion* must be understood in light of several preoccupations: the "Red Menace," which crystallized around the activities of Senator Joseph McCarthy and the somewhat less spectacular blacklisting of figures in the communications and entertainment industry, who were seen as a nefarious, subversive element undermining the entire fabric of American society; learning to cope with the consequences of a modern, urban, technologically bureaucratized society; and the pervasive fear of atomic annihilation. All these factors undermined the traditional American myth of individual action. The experience of the Depression, the rise and threat of totalitarianism, the loss of American insularity, the growth of technocracy all in one form or another challenged the integrity of the individual. It is therefore not surprising to note that film genres like science fiction or horror films proliferated in the 1950s. The central themes of these films show a preoccupation with depersonalization and dehumanization. Moreover, as Susan Sontag has suggested, it is by no means coincidental that at a time when the moviegoing public had for over ten years been living under the constant threat of instant atomic annihilation films of the 1950s should be concerned with the confrontation of death. As Sontag expressed it: "We live[d] under continued threat of two equally fearful, but seemingly opposed destinies: unremitting banality and inconceivable terror." On the surface there existed a complacency that disguised a deep fear of violence, but conformity silenced the cries of pain and feelings of fear.

In response to the threats of social banality and universal annihilation, three concepts dominated the decade: (1) conformity, (2) paranoia, (3) alienation. Each concept had its keywords. Conformity: "silent generation," "status seekers," "lonely crowds," "organization men," "end of ideology," "hidden persuaders." Paranoia: "red decade," "dupes," "front organization," "blacklisting," "un-Americanism," "fifth column," "fellow travelers," "pinkos." Alienation: "outsiders," "beats," "loners," "inner-directed men," "rebels." For the most part, the decade celebrated a suburbanized, bureaucratized, complacent, secure, conformist, consensus society in opposition to an alienated, disturbed, chaotic, insecure, individualistic, rebel society. Each of those three concepts dominating the 1950s finds obvious expression in *Invasion of the Body Snatchers*. First—conformity.

During the 1950s a concern for respectability, a need for security and compliance with the system became necessary prerequisites for participation in the reward structure of an increasingly affluent society. Conformism had replaced individuality as the principal ingredient for success. This standard extended to all aspects of life.

Tract-built, identical, tidy little boxlike ranch houses on uniform fifty-foot plots bulldozed to complete flatness were the rage. Conformity dictated city planning in the form of Levittowns, the same way it silenced political dissidents in Congress. Creativity meant do-it-yourself painting-by-numbers. One created great artistic masterpieces by following directions.

The concern with conformity grew out of a need to escape from confusion, fear, worry, tension, and a growing sense of insecurity. It was accentuated by a sense of rootlessness and increased mobility. Consensus mentality offered a refuge in an anxious and confusing world. It represented an attempt to shift the burden of individual responsibility for one's fate to an impersonal monolithic whole. Excessive conformity, as in the 1950s, was a salve to smooth over obvious conflict and turmoil. A country that emerged from war victorious around the globe feared internal subversion at home; a society powered by a new technology and a new structure (corporate bureaucracy) feared a loss of personal identity. In the White House was a person whose great appeal was that he represented a politics of consensus, classlessness, and conformism—Eisenhower.

By the time *Invasion* was released (May, 1956) the intensity of the drive for consensus politics had diminished—the Korean War had ended, McCarthy had been censored, Stalin was dead, the spirit of Geneva had thawed the Cold War, the imminent threat of atomic annihilation had subsided, witch hunting had lost its appeal, and the threat of internal subversion had lessened. But the context of fear was still active. The political reality might not seem as frightening, but the mind-set of the period was always ready at any moment to raise its repressive head. To many people, the fact that the enemy appeared less threatening only meant that he was better at concealing his subversion and that the eternal vigilance of good Americans had to be even more effective.

David Riesman's *The Lonely Crowd* (1955) spoke of a society obsessed by conformity. His now-famous formulation about inner-directed and other-directed men, focuses on the same conflicts outlined by Siegel in *Invasion*. Miles Bennell is "inner directed"—a self-reliant individualist who has internalized adult authority, and judged himself and others by these internalized self-disciplined standards of behavior. The "pods" are "other-directed" beings whose behavior is completely conditioned by the example of their peers. While inner-directed individuals like Miles felt concern and guilt about violating their inner ideals—in fact were driven by them—the other-directed pods had no inner ideals to violate. Their morality came from the compulsion to be in harmony with the crowd. Their guilt developed in direct proportion to how far they deviated from group consensus. The other-directed pods were uncritical conformists. It was no coincidence that the most popular adult drug of the 1950s was not alcohol or aspirin, pot or cocaine—but Miltown and Thorazine—tranquilizers.

The second basic concept in 1950s America, the natural corollary to the drive toward conformity, was the notion of conspiracy. Conformity is based on the idea that there is a clear-cut division between them and us. In periods of overt conflict, like wars or economic crises, the division between the good and the bad is obvious. But in periods of confusion, the identification of enemies becomes more problematic. Covert expressions of subversion are more common than overt challenges; the enemy attacks—whether real or imagined—through subversion and conspiracy rather than war. In the 1950s subversion seemed to be everywhere. Appearances were deceptive; to many, nothing was what it appeared to be. Schools named after American heroes like Jefferson, Lincoln, Walt Whitman, Henry George were rumored to be fronts for communists, calls for free speech were seen as pleas for communism, and racial unrest as being fomented by party activists. To many, taking the Fifth Amendment in order not to incriminate oneself was just another way of disguising one's political treason.

Threats to social order in the 1950s were not so much associated with personal violence as with an indefinable, insidious, fiendishly cold undermining of the normal. Conspiracy theories feed off the idea of the normal being deceptive. In *Invasion,* the pods, the alien invaders, take on the appearance of normal people. It becomes physically impossible to tell the difference between the aliens and the normals. In *Invasion* all forms of normalcy are inverted. Friends are not friends, "Uncle Ira" is not Uncle Ira, the police do not protect, sleep is not revivifying, telephones are no longer a way of calling for help but a device to tell the pod-people where the remaining non-pod-people are. Even the name of the town is paradoxical. Mira in Spanish means "to look," but the people of Santa Mira refuse to look; they stare blankly into the unknown.

A patina of normalcy hides a deep-seated violence. A man holds a giant seed pod and calmly asks his wife, "Shall I put this in with the baby?" "Yes," she replies, "then there'll be no more crying." In another scene, what appears to be a quiet Sunday morning gathering in the town square turns out to be a collection point where fleets of trucks filled with pods quietly dispense these "vegetables" to people who carry them to their cars and buses, ready to spread the invasion to neighboring towns. It is during a typical home barbeque among friends that Miles finds the pods in his greenhouse.

At the end of the film, when all avenues of help seemed closed, Miles and Becky, hiding in an abandoned cave, hear sweet, loving music—a Brahms lullaby. Miles decides that such beauty and feeling could not possibly be the singing of unemotional pods. He scrambles off to find out where this music is coming from— only to discover that its source is a radio in a large truck being loaded by robotlike people with seed pods destined for far-off towns. The familiar is fraught with danger. It is no wonder that Miles comes to the edge of madness, no wonder that he treats people with a paranoid suspicion. Paranoia becomes the logical alternative to podlike conformism.

Finally, conformism and conspiracy signaled a new age of personal alienation. From the very beginning of our history, one of the most persistent myths about American society has been the myth of natural harmony. The idea is derived from the notion made popular by Adam Smith and John Locke that there is a natural and harmonious relationship between the desires of individuals and the demands of social necessity, that individuals who act out of self-interest will automatically move the society as a whole in the direction of natural perfection. At the heart of this notion was the belief that nothing in the system prevented people from achieving their own individual goals, and that the traditional barriers of class, religion, and geography were absent in the American experience. The concept of natural harmony is further based on the belief of abundance. Individual failure had to be due to personal shortcomings because a society of abundance offered opportunity to anyone capable of grasping it—conflict was not built into the system. People were basically good. Solutions were always within grasp. Control was inevitable. Progress was assured.

This underlying belief in natural harmony was one of the casualties of the post-1945 world. In the 1930s American films had portrayed people ordering their environment. "The people," the Mr. Smiths, the Mr. Deeds, the Shirley Temples, and the Andy Hardys saw to it that control and harmony were restored. Individual "good acts" reinforced "social good" in the desire to control life. In the 1940s the theme of conquest, control, and restoration of the natural was the underlining statement of war films. Commitments to courage, self-sacrifice, and heroism were shown instead of Senate filibusters, talks with Judge Hardy, or faith in "the people." Depictions of failure, helplessness, and feelings of inadequacy were introduced as muted themes in the postwar films. Although we had won the war, conquered the Depression, and tamed nature by splitting the atom, things seemed out of control in the 1950s as conflict emerged between the desire for personal autonomy and the pressures for collective conformity. Individual acts of heroism were suspect. Group work and group think were the ideals. Success was measured by how much individuals submerged themselves into some larger mass (society, bureaucracy) over which they had little individual control. The rewards of status, popularity, and acceptance came with conformity to the group. In the films of the period, people who did not sacrifice individual desires for general social needs were fated to die, commit suicide, be outcast, or simply go mad.

Popular books like Riesman's *The Lonely Crowd,* William Whyte's *The Organization Man,* and Vance Packard's *The Status Seekers* showed how the traditional model of the hardworking, rugged individualist was being rejected for a world of the group—big universities, big suburbs, big business, and big media. Such harmony as existed resulted from the artificial ordering to an agreed upon surface norm. After the scarcity of the Depression came the affluence of the 1950s—complete with its never-ending routine of conspicuous consumption. Out of the victory for democracy and freedom came a society more standardized, less free, more conformist, and less personal. Out of splitting the atom came the threat of instant annihilation.

The mid-1950s films portrayed people trying desperately to ward off failure in the face of overwhelming destructive forces of nature (horror films), technology (science fiction films), and human imperfection (film noir). There were films about people being taken over or reincarnated: *The Search for Bridie Murphy* (1956), *I've Lived Before* (1956), *Back from the Dead* (1957), *The Undead* (1957), *Vertigo* (1956), *Donovan's Brain* (1953); about individuals in conflict with their societies: *High Noon* (1952), *The Phenix City Story* (1955), *No Place to Hide* (1956), *Not of this Earth* (1957); about superior forces beyond man's control: *Them* (1954), *Tarantula* (1956), *The Beast from 20,000 Fathoms* (1953), *This Island Earth* (1955), *Earth versus the Flying Saucers* (1956); about the apocalypse: *20,000 Leagues Under the Sea* (1954), *On the Beach* (1959), *The Thing* (1951). In these films, the world seemed menacing, fluid, chaotic, impersonal, composed of forces which one seldom understood, and certainly never controlled. Fear is centered on the unknown, unseen terrors that lurk beneath the surface normality.

Invasion's podism is depicted as a malignant evil, as a state of mind where there is no feeling, no free will, no moral choice, no anger, no tears, no passion, no emotion. Human sensibility is dead. The only instinct left is the instinct to survive. Podism meant being "reborn into an untroubled world, where everyone's the same." "There is no need for love or emotion. Love, ambition, desire, faith—without them, life is so simple." A metaphor for communism? Perhaps! But, more directly, podism spoke to a society becoming more massified, more technological, more standardized.

The motto of the pods was "no more love, no more beauty, no more pain." Emotionless, impersonal, regimented, they became technological monsters. But they were not the irrational creatures of blood lust and power—they were just nonhuman. They became tranquil and obedient. They spoke to the fear of the 1950s—not the fear of violence, but the fear of losing one's humanity. As Susan Sontag argued, "the dark secret behind human nature used to be the upsurge of the animal—as in *King Kong* (1933). The threat to man, his availability to dehumanization, lay in his own animality. Now the danger is understood to reside in man's ability to be turned into a machine." The body is preserved, but the person is entirely reconstituted as the automated replica of an "alien" power.

The attraction of becoming a pod in the 1950s was all too real. But although dangling the carrot of conformity, *Invasion* opts ultimately for the stick of painful individuality. The possibility of moral uncertainty was the price we must pay for continued freedom. As Miles says: "Only when we have to fight to stay human do we realize how precious our humanity is." Podism, an existence without pain or fear or emotion, is seen as no existence at all. The fear of man becoming a machinelike organism, losing his humanity, was centered around the ambiguous dual legacy of an increasingly technological civilization. The atomic bomb was both a testament to man's increased control over his universe and a clear symbol of man's fallibility. *Invasion* mirrors this duality. It praises the possibility of a society without pain, yet it raises the spectre of a society without feeling. Security at what price?—the price of freedom and individualism. The rise of technology at what costs?—the cost of humanness itself. Although *Invasion* is ambiguous on this issue, demonstrating the positive effects of "podism" at the same time as condemning its consequences, this confusion, this ambiguity, is very much at the heart of the American cultural issues of the period—the internal conflict between the urge for conformity and the painful need for individuality, between an antiheroic loner and an institutionalized, bureaucratized system of mindless automated pods.

In his struggle to remain his own master, Miles fights against control by first falling back on the traditional notions inherited from the past. He appeals to friends—only to be betrayed. He appeals to the law—only to be pursued by it. He appeals to the system—only to be trapped by it. He appeals to love—only to be disappointed by losing it. All betray him. All become his enemy. Not because they are corrupt, or evil, but because they have become pods, because they have given up their individuality, their ability to choose.

If there is a 1950s vision of historical reality in *Invasion,* there is also a system of film technique designed to reinforce this vision. The language and technique of *Invasion* come out of the social reality of the period and speak directly to that context.

One of the major themes of life in the 1950s was the feeling of constraint—people feeling enclosed within boundaries. People were cut off from options, limited in their choices. There was a closing down of dissent, a shrinking of personal freedom. Silence became the acceptable response to oppression.

Invasion is a film about constraints. It is the story of a man whose ability to make sense of the world decreases and diminishes to the point of madness and frenzy. The film's action takes place within enclosed physical spaces and the physical spaces in the film induce a sense of isolation and constraint. The sleepy California town of Santa Mira is surrounded by hills. When Miles tries to escape he must run up a series of ladderlike stairs to flee the pod-people and reach the open highway that separates the town from the outside world. Miles and Becky are constantly running—in and out of small rooms, darkened cellars illuminated only by matches, large but empty nightclubs, miniature greenhouses, closets, low-ceilinged dens abandoned caves. The giant seed pods are found in basements, closets, car trunks, greenhouses. The main actors are claustrophobically framed by doorways and windows photographed from low angles, and spend much of their time running down and up endless stairs, into locked doors, and beneath towering trees. The narrative structure of *Invasion* resembles a series of self-contained Chinese boxes and is designed to tighten the tension of the story at every step. Though Miles returns from his convention on a sunny morning and the film ends in a confused mixture of daylight and darkness, the main section of the film takes place in darkness—at night.

The whole film is enclosed within a framing device of prologue and epilogue. Siegel's original version had not included this frame, but the addition of a prologue and epilogue, making the film narrative appear as an extended flashback, has the unintended effect of constricting the narrative—itself contained in a rigidly enclosed time frame—even further. Within this framing device, Siegel also uses the technique of repeating a situation at the end of the film that mirrors a sequence presented at the beginning. In the final flashback episode, Siegel has Miles running in panic down the road and being pursued by a whole town of pod-people. This scene mirrors the opening scene when we see little Jimmy Grimaldi running down the road being pursued by his "podized" mother.

The effect of these devices is to keep the narrative tight in order to heighten tension and suspense. The use of flashback, prologue and epilogue, repeated scenes, interplay of lightness and darkness, all keep the narrative constrained within a carefully defined filmic space. The unbelievable tension is released only in the epilogue, when Miles finally finds someone who believes his story. The ending is not about the FBI's ability to counteract the threat of the pods but about the fact that Miles has finally made contact with another human—and that he is not alone. The film is more about being an alien, an outsider, an individualist, than about the "invasion" by aliens. When Dr. Bassett and his staff finally believe Miles's story, the enclosing ring of constraint is broken, and Miles collapses, relaxing for the first time in the film, knowing that at least he has been saved from a horror worse than death—the loss of identity. The final line—"Call the F.B.I."—is the signal that he is not alone and acts as an affirmative answer to the shout heard at the opening of the film—"I'm not insane." Up to the point when the doctor finally believes Miles's story, the film is actually about a man going insane.

Time is also a constant constraint on humanity, and Siegel emphasizes the fact that time is running out for Miles. The whole film is not only a race against madness, but also against time—of time slipping away. Time in *Invasion* is circumscribed by the fact that sleep is a danger. Miles needs to escape Santa Mira before he falls asleep. He takes pills, splashes his and Becky's face in a constant battle to stay awake. Sleep is not comfort and safety but the instrument of death.

Siegel uses a whole arsenal of filmic techniques to reinforce the feelings of enclosure, isolation, and time running out. His shot set-ups focus on isolated action. People are photographed in isolation standing beneath street lamps, in doorways, alone at crowded railway stations. A background of black velvet darkness and a direct artificial light are used to highlight objects which in isolation take on an "evil clarity." In the film, objects are always illuminated, people's faces are not. Shadows dominate people's space and obscure personality. Diagonal and horizontal lines pierce bodies.

Darkness is combined with a landscape of enclosure to increase the feeling of fear. There is a stressed relationship between darkness and danger, light and safety. Those who wish to remain free of the pods must not only keep awake, but must constantly keep themselves in direct light. For example, when Miles discovers Becky's pod-like double in the basement of her home, he hurries upstairs into her darkened bedroom and carries her out of the dark house into his car which is parked directly beneath a bright street lamp.

Tension in the film is not only created by lighting techniques and camera set-ups, but most significantly by the contrast in how the actors play their roles. Miles is frenzied, harried, hard-driving, always running. The robot-like, affectless pod people stare out at the camera with vacant eyes, openly unemotional, unbelievably calm, rational, logical. They appear to be normal, and Miles appears to be insane; however, the reverse is true. The pods' blank expression, emotionless eyes mask their essential nature.

The whole film texture is based on the internal contrast between normal and alien. The hot dog stands, used-car lots, small office buildings, friendly cops, sleepy town square, and neighborhood gas stations only create the illusion of normalcy played against mounting terror.

The mise-en-scène, lighting, acting styles, physical presence, props, and Carmen Dragon's unrelenting, spine-chilling musical score keep the audience in a constant state of tension. The same is true of the constant introjection of siren sounds, cuckoo clocks, screams in the middle of the night, and the use of distorting lenses, claustrophobic close-ups, juxtaposed long shots, and low-angled shots that establish a mood of vague disquiet. All help to create a basic tension between the normal and the fearful, the familiar and the sinister, and to result in a film designed to give the audience a sense of isolation, suspense, and feeling of constraint.

Historians will debate the actual nature of the 1950s for a long time. But through the films of a period we can see how a particular society treated the period, viewed it, experienced it, and symbolized it. Few products reveal so sharply as the science fiction/horror films of the 1950s the wishes, the hopes, the fears, the inner stresses and tensions of the period. Directly or indirectly, *Invasion* deals with the fear of annhilation brought on by the existence of the A-bomb, the pervasive feeling of paranoia engendered by an increasing sense that something was wrong, an increasing fear of dehumanization focused around an increased massification of

American life, a deepseated expression of social, sexual, and political frustration resulting from an ever-widening gap between personal expectation and social reality, and a widespread push for conformity as an acceptable strategy to deal with the confusion and growing insecurity of the period. It is a film that can be used by historians, sociologists, and psychologists to delineate these problems and demonstrate the way American society experienced and symbolized this crucial decade.

6

THE WESTERN AS COLD WAR FILM

Gunfighters and Green Berets:
The Magnificent Seven and the Myth of Counter-Insurgency
Richard Slotkin

One of America's most significant contributions to film, the Western has long been one of the most popular and influential film genres. In this essay, Richard Slotkin analyzes the political ideologies that Westerns expressed during the Cold War era.

In this study, I want to account for the Western's special role in the culture of the American 1950s and '60s, and to interpret the genre's effect on ideological discourse, by looking closely at a single film, John Sturges' *The Magnificent Seven* (1960). The film was an epic rendition of the traditional "gunfighter" Western, but it was also a seminal film of the new subgenre of "Mexico Westerns"—and although it predates our military intervention, it was also in many respects the first "Vietnam Western." Before we can interpret the special uses to which Sturges put the language of the genre, however, we need to review the genre's history and its relation to the development of American myth and ideology.

Myths are stories drawn from a society's history, which have acquired through persistent usage the power of symbolizing that society's ideology and dramatizing its moral consciousness, with all of the complexities and contradictions that consciousness may contain. Mythic versions of history transform accepted "facts" into ideological imperatives for belief and action. The myths of Custer's Last Stand, the Alamo, and Pearl Harbor are all based on historical events, but we use them as symbols and metaphors, interpreting crises different in character and time according to these mythic models, and deriving from the models sanctioned scenarios of political response.

The Myth of the Frontier is one of our oldest myths, expressed in a body of literature, folklore, ritual, historiography and polemics produced over a period of three centuries. Its symbols and concerns shaped the most prevalent genres of both nineteenth-century literary fiction and twentieth-century movies. The myth celebrates the conquest and subjugation of a natural wilderness by entrepreneurial individualists, who took heroic risks and so achieved windfall profits and explosive growth at prodigious speeds.

Violence is central to both the historical development of the frontier and its mythic representation. The Anglo-American colonies grew by displacing Amerindian societies and enslaving Africans to advance the fortunes of white colonists. As a result, the Indian war became a characteristic episode of each phase of westward expansion; the conflict of cultural and racial antagonists became the central dramatic structure of the Frontier Myth, providing the symbolic reference points for describing and evaluating other kinds of conflict, such as those between different generation or classes of settlers.

In the myth, both material and moral progress depend on success in violent enterprises. Conquest of the natural wilderness makes Americans "better off," but the struggle against the Indians and over the analogous classes of "savages" within civil society makes the American a "better man." The moral problem, and its triumphant solution, is embodied in the Frontier's mythic heroes: the scouts and Indian fighters of popular history and literature, "living legends" like Daniel Boone and literary myths like James Fenimore Cooper's Hawkeye. Their fables teach the necessity of racial solidarity against a common enemy, which cements a social compact that is otherwise imperiled by the ideology of self-interest. These figures stand on the border between savagery and civilization; they are "the men who know Indians," and in many ways their values and habits of thought mirror those of the savage enemy. Because of this mirroring effect, the moral warfare of savagery and civilization is, for the heroes, a spiritual or psychological struggle, which they win by learning to discipline or suppress the savage or "dark" side of their own human nature. Thus they are mediators of a double kind, who can teach civilized men how to defeat savagery on its native grounds: the natural wilderness, and the wilderness of the human soul.

By the time movie-makers took up the subject, the West—as the Frontier—had already become a thoroughly mythologized space, defined by an elaborate system of cultural illusions and ideological formulae. In 1903, when Porter's *The Great Train Robbery* became the first Western and the pattern-setter for the development of narrative cinema, the Myth of the Frontier had become the dominant formula of American historiography and geopolitics. Frederick Jackson Turner's "Frontier Hypothesis" explained all of American history as the consequence of frontier experiences; Theodore Roosevelt, the philosopher John Fiske, and the Social Darwinist spokesmen for Manifest Destiny extended the metaphor into a model of world race history and used it to justify America's assumption of world power.

From 1903 to 1929 the silent Western developed distinctive generic patterns in its handling of Frontier stories. This development was interrupted by the advent of sound and the Depression; beginning in 1931 the genre went into a nine-year eclipse, during which few feature-length Westerns were produced. But in 1939 the Western experienced a "renaissance," which inaugurated a 30-year period in which Westerns were the most consistently popular form of action movie, with both audiences and producers, in the theater and in the new medium of television. These Westerns were resolutely "historical" in their references, and they succeeded in establishing a powerful association between the imagery of the West and the idea of a heroic age of American progressive enterprise. The pastoral and wilderness imagery of the Western invested these fables of power and achievement with an aura of natural innocence. The narrative structure of the Western story, however, insisted that whatever the nominal historical setting, violence was the necessary and justified determinant of the outcome. Every variety of Western has its characteristic form of violent resolution: the cavalry Western has its Indian massacre or charge into battle, the gunfighter or town-tamer movie has its climactic shoot-out in the street, the outlaw movie has its disastrous last robbery or assassination, the romantic Western has its bullet-riddled rescue scene. Moreover, because the Western has been seen as a representation of American history, the genre's insistence on the necessity of violence amounts to a statement about the nature of history and of politics.

By the Korean War, the symbolic language of the Western had been developed by its practitioners to a level of high sophistication and formal economy. Narrative formulae and characterizations were so well understood as to constitute a kind of media folklore; and in this form they invited all sorts of virtuosi and allegorical play with forbidden or difficult subjects: coexistence, civil rights, homosexuality, psychoanalysis. But because the genre's material had been so heavily encoded as referring to history and politics, this artistic play was actually quite serious as both a reflection and an influence on the ideologies of Cold War liberalism and conservatism in the years preceding the Vietnam War.

One of the most important subgenres of the Western had been the so-called "Cult of the Outlaw," derived from Henry King's epic version of Jesse James in 1939. These films had taken a Depression era view of the outlaw as social bandit, rooting his outlawry in an experience of social oppression at the hands of corporate tyrants (railroads) or military despots (Reconstruction officers). Outlaw Westerns embodied the most explicitly populist reading of the West, and functioned as vehicles for social and political criticism.

Starting in 1950, however, with Henry King's *The Gunfighter,* the outlaw character was reduced to the simple elements of his screen persona: his loneliness and alienation, his living outside the law, and his skill with a gun. In place of the elaborately narrated social motives of outlawry, the gunfighter appeared as a man almost entirely lacking in a past, or in the social motives that drove the outlaw. This tendency reached its most extreme development in Clint Eastwood's Westerns of the early '70s, in which the hero is so abstracted from history of any kind that he is called "The Man with No Name."

The ideological significance of the shift from outlaw to gunfighter can be seen in the contrast between King's *Jesse James* and George Stevens' *Shane* (1953). King's movie spends most of its narrative describing and analyzing the outlaw's response to oppression and injustice; and relates these concerns to the life of the outlaw's community, showing how Jesse emerges from the heart of that community, serves it, then goes too far and is cast out of it. The hero of *Shane* is also a skilled fighter who assists small farmers against a tyrannical proprietor. But Shane arrives from outside, and his past is concealed. His style, manners and speech mark him as an aristocrat of some kind, and the deference with which he is treated is due to both his air of refinement and his skill with a gun. He is the only character in the movie who never acts (or hesitates to act) from self-interested motives. But because Shane's motives for helping the farmers are unique, and arise from no visible history or social background, they appear to be expressions of his nature, signs of a chivalric nobility which is independent of history, like the attributes of a "higher race." Shane is never part of the community, and his superior values are not seen as belonging to that community. He is an aristocrat of violence, an alien from a more glamorous world, who is better than those he helps and is not accountable to those for whom he sacrifices himself.

Shane's popularity was exploited in a wave of Westerns that developed the figure of the gunfighter as chivalric rescuer. In order to get new stories out of well-used material, these films queried the romantic idealism of Shane, played variations on the opposition of economic and chivalric motives for violence, and raised new issues out of the original problem of the hero's proper elation to the erotic life and the cash nexus. A more naturalistic version of the gunfighter appeared, in which the hero begins as a mercenary professional, and experiences a kind of "conversion" to the chivalric ideal in the course of the action. The means to this conversion is usually the love of a woman who promises both the fulfillment of romantic desire and reconciliation with a social code that demands self-sacrifice. One of the earliest and most spectacular exercises in this vein was also the first of the "Mexico Westerns," *Vera Cruz* (1954), directed by Robert Aldrich and starring Burt Lancaster and Gary Cooper. The film drew criticism for its lavish and humorous display of cynical and self-interested motives in both hero and heavy. But its strong association of heroic competence with mercenary pragmatism set the pattern for future "adult" Western. . . .

Which brings us to *The Magnificent Seven,* which tells the story of a group of American gunfighters—professionals and technicians of violence, rugged individualists all—who go into Mexico to aid a peasant village against a predatory warlord or bandit who controls their region. Before Kennedy took office, before the Special Forces landed in Saigon, movie-makers had begun to imaginatively explore and test out the mythological and ideological premises that lay behind the counterinsurgency of the New Frontier. The movie is a complex reflecting mechanism, not simply a device for propagating Cold War values. By combining the political concerns of the new Cold War with the traditional terms of the Western, *Magnificent Seven* frames a vision which on the one hand rationalizes and justifies counter-insurgency, but which also exposes the contradictions and weaknesses of that ideology, and the military practices the policy begot.

John Sturges' *The Magnificent Seven* was released several months before Kennedy's inauguration, and had begun production long before the 1960 presidential campaign. Obviously, we are not dealing with a case of direct influence (unless the film influenced the President). Rather, film and President share a common set of ideological premises, a common mythology, and a common conception of heroic style.

Sturges' film was officially an American remake of Akira Kurosawa's *Seven Samurai*—a film which itself owed a great deal to American Westerns, and which had enjoyed both commercial success and critical prestige during its run in the States. *The Magnificent Seven* was successful in ways that go beyond its considerable box office: it became the basis of imitation and a rich source of popular icons. The musical score by Elmer Bernstein became the Marlboro cigarette theme-song, and thus part of one of the major advertising triumphs of the era, which ended by identifying the whole West as "Marlboro country." Yul Brynner and Eli Wallach revived and redirected their flagging careers from the film's success. Supporting player Steve McQueen emerged immediately as a major star, to be followed by others of the Seven: Horst Buchholz, James Coburn, Robert Vaughn and Charles Bronson. Several sequels and innumerable imitations of the film have been made in both Europe and the United States over the last 25 years, in the combat and science fiction genres as well as the Western, many starring one or more of the original players.

A poor Mexican village is being raided and tyrannized by Calvera (Wallach), a brutal and complex villain who acts like a bandit, but speaks the language of paternal authority—"I am a father to these men; they depend on me"—to justify his rape of the village. Driven at last to resist, the villagers send a delegation to the United States to buy guns, but they discover that in the US, guns are expensive while "men are cheap." Apparently the end of the wild west phase of the frontier has thrown a lot of gunfighters into unemployment. The peasants show their amenability to modernization by the speed with which they learn to think like capitalists, and take advantage of the situation. They decide to hire an American mercenary.

The peasants' decision is aided by a moral drama to which they are an audience. The town drunk has died—an Indian named "Old Sam"—and the town's bigots will not let him be buried in Boot Hill. True to the canons of the outlaw and the Indian-centered Westerns of the '40s and early '50s, the film invokes a kind of pastoral nostalgia as the basis for a critique of American social hypocrisy. But the scene also invokes current history, specifically the civil rights battles of the previous five years, some of which concerned the integration of southern military graveyards.

At this point two gunfighters step forward, drive the hearse to the cemetery, stand off the bullies, and bury the Indian. These are Chris and Vin (Brynner and McQueen)—Chris is a solemn, blackclad figure, Vin a laid-back, easy man with a Mark Twain style, full of folk-sayings, irony and tall tales. It is not clear why they do it; not a word is said about integration or racism, nor do they accept money, though both are out of funds. It appears that the sight of injustice, and of an important job undone, is more than they can resist: ask not what your country can do for you, but what you can do for your country.

Old Sam's funeral highlights the central importance of racial imagery in the adaptation of Kurosawa's film to American and Western-movie terms. *Seven Samurai*'s narrative counterpoints two kinds of conflict: the tactical struggle of the samurai to save the peasants from the bandits, and the class conflict between the values and practices of the fading military aristocracy and the peasantry. The ideological tradition of the Frontier Myth, even in its most sophisticated historiographical formulations, had always insisted on American exceptionalism and our exemptions from the class conflicts of the Old World. The gestures toward the mythic representation of class conflicts made during the Depression were very tentative; even in the "outlaw" Westerns of 1939–50, the oppressed farmers are seen as a mistreated interest group rather than a peasantry. Now, in 1960, the only way the American producers can imagine American engagement with the issues of class raised by *Seven Samurai* is to identify class with race, and project the conflict beyond the borders, into the Third World.

The contrasting motives that impel gunfighters and peasants are presented as the signs of both class and racial difference. The peasants try to persuade Chris to help them by using a naive and inconsistent mixture of crass materialism ("We can pay you well") and a sentimental appeal to his sympathies. In fact, the money they offer is inadequate by Chris' professional and American standards, and Chris has already demonstrated his contempt for mere sentiment by dismissing the effusive praise an eastern "drummer" offers for his burial of Old Sam. The American's moral choices are determined by a mix of motives more complex and "sophisticated" than the Mexican peasants can imagine. Accessibility to the appeal of human sympathy and the needs of the weak is balanced and offset by the hard-headed materialism and tactical pragmatism of the mercenary, and the pride of the professional man of arms, for whom violence is a calling, a discipline and an art. What tips Chris' balance is his discovery that the little bag of coins and the gold watch the Mexicans offer are their sole possessions. He squares his chivalric sympathies with professional hard-headedness by saying, "I have been offered a lot for my services before, but never everything."

Chris then recruits six other gunfighters, through an elaborate series of tests and rituals. The narrative thus makes clear that the force that must aid the Mexicans is an elite one, carefully chosen by means that are technically and morally sophisticated. But the group which is put together is designed to emphasize the range and variety of skills and motives that compose such a killer elite. The common denominator is tough-mindedness and professionalism; the test for this is adherence to the formulas of self-interest. The good work of saving the Third World is not to be undertaken in the sentimental or idealistic spirit of romantic missionaries; it is to be firmly based in realism and a sense of self-interest, the implication being that pure idealism is too rare and perishable a quality to sustain a long twilight struggle.

There is only one pure mercenary in the crowd, however—Chris' oldest friend, Harry, who refuses to believe that there is not some hidden treasure Chris is angling for. For the rest, professionalism (as an ideal and a social status) weighs equally with cash values: Vin joins up because he is out of money, and must choose between killing for low wages or clerking in a store—"good, steady work," one of the Mexicans tells him. But Vin despises that kind of work, and the loss of status and dignity that it suggests, and he paradoxically demonstrates his contempt for the Mexican's values by immediately enlisting in the villagers' cause. The maintenance of professional status outweighs the peasant (actually, the bourgeois) considerations of cash value and security.

From the first, then, we see that the differences between Mexicans and Americans have both a racial and a class aspect: the Americans are a white aristocracy or elite, whose caste-mark is their capacity for effective violence; the Mexicans are non-white peasants, technologically and militarily incompetent. Professionalism is thus a metonymy of the class and ethnic superiority of Americans to Mexicans. As more gunfighters are recruited, this definition is developed and extended. The most professional of the crew, Reb (James Coburn), is like a Zen master gunfighter; he joins because he sees an occasion to test himself and exercise his skills, and this compensates for the low pay—professionalism here is a form of religious discipline or calling. Lee (Robert Vaughan) is the neurotic gunfighter, who joins up to get away from his past, and from the vengeful Johnson brothers—professionalism is the last virtue of a failure, the last strength of the psychically damaged. The youngest and least competent of the gunfighters, Chico or "The Kid" (Horst Buchholz), is a child of Mexican peons (who may have been killed by bandits or gringo gunfighters), who wants desperately to be one of the elite—professionalism is the means to Americanization, higher status, self-transformation. This theme is emphasized by the role of Bernardo Riley (Bronson), the child of a Mexican mother and an Irish father, whose identity is split between pride in his status as American killer-professional, and nostalgia for the maternal and familial values represented by Mexico.

In these seven, Sturges gives us a sampling of the major types of gunfighter developed by the movies in the preceding decade: the wild kid, the crazed neurotic, the aristocratic loner, the folksy populist, the ethnic outsider seeking acceptance. By multiplying heroes in this way, Sturges enlarges a form that had canonically focused on the single gunfighter. He gives us a platoon of lonely men, whose motives map the range of heroic motives, and even take in a range of ethnic possibilities: Reb is a Southerner, Chris a Cajun, Riley is Irish and Mexican, Chico is Mexican. In effect, Sturges has merged the conventions of the Western and the combat movie—the adventure of the lonely man blends with the adventure of the representative platoon. Although these men are gunfighters, the form of their recruitment and association suggests that they are also commandos, or Green Berets.

Once in the village, the gunfighters begin to train the Mexicans in self-defense. As in the combat film, there is comic contrast between the incompetence and innocence of the peons (recruits) and the expertise and professionalism of the gunfighters (sergeants). There is also ethnic tension and mutual suspicion: the farmers hide their wives and daughters, and otherwise show their distrust, until action proves the worth of the gunfighters. Likewise, the gunfighters maintain a professional reserve; they will help only as long as the peasants keep their bargain and obey orders. They keep reminding themselves that it is a canon of their professional code not to get emotionally involved with their work. Each party modifies the other, however. Association with the tribal life of the village softens the gunfighters, specifically by evoking paternal feelings. The key figure here is Riley, who becomes a father-figure to a group of children, and who will be killed at the end because of that. For Riley, acceptance of the children means accepting the part of himself that is Mexican, but he does this in a style that affirms his own higher paternalism—the paternalism of violence—even while he denies it. When the children ask to go with him, because they despise the cowardice of their peasant fathers, Riley spanks them, and orders them to believe that their fathers are not cowards because they cannot fight, that it takes more courage to be a good father and breadwinner than to be a gunfighter.

This nominal ideology, however, is undercut by the film's entire structure, which shows frame by frame that the gunfighter is both technically and morally superior to the farmer. This clash of nominal and actual ideology is brought to full articulation in a scene late in the film, in which the gunfighters, questioned by Chico, voice their code in a formal chorus. The gunfighters begin to get sentimental about the village and its families; lonely technocrats dreaming of a lost pastoral. But Chico breaks into the mood, reminding them that "you owe everything to the gun—no false pastoral for Chico, he knows the dark side of peon life all too well. Chico's question provokes the gunfighters to think things over, and each answers him in turn, at first emphasizing the emptiness of their life—"Home? None. Wife? None.

Kids? None." Then Chris and the others chime in, and the balance shifts towards the pride and power of their calling—"Places tied down to? None. Men you step aside for? None." Although the passage is meant to underline the ideological premise that the solid family life and working-class virtues of the Mexicans are morally superior to gunfighting, it becomes a paean to rugged individualism. The audience's emotional response is voiced by Chico, the peon who would be a gunfighter: "This is the kind of arithmetic I like!"

Thus the film's visual and stylistic apparatus valorize the gunfighter ethic of violence, mobility and individualism at the expense of the farmer-values, the peon-values. The gunfighters are "good paternalists," whose order conforms to the Camelot slogan, which described the ideal world order as one in which "the strong are just, and the weak are protected." But the movie is consciously ironic in its deployment of this chivalric/paternalistic structure, because the most eloquent spokesman in the movie for paternalistic ideology, the most eloquent sloganeer for the party of order, is none other than Calvera the bandit.

The characterization of Calvera is very different from Kurosawa's bandit chief. The latter is virtually an abstraction of evil ferocity; Calvera has complexity and irony, and sardonic humor of a kind that has great appeal on the screen. There is even a kind of perverse innocence in his belief that all men, and especially all thieves and professional mercenaries, can be trusted to act on a rational calculation of self-interest. When he first arrives to rape the village, he says he must do so because he is "a father to his men," who depend on him; and he praises the village for its old-fashioned piety and hard work. He has a mouth full of cynical proverbs: "If God did not mean them to be sheared, he would not have made them sheep."

He is more than a simple bandit, then. The movie's imagery links him to figures like Villa and Zapata, who (in their movie biographies) are transformed from horse-back bandits to social revolutionaries. If Calvera looks like Villa or Zapata, he talks like Porfirio Diaz or General Huerta, cynically mouthing paternalistic slogans and religious pieties while he "taxes" the village. Clearly he is more accurately described as a "warlord" than as a bandit, but since we cannot limit Calvera's type specifically to either the revolutionary left or the patriarchal right, he becomes an abstraction of the tyrannical potential inherent in the "extremes." This paradoxical combination makes Calvera the perfect enemy: the enemy counterinsurgency always sought and never found, the enemy who is native, but more hated by the people than the alien Americans, who represents simultaneously the principle of excessive order (tyranny) and excessive disorder (banditry, revolution), who embodies two "extremes," leaving the center to the Americans.

Calvera is a savage parody of paternalism, but as such, he also offers a critique—implied and stated—of the character and motives of the Americans. Like them, he is a professional, which is to say a man whose actions are motivated by pure pragmatism, self-interest and an advanced understanding of weapons and tactics. This parallel is perceived by every Mexican, from Calvera to Chico to the townspeople themselves. When Calvera appeals to the understanding of self-interest and pragmatism common to all professionals, he expects the Seven to understand, and is mystified when they persist in acting "unprofessionally." "We are in the same business," Calvera says. They are thieves—why do they pretend to be policemen?

The parallel becomes sharper as the plot moves toward its crisis. After Calvera's first attack is repulsed, the villagers realize that they will have to fight to the death against the outraged bandit. A party of appeasement arises, and Chris suppresses it by demanding that the peasants choose now between fighting and surrender. He holds a kind of false plebiscite right there in Sotero's bar; and when those present (some of whom are intimidated by his glare) choose to fight, he tells them that they are now committed, and if anyone backs off or tries to get out of it, Chris will shoot him. Chris deals with Sotero and the Mexican fathers as Riley deals with the children: he "spanks" and disciplines them coercively, replacing their authority with his own in everything but name; he asserts that this paternalistic coercion will make them free and independent adult men.

The paradox in Chris's response to Sotero mirrors the contradiction on which the Green Beret approach to counter-insurgency foundered. At the center of the counter-insurgency ideology was the assumption of American superiority, not merely at the level of technology and technique, but at the level of political culture, consciousness and commitment. According to Cable's study, between 1956 and 1962 American counter-insurgency doctrine held that "the organic and unsponsored insurgency was not a viable possibility." It was "the American political shibboleth that insurgency could not be organic," but must absolutely depend upon an external sponsor," not only for the material of war, but for political will, for the motivation that initiates and sustains purposeful political action over a period of years and decades.

This belief blinded policy-makers not only to the political character of the North Vietnamese regime, but also to the existence of an indigenous political culture in the South. If the native political culture was null, it followed that the American task would be to supply something in the place of nothing: to inscribe the forms of national organization on the "blank slate" of a pre-nationalist culture. Like Fenimore Cooper's Hawkeye, the Green Beret "knows Indians" and mirrors their qualities, but his mission (after all) is not to vindicate and protect their culture, but to discredit, transform, and replace it with a "more civilized" model. Thus the various programs of "reform" and "nation-building" tended to become programs of Americanization. Since there was in fact a strong and intractable political culture in Vietnam, however, Americanization of the war served only to alienate the people it was intended to protect, and to allow the Communists to identify themselves with the defense of the indigenous culture.

At the moment when Chris asserts his dominance, the narrative of *Magnificent Seven* departs radically from the plot of Kurosawa's *Seven Samurai*. The samurai and villagers achieve a kind of comradeship, and their solidarity is never broken. But the gunfighters dictate to the villagers; and the villagers betray the Seven to Calvera. For at least some in the village, Chris and Calvera are morally equivalent, and Calvera is in some ways preferable—or at least, he seems the more powerful and inescapable of the two. This moral equivalency is voiced again by Calvera, who says that "A thief who robs from a thief is pardoned for a thousand years . . . I pardon you." He allows them to live, and returns their guns to them, in return for their promise to leave Mexico. His reasons are thoroughly professional—he recognizes that the Seven probably have friends in the States who would avenge them. Calvera doesn't want gringo trouble; he's won his point, proven the enterprise futile. He expects men of similar professional expertise to recognize the facts and bow to them in a rational and disinterested spirit.

Calvera's version of a "Geneva settlement" offers the gunfighters peace at the expense of their honor, and it is clear that they are humiliated by his terms. But Chris' behavior, and his discussion with the most mercenary of the gunfighters (Harry), confirms Calvera's assertion that the arrangement is rational and in perfect accord with the code of more-or-less-enlightened self-interest by which the professional, modern man determines his actions. Indeed, Calvera's treaty is just the sort of pragmatic stick-and-carrot deal which President Johnson offered the North Vietnamese in his speech at Johns Hopkins in April 1965. The logic behind the offer derived from the deterrent aspect of counter-insurgency doctrine which aimed at deterring future guerrilla wars by demonstrating a will to impose "excessively high" costs on the enemy.

The Seven are "magnificent" because they follow the imperatives of pride and "honor," rather than the ethic of rational self-interest. Rational self-interest, as a principle of action, is rendered morally questionable by its association with Calvera. At work here is an ideological double-standard, which sees Americans and their (non-white) enemies as governed by fundamentally different motives and standards. What is sanity and reason for the enemy is madness and dishonor for us; what is "selfless idealism" in the Seven would appear as irrational fanaticism in an enemy. Moreover, it is clear that the American chivalric standard is the higher of the two: carrots and sticks appeal only to a lower order of moral intelligence. Americans ask not what their country can do for them (nor fear what it may do to them), but ask what they can do for their country.

The decision of the Seven to return to the village heightens the distinction between hapless Mexicans and powerful Americans. The gunfighters will go back and redeem the village in spite of the villagers' betrayal, in the teeth of evidence that the village polity does not fully sustain them, and that its culture is alien to them. Their motives are again mixed: Chris, Vin and Riley have learned to care about the little people of the town; Chico wants to vindicate his race. The common denominator is that their reasons are personal: they will finish the fight to resolve moral dilemmas which arise more from their character as Americans and professionals than from any real tie to the village. They return because their feelings of affection for the village and their desire for symbolic vindication now coincide precisely; there is no choice between making love and making war—pragmatically, they have become the same thing.

Again, the movie reads accurately the mix of values in the political ideology of the Green Beret moment in foreign affairs. More than this, it predicts the direction in which that ideology would move: from an assertion that Vietnam must be defended for material reasons of national interest, to the assertion that the war is necessary as a "symbol" of American determination, down to the strident and pathetic demands of Nixon and Kissinger that the war must be continued and extended—through bloody infantry assaults on symbolic targets, through signals in the form of massive bombing campaigns—to prevent our being perceived as "a pitiful helpless giant."

In the movie, what follows this shift is a massacre scene which, had it been filmed a few years later, would have raised echoes of My Lai. The Seven stage a commando-style attack on the village, in which bandits and townsfolk are completely intermingled, yet so expert is their technique that they never kill any townspeople, they only and precisely kill bandits. The mythical "surgical strike," so central to the fantasies of military scenario-makers, and the counter-insurgency fantasy of killing the guerillas without harming any of the peasants, are visualized here. But the literal representation of the attack as an extermination of the bandits is offset by the visual impression that this is indeed an attack on the village which has betrayed them. The contrast with Kurosawa's movie throws this point into high relief: Kurosawa's samurai are never outside the village, and in the last attack samurai and peasants fight as comrades. Sturges goes out of his way to show that, in the crisis the peasants are helpless, dependent on the violent incursion of the Americans outside—and on the chivalric caritas of men who owe them nothing, except perhaps contempt. Only when the Americans have begun their act of self-sacrifice do the peasants join them.

The surviving gunfighters do not remain in the village after their triumph, however. Only Chico stays behind, to marry a local girl—the film's only bit of sexual romance. The Americans help this world, but literally have no interest in it; they are not hewers of wood and drawers of water, but professionals. This ending also fulfills in fantasy the scenario of counter-insurgency, which envisioned the victorious Green Berets—like Washington after the Revolution—declining the mantle of imperial rule. With the old colonial power gone, and the new Communist takeover defeated, the Green Berets could safely turn power back to the natives, or rather to a new class of Americanized leaders—that elusive "Third Force" envisioned by policy makers, that would be neither communist nor reactionary, neither peasant nor landlord. The war done, the Americans leave the scene, either to go back home or, like the Lone Ranger, to ride on to similar adventures in yet another imperilled town. . . .

6

PRIMARY SOURCES

A.   *United States* v. *Paramount Pictures, Inc.* (1947)

In its 1947 Paramount antitrust ruling, the U.S. Supreme Court deprived the major Hollywood studios of their guaranteed domestic market.

We have no doubt that moving pictures, like newspapers and radio, are included in the press whose freedom is guaranteed by the First Amendment. . . . The main contest is over the cream of the exhibition business—that of the first-run theatres. . . . The question here is not *what* the public will see or *if* the public will be permitted to see certain features. It is clear that under the existing system the public will be denied access to none. If the public cannot see the features on the first-run, it may do so on the second, third, fourth, or later run. The central problem presented by these cases is which exhibitors get the highly profitable first-run business. . . .

The controversy over monopoly relates to monopoly in exhibition and more particularly monopoly in the first-run phase of the exhibition business.

The five majors in 1945 had interests in somewhat over 17 percent of the theatres in the United States—3,137 out of 18,076. Those theatres paid 45 percent of the total domestic film rental received by all eight defendants.

In the 92 cities of the country with populations over 100,000 at least 70 per cent of all the first-run theatres are affiliated with one or more of the five majors. . . . In 38 of those cities there are no independent first-run theatres. . . .

The District Court . . . found that the five majors . . . "do not and cannot collectively or individually, have a monopoly of exhibition." The District Court also found that where a single defendant owns all of the first-run theatres in a town, there is no sufficient proof that the acquisition was for the purpose of creating a monopoly. It found rather that such consequence resulted from the inertness of competitors, their lack of financial ability to build theatres comparable to those of the five majors, or the preference of the public for the best equipped theatres. . . .

The District court . . . did find an attempt to monopolize in the fixing of prices, the granting of unreasonable clearances, block booking, and other unlawful restraints of trade. . . .

B.   Hearings Regarding the Communist Infiltration of the Motion-Picture-Industry Activities in the United States, U.S. House of Representatives Committee on Un-American Activities, 1947

In 1947, the House Un-American Activities Committee conducted its first investigation of Communist infiltration in the film industry. It called a group of radical screen writers and producers to testify about their political beliefs.

[Hon. J. Parnell Thomas (chairman) presiding]

The committee is well aware of the magnitude of the subject which it is investigating. The motion-picture business represents an investment of billions of dollars. It represents employment for thousands of workers, ranging from unskilled laborers to high-salaried actors and executives. And even more important, the motion-picture industry represents what is probably the largest single vehicle of entertainment for the American public—over 85,000,000 persons attend the movies each week.

However, it is the very magnitude of the scope of the motion-picture industry which makes this investigation so necessary. We all recognize, certainly, the tremendous effect which moving pictures have on their mass audiences, far removed from the Hollywood sets. We all recognize that what the citizen sees and hears in his neighborhood movie house carries a powerful impact on his thoughts and behavior.

With such vast influence over the lives of American citizens as the motion-picture industry exerts, it is not unnatural—in fact, it is very logical—that subversive and undemocratic forces should attempt to use this medium for un-American purposes.

C.   Hearings Regarding the Communist Infiltration of the Motion-Picture-Industry Activities in the United States, U.S. House of Representatives Committee on Un-American Activities, 1951

In 1951, HUAC went back to Hollywood and called hundreds of witnesses from both the political right and political left.

Testimony of Larry Parks, Accompanied by His Counsel, Louis Mandel

MR. TAVENNER (HUAC Counsel). Mr. Parks, when and where were you born?

MR. PARKS. I was born in Kansas on a farm. I moved when I was quite small to Illinois. I attended the high school in Joliet, Ill., and I also attended and graduated from the University of Illinois, where I majored in chemistry and minored in physics. I sometimes wonder how I got in my present line of work. . . .

MR. TAVENNER. Now, what is your present occupation?

MR. PARKS. Actor. . . .

MR. TAVENNER. You understand that we desire to learn the true extent, past and present, of Communist infiltration into the theater field in Hollywood, and the committee asks your cooperation in developing such information. There has been considerable testimony taken before this committee regarding a number of organizations in Hollywood, such as the Actors' Laboratory; Actors' Laboratory Theater; Associated Film Audiences-Hollywood Branch; Citizens' Committee for Motion-Picture Strikers; Film Audiences for Democracy or Associated Film Audiences; Hollywood Anti-Nazi League or Hollywood League Against Nazism; Hollywood Independent Citizens' Committee of the Arts, Sciences, and Professions; Hollywood League for Democratic Action; Hollywood Motion-Picture Democratic Committee; Hollywood Peace Forum; Hollywood Theater Alliance; Hollywood Writers' Mobilization; Motion Picture Artists' Committee; People's Educational Center, Los Angeles; Mooney Defense Committee-Hollywood Unit; Progressive Citizens of America; Hollywood Committee of the Arts, Sciences, and Professions; Council of the PCA; Southern California Chapter of the PCA; Workers School of Los Angeles.

Have you been connected or affiliated in any way with any of those organizations?

MR. PARKS. I have. . . .

MR. TAVENNER. Will you tell the committee whether or not in your experience in Hollywood and as a member of these organizations to which you have testified there were to your knowledge Communists in these various organizations which I have referred to, particularly those that you were a member of?

MR. PARKS. I think I can say "Yes" to that.

MR. TAVENNER. Well, who were these Communists?

MR. PARKS. There were people in the Actors' Lab, for instance—this, in my opinion, was not a Communist organization in any sense of the word. As in any organization, it has all colors of political philosophy. . . .

MR. TAVENNER. Well, were there Communists attached to these other organizations which you say you were a member of?

MR. PARKS. This I'm not familiar with. I don't know. I don't know who else was a member of them besides myself.

MR. TAVENNER. Your answer is because you do not recall who were members of these other organizations?

MR. PARKS. I think that is the gist of my answer; yes. . . .

MR. TAVENNER. Well, what was your opportunity to know and to observe the fact that there were Communists in [the Actors' Laboratory]?

MR. PARKS. May I answer this fully and in my own way?

MR. TAVENNER. I would like for you to. . . .

MR. PARKS. I am not a Communist. I would like to point out that in my opinion there is a great difference between—and not a subtle difference—between being a Communist, a member of the Communist Party, say in 1941, 10 years ago, and being a Communist in 1951. To my mind this is a great difference and not a subtle one. . . .

As I say, I am not a Communist. I was a member of the Communist Party when I was a much younger man, 10 years ago. I was a member of the Communist Party. . . .

Being a member of the Communist Party fulfilled certain needs of a young man that was liberal in thought, idealistic, who was for the underprivileged, the underdog. I felt that it fulfilled these particular needs. I think that being a Communist in 1951 in this particular situation is an entirely different kettle of fish when this is a great power that is trying to take over the world. This is the difference. . . .

MR. TAVENNER. In other words, you didn't realize that the purpose and object of the Communist Party was to take over segments of the world in 1941, but you do realize that that is true in 1951? Is that the point you are making?

MR. PARKS. Well, I would like to say this: That this is in no way an apology for anything that I have done, you see, because I feel I have done nothing wrong ever. Question of judgment? This is debatable. I feel that as far as I am concerned that in 1941, as far as I knew it, the purposes as I knew them fulfilled . . . certain idealism, certain being for the underdog, which I am today this very minute. . . .

I wasn't particularly interested in it after I did become a member. I attended very few meetings, and I drifted away from it the same way that . . . I drifted into it. . . . To the best of my recollection, I petered out about the latter part of 1944 or 1945. . . .

REPRESENTATIVE CHARLES E. POTTER (HUAC Committee Member). Who would call these meetings together? . . .

MR. PARKS. I would prefer not to mention names under these circumstances. . . .

REPRESENTATIVE JOHN S. WOOD (HUAC Committee Chairman). Mr. Parks, in what way do you feel it would be injurious, then, to them to divulge their identities, when you expressed the opinion that at no time did they do wrong?

MR. PARKS. This brings up many questions on a personal basis, Mr. Congressman, as an actor. . . . One of the reasons is that as an actor my activity is dependent a great deal on the public. To be called before this committee at your request has a certain inference, a certain innuendo that you are not loyal to this country. This is not true. I am speaking for myself. This is not true. But the inference and the innuendo is there as far as the public is concerned. . . .

MR. WOOD. Don't you feel the public is entitled to know about [communist infiltration of the motion picture industry]?

MR. PARKS. I certainly do, and I am opening myself wide open to any question that you can ask me. I will answer as honestly as I know how. And at this particular time, as I say, the industry is—it's like taking a pot shot at a wounded animal, because the industry is not in as good a shape today as it has been, economically I'm speaking. It has been pretty tough on it. And, as I say, this is a great industry, and I don't say this only because it has been kind to me. It has a very important job to do to entertain people, in certain respects to call attention to certain evils, but mainly to entertain, and in this I feel that they have done a great job. Always when our country has needed help, the industry has been in the forefront of that help. . . .

On the question of naming names, it is my honest opinion that the few people that I could name, these names would not be of service to the committee at all. I am sure that you know who they are. These people I feel honestly are like myself, and I feel I have done nothing wrong. Question of judgment? Yes, perhaps. And I also feel that this is not—to be asked to name names like this is not—in the way of American justice as we know it, that we as Americans have all been brought up, that it is a bad thing to force a man to do this. I have been brought up that way. I am sure all of you have.

And it seems to me that this is not the American way of doing things—to force a man who is under oath and who has opened himself as wide as possible to the committee—and it hasn't been easy to do this—to force a man to do this is not American justice. . . .

My people have a long heritage in this country. They fought in the Revolutionary War to make this country, to create this Government, of which this committee is a part. . . .

I don't think I would be here today if I weren't a star, because you know as well as I, even better, that I know nothing that I believe would be of great service to this country. I think my career has been ruined because of this, and I would appreciate not having to—don't present me with the choice of either being in contempt of this committee and going to jail or forcing me to really crawl through the mud to be an informer, for what purpose? I don't' think this is a choice at all. I don't think this is really sportsmanlike. I don't think this is American. I don't think this is American justice. I think to do something like this is more akin to what happened under Hitler, and what is happening in Russia today.

I don't think this is American justice for an innocent mistake in judgement, if it was that, with the intention behind it only of making this country a better place in which to live. I think it is not befitting for this committee to force me to make this kind of choice. . . .

D.   The Miracle Decision
Joseph Burstyn, Inc. v. Wilson, Commissioner of Education of New York, et al. (1952)

The Italian film The Miracle *had been banned in New York for "blasphemy." In this landmark decision, the Supreme Court extended to the movies First Amendment protections of freedom of speech.*

The issue here is the constitutionality, under the First and Fourteenth Amendments, of a New York statute which permits the banning of motion picture films on the ground that they are "sacrilegious"....

Appellant is a corporation engaged in the business of distributing motion pictures. It owns the exclusive rights to distribute throughout the United States a film produced in Italy entitled "The Miracle." On November 30, 1950, the motion picture division of the New York education department . . . issued . . . a license authorizing exhibition of "The Miracle," with English subtitles. . . .

The New York State Board of Regents, which by statute is made the head of the education department, received "hundreds of letters, telegrams, post cards, affidavits, and other communications" both protesting against and defending the public exhibition of "The Miracle." The Chancellor of the Board of Regents requested three members of the Board to view the picture and to make a report to the entire Board. After viewing the film, this committee reported . . . that in its opinion there was basis for the claim that the picture was "sacrilegious". . . . On February 16, 1951, the Regents, after viewing "The Miracle," determined that it was "sacrilegious" and . . . ordered the Commissioner of Education to rescind appellant's license to exhibit the picture. . . .

After the *Mutual* decision [1915], the present case is the first to present squarely to us the question of whether motion pictures are within the ambit of protection which the First Amendment, through the Fourteenth, secures to any form of "speech" or "the press."

It cannot be doubted that motion pictures are a significant medium for the communication of ideas. They may affect public attitudes and behavior in a variety of ways, ranging from direct espousal of a political or social doctrine to the subtle shaping of thought which characterizes all artistic expression. The importance of motion pictures as an organ of public opinion is not lessened by the fact that they are designed to entertain as well as to inform. As was said [in 1948] . . .

> The line between the informing and the entertaining is too elusive for the protection of that basic right [a free press]. Everyone is familiar with instances of propaganda through fiction. What is one man's amusement, teaches another's doctrine.

It is urged that motion pictures do not fall within the First Amendment's aegis because their production, distribution, and exhibition is a large-scale business conducted for private profit. We cannot agree. That books, newspapers, and magazines are published and sold for profit does not prevent them from being a form of expression whose liberty is safeguarded by the First Amendment. We fail to see why operation for profit should have any different effect in the case of motion pictures.

It is further urged that motion pictures possess a greater capacity for evil, particularly among the youth of a community, than other modes of expression. Even if one were to accept this hypothesis, it does not follow that motion pictures should be disqualified from First Amendment protection. If there be capacity for evil it may be relevant in determining the permissible scope of community control, but it does not authorize substantially unbridled censorship such as we have here. . . .

It is not the business of government in our nation to suppress real or imagined attacks upon a particular religious doctrine, whether they appear in publications, speeches, or motion pictures.

Since the term "sacrilegious" is the sole standard under attack here, it is not necessary for us to decide, for example, whether a state may censor motion pictures under a clearly drawn statute designed and applied to prevent the showing of obscene films. That is a very different question from the one now before us. We hold only that under the First and Fourteenth Amendments a state may not ban a film on the basis of a censor's conclusion that it is "sacrilegious."

PART V

Bonnie and Clyde

HOLLYWOOD SINCE VIETNAM

1

INTRODUCTION

Bonnie and Clyde

Few films have ever aroused such intense controversy. *The New York Times* called it immoral: "a cheap piece of boldfaced slapstick comedy that treats the hideous depredations of thatsleazy moronic pair as though they were as full of fun and frolic as the jazz-age cut-ups in *Thoroughly Modern Millie*." But many others responded much more positively. Bonnie and Clyde dress styles became the rage. A song, "The Ballad of Bonnie and Clyde," climbed to the top of the pop charts.

Set in Texas in 1931, the film tells the story of the Barrow Gang, a group of Depression-era bank robbers. The film portrays the gang's leaders, Bonnie Parker and Clyde Barrow, as sensitive young people—"drifters, nobodies, yearning to be any kind of somebodies." They are depicted as latter-day Robin Hoods, who rob banks—not their customers—and only kill reluctantly, when forced to. In real life, they were small-time criminals, who held up gas stations and grocery stores as well as banks. Their largest haul was about $1,500 and they killed 13 people—including two Texas highway patrolmen whom they shot from an ambush.

As played by Warren Beatty, Clyde Barrow is a sympathetic figure, cocky and reckless, who suffers from sexual impotence. In actuality, he was a vicious, sadistic killer. He was described at the time as "a shifty-eyed young Texas thug," "a snake-eyed murderer who killed without giving his victims a chance to draw." The film also treats Bonnie with compassion, depicting her as a sensitive figure who describes the gang's exploits in poetry. The real life Bonnie Parker was a married Dallas waitress who killed three people.

Of course, the film's appeal does not lie in any claims of historical accuracy. Rather, the film successfully transforms Bonnie and Clyde into folk heroes, into rebels who might serve as precursors of the counterculture of the late 1960s. They are treated as underdogs who attack symbols of the establishment, defend the poor, and are ultimately gunned by lawmen who riddle them over and over with bullets from ambush when they stop to help a driver change his tire. The movie's advertising slogan—"They're young, they're in love, they kill people"—expressed the spirit of youthful rebellion that characterized the counterculture.

2

A SHIFTING SENSIBILITY

Dr. Strangelove:
Nightmare Comedy and the Ideology of Liberal Consensus
Charles Maland

Dr. Strangelove struck America like a bolt of lightning on a dark night. It threw a flash of light on the country's foreign policy and called into question stock beliefs and assumptions about the nature of the Cold War and the prospects of nuclear war. In the following essay, Charles Maland discusses a film that lingered on the minds and troubled the conscience of many Americans.

Dr. Strangelove Or How I Learned to Stop Worrying and Love the Bomb (Stanley Kubrick, 1964) is one of the most fascinating and important American films of the 1960s. As a sensitive artistic response to its age, the film presents a moral protest of revulsion against the dominant cultural paradigm in America—what Geoffrey Hodgson has termed the Ideology of Liberal Consensus. Appearing at roughly the same time as other works critical of the dominant paradigm—*Catch 22* is a good literary example of the stance—*Dr. Strangelove* presented an adversary view of society which was to become much more widely shared among some Americans in the late 1960s. This essay will examine the Ideology of Liberal Consensus, demonstrate how *Dr. Strangelove* serves as a response to it (especially to its approach to nuclear strategy and weapons), and look at how American culture responded to its radical reassessment of the American nuclear policy in the early 1960s.

The American consensus to which *Dr. Strangelove* responds was rooted in the late 1930s and in the war years. When Americans in the late 1930s began to feel more threatened by the rise of foreign totalitarianism than by the economic insecurities fostered by the stock market crash, a previously fragmented American culture began to unify. A common system of belief began to form, a paradigm solidified during World War II, when American effort was directed toward defeating the Axis powers. Fueled by the success of the war effort and the economic prosperity fostered by the war, this paradigm continued to dominate American social and political life through the early 1960s.

The 1950s are commonly remembered as an age of conformity typified by the man in the gray flannel suit, the move to suburbia, and the blandness of the Eisenhower administration. There were, of course, currents running counter to the

252

American consensus in the 1950s—C. Wright Mills challenging the power elite and the era's "crackpot realism"; James Dean smouldering with sensitive, quiet rebellion; the Beats rejecting the propriety and complacency of the era—yet most people remained happy with America and its possibilities. Much more than a passing mood or a vague reaction to events, this paradigm—the Ideology of Liberal Consensus—took on an intellectual coherence of its own. According to Geoffrey Hodgson, the ideology contained two cornerstone assumptions: that the structure of American society was basically sound, and that communism was a clear danger to the survival of the United States and its allies. From these two beliefs evolved a widely accepted view of America. That view argued its position in roughly this fashion: the American economic system has developed, softening the inequities and brutalities of an earlier capitalism, becoming more democratic, and offering abundance to a wider portion of the population than ever before. The key to both democracy and abundance is production and technological advance; economic growth provides the opportunity to meet social needs, to defuse class conflict, and to bring blue-collar workers into the middle class. Social problems are thus less explosive and can be solved rationally. It is necessary only to locate each problem, design a program to attack it, and provide the experts and technological know-how necessary to solve the problem.

The only threat to this domestic harmony, the argument continued, is the specter of Communism. The "Free World," led by the United States, must brace itself for a long struggle against Communism and willingly support a strong defense system, for power is the only language that the Communists can understand. If America accepts this responsibility to fight Communism, while also proclaiming the virtues of American economic, social, and political democracy to the rest of the world, the country will remain strong and sound. Hodgson sums up the paradigm well when he writes: "Confident to the verge of complacency about the perfectibility of American society, anxious to the point of paranoia about the threat of Communism—those were the two faces of the consensus mood.

These two assumptions guided our national leadership as it attempted to forge social policy in an era of nuclear weapons. After the Soviet Union announced in the fall of 1949 that it had successfully exploded an atomic bomb, President Truman on January 31, 1950 ordered the Atomic Energy Commission to go ahead with the development of a hydrogen bomb. By late 1952 the United States had detonated its first hydrogen bomb, 700 times more powerful than the atomic bomb dropped on Hiroshima. Less than a year later, on August 8, 1953, the Soviets announced that they, too, had a hydrogen bomb. The arms race was on.

About the time that Sputnik was successfully launched in 1957—leading to national fears about the quality of American science and education—some American intellectuals began to refine a new area of inquiry: nuclear strategy. Recognizing that nuclear weapons were a reality, the nuclear strategists felt it important to think systematically about their role in our defense policy. Henry Kissinger's *Nuclear War and Foreign Policy* (1957), one of the first such books, argued that the use of tactical nuclear weapomust be considered by decision makers. More widely known was the work of Herman Kahn, whose *On Thermonuclear War* (1960) and *Thinking About the Unthinkable* (1962) presented his speculations on nuclear war and strategy, most of which stemmed from his work for the RAND Corporation during the 1950s. Kahn was willing to indulge in any speculation about nuclear war, including such topics as the estimated genetic consequences of worldwide doses of radioactive fallout, the desirable characteristics of a deterrent (it should be frightening, inexorable, persuasive, cheap, non-accident prone, and controllable), and the huge likelihood of vomiting in postwar fallout shelters.

Though the professed intent of the nuclear strategists was to encourage a rational approach to foreign policy in a nuclear age, the mass media seemed intent on making the public believe that thermonuclear war might be acceptable, even tolerable. A few examples illustrate that some mass magazines believed that nuclear war would not really be that bad. *U.S. News and World Report* carried a cover article, "If Bombs Do Fall," which told readers that plans were underway to allow people to write checks on their bank accounts even if the bank were destroyed by nuclear attack. The same issue contained a side story about how well survivors of the Japanese bombings were doing. *Life* magazine placed a man in a reddish fallout costume on its cover along with the headline, "How You Can Survive Fallout. 97 out of 100 Can Be Saved." Besides advising that the best cure for radiation sickness "is to take hot tea or a solution of baking soda," *Life* ran an advertisement for a fully-stocked, prefabricated fallout shelter for only $700. The accompanying picture showed a happy family of five living comfortably in their shelter. I.F. Stone suggested in response to this kind of writing that the media seemed determined to convince the American public that thermonuclear warfare was "almost as safe as ivory soap is pure." While all this was going on, a RAND corporation study released in August 1961 estimated that a 3000 megaton attack on American cities would kill 80 percent of the population.

This paradoxical, bizarre treatment of the nuclear threat can be explained in part as an attempt by journalists to relieve anxiety during a time when the Cold War was intensifying. A number of events from 1960 to 1963 encouraged this freeze in the Cold War. Gary Powers, piloting a U-2 surveillance plane, was shot down over the Soviet Union in May 1960. In 1961, the Bay of Pigs fiasco occurred in May, President Kennedy announced a national fallout shelter campaign on television in July, and in August, the Berlin Wall was erected and the Soviet Union announced that they were resuming atmospheric testing of nuclear weapons. Worst of all, the Cuban Missile Crisis of October 1962 carried the world to the brink of nuclear war, thrusting the dangers of nuclear confrontation to the forefront of the public imagination. Though the crisis seemed to be resolved in favor of the United States, for several days nuclear war seemed imminent.

One result of this intensification was to erode the confidence of some Americans in the wisdom of American nuclear policy. Though there had been a small tradition of dissent regarding American nuclear policy in the 1950s—led by people like J. Robert Oppenheimer, Linus Pauling, Bertrand Russell, and C. Wright Mills, and groups like SANE (the National Committee for a Sane Nuclear Policy)—these people were clearly a minority, prophets crying in the wilderness. But Edmund Wilson's warning in 1963 that our spending on nuclear weapons may be one of mankind's final acts, and H. Stuart Hughes' impassioned challenge to deterrence strategy and his support of disarmament in the same year, were both symptomatic of a growing dissatisfaction of some Americans with the federal government's nuclear policy. Judged from another perspective, outside the assumptions of the Ideology of Liberal Consensus, the threat posed by the Soviet Union did not at all warrant the use of nuclear weapons. In the same vein, the realities of America itself—as the defenders of the Civil Rights movement were pointing out—did not live up to the rhetoric about the harmonious American democracy so prevalent in the 1950s. By 1962 and 1963, when *Dr. Strangelove* was being planned and produced, the Ideology of Liberal Consensus seemed increasingly vulnerable. In fact, it is not unfair to say that an adversary culture opposed to the hypocrisies and inconsistencies of the dominant paradigm was beginning to form.

Stanley Kubrick, director of *Dr. Strangelove,* played a part in extending that adversary culture. Born in 1928 to a middle-class Bronx family, Kubrick was from an early age interested in chess and photography. It is not hard to move from his fascination with chess, with the analytical abilities it requires and sharpens, to the fascination with technology and the difficulties men have in controlling it which Kubrick displays in *Dr. Strangelove* and *2001: A Space Odyssey*. Photography became a pastime when Kubrick received a camera at age thirteen, and a profession when *Look* magazine hired him at age eighteen as a still photographer. From there Kubrick became interested in filmmaking and made a short documentary on middleweight boxer Walter Cartier called *Day for the Fight* (1950). He followed this with a second documentary for RKO, *Flying Padre* (1951), after which he made his first feature film, *Fear and Desire* (1953). From then on Kubrick was immersed in making feature films.

In his mature work Kubrick has returned constantly to one of the gravest dilemmas of modern industrial society: the gap between man's scientific and technological skill and his social, political, and moral ineptitude. In Kubrick's world view, modern man has made scientific and technological advances inconceivable to previous generations but lacks the wisdom either to perceive how the new gadgetry might be used in constructive ways or, more fundamentally, to ask whether the "advance" might not cause more harm than good. Kubrick first faced this problem squarely in *Dr. Strangelove*.

Kubrick's films before 1963 do hint at interests which he was to develop more fully in *Dr. Strangelove*. *The Killing* shows a group of men working toward a common purpose under intense pressure and severe time limitations. *Paths of Glory*—one of a handful of classic anti-war films in the American cinema—vents its anger at the stupidity of military leaders, their callous disregard for other human lives, and their own lust for power. Released in 1957 in the midst of the Cold War, *Paths* was a courageous film made slightly more palatable for audiences because of its setting and situation World War One and the evils of French military leaders.

It is not totally surprising, then, that Kubrick should make a film about military and civilian leaders trying to cope with accidental nuclear war. Actually, Kubrick had developed an interest in the Cold War and nuclear strategy as a concerned citizen in the late 1950s, even before he thought of doing a film on the subject. In an essay on *Dr. Strangelove* published in mid-1963, a half year before the release of the film, Kubrick wrote: "I was very interested in what was going to happen, and started reading a lot of books about four years ago. I have a library of about 70 or 80 books written by various technical people on the subject and I began to subscribe to the military magazines, the Air Force magazine, and to follow the U.S. naval proceedings." One of the magazines he subscribed to was the *Bulletin of the Atomic*

Scientist which regularly published articles by atomic scientists (Oppenheimer, Edward Teller, and Leo Szilard) and nuclear strategists (Kahn, Bernard Brodie, and Thomas Schelling). The more he read on the subject, the more he became engrossed in the complexities of nuclear strategy and the enormity of the nuclear threat.

> I was struck by the paradoxes of every variation of the problem from one extreme to the other—from the paradoxes of unilateral disarmament to the first strike. And it seemed to me that, aside from the fact that I was terribly interested myself, it was very important to deal with this problem dramatically because it's the only social problem where there's absolutely no chance for people to learn anything from experience. So it seemed to me that this was eminently a problem, a topic to be dealt with dramatically.

As his readings continued, Kubrick began to feel "a great desire to do something about the nuclear nightmare." From this desire came a decision to make a film on the subject. In preparation, he talked with both Thomas Schelling and Herman Kahn, gradually coming to believe that a psychotic general could engage in what Kahn termed "unauthorized behavior" and send bombers to Russia.

Kubrick found the literary work upon which his film was based almost by accident. When he requested some relevant readings from the Institute of Strategic Studies, the head of the Institute, Alastair Buchan, suggested Peter George's *Red Alert,* a serious suspense thriller about an accidental nuclear attack. The book contained such an interesting premise concerning accidental nuclear war that even a nuclear strategist like Schelling could write of it that "the sheer ingenuity of the scheme . . . exceeds in thoughtfulness any fiction available on how war might start." Kubrick, likewise impressed with the involving story and convincing premise, purchased rights to the novel.

However, when author and screenwriter started to construct the screenplay, they began to run into problems, which Kubrick describes in an interview with Joseph Celmis:

> I started work on the screenplay with every intention of making the film a serious treatment of the problem of accidental nuclear war. As I kept trying to imagine the way in which things would really happen, ideas kept coming to me which I would discard because they were so ludicrous I kept saying to myself: "I can't do this. People will laugh." But after a month or so I began to realize that all the things I was throwing out were the things which were most truthful.

By trying to make the film a serious drama, Kubrick was accepting the framework of the dominant paradigm, accepting Cold War premises and creating the gripping story within these premises. This was the approach of *Red Alert* as well as of *Fail Safe,* a popular film of late 1964 adapted from the Burdick and Wheeler novel. But after studying closely the assumptions of the Cold War and the nuclear impasse, Kubrick was moving outside the dominant paradigm. Kubrick's fumbling attempts to construct a screenplay provide an example of what Gene Wise, expanding on Thomas Kuhn, has called a "paradigm revolution" in the making: a dramatic moment when accepted understandings of the world no longer make sense and new ones are needed.

Kubrick describes in an interview how he resolved his difficulties with the screenplay: "It occurred to me I was approaching the project in the wrong way. The only way to tell the story was as a black comedy, or better, a nightmare comedy, where the things you laugh at most are really the heart of the paradoxical postures that make a nuclear war possible." After deciding to use nightmare comedy in approaching his subject, Kubrick hired Terry Southern to help with the screenplay. This decision connects Kubrick to the black humor novelists of the early 1960s. Writers like Southern, Joseph Heller *(Catch 22),* Kurt Vonnegut *(Mother Night),* and Thomas Pynchon *(V* and *The Crying of Lot 49)* shared with Kubrick the assumption of a culture gone mad, and responded to it with a similar mixture of horror and humor. Morris Dickstein's comment that "black humor is pitched at the breaking point where moral anguish explodes into a mixture of comedy and terror, where things are so bad you might as well laugh," describes quite accurately the way Kubrick came to feel about the arms race and nuclear strategy.

The premise and plot of the film are, paradoxically, quite realistic and suspenseful, which in part accounts for why the nightmare comedy succeeds. At the opening of the film an actor tells us that the Russians have built a Doomsday device which will automatically detonate if a nuclear weapon is dropped on the Soviet Union, destroying all human life on the planet—a case of deterrence strategy carried to the absurd. A paranoid anti-Communist Air Force general, unaware of the Russian's ultimate weapon, orders a fleet of airborne SAC B-52s to their Russian targets. The President of the United States finds out, but soon learns that the jets cannot be recalled because only the general knows the recall code. Moving quickly into action, the President discusses the problem with his advisors, calls the Russian Premier, and assists the Russians in their attempts to shoot down the B-52s. Finally, all the planes are recalled but one, which drops its bombs on a secondary target, setting off the Russian retaliatory Doomsday device. *Dr. Strangelove* concludes in apocalypse.

After the narrator's initial mention of a Doomsday device, Kubrick subtly begins his nightmare comedy by suggesting that man's warlike tendencies and his sexual urges stem from similar aggressive instincts. He does this by showing an airborne B-52 coupling with a refueling plane in mid-air, while the sound track plays a popular love song, "Try a Little Tenderness." The connection between sexual and military aggression continues throughout the film, as when an otherwise nude beauty in a *Playboy* centerfold has her buttocks covered with a copy of *Foreign Affairs,* but it is most evident in the names given the characters by the screenwriters. Jack D. Ripper, the deranged SAC general, recalls the sex murderer who terrorized London during the late 1880s. The name of Army strategist Buck Turgidson is also suggestive: his first name is slang for a virile male and his last name suggests both bombast and an adjective meaning "swollen." Major King Kong, pilot of the B-52, reminds viewers of the simple-minded beast who fell in love with a beautiful blonde. Group Captain Lionel Mandrake's last name is also the word for a plant reputedly known for inducing conception in women, while both names of President Merkin Muffley allude to female genitals. Appropriately, Ripper and Turgidson are hawks, while Muffley is a dove. Other names—*Dr. Strangelove,* the Soviet Ambassador DeSadesky, and Premier Dmitri Kissov—carry similar associations. These sexual allusions permeate the film, providing one level of the film's nightmare comedy.

More important than these sexual allusions, however, is *Dr. Strangelove*'s frontal assault on the Ideology of Liberal Consensus. Above all else, *Dr. Strangelove* uses nightmare comedy to satirize four dimensions of the Cold War consensus: anti-Communist paranoia; the culture's inability to realize the enormity of nuclear war; various nuclear strategies; and the blind faith modern man places in technological progress.

The critique of American anti-Communist paranoia is presented primarily through General Ripper, played by Sterling Hayden. Kubrick portrays Ripper as an obsessed member of the radical right. Convinced that the Communist conspiracy has not only infiltrated our country but also, through fluoridation, contaminated our water, Ripper decides to take action by sending the B-52s to bomb Russia. Cutting off all communication to the outside world, he then orders his men to fight anyone attempting to capture the base.

The most grimly ominous character in the film, Ripper dominates its action in the first half, and Kubrick underlines this action stylistically, often shooting Ripper from a low camera angle. But Ripper's words also characterize his paranoia. Kubrick once agreed that whereas *2001* develops its focus visually, *Dr. Strangelove* does so much more through its dialogue. Early in the film, Ripper reveals his fears to Mandrake (Peter Sellers, in one of his three roles):

> Mandrake, have you ever seen a Communist drink a glass of water? Vodka, that's what they drink, isn't it? Never water—on no account will a Commie ever drink water, and not without good reason . . . Mandrake, water is the source of all life: seven-tenths of this earth's surface is water. Why do you realize that 70 percent of you is water? And as human beings, you and I need fresh, pure water to replenish our precious bodily fluids. . . . Have you never wondered why I drink only distilled water or rain water and only pure grain alcohol? . . . Have you ever heard of a thing called fluoridation? Do you realize that fluoridation is the most monstrously conceived and dangerous Communist plot we've ever had to face?

Later Ripper mentions that fluoridation began in 1946, the same year as the postwar international Communist conspiracy. By portraying this paranoid officer willing to obliterate the world because of fluoridation Kubrick lays bare the irrational American fear of Communism as one source of the cultural malaise of the early 1960s.

The second object of attack through satire—the failure to realize how nuclear weapons have changed the nature of war—is carried out primarily on one of General Ripper's B-52s. The pilot of the plane, Major King Kong (Slim Pickens), gives evidence of outmoded notions about war in his pep talk to the crew after they have received the "go" code:

> Now look boys—I ain't much of a hand at makin' speeches . . . I got a fair idea of the personal emotions that some of you fellas may be thinking. Heck. I reckon you wouldn't even be human bein's if you didn't have some pretty strong feelin's about nuclear combat. But I want yall to remember one thing. The folks back home is a-countin on you and, by golly, we ain't about to let 'em down. I'll tell you something else: if this thing turns out to be half as important as I figger it just might be, I'd say your all in line

for some important promotions and personal citations when this thing's over with. And that goes for every one of you, regardless of yer race, color, or yer creed.

Such a pep talk might be appropriate for a World War II film—in fact, most films about that war contained some such scene—but Kong's blindness to what he is being asked to do is almost complete. The fact that Kong wears a cowboy hat while making the speech, connecting him to the frontier heritage, and that "When Johnny Comes Marching Home"—a patriotic American war tune—plays on the sound-track in the background, reinforces the conception of Kong as a dangerous anachronism.

To drive this point home, Kubrick has Kong go through the contents of a survival kit. It includes, among other items, a pistol, nine packs of chewing gum, several pairs of nylon stockings, a miniature combination Bible and Russian phrase book, and, of course, an issue of prophylactics. Besides parodying what every soldier shot down over enemy territory might need, the scene reasserts that Kong is fighting another war at another time, never having realized that if his bomber goes down after dropping its atomic load, the crew will not have to worry much about survival, to say nothing of survival kits. Kubrick, perhaps responding to the media articles which made light of the nuclear threat, attacks the shortsightedness of those who think nuclear war may not actually be that bad.

National strategies also come under attack. Here the satire is particularly pointed; the various strategic positions taken by characters in the War Room correspond quite closely to positions taken by military and civilian strategists.

General Turgidson (George C. Scott) is a "hardliner." His position is even more severe than that of John Foster Dulles, who announced the policy of "massive retaliation" in 1954. Turgidson secretly favors a first-strike policy—he would like to see the U.S. obliterate the Russians offensively. After learning that the planes have been accidentally sent to their Russian targets, Turgidson urges the President to intensify the attack with even more planes:

> T: It is necessary now to make a choice, to choose between two admittedly regrettable but nevertheless distinguishable postwar environments. One, where you got twenty million people killed and the other where you got 110 million people killed.
>
> M: (Shocked) You're talking about mass murder, general, not war,
>
> T: I'm not saying we wouldn't get our hair mussed. But I do say no more than ten to twenty million killed, tops—depending on the breaks.
>
> M: (Angrily) I will not go down in history as the greatest mass murderer since Adolph Hitler.
>
> T: Perhaps it might be better, Mr. President, if you were more concerned with the American people than with your image in the history books.

Scott delivers these lines with zestful enthusiasm, and his animated features suggest that he can hardly wait for the annihilation to begin. In rhetoric distressingly similar to the arguments occurring occasionally in the journals, Turgidson advises "total commitment," sacrificing a "few lives" for what he believes would be a more secure and satisfactory "post-war environment."

President Muffley's position is the most reasonable of any in the War Room. He is neither a fanatic nor a warmonger. Unfortunately, he's also neatly totally ineffectual as he tries to implement his goal: attempting to avoid catastrophe at all costs through communication with the Soviets. Peter Sellers plays this role with a bald wig, in part to differentiate himself visually from his other two roles, in part to remind audiences of Adlai Stevenson, the quintessential liberal of the 1950s, twice-unsuccessful candidate for the Presidency. When Muffley negotiates with Premier Kissov over the hot line to Moscow, he appears ridiculous. After Kissov says Muffley should call the People's Central Air Defense Headquarters at Omsk, Muffley asks, "Listen, do you happen to have the phone number on you, Dmitri? . . . What? . . . I see, just ask for Omsk information." Muffley argues with Kissov about who is sorrier about the mistake, insisting that he can be just as sorry as Dmitri. Such small talk amidst the enormity of the crisis is ludicrous. By appearing both ridiculous and ineffectual, Muffley furthers Kubrick's nightmare comedy. For if the person who has the most rational strategy (and who also happens to be the commander in chief) is unable to control nuclear weapons and his military advisors, citizens really have something to worry about.

Although Dr. Strangelove does not speak until the last third of the film, the creators seem to have taken a great deal of care in creating Strangelove as a composite of a number of pundits in the new "science" of nuclear strategy. As a physicist involved in weapons research and development, he invites comparisons to Edward Teller. Not only was Teller involved in the creation of the atomic bomb, but he was also a strong anti-Communist who pushed hard for the development of the much more powerful hydrogen bomb in 1949 and 1950. In his background, accent, and some of his dialogue, Strangelove suggests Henry Kissinger. Like Kissinger, Strangelove came from Germany in the 1930s and still speaks with a German accent. With his wavy dark hair and sunglasses, he also bears a physical resemblance to Kissinger. Even his definition of deterrence—"the art of producing in the mind of the enemy the fear to attack you"—sounds remarkably like the definition Kissinger offered in his *Nuclear Weapons and Foreign Policy* (1957). Finally, Herman Kahn plays a part in the Strangelove composite, primarily as related to the Doomsday device. Strangelove tells the President that he recently commissioned a study by the Bland corporation (Kahn worked for RAND) to examine the possibility of a Doomsday device. The study found the device technologically feasible; it would be hooked to a computer and programmed to detonate under certain prescribed circumstances. However, Strangelove found the machine impractical as a deterrent because it would go off even if an attack was accidental. All these details are similarly discussed in Kahn's *On Thermonuclear War,* with Kahn similarly concluding that though the device would contain most of the characteristics of a deterrent, it would not meet the final characteristics of being controllable. As a mixture of Teller, Kissinger, Kahn, and probably a number of others (Werner Von Braun is another possibility), Strangelove becomes a significant symbol. Essentially, he is the coldly speculating mind, not unlike one of Nathaniel Hawthorne's calculating and obsessed scientists. Like them, Strangelove is devoid of fellow feeling. He proves this near the end of the film: even after the American B-52 gets through to bomb its target, Strangelove has ideas. He offers a plan to take all military and political leaders (along with attractive women at a ratio of ten women to one man) into a mine shaft in an effort to survive the virulent radio-activity produced by the Doomsday device. Clearly, none of the strategic postures presented by Kubrick—Turgidson's militarism, Muffley's tender-minded rationality, or Strangelove's constant speculations—are able to control the inexorable march of nuclear holocaust.

Although *2001* is more famous for its exploration of technology, Kubrick shows a fascination with machines in *Dr. Strangelove*. Most prominent is the simulation of the B-52 cockpit, which Kubrick—after the Air Force denied him any assistance in making the film—had built from an unauthorized photograph he discovered in an aviation magazine. Throughout the B-52 scenes, Kubrick keeps viewer interest by alternating close-ups of various panel controls with shots of crew members expertly carrying out their orders. Besides those in the B-52, many other machines—telephones, radios, the electronic wall chart in the War Room—play important parts in the film.

Kubrick develops his attitude toward technology in *Dr. Strangelove* by making use of both machines of destruction and machines of communication; the problem in the film is that while people handle the machines of destruction with great alacrity, the more neutral machines of communication are either ineffectual or turned toward destructive purposes. Through a misuse of radio codes, Ripper sends the B-52s on their destructive mission; DeSadesky uses a camera to take pictures of the War Room, presumably for purposes of intelligence. When people try to use the neutral machines to prevent destruction, however, they prove to be ineffective. During President Muffley's call to Kissov, for example, social amenities and small talk hinder attempts to stop the B-52s, as does the slowness of the process. Likewise, when Mandrake tries to call the President after he has discovered the recall code, he cannot because he does not have a dime for the pay phone.

Though people can't use neutral machines effectively, they handle the machines of destruction with deadly efficiency. This includes not only the conventional weaponry at the Air Force base, where Army infantry and artillery attempt to take over the base, but also, more distressingly the nuclear weapons. The whole crew of the B-52 expertly manipulate their machines, even after the explosion of an anti-aircraft missile damages the plane. Kong, to the dismay of the audience, shows great ingenuity in repairing damaged circuits in time to open the bomb doors over the target. Kubrick is not really suggesting that machines are dominating men. Rather, he seems to perceive a human death instinct. Arising from a nearsighted rationality, this death instinct leads man first to create machines, then to use them for destroying human life. In questioning the "progress" inherent in technology, Kubrick was challenging a fundamental assumption of the dominant paradigm. This challenge to technology—both to the stress on technique in society and to the increasing importance of machines in modern life—was to become a dominant theme in the late 1960s, important in several works of social criticism during that era, including Theodore Roszak's *The Making of A Counter Culture* (1969), Lewis Mumford's *The Myth of the Machine: The Pentagon of Power* (1969), and Philip Slater's *The Pursuit of Loneliness* (1970).

The film's final scene underlines Kubrick's attack on the Ideology of Liberal Consensus. Mushroom clouds billow on the screen, filling the sky, exuding both an awesome power and a perverse beauty. Simultaneously, a light, sentimental love song from the late 1940s—Vera Lynn's "We'll Meet Again"—provides a contrasting aural message in an excellent use of film irony. Its opening lines are: "We'll meet again, don't know where, don't know when, but I know we'll meet again some sunny day." If we go on with the world view of the postwar era, Kubrick ironically suggests, we will never meet again, because there will be no one left on earth. Retaining the conflict between image and sound throughout the final credit sequence, Kubrick hopes to prod his viewers to reflect on all that they have seen.

Taken as a whole, *Dr. Strangelove* fundamentally challenges The Ideology of Liberal Consensus by attacking anti-Communist paranoia, American adherence to outmoded notions of heroism, various nuclear strategies, and faith in social salvation through technological expertise. The Cold War foreign policy so strongly supported by Americans in the late 1940s and 1950s rested on the belief that America was a fundamentally just society threatened only by the germs of "Godless Communism." *Dr. Strangelove,* though it certainly does nothing to imply that the Soviet leaders are any wiser than their American counterparts, suggests that no nation-state has a monopoly on foolishness and that the backstage strategies of military and political leaders are simply exercises in paranoia. The nightmare comedy presented a disturbing and deeply wrought challenge to America in 1963 and 1964.

The film would not be so important were it not so uncharacteristic in the way it treated the Cold War. The House Un-American Activities Committee investigated Hollywood in two waves, once in 1947 (resulting in the infamous Hollywood Ten trials) and later in the early 1950s. Hollywood responded not by fighting government interference—as it had in the mid-Thirties censorship controversies—but by cooperating, blacklisting people who were suspected of leftist affiliations in the Thirties and making a spate of films which overtly or covertly supported the dominant paradigm.

The paradigm was overtly supported by a good number of anti-Communist melodramas from the late 1940s and early 1950s, of which *My Son John* (1952) may be the most famous example. These films were most popular between 1940 and 1953: in 1952 alone, twelve of them were released. Films about World War II, portraying the Nazis or the Japanese as villains, tended also to divide the world into good (the Allies) and evil (the Axis powers) and thus to support the dominant paradigm. Here Kubrick's anti-war *Paths of Glory* (1957) was clearly an anomaly. Even science fiction films, like *The Thing* (1951) or *War of the Worlds* (1952), by using threats from outer space as a metaphor of the Communist threat, covertly supported this conventional way of looking at and understanding the world. More directly related to *Dr. Strangelove* are a series of films through the 1950s and into the 1960s dealing with the bomb and especially with the Strategic Air Command.

Dr. Strangelove seems all the more amazing when one contrasts its iconoclasm and sharp satire with *Above and Beyond* (1952), *Strategic Air Command* (1957), *Bombers B-52* (1957), *A Gathering of Eagles* (1963), and *Fail Safe* (1964). The first of these films concerns the story of Paul Tibbetts, commander of the group which actually dropped the first atomic bombs on Hiroshima and Nagasaki. Much of the story concerns Mrs. Tibbetts' gradual acceptance of her husband's secret yet important work. *Strategic Air Command* follows much the same vein. In it a major league baseball star and former World War II pilot, played by Jimmy Stewart, gives up the last years of his prime to return to active duty. Stewart's wife, at first upset at her husband's decision, realizes that it is necessary for the peace and well-being of the nation. Produced in the same year, *Bombers B-52* concerns a sergeant who resists the temptation to take a higher paying civilian job, and thus retains his wonderful existence as an enlisted man.

Both *A Gathering of Eagles* and *Fail Safe* were released about the time of *Dr. Strangelove,* yet their approaches to their subjects are light years from that of *Strangelove.* General Curtis LeMay, commander of SAC, took a personal concern in *A Gathering of Eagles:* he stressed the need to explain how many safeguards had been created to prevent accidental war. The film concerns a young colonel who takes over a SAC wing that has failed a surprise alert and gradually trains his men so they are ever ready to go to war if the necessity arises. LeMay was pleased with the film, judging it "the closest any of the Air Force films ever came to showing the true picture of what the military was all about."

Fail Safe, released less than a year after *Dr. Strangelove* first seemed quite similar to *Dr. Strangelove* in that in both films, nuclear weapons are detonated by accident. But *Fail Safe* does nothing to suggest, as *Strangelove* does, that national policy is ridiculous. Instead it portrays the President (Henry Fonda) as a responsible and competent man caught in a tragic, yet controllable circumstance. His decision— to obliterate New York City in exchange for the accidental destruction of Moscow— prevents the destruction of the world and is powerfully rendered without a touch of irony: in the final moments, we see freeze frames of people on New York streets just before the bomb explodes. Despite its powerful cinematic ending, the film is, as Julian Smith has suggested, "a morally and intellectually dangerous film because it simplifies and romanticizes the issues of national responsibility."

All these films present a common respect for national and military leaders. Though bad apples may show up occasionally, though accidents may cause some difficulties, each film ends with control being reestablished, the viewer reassured that the American way is the best course and that the military is doing the best job possible to shield us from the Communist menace. None hint, as does *Dr. Strangelove,* that we may need protection against ourselves.

A look at how reviewers and the public responded to *Dr. Strangelove* can give us some indication of how Kubrick's adversary views were accepted. Since a feature film most often must reinforce the cultural values and attitudes of its viewers if it expects to be popular, it is understandable that neither critics nor the public were swept away by the film. Though few critics of mass magazines or political journals panned the film, a number of them, thinking within the bounds of the dominant paradigm, came up with strange interpretations. The critic for the right-wing *National Review,* for example, suggested that *Dr. Strangelove*'s theme was that all ideology should be abandoned. He went on to defend American ideology "with its roots thrust deep in Greek political thought," closing curiously with a hope that Kubrick might make a film criticizing Stalinism. *Saturday Review*'s Hollis Alpert gave a generally favorable review, concluding with these comments: "No one thinks our ingeniously destructive world-destroying bombs are a laughing matter. Certainly director Kubrick doesn't. But on some fairly safe planet out of view, maybe this is the way they would view our predicament." Alpert seems to miss Kubrick's point. No one accepting the dominant paradigm would see nuclear weapons as a laughing matter, but Kubrick, after studying the arms race, the Cold War, and the idea of deterrence carefully, realized the insanity of the situation and found that the only way he could possibly approach the material was through the satirical thrust of nightmare comedy. By having his audience laugh at the situation, he hoped not that they would realize its seriousness but rather that they would perceive its absurdity. Alpert, evidently, misunderstood the social rhetoric.

Two observers who thought highly of the film were Stanley Kauffmann and Lewis Mumford. Writing for *The New Republic*, Kauffmann—a critic notoriously harsh on most American films—thought *Dr. Strangelove* the best American film in fifteen years. The film showed "how mankind, its reflexes scored in its nervous system and its mind entangled in orthodoxies, insisted on destroying itself."

Dr. Strangelove

3

FILMS OF THE LATE SIXTIES AND EARLY SEVENTIES

From Counterculture to Counterrevolution, 1967–1971
Michael Ryan and Douglas Kellner

The late 1960s represented one of Hollywood's most creative periods, as filmmakers experimented with new narrative and stylistic techniques and used film to present searching reexaminations of American values and history. In sharp contrast during the early 1970s there occurred a sharp reaction against many of the values glorified in the films of the late 1960s.

In the late 1960s many Hollywood films, responding to social movements mobilized around the issues of civil rights, poverty, feminism, and militarism that were cresting at that time, articulated critiques of American values and institutions. They transcoded [expressed] a growing sense of alienation from the dominant myths and ideals of U.S. society. Film served as both an instrument of social criticism and a vehicle for presenting favorable representations of alterative values and institutions. "New Hollywood" films like *The Graduate, Bonnie and Clyde, Midnight Cowboy,* and *Easy Rider* were important not only for their social content. Some subverted the traditional narrative and cinematic representational codes of Hollywood filmmaking. Many employed a disjunctive editing that undermined passive viewing *(The Graduate, Point Blank),* used experimental camera techniques as thematic correlates *(Midnight Cowboy),* mixed genres like slapstick and tragedy *(Bonnie and Clyde),* employed color as an ironic or critical rather than expressive correlate of meaning *(They Shoot Horses, Don't They?),* broke down the classical narrative patterns that had dominated the 1950s and early 1960s *(Little Big Man),* introduced camera and editing techniques derived from television that significantly altered the pace and format of film *(M*A*S*H),* and underlined the mixture of blithe cynicism, complacent naivete, and strained optimism that characterized the Cold War period (in some respects, a "Restoration Period" in Hollywood).

These films provided audiences with a new set of representations for constructing the world, new figures of action, thought, and feeling for positing alternative phenomenal and social realities, sometimes apart from, sometimes within the interstices of the dominant social reality construction. These alternative representations and figures were as important as the new institutions and laws brought into being by the direct actions of blacks, students, and women in the streets and legislatures during the period. Even though the social movements themselves could be repressed or contravened, those new figures of social understanding and behavior would become a permanent part of American culture. Perhaps the most important of these representations was that of the self or subject in rebellion against conservative authority and social conformity. It was the figure that marked the end of the fifties ideal of functional selflessness. Related representations included that of the "Establishment" as a set of outdated conservative values, of the police as an enemy rather than a friend, of the patriarchal family as an institution for the oppression of women, of the liberal ideal of consensus as a cloak for white racial domination, of the government as the slave of economic interests, especially war industry interests, of foreign policy as a form of neoimperialism, of Third World liberation struggles as heroic, of the value of subjective experiences related to mysticism and drugs, of the importance of the preservation of nature, of sexuality as a rich terrain of possibility rather than as an evil to be repressed, and of capitalism as a form of enslavement instead of a realm of freedom. This transformation of the dominant representations which determined how the commonly held sense of social reality was constructed would have lasting, indeed permanent effects. It would be impossible to return unquestioningly to the imposed discipline of the fifties or to restore the conservative order of sexual and moral propriety that prevailed prior to the sixties. A radical alternative culture came into being, one immune to the sort of McCarthyite repression that had silenced the radical culture of the twenties and thirties, because the new radicalism was as critical of the Soviet Union as it was of the United States. And that meant that the impunity with which the business-government class had acted, especially overseas, could no longer be assumed without opposition. Resistance had become a staple of American culture.

Alienation and Rebellion

The major movements of the sixties were the black struggle for civil rights, the struggle against the Vietnam War, the feminist movement, and the New Left student movement. The sixties were also characterized by a high level of disaffection on the part of white middle-class youth from the values and ideals of fifties America, the world of suburban houses, corporate jobs, "straight" dress and behavior, sexual repression, and social conformity. These alienated and rebellious youth took to the roads, dropped out of school, started communes, grew long hair, listened to rock music, took drugs, and engaged in the creation of alternative lifestyles to those associated with the bourgeois "Establishment." We will begin our consideration of the sixties by looking at the phenomenon of alienation from and rejection of the "American Dream."

The American ideology which came to be rejected by so many during this period consisted of a set of codes for understanding the world and living in it that derived from American institutions and helped reproduce and legitimate them. Those codes provided an essentially metaphoric version of U.S. history and society. A metaphoric representation is one which replaces a real version of events or an accurate account of social reality with an elevated ideal. An understanding of the phenomenon of alienation from and rebellion against such ideals is therefore insepa-rable from an understanding of the representational strategies used to undermine such ideological idealizations.

Crucial among these representations is the individualist male hero, the ideal of the just American war, a righteous vision of U.S. history, and the frontier myth of expanding possibilities for achievement and wealth that are available to all. Many revisionist films criticize the myth of the traditional American hero through reconstructive representations that clash with the hitherto prevalent Hollywood conventions. For example, in *Little Big Man,* one of the most popular films of 1970, General Custer is portrayed as a megalomaniacal butcher who deserved his fate. The critical representational strategy of the film consists of adopting the position of the Native Americans and of depicting the U.S. soldiers from outside as the enemy. At a time when domestic opposition to the Vietnam War was on the rise, a number of satiric and tragic films like *M*A*S*H* and *Johnny Got His Gun* departed from the tradition of the just American war by representing war as something stupid and inhumane. The mythic representation of the frontier is undermined in films like *Soldier Blue* and *McCabe and Mrs. Miller,* which depict it as brutal. And the traditional representation of the ladder of individual success open to all talents is revised in critical films like *Midnight Cowboy* and *They Shoot Horses, Don't They?*—a film based, like *Johnny,* on a Depression-era novel. The revival of thirties leftism is also signaled by three critical films by directors from the heyday of the social problem film—Dassin's *Uptight,* Biberman's *Slaves,* and Polonsky's *Tell Them Willie Boy Is Here*—all of whom had been blacklisted.

The development of new narrative strategies in a number of these films is inseparable from their critiques of the major tenets of the American imaginary. The theme of individual success, like that of the great American patriotic tradition, is based in a narrative form. It is a story that entails a character, a plot, and a conclusion. Similarly, American history is a narrative with good and bad characters projected over actual events that moves from a happy beginning (the Founding Fathers) to an even happier conclusion (the present, or if that doesn't work, the future). The frequent use of discontinuous, reflexive, and interrupted narratives in these films is thus not only a playful formal device. It gets at the heart of the American imaginary, inasmuch as that is based in narratives (of individual success, of American history, and so on). . . .

The Graduate (1967), one of the first alienation films, is the story of a college graduate who rejects his parents' upper-class career track, has an affair with a much older woman, and finally flees with her daughter. Images of immersion in water suggest the claustrophobia of the bourgeois world, the cloying sense of its hypocrisy and emptiness, which many young people of the time were experiencing. And the career advice Ben (Dustin Hoffman) receives—"Plastics"—sums up what many young people of the era thought of the fifties world of their parents and of the career imperatives of the American Dream—that they were crass and artificial. Directed by Mike Nichols, *The Graduate* was a key alienation film of the period and was also the biggest box-office success of the late sixties. It was innovative in style, relying on imported French New Wave techniques—jump cuts, long takes with handheld cameras, tight close-ups—to render the experience of alienation from the American ideal of material success. Though weighted down by Christian imagery (Ben uses a cross to fight for his beloved Elayne) and a traditionalist romantic conclusion, the film nonetheless expanded the lexicon of the American cinema through editing and music primarily. In the credit sequence, Ben's air of passivity as he is carried along an airport conveyor belt while a loudspeaker issues recorded instructions is reinforced by Simon and Garfunkel's song "The Sounds of Silence." The music and the imagery suggest he is a cipher in a world of mass conformity and social control, the mode of being alienated young people claimed a technological and technocratic society was imposing on them. The film's critique is also executed through editing. Nonrealist transitions permit Ben to walk out of one space (his parents' outdoor pool) and into another quite different one (the hotel room where he carries on his affair), thus establishing contiguous links that suggest the interchangeability of upper-class luxury and cynical adultery. The [challenge to the ideal of] bourgeois success is realized fully at the end when the escaping young couple ride a common bus to freedom and leave behind their parents' wealth.

In the other great rebellion film of 1967, *Bonnie and Clyde,* the story of two young Depression-era outlaws who are ultimately murdered by the police, images of imprisonment and confinement (the bars of a bed which represent the constraints a young woman feels in her working-class world) are juxtaposed to images of the open fields of nature to establish a simple trajectory of escape. Contrasts in visual texture and tempo code the escape as one from confinement and fragmentation to openness and continuity. Throughout the film, images of open fields, single tone colors, an expansive camera frame for exterior shots, and jaunty banjo music suggest liberation from the tight focus shots in small-town settings. While the young rebels are associated with brown earth, blue sky, freedom of movement, and dynamic music, the figures of Establishment authority are represented negatively in association with bleak, whitewashed prison settings and images of urban confinement. The film thus evokes the romanticism that was prevalent in the late sixties, which counterposed nature as a realm of freedom and equality to the authoritarianism of the Establishment. . . .

Yet both *The Graduate* and *Bonnie and Clyde* evidence the limitations of the sixties version of alienated white middle-class rebellion. The alternatives posed to bourgeois conformity frequently took the form of a search for more personal, self-fulfilling experiences. The self ("doing one's own thing") became a criterion of authenticity, and in many ways this representation cohered perfectly with traditional American individualism. . . .

Alienation from the "American Dream" assumed its most striking form during the period in the hippie counterculture. Founded on the values of a return to nature, of the virtue of preindustrial social forms like the commune, of the need to liberate oneself from "straight" behavior, especially regarding sexuality, of the ideal of a simple and more authentic life experience, usually gained with the aid of drugs, the counterculture seemed for a time to be in the process of constituting a genuine and permanent alternative to bourgeois life. But the effort was itself dependent on a well-fueled capitalist economy, which began to fizzle out in 1970, and dropping out soon gave way to caving in. Law school followed a quick shave and haircut for many former hippies.

Easy Rider (1968) was produced by Bert Schneider and Bob Rafelson's BBS company, which also was responsible for other alienation classics of the time like *Five Easy Pieces* (1970) and *The Last Picture Show* (1971). The story of two motorcycle-riding hippies who travel from Los Angeles to New Orleans to sell drugs and who are murdered by rural rednecks in the end, the film turned a small budget into a large profit and helped launch the "New Hollywood" of more "personal" and artistic independent films. It is in this film that the ambivalent ideology of sixties individualism is most evident. Such individualism is usually male and highly narcissistic. Consequently, the ride into nature which the bikers undertake is both a metaphor for the escape from urban oppression into the freedom of self-discovery and a synecdoche for male narcissistic regression to a warm, comforting maternal environment in the face of the constraints of modern mass life (signaled by the metal structures that seem to be devouring the bikers in a scene just before their death). Women are noticeably marginalized in the film; they appear as compliant sexual partners, prostitutes, or devoted wives. Moreover, although the hippie quest permits a critique of small-town southern provincialism, it is also essentially aimed toward an ideal of freedom that is highly traditional. Indeed, it recalls the Jeffersonian yeoman ideal of small rural capitalism. For example, at one point the bikers are compared to cowboys shoeing a horse in a medium shot which includes both within the frame. In a certain sense, the bikers' ride is as much into the past as it is into the heartland. . . .

While hippie romanticism can be conservative, it also helped spawn the ecology movement, legislation to protect the environment, and the rediscovery of natural agriculture and foods. In its benign progressive forms, the counterculture became a culture of alternative values based in nature that led eventually to such important later social movements as the antinuclear campaigns of the late seventies and Greenpeace. In light of the value of "nature," some of the more negative aspects of conservative capitalist life came into focus—toxic waste, pollution, etc.—and became objects of social opposition. Thus, hippie romanticism was not univocal. Even though its inflection in *Easy Rider* is male individualist and narcissistic, it also gave rise to a mental health movement which questioned the prevailing definitions of psychological normality, emphasized the psychological costs of living in a capitalist society, and promoted ideals of self-expression as a way of gaining mental health. The very important subjective psychology movement of the seventies (the so-called "culture of narcissism") derives from the counterculture's emphasis on expressivity. Although it was often limited to white professionals, that movement pointed toward the necessity of a focus on issues of mental health in any progressive vision of social reconstruction.

We have concentrated on films celebrating the values of alienation and rebellion, but many films of the era cast both the counterculture and the new hip rebelliousness in a somewhat more critical light. Richard Lester's *Petulia* (1968) and Paul Mazursky's *Bob and Carol and Ted and Alice* (1970), for example, criticized the alternative lifestyles of the new sexual revolution. And films like *Panic in Needle Park* (1971) and Arthur Penn's *Alice's Restaurant* (1969) depicted the countercultural use of drugs negatively. Penn's film also suggested the fragility of the communal experience. By 1971, the dark side of the counterculture would be revealed for many in *Gimme Shelter,* the film of the Rolling Stones concert at Altamont which culminated in violent death. Film itself contributed to the standardization of the counterculture. The "capturing" of the experience of Woodstock, the major commercial "happening" of the late sixties, in a film of 1970 was also a freezing of the supposed spontaneity of the occasion. What could be filmed and commercialized was to a certain extent already inimical to the countercultural rejection of bourgeois values in favor of more noncommercial and natural ideals. To be "counter" cultural was to place oneself at odds with the mainstream of American culture, and while taking advantage of so commercial a form as the rock concert or the rock movie could help spread the countercultural message, it also necessarily contradicted the essential values of the counterculture. . . .

The Hollywood Counterrevolution

The struggles and movements of the sixties began to provoke a conservative backlash by the early seventies. Polls indicated a change during this period toward more "conservatism" and toward more concern with material self-satisfaction. Whereas only 1% of the people listed national unity as a major concern in 1959, the figure had risen to 15% by 1971. Adults also registered a reduced sense of integration into the social structure, more anxiety accompanied by an increased search for intimacy, an increased concern about an uncertain future, and a move to less social, more personal and individuated integration and well-being. There seems to be a relation between the new conservatism and the onset of the first major economic recession of the period at the same time. But the social struggles of the sixties also took their toll, giving rise to a countertendency desirous of unity, order, and peace. The demolition in the sixties of the cultural representations essential to the traditional order seemed to lead to a search for alternative forms of representational security and ego-integrity. But the sixties' assault on traditional values also provoked a reassertion of exaggerated versions of conservative ideals. The fearful retreat from the public world of disharmony and conflict was accompanied by a resuscitation of security-providing patriarchal representations. One finds evidence of the turn to personalism in the great popularity of *Love Story* (the top grossing picture of 1970) and of the desire for patriarchal unity in the success of right-wing police dramas like *The French Connection,* the Oscar winner in 1971, and *Dirty Harry* (1971), one of the most notorious films of the period.

Conservative films had been made during the late sixties. But on the whole, conservatives were then on the defensive, and the terrain of social struggle was determined by the insurgent liberal and radical social forces. The killing of student radicals at Kent State and Jackson State by National Guardsmen and police in 1971 marked a turning point in the limits of conservative tolerance for social revolt. By 1972, the Nixon counterrevolution was in full force, and the Nixon administration successfully mobilized conservative sentiments against young radicals, minorities, and feminists in the 1972 election by painting liberal Democrat George McGovern as the candidate of the three A's—abortion, acid, and amnesty for draft resisters. A meaner, more cynical discourse began to emerge as the dominant mode of Hollywood film. In 1971 alone, *The French Connection, Dirty Harry,* and *Straw Dogs* articulate an antiliberal value system that portrays human life as predatory and animalistic, a jungle without altruism.

At stake in Peckinpah's *Straw Dogs* is the law of the patriarchal family. In the late sixties, women were striking out for independence from male law in the home, and sexuality, long a secure domain of male power, became problematic. *Straw Dogs* sets the tone for the antifeminist counterrevolution of the seventies. The woman in the film is depicted as a treacherous sex kitten who betrays her "wimpy" husband, David, and entices men who finally rape her, an act she is portrayed as enjoying. In the final segment of the film, the same men attack their house, and she attempts to join them but is prevented from doing so by her husband, who is eventually transformed into a warrior who ultimately kills the attackers. His ascent to true manhood is associated with learning that liberal civility and law are useless against brute force and that women need to be disciplined if they are not to go astray. At one point he calls out to his attackers that what they are doing is against the law, but of course his plea is ineffective. The local constable, whose ineffectuality is signaled by his lame arm, ultimately hands power over to David, telling him he is "the law here now." The benediction seems also to apply to the domestic sphere. David immediately tells his wife, "Do as you're told," and smiles beatifically. In the end, he separates out from her altogether and rides off into the night with another man, a sign of the homosocial origins of misogyny.

Peckinpah's style earnestly expresses the ideal of male redemption through violence. The color tones suggest a dark nature of instinct and passion, and the violence has all the frenzy of a sexual encounter; indeed this is a telling feature for understanding its origins. *Straw Dogs* opens with a shot of children playing against gravestones, a scene reminiscent of the juxtaposition of innocence and violence that opens *The Wild Bunch*—children tormenting a scorpion with ants, then setting it on fire. Even the innocent harbor bestial desires and violent instincts, the film suggests. *Straw Dogs,* therefore, concerns regression, the falling back upon a supposedly more basic or natural reality of violence when social order breaks down. Yet the film can also be said to undermine or deconstruct its own premises.

David is educated in the process of the film. He learns to be violent, to regress from civility to bestiality, and to be a "man." The film presents this metaphorically as a recognition of primordial realities (through the metaphors of primitive hunting devices), but it depicts the regression as a process of training or socialization, a random, contingent, and metonymic process, in other words. The constable's benediction is the most telling evidence of the initiatory or artificially induced character of David's learning experience. Moreover, his relation to his wife is characterized by a mixture of fear and dependence that situates his aggressive domination of her and his ultimate flight into the night with another man as further evidence of the social origins of this particular male "nature." In the penultimate scene, David is about to be overwhelmed by one of the aggressors. He lies on his back, with the other man on top, an explicitly "feminine" pose. He is passive and helpless, and his wife has to save him with a shotgun blast. She stands at the top of the stairs, he at the bottom, a curious literal denial of all the film figuratively asserts. The passive male's rage against woman is in fact an anger against dependence, against the possibility of being "on the bottom," that is linked to fears of passivity in regard to other men in a competitive male world. Violence permits an escape from those feelings, as well as an overthrowing of female power and potential independence. What is really regressed to is an earlier stage of psychic development when women have power over men as their primary caretakers. That power must be purged in order for the man to acquire a patriarchally defined male identity. But male anxiety is not limited to an abreaction of earlier experiences of female power, a metaphor of a narcissistic, atemporal simultaneity or fusion. It also concerns female sexuality. When David's wife almost leaves to join the other men, she displays the origin of male sexual anxiety in a female sexuality which is not ultimately beholden to male power, which, like the literal metonymic associations that trouble self-idealizing metaphors, can "go astray." Violence also cures this threat to impropriety.

The other major conservative films of 1971—*Dirty Harry* and *The French Connection*—were crime dramas. These "law and order" thrillers transcoded discourse of the campaign against crime and drugs waged by Nixon and Agnew in the early seventies. They are also vehicles for conservative counterattacks against the liberalism that many conservatives blamed for the crisis in domestic order brought about by the sixties. Both films contest the liberal theories of criminal justice, exemplified in the Miranda decision, that gave more rights to criminal suspects and curtailed the powers of the police. In this vision, liberal criminal justice is unjust because it prevents good cops from doing their job, and it lets criminals go free to commit more crimes. Cops are portrayed as heroes whose zeal to protect the innocent and society is misinterpreted as brutality by liberals. Like *Straw Dogs* and *Clockwork Orange,* these films portray conservatism as a regression to primary process thinking, to a privileging of force and instinct over civil procedure. Unsublimated drives such as competition and domination are presented as more fundamental than such liberal civil modes as negotiation, mediation, and cooperation—all connective or metonymic ways of proceeding which encroach upon the firmly boundaried identities that conservative metaphors establish.

In *The French Connection,* a tough cop named Popeye Doyle (Gene Hackman) manages to crack a heroin smuggling operation, but all the criminals are let go in the end for lack of evidence. The suggestion is that liberals are responsible for the failure of the system, while the individualist cop is a better solution. The film is metaphoric to the extent that it presumes certain axioms that are not open to negotiation; the narrative obliges the audience to agree with the premises of the film because there are no spaces where reflection is possible. The cop reacts instinctively to the "problem" of crime (which, significantly, has not yet been committed), and the audience is given little time to do anything but react with equal rapidity to his actions, thus assuming guilt without judicial process. This is made clear in the famous chase scene. The subjective camera lodged in Popeye's car identifies the audience with his point of view in a way that works against reflection on the motivations and consequences of his actions. The audience's desires are manipulated into supporting a restoration of order or the achievement of the goal of catching the criminal, no matter what the cost in life or liberty (and Popeye almost does harm a number of people during the chase). When he finally does kill the hit man (unnecessarily; he could just as easily have wounded the disarmed man), the audience is prepared to desire the release of tension that ensues. Police brutality is thus legitimated stylistically.

A more overt and articulated statement against the sixties in general and against liberal criminal justice in particular is made in Don Siegel's *Dirty Harry*. Liberalism in crime prevention is outrightly condemned, and the evil figure in the film is a fanatical and "effeminate" killer named Scorpio who is associated with peace symbols, long hair, and other countercultural paraphernalia. The rhetorical procedure of this film is to position the audience as being knowledgeable of the criminal's guilt, then to show liberals letting him go after Harry has risked his life to capture him. When Scorpio kills again, the audience knows that Harry's only choice is to sidestep the liberal criminal system and use force. The style of the film is designed to produce both repulsion and idealization (two conjoined attitudes that reappear in a number of conservative films). It mixes naturalistic representations of violence and brutality (a raped adolescent girl being removed from a hole in the ground where she has been allowed to suffocate) with monumentalizing celebrations of white male individualist power (Harry standing alone against the sky overlooking the city like a Hobbesian sovereign). The representational mix is significant because such metaphoric idealization (which establishes Harry's higher meaning as a savior while separating him from the mass) is often a means of turning away from or denying something threatening or repulsive. In this case, the idealization is of extremely "male" traits such as aggressivity, toughness, lack of affect, and individualism. What is repulsive is "feminine" or, worse, indeterminate. Scorpio is associated with gays ("My, that's a big one," he remarks of Harry's gun, after Harry has mistaken a gay for Scorpio), and he is depicted as whining, weak, and very un-"manly." What this suggests is that male-defined ideals of conservative law and order are bound up with the representational dynamics that construct male sexual identity. Metaphoric male idealization comes down to an insecurity in males over the determinacy of sexual identity, over being a "man" and not being confused with a "woman," an insecurity associated with representational patterns that are metonymic, that is, that break down male boundaries and male identity by establishing empathetic connections with people or differential relations between supposedly hermetic [separate] realms. Because Scorpio represents such a breakdown, he must be eliminated. . . .

Dirty Harry was not a significantly popular film, at least in regard to box office receipts. Its sequels would fare much better. Our audience survey also suggests that it wasn't successful in winning large segments of the population over to its viewpoint: 77% of our sample felt Harry's methods were the wrong way to deal with crime, and 73% felt that the D.A. represented necessary constitutional protections as opposed to unnecessary red tape. While 40% perceived Harry as a rebel against American society, a significant 68% characterized him as a reactionary. It may be important as well that nearly 30% of our sample had not seen the film, though some of these no-views may be due to the age of the film. While our survey suggests that many viewers rejected the film's vision of the world, we should also note that in our oral interviews we encountered a number of people who fully held the position of the film, and in a number of cases where people disagreed with the solution to crime, they nonetheless confessed to buying in temporarily to the action format and the plot premises of the film. This splitting of the ego between a reserved judgment and participation in the spectacle characterizes a number of audience response patterns to different films. It suggests that the popularity of right-wing films is not necessarily a testament to the prevalence of right-wing opinions in the film audiences. But it also points to the possibility of false consciousness and of unconscious influences. It is noteworthy, for example, that 79% of those polled also support stronger punishment for criminals.

French Connection and *Dirty Harry* are reactionary films, yet they also contain immanent critiques of American society. To be able to proclaim their right-wing solutions, they must inadvertently describe a disintegrating society which is incapable of finding real solutions to its fundamental problems of economic, political, and social inequality. The films depict the failure of liberal solutions to the problems of crime and poverty generated by capitalism. More accurately than liberal films, they portray the real exercise of force that underlies seemingly apolitical problems like crime. Right-wing films in certain ways portray the harsh truth of a society which must rely on authoritarian and repressive police force, generally directed overwhelmingly at minorities, in order to avoid coming undone as a result of its structural imbalances. . . .

4

REAFFIRMING TRADITIONAL VALUES

The Blue Collar Ethnic In Bicentennial America: *Rocky* (1976)
Daniel J. Leab

Years after it first appeared, Rocky *remains one of the most popular films made during the 1970s. In this essay, the historian Daniel J. Leab locates the film in the context in which it was originally made, and shows how it reflected shifting cultural attitudes toward race, class, and ethnicity, and a broad cultural impulse to reaffirm traditional values that took place in the middle and late 1970s.*

The very foundations of the American Dream had been severely shaken during the first half of the 1970s: the Watergate crisis had resulted in the resignation of a President of the United States and criminal prosecution of high-ranking federal officials; the armed forces had been defeated in combat by an Asian people; the Arab oil embargo forced recognition that the United States no longer enjoyed unlimited natural resources; the economy floundered between the seemingly irreconcilable forces of increasing unemployment and inflation; a vocal and alien counterculture had challenged successfully various traditional values; "crime-in-the-streets" as well as rioting in the inner city and on campus threatened permanent damage to domestic tranquility; various minority groups through escalating, sometimes violent, demands seemed to have irreparably rent the fabric of American society. So dour, indeed, did everyday American life appear that in 1974 a positive and hopeful assessment of the United States in the 1970s characterized the decade thus far as "the age of the rip-off."

Suddenly, in 1976, with the celebration of the two hundredth anniversary of the Declaration of Independence and the creation of the United States, the nation's mood changed perceptibly. Bicentennial America, almost overnight, put behind it Watergate, Vietnam, stagflation, and many other problems. The media—which for so long had highlighted the negative side of American life—now spoke of "the ongoing resilience of what used to be called The American Dream." Even *U.S. News and World Report,* well known for its weekly prophecies of doom and analyses of the various malaises troubling the United States, now unabashedly declared that "nowhere on earth . . . do the hopes for the future appear more exciting than they do in the U.S., rich in spirit . . . power . . . and people." A German observer of the American scene found that concern over America's problems had given way, at least for the moment, to celebration of the bicentennial.

Rocky is an integral if somewhat unusual part of that bicentennial binge. Set in the white ethnic working-class slums of South Philadelphia, *Rocky* deals with such unappetizing aspects of current life in the United States as organized crime, professional boxing, media exploitation, and the hard-scrabble world of the working-class, blue-collar ethnic. Yet, even though dealing with the underside of contemporary America, *Rocky* is a celebration of the American Dream. Movie critic Frank Rich perceptively analyzed the film's wide appeal when he described *Rocky* as a "fairy tale" that "tapped the popular spirit of the present: . . . the old-fashioned, Bi-Centennial vision of America."

At first glance the film's eponymous protagonist seems an unusual hero for bicentennial America. Rocky Balboa (Sylvester Stallone)—self-styled "The Italian Stallion"—is a dim-witted, fourth-rate, thirty-year-old club fighter of no particular distinction, except perhaps for the fact (of which he proudly boasts) that in ten years of fighting his nose has never been broken. Professional boxing has netted him nothing. He earns his keep working as a muscle man for Gazzo, a loan shark. Rocky's life is bleak. He seems to have no future. He lives alone, in squalor. Drunks, bums, and seedy layabouts line the streets of his rundown Philadelphia neighborhood. His friends and acquaintances are corrupt, moronic, or venal. Avuncular advice to a young teenage girl about "hanging out" at night "with them coconuts on the corner [older boys]" earns Rocky a derisive "Screw you, Creepo ! ! !"

Whatever the drawbacks of Rocky's world, the film makes clear in that peculiar cinematic shorthand so well understood by movie audiences all over the world—that although he may he a bum, he is a bum with heart. Rocky (to use one reviewer's exaggerated but apt words) is presented as "an innocent . . . an earth child from the streets of a slum." He likes animals: his confidantes are two pet turtles named Cuff and Link. He cares about people: on a cold night he takes a drunkard out of the gutter and carries him into the corner saloon. He is not mean: even though ordered to break the thumb of one of Gazzo's clients, Rocky refrains from so doing.

Happenstance lifts Rocky out of his nether world. A bicentennial world heavyweight championship match has been scheduled for Philadelphia. A few weeks before the match, the contender is injured and the champion, Apollo Creed (Carl Weathers playing a nasty caricature of Muhammad Ali), decides that rather than scrap the intricate and profitable arrangements that already have been made, he will fight a "local boy." Creed chooses Rocky, in part because Rocky seems easily beatable, and in part because the champion believes that the "Italian Stallion" nickname should make good media copy and help maintain interest in the fight. A surprised Rocky is offered 150,000 dollars and a chance at the title. He accepts and trains to win. On the eve of the fight Rocky recognizes that he has been deceiving himself, but he resolves to prove his worth nevertheless by going the distance with Creed. And in a bruising, gritty, fifteen-round brawl Rocky does just that—even managing to knock down the champion several times. The decision goes to Creed, but Rocky has won personally, having proven that he is not "just another bum from the neighborhood."

As important as the title match for Rocky's growth in self-esteem is his romantic involvement with Adrian (Talia Shire), his friend Paulie's (Burt Young) painfully shy spinster sister. Adrian works in the pet shop that Rocky frequents. However, their first date comes about at the instigation of Paulie, who virtually orders Rocky to ask out Adrian and forces her to accept. Initially she appears on screen as an unattractive, mousey, withdrawn drudge who forlornly lives with and looks after her brother. But then Rocky takes her out, takes down her hair, takes off her glasses, and takes her to bed. As their romance blossoms she becomes a new person in the best traditions of Hollywood's Golden Age. And by the end of the film she has become a graceful, attractive, spirited young woman. After an argument with Paulie about his attempts to use Rocky, she moves out of her brother's home and in with the fighter. This concession to modern mores notwithstanding, the relationship between Rocky and Adrian is presented as sentimental and uplifting. In an age of sexually blatant movies, *Rocky*'s love scenes are discreet: the sexual overtones are there, but only romance is made explicit; nudity and copulation are left to the audience's imagination.

Rocky's story is essentially the work of Sylvester Stallone. He began writing it in the early spring of 1975. He was in his late twenties and after six years of brash effort seemed to have failed as an actor. His one big part had been in *The Lords of Flatbush,* a 1974 artistic success/commercial flop. The majority of his roles had been small and/or forgettable in movies like *The Prisoner of Second Avenue* (1975), *Capone* (1975), and *Death Race 2000* (1975). He also had tried writing movie and television scripts but won little recognition—the major exception being a credit he earned for "additional dialogue" on *The Lords of Flatbush.*

Stallone got the idea for *Rocky* after watching the March, 1975, title bout between Muhammed Ali and Chuck Wepner for the heavyweight championship. Wepner, "a guy on the skids" known as "the Bayonne Bleeder," not only managed to knock Ali down, but also (unlike most of the champion's previous opponents) almost went the distance—the fight being stopped nineteen seconds from the end of the fifteenth and final round. Stallone and Gene Kirkwood, a "fledgling producer" (to use *Newsweek*'s description) had been discussing various movie possibilities before the Ali-Wepner match. Inspired by the fight, Stallone in three and a half days of almost nonstop effort drafted the screenplay that became *Rocky.* An interesting sidelight to current moviemaking is Stallone's comment that this "script was about 122 pages long and went to more than 330 or 340 pages of revisions and we barely altered it from the original concept." Kirkwood interested the independent producing team of Robert Chartoff and Irwin Winkler in Stallone's script. They in turn offered it to United Artists, who ultimately agreed to undertake the production. Shooting began in December, 1975.

Stallone was determined to play Rocky. The producers recognized the quality of the script but wanted a name star for the title role. They offered Stallone well over $100,000 to sell the script and "to bow out." He refused, even though, as Kirkwood recalls, Stallone was "hard up for bucks": he had a bank balance of $106, a pregnant wife, and few other foreseeable prospects. Stallone later recalled telling his wife "if you don't mind going out in the backyard and eating grass, I'd rather burn this script than sell it to another actor." She agreed, but the need to eat grass never arose. Stallone played Rocky. He won critical acclaim as well as Oscar nominations for his script and his performance—placing him in very select company, as only Orson Welles and Charlie Chaplin had received these dual nominations before.

Stallone made good media copy, and understandably he received far more publicity than anyone else connected with the film. However, as critic James Monaco pointed out, "while *Rocky* has been advertised as the protean conception of its star-writer, director John Avildsen's contributions are essential to its success and should not be overlooked. Avildsen has a flair for the kind of working-class milieu portrayed in *Rocky*. Indeed, he first came to prominence in 1970 as director and photographer of *Joe,* whose central character was also lower class—albeit very different from the good-natured *Rocky*. Joe was a foul-mouthed, beer-drinking, hippie-hating factory worker, who joined with an upper-middle-class "friend" to murder some Greenwich Village "drop outs." The film's phenomenal box-office success stemmed in part from Avildsen's ability to present Joe so realistically and dramatically that there were "recorded incidents of kids shouting 'We'll get you, Joe!' at the screen." *Joe*'s success enabled Avildsen to escape making exploitation pictures such as *Turn On To Love,* and in the next few years he directed a variety of films, including the 1973 Paramount release *Save the Tiger,* whose star, Jack Lemmon, won the Oscar for Best Actor.

Avildsen, noted for his economy and speed, shot *Rocky* in twenty-eight days (two under schedule) and did not overspend his budget. Critical response to Avildsen's direction of *Rocky* varied considerably. Pauline Kael found his approach to be "strictly-from-hunger." Andrew Sarris asserted that Avildsen provided "no glow, no aura for his hero." *Newsweek*'s Janet Maslin, on the other hand, maintained that the film had been "crisply directed." In *Time,* Richard Schickel argued that in *Rocky* the director showed a "stronger naturalistic gift than in *Joe* or *Save the Tiger*."

Certainly the film benefitted from Avildsen's ability to capture the gritty atmosphere of South Philadelphia's garbage-strewn, joyless streets and seedy, worn, row houses. English critic Tom Milne waxed rhapsodic over Avildsen's ability to film the "extraordinary nocturnal landscapes of strangely dislocated urban geometry . . . in which the human figures seem both estranged and yet as much a natural part of the scene as the tenuously impermanent structures themselves." Milne argued that Avildsen and his cameraman had turned the Philadelphia exteriors "into something very close to a series of Magritte paintings." Amidst all the justified praise for Stallone, it should be remembered that Avildsen won an Academy Award for his direction of *Rocky*.

Both the much-publicized genesis of the film and Stallone's insistence on playing Rocky had Horatio Alger overtones that appealed to bicentennial America. But the production of the film reflects no sentiment, only the hard-headed economic realities of the American movie industry in the 1970s. Chartoff and Winkler are not producers in the traditional sense; they are "packagers" and as such part of what the film journalist Axel Madsen has dubbed "the New Hollywood." They do not work with any one studio. They put packages together and then look to the studios for financing. As Chartoff has explained: "We go to Warner's and say 'Look, we have such and such a project that so and so is interested in . . . ; the whole thing can be made for so and so much money. . . .' " If Warner's is not interested, "United Artists, Columbia, or any of the other majors then look at it and say yes or no, sometimes no . . . or yes, if we can bring it down to such a figure." Chartoff, a theatrical lawyer, and Winkler, a television agent, met "by accident," became one of the first independent producing teams in Hollywood in the mid-1960s, and prior to *Rocky* had produced eighteen movies, including such interesting ones as *Point Blank* (released by MGM in 1967) and such clinkers as the Charles Bronson melodrama *Breakout* (distributed by Columbia in 1975).

After *Rocky* had proved itself, the head of West Coast production for United Artists gloated over "the excitement" provoked both by the film and by Stallone. But when Chartoff and Winkler initially sought approval from United Artists to meet Stallone's demand that he himself play Rocky, the company set some hard conditions. The film's budget was cut almost in half to one million dollars; Stallone was to be paid a minimal salary of twenty thousand dollars (albeit also a percentage of the possible profits); Chartoff and Winkler had to guarantee to make up any budget overruns. Just before the film was released, Winkler told an interviewer "everyone sacrificed for potential profits. We hope it pays off—we think it will . . ."

And it did, probably far beyond his expectations. Financially the film turned out to be a bonanza, "one of the biggest movie winners of all time," according to *Newsweek*. Its one-million-dollar budget was very modest in terms of 1975–76 feature film production, "peanuts in today's movie world," to use critic David Sterritt's clichéd but apt description. By the end of April, 1977—five months after the film had been released—*Rocky* had grossed over fifty million dollars in the United States and Canada. And in August, 1977, *Variety* estimated that thus far *Rocky* had grossed over one hundred million dollars in the United States and Canada, and that the film still had considerable earning potential in those markets. *Rocky* had proved to be one of the highest grossing films ever made, on a par in terms of impact and drawing power with films like *Gone With the Wind* (1939), *The Sound of Music* (1965), and *Jaws* (1975).

Critically, *Rocky* also scored a major triumph—albeit one less overwhelming than its box-office success. Film reviewers used words like "schmaltz" and "cliché" in discussing *Rocky,* and there was criticism of some aspects of the film in most reviews, but overall, few reviewers failed to respond positively to it. Even the tough-minded and unsentimental Pauline Kael found much to praise in *Rocky,* and although alert to its shortcomings she described the film as "engaging" and "emotionally effective." Vincent Canby of the *New York Times* was a notable exception to the generally favorable critical response; he found the film lacking in verve, seemingly fraudulent, and he thought it "never quite measured up." But his comments had little effect. *Rocky* won a wide variety of awards, including ten Oscar nominations and three Academy Awards (Best Director, Best Picture, and Best Editing).

To what can one attribute *Rocky*'s extraordinary commercial success and generally favorable critical reception? An extensive, hard-hitting, intelligent publicity campaign played a significant role. A seemingly untiring Stallone, for example, made himself available for interview after interview by representatives from every branch of the media. Indeed, so ubiquitous was Stallone that one commentator claimed that *Rocky*'s creator "has granted more interviews in recent months than any American short of Lillian Carter." The *Variety* review of *Rocky,* written almost a month before the film went into release, noted that "the p.r. juggernaut is already at high speed." Vincent Canby in his *New York Times* review expressed uneasiness and displeasure at "the sort of highpowered publicity . . . that's been attending the birth of *Rocky* . . ." The extent of this high-powered publicity campaign is emphasized by the many echoes of Canby's attitude among reviewers. A trade journalist examining the selling of the film found that "whether rave, pan, or . . . 'no opinion,' review after review of *Rocky* tore into the crescendo of advance comment. . . ."

Hype alone, however, cannot account for the wildly enthusiastic response that many movie audiences afforded the film. They cheered Rocky, booed Creed, and at the end of the film, with tears in their eyes, applauded the credits. Critic Roger Greenspan reported that "the two times I saw *Rocky* people in the audience stood up and cheered at the end." Another reviewer detailed the reactions of an "Italian friend" at a screening of the film: "when the 'Italian Stallion' landed a savage right hook on the . . . chin of Apollo Creed . . . my friend let out a 'Whoop' as if he had a week's salary riding on the punch." Frank Rich expressed amazement at the number of usually blasé New York City moviegoers who after seeing *Rocky* left "the theater beaming and boisterous, as if they won a door prize rather than parted with the price of a first-run movie ticket, and they volunteer ecstatic opinions of the film to the people waiting on line for the next show."

Viewing *Rocky* was an emotion-charged experience for many American movie-goers. The film touched "a live nerve with the public," as Frank Rich put it. American audiences, influenced by the bicentennial's strong emphasis on the validity of the American Dream, had lost interest in downbeat themes, in bleak reality, in attacks on old-fashioned values—all subjects which as films of one sort or another had recently done well at the box office. Stallone rather perceptively touched on the changing interests of moviegoers in one of his many interviews: "I believe the country as a whole is beginning to break out of this . . . anti-everything syndrome . . . this nihilistic, Hemingwayistic attitude that everything in the end must wither and die. . . ."

In discussing *Rocky's* appeal (as well as its positive outlook) reviewers and other commentators referred over and over again to the optimistic, idealistic, senti-mental, 1930s movies of director Frank Capra. Even Avildsen announced that he was fond of the comparison: "Capra's my idol. I love the emotionalism and idealism in what he was doing. . . ." Capra himself said about *Rocky:* "Boy, that's a picture I wish I had made." But "Capra-corn" as evidenced by such films as *Mr. Deeds Goes to Town* (1936) or *Mr. Smith Goes to Washington* (1939) will not and should not serve as points of reference for *Rocky*. In the Capra productions, as film histo-rian Richard Griffith has astutely pointed out, "a messianic innocent, not unlike the classic simpleton of literature . . . pits himself against the forces of entrenched greed . . . his gallant integrity in the face of temptation calls forth the good will of the 'little people' and through combined protest, he triumphs." Rocky may be an innocent, but he is not messianic, and the "little people" he associates with are not the middle class on which Capra dotes. It is not surprising that Capra, when discussing his films at an AFI seminar in 1971, declared that Ralph Nader "would make a perfect Capra hero." And Rocky certainly is not a Nader type.

Just as *Rocky* owed little to the Capra films, so too did it owe little to previous Hollywood treatments of boxing. These in the main had concentrated on exposing the ills of "the fight game." But *Rocky* had none of the bleak cynicism of *Champion* (1949), the oppressive social consciousness of *Golden Boy* (1939), the vicious corruption of *The Harder They Fall* (1956), or the sleazy hopelessness of *The Set-*

Up (1949). However, *Rocky* does not exist in a vacuum. It does owe something to the ingratiating style of *Somebody Up There Likes Me,* the enthusiastic 1956 screen biography of one-time middle-weight champion Rocky Graziano. And *Rocky's* love story obviously owes something to *Marty,* the poignant 1955 film about two lonely people who expect never to find love, but come together. In one respect, however, *Rocky* is almost unique, and that is its working-class perspective.

As James Monaco has pointed out, "the intellectual, middle class establishment has always felt quite comfortable with films whose *subjects* were workers. . . ." But *Rocky* is not presented from a middle-class point of view; the film speaks for the working class, albeit as columnist Pete Hamill acidly commented: "nobody calls it the working class any more . . . ; the bureaucratic, sociological phrase is white lower-middle class," sometimes referred to as "the ethnics." *Rocky* obviously was palatable to the American middle class, but its success rests on the film's appeal to the white ethnic American (once succinctly described by a magazine writer as "perhaps the most alienated person" in the United States). *Rocky* endorsed the ethnic's prejudices, deferred to his fantasies, and highlighted his lifestyle.

The film's treatment of blacks accords with the racial attitudes that, in the view of many social scientists, govern the thinking of the white ethnic American. Their conventional wisdom holds that these white ethnics believe that they have "paid the costs" of American society's attempts to redress black grievances, that "the poorest, least secure, least educated, and least tolerant" in the white community believe they have been sacrificed by a liberal elite anxious to ensure "responsible social change." And, it is argued, the ethnics bitterly resent this attempt at change. Thus, a sociologist surveying the attitudes of a group of blue-collar workers about contemporary America in the early 1970s argues that except for the Vietnam war "the most explosive issue was the demand for black equality." And in this context he quotes as representative a carpenter who angrily declared, "I realize that something has to be done for the black bastards, but I sure as hell don't want them living next to me. I don't care to work with them either."

Rocky plays on these old prejudices and new fears. The film's racism is not overtly stated, but if not explicit, it is still vividly (and visually) implicit. At one point in the film Rocky is shown training in the meat-packing plant where Paulie works. He is training for the fight with Creed by using a carcass of beef as a punching bag, hitting the carcass until his hands are blood red from the juice of the meat. A local television station has sent a crew to film this unusual method of training. The reporter is an arrogantly glib, fashionably dressed, light-skinned black woman, who oozes condescension and contempt during her dealings with Rocky (and Paulie). In many ways she is an unpleasant burlesque of the female reporters found on television newscasts across the country. One can, of course, attribute her presence in the film to a hostility to television news programming or to the women's liberation movement. But one must also ask why a black woman, why that particular kind of arrogant black woman, who patronizes Rocky and Paulie. Here we must remember the words of a literary critic in dealing with another movie genre: "everything in a film is there because somebody wanted it there, although it is often hard to know why or even who that somebody was."

That "somebody" must also claim credit for the nasty, smarmy depiction of Apollo Creed. In public Creed acts the clown, satirizing traditional American values. He enters the arena for his fight with Rocky to the tune of "Yankee Doodle Dandy," and he prances around the ring in an elaborate Uncle Sam costume before stripping to star-spangled trunks. If publicly Creed mocks the bicentennial, privately he expresses contempt for the American Dream and views public belief in it as one more means of making money. Explaining his choice of Rocky as a substitute for the injured challenger, a mocking Creed says "I'm sentimental, and lots of people in this country are just as sentimental." The articulate, well-groomed, business-minded Creed stands in obvious contrast to Rocky—so much so that as Andrew Sarris points out, the "Italian Stallion" becomes "the most romanticized Great White Hope in screen history." Nor, despite over a decade of black heavyweight champions, should the White Hope feeling be ignored. Ali, for example, in his autobiography touches on "the racial issue" in boxing and asks "who put it there and who keeps it there." His answer is given by a veteran reporter who tells him, "they want your ass whipped in public, knocked down, ripped, stomped, clubbed, pulverized, and not just by anybody, but by a real Great White Hope."

The makers of *Rocky* had a feel for ethnic America. Somber authenticity marks the film's settings indoors and out. The home of Paulie and Adrian, for example, is in a row house with a tiny front yard in a decayed inner-city neighborhood. The furniture is neat but worn, the rooms are small, the lamps are chintzy, the living room is dominated by an old television set. The outdoor Christmas decorations, or lack of them, on various houses are just right for South Philadelphia, or Hamtramck, or Corona, or any one of a hundred ethnic neighborhoods.

Paulie is presented as "pathetically brutish" (to use Judith Crist's apt phrase). A picture of him in uniform on the mantel hints at his only and temporary escape from the neighborhood. Paulie desperately wants to get away from the meat-packing plant and almost pleadingly asks Rocky for an introduction to Gazzo the loan shark. Paulie feels he could certainly do as good a job for Gazzo as Rocky. Michael Novak has commented that one of the reasons for "the new ethnicity" is the "suppressed anger" of the white lower-middle class. In a remarkable scene Paulie lets loose that anger, and stalking around his home strikes out wildly, viciously, forcefully with a baseball bat. He smashes doors, furniture, walls, as he rants against the dead-endedness of his life. Paulie, in Stallone's words, is "a symbol of the blue collar, disenfranchised, left-out mentality, a man who feels life has given him an unfair amount of cheap shots. . . ."

But in the final analysis neither racism nor reality brought people to the box office in such large numbers. *Rocky* succeeded because of its mythic qualities which neatly dovetailed with the imagery that had been sold by the bicentennial. The sociologist Andrew Greeley has argued that "ethnicity has become almost fashion-able." But it was not that fashion which sold *Rocky*. The movie, as Frank Rich said, "can hold its own with Cinderella," as it sets forth that a bum can become a real contender overnight, that riches can come from nowhere, that hard work and the will to make good can still succeed in the United States, that "a shy and unattractive heroine can blossom into a worldly beauty by getting contact lenses and losing her virginity," and that happy endings still exist. And it is to such myths that *Rocky*'s audiences responded so enthusiastically.

Historian William Hughes contends that the feature film does not just "reveal popular attitudes," but "like other forms of cultural expression, can reveal more than they intend." *Rocky* is an excellent manifestation of this "covert-overt" approach to looking at feature films. On the surface it is a "fairy tale," and quite an ingratiating one at that. But *Rocky* also provides strong clues to the public mood in the United States in the mid-1970s. *Rocky* could do this because as a French commentator on American film points out, "the freedom of the Hollywood director is not measured by what he can openly do within the . . . system, but rather by what he can imply about American society in general. . . ." John Avildsen wove Stallone's story into a richly textured film, shot through with social implications, reactionary as some of them may be.

The film itself and the public's response to it speak volumes about how Americans saw themselves in 1976. *Rocky* captured the mood of bicentennial America, a mood which saw the reaffirmation of many traditional values, including racial prejudices that seemed rejuvenated by the economic and social pressures of the 1970s. *Rocky* also highlighted America's changing attitude toward the white lower-middle class and toward ethnic blue-collar America. Stallone hit at the core of the matter in his comments on audience response to the film: "when they're cheering for Rocky, they're cheering for themselves."

5

COMING TO TERMS WITH THE VIETNAM WAR

Distorted Images, Missed Opportunities

James S. Olson and Randy Roberts

Since the John Wayne epic The Green Berets *appeared in 1968, Hollywood has released more than twenty-five films examining the Vietnam War. In this essay, two historians examine the variety of ways that Hollywood moviemakers have dealt with the American experience in Vietnam.*

It was not at all like the Iwo Jima monument. On that point nearly everyone agreed. Probably the most famous American war monument, the Iwo Jima statue stands proud in Arlington, Virginia, an eloquent reminder of a simpler, more straightforward war. Frozen in bronze are the five marines thrusting the American flag into the soil on top of Mount Surabachi. Its style is heroic realism, a faithful attempt to reproduce the award-winning photograph. It traffics in uncomplex emotions that border on clichés: the "good war," John Wayne in the Pacific, go get 'em boys, "I shall return." Not far from the Iwo Jima monument, across the Potomac River, broods the Vietnam War Memorial. Between the Washington Monument and the Lincoln Memorial, the Vietnam Memorial rises out of a depression in the ground, shifts direction a bit, and then descends back into the ground. Its surface is polished black granite, an inscrutable veneer that reflects the image of the viewer and the landscape that faces it. Cut into the granite are the names of the more than 58,000 men and women who died in the war. What did they die for? What caused the war? What was the nature of the conflict? If you look for the answers in the silent black stone, all you will see is yourself.

From its inception the memorial generated controversy. It was too vague, some said, too abstract, not heroic enough. Others complained loudly and bitterly about the architect, Yale student Maya Ying Lin. The war had been against Asians. Students had been the most outspoken opponents of the war. Should an Asian-American student memorialize the war? Many veterans answered no. Emotion ran high. The memorial, meant to commemorate sacrifice, opened old wounds. The questions about the meaning of the war returned with fresh force. To satisfy veterans' protests, another sculpture was commissioned. This one, the work of Frederick Hart, is a realistic rendition of soldiers. Both memorials were dedicated on November 13, 1982.

The controversy died quickly. Good for a few stories on nightly news shows

284

and a handful of editorials, by 1983 it had become old news. The polished black stone took its place near the other stones—some polished, some not—which memorialize other events and other wars and other men. Tourists dutifully visited it along with the others. Most were pleased by what they saw, agreeing that it was "a pretty nice" memorial after all. They came, they saw, they passed judgment, and they left. Their reflections lasted only a moment. In some very special way, the memorial was like the war itself—so misunderstood and complex and even abstract. Americans went to a land few understood. They fought a war full of sound and fury. And then they returned home. And within a short time Vietnam left the news shows and the news magazines, replaced by other stories.

The struggle of Americans to come to terms with the Vietnam War was contested largely outside the corridors of power. Politicians, diplomats, and military leaders lost their chance to influence popular opinion. Many Americans no longer trusted their answers to fundamental questions. With the war lost and the peace concluded, politicians gave way to intellectuals and artists and media executives, a diverse collection of historians, writers, and film and television producers. It was now their turn to explain the war and its impact upon American society. The time to ask, "What should we do?" had passed. Now the questions "What did we do?" and "Why did we do it?" occupied center stage.

Americans struggled with three central issues. First, the veterans of the war. How did Vietnam change them? Could they peacefully return to American society? How did their experiences scar them? Second, the war itself. What did it accomplish? What did it mean? How did it change America? Third, the loss of the war. Why did the United States lose? Who or what was to blame? How did that experience change America?

Vietnam War

At first the Vietnam veteran had loomed large in American popular culture. He came to symbolize the war that the nation wished to forget, and far from being portrayed as a hero he was transformed into a villain. Somehow his participation in the "immoral" war, even if it had not been voluntary, set him apart from the civilians at home and made him a misfit. Often he was seen as a person not to pity or hate or love but to fear, for he was a ticking time bomb waiting to explode, waiting to carry the war home.

This presentation of the returning veteran was not unique to the Vietnam War. In Edward Dmytryk's film *Crossfire* (1947), Robert Ryan plays a psychotic returning veteran consumed by his hatred for Jews. Palpable violence pervades the film. A civilian correctly notes, "You can feel the tension in the air. A whole lot of fight and hate that doesn't know where to go." Ryan clearly does have deadly potential, and he can and does kill. But he is not portrayed as the typical returning GI.

His hate is deeper; it is the fruit of a lifetime of psychological trouble, not the product of the war. Other veterans might have some difficulty adjusting to civilian life—as they do in *The Best Years of Our Lives* (1946)—but if they threaten anyone it is only themselves. And by the end of the films the returning veterans do adjust; they are successfully reintegrated into civilian society.

Few people doubted the moral fiber of the World War II veteran. After all, he had fought in the "good war," and his cause was just. Korean War veterans faced greater difficulties. The war was more ambiguous; the peace, less satisfying. In fact, was it a war at all? Or was it a "police action" or simply a "conflict"? The veterans knew the answer, but civilians had called into question their very performance. Reports that the communists had successfully "brainwashed" POWs frightened civilians and led to speculation that some of the returning soldiers might be spies. The novel (1959) and later the film (1962) *The Manchurian Candidate* centered on the idea that communists had programmed some returning POWs to kill. But even in the case of the brainwashed killer—the Manchurian Candidate—psychological problems are rooted more in his relationship with his mother than in his wartime experiences. On this point the novel and the film are clear: The war did not create misfits and psychotics; only a lifetime of maladjustment—and perhaps a dash of communist "brainwashing"—could produce an unbalanced veteran.

The psychotic or maladjusted Vietnam War veteran, however, was portrayed as a product of the war. In most cases, he is a man without a background, a man without a home or parents or life before his service in Vietnam. It is almost as if he were bred in the country's steamy jungles and fertile rice fields. All he knows is war, and when he returns to the United States he continues to ply his trade. Sometimes he joins an outlaw motorcycle gang in which violence is a way of life and a reason for being. Such B-movies as *Angels from Hell* (1968), *Satan's Sadists* (1969), *Chrome and Hot Leather* (1971), and *The Losers* (1971) transport the veteran from a helicopter to a Harley. Other times the veteran remains a loner. But once again the potential for violence seethes beneath the surface. In *Taxi Driver* (1976) Travis Bickle (Robert De Niro) ticks quietly in New York City. He has no past and no future; he seems to invent both out of thin air. Although he writes his parents, he fills his letters with lies, and one suspects that his parents are part of his fantasy life. The only reality in his life is the war that he cannot articulate but that drives him toward violence as surely as he drives his taxi. As Seth Cagin and Philip Dray observe: "Travis Bickle is the prototypical movie vet: In ways we can only imagine, the horror of the war unhinged him. He's lost contact with other human beings, he doesn't hear them quite properly, and his speaking rhythms are off. He's edgy; he can't sleep at night, not even with the help of pills, so he takes a job as a taxi driver on the night shift." And he waits to explode. That in the end he kills a pimp is irrelevant. He might just as easily have killed a politician or anyone else, including himself. His violence knows no reason. It is not directed toward society or politicians or any particular person. It just is.

Violence is given greater direction and logic in *Tracks* (1976), a low budget film directed by Henry Jaglom. In the film an army sergeant, played by Dennis Hopper, escorts the body of a friend killed in Vietnam back to the soldier's home for burial. On the cross-country train trip he tries to tell his fellow passengers about the dead soldier, a black hero who saved his life. He asks the civilians about the war and wonders why the United States was in Vietnam. Most of the other passengers are not interested in the sergeant, his dead comrade, or his questions; some are hostile, a few embarrassed. His war is not their war; his sufferings are not their sufferings. The film ends with the burial. Alone, the sergeant watches the coffin being lowered into the ground. Then he jumps in after it. When he emerges from the hole he is dressed for battle and fully armed. "You want to go to Nam?" he cries out. "I'll take you there." A sympathetic character has once again been transformed into violence incarnate. Avenging angel or not, violence is implicit in his being, the answer to an uncaring nation.

Even when the veteran wishes to avoid violence it follows him like an albatross. In Karel Reisz's *Who'll Stop the Rain* (1978), based on Robert Stone's novel *Dog Soldiers* (1974), the action centers on a veteran who is involved in smuggling a shipment of heroin into the United States. Not only does he bring the corruption of Saigon back home with him—for the heroin will ruin civilians just as it did soldiers—but violence and death follow in his wake. As in the other films, the ultimate threat of the veterans is the Vietnamization of the United States.

Occasionally the Vietnam veteran made it to prime-time television. Here, too, he is often portrayed as a potential or actual killer. Normally there is an attempt to explain his problems and to help him. More often than in Hollywood films, he is characterized as a basically good person corrupted and turned violent by the war. If not consumed by violence, the veteran stands apart from the civilian population in some other way. Perhaps he is a loner or a drug addict, a perfectionist or a malcontent. Almost never does he have a family or enjoy "normal" relations with other people. In her article on the changing image of the Vietnam veteran, Lisa M. Heilbronn comments, "Service in Vietnam most often served to explain the sociopathic or homicidal behavior of a criminal. It was used to explain a personal crisis, alcoholism, drug use, or the psychological problems of a character whom the series' regulars would aid."

Lieutenant Howard Hunter, the leader of a SWAT team in the popular "Hill Street Blues," was one of the few Vietnam veterans who was fully integrated into a series. Competent at his job, Hunter is nonetheless emotionally crippled. He is portrayed as a lonely man, living an isolated existence except for work and his dog. Inept with women, he is also stiff and uncomfortable around men. In one episode he even attempts suicide. Although rigidly moralistic, he is also reactionary and prejudiced and prone toward the most violent solution to the problems he faces. During the years that the series was on television, Hunter's character evolved and he was given more "human" qualities. But he remained a man living close to his emotional limits, a spring wound a bit too tight.

Starting in the late 1970s the image of the Vietnam veteran began to change. Hollywood signaled the shift with two successful movies—*Coming Home* (1978) and *The Deer Hunter* (1978). In *Coming Home,* director Hal Ashby continued his interest in Vietnam. Three years earlier he had directed *Shampoo,* a film about wealthy Southern Californians set during the 1968 presidential election. As the characters in *Shampoo* get ready for a Nixon victory party, news of the horrors of Vietnam assaults them from radios and televisions. But they pay no mind; it is not their war, not their concern. *Coming Home* brings the war to southern California. Its central characters are Luke Martin (Jon Voight), a bitter paraplegic, and Sally Hyde (Jane Fonda), the wife of a marine captain (Bruce Dern) serving a tour in Vietnam. Viewed from the perspective of the early 1990s, *Coming Home* is sentimental stuff. It is too pat. During the course of the film the conservative, sexually repressed Sally flowers into a liberal, liberated woman. She puts on Levis, allows her hair to follow its natural frizzy disposition, and experiences an orgasm—with Luke—for the first time in her life. Luke also is transformed. Bitter and angry at the start of the film, he becomes introspective and gentle. *Coming Home* suggests that love can cure the trauma of Vietnam, that understanding can erase the pain of bad memories.

In 1978, however, *Coming Home* was an original film. Frank Rich of *Time* magazine called it "one long, low howl of pain," and other reviewers agreed that it was an important statement. It also showed Hollywood that a film about the Vietnam War could be political and profitable. At the same time it contributed to the rehabilitation of the popular image of the Vietnam veteran. Influenced by paraplegic Ron Kovic's *Born on the Fourth of July* (1976), *Coming Home* portrays the veteran as not only someone who needs to be healed but also as a healer. Luke is not a loner; he is not a ticking bomb; he is not a threat to society. His anger flows from the unwillingness of America to recognize his plight. "When people look they don't see me," Luke tells Sally. He wants America to take notice and to remember, for his crippled body is an important legacy of Vietnam. Toward the end of the film he tells a group of high school students, "There was a lot of shit over there I find fucking hard to live with. But I don't feel sorry for myself. I'm just saying that there's a choice to be made." And that choice is as present in the United States as it was in Vietnam. Luke has to decide whether he will live consumed by bitterness or use his pain to help others. He chooses the latter course and is reintegrated into society.

The Deer Hunter contains the same message. Directed by Michael Cimino, the film shows how the war changed the lives of three men from a western Pennsylvania steel town. Of the three, the most important is Michael (Robert De Niro). He begins the film as a loner, and violence seems an integral part of his character. He kills a deer with one shot and is intolerant of his friends' shortcomings. In Vietnam, it seems, surrounded by death and terror, he finds compassion. He saves the lives of his two friends, and when one becomes addicted to heroin and Russian roulette, Michael even risks his own life in an attempt to reach him. "I love you," he says just before Nicky's (Christopher Walken) luck runs out and he loses his final game of Russian roulette.

Vietnam changes Michael for the better. It purges him of his aggression and anger. He no longer wants to kill deer or any other living animals. He is at peace with himself and his surroundings. He can even love and now is able to relate to women. The film ends on a note of affirmation. After Nicky's funeral, Michael joins his other friends—women as well as men—in singing "God Bless America." He is finally a whole person, reconciled with himself, his community, and his country. That same message comes through in Oliver Stone's 1990 film *Born on the Fourth of July,* in which Tom Cruise portrays Ron Kovic, a crippled Vietnam veteran who finally comes to terms with the war.

After 1980 the popular image of the Vietnam veteran began to change on television. Like Michael in *The Deer Hunter* and Luke in *Coming Home,* the veteran was transformed into a figure of compassion and imbued with a sense of justice. Rather than threaten society, the new television veteran defends society, upholds justice, and restores order. In Vietnam he learned how to fight, use sophisticated weapons, and function in a tight-knit group, but the experience did not rob him of his compassion. Indeed, it is suggested that the very traits that led him to Vietnam now compel him to battle evil and injustice in the United States. Television showcased this new veteran in such shows as "Magnum, P.I.," "The A-Team," "Riptide," and "Air Wolf." Most of the heroes of these shows are unmarried, but their bachelorhood is not viewed as negative. The group functions as their family, and they display a healthy attraction to women that is amply reciprocated. Furthermore, they are not scarred emotionally or physically by their service in Vietnam. No guilt troubles their thoughts, no injuries plague their days.

Although these heroes were once in the military, they no longer act on behalf of the government. Crippled by red tape and bureaucratic lethargy, the modern state seems unable to act with speed and justice. The veteran heroes are part of the private sector—the United States of Ronald Reagan—and they function outside official channels. But they always get the job done; they ensure justice. As the viewer is told each week at the beginning of "The A-Team," "If you have a problem, if no one else can help, and if you can find them . . . you can hire the A-Team." But if the veteran heroes work outside of the government, they are still willing to fight for their country. Often they combat external threats—drug smuggling, terrorism, and spying. Occasionally they travel outside the United States to solve problems. This they willingly do, for their cause is always just and on television ends justify means. Perhaps, as Lisa M. Heilbronn writes, they "represent a desire on the part of the public to see our control secured beyond the boundaries of the United States."

The transformation of the Vietnam veteran on television since 1980 is part of the more general rehabilitation of the popular image of the United States military. During the 1970s films and television portrayed the military as a corrupt, bloodthirsty institution. Although enlisted men were occasionally presented as decent people, officers were invariably pictured as incompetent, self-serving, and destructive. "The bullshit piled up so fast in Vietnam you needed wings to stay above it," Captain Willard remarks in *Apocalypse Now* (1979). And in the same movie, Lieutenant Colonel Kilgore orders his men into battle to secure a strip of beach that has "good surf." In such films as *An Officer and a Gentleman* (1982), *Taps* (1981), *Lords of Discipline* (1983), *Private Benjamin* (1980), and *Stripes* (1981),

Hollywood revitalized the military. Instead of being an institution that kills boys, it is viewed as a place where boys become men, or in the case of *Private Benjamin,* spoiled girls become independent women.

At the start of *An Officer and a Gentleman,* Zack Mayo (Richard Gere) is a self-centered punk. He wants to be an officer but cares nothing for discipline or traditions and exploits his fellow officer candidates. During the course of the film he learns to respect and love the navy. "I will never forget you," he tells his ruthless drill instructor (DI) upon completing officer candidate school. For him the navy has become the home he never had. His spit-and-polish black DI becomes his true father, replacing his drunken, prostitute-chasing biological father. Mayo and his classmates are ideal types—clean, honorable, and disciplined. By contrast, civilians in the film are portrayed as beer-swilling, pool-shooting troublemakers. They provoke fights—which they promptly lose—and generally exist to envy the officer candidates. As for the candidates who do not have the "right stuff," life appears bleak. Mayo's friend who quits just before graduation informs his fiancee that he can return to Oklahoma and get his old job back at J. C. Penney. Faced with that prospect, she dumps him and he commits suicide.

In part, the promilitary films reflect the economy of the late 1970s and early 1980s. High-paying jobs in heavy industry were becoming scarce, and there was little glamour or money in flipping hamburgers at McDonald's. For many young Americans the military became "a great place to start." Enlistments in the armed forces jumped in the 1980s, and enrollment in ROTC programs doubled. The mood of Reagan's era—with its overt patriotism and promise of restored greatness— contributed to the popularity of the films. It contrasted especially with the malaise and perceived impotency of the Carter years. Americans yearned for a return to greatness. They wanted a military with teeth, equipped to act and fortified by a commitment to a higher code.

As Americans reappraised the Vietnam veteran and the military, they also attempted to understand the war itself. Historians sifted through the "facts" of the war. Aided by the illegally released Pentagon Papers, they searched for its causes. During the 1960s and most of the 1970s two schools of thought emerged. The first believed that the war, in Arthur Schlesinger, Jr.'s words, was a "tragedy without villains." It resulted from unfortunate decisions made by well-meaning officials. The second school rejected this benign view and asserted that the war was the result of an imperialistic American foreign policy. Such historians as William Appleman Williams, Walter LaFeber, and Gabriel Kolko claimed that the United States had a history of expansion and domination and that at least since the turn of the century it had been establishing its hegemony over the Pacific. The Vietnam War marked a setback in this policy of expansion, but the decision to fight in Vietnam was very much a part of the policy.

During the 1980s a third school of historical thought gained ascendancy. It maintained that the war was a "noble crusade" against communism, a shining expression of American commitment to democracy and liberty. Not only did these historians believe that the United States should have fought in Vietnam, they argued that the military could have won the war. These historians absolve the military of all guilt. As Guenter Lewy writes in *America in Vietnam* (1978), "The sense of guilt created by the Vietnam War in the minds of many Americans is not warranted and the charges of officially condoned illegal and grossly immoral conduct are without substance." Instead of being the villains, the soldiers who fought the war were the heroes; they did their duty under taxing circumstances. That the war was ultimately lost was not their fault. Rather civilians back home—both inside and outside the government—failed to understand what the war was about and refused to live up to their country's honorable commitment to South Vietnam. Of course, this perception reflected the changing political face of the United States. By 1980 politicians were once again talking about falling dominoes and the obligations the United States had to countries struggling to stay free. In 1980 Ronald Reagan said that the United States had "an inescapable duty to act as the tutor and protector of the free world."

This academic search for an understanding of the Vietnam War was expressed in popular culture. Many of the novelists who wrote about the war had served in Vietnam, and for them the war was a morass. Raised on World War II films that ooze moral certainty and enshrine a sporting ethos and the notion of fair play, these writers confront in Vietnam a world of shadows and moral ambiguities. Their schoolboy rules belonged to a distant continent. "It was the dawn of creation in the Indochina bush," writes Philip Caputo in *A Rumor of War* (1977), "an ethical as well as a geographical wilderness. Out there, lacking restraints, sanctioned to kill, confronted by a hostile country and a relentless enemy, we sank into a brutish state." The same sense of uncertainty is expressed in Tim O'Brien's *Going after Cacciato* (1978). His protagonist

> didn't know who was right, or what was right; he didn't know if it was a war of self-determination or self-destruction, outright aggression or national liberation; he didn't know which speeches to believe, which books, which politicians; he didn't know if nations would topple like dominoes or stand separate like trees; he didn't know who started the war, or why, or when, or with what motives: he didn't know if it mattered.

This profound sense of confusion about the meaning of and the reasons for the war also found its way into the films about the war. Francis Ford Coppola's *Apocalypse Now* attempted to translate that confusion into a narrative film. "The most important thing I wanted to do in the making of *Apocalypse Now*," Coppola wrote in the program notes for the film, "was to create a film experience that would give the audience a sense of the horror, the madness, the sensuousness, and the moral dilemma of the Vietnam War." Captain Willard's voyage up the river into the "heart of darkness" is as much a quest for answers as it is a mission of death. In trying to understand the sanity behind Colonel Kurtz's insanity, Willard is attempting to fathom the logic of the illogical conflict. Everywhere there is madness. The coldly unemotional military and civilian officials who tell Willard that Kurtz's command must be "terminated with extreme prejudice" are mad. They speak the language of madness; the meanings of their words cannot be found in a dictionary. Kilgore is mad. He attacks the enemy not to win the war but to secure a good surfing beach. Even Willard remarks, "After seeing the way Kilgore fought the war, I began to wonder what they had against Kurtz." And Kurtz, well, he is quite mad. He is like a computer thrown into an Alice-in-Wonderland world and fed bits of illogical data. His response to his environment is to become insane, for as the film demonstrates, only the insane survive.

Apocalypse Now may be the best film about the war, and its theme of madness may be accurate on a psychological level, but it does not help the viewer understand how or why the United States became involved in the war. It does not deal with what the war accomplished or how it changed the country. Its major political criticism is aimed not at the war itself but at the management of the war. Willard describes his superior officers as "a bunch of four star clowns who are giving the whole circus away." He openly sympathizes with the outlaw Kurtz: "Charging someone with murder in a place like this is like handing out speeding tickets at the Indianapolis 500."

Platoon (1986) similarly does not address questions of causation or results. Instead, it revolves around a conflict of good and evil. The war becomes a stage, and although there is an attempt to relate something of the combat experience, the meaning of the war is irrelevant. In one voice-over, Chris Taylor (Charlie Sheen), the leading character in the film, remarks, "I think now, we did not fight the enemy, we fought ourselves. And the enemy was in us." This is the soul of the film—the enemy within. It happens to be set in Vietnam. It just as easily could have been set in World War II or peacetime. Like *Apocalypse Now, Coming Home,* and *The Deer Hunter, Platoon* is about self-discovery, not war.

Films that have taken a political stand have not been particularly successful at the box office. *Go Tell the Spartans* (1978) deals with the early years of the American combat presence in Vietnam. In theory these were years of youthful innocence, a time when the struggle for "hearts and minds" was taken seriously by Americans in Vietnam and in the United States. But as the film illustrates, the war was already over. The United States had lost but had not yet realized the fact. The film's final scene—a long shot of a cemetery of war dead—suggests that the only act remaining in the war was death, futile, meaningless death.

If filmmakers dealt poorly with the origins and meaning of the war, they were even worse at coming to terms with defeat. To be sure, most of the films depict a thoroughly corrupt or stupid officer corps. But beyond this limited explanation of failure few producers were willing to go. Part of the reason was financial; industry leaders maintained that Americans would not pay to watch a film about their country's losing a war. During the 1970s when there was a mood of self-criticism in the country, few films about the war were made. And when producers turned to the subject of the war, the age of self-criticism had passed. The Reagan years affirmed patriotic values. Heroes dominated popular culture. Rock star Bruce Springsteen, at his 1986 concert in Dallas, expressed frustration that his anti-Vietnam megahit "Born in the U.S.A." had actually become, in the popular mind, a patriotic anthem.

The best expression of this new mood was Sylvester Stallone's film *First Blood* (1982) and *Rambo: First Blood II* (1985). In the first film John Rambo is an ex-Green Beret who is mistaken for a hippie. By nature a loner and even a peaceful man, he is forced by a series of inept government officials to defend his freedom in the wilds of the Pacific Northwest. The movie suggests that men like John Rambo did not lose the war; politicians back home did. In the climactic scene Rambo tells his former Special Forces commanding officer: "Nothing is over, nothing! You just don't turn it off. It wasn't my war—you asked me, I didn't ask you . . . and I did what I had to do to win—but somebody wouldn't let us win." Yet there is no examination of just what "winning" in the context of the war in Vietnam means. It is enough for Rambo and his audience that the war could have been won.

In the second film Rambo returns to Vietnam to find and rescue Americans missing in action (MIAs) from Vietnam—a popular scenario in the mid-1980s that was central to such films as *Uncommon Valor* (1983), *Missing in Action* (1984), *Missing in Action II* (1985), *P.O.W.: The Escape* (1986), and *The Hanoi Hilton* (1987). But Rambo was really returning to Vietnam to win the war. When Colonel Trautman (Richard Crenna), his former commander, tells him, "The old war's dead, John," Rambo replies, "I'm alive. It's still alive." And later Rambo asks, "Do we get to win this time?" Trautman answers, "This time it's up to you." And since winning is again never defined, Rambo rewrites history. He "wins."

While American filmmakers "Ramboized" the conflict, Vietnam labored to construct a viable nation out of the rubble of war. As the last American helicoptered from the roof of the United States Embassy in Saigon in 1975, North Vietnamese troops crashed through the gates. Saigon, whose very name was associated with American domination, was renamed Ho Chi Minh City, a salute to the dead Vietnamese hero. North Vietnamese and Vietcong celebrated the creation of a new country, the fulfillment of the centuries-old dream.

The war of liberation had ended, but the struggle continued. The Socialist Republic of Vietnam (SRV), as the united nation was named, faced pressing problems. At the core of the new struggle was a nation battered by three decades of fighting. American bombing had destroyed the infrastructure of Vietnam. Roads and bridges, power plants and factories lay in ruins. Ports suffered from damage and neglect. For a generation the resources of Vietnam had been used to fuel the war machines, and with the war over, conversion to a peacetime economy presented difficult, at times almost insurmountable, problems. Raw materials were in short supply, and investment capital had left with the Americans. Machines that had been imported from the United States broke down, and spare parts were impossible to obtain. If peace brought hope, it also brought the specter of economic ruin.

Vietnamese communism smothered the country with a stifling bureaucracy. The communists tried to implement Ho's dream—political reunification of the two Vietnams and imposition of a socialist economic order. North Vietnamese cadres and Vietcong took control of South Vietnam, seized private property, collectivized plantations and farms, squeezed out small businesses, and hunted down South Vietnamese political and military officials. The government forcibly moved nearly 1 million civilians from Ho Chi Minh City, Hue, Danang, and Nha Trang to "New Economic Zones" in abandoned sections of South Vietnam. The SRV—blessed with a strategic location, a huge capacity for producing rice, and an enterprising people—declined into Third World poverty complete with high unemployment, crippling food shortages, and starvation. Along with the direct results of the war— hundreds of thousands of orphans, paraplegics, and amputees, and the physical destruction wrought by the American military—the ideology of communism transformed Vietnam into one of the poorest countries in the world. The average worker made the equivalent of 300 dong a month in 1980. That same year a pair of cotton trousers cost 400 dong and a new bicycle 20,000 dong. Malnutrition became a normal condition. As one Soviet professor in Vietnam privately confided, "How much poverty in Vietnam? We have nothing like this in Moscow. Their party has made so many mistakes."

The SRV also failed in its attempt to de-Westernize the country. Western ideas and aspirations lingered in the south. Reeducation along socialist lines failed to alter old habits. A number of critics even contended that southerners "Westernized" northerners. The official party newspaper Nhan Dan warned that the "neo-colonial culture" of the south was "expanding to the north" and threatened to "spoil our younger generation and wreck our revolution." French food, American beer, and Western ideas became black market commodities. Governmental corruption, always a staple in the south, wound its way north. As one loyal northerner admitted, "I've been a Communist all my life. But now, for the first time, I have seen the realities of Communism. It is a failure—mismanagement, corruption, privilege, repression. My ideals are gone."

As conditions in Vietnam worsened, hundreds of thousands of Vietnamese fled the food and electricity rationing, de-Westernization, grinding poverty, and countless other daily hardships. Ethnic Chinese, the business leaders and merchants in Ho Chi Minh City, left the country in droves. The "boat people"—desperate Vietnamese willing to flee the SRV at all costs—risked the dangers of the South China Sea to find a new home. Tens of thousands drowned at sea when their rickety ships sank, and thousands more were killed by pirates. Tens of thousands were caught by Vietnamese authorities before they had gone very far. Indonesia and Malaysia frequently rejected them when they did make landfall. Although exact statistics are difficult to obtain, as many as 250,000 Vietnamese boat people died during their escape attempt.

Diplomatic woes compounded domestic unrest. In 1977 President Jimmy Carter cautiously extended the olive branch to the SRV. Determined to improve the image of the United States among Third World countries, soon after his election Carter announced that he "Would be perfectly glad to support the admission of Vietnam to the United Nations and to normalize relations with Vietnam." That autumn he made good on his promise, and the two countries allowed academic and other cultural exchanges. At that moment what the SRV most needed was the investment capital and technological expertise of the United States. But in 1978 the SRV committed several critical mistakes, the most important of which was to demand reparations as a precondition for normalization. This demand prompted a quick reaction in Congress, opening still fresh psychological wounds. Carter's decision to extend amnesty to all Americans who had fled to Canada during the war to avoid the draft and to all those who had deserted from the armed forces had a similar effect. Carter's initiatives—Vietnam's best hope of recovery and economic stability—died on the floor of Congress.

In 1978 the SRV made a second disastrous mistake. It invaded Kampuchea (formerly Cambodia). In comparison with Kampuchea, Vietnam's problems seemed insignificant. Recalling the mid-1970s, the *New York Times* correspondent Sydney H. Schanberg remarked: "Everybody, Cambodians and foreigners alike, looked with hopeful relief to the collapse of the city, for they felt that when the Communists came and the war finally ended, at least the suffering would be over. All of us were wrong." When Pol Pot and the Khmer Rouge roared into downtown Phnom Penh in armored personnel carriers and trucks in April 1975, they brought a demanding, ruthless ideology with them. They began emptying the cities of Cambodia, forcing people into the countryside for reeducation. For Pol Pot it was the beginning of a new age—"Year Zero" for the new country of Kampuchea.

Dreaming of a preindustrial, agricultural utopia, he launched an assault on cities, teachers, intellectuals, professionals, and the middle class. He completely evacuated Phnom Penh, turning the city of 3 million people into a ghost town. He ordered the destruction of libraries, temples, schools, colleges, businesses, and whole cities. He transformed Kampuchea into a concentration camp, a huge "killing field" where 2 million Kampucheans lost their lives.

The Vietnamese watched the horrors with growing anxiety. A revolt in eastern Cambodia in 1977 sent hundreds of thousands of frightened Kampucheans fleeing across the border into Vietnam. By 1978 the SRV had had enough of Pol Pot's megalomania. Vietnamese troops invaded Kampuchea, drove Pol Pot and the Khmer Rouge into the jungles, and established the People's Republic of Kampuchea. But the invasion did not end the suffering. Coming as it did during the planting season, peasant farmers lost their rice crop, and widespread starvation resulted. Pol Pot regrouped his forces and, with 35,000 troops, began a guerrilla action against the invasion. The Khmer People's National Liberation Front, supplied by the United States, fielded 15,000 of its own guerrillas, and there was another 9,000-person guerrilla army loyal to Prince Norodom Sihanouk. The three groups fought guerrilla wars against one another and the Vietnamese. With the Vietnamese in Kampuchea, the premeditated killing of civilians stopped, but once again the flames of war swept across Indochina.

The centuries-old animosities between Vietnamese and Kampucheans stirred other ancient hatreds and fears. China did not want to see the SRV extend its influence. On February 17, 1979, Deng Xiaoping sent the People's Liberation Army across the border into Tonkin. The bloody war lasted less than one month, but 35,000 people died before it was over. On their way out of Tonkin, the Chinese destroyed several towns, blew up vital railway links, and obliterated important power plants and a phosphate mine responsible for most of Vietnam's fertilizer.

The border war against China and the guerrilla war against Kampuchea further strained the Vietnamese economy. Before the two wars the SRV had been attempting to secure desperately needed loans from China, Japan, and several Western countries. As the fighting became hotter, the international financial community became colder. To make matters worse, the SRV had the added cost of maintaining a standing army of more than 1 million men and stationing 140,000 troops in Kampuchea. By the mid-1980s the SRV had become one of the poorest nations in the world, but its army was the fourth largest in the world. In 1989 Vietnam withdrew its troops from Kampuchea, raising the specter of the return of Pol Pot and Khmer Rouge to power. Visions of genocide, of the holocaust portrayed in David Putnam's 1984 film *The Killing Fields,* once again plagued the people of Indochina. The American war in Vietnam was over. The older war, with origins in the ancient past, continued.

For the money needed to keep its country solvent, Vietnam turned to the Soviet Union. The loans the Soviet Union provided—$1.5 billion annually—carried strings that stretched back to Moscow. To many people inside and outside of Vietnam, it soon appeared that Soviet domination had simply replaced American domination. Just as American advisers and experts flocked to Vietnam twenty years earlier, so now the Soviets came. "Americans without dollars," the Vietnamese called them. One Vietnamese joke reflected the new relationship with the Soviet

Union: After appealing to the Soviets for loans, Vietnam receives the cable: "Tighten your belts." Vietnam replies: "Send belts."

By the mid-1980s the SRV had sunk to its lowest point. Economic reorganization had failed. Emigrants—often valuable professionals whom the country needed—continued to leave. The guerrilla war in Kampuchea dragged on. And Soviet advisers worked to turn the SRV into Cuba East. Finally, in 1986 the SRV committed itself to a radical change. At the Sixth Communist Party Congress, party leaders admitted that their experiment in communism had failed. The old guard retired and a new set of leaders, led by Nguyen Van Linh, took office. Linh, who had been born in Hanoi but had lived the majority of his life in the south, symbolized the desire for true national unification. He realized that the economic and foreign policies of Pham Van Dong were bankrupt. Boldly, and with a firm sense of resolve, he once again looked West.

Undoubtedly influenced by the ideas and actions of Mikhail Gorbachev, Linh opened Vietnam to increasing amounts of democracy and capitalism. He permitted politicians to openly contest for assembly seats, and he released political prisoners. He sanctioned limited free enterprise and trimmed the glutted governmental bureaucracy. He even opened up Vietnam to Western goods. As the historian Terry H. Anderson notes, "Western T-shirts and tapes of Madonna" were sold on the streets of Hanoi. Where a few years earlier the SRV had frightened away Western investment capital, it now courted Western bankers and industrialists by enacting a liberal foreign investment code. "An underdeveloped nation such as Vietnam," Linh emphasized, "needs even more to look to the capitalist world for lessons."

The emergence of new forms in popular culture reflected Vietnam's political and economic changes. Such American films as *Platoon* played to crowded houses in Ho Chi Minh City and Hanoi. And the Vietnamese film industry started to make films that showed the emotional complexity of the war. In *Ahn va em* (*Brothers and Relations,* 1986) a veteran returns from war to find a changed Vietnamese society. Hanoi is wallowing in consumerism, his family has betrayed the ideas of socialism, and government corruption hampers efforts to reconstruct Vietnam. The veteran questions why he fought. In the end of the film, he turns away from the modern Vietnam and withdraws to the traditional, "unprogressive" life of the rural village.

The image of Americans is also revamped in the recent Vietnamese films. American soldiers are portrayed as victims of a senseless and unjust war—confused, frustrated, and angry but not evil. Films such as Hong Sen's *The Abandoned Fields—Free Fire Zone* (1979) endow the machines of war, not the soldiers, with evil intentions. The filmmaker anthropomorphizes helicopters, giving them malevolent qualities. They drop from the sky like prehistoric birds of prey. They, not their pilots, are blamed for the destruction. In the last scene of the film the Vietnamese shoot down a helicopter. In the wreckage they discover a dead pilot. "It is a sad moment," notes film critic Karen Jaehne, made "all the sadder for a photo of the pilot's family carried away from the carnage on the wind."

Altogether the films signal a shift in Vietnam's attitude toward the United States. Since 1986 the SRV has promoted cultural exchanges with the United States by liberalizing its visa policy and allowing American writers and journalists greater access to Vietnam. American tourists can now visit Hue, Dienbienphu, and the Cu Chi tunnels. The government has allowed Vietnamese Amerasian children to emigrate to the United States to reunite with their parents. Through actions and words, the SRV has conveyed the simple message that the war is over and the time to forgive is at hand.

The message, however, was at odds with American foreign policy in the 1980s. During his two terms as president, Ronald Reagan consistently ignored Vietnamese efforts to normalize relations between the two countries. Rather than emphasize areas of agreement, he stressed fields of discord. Reagan focused on two issues: Vietnam's continued occupation of Kampuchea and the POW-MIA controversy. The first was a concrete problem. The SRV expressed a willingness to withdraw from Kampuchea—and in fact began to withdraw in 1988—but the prospect of the return of Pol Pot to power complicated matters. Given the centuries of hostilities between the Vietnamese and the Khmer, the SRV was not anxious to see the Khmer Rouge extend its power. In addition, other world powers feared the return of Pol Pot would initiate a new phase in his genocidal war against all Western influences within Kampuchea. Nevertheless, the Vietnamese completed their withdrawal from Kampuchea in 1989.

The POW-MIA issue was largely imaginary. Fueled by a series of POW-MIA movies and the incendiary rhetoric of the Reagan administration, a large portion of the American public became convinced that there were thousands of prisoners of war and other American soldiers listed as missing in action still alive in Vietnam. This emotionally charged issue blocked talks between the United States and the Socialist Republic of Vietnam for almost a decade. It also defied logic and impartial investigation. Although several government investigations of the issue reached the conclusion that there are no live POWs or MIAs in Vietnam, still the suspicion lingers. Criticizing the Reagan administration for its intractable stand, Terry H. Anderson observes:

> Technically, it is impossible for any Vietnamese government to find "all recoverable remains" under fifteen years of jungle growth. . . . Also MIAs are not just an American problem. The French still have 20,000 MIAs from their war in Indochina, and the Vietnamese list over 200,000. Furthermore, the United States still has 80,000 MIAs from World War II and 8,000 from the Korean War, figures that represent 20 and 15 percent, respectively, of the confirmed dead in those conflicts; the percentage is 4 percent for the Vietnam War. . . . The real "noble cause" for [the Reagan] administration is not the former war but its emotional and impossible crusade to retrieve "all recoverable remains."

Since 1988 the SRV has attempted to improve its foreign relations. It completed the withdrawal from Kampuchea and tried to address the POW-MIA charges. It has even moved to weaken its ties with the Soviet Union. Still, during the late 1980s, American policy was influenced less by Vietnam's recent actions than by the films of Sylvester Stallone and Chuck Norris—two actors who were of draft age during the war but never served—and Reagan's rhetoric labeling Vietnam as part of the Soviet's "evil empire." Indeed, even as glasnost changed Reagan's and Bush's attitudes toward the Soviet Union, Vietnam has remained a country untouchable. Neither rice bug infestations nor droughts, nor typhoons, nor starvation, nor suffering has altered the official policy. Vietnam may have won the war, but it has not won peace.

6

FILMS OF THE EIGHTIES

The Yuppie Texts
William Joe Palmer

A new character type appeared in the films of the 1980s: the young urban professional, better known as the yuppie. Born during the baby boom of the 1950s and early 1960s, a period of unprecedented economic growth, holding high expectations for their material success and personal self-fulfillment, yuppies assumed a disproportionate place in the popular culture of the 1980s. In this essay, William Joe Palmer examines the various ways that Hollywood depicted yuppies, their values, virtues, and vices.

In the action comedy *Burglar* (1987), Whoopie Goldberg and Bob Goldthwaite steel themselves to enter a crowded fern bar to gather information, when Goldthwaite panics and babble-screams: "I can't go in there! I can't go in there! It's full of crazed yuppies from hell!" While the Hell's Angels of the biker films of the fifties and early sixties have not really been replaced by the Hell's yuppies of the eighties, Goldthwaite's terror at the specter of America's cities being taken over by roving gangs of young urban professionals wearing three-piece suits, driving Volvos, BMWs, and Mercedes, and flaunting their Gold Card wealth in an orgy of material acquisitiveness certainly seemed the case in the films of the eighties.

Residing at the opposite end of the spectrum from the Mid-American, rural, feminism of the farm crisis films, the text of urban yuppie materialism also exhibited a neoconservative style fostered by Reaganomics. The yuppie drives to make large amounts of money quickly, to succeed in a ruthless competitive world, to acquire the most expensive material goods, to spend rather than save, to party extremely hard as a reward for working extremely hard, to sacrifice (especially human relationships) for one's job, mirrored the Reagan administration's deficit spending policies and hi-tech defense system acquisitions. Eighties yuppies saw their ruthless competitive work ethic and their consumptive materialism as hedges and buffers against an increasingly unstable terrorist- and nuclear- and deficit-threatened world. Yuppieness became a form of protective coloration against the economic and status threats from ethnic minorities and the poor, from a questionable national economy, from an increasingly competitive world. Yuppies saw themselves as a uniformed cavalry circling the wagons around what was left of the American dream, that dream's material icons: the job with a chance for advancement, the house (in its new condo form), the car, the status goods, perhaps even a controlled and economically justi-fied family. The films of the eighties were acutely aware not only of the stereotypes and accoutrements of the yuppie lifestyle but also of the insecurity of the dying American dream.

For example, in the eighties, the heroes of films were less likely to be cowboys or spacemen with the right stuff or loner cops like Dirty Harry Callahan (Clint Eastwood) than they were businessmen or marketing executives or advertising geniuses. In films like *Kramer vs. Kramer* (1979), *Nothing in Common* (1986), *Baby Boom* (1986), *Planes, Trains and Automobiles* (1987), *The Secret of My Success* (1987), *Parenthood* (1989), *When Harry Met Sally*, and *Crazy People* (1990), the central characters are all advertising executives, while in *Wall Street* (1987), *Dad* (1989), and *Rollover* (1981), the central characters are all aggressive urban money men.

"So what are all those work-obsessed, amoral advertising and marketing men doing in today's movies?" One industry observer asks: "Studio executives relate to them," insists a marketing executive who requests anonymity. "It's a high-pressure, brutally competitive environment that mirrors the style and workings of making movies." Yuppie filmmakers like Steven Spielberg, George Lucas, and Ron Howard reached their positions of power in eighties Hollywood, according to industry analyst Tony Hoffman, because "they're going to make commercial hits . . . movies that gross over $100 million." The demographic definition of the yuppie lifestyle would seem to support this industry view. A report based on twenty years of polling data on six million college freshmen noted a sharp rise in conservatism, in an interest in material success, and in business majors, as opposed to a steady decrease in people interested in developing a philosophy of life or pursuing English, math, and science majors. By the end of the eighties decade, yuppies were so prominent and accepted as part of the American landscape that none of the reti-cence of TV critic Harry F. Waters, writing about a new show at mid-decade, any longer existed: "Its creators are reportedly touting 'Sara,' a sitcom about a career woman working in a San Francisco law office, as 'The Mary Tyler Moore Show' of the Eighties. The difference between Mary and Sara is that the latter is—let's come right out and say it—a yuppie." By the end of the eighties yuppies were accepted, not without some contempt but with lessening ridicule and caricature, as the movers and go-getters of American society, and their image—the way they dressed, the cars they drove, the things they valued (or did not)—had itself become a recognizable uniform. Perhaps the most symbolic precursor of the eighties yuppie films was *Urban Cowboy* (1980). In a highly ironic myth, the film chronicles how the old West of cowboys and bucking bronchos has been replaced by a new yuppie West of designer-dressed cowboys riding mechanical bulls. *Urban Cowboy* is the death knell of the Western, of an American mythology that has been superceded by a new species of Wall Street gunslingers. The yuppie films of the eighties all explore the contours and the effects of the new myth of the American dream and measure it against the old.

The eighties yuppie film text took two separate forms. The first, the yuppie angst text, portrayed and critiqued the yuppie lifestyle from a skeptical perspective, focusing upon its flaws, excessiveness, the obsession with success and the rejection of spiritual fulfillment for material acquisitiveness. It was most often occasioned by the insecurity of maintaining their position in society and their fast-lane lifestyle as well as by their own doubts and dissatisfactions with the superficiality of their existence. The second yuppie text, much like the feminist issue texts, confronted a spectrum of yuppie issues from sex to babies to sports to houses. In eighties films, the characters were more likely to inhabit the milieu and the economic strata of the yuppie than any other segment of the American public.

Yuppie Angst

The major eighties document, in both its novel and film forms, was Jay McInerney's 1984 best seller and film adaptation *Bright Lights, Big City* (1988). Early in the film, Alex Hardy (Jason Robards), a drunken writer-editor at *Gotham* magazine tipsily counsels Jamie Conway (Michael J. Fox) over a three-martini lunch:

> ALEX: Have you ever considered getting an MBA?
>
> JAMIE: Absolutely not.
>
> ALEX: Well, I'm not necessarily saying go into business. No, no, but write about it. That's the stuff now. The guys that understand business are writing the new literature. Money is poetry now.
>
> JAMIE: I don't wanna believe that. It may be true, but I don't wanna believe that.
>
> ALEX: Don't be seduced by all that crap about writing in a garret like I was. Write about money.

In the eighties the yuppie moneymongers not only are taking over literature but are insinuating their acquisitive lifestyle into every corner of American society. *Bright Lights, Big City* is a sewer guide to the underside of the yuppie American dream. Almost clinically it dissects the angst attached to the eighties. Lust for money, fame, social acceptance; how the yuppie's social struggle, because it pursues purely material goals, causes a gradual disintegration, or at least disorientation, of the existential self.

Bright Lights, Big City is a declawed eighties version of Dr. Jekyll and Mr. Hyde. See cute little conservative materialistic Alex Keaton (also Michael J. Fox) of the long-running eighties TV sitcom *Family Ties* turn into guilty, confused cokehead and undersized playboy of the New York disco scene. Jamie's friend Ted Allegash (Kiefer Sutherland) describes their dark yuppie Hyde-like quest: "Into the heart of the night. Wherever there are dances to be danced, drugs to be hoovered, girls to be Allegashed."

As in the *Dr. Jekyll and Mr. Hyde* original, one central stream of imagery in *Bright Lights, Big City* is that of mirrors. Jamie spends much of his time either snorting coke off of them or trying to find his lost self in them. Much of the film, in fact, is spent in unisex disco restrooms where men and women share their coke in the stalls and then check out their noses in the mirrors before returning to the yuppie fray. But at other times, Jamie looks into bathroom mirrors in hopes of finding a self that the coke, the loss of his wife, his mother, his job, have all blurred. In fact, much of the film, its night scenes, are shot in a yellow neon blur, a drug blur that sends Jamie off into memory flashbacks and *National Enquirer* hallucinations of "coma babies" (the film's embarrassingly obvious controlling metaphor) refusing to come out of a drug womb. The film's visual blurring of reality is ironically paralleled by Jamie's job as fact-checker at *Gotham* magazine. The coke, the late nights, the guilt, and insecurity of his yuppie lifestyle are all blurring his ability to see the facts both on the job and in his own life. In his job performance, Jamie becomes a close parallel to Buddy Fox (Charlie Sheen) in *Wall Street* (1987). Both deceive themselves in thinking that they can get away with the shortcuts of their fast-lane lifestyles.

But *Bright Lights, Big City* also provides a checklist of the yuppie image. It defines the uniform—button-down shirt, tie, three-piece suit—or more casually— shirt, tie, sports jacket, jeans—and, of course, no self-respecting yuppie ever sleeps in anything but an Ivy League T-shirt—Jamie is a Dartmouth grad. The yuppie uniform is this confused mix of the formal and the casual; Dustin Hoffman wore it in *Kramer vs. Kramer* (1979), Michael Murphy in *Manhattan* (1979), and Steve Martin in *Roxanne* (1987). Drugs serve as the anaesthetic to the confusion of this life; they create the illusion that all of this imagery means something.

The Job Battle

Most often, the workplace became the yuppie battlefield. Their jobs took precedence over all other areas of their lives: self, relationships, family, morality. The competition for success, power, status, money, in the workplace and in society became an unhealthy obsession. Whereas young Jamie Conway in *Bright Lights, Big City* looks at the Manhattan skyline at the end and vows to fight his way back, in *Wall Street* young Huckleberry Fox (Charlie Sheen) cannot just wipe the slate clean with a firm purpose of amendment as he stands on the balcony of his million-dollar condo overlooking the Manhattan skyline. Rather, Bud Fox has participated in the criminal defrauding of thousands of people and must pay in loss of reputation, in court, and in prison. In both films, these innocents are abroad in the fast-lane world of their jobs and are not able to handle the pressure.

Broadcast News (1988) and *Switching Channels* (1988) both went behind the scenes in the world of TV news to study the job-generated yuppie angst of the high-pressure media world, while *Street Smart* (1987) examined the loss of ethics of a yuppie print journalist. In all three, the pressure, the competition, and the frantic pace of the news-gathering profession force the characters caught in this vortex to take shortcuts, sacrifice their ethics for the scoop, the exclusive. Unfortunately the sacrifice of their ethics seems to come fairly easy to these characters and the rewards for their dishonesty are huge in terms of young urban professional success.

Right up there next to the media as a favorite yuppie profession in film texts of the eighties were the legal profession and Wall Street. In *Legal Eagles* (1986), *Suspect* (1987), and *The Accused* (1988), yuppie lawyers plied their trade. These lawyers, most of them women, wear the three-piece yuppie uniform and carry their briefcases with grace and assertiveness. *Legal Eagles* especially highlights the yuppie accoutrements. Set amidst the high-rent rehabs of Greenwich Village and the Tribeca area of Manhattan, it wanders through the expensive world of the New York art gallery scene as well as the trendy world of performance artists. Both the TV news people and these lawyers work hard at their jobs and are remunerated well, but not nearly as well as the kamikaze kids of Wall Street, the brokers, the junk bond salesmen, the investment bankers and the corporate raiders, the Ivan Boeskys and the Michael Milkens and the Boone Pickens who made the megabucks and catapulted the yuppie lifestyle into the materialist stratosphere.

Wall Street (1987) is the ultimate film text of the workplace battlefield. It inventories the ammunition that loads up the yuppie dream, tracks the quick and easy money that fires that dream off. In *Wall Street,* Gordon Gekko (Michael Douglas), microphone in hand and working the room like a rock star, addresses a corporate stockholders' meeting and delivers the Gettysburg Address of the yuppie philosophy:

> Well, ladies and gentlemen, we're not here to indulge in fantasy, but in political and economic reality. America, America has become a second rate power. Its trade deficit and its fiscal deficit are at nightmare proportions. . . . Today, management has no stake in the company. . . . You own the company and you are being royally screwed over. . . . Well in my book you either do it right or you get eliminated. In the last seven deals that I have been involved with, there were 2.5 million stockholders who have made a pre-tax profit of 12 billion dollars. [applause] Thank you. I am not a destroyer of companies; I am a liberator of them. The point is, ladies and gentlemen, that greed, for lack of a better word, greed is good. Greed is right. Greed works. Greed clarifies, cuts through and captures the essence of the evolutionary spirit. Greed, in all its forms, greed for life, for money, for love, for knowledge, has marked the upward surge of mankind and, greed, you mark my words, will not only save Teldar Paper, but that other malfunctioning corporation called the USA. Thank you very much.

Gekko's speech, his preposterous paean to greed, rings with a kind of evangelistic fervor. It is delivered in a setting similar to the UBS stockholders' meeting in *Network* presided over by the snakelike Frank Hackett (Robert Duvall) and the charismatic corporate evangelist Diana Christiansen (Faye Dunaway). In his address, Gekko offers an absolution to all the yuppies in the audience who are suffering guilt over their materialism. Though addressing the shareholders of Teldar Paper, a corporation he is raiding, Gekko begins his Sermon on the Mount by defining how the American dream has turned into a nightmare due to bad management. For Gordon Gekko, America is no longer an idea, it is merely another large corporation being mismanaged by bureaucrats and suffering from cash flow problems. Gekko uses the nation as a macrocosmic metaphor for Teldar and offers his panacea for the problems of both troubled corporations, greed. Greed, one of the Seven Deadly Sins, takes on moral stature (it is "good" and "right"), pragmatic efficiency (it "works"), rhetorical power (it "clarifies" and "cuts through and captures the essence"), and progressive force ("it marks the upward surge of mankind"). Greed, literally, becomes a savior for both Teldar Paper and for the USA, and Gekko's speech becomes a fervent absolution of the yuppie angst that clouds the hardhearted decision making of corporate raiding.

Wall Street is the ultimate yuppie nightmare. It portrays the crash of the yuppie ideal of money, power, and status. The dialogue of *Wall Street* is a constant rollercoaster of buying and selling. The film's most prominent icons are cellular phones and computer terminals. Much of the action takes place at desks. The film issues a backstage pass to America's longest running economic repertory theater where comedy and tragedy alternate on a daily basis.

Buddy Fox (Charlie Sheen) is an American innocent from Queens who has worked his way into the inner circle of stock brokerage trading, hostile takeover deals, and the Manhattan yuppie rat race. It is no wonder that his father Carl (Martin Sheen), the representative of an airplane mechanic's union, has nicknamed him Huckleberry. By a lot of toadying, Buddy becomes the protege and soon-to-be fall guy for Gordon Gekko, the most ruthless of the Wall Street corporate raiders. To use the metaphoric language of actual corporate raiding, the plot of *Wall Street* is like a medieval joust. Gekko, the black knight, and Sir Laurance Wildman (Terence Stamp), the white knight, fight it out with telephones mounted on stretch limos attended by their squires who are either Brooks Brothers lawyers or innocent young stockbrokers like Fox.

The plot of *Wall Street,* however, is much less engaging than the momentum that the film's language creates, its fast-paced rhetoric of the art of the deal featuring two recurring metaphors: of war and of sex. The rhetoric of Gordon Gekko's deal making is violent and bloodthirsty and seems to emanate more appropriately from the grunts in director Oliver Stone's previous film *Platoon* than from a suspendered, manicured, and slicked-back businessman talking on the phone in an upholstered office overlooking Manhattan. Gordon Gekko's office is the computerized control center of a battlefield. He barks the macho language of war on his speaker phones as he triggers his deals:

> I loved it at 40, it's an insult at 50. Their analysts, they don't know preferred stock from livestock. See, wait'll they head south and then we'll raise the sperm count on the deal. Get back at ya. [Hangs up phone. Turns to Bud Fox.] This is the kid. Calls me 59 days in a row. Wants to be a player. Oughta be a picture of you in the dictionary under "PERSISTENCE," kid. [Phone rings. He picks up and swivels away from Bud.] Listen Jerry, all I want is negative control. No more than 30–35 percent. Just enough to blow anyone else's merger plans and find out from the inside if the books are cooked. If it looks good as on paper, we're in the kill zone pal, lock and load. Lunch? What, are you kiddin for wimps.

His rapid-fire patter toys momentarily with a macho sexual metaphor—"we'll raise the sperm count on the deal"—but quickly drops more violent rhetoric of war. In the steam room after destroying Bud at racquet ball, Gekko returns to his war metaphor to define the tactics of the yuppie battlefield:

GEKKO: The most valuable commodity I know of is information, wouldn't you agree?

BUD: Yea.

GEKKO: The public's out there throwing darts at a board, sport. I don't throw darts at a board. Read Sun Soo, *The Art of War*. Every battle is won before it's fought.

Later, Bud Fox quotes Sun Soo word for word back to Gekko as evidence that he is man enough to join the battle. In the eighties, Oliver Stone made his reputation portraying the decade's battlefields. From *Salvador* to *Platoon* to *Wall Street* to *Talk Radio* (1989) he moved from the terrorist war of Central America to the shooting war of Vietnam to the yuppie battlefields of the stockbrokers and the media stars.

Gordon Gekko relishes his macho battle rhetoric, but Bud Fox is defined in terms of more human metaphor, that of sex. In the world of *Wall Street,* the human emotions of love and the excitement and release of sexuality are overshadowed by the making of money. Making money becomes a twisted form of sex, an almost orgasmic thrill. After buying a painting for $2.5 million, Gekko invites Darien (Darryl Hannah) Bud's upscale decorator girl friend, to share a room at the Carlyle Hotel for the afternoon. "You and I are the same, Darien," Gekko argues. "We are smart enough not to buy into the oldest myth running, love—a fiction created by people to keep them from jumping out of windows." Darien laughs off his proposition with "you know, sometimes I miss you Gordon. You're really twisted." That is what this yuppie drive for money and power and status does to natural human emotions, twists them into deformity. The yuppie dream replaces the human with the purely material, sexuality with money and power. "See that building over there," Gekko brags to Bud Fox. "It was my first real estate deal. I bought it eight years ago. Two years later I sold it for an $800,000 profit. It was better than sex."

The Yuppie Issues

If the yuppie uniform, the yuppie materialism, the yuppie obsession with success in the workplace, the yuppie exclusiveness all opened themselves up to caricature, there were also serious issues that attached themselves to the yuppie lifestyle. A broad range of yuppie-specific issues arose out of the yuppies' own existential questionings. Caught in the competitiveness, materialism, and superficiality of yuppiness, members began examining their problems. Rarely did the obvious alterative of rejecting the yuppie lifestyle arise as a viable option, rather yuppies attempted to accommodate the specific problems that the lifestyle occasioned. Thus yuppiness was accepted, but not unequivocally. Issues that needed to be resolved were recognized and confronted both in society and in eighties films.

The major equivocative issues of the yuppie lifestyle were:
1. The loss of idealism and social consciousness in the face of materialism and selfishness
2. The fragility and superficiality of sexual relationships in the face of the pressures of the lifestyle
3. The redefinition of the family in terms of the lifestyle.

Each issue had both a social and a personal side. For example, had the yuppie ideals eroded all possibility for social consciousness in a whole generation of young Americans and made it impossible to become involved in either social or personal relationships? Or had the yuppie lifestyle not only taken passion out of sex but once and for all destroyed the institution of the family? Yuppies were adamantly unwilling to give up their lifestyle, but they were also innovative in finding ways to accommodate solutions to these problems to that lifestyle. The films of the eighties, most often in serious dramatic explorations, but frequently in witty social comedies, observed these yuppies facing up to these lifestyle issues.

Can Yuppies Have a Social Consciousness?

Of course they can, but often they have to seek it out rather than having it thrust upon them, as was the case in the sixties. Roger Baron (Robert Downey, Jr.) is doing exactly that sort of seeking in *True Believer* (1989), which is an exploration of the lost idealism of the sixties generation in the cynical eighties. But in its subtext, centered in the character of Roger Baron, *True Believer* is a film of the eighties generation's need to rekindle the fire of the sixties idealism doused by Vietnam, Watergate, and the social austerity of the Reagan eighties. *True Believer* is about two generations, the hippies of the sixties and the yuppies of the eighties, both trying to find their social consciousness.

In the sixties, Eddie Dodd (James Woods) was right there when it all was happening. A radical lawyer a la William Kunstler, Eddie defended and won the biggest cases of the antiwar and civil rights movements. In the eighties, however, all that is left of Eddie Dodd's sixties idealism is his long hair. His practice is defending drug dealers, because they pay in cash that is never reported to the IRS. He is a classic burnt-out case until young Roger Baron comes along. Roger comes off the *University of Michigan Law Review* with civil liberties stars in his eyes and a yuppie wardrobe of pinstriped suits and class ties. James Woods's Eddie Dodd burns up the screen in *True Believer,* but the film is also about the young yuppie Roger and his quest for idealism in the midst of the disengagement of his generation. Roger Baron, with all of his exterior yuppie trimmings, goes against the stereotype of the social apathetic, cynical, money-possessed, and ideologically barren eighties generation. *True Believer* is two parallel generational quests. Pauline Kael argues that the real social theme of *True Believer* addresses the inadequacy of the American legal system in the eighties, "how legal trade-offs violate the system of justice." That theme of trade-offs, plea bargains, deals, symbolically represents what is wrong with the yuppie lifestyle. In the age of Donald Trump, "the art of the deal" is the shortcut away from social engagement. What Roger tells Eddie is that you just cannot make deals about right and wrong. If your client is innocent, you ought to get him out of jail not deal for a shorter term. The yuppie generation has made too many material trade-offs and has ignored their social responsibility too long, Roger Baron repeatedly emphasizes.

Can Yuppies Maintain Sexual Relationships?

That depends, but even when they manage to establish relationships it is a real struggle. Perhaps the single most frightening bugaboo of the yuppie lifestyle is the specter of involvement. That scary spook haunts the title characters in *When Harry Met Sally* (1989). They are yuppies to their eyebrows, and the film tracks their relationship over twelve years—1977 to 1989—in New York. In a sense, *When Harry Met Sally* is a social history of this single issue—fear of relationships—across the whole yuppie era.

Harry is a fast-talking, witty advertising man, while Sally (Meg Ryan) is an emotional, picky, highly ironic careerwoman. The film focuses upon their talk—in cars, in restaurants, in airplanes, in Central Park, on the telephone in separate beds—about the ironies of yuppie sexual insecurity. Each generation has its own version of this film—in the fifties it was *Pillow Talk* (1959); in the sixties Audrey

Hepburn and Albert Finney were *Two for the Road* (1967); for the seventies it was Barbara Streisand and Robert Redford analyzing *The Way We Were* (1973)—and *When Harry Met Sally* is the eighties decade's romantic chronicle. Laughing at the byzantine intricacies of yuppie insecurities, *When Harry Met Sally* is about the difference between friendship and relationship. Of course, the difference is sex. The film fixates on twelve years of a single couple trying to sort out the stresses of being friends or lovers or both. If they are representative of the yuppie generation, then it is a miracle that the concept of marriage still exists and celibacy is not universal. It is no coincidence that the funniest scene in the film is a faked orgasm. The film is about coitus interruptus, about sacrificing an inner life for an outer life of simulation and show.

St. Elmo's Fire (1985) and *About Last Night* (1986) were earlier, serious versions of *When Harry Met Sally*. These two films also agonized over what sex means and how much of a sacrifice love is among yuppies. Both films observe control groups of new college graduates trying to gain entry into the real world while simultaneously trying to cope with the attractions and demands of sexual relationships. What both films emphasize most strongly is the terrible fear of commitment.

St. Elmo's Fire provides a rogue's gallery of interpersonally screwed-up yuppies. How can these Georgetown graduates have been so successful in their studies and in their new jobs, yet be so terribly confused in their personal lives? Alex (Judd Nelson) is a ruthless congressional aide and Kirbo (Emilio Estevez) is a law student, but both, in the presence of women they are trying to impress, make complete fools of themselves. Billy (Rob Lowe), a talented sax player, has exactly the opposite problem. Though he is married and has a child, he still chases women and flees the commitment of his family. Kevin (Andrew McCarthy) is a would-be writer whose Byronic poutiness covers his insecurities. The women in this rogue's gallery are no less yuppie and no more stable than the men. Wendy (Mare Willingham) is a Washington, D.C., welfare worker, but she must be a rigorously sheltered one because she falls for the narcissistic self-absorption of Billy. Leslie (Ally Sheedy), an architect, is smart enough to see through the utterly dishonest Alex but falls for the moody Kevin. The most self-deceived is Jules (Demi Moore) whose cocaine habit turns her into "a sad and funny yuppy slut." Ultimately, St. Elmo's fire is about the paralyzing insecurity that these otherwise decisive, intelligent, and successful young professionals feel in their private lives.

About Last Night is a more focused study of the chronic inability of yuppies to commit to each other. Adapted from David Mamet's play *Sexual Perversity in Chicago,* the dirtiest of the legions of dirty words in this film is "love." In *St. Elmo's Fire,* all the stilted couples were still holding out hope that they could actually find love. In *About Last Night,* as its title implies, we must apologize for even seeking it. One couple, Danny (Rob Lowe) and Debbie (Demi Moore), try to love each other but are too afraid of commitment. The other couple, Bernie (James Belushi) and Joan (Elizabeth Perkins), openly despise each other from the outset. Both are utterly cynical in their taunting of the two serious lovers and instrumental in dooming any of Danny and Debbie's sincere attempts at relationship. For *About Last Night*'s yuppies, the sex is good, the specter of commitment frightening, and the city's single bars the barren, loveless refuges of the cynical and insecure.

But if these two brat-pack films are the most serious anatomies of the yuppie fear of commitment, *Key Exchange* (1985) may be the most Mickey Mouse treatment of that theme. Somehow it was inconceivable that anyone would consider making a film about the momentousness of boy and girl yuppies trying to decide whether or not to exchange keys to their apartments. Lisa (Brooke Adams) is similar to Debbie in *About Last Night* and Philip (Ben Masters) is a clone of Billy in *St. Elmo's Fire*. Both are card-carrying yuppies trying to fit what they think might possibly maybe somehow perhaps potentially be a relationship into their business work lives and their self-absorbed conceptions of themselves. Lisa is a TV producer who wants Philip to move in and pay attention to no one but her. Philip is a mystery writer with a flexible, self-employed work life that he enjoys employing for the self-gratification of casual sexual affairs with other women besides Lisa. Both characters' mobility of commitment is symbolized by the bicycles they ride through New York. Their yuppie lives are moving so fast that they just cannot slow down enough to touch each other.

But fear of commitment was not the only relationship problem that plagued the yuppies of the eighties. Two yuppie horror films, *Heartburn* (1986) and *Fatal Attraction* (1987), focus upon the ravages of commitment in a world where the cynical warning of *About Last Night* about the death of love has gone unheeded. Both films are about marriages that, because of infidelity, go violently awry. Their violence ranges from a key lime pie in the face to a huge butcher knife in the bathroom, but both make the same point: that in a high-pressure yuppie world where the ego must be continually reinflated, monogamy is not a strong enough support structure.

In *Heartburn,* Rachel (Meryl Streep) is a magazine food writer and Mark (Jack Nicholson) is a Washington political columnist. These two yuppie characters are based on real life yuppies Nora Ephron and Carl Bernstein, and the film is adapted from Ephron's revenge novel about their breakup. Rachel and Mark's nice yuppie marriage seems to be going along just fine. The only real problem is communicating with their Hungarian contractor who is renovating their Georgetown townhouse. The first half of the film seems to be an anatomy of a happy, healthy yuppie marriage, but then Rachel finds out that Mark is having an affair with a Washington socialite, and suddenly it is as if their whole lives have caught cancer. Little attempt is made to salvage the marriage. Rachel flees back to the workplace, where she is consoled by her old editor. He promises her old job back and that seems to make everything fine again. The moral of the story seems to be that for a yuppie, as long as one has a good job there is really no personal betrayal or emotional hurt or psychological pain that can undermine one's basic position of strength. For the yuppie, the public life is all that counts and a fulfilling private life is never anything but a romantic illusion. David Ansen, reviewing *Heartburn,* hits the film dead center when he writes, "it's less a slice of life than a slice of lifestyle." While *Heartburn* is a harmless gloss over the fragility of a yuppie marriage, *Fatal Attraction* is the ultimate yuppie marriage horror story. As in the old vampire and werewolf movies, the two central characters of *Fatal Attraction,* Dan Gallagher (Michael Douglas), a successful New York lawyer with a lovely wife and small daughter, and Alex Forest (Glenn Close), an unmarried publishing house executive, are easily recognizable contemporary types. He is a model yuppie family man. She is an intelligent, successful, liberated, extremely attractive career woman. Yet both, when crowded by circumstances, become monsters. Each is flawed; each is guilty. Both are victims. Happy in his marriage, loving toward his family, adept in his job, Dan is momentarily seduced by Alex's style and freedom. Given the seductive opportunity, he indulges himself in a one-night stand with Alex, which he immediately regrets and from which he flees the following morning. Alex, who has been exploited by men all her life, at first enjoys controlling the naive Dan, but then breaks down: first as someone once again a victim of sexual exploitation; and then, as a vengeful monster driven by her sexual obsession for possessing Dan.

The primary text of *Fatal Attraction* is similar to that of *Wall Street*. It is a film about the wages of opportunism, about the dangers of greed. Dan Gallagher has it all: he possesses the yuppie uniform with all its accessories, yet he grabs for more in the form of Alex Forest. The visual characterization of Alex focuses upon her long, wild tangle of curls that signal the film's controlling myth. Alex and the greedy, self-absorbed, instant gratification ideal that she represents is the Medusa curse of the yuppie lifestyle. It is tremendously attractive, but in order to attain and sustain it one must give up the self. Subtexted within this primary text is also an elaborate metaphor for the threat of AIDS in a one-night stand yuppie society. As a film about contemporary sexual responsibility, *Fatal Attraction* is like *Kramer vs. Kramer* (1979) gone berserk. Here, the yuppie family is threatened by something much more tangible, physical, than simply the ravages of divorce. Alex Forest descends upon the Gallaghers like a plague.

7

OUR MOVIE-MADE PRESIDENT

No Method to His Madness
Richard Schickel

In this 1987 essay, the film critic Richard Schickel examines how President Ronald W. Reagan's experience in Hollywood shaped his ideology and outlook.

It will help if we radically reformulate the terms of our bemusement. The problem is not that the President of the United States, the Leader of the Free World, the Occupant of the World's Loneliest office, etc., used to be a movie actor, a creator of make-believe. The problem is that he used to be—probably still is—a movie fan, a consumer of make-believe, even an addict of it.

This is a disturbing conclusion. So much so that even bold Garry Wills, whose *Reagan's America: Innocents at Home* leads one inescapably toward it, stops short of baldly setting it forth. And for good reason: it implies the most depressing things not only about Ronald Reagan but about ourselves and our infinite capacity for delusion, political and otherwise.

Like the rest of us, Wills has learned to stop worrying and live with the idea of an actor-president. This is no small matter. It is, in fact, an aspect of one of the more interesting unremarked social phenomena of postwar American life: the general acceptance of the idea that acting is a profession, demanding of its practitioners a training, discipline, and sobriety comparable to that required of lawyers, doctors, and the other grown-up occupations.

To earlier generations, this notion would have been unimaginable, dumbfounding. But there it is. Three decades of journalistic and talk-show debates about The Actors Studio and The Method; a similar span of general concern about Marlon Brando's integrity; the rise of graduate education in the theatrical arts and crafts, and the decline of the term contract in Hollywood, which freed performers to pursue highly personal projects at the same time they were freed to express themselves with impunity on public issues and, for that matter, private morals—all of this encouraged movie actors to take their work, and their duties as citizens, more seriously. And encouraged the general public to join them in this activity. It is ironic that Ronald Reagan, that least serious and least actorish of actors, a man no one ever really thought of as a major talent or screen presence, should be the chief beneficiary of this change in our attitudes.

This point, quite correctly, worries Wills: "On the one hand, some try to explain Reagan's extraordinary succcess in politics by saying he gets by because he is 'just an actor.' On the other hand, we are told he was not even a good actor—which seems to make his political success more mysterious. Which is it to be? Is he just reading lines, following his script, using theatrical skills, as President? Or did a man lacking the depth for great roles in the theater somehow acquire a knack for filling the most responsible role in the world?". . .

Wills' rhetorical questions are quite unanswerable as posed. Reagan was clearly not a distinguished actor, and though he was sometimes a respectable one, he was just as often an incompetent one. Similarly, it is hard to find any evidence that he possessed a genius for the political gesture that awaited unlocking by changing times and circumstances. No, you cannot get hold of this character with questions as convenient as those posed by Wills. Reagan's astonishing success, in not one but two careers that have defeated men with far higher gifts and far more ferocious ambitions, begins to make sense only if you view it in utterly unconventional, indeed in utterly un-American terms. This way:

He succeeded as an actor, in the theatrical sense of the word, precisely because he refused to act, in the general sense of the word. He refused to try to impose himself on events, to shape them to his uses. Rather, he succeeded because he correctly saw his movie career as a lucky opportunity proffered him by rich and powerful men, men much cleverer than he was, to live within one of the most delicious American fantasies. All he had to do, as he saw it, was go along with them agreeably—show up on time, learn his lines, submit to the publicity process, and above all, not question the wisdom of their decisions about his career.

The result was little short of miraculous. In his rise, as Wills nicely put it, he was "a winner, not a stunner; in his fall he was a fader, not a loser." And when he had reached near-ectoplasmic status as a movie star, his mentors, having accumulated no grievances against him, had no reason to indulge the usually irresistable Hollywood habit to punish the weakened star for his past arrogances. Instead, they pointed Ron in a new direction, toward the political illusion, within which one may also succeed simply by showing up on time, learning one's lines, etc., etc.

I do not wish to imply that Ronald Reagan was without gift. In fact, he was hugely gifted—as a fantasist. Which is an occupation that, until he showed us the way, no one had ever regarded as likely to lead anybody anywhere very exalted. But which now, perhaps, we might find a certain profit in re-examining.

We can begin, prosaically enough, with Wills' observation that Reagan was of the generation that came of age as the movies came of age. He was born the year the first studio opened in Hollywood; he was graduated from high school the year talkies came in. His crowd was the one on which the myth-making power of the movies shone with the piercing power of the new. He was also of a place (small-town middle America) and of a class (the lumpen bourgeoisie) that had particular need for the transfiguring power of this mythology. In other words, the kind of glory-dreaming he has his whole long life indulged himself in was by no means unique to him. . . .

Reagan somehow contrived to remain what he was long before he came to the movies: profoundly suggestible. We all know that he entered showbiz as a radio sports reporter for small stations in Iowa, where his specialty was, to use the polite contemporary word, "visualization" of baseball games. The facts of a game proceeding in far-off Chicago were telegraphed to him, and he was required to create, on the spot, a full word picture of the game, right down to little red-haired boys making spectacular catches of balls fouled into the stands.

In later years one of Reagan's favorite anecdotes has the line going dead as a ball left the pitcher's hand, leaving silver-tongued Dutch Reagan to improvise many, many foul balls—utterly untraceable in the next day's box score—until service was restored. Harmless fun, of course, and arguably a service to the higher truth. That is to say, Reagan's fictive embroidery did not distort the account of the

Ronald Wilson Reagan

game as it progressed—the hits, runs, and errors were all present and accounted for—and the rest was just entertainment. Also, possibly, good training in those on-your-feet skills requisite to the successful conduct of a Presidential press conference.

In any case, as Wills observes, Dutch Reagan became in those years an uncritical admirer of that school of sports reporting . . . which could not resist improving on the historical record, particularly if their inventions would lend an uplifting moral point to an anecdote. It was at this stage that Reagan began his fascinating lifelong association with George Gipp by retelling [Grantland] Rice's basic "win one for the Gipper" legend on one of his radio shows. The story stayed with him so powerfully that he proposed it as a screenplay soon after signing his Warner Bros. contract and well before he was himself cast as Gipper in *Knute Rockne—All American*. He was still telling it, essentially unchanged, when he received an honorary degree from Notre Dame in 1981.

A little research of the kind that White House staffs can easily command—and which, indeed, Reagan himself might have conducted at any point in his half-century's obsession with the Gipper—would have revealed a number of interesting points about his story. The first is that Gipp himself was a thoroughly undesirable character, a pool hustler who smoked, drank, played pro football on the side, and regularly bet on Notre Dame games in which he played. In life he was never referred to as "the Gipper"; and his death, before graduation, appears to have been hastened by his dissipations, which he never recanted.

Still more interesting: no one ever heard of his deathbed request—that Rockne invoke his name sometime when a Notre Dame team was in need of inspiration—until the coach brought his weakest team into New York for the Army game of 1928. He spent the evening before it with Rice, trying out this preposterous inspirational yarn on the sportswriter before feeding it to his team the next day. This may have been Rockne's biggest whopper, but it was by no means his only inspiring invention. For this most sacred icon of the American sports pantheon, this legendary builder of youthful character, was a congenital liar, or (if you prefer the politer term, suitable to presidents as well as folk heroes) a mythomaniac. But, as the Leader of the Free World himself inquired at Notre Dame, "Is there anything wrong with young people having an experience, feeling something so deeply, thinking of someone else to the point where they can give . . . completely of themselves?"

Well . . . er . . . um . . . gosh. One wonders: Are these higher truths, arrived at by climbing a ladder of smaller untruths, really worth the cynicism they will inevitably engender? And how high, really, are these higher truths? They are not exactly Olympian in their richness, are they? Not exactly the sort of legends around which you would want to organize your life or your society. At best, they are fables for a high school sports banquet.

But Reagan has a million of them, and he goes on telling them to this day. One favorite has a World War II B-17 pilot ordering his crew to bail out after their plane has been crippled by anti-aircraft fire, then finding one of his gunners wounded and immovably trapped as the plane starts to spiral earthward. The boy is frightened, but the pilot cradles him in his arms and says, "Never mind, son, we'll ride it down together." The Leader of the Free World likes to use the story as evidence of how our political system creates a morality superior to that of the Communist system.

Terrific. But if the only two witnesses to this exchange indeed ride their crippled plane down together, who survived to recount their dialogue? Is it from some old war movie the rest of us have forgotten, or a radio drama or a pulp story? No one seems to know, and the tale's provenance is a matter of curiosity nowhere near as spectacularly compelling—or as enigmatic—as the sources of Reagan's fondness for it.

Be that as it may, one does feel confident in observing that his taste for these slices of life according to *Reader's Digest* has obviously had an influence on his autobiographical impulse. His life, as he likes to retell it, is at every stage illuminated by similarly shapely and instinctive dramatic sequences. For example: He is playing football for Dixon High School and at a crucial juncture in the game commits an infraction undetected by the officials but protested by the opposing players. One of the zebras puts it to young Dutch—did he or didn't he perpetrate a foul? Alas, "truth telling had been whaled into me," so Reagan fesses up, apparently costing his team a chance for the touchdown by which it ultimately lost the game. We owe to the relentlessly researching Wills the information that no game with an outcome of the kind Reagan describes took place while he was playing for Dixon.

As he grows older, the line between provable and improvable truth grows ever more blurry—and possibly, ever more important in evaluating his character and his "performances." Another example: He has honorably served his country in war, abandoning his screen career just as he was making the transition from B pictures to A's. "By the time I got out of the Army Air Corps, all I wanted to do—in common with several million other venterans—was to rest up for a while, make love to my wife, and come up refreshed to a better job in a better world." Right. Unexceptional sentiments. Except that they imply lengthy service far from the comforts of home. But Reagan passed the war entirely in Hollywood, assigned to "Fort Roach" (normally Hal Roach's Culver City studio) where he worked on air corps training films. He went home to his wife Jane Wyman every night, except for a period when she was away on a bond-selling tour. Indeed, her wartime duties likely took her away from home for a longer period than his did.

And now memory grows even loopier. It is 1983, and President Reagan is entertaining the Prime Minister of Israel and implies, or seems to imply, that he was part of a Signal Corps unit filming the Nazi death camps as they are liberated. Moreover, he moreovers, there was this one particularly moving piece of footage that he felt he ought to sequester, because he felt someday people would question the authenticity of the Holocaust and—sure, sure, that's the ticket—one day someone did exactly that in his presence and he had this footage and . . .

Mr. Shamir was duly moved and impressed. So were Simon Wiesenthal and Rabbi Marvin Hier when they visited the White House and were treated to the same story. It was only after it was repeated in the Israeli press and people here and elsewhere started checking on it that Reagan's staff had to launch the most strenuous "containment" effort of his presidency up to that time. Ahem. Cough-cough. You see. What he meant to say was. And perhaps the visiting dignitaries misunderstood Reagan: after all, English is not their native language. Obviously, if Reagan passed the war entirely in Hollywood it would have been a little difficult for him to be with a Signal Corps unit as the camps were freed. . . .

Outrageous, on the face of it. Yet neither Wills, collecting and recounting these stories, nor I, fascinatedly reading them, can quite summon the appropriate outrage. For we recognize in Reagan something we indulge in ourselves and in our friends. It is our not-entirely-conscious, not-entirely-unconscious desire to reshape the maddening ambiguities of reality into the form of an old-fashioned movie: narratively neat, psychologically gratifying, with a beginning, a middle, and an end, and above all, a central figure we have no trouble rooting for—ourselves. . . .

Ronald Reagan did not break a sweat breaking in. He was out covering the Chicago Cubs' spring training season on Catalina Island, off Los Angeles, where he took a few hours off for screen tests and obtained for himself a modest Warner Bros. contract that was to be his first step on the road to the White House. He seems to have found life around the studio fun, and both his own accounts and those of others show him in these days to be a young man of no temperament and no image of himself as an actor at all. This would be his salvation, of course. For, Warners in the days of his apprenticeship was a-roil with rebellion. James Cagney (Reagan's latter-day pal), Bette Davis, Olivia de Havilland, Humphrey Bogart, Erroll Flynn, even, yes, Joan Leslie were in constant, noisy conflict with Jack Warner, seeking better parts, more money, a role in the choice of their roles.

Not young Ron. He unassumingly did leads in program features, small parts in a few A's. He established himself most usefully as Brass Bancroft, in the four pictures comprising the Secret Service of the Air series that Brynie Foy's B picture unit ground out. These pictures, Wills hints, prepared Reagan emotionally for his later role as a real-life FBI informer against suspected Communists; Brass did a bit of undercover work in his time. Wills also suggests that the Bancroft series may account for Reagan's devotion to the Star Wars concept. In the last of these pictures Brass must defend from enemy agents the "Inertia Projector," a device capable of knocking enemy planes out of the air from a distance of four miles. Life may occasionally imitate art for everyone, but it did so repeatedly in Ronald Reagan's career.

In any event, he had no cause for complaint. His career was moving ahead at a nice, but not unnerving pace. It did not cost him sleep or recreation time—loss of which are kown to make him cranky, even now. He got his good showy bit, in *Knute Rockne* and immediately thereafter an excellent second lead as George Armstrong Custer vying anachronistically with Flynn's Jeb Stuart for de Havilland's hand in *Santa Fe Trail*. The thing was not at all the Western it sounds, but rather a preparedness preachment, in which the two are in pursuit of Raymond Massey's John Brown, who is made to stand in for Hitler, with good men being urged to stand up to his raving bigotry before it is too late. *Santa Fe Trail* was also, about half the time, a romantic comedy, with Flynn playing the smooth seducer and Reagan playing Custer as the one thing he surely was not, an amiable goof, the butt of Flynn's jokes and schemes, and ultimately the loser to him in their contest for the girl. . . .

Two years later he got his best role, the one that stays everyone's hand in the attempts to evaluate his acting career, that of Drake McHugh in *King's Row*. His next good part, and his last before entering the service himself, was again with Flynn and Massey in Raoul Walsh's *Desperate Journey*, in which he was a Yank in an RAF crew, downed in occupied Europe and trying to fight its way back to England. Much of the film was played as knockabout comedy, and rather refreshingly so. Aside from *This is the Army,* for which Warners was able to borrow him back from the Air Corps to play the romantic lead, that was it for Reagan until 1947 and *Stallion Road.*

Reagan's prewar movies repay study. They are the ones that define the limits of the untutored talent that, once he had asserted it, he did nothing to develop or refine. Obviously, *King's Row* is central to this consideration, for though it must tiptoe around the incest theme that was crucial to the success of the best-seller on which it was based, and though poor, bland Robert Cummings was a hopeless leading man, it was an energetic and memorable picture. . . . Above all, it gave Reagan what everyone pretending to movie stardom must somehow obtain, a riveting scene, with a line as unforgettable as "Where's the rest of me" when he wakes up to discover that a sadistic doctor has needlessly ambutated both his legs after an accident in a railyard.

In his reading of this movie, Wills, I think, errs seriously. He wants to take even this one thespic triumph away from Reagan, and so he insists that his big scene is really Ann Sheridan's. . . . But I ran it over and over the other night, and it is just not so. To be sure, the preparation for it is all Sheridan's. The camera is long on her as she anxiously awaits Drake's awakening from shock and anethesia and his discovery that he has been crippled. But once she responds to his first cry, mounts the stairs, and enters his room, they share the scene equally. She has three close-ups, he has two, and there are three two-shots, two of which distinctly favor him. Moreover, he does his famous line unimprovably: anguish and panic in his voice, in his facial expression, in his thrashing movements under the covers. And one gets no sense that the director, Sam Wood, had to cheat to cover for Reagan. Hard to ask more from any actor.

No. Reagan's problems in *King's Row* occur earlier, when he is called to represent hismelf as a careless womanizer and ne'er-do-well heir to a small fortune. He is supposed to provide the contrast to Cummings, who plays an earnest, idealistic medical student. At this stage of the movie Drake McHugh is not a nice guy, and Reagan is visibly uncomfortable, straining, in these passages. He does not exhibit the born actor's relish at playing a heel; he exhibits the born politician's discomfort at being mistaken for one. He has no technique to help him get under this character's skin, or to distract us from his own discomfort. Before he loses his legs, Drake loses his inheritance, and that returns Reagan's character to the emotional range where he was—and is—comfortable in reality. It is the only realm where he ever learned to live persuasively, on the screen.

His other work in the period reinforces this point. Take his Custer, for example. The relationship with Jeb Stuart is not the only anachronism in *Santa Fe Trail.* Reagan plays his role as a modern youth improbably dressed up in a 19th-century soldier suit, and though he is kind of funny sometimes, he is kind of jarring, too. Things work out for him a little better in *Desperate Journey*. He is supposed to be a breezy American kid who, under interrogation by Massey (playing a Gestapo officer), resorts to jive talk in order to evade awkward questions, and he is genuinely funny in the scene. Timing was the experienced radio performer's strong suit, his only reliable technical skill, and he used it to good effect here. As for *This is the Army,* he was straight man to a vast troupe putting on a soldier show. As the movie's only male romantic interest, he tries to evade Joan Leslie's advances on the ground that it was irresponsible to marry while there was a war and he might be killed—yes, that one. But again, the part was comfortably within his modest range. . . .

Real actors are in essence escape artists, or maybe quick-change artists. It is the opportunity to strut that gift that provides such fascination and payoffs, the thing that makes a difficult and frustrating business occasionally worthwhile. It is also, of course, the thing that goads actors, makes them difficult, hard for the studio manager to manage. They are, in effect, junkies ever in search of their fix, their passage out of entrapping reality.

For Reagan, lacking the gift of transcendence, acting could only provide an extension of reality, not an escape from it. Like the rest of us "non-pros" (to borrow *Variety*'s old, contemptuous term), he had to rely on private fantasies to make his way out of the quotidian. And as with the rest of us, his dreams were fed, polluted perhaps, by mechanized dream works, in movies of the very kind he unimaginatively worked in. And by the movielike fantasies that the rest of the media provided—sportscasters, political commentators, storytellers of every "non-fictional" kind who had mastered the basic American movie trick, which is to tell whoppers in a realistic-seeming manner, tell whoppers of the kind Reagan is still genially telling and believing. Oh, yes, absolutely believing, as Colonel [Oliver] North and Adm. [John] Poindexter discovered to their delight. They looked like old-fashioned heroes to him and so they could tell him just about anything and make him believe it—especially spy stories that must have sounded a lot like movie treatments as they outlined them to him, keeping them brief and punchy, the way Jack Warner used to like them.

It was not so important back before the war, this limit under which he worked. He was a cute guy, and young. And, as noted, a pleasant relief from all those artist types yearning to breathe free. After the war, though, it was different. He wasn't so young anymore, and the movies were changing. Genre films, the conventions of which had done a lot of the actors' work for them, were losing their hold on the public. Now you had to bring something of your subtler awarenesses of self and world to the party up there on the screen. Hard for everybody, especially hard for Reagan.

His wife of the time caught this drift early. "Button-Nose," better known as Jane Wyman, came from a background similar to, and not more tony than, Reagan's. When they were courting she was making B's at Warners too, and she fit in chipperly with a gang of midwestern transplants, non-pros the lot of them, with whom Reagan ran socially—mostly to the beach (odd for movie folk), to the movies, where they paid their money and took their place with the other non-pros in the audience. But instinctively, the starlet sniffed the profession's possibilities for healthy escape from self and the quotidian. By 1945 she had *The Lost Weekend*, by '47 her first Oscar nomination (for *The Yearling*), a year later the big prize itself, for *Johnny Belinda*. Hubby was left behind to make a better quip, that he should name *Belinda* as co-respondent in his divorce action. In other words, Wyman had found and entered the country of the imagination—one feels like writing "the healthy imagination"—that Reagan could never locate.

They tried to help him, the people who ran the town. Unlike most of the other actors, he had always treated them politely, gratefully, according them respect he had never been able to grant his alcoholic father, the shiftless shoe salesman who

had more than once shamed him. He had been loyal to Jack Warner. More important, he had remained faithful to the only agency he had ever had. Lew Wasserman's
increasingly powerful MCA. They all saw him as an actor who had to stay within
himself—these people really are not stupid about their business; it's all they ever
think about. Basically, that meant light comedy and romance, contemporary stuff.
It also meant perpetual youth, which is actually easier to maintain and project in
real life (and on television, where presidents star) than it is on the cruelly magnifying
big screen, which makes all the wrinkles and wattles loom large.

For a while he could get away with it. In later years *Bedtime for Bonzo* served
him as *The Horn Blows at Midnight* served Jack Benny; it was a funny-sounding
title around which gag writers could cluster deflationary jokes about his career, the
film that put ironic quotation marks around his "stardom." Also, of course, liberals
and other cruel people could use it as a symbol of his fundamental lack of seriousness. ("Doesn't it bother you," asks a stoned journalist in Oliver Stone's *Salvadore,*
"that this straight man to a chimp is gonna be the next President?") Actually, *Bonzo*
is an agreeable farce, and he is expert as the professor of behavioral psychology
trying to maintain his dignity while raising a baby chimp as a human baby.

He was 40 the year it was released. And it was obvious to him, if not to anyone
else, that he could not perpetually sham youth. He needed to do grown up roles,
roles without jokes. He loved the outdoors, was proud of his skills as a horseman
(that would be director Allan Dwan's chief memory of him), and from youth, and
like just about every other male of his age, he had wanted to encompass the Western
myth, internalize and then project it. Maybe he could resume his career as another
aging juvenile had done, by embodying that myth onscreen. But though he now
had the crags to match the landscape's, Ronny Reagan was no Jimmy Stewart.
Watch him in *Cattle Queen of Montana*. He lacks the *gravitas* one expects of the
classic westerner. He seems to float above this countryside, unrooted in it or in its
history. Above all, he is innocent of that radical self-sufficiency that is the essence
of the heroic westerner.

It is the same way with most of his other attempts to break away from the
selfhood that he was at last beginning to see as a professional imprisonment. Maybe
he should have played more soldiers and sailors. *Hellcats of the Navy,* the picture
now famous because Nancy [his wife] was his co-star in it, is interesting not merely
because it reveals what prevented her from becoming a star—coarse jawline—but
a signpost of a road not taken by him. Somehow, in a uniform, going by the military
book, he is granted an authority, a maturity, unexpressed in his other postwar roles.
This costume does a job for him that westerner's garb cannot. For to borrow from
David Riesman, whose terms were much on everyone's lips in those days, a military
man is classically other-directed (like Reagan himself), while a westerner is classically inner-directed (utterly unlike him).

In any event, a trip to the corner video parlor will demonstrate to anyone that
off-casting him was not the answer for him. His last picture, *The Killers,* was his
most ludicrous. He's supposed to be this mysteriously crooked businessman,
keeping Angie Dickinson, hinting at off-screen sadism in his relationship with her
while he plots the mail heist that will bring him the wealth with which he intends to
buy respectability. But he cannot project menace in 1964 any better than he could
project sexual banditry in 1941 as Drake McHugh. *The Killers* offers him only one

scene within his range. For purposes of plot he has to dress up as a cop and direct traffic away from the scene of his crime. He has to be chatty, amiable, as he misdirects motorists, and he is as relaxed and agreeable as can be. A nice and totally believable liar. In short, he is positively presidential in the scene. Presidential, that is, as he has redefined the term in recent years.

By the time he made *The Killers,* solutions to the Ronald Reagan problem were in sight. He had made his own significant contributions to this effort. In showbiz the unions are generally presided over by either has-beens or never-weres, people who take themselves seriously and thus seriously feel it when they are denied proper stages on which to assert their gifts. Reagan was not a dynamic Screen Actors Guild prexy. In Doug McClelland's useful compilation of eyewitness accounts of his rise and decline in the business, *Hollywood on Ronald Reagan,* Olivia de Havilland is quoted thus on his leadership: "What comes to mind is his affability and his gift for conducting Screen Actors Guild meetings with adroitness and good humor. I think he was always an instinctive politician, and a genial one."

Yes. Sounds right. He was finding a way to play a president that was within his range. He was not taking charge of that presidency any more than he could be said to have taken charge of his subsequent governorship or his larger presidency. He was substituting agreeableness for authority, letting the mantle of office—the generic conventions of the role, as it were—substitute for true characterization. It is the *Hellcats of the Navy* illusion writ large.

There is, piled up in Wills's book, a huge body of evidence that Reagan's grasp of the complex issues confronting SAG was no more subtle than it was in the White House. Talking with a paid union staffer, Reagan wonders why they need to go on insisting on a union shop in their negotiations with employers. He thought the union was so popular, was doing such a good job, that it could prosper as a purely voluntary organization. We know, of course, that Reagan vastly simplified—recast in starkly melodramatic terms, B-movie terms, if you will—the whole issue of Communist penetration of the unions. We know, too, that he was instrumental in granting the SAG waiver that permitted his own agency, MCA, to enter film and TV production, thus facilitating its rise to its present eminence as the most powerful—and stable—institution in the moving-image industry. We know that ultimately it was MCA functionaries who arranged the real-estate transactions that provided him with the wealth to run for the presidency.

But the real payoff was both more subtle and more immediate. His agent looked upon his performance as SAG's leader and saw that it was good. If it played for an audience of professionals like de Havilland, it would play for a broader, less demanding audience. Reagan did not object or disbelieve. These men had been good to him for so long, had been so, well fatherly (in a way that his own father never had been), so gently undisruptive of his dreamy ways—why should he not follow the drift they pointed out for him now? Why not give up the exhausting effort to be something other than himself, which is what his late screen career kept demanding of him? Why not relax back into the old, simple, perpetually youthful self he had been so contented playing in his earlier movie days? Obivously, they had the right of it. Reagan's too-temperate naturalism, his lack of imaginative fire, may have limited his screen career, but these very deficiencies had, his agents could sense, limitless possibilities in different venues. TV hosting, for starters. And after that . . .

No. Not even Lew Wasserman is that smart. He was clearly a great agent in his day—who else can we imagine getting a million-dollar contract for Reagan out of Jack Warner?—but not even he could have imagined that politics was about to become a branch of television in a wink of history's eye. . . .

This much, however, Wasserman knows, Reagan knows, everyone in showbiz knows: "Yesterday, they told you you would not go far . . . Next day on your dressing room they've hung a star." In other words, the art of showbiz survival consists largely in riding the ups and downs patiently—gracefully, if you can manage it. . . .

Now, of course, Reagan got and-how lucky. Until a couple of minutes ago. When it was rather forcefully borne in on him [during the Iran-Contra Affair] that, once in a while, Presidents really must behave presidentially. What a rude and puzzling awakening. For most of his adult life, he had operated under the unspoken, but very firm, agreement that rules the relationship between "talent" and its agents and managers. It holds the former is to be spared all the unpleasant details of career management. The idea is to free creative people from those distractions that might dilute or divert their creative energies. Or from just having fun or dreaming along, enjoying one's fame and fortune, if, as it was with Reagan, creativity was not a high priority—or, truth to tell, much of a possibility.

The business types like this arrangement. They are pleased to think of their clients as willful children in need of practical advice. And they are inclined to believe that if these clients mix too assertively into business affairs they blunt the creativity of the deal-making process. Modern movie stars tend to get a bit scratchy with this arrangement, but a lot of old-timers like Reagan got used to it. One imagines him feeling he could leave things to [White House Chief of Staff] Don Regan the same way he used to leave things to Lew Wasserman. One imagines Reagan even less prepared for characters like Poindexter and North, with their hidden ideological agendas, not to mention the starring roles they were intent on playing in the phantasmagoric spy movies running in their heads. Showbiz agents, the good ones, do not have hidden agendas—not where their clients' interests are concerned.

One is saddened. To be awakened so close to the end of this long-running dream work of Reagan's, and to have the instrument of his awakening be the yawping and baying of the press, which Lew and his crowd had always been so good at tranquilizing. No movie fan—and who among us is not?—can be anything but touched by his plight as he stands, at last, outside the theater, blinking at the light, trying to recapture the sweet cheats he had so long and happily enjoyed inside. My God! At last he looks, and acts, his age.

Still, he has a mighty consolation. His picture ran longer and prospered better than any other mind's eye ever contemplated. And none of us had plot devices to match the boldness of his: a mental movie in which the star becomes a real movie star. And then President! He is to this form of dreaming what Alexander Portnoy was to another, less dangerous, and less interesting kind.

8

PRIMARY SOURCE

The Hollywood Rating System, 1968

In 1968, the film industry found a successful way to balance artistic independence with public demands that the movies exercise moral responsibility. The new rating system offered moviegoers an indication of the appropriate audience for a particular film.

This Code is designed to keep in close harmony with the mores, culture, the moral sense and change in our society.

The objectives of the Code are:

1. To encourage artistic expression by expanding creative freedom.
2. To assure that the freedom which encourages the artist remains responsible and sensitive to the standards of the larger society.

Censorship is an odious enterprise. We oppose censorship and classification by governments because they are alien to the American tradition of freedom.

Much of this nation's strength and purpose is drawn from the premise that the humblest of citizens has the freedom of his own choice. Censorship destroys this freedom of choice.

It is within this framework that the Motion Picture Association continues to recognize its obligation to the society of which it is an integral part.

In our society parents are the arbiters of family conduct. Parents have the primary responsibility to guide their children in the kinds of lives they lead, the character they build, the books they read, and the movies and other entertainment to which they are exposed.

The creators of motion pictures undertake a responsibility to make available pertinent information about their pictures which will assist parents to fulfill their responsibilities.

But this alone is not enough. In further recognition of our obligation to the public, and most especially to parents, we have extended the Code operation to include a nationwide voluntary film rating program which has as its prime objective a sensitive concern for children. Motion Pictures will be reviewed by a Code and Rating Administration which, when it reviews a motion picture as to its conformity with the standards of the Code, will issue ratings. It is our intent that all motion pictures exhibited in the United States will carry a rating. These rating are:

(G)   SUGGESTED FOR GENERAL AUDIENCES

This category includes motion pictures that in the opinion of the Code and Rating Administration would be acceptable for all audiences, without consideration of age.

(M)   SUGGESTED FOR MATURE AUDIENCES
—ADULTS & MATURE YOUNG PEOPLE

This category includes motion pictures that in the opinion of the Code and Rating Administration, because of their theme, content and treatment, might require more mature judgment by viewers, and about which parents should exercise their discretion.

(R)   RESTRICTED—PERSONS UNDER 16 NOT ADMITTED
UNLESS ACCOMPANIED BY PARENTS OR ADULT GUARDIAN

This category includes motion pictures that in the opinion of the Code and Rating Administration, because of their theme, content or treatment, should not be presented to persons under 16 unless accompanied by a parent or adult guardian.

(X)   PERSONS UNDER 16 NOT ADMITTED

This category includes motion pictures submitted to the Code and Rating Administration which in the opinion of the Code and Rating Administration are rated (X) because of the treatment of sex, violence, crime or profanity. Pictures rated (X) do not qualify for a Code Seal. Pictures rated (X) should not be presented to persons under 16.

The program contemplates that any distributors outside the membership of the Association who choose not to submit their motion pictures to the Code and Rating Administration will self-apply the (X) rating.

The ratings and their meanings will be conveyed by advertising; by displays at the theaters; and in other ways. Thus, audiences, especially parents, will be alerted to the theme, content, and treatment of movies. Therefore, parents can determine whether a particular picture is one which children should see at the discretion of the parent; or only when accompanied by a parent; or should not see.

We believe self-restraint, self-regulation, to be in the American tradition. The results of self-discipline are always imperfect because that is the nature of all things mortal. But this Code, and its administration, will make clear that freedom of expression does not mean toleration of license. . . .

Standards for Production

In furtherance of the objectives of the Code to accord with the mores, the culture, and the moral sense of our society, the principles stated above and the following standards will govern the Administrator in his consideration of motion pictures submitted for Code approval:

—The basic dignity and value of human life shall be respected and upheld. Restraint shall be exercised in portraying the taking of life.

—Evil, sin, crime and wrong-doing shall not be justified.

—Special restraint shall be exercised in portraying criminal or anti-social activities in which minors participate or are involved.

—Detailed and protracted acts of brutality, cruelty, physical violence, torture and abuse shall not be presented.

—Indecent or undue exposure of the human body shall not be presented.

—Illicit sex relationships shall not be justified. Intimate sex scenes violating common standards of decency shall not be portrayed.

—Restraint and care shall be exercised in presentations dealing with sex aberrations.

—Obscene speech, gestures or movements shall not be presented. Undue profanity shall not be permitted.

—Religion shall not be demeaned.

—Words or symbols contemptuous of racial, religious or national groups, shall not be used so as to incite bigotry or hatred.

—Excessive cruelty to animals shall not be portrayed and animals shall not be treated inhumanely.

9

PRESENTING AFRICAN AMERICANS ON FILM

THE RISE AND FALL OF SIDNEY POITIER
Aram Goudsouzian

Sidney Poitier was one of the first successful black movie stars to step outside of negative racial stereotypes. Later in his career essentially integrationist roles—he often played opposite to white actors and actresses—brought him censure from black militants and their white admirers. But he never deviated in any major way from the roles that defined his integrity.

"Why Does White America Love Sidney Poitier So?" asked a *New York Times* headline in September of 1967. It was a good question. Earlier that year, an imprint of the actor's hands and feet had joined Hollywood's elite at the famous forecourt of Grauman's Chinese Theater. Now, two of his films—*To Sir, With Love* and *In the Heat of the Night*—were trading the top spot back and forth in box-office surveys. Poitier was the highest paid actor in Hollywood, and a Gallup poll found that he headed a list of stars—including Julie Andrews, Steve McQueen, Elizabeth Taylor, and Paul Newman—whose name could sell an otherwise unknown movie. He was a confirmed superstar, the first black actor to reach such heights.

But the article underneath that headline was no celebration of the actor's feats. Clifford Mason, a black playwright and drama critic, argued that Poitier constantly played an "antiseptic, one-dimensional hero." His roles were "merely contrivances, completely lacking in artistic merit." Mason criticized Poitier for soothing white consciences during an era of black political stridency. He rejected the notion that "the Negro is best served by being a black version of the man in the gray flannel suit, taking on white problems and a white man's sense of what's wrong with the world." *To Sir, With Love*, Mason went on, "had the all-time Hollywood reversal act. Instead of putting a love interest into a story that had none, they took it out." *In the Heat of the Night* exhibited "the same old Sidney Poitier syndrome: a good guy in a totally white world, with no wife, no sweetheart, no woman to love or kiss, helping the white man solve the white man's problem." Poitier did not reflect dignity or manhood; his passive sterility precluded it. He was a tool of the white establishment—in Mason's cruelest words, a "showcase nigger."

The essay joined a critical chorus denouncing Poitier as a passive attendant to his white co-stars, a neutered accomplice to stereotypes of black sexuality, and a too-perfect symbol of black martyrdom. The showers of scorn provided an ironic juxtaposition to Poitier's escalating mainstream appeal. In December of 1967 Columbia Pictures released *Guess Who's Coming to Dinner*, the actor's third blockbuster movie of the year. It showcased the same icon as the other two films: an educated, articulate, dignified black man who teaches and befriends whites. It also imposed the same limitations—he shows no sexual passion, lets white characters determine the scope of their relationship, and displays little connection to the issues that dominated the lives of most African Americans. *Guess Who's Coming to Dinner* became Poitier's most popular film ever, and it inspired the most critical abuse.

The contradictory reaction spoke to Poitier's unique position in American film history. He was the only black actor consistently to win lead roles in movies from the late 1950s to the late 1960s, the era of nonviolent mass protest that began with the Montgomery bus boycott and ended with the assassination of the Reverend Martin Luther King, Jr. The integrationist themes of his films helped win the hearts and minds of Americans during this quest for black equality. Like other Hollywood stars, Poitier constructed a lasting screen image—in his case, a mannered, humane, intelligent advocate of interracial cooperation.

Unlike other stars, Poitier had an image wrapped in rapidly shifting political realities. By the time of *Guess Who's Coming to Dinner*, America had reached a crossroads both in black politics and in black film representations. Urban riots, the emergent popularity of black radicals, and King's assassination suggested that the foundation of liberal political consensus underneath Poitier's career was crumbling. Yet the black rebellion that rejected Poitier simultaneously provoked fear among political moderates. Soothed by his restrained dignity, hordes of Americans flocked to his films, celebrating Hollywood's sole representative of the civil rights movement with one last, great hurrah.

The poor, nearly illiterate Bahamian child whose rise to screen exemplar of black middle-class polish is a remarkable story in its own right. Poitier grew up on Cat Island, a thin strip on the western edge of the Bahamas, unfettered by physical or racial boundaries. Very few whites lived on the island, and until he was old enough to help his parents and six older siblings with their small tomato farm, he roamed the island, swam the ocean, and daydreamed. By the time he was eleven, the Great Depression had ravaged the tomato market. His family sailed for the capital city of Nassau, moving into a crowded neighborhood of Out Island migrants called Over-the-Hill. They joined the large black underclass that serviced British colonial administrators and wealthy American tourists. After four years receiving only the most rudimentary of educations, working a few World War II-era construction projects, and sinking into petty crime and idle mischief, Poitier left Nassau for his older brother's house in Miami.

The headstrong, impulsive teenager collided with Southern racial codes. The Bahamian racial system never assumed social deference on the part of blacks, and Jim Crow grated on Poitier. After a three-month stay that included threats from the Ku Klux Klan (after he delivered a package to a white woman's front door) and a Miami sheriff (after he hitchhiked in a white neighborhood), he left for New York City. Fifteen and friendless in the booming metropolis, he further floundered. He slept in pay toilets and on the roof of the Brill Building, worked as a dishwasher by night and wandered the city by day, suffered through loneliness and withered in the harsh winter. He even joined the Army for an unsatisfying one-year stint at a Long Island psychiatric hospital. He considered returning to Nassau until he stumbled across an audition for the American Negro Theater (ANT).

At Poitier's original audition, ANT co-founder Frederick O'Neal—a giant with a withering glare and intimidating goatee—berated him for his slow, heavily accented reading. The rejection somehow galvanized the directionless youth. He trained himself by devouring newspapers and imitating the voices on the radio. He returned to ANT six months later for a second audition and joined its School of Drama. By then Broadway producer Douglas Wildberg had bought the ANT play *Anna Lucasta*, exposing black actors to more commercial success and opening doors for the younger actors such as Poitier. A quick study who enjoyed the sense of self-worth and camaraderie acting afforded him, Poitier capitalized on these opportunities, appearing on Broadway for an all-black, ill-fated 1947 production of *Lysistrata* before joining a touring cast of *Anna Lucasta*. He saw the country and honed his acting chops, and then returned to New York City in 1949. After a brief spell of unemployment, he landed a role in his first film, the Twentieth Century Fox production *No Way Out*.

A cycle of "message movies" addressing racial prejudice had begun in 1949 with *Home of the Brave, Lost Boundaries, Pinky*, and *Intruder in the Dust*. After the sacrifices of African Americans in World War 11, blacks were beginning to be included in the democratic tradition. *No Way Out*, released in 1950, took the message movie genre to new lengths, presenting Poitier in the central role as a sympathetic medical intern who fends off a fanatical white racist. Building off the scattered positive minor characters of the World War 11 era and the themes of the message movies, *No Way Out* contradicted the historical burden of blacks on screen: docile slaves, pancake-flipping mammies, grinning song-and-dance men, and comic Stepin Fetchit types. Poitier's middle-class iconography (he played a doctor who has a family, and tries to defuse a race riot) suggested that at least some white Americans were willing to consider blacks as more complete, three-dimensional characters, not consigned to dancing or inanity. Poitier reinforced this perception in his next project, when in 1951 he played a virtuous South African priest in the film adaptation of Alan Paton's novel *Cry, the Beloved Country*.

He received fine reviews for both performances, and in other circumstances, he might have been on the cusp of stardom. But over the next three years, he appeared only in supporting roles in two minor films. It was the era of the blacklist, following HUAC's second Hollywood visit in four years. Already in the midst of crisis following the 1947 Paramount decision, the suburban migration and baby boom, and the impending threat of television, studios shunned pictures with liberal social messages—including nearly all films with racial themes—out of fear of negative publicity. Poitier hurt his own prospects by traveling in America's most radical social circles, joining the small circle of black artists and intellectuals who openly admired Paul Robeson, the famous black performer vilified by the mainstream for his Communist Party ties. The anti-Communist watchdog *Counterattack* later reported that during the early 1950s, Poitier spent "considerable time sponsoring, entertaining at, and otherwise supporting Communist front causes," including the Committee for the Negro in the Arts. Though he had no direct connection to organized radical politics, he had associated his talents with allegedly subversive plays and events.

Poitier's breakthrough role came in 1955, with *Blackboard Jungle.* The picture features violent scenes in an urban high school, sparking vigorous media debates over its accuracy. Cities and small towns throughout the United States banned or cut scenes from the film. Senator Estes Kefauver's subcommittee on juvenile delinquency investigated the film industry, paying particular attention to *Blackboard Jungle.* Months later Italian ambassador Clare Boothe Luce ignited an international controversy when she boycotted the picture at the Venice Film Festival. The furor centered around the explicit violence, but Poitier's cool menace lent an added subtext of black anger. His character does aid the white hero played by Glenn Ford at film's end, however, a pattern he would recreate in 1957 in his next major role, *Edge of the City.* Nevertheless, Poitier carried a reputation as a Hollywood maverick. Both for *Blackboard Jungle* and the live television version of *Edge of the City,* (entitled *A Man is Ten Feet Tall*), lawyers implored Poitier to sign a loyalty oath denouncing his radical mentors Paul Robeson and Canada Lee. At risk to his career, he refused.

In the late 1950s, Poitier was not yet typecast into the staid middle-class image that characterized both his first films and his most popular pictures from the 1960s. Like his friend Harry Belafonte, who captained a fervent but short-lived Calypso Craze, Poitier conveyed elements of black exoticism: in 1957 a Mau Mau terrorist in *Something of Value,* and a cocksure slave in *Band of Angels,* the following year an African diplomat married to the steamy Eartha Kitt in *Mark of the Hawk* and a robust West Indian in *Virgin Island.* He also used his celebrity for political ends, speaking in Washington at the 1957 Prayer Pilgrimage and in New York City at a 1959 rally celebrating the fifth anniversary of the decision in *Brown vs. Board of Education.* Columnists tied his films to the civil rights movement. Black newspapers constantly celebrated his demand to portray a positive black image, Dorothy Masters of the *New York*

Daily News implied a connection between the actor and the ministers of the Montgomery bus boycott, and Barry Gray of the *New York Post* equated the hardships faced by the Little Rock Nine with his struggle to rise from poverty.

But Poitier's burgeoning notoriety caused complications. The legendary independent producer Samuel Goldwyn manipulated him into participation in *Porgy and Bess*, despite the actor's public dismissal of the Gershwin folk opera depicting the crap-shooting, razor-toting, dialect-speaking denizens of Catfish Row. His character Porgy, moreover, is an emasculated cripple. After one of Poitier's agents mistakenly promised him for the project, Goldwyn threatened legal action if Poitier instead accepted a role in the Stanley Kramer film *The Defiant Ones*, a story of a black and a white fugitive chained together. Poitier in 1959 compromised his image in *Porgy and Bess*, but the previous year's film *The Defiant Ones* had proved a career boon by providing him with his first star role in a commercially successful picture. Yet even that film revealed the limitations of the white liberal perspective that governed most Poitier films. James Baldwin reported that the movie's final scene, when Poitier leaps off a train to tend Tony Curtis and await certain capture, inspired tears and hosannas among white audiences. But black audiences howled: "*Get back on the train, you fool!*"

The actor left the entanglements of Hollywood for a six-month run on stage in *A Raisin in the Sun*, a milestone for blacks on Broadway. Lorraine Hansberry's play—with the black director Lloyd Richards, a predominantly black cast including Claudia McNeil and Ruby Dee, and Poitier as Walter Lee Younger—explores the struggles of a working class black family through a riveting, emotional drama. The winner of the 1959 Drama Critics Circle Award, the play inspired heartfelt laughter, teary catharsis, and proclamations that it was not a "Negro play," but about people "who happened to be Negroes." This interpretation (or misinterpretation) spoke to the pervasiveness of black stereotypes on stage and screen, and *A Raisin in the Sun*'s ability to transcend them. The play and its 1961 film adaptation, the publicity from *Porgy and Bess*, Poitier's Academy Award nomination for *The Defiant Ones*, and his upcoming roles in the 1960 release *All the Young Men* and *Paris Blues* in 1961 generated countless media profiles of him. Always, he presented a humble yet thoughtful image, speaking eloquently on the necessity of including blacks in the American democratic tradition and emphasizing his own childhood poverty, work ethic, and middle class ideology.

By the early 1960s, as the Greensboro sit-ins launched an era of continued nonviolent direct action in the South, Poitier had become an important representative of black America. He played a valuable fundraising role for civil rights organizations, attended the 1963 March on Washington, and even joined Belafonte on a dangerous 1964 mission to deliver money to civil rights workers in Greenville, Mississippi. He also spoke often on race and Hollywood. "Except for the coffee boy, I am the only Negro on the set," he told the House Labor Committee in 1962, "I have made 17 pictures, but it is no joy to me that I am used as an example to prove they really don't discriminate." As an additional frustration, he seemed unable to launch his career to the next level. Plans for his own production company, an opportunity to direct, and numerous film projects all failed to materialize.

His breakthrough came in the most unlikely of films, a 1963 low-budget production entitled *Lilies of the Field*. It featured Poitier as an itinerant handyman who builds a church for five German nuns, and its sweet message and endearing hero charmed audiences. The film made Poitier rich, as he negotiated one of the first deals that awarded an actor a percentage of the gross. And in 1964, the same year of the Civil Rights Act and Martin Luther King, Jr.'s Nobel Peace Prize, Poitier won the Academy Award for Best Actor. "It has been a long journey," he told the audience.

The Oscar opened opportunities. In 1964 Poitier had already filmed *The Long Ships*, roundly considered his most execrable movie, but he now chose roles that reinforced the proper, buttoned-down image he had exhibited in the 1962 film *Pressure Point*, when he played a psychiatrist. He was a journalist in both *The Bedford Incident* and *A Patch of Blue*, both of them appearing in 1965, and next year a volunteer at a crisis center in *The Slender Thread*. In each case, he embodied reason and virtue, warning crazed sea captains against Cold War paranoia, befriending a blind girl tormented by an abusive mother, and counseling a woman on the brink of suicide. Each, in its own way, served as an advertisement for racial integration. Like the civil rights demonstrators in Birmingham, Selma, and throughout the South, Poitier's characters embodied nonviolence and love for fellow man. The pictures were generally successful, capturing a broad middle-class audience.

Yet Poitier increasingly inspired groans among many intellectuals and black critics, who anticipated the nation's shifting racial climate. The media took note that for both *The Bedford Incident* and *The Slender Thread*, Poitier played roles not specifically designated for black actors. This was another milestone, but some regarded Poitier's acceptance of these roles as an abandonment of black identity. Moreover, he continued to play the sacrificial lamb: dying in a baling hook fight in *Edge of the City*, falling into an elephant pit in *Something of Value*, jumping off the train in *The Defiant Ones*, and so on. In each case, his suffering enlightens his white co-star. Finally, Poitier rarely played the romantic lead typical of handsome Hollywood stars. In most every movie, he was in an all-male setting, married to a prim housewife *a la* Ruby Dee, or explicitly (and creatively) desexualized. His lust for a mulatto woman was written out of *Band of Angels*, and his Moorish villain takes a bizarre oath of celibacy in *The Long Ships*. In *A Patch of Blue*, he finally kisses a white girl—but she is blind.

It was unfair to lay the burden entirely at the actor's feet. The bulk of the criticism stemmed from his being the film industry's sole black leading man. "We don't make race films," went a common adage. "We make Sidney Poitier films." But by 1967, as ghettos erupted in riots and radical voices such as Stokely Carmichael and H. Rap Brown became media darlings, either a revamping of Poitier's image or his fadeout from Hollywood might have been predicted. Instead, three films intensified every aspect of the Sidney Poitier stereotype, prompted the criticisms of intellectuals and black radicals, and—perhaps most remarkably—boosted Poitier's popularity even higher.

To Sir, With Love opened first, and it provided a soothing balm on national wounds of racial fracture and urban discontent. In a reversal of *Blackboard Jungle*, and an apt illustration of Poitier's career arc, he now played the new teacher sent to tame rowdy students—this time, in London's East End. After floundering at first, he throws out his books and teaches the students about practical issues they will face upon graduation, all the while injecting lessons of manners, tolerance, and nonviolence. The classroom abruptly transforms from clamorous to captivated. By the end, the students brim with excitement over finding jobs, and Poitier decides to remain a teacher. With a splash of Mod style and the debut of pop star Lulu, it became a sleeper hit that summer.

Appearing almost simultaneously in theaters was *In the Heat of the Night*. Poitier played a proud Philadelphia detective thrust into aiding an arrogant Southern sheriff played by Rod Steiger. The actual murder mystery is secondary to the tense relationship between the two outstanding actors. Poitier proves his detective skill and wins grudging acceptance of his status from the racist sheriff. They develop a prickly understanding. When an aristocratic cotton magnate slaps Poitier, he slaps back, and Steiger remains impassive. Later Steiger saves Poitier when the black detective is surrounded by armed vigilantes. After Poitier solves the case, Steiger walks him to the train station and tells him to "Take care, you hear?" With those final words, a human connection is established.

September 1967, when audiences swarmed to the two pictures, *Variety* called "Sidney Poitier Month." *In the Heat of the Night* proved instantly successful, and *To Sir, With Love* recovered from an unambitious marketing campaign to surge atop box-office surveys well into October. After a summer of bloody riots, the middle class appreciated Poitier's restrained black superhero. The substantial, even disproportionately large black audience supported Poitier's films because there were no alternatives with blacks in lead roles. Also, his integrationist values still served some good. *Variety* called him "The Useful Negro." "Poitier on the screen," it surmised, "is the only Negro which myriads of Americans feel they know and understand."

That was a heavy burden. Since his first acting job, Poitier had accepted the responsibility of presenting a positive black image, both on screen and in print. But this position of solitary racial spokesman tore at him. As the keynote speaker for the 1967 conference of the Southern Christian Leadership Conference, reporters peppered him with questions about the summer riots. He exploded. "There are many aspects of my personality that you can explore very constructively," he seethed. "But you sit here and ask me such one-dimensional questions about a very tiny area of our lives. You ask me questions that continually fall within the Negroness of my life." He also called Hollywood "a hostile community" that sacrificed complete black depictions for broader appeal. But in the wake of his fantastic success, he insisted on playing the noble hero. "I'm the only one," he argued. "I represent 10,000,000 people in this country and millions more in Africa; I'm the only one for these people to identify with on the screen." He carefully chose his roles, and insisted that "if the fabric of society were different I would scream to high heaven to play villains and to deal with different images of Negro life that would be more dimensional. But I'll be damned if I do that at this stage of the game."

Poitier's persistent typecasting and isolation nettled some some veteran critics. Stephen Farber called him "the suburban audience's dream of a well-adjusted Negro." Pauline Kael added that he "has been playing the ideal boy-next-door-who-happens-to-be-black for so long that he's always the same." In both *In the Heat of the Night* and *To Sir, With Love,* Poitier was less a real person than a vehicle through which whites question their belief system. He restrains himself from intimacy with an admiring white teacher in *To Sir, With Love.* He bathes in isolated righteousness during *In the Heat of the Night.*

Then came *Guess Who's Coming to Dinner.* The picture carried the Poitier archetype to its logical end—and beyond. His character is not just a doctor: he has taught at Yale Medical School and the London School of Tropical Medicine, served as the assistant director of the World Health Organization, and been featured in *Commonweal.* He falls in love with a white woman—the daughter of a liberal San Francisco newspaper publisher and his equally liberal wife—and arrives at their doorstep seeking her parents' blessing. The audience identifies with the father, played by Spencer Tracy, who must decide whether he can abide by the racial liberalism he has so long preached. As director and producer Stanley Kramer himself said, "The film is an adventure into the ludicrous—the characters so perfect that the only conceivable objection to this marriage could be ludicrously enough, the pigmentation of a man's skin."

But in its mission to expunge him of the slightest shard of negative black cultural stereotype, the picture strips Poitier of his humanity. His racial colorblindness, which even five years earlier would have made him a progressive, seems outdated by 1968. It is dramatic only in opposition to the obsolete political stance of the other black characters, his parents and a sassy maid. Moreover, only Spencer Tracy's approval carries any weight; Poitier even informs her parents that he will not marry their daughter if they disapprove. Finally, Poitier displays a debasing sexual priggishness, almost consciously avoiding physical contact with his fiancée, covering his bare chest with a towel when the maid enters his room, and refusing to sleep with his fiancée until they are married. He kisses her only once, briefly, during a cab ride. But even that scene is compromised: the camera captures the moment through the cab driver's rear view mirror.

The picture disgusted an increasingly assertive segment of the population. "Even George Wallace would like that nigger," grumbled H. Rap Brown. College students lambasted Kramer when he traveled to campuses defending his picture. The theater critic Lindsay Patterson called the film "a perfect example in Hollywood's escapism, blithely disregarding the genuine and maybe altogether unendurable problems to be encountered in a mainland interracial marriage." Even mainstream publications ridiculed the outdated political message and subject. *Newsweek* wrote: "When this film was conceived several years ago, the problems of love among the comfortable middle classes may have still seemed more dramatic than the passions of ghetto blacks, but it was ill-conceived even then." "Now," the magazine concluded, "it seems an absolute antique."

Yet the film presented a message of racial integration that captured a broad segment of the population, illustrated by its box-office dominance in the winter of 1968. The film's massive appeal suggested that the majority of the American people, at least theoretically, embraced liberal racial attitudes. James Baldwin hated the movie, but presciently forecast its implications: "*Guess Who's Coming to Dinner* may prove, in some bizarre way, to be a milestone, because it is really quite impossible to go any further in that particular direction. Next time, the kissing will have to start." And as removed as the picture seemed from the emergent black ethic seeking racial confrontation and fixed on the problems of the urban poor, it still rankled the nation's staunchest white conservatives. A number of southern theaters endured Ku Klux Klan protests and cut out the interracial kiss scene. The picture's popularity, combined with the scathing attacks from each end of the political spectrum, illuminated the inability of Americans in 1968 to achieve any sort of consensus on racial politics. When that consensus disintegrated, so did Poitier's status of Hollywood leading man.

On April 4, 1968, just as the box-office momentum of *Guess Who's Coming to Dinner* began to wane, Martin Luther King, Jr. was assassinated. As the nation confronted racial uncertainty, the entertainment world struggled to respond appropriately. Columbia called back all copies of *Guess Who's Coming to Dinner* and edited out a scene where Poitier's fiancée asks the maid to "guess who's coming to dinner." "The Reverend Martin Luther King Jr.!" she sasses back. Poitier, Diahann Carroll, Sammy Davis Jr., and Louis Armstrong announced that out of respect for Dr. King, they could no longer participate in the upcoming Academy Awards.

The board of directors of the Academy of Motion Picture Arts and Sciences quickly agreed to postpone the ceremony for two days, and the black performers reconsidered. In the shadow of King's death, the ceremony included musings on entertainment's role in race relations. Hollywood equated Poitier with the King legacy; when he rose to present the award for Best Actress, he received the evening's biggest ovation. The Academy president Gregory Peck declared of the Poitier films: "One measure of Dr. King's influence on the society in which we live is that of the five films nominated for best picture of the year, two dealt with the subject of understanding between the races." Those films were *In the Heat of the Night* (which won the award) and *Guess Who's Coming to Dinner*. Peck called for more films "which celebrate the dignity of man, whatever his race or color or creed." Rod Steiger ended his acceptance speech for Best Actor with the words, "We Shall Overcome."

But King's death represented the end of an era of nonviolent protest for racial integration, and it was the hinge upon which Poitier's career turned. Two years later, the *New York Times* was asking, "is Sidney Poitier obsolete?" It explained: "The terrible thing about being a political point of view and a social symbol is that time, even before age, may suddenly overtake you." Poitier's responses to changing racial sensibilities appeared calculated and lame. His role in 1969 of black radical in *The Lost Man* was unconvincing and politically ambiguous. His reprise of his character from *In the Heat of the Night—They Call Me Mister Tibbs!* in 1970 and the next year *The Organization*—lacked the racial friction of the original, turning his character into a banal supercop. In *Brother John*, also in 1971, the first project of his production company, he starred as a mystic archangel in what seemed a clumsy exercise in self-deification.

The shifting winds of black politics had sucked Poitier into a curious trap: unable to portray his trademark virtuous emblem of dignity, and unconvincing in a departure from that image. The times demanded a calculated reversal of the Poitier stereotype, embodied in a new generation of black films—*Shaft, Super Fly, Sweet Sweetback's Baadasssss Son*—that celebrated a novel black hero who uses violence, sleeps with white women, and dresses and speaks in urban styles. For an audience frustrated with the slow pace of racial progress, the new film icon offered blacks an emotional satisfaction that Poitier's characters could never approach.

Poitier never disappeared from Hollywood. In fact, he remained at the forefront of black progress in the film industry. In 1969 he founded, along with Paul Newman and Barbra Streisand, the First Artists Production Company to finance production and distribution of films they would each star in and produce. In 1972 he directed his first film, the western *Buck and the Preacher*. He directed and co-starred in a trio of successful comedies, *Uptown Saturday Night* in 1974, *Let's Do It Again* in 1975, and *A Piece of the Action* two years later. He addressed the conditions that he had complained about to the House Labor Committee a decade earlier, hiring black actors, writers, and technicians. But for many in the younger generation, Poitier seemed a relic, an apologetic accommodationist constructed by white liberals and stripped of black autonomy. Few remembered just how important, and just how controversial, Sidney Poitier had once been.

A BIBLIOGRAPHY OF FILM HISTORY

REFERENCE WORKS

BIBLIOGRAPHIES

Bowles, Stephen E. *The Film Anthologies Index*. Metuchen: Scarecrow, 1994.

Ellis, Jack C. et al. *The Film Book Bibliography, 1940–1975*. Metuchen: Scarecrow, 1979.

Manchel, Frank. *Film Study:Analytical Bibliography*. Rutherford: Fairleigh Dickinson, 1990.

Morgan, Jenny. *Film Researcher's Handbook*. London: Routledge, 1996.

BIOGRAPHICAL DICTIONARIES

Andrew, Geoff. *The Director's Vision: A Concise Guide to the Art of 250 Great Filmmakers*. Chicago: A. Cappella, 1999.

Herbert, Stephen and Luke McKernan. *Who's Who of Victorian Cinema*. London: BFI, 1996.

Liebman, Roy. *From Silents to Sound: A Biographical Encyclopedia of Performers Who Made the Transition to Talking Pictures*. Jefferson, NC: McFarland, 1998.

Petrikin, Chris, Andrew Hindes, and Dan Cox, eds. *Variety Power Players 2000: Movers and Shakers, Power Brokers, and Career Makers in Hollywood*. New York: Perigee Books, 1999.

Quigley, Martin S. *First Century of Film*. New York: Quigley, 1995.

Stephens, Michael L. *Art Directors in Cinema: A Worldwide Biographical Dictionary*. Jefferson, NC: McFarland, 1998.

Thomson, David. *A Biographical Dictionary of Film*. 3rd ed. London: A. Deutsch, 1994.

Vazzana, Eugene Michael. *Silent Film Necrology*. Jefferson, NC: McFarland, 1995.

Walker, John, ed. *Halliwell's Who's Who in the Movies*. 13th ed. London: HarperCollins, 1999.

Wise, James E., Jr. and Anne Collier Rehill. *Stars in the Corps: Movie Actors in the United States Marines*. Annapolis: Naval Institute Press, 1999.

CHRONOLOGIES

Brown, Gene. *Movie Time*. New York: Macmillan, 1995.

DICTIONARIES

Bognar, Desi K. *International Dictionary of Broadcasting and Film*. 2nd ed. Boston: Focal, 2000.

Busby, Alex. *A–Z of Film, Television, and Video Terms*. London: Blueprint, 1994.

International Dictionary of Films and Filmmakers. 3rd ed. Detroit: St. James, 1997.

Jackson, Kevin. *The Language of Film*. Manchester: Carcanet, 1998.

Konigsberg, Ira. *The Complete Film Dictionary*. 2nd ed. New York: Penguin, 1997.

Slide, Anthony. *The New Historical Dictionary of the American Film Industry*. Lanham, MD: Scarecrow Press, 1998.

DOCUMENT COLLECTIONS

Brown, Gene. *New York Times Encyclopedia of Film*. New York: New York Times, 1984.

Gardner, Gerald. *Censorship Papers: Movie Censorship Letters from the Hays Office, 1934–1968*. New York: Dodd, Mead, 1987.

Mast, Gerald. *The Movies in Our Midst: Documents in the Cultural History of Film in America*. Chicago: University of Chicago, 1982.

ENCYCLOPEDIAS AND REFERENCE GUIDES

Curran, Daniel. *Guide to American Cinema, 1965–1995*. Westport, CT: Greenwood Press, 1998.

Hayward, Susan. *Key Concepts in Cinema Studies*. 2nd ed. New York: Routledge, 2000.

Hunter, Allan. *Chambers Film and Television Handbook*. Edinburgh: Chambers, 1991.

Katz, Ephraim. *Film Encyclopedia*. 3rd ed. New York: HarperPerennial, 1998.

Krautz, Alfred. *Encyclopedia of Film Directors in the United States and Europe*. Munchen: K.G. Saur, 1993–.

Law, John. *Cassell Companion to Cinema*. London: Cassell, 1997.

Monaco, James. *The Encyclopedia of Film*. New York: Perigee, 1991.

Tibbetts, John C. and James M. Welsh. *Encyclopedia of Novels into Film*. New York: Facts on File, 1998.

Whissen, Thomas R. *Guide to American Cinema, 1930–1965*. Westport, CT: Greenwood Press, 1998.

Winnert, Derek. *Virgin Encyclopedia of the Movies*. London: Virgin, 1995.

FILM GUIDES

Curran, Daniel. *Guide to American Cinema, 1965–1995*. Westport, CT: Greenwood Press, 1998.

Film Index International. Paris: Chadwyck-Healey-France, n.d.

Goble, Alan. *International Film Index on CD-ROM*. West Sussex: Bowker-Saur, 1996.

Halliwell, Leslie. *Halliwell's Filmgoer's Companion*. 12th ed. London: HarperCollins, 1997.

Magill, Frank N. *Magill's Survey of Cinema*. Englewood Cliffs: Salem, 1980, 1981, 1985.

Whissen, Thomas R. *Guide to American Cinema, 1930–1965*. Westport, CT: Greenwood Press, 1998.

FILMOGRAPHY

Fetrow, Alan G. *Feature Films, 1950–1959: A United States Filmography*. Jefferson, NC: McFarland, 1999.

Klotman, Phyllis Rauch and Gloria J. Gibson. *Frame by Frame II: A Filmography of the African American Image*. Bloomington: Indiana University, 1997.

Martin, Len D. *The Republic Pictures Checklist*. Jefferson, NC: McFarland, 1998.

Ranucci, Karen and Julie Feldman, eds. *A Guide to Latin American, Caribbean, and U.S. Latino Made Film and Video*. Lanham, MD: Scarecrow Press, 1998.

Richards, Larry. *African American Films Through 1959*. Jefferson, NC: McFarland, 1998.

JOURNALS

American Film
Cineaste
Cinema Journal
Classic Images
Film & History
Film Comment
Film in Review
Film Quarterly
Film Reader
Historical Journal of Film, Radio, and Television
Image
Journal of Popular Film and Television
Journal of the University Film and Video Association
Jump Cut
Literature/Film Quarterly
Marquee
Quarterly Review of Film Studies
Screen
Sight and Sound
SMPTE Journal (Society of Motion Picture and Television Engineers)
Variety
Velvet Light Trap
Wide Angle

QUOTATIONS

Bloch, Jeff. *Women's Book of Movie Quotes*. Secaucus: Carol, 1995.

Corey, Melinda. *Dictionary of Film Quotations*. New York: Crown, 1995.

Nowlan, Robert A. and Gwendolyn W. Nolan. *Film Quotations*. Jefferson, NC: McFarland, 1994.

RESEARCH GUIDES

Mehr, Linda. *Motion Pictures, Television, and Radio: A Union Catalogue of Manuscript and Special Collections in the Western United States*. Boston: G.K. Hall, 1977.

Rowan, Bonnie G. *Scholars' Guide to Washington D.C. Film and Video Collections*. Washington: Smithsonian, 1980.

TOPICS IN AMERICAN FILM HISTORY

ACTORS AND ACTRESSES

Baty, S. Paige. *American Monroe: The Making of a Body Politic*. Berkeley: University of California, 1995.

Kurtzen, Michaela. *The Most Beautiful Woman on the Screen: The Fabrication of the Star Greta Garbo*. New

York: P. Lang, 1992.

Sklar, Robert. *City Boys: Cagney, Bogart, Garfield*. Princeton: Princeton, 1992.

Smith, Paul. *Clint Eastwood: A Cultural Production*. Minneapolis: University of Minnesota, 1993.

AESTHETICS

Aitken, Stuart C. and Leo E. Zonn. *Place, Power, Situation, and Spectacle: A Geography of Film*. Lanham, MD: Rowman & Littlefield, 1994.

Armes, Roy. *Action and Image: Dramatic Structure in Cinema*. New York: Manchester, 1994.

Bordwell, David. *On the History of Film Style*. Cambridge: Harvard, 1997.

Bordwell, David, Janet Staiger, and Kristin Thompson. *The Classical Hollywood Cinema*. New York: Columbia, 1985.

Bordwell, David and Kristin Thompson. *Film Art: An Introduction*. 4th ed. New York: McGraw Hill, 1993.

Fell, John L. *Film and the Narrative Tradition*. Norman: University of Oklahoma, 1974.

Hollander, Anne. *Moving Pictures*. Cambridge: Harvard, 1991.

Jameson, Frederic. *The Geopolitical Aesthetic: Cinema and Space in the World System*. Bloomington: Indiana University, 1992.

McGee, Patrick. *Cinema, Theory, and Political Responsibility in Contemporary Culture*. New York: Cambridge, 1997.

Mitry, Jean. *Aesthetics and Psychology of the Cinema*. Bloomington: Indiana University, 1997.

Montgomery, Michael V. *Carnivals and Commonplaces: Bakhtin's Chronotope, Cultural Studies, and Film*. New York: P. Lang, 1993.

Nichols, Bill. *Ideology and the Image*. Bloomington: Indiana University, 1981.

Orr, John. *The Art and Politics of Film*. Edinburgh: Edinburgh University, 2000.

———. *Cinema and Modernity*. Cambridge: Polity, 1993.

Peucker, Brigitte. *Incorporating Images: Film and the Rival Arts*. Princeton: Princeton, 1995.

Rabiger, Michael. *Directing: Film Techniques and Aesthetics*. Boston: Focal Press, 1997.

Ray, Robert. *A Certain Tendency in the Hollywood Cinema, 1930–1980*. Princeton: Princeton, 1985.

Sennett, Robert S. *Setting the Scene: The Great Hollywood Art Directors*. New York: H.N. Arams, 1994.

Shaviro, Steven. *The Cinematic Body*. Minneapolis: University of Minnesota, 1993.

Staiger, Janet. *Interpreting Films: Studies in the Historical Reception of American Cinema*. Princeton: Princeton, 1992.

Taylor, Clyde R. *The Mask of "Art": Breaking the Aesthetic Contract*. Bloomington: Indiana University, 1998.

ALCOHOLISM AND FILM

Cook, Jim and Mike Lewington. *Images of Alcoholism*. London: BFI, 1979.

Denzin, Norman K. *Hollywood Shot by Shot*. New York: A. de Gruyter, 1991.

ARCHITECTURE AND FILM

Fear, Bob, ed. *Architecture and Film II*. London: Wiley-Academy, 2000.

Lamster, Mark, ed. *Architecture and Film*. New York: Princeton Architectural Press, 2000.

ARCHIVAL PROJECTS

Usai, Paolo Cherchi, ed. *The Griffith Project*. London: British Film Institute, 1999–.

ART DESIGN

Affron, Charles. *Sets in Motion: Art Direction and Film Narrative*. New Brunswick: Rutgers, 1995.

Ettedgui, Peter. *Production Design and Art Direction*. Woburn, MA: Focal Press, 1999.

Neumann, Dietrich. *Film Architecture*. Munich: Prestel, 1996.

Schaal, Hans Dieter. *Learning from Hollywood: Architecture and Film*. Fellbach: Ed. Axel Menges, 1996.

Tashiro, C. S. *Pretty Pictures: Production Design and the History Film*. Austin: University of Texas, 1998.

AUDIENCES

Barker, Martin. *Knowing Audiences: Judge Dredd, Its Friends, Fans and Foes*. Luton: University of Luton, 1998.

Casetti, Francesco. *Inside the Gaze: The Fiction Film and Its Spectator*. Bloomington: Indiana University, 1998.

Dixon, Wheeler W. *It Looks at You: The Returned Gaze of Cinema*. Albany: SUNY, 1995.

Scheiner, Georganne. *Signifying Female Adolescence: Film Representations and Fans, 1920–1950*. Westport, CT: Praeger, 2000.

Sedgwick, John. *Popular Filmgoing in 1930s Britain: A Choice of Pleasures*. Exeter: University of Exeter, 2000.

Staiger, Janet. *Perverse Spectators: The Practices of Film Reception*. New York: New York University, 2000.

Stempel, Tom. *American Audiences on Movies and Moviegoing*. Lexington: University of Kentucky, 2001.

Stern, Lesley and George Kouvaros, eds. *Falling for You: Essays on Cinema and Performance*. Sydney:

Power, 2000.

Stokes, Melvyn and Richard Maltby. *Identifying Hollywood's Audiences: Cultural Identity and the Movies.* London: British Film Institute, 1999.

CENSORSHIP

Aldgate, Anthony. *Censorship and the Permissive Society: 1955–1965.* Oxford: Oxford University, 1995.

Black, Gregory D. *The Catholic Crusade Against the Movies, 1940–1975.* Cambridge: Cambridge, 1998.

———. *Hollywood Censored: Morality Codes, Catholics, and the Movies.* Cambridge: Cambridge, 1994.

Burns-Bisogno, Louisa. *Censoring Irish Nationalism: 1909–1995.* Jefferson, NC: McFarland, 1997.

Couvares, Francis G. *Movie Censorship and American Culture.* Washington: Smithsonian, 1996.

Jacobs, Lea. *The Wages of Sin: Censorship and the Fallen Woman Film, 1928–1942.* Berkeley: University of California, 1997.

Johnson, Tom. *Censored Screams: The British Ban on Hollywood Horror in the Thirties.* Jefferson, NC: McFarland, 1997.

Leff, Leonard J. and Jerold L. Simmons. *The Dame in the Kimono: Hollywood, Censorship, and the Production Code.* New York: Grove Weidenfeld, 1990.

Lyons, Charles. *The New Censors: Movies and the Culture Wars.* Philadelphia: Temple, 1997.

Petrie, Ruth. *Film and Censorship.* Washington: Cassell, 1997.

Robertson, James C. *The Hidden Cinema: British Censorship.* London: Routledge, 1993.

Skinner, James M. *The Cross and the Cinema: The Legion of Decency and the National Catholic Office for Motion Pictures.* Westport, CT: Praeger, 1993.

Vasey, Ruth. *The World According to Hollywood, 1918–1939.* Madison: University of Wisconsin, 1997.

Walsh, Frank. *Sin and Censorship: The Catholic Church and the Motion Picture Industry.* New Haven: Yale, 1996.

CHILDREN AND FILM

Ayesworth, Thomas G. *Hollywood Kids: Child Stars of the Silver Screen.* New York: Dutton, 1987.

Bazalgette, Cary and David Buckingham. *In Front of the Children: Screen Entertainment and Young Audiences.* London: BFI, 1995.

Bell, Elizabeth et al. *From Mouse to Mermaid: The Politics of Film, Gender, and Culture.* Bloomington: Indiana University, 1995.

Cantor, Joanne. *Mommy, I'm Scared: How TV and Movies Frighten Children and What We Can Do to Protect Them.* New York: Harcourt Brace, 1998.

Jackson, Kathy Merlock. *Images of Children in American Film.* Metuchen: Scarecrow, 1980.

Keller, Marjorie. *The Untutored Eye: Childhood in the Films of Cocteau, Cornell, and Brakhage.* Rutherford: Fairleigh Dickinson, 1986.

Kinder, Marsha. *Playing with Power in Movies, Television, and Video Games.* Berkeley: University of California, 1991.

Moss, Joyce and George Wilson. *From Page to Screen: Children's and Young Adult Books on Film and Video.* Detroit: Gale, 1992.

Pecora, Norma Odom. *The Business of Children's Entertainment.* New York: Guilford, 1998.

Sinyard, Neil. *Children in the Movies.* London: Batsford, 1990.

Staples, Terry. *All Pals Together: The Story of Children's Cinema.* Edinburgh: Edinburgh, 1997.

CITIES AND TOWNS IN FILM

Clarke, David B. *The Cinematic City.* London: Routledge, 1997.

Levi, Emanuel. *Small-Town America in Film: The Decline and Fall of Community.* New York: Continuum, 1991.

MacKinnon, Kenneth. *Hollywood's Small Towns.* Metuchen: Scarecrow, 1984.

DIRECTORS

Bliss, Michael. *Justified Lives: Morality and Narrative in the Films of Sam Peckinpah.* Carbondale: Southern Illinois University, 1993.

Durgnat, Raymond and Scott Simmon. *King Vidor.* Berkeley: University of California, 1988.

Gehring, Wes D. *Populism and the Capra Legacy.* Westport, CT: Greenwood Press, 1995.

Girgus, Sam B. *Hollywood Renaissance: The Cinema of Democracy in the Ear of Ford, Capra, and Kazan.* Cambridge: Cambridge, 1998.

Gunning, Tom. *D.W. Griffith and the Origins of American Narrative Film.* Urbana: University of Illinois, 1991.

Jacobs, Diane. *Christmas in July: The Life and Art of Preston Sturges.* Berkeley: University of California, 1992.

Kapsis, Robert E. *Hitchcock: The Making of a Reputation*. Chicago: University of Chicago, 1992.

Kolker, Robert Phillip. *A Cinema of Loneliness: Penn, Kubrick, Coppola, Scorsese, Altman*. New York: Oxford, 1980.

Koszarski, Richard. *Hollywood Directors, 1914–1940*. New York: Oxford, 1976.

———. *Hollywood Directors, 1941–1976*. New York: Oxford, 1977.

Lourdeaux, Lee. *Italian and Irish Filmmakers in America: Ford, Captra, Coppola, and Scorsese*. Philadelphia: Temple, 1990.

Morrison, James. *Passport to Hollywood: Hollywood Films, European Directors*. Albany: SUNY, 1998.

Phillips, Gene D. *Major Film Directors of the American and British Cinema*. Bethlehem: Lehigh, 1990.

Quarles, Mike. *Down and Dirty: Hollywood's Exploitation Filmmakers and Their Movies*. Jefferson, NC: McFarland, 1993.

Sikov, Ed. *On Sunset Boulevard: The Life and Times of Billy Wilder*. New York: Hyperion, 1998.

Studlar, Gaylyn and David Desser. *Reflections in a Male Eye: John Huston and the American Experience*. Washington: Smithsonian, 1993.

DISABILITY AND FILM

Fleming, Michael and Roger Manvell. *Images of Madness*. Rutherford: Fairleigh Dickinson, 1985.

Klobas, Lauri E. *Disability Drama in Television and Film*. Jefferson, NC: McFarland, 1988.

Norden, Martin F. *The Cinema of Isolation: A History of Physical Disability in the Movies*. New Brunswick: Rutgers, 1994.

Schuchman, John S. *Hollywood Speaks: Deafness and the Film Entertainment Industry*. Urbana: University of Illinois, 1988.

EDITING

Bouzereau, Laurent. *The Cutting Room Floor*. Secaucus: Carol, 1994.

Clark, Barbara and Susan J. Spohr. *Guide to Post Production for TV and Film*. Boston: Focal, 1998.

LoBrutto, Vincent. *Selected Takes: Film Editors on Editing*. New York: Praeger, 1991.

Murch, Walter. *In the Blink of an Eye*. Sydney: Australian Film, Television & Radio School, 1992.

Oldham, Gabriella. *First Cut: Conversations with Film Editors*. Los Angeles: University of California, 1992.

ETHNOCENTRISM AND FILM

Shohat, Ella and Robert Stam. *Unthinking Eurocentrism: Multiculturalism and the Media*. London: Routledge, 1994.

ETHNOGRAPHY

Heider, Karl G. *Seeing Anthropology: Cultural Anthropology Through Film*. 2nd ed. Boston: Allyn and Bacon, 2001.

MacDougall, David. *Transcultural Cinema*. Princeton: Princeton University, 1998.

Ruby, Jay. *Picturing Culture: Explorations of Film and Anthropology*. Chicago: University of Chicago, 2000.

Russell, Catherine. *Experimental Ethnography in the Age of Video*. Durham: Duke University Press, 1999.

EUROPEAN INFLUENCE ON AMERICAN FILM

Langman, Larry. *Destination Hollywood: The Influence of Europeans on American Filmmaking*. Jefferson, NC: McFarland, 2000.

Morrison, James. *Passport to Hollywood: Hollywood Films, European Directors*. Albany: State University of New York, 1998.

FAMILY AND FILM

Harwood, Sarah. *Family Fictions: Representations of the Family in 1980s Hollywood Cinema*. Basingstoke: Macmillan, 1997.

Leibman, Nina C. *Living Room Lectures: The Fifties Family in Film and Television*. Austin: University of Texas, 1995.

Rueschmann, Eva. *Sisters on Screen: Siblings in Contemporary Cinema*. Philadelphia: Temple, 2000.

Williams, Tony. *Hearths of Darkness: The Family in the American Horror Film*. Madison: Fairleigh Dickinson, 1996.

FICTIONAL TREATMENTS OF HOLLYWOOD

Spatz, Jonas. *Hollywood in Fiction*. Brussels: Moulton, 1969.

Vidal, Gore. *Hollywood: A Novel of America in the 1920s*. New York: Modern Library, 1999.

Wells, Walter. *Tycoons and Locusts: A Regional Look at Hollywood Fiction in the Thirties*. Carbondale: Southern Illinois University, 1973.

FILM CRITICISM

Agee, James. *Agee on Film: Criticism and Comment on the Movies*. New York: Modern Library, 2000.

Bromley, Carl. *Cinema Nation: The Best Writing on Film from the Nation, 1913–2000*. New York: Thunder Mouth Press, 2000.

Canby, Vincent et al. *The New York Times Guide to the Best 1,000 Movies Ever Made*. New York: Times Books, 1999.

Champlin, Charles. *Hollywood's Revolutionary Decade: Charles Champlin Reviews the Movies of the 1970s*. Santa Barbara: John Daniel, 1998.

Farber, Manny. *Negative Space: Manny Farber on the Movies*. New York: Da Capo Press, 1998.

Malcolm, Derek. *A Century of Films*. London: Tauris Parke Paperbacks, 2000.

Penman, Ian. *Vital Signs: Music, Movies, and Other Manias*. London: Serpent's Tail, 1998.

FILM HISTORY

Basinger, Jeanine. *American Cinema: One-Hundred-Years of Filmmaking*. New York: Rizzoli, 1994.

Belton, John. *American Cinema/American Culture*. New York: McGraw-Hill, 1994.

Bilbow, Tony and John Gau. *Lights, Camera, Action! A Century of the Cinema*. Boston: Little Brown, 1995.

Bohn, Thomas W. and Richard L. Stromgren. *Light and Shadows: A History of Motion Pictures*. 2nd ed. Sherman Oaks: Alfred, 1978.

Brewster, Ben and Lea Jacobs. *Theatre to Cinema: Stage Pictorialism and the Early Feature Film*. Oxford: Oxford University, 1997.

Burch, Noel. *Life to Those Shadows*. Berkeley: University of California, 1990.

Christie, Ian. *The Last Machine: Early Cinema and the Birth of the Modern World*. London: BBC, 1994.

Cook, David A. *A History of Narrative Film*. 3rd ed. New York: W.W. Norton, 1996.

Cripps, Thomas. *Hollywood's High Noon: Moviemaking and Society before Television*. Baltimore: Johns Hopkins, 1997.

Davies, Philip John. *Representing and Imagining America*. Keele: Keele University, 1996.

Ellis, Jack C. *A History of Film*. 4th ed. Boston: Allyn and Bacon, 1995.

Elsaesser, Thomas. *Early Cinema: Space, Frame, Narrative*. London: BFI, 1990.

Giannetti, Louis D. *Flashback: A Brief History of Film*. 3rd ed. Englewood Cliffs: Prentice Hall, 1996.

Holston, Kim R. *English-Speaking Cinema: An Illustrated History, 1927–1993*. Jefferson, NC: McFarland, 1994.

Jowett, Garth. *Film: The Democratic Art*. Boston: Little, Brown, 1975.

Kupsc, Jarek. *The History of Cinema for Beginners*. New York: Writers and Readers Publishing, 1998.

Maltby, Richard. *Hollywood Cinema: An Introduction*. Oxford: Blackwell, 1995.

Mannoni, Laurent. *Light and Movement: Incunabula of the Motion Picture, 1420–1896*. Gemona, Italia: Giornate del cinema muto, 1995.

Mast, Gerald and Bruce F. Kawin. *A Short History of the Movies*. 6th ed. Boston: Allyn and Bacon, 1996.

Nowell-Smith, Geoffrey. *Oxford History of World Cinema*. New York: Oxford, 1996.

Parkinson, David. *History of Film*. London: Thames and Hudson, 1996.

Ponti, James. *Hollywood East: Florida's Fabulous Flicks*. Orlando: Tribune, 1992.

Schechter, Harold. *For Reel: The Real-Life Stories that Inspired Some of the Most Popular Movies of All Time*. New York: Berkley-Boulevard Books, 2000.

Shipman, David. *Cinema: The First Hundred Years*. London: Weidenfeld and Nicolson, 1993.

Sklar, Robert. *Film: An International History of the Medium*. New York: H.N. Abrams, 1993.

―――. *Movie-Made America: A Cultural History of American Movies*. Rev. ed. New York: Vintage, 1994.

Thompson, Kristin and David Bordwell. *Film History*. New York: McGraw-Hill, 1994.

Vidal, Gore. *Screening History*. Cambridge: Harvard, 1992.

FILM INDUSTRY

Balio, Tino. *Grand Design—Hollywood as a Modern Business Enterprise, 1930–1939*. New York: Scribner, 1993.

―――. *United Artists*. Madison: University of Wisconsin, 1976, 1987.

Bart, Peter. *The Gross: The Hits, the Flops—the Summer That Ate Hollywood*. New York: St. Martin's Press, 1999.

Daniels, Bill, David Leedy, and Steven D. Sills. *Movie Money: Understanding Hollywood's (Creative) Accounting Practices*. Los Angeles: Silman-James Press, 1998.

Gomery, Douglas. *Hollywood Studio System*. New York: St. Martin's, 1986.

Klawans, Stuart. *Film Follies: The Cinema Out of Order*. London; New York: Cassell, 1999.

Prince, Stephen. *A New Pot of Gold: Hollywood Under the Electronic Rainbow, 1980–1989*. New York: Charles Scribner's Sons, 2000.

Shorris, Sylvia and Marion Abbott Bundy. *Talking Pictures.* New York: New Press, 1994.

FILM STUDIES

Gledhill, Christine and Linda Williams, eds. *Reinventing Film.* London: Arnold; New York: Co-published in the United States by Oxford University Press, 2000.

FILM TECHNOLOGY

Fielding, Raymond. *A Technological History of Motion Pictures and Television.* Berkeley: University of California, 1967.

Geduld, Harry M. *The Birth of the Talkies.* Bloomington: Indiana University, 1975.

FILM THEORY

Bellour, Raymond. *The Analysis of Film.* Bloomington: Indiana University, 2000.

Casetti, Francesco. *Theories of Cinema: 1945–1995.* Austin: University of Texas, 1999.

Miller, Toby and Robert Stam, eds. *A Companion to Film Theory.* Malden, MA: Blackwell, 1999.

Stam, Robert. *Film Theory: An Introduction.* Malden, MA: Blackwell, 2000.

FILMMAKERS

D'Agostino, Annette M. *Filmmakers in the Moving Picture World: An Index of Articles, 1907–1927.* Jefferson, NC: McFarland, 1997.

Lee, C. P. *Like a Bullet of Light: The Films of Bob Dylan.* London: Helter Skelter, 2000.

Lippy, Tod, ed. *New York Film-Makers on Film-Making.* London: Faber and Faber, 2000.

GAYS AND LESBIANS IN FILM

    GUIDES

    Jackson, Claire and Peter Tapp, eds. *The Bent Lens: A World Guide to Gay and Lesbian Film.* St. Kilda, Australia: Australian Catalogue Co., 1997.

    Olson, Jenni, ed. *The Ultimate Guide to Lesbian and Gay Film and Video.* New York: Serpent's Tail, 1996.

    Parish, James Robert. *Gays and Lesbians in Mainstream Cinema.* Jefferson, NC: McFarland, 1993.

    HISTORY AND INTERPRETATION

    Benshoff, Harry M. *Monsters in the Closet: Homosexuality and the Horror Film.* Manchester: Manchester University, 1997.

    Berry, Chris. *A Bit on the Side: East-West Topographies of Desire.* Sidney: EmPress, 1994.

    Bourne, Stephen. *Brief Encounters: Lesbians and Gays in British Cinema, 1930–1971.* London: Cassell, 1996.

    Burston, Paul. *What Are You Looking At? Queer Sex, Style, and Cinema.* London: Cassell, 1995.

    Corber, Robert J. *Homosexuality in Cold War America: Resistance and the Crisis of Masculinity.* Durham: Duke, 1997.

    ———. *In the Name of National Security: Hitchcock, Homophobia, and the Political Construction of Gender in Postwar America.* Durham: Duke, 1993.

    Davies, Jude and Carol R. Smith. *Gender, Ethnicity, and Sexuality in Contemporary American Film.* Edinburgh: Keele University, 1997.

    Doty, Alexander. *Flaming Classics: Queering the Film Canon.* New York: Routledge, 2000.

    Dyer, Richard. *The Matter of Images: Essays on Representations.* London: Routledge, 1993.

    ———. *Now You See It: Studies on Lesbian and Gay Film.* London: Routledge, 1990.

    Ehrenstein, David. *Open Secret: Gay Hollywood, 1928–1998.* New York: William Morrow, 1998.

    Farmer, Brett. *Spectacular Passions: Cinema, Fantasy, Gay Male Spectatorships.* Durham: Duke University, 2000.

    Gever, Martha et al. *Queer Looks: Perspectives on Lesbian and Gay Film and Video.* New York: Routledge, 1993.

    Hadleigh, Boze. *The Lavender Screen: The Gay and Lesbian Films.* Rev. ed. Secaucus: Carol, 1997.

    Hanson, Ellis, ed. *Out Takes: Essays on Queer Theory and Film.* Durham: Duke University, 1999.

    Hart, Lynda. *Fatal Women: Lesbian Sexuality and the Mark of Aggression.* Princeton: Princeton University, 1994.

    Heathcote, Owen, Alex Hughes, and James S. Williams, eds. *Gay Signatures: Gay and Lesbian Theory, Fiction, and Film in France, 1945–1995.* Oxford: Berg, 1998.

    Horrigan, Patrick E. *Widescreen Dreams: Growing Up Gay at the Movies.* Madison: University of Wisconsin, 1999.

    Howes, Keith. *Broadcasting It: An Encyclopedia of Homosexuality in Film, Radio and TV in the UK.* London: Cassell, 1993.

    Jackson, Earl, Jr. *Strategies of Deviance: Studies in Gay Male Representation.* Bloomington: Indiana

University, 1995.

Kuzniar, Alice A. *The Queer German Cinema*. Stanford: Stanford University, 2000.

Moon, Michael. *A Small Boy and Others: Imitation and Initiation in American Culture*. Durham: Duke, 1998.

Murray, Raymond. *Images in the Dark: An Encyclopedia of Gay and Lesbian Film and Video*. London: Titan, 1998.

Murray, Timothy. *Like a Film: Ideological Fantasy on Screen, Camera, and Canvas*. London: Routledge, 1993.

Parish, James Robert. *Gays and Lesbians in Mainstream Cinema*. Jefferson, NC: McFarland, 1993.

Price, Theodore. *Hitchcock and Homosexuality*. Metuchen: Scarecrow, 1992.

Ringer, R. Jeffrey. *Queer Words, Queer Images: Communication and the Construction of Homosexuality*. New York: NYU, 1994.

Russo, Vito. *Celluloid Closet: Homosexuality in the Movies*. New York: Harper & Row, 1981.

Saunders, Michael Willliam. *Imps of the Perverse: Gay Monsters in Film*. Westport, CT: Praeger, 1998.

Smith, Paul Julian. *Laws of Desire: Questions of Homosexuality in Spanish Writings and Film, 1960–1990*. Oxford: Clarendon Press, 1992.

Somerville, Siobhan. *Queering the Color Line: Race and the Invention of Homosexuality in American Culture*. Durham: Duke University, 2000.

Straayer, Chris. *Deviant Eyes, Deviant Bodies: Sexual Re-Orientations in Film and Video*. New York: Columbia, 1996.

Suarez, Juan Antonio. *Bike Boys, Drag Queens and Superstars: Avant-Garde, Mass Culture, and Gay Identities in the 1960s Underground Cinema*. Bloomington: Indiana University, 1996.

Tyler, Parker. *Screening the Sexes: Homosexuality in the Movies*. New York: Da Capo, 1993.

Van Leer, David. *The Queening of America: Gay Culture in Straight Society*. New York: Routledge, 1995.

Waugh, Thomas. *The Fruit Machine: Twenty Years of Writings on Queer Cinema*. Durham: Duke University, 2000.

———. *Hard to Imagine: Gay Male Eroticism in Photography and Film*. New York: Columbia, 1996.

HISTORIOGRAPHY

Adair, Gilbert, ed. *Movies*. London: Penguin, 1999.

Allen, Robert C. and Douglas Gomery. *Film History: Theory and Practice*. New York: Knopf, 1985.

Hill, John and Pamela Church Gibson. *American Cinema and Hollywood: Critical Approaches*. New York: Oxford University, 2000.

———. *World Cinema: Critical Approaches*. New York: Oxford University, 2000.

McDonnell, Brian. *Fresh Approaches to Film*. Auckland: Longman, 1998.

HOLLYWOOD

Silvester, Christopher, ed. *The Penguin Book of Hollywood*. London: Viking, 1998.

Springer, John Parris. *Hollywood Fictions: The Dream Factory in American Popular Literature*. Norman: University of Oklahoma, 2000.

Wallace, David. *Lost Hollywood*. New York: St. Martin's Press, 2001.

Webb, Michael. *Hollywood: Legend and Reality*. Boston: Little, Brown, 1986.

HOLOCAUST AND FILM

Avisar, Ilan. *Screening the Holocaust: Cinema's Images of the Unimaginable*. Bloomington: Indiana University, 1988.

Bartov, Omer. *Murder in Our Midst: The Holocaust, Industrial Killing, and Representation*. New York: Oxford, 1996.

Colombat, Andre. *The Holocaust in French Film*. Metuchen: Scarecrow, 1993.

Davis, Jonathan, ed. *Film, History, and the Jewish Experience: A Reader*. London: National Film Theatre, 1986.

Doneson, Judth E. *The Holocaust in American Film*. Philadelphia: Jewish Publication Society, 1987.

Fensch, Thomas, ed. *Oskar Schindler and His List: The Man, the Book, the Film, the Holocaust and Its Survivors*. Forest Dale, VT: Paul S. Eriksson, 1995.

Flanzbaum, Hilene, ed. *The Americanization of the Holocaust*. Baltimore: Johns Hopkins University, 1999.

Insdorf, Annette. *Indelible Shadows: Film and the Holocaust*. 2nd ed. Cambridge: Cambridge University, 1983.

Kirtizman, Lawrence D. *Auschwitz and After: Race, Culture, and ""the Jewish Question" in France*. New York: Routledge, 1995.

Lewis, Stephen. *Art Out of Agony: The Holocaust Theme in Literature, Sculpture, and Film.* Montreal: CBC Enterprises, 1984.

Loshitzky, Yosefa. *Spielberg's Holocaust: Critical Perspectives on Schindler's List.* Bloomington: Indiana University, 1997.

Santner, Eric L. *Stranded Objects: Mourning, Memory and Film in Postwar Germany.* Ithaca: Cornell, 1990.

IMMIGRANTS AND FILM

Naficy, Hamid. *Home, Exile, Homeland: Film, Media and the Politics of Place.* New York: Routledge, 1998.

INDEPENDENT CINEMA

Aberdeen, J. A. *Hollywood Renegades: The Society of Independent Motion Picture Producers.* Los Angeles: Cobblestone Entertainment, 2000.

Ferncase, Richard K. *Outsider Features: American Independent Films of the 1980s.* Westport, CT: Greenwood Press, 1996.

Klawans, Stuart. *Film Follies: The Cinema Out of Order.* London: Cassell, 1999.

Levy, Emanuel. *Cinema of Outsiders: The Rise of American Independent Film.* New York: New York University, 1999.

Lyons, Donald. *Independent Visions: A Critical Introduction to Recent Independent American Film.* New York: Ballantine, 1994.

Merritt, Greg. *Celluloid Mavericks: The History of American Independent Film.* New York: Thunder's Mouth Press, 2000.

Pierson, John. *Spike, Mike, Slackers, and Dykes: A Guided Tour Across a Decade of American Independent Cinema.* New York: Miramax Books, 1997.

Stubbs, Liz and Richard Rodriguez. *Making Independent Films: Advice from Filmmakers.* New York: Allworth Press, 2000.

Vachon, Christine. *Shooting to Kill: How an Independent Producer Lasts Through the Barriers to Make Movies that Matter.* London: Bloomsbury, 1998.

INDICES

D'Agostino, Annette M. *Filmmakers in the Moving Picture World, 1907–1927.* Jefferson, NC: McFarland, 1997.

INFLUENCE OF FILM

Casetti, Francesco. *Inide the Gaze: The Fiction Film and Its Spectators.* Bloomington: Indiana Univeristy, 1998.

Dixon, Wheeler W. *Disaster and Memory: Celebrity Culture and the Crisis of Hollywood Cinema.* New York: Columbia University, 1999.

Hirschman, Elizabeth. *Heroes, Monsters and Messiahs: Movies and Television Shows as the Mythology of American Culture.* Kansas City: Andrews McMeel Pub., 2000.

Massey, Anne. *Hollywood Beyond the Screen: Design and Material Culture.* Oxford: Berg, 2000.

Turner, Graeme. *Film as Social Practice.* 3rd ed. London: Routledge, 1999.

Wolf, Michael J. *The Entertainment Economy: How Mega-Media Forces Are Transforming Our Lives.* New York: Times Books, 1999.

INTERVIEWS

Anderson, Jo. *Sundancing: Hanging Out and Listening in at America's Most Important Film Festival.* New York: Spike, 2000.

Falsetto, Mario. *Personal Visions: Conversations with Independent Film-Makers.* London: Constable, 1999.

Grobel, Lawrence. *Above the Line: Conversations About the Movies.* Cambridge, MA: Da Capo Press, 2000.

Kagan, Jeremy. *Directors Close Up.* Boston: Focal Press, 2000.

Lane, Christina. *Feminist Hollywood.* Detroit: Wayne State University, 2000.

Lippy, Tod. *New York Film-Makers on Film-Making.* London: Faber and Faber, 2000.

Lowenstein, Stephen. *My First Movie.* New York: Pantheon, 2001.

Macklin, Tony and Nick Pici. *Voices from the Set: The Film Heritage Interviews.* Lanham, MD: Scarecrow Press, 2000.

Singer, Michael. *A Cut Above: 50 Film Directors Talk about Their Craft.* Los Angeles: Lone Eagle, 1998.

Weaver, Tom. *Return of the B Science Fiction and Horror Heroes.* Jefferson, NC: McFarland Classics, 2000.

JOURNALISM AND FILM

Good, Howard. *Girl Reporter: Gender, Journalism and the Movies.* Metuchen: Scarecrow, 1998.

Langman, Larry. *The Media in the Movies.* Jefferson, NC: McFarland, 1998.

Ness, Richard R. *From Headline Hunter to Superman: A Journalism Filmography.* Lanham: Scarecrow, 1997.

LABOR RELATIONS IN THE MOTION PICTURE INDUSTRY
Home, Gerald. *Class Struggle in Hollywood, 1930–1950*. Austin: University of Texas, 2001.
LAW AND FILM
Denvir, John. *Legal Reelism: Movies as Legal Texts*. Urbana: University of Illinois, 1996.
LITERATURE AND FILM
Bignell, Jonathan, ed. *Writing and Cinema*. Longman: Pearson Education, 1999.
Cartmell, Deborah and Imelda Whelehan, eds. *Adaptations: From Text to Screen, Screen to Text*. London: Routledge, 1999.
Cartmell, Deborah, ed. *Classics in Film and Fiction*. London: Pluto Press, 2000.
Chipman, Bruce L. *Into America's Dream-Dump: A Postmodern Study of the Hollywood Novel*. Lanham, MD: University Press of America, 1999.
Corrigan, Timothy. *Film and Literature: An Introduction and Reader*. Upper Saddle River, NJ: Prentice Hall, 1999.
Giddings, Robert and Erica Sheen. *Screening the Novel: The Theory and Practice of Literary Dramatization*. Houndmill: Macmillan, 1990.
Goldstein, Laurence. *The American Poet at the Movies: A Critical History*. Ann Arbor: University of Michigan, 1994.
Hellerstein, Marjorie H. *Inventing the Real World: The Art of Alain Robbe-Grillet*. Selinsgrove, PA: Susquehanna University, 1998.
Hitt, Jim. *Words and Shadows: Literature on the Screen*. Secaucus: Carol, 1992.
Larson, Randall. *Films into Books: An Analytical Bibliography of Film, Novelizations, Movie and TV Tie-Ins*. Metuchen: Scarecrow, 1995.
Lothe, Jakob. *Narrative in Fiction and Film: An Introduction*. Oxford: Oxford University, 2000.
Lupack, Barbara Tepa. *Nineteenth-Century Women at the Movies: Adapting Classic Women's Fiction to Film*. Bowling Green: Bowling Green State University, 1999.
———. *Take Two: Adapting the Contemporary American Novel to Film*. Bowling Green: Bowling Green State University, 1994.
Morris, Timothy. *You're Only Young Twice: Children's Literature and Film*. Urbana: University of Illinois, 2000.
Naremore, James, ed. *Film Adaptation*. New Brunswick: Rutgers University, 2000.
Sennett, Robert S. *Hollywood Hoopla: Creating Stars and Selling Movies in the Golden Age of Hollywood*. New York: Billboard Books, 1998.
Springer, John Parris. *Hollywood Fictions: The Dream Factory in American Popular Literature*. Norman: University of Oklahoma, 2000.
Tibbetts, John C. and James M. Welsh. *The Encyclopedia of Novels into Film*. New York: Facts on File 1998.
Troost, Linda and Sayre Greenfield, eds. *Jane Austen in Hollywood*. Lexington: University Press of Kentucky, 1998.
Weissenborn, Ulrike. *"Just Making Pictures": Hollywood Writers, the Frankfurt School, and Film Theory*. Tubingen: G. Narr, 1998.
Willson, Robert Frank. *Shakespeare in Hollywood, 1929–1956*. Madison, NJ: Fairleigh Dickinson University: 2000.
MARKETING
Gore, Chris. *The 50 Greatest Movies Never Made*. New York: St. Martin's Griffin, 1999.
Jarvie, I. C. *Hollywood's Overseas Campaign: The North Atlantic Movie Trade, 1920–1950*. Cambridge: Cambridge, 1992.
Rosenbaum, Jonathan. *Movie Wars: How Hollywood and the Media Conspire to Limit What Films We Can See*. Chicago: A. Capella, 2000.
Segrave, Kerry. *American Films Abroad: Hollywood's Domination of the World's Movie Screens from the 1890s to the Present*. Jefferson, NC: McFarland, 1997.
Thompson, Kristin. *Exporting Entertainment: America in the World Film Market, 1907–1934*. London: BFI, 1985.
MASCULINITY AND FILM
Bingham, Dennis. *Acting Male: Masculinities in the Films of James Stewart, Jack Nicholson, and Clint Eastwood*. New Brunswick: Rutgers, 1994.
Cohan, Steven. *Masked Men: Masculinity and the Movies in the Fifties*. Bloomington: Indiana University, 1997.

Cohan, Steven and Ina Rae Hark. *Screening the Male: Exploring Masculiniities in Hollywood Cinema.* New York: Routledge, 1993.

Hendershot, Cyndy. *The Animal Within: Masculinity and the Gothic.* Ann Arbor: University of Michigan, 1998.

Jeffords, Susan. *Hard Bodies: Hollywood Masculinity in the Reagan Era.* New Brunswick: Rutgers, 1994.

Kirkham, Pat and Janet Thumim. *You Tarzan: Masculinity, Movies, and Men.* London: Lawrence & Wishart, 1993.

Lehman, Peter. *Running Scared: Masculinity and the Representation of the Male Body.* Philadelphia: Temple, 1993.

Penley, Constance and Sharon Willis. *Male Trouble.* Minneapolis: University of Minnesota, 1993.

Siegel, Carol. *Male Masochism: Modern Revisions of the Story of Love.* Bloomington: Indiana University, 1995.

Studlar, Gaylyn. *This Mad Masquerade: Stardom and Masculinity in the Jazz Age.* New York: Columbia, 1996.

MEDIA INFLUENCE

Jowett, Garth et al. *Children and the Movies: Media Influence and the Payne Fund Controversy.* New York: Cambridge, 1996.

Langman, Larry. *The Media in the Movies: An Illustrated Catalog of American Journalism Films, 1900–1996.* Jefferson, NC: McFarland, 1998.

MOTHERHOOD IN FILM

Fischer, Lucy. *Cinematernity: Film, Motherhood, Genre.* Princeton: Princeton University, 1996.

MUSIC AND FILM

BIBLIOGRAPHIES AND DIRECTORIES

Craggs, Stewart R. *Soundtracks: An International Dictionary of Composers for Film.* Brookfield, VT: Ashgate, 1998.

Marill, Alvin H. *Keeping Score: Film and Television Music, 1988–1997.* Lanham, MD: Scarecrow Press, 1998.

HISTORY AND INTERPRETATION

Anderson, Gillian. *Music for Silent Films.* Washington: Library of Congress, 1988.

Buhler, James, Caryl Flinn, and David Neumeyer, eds. *Music and Cinema.* Hanover, NH: University Press of New England, 2000.

Cook, Nicholas. *Analyzing Musical Multimedia.* Oxford: Clarendon Press, 1998.

Fehr, Richard. *Lullabies of Hollywood: Movie Music and the Movie Musical.* Jefferson, NC: McFarland, 1993.

Gabbard, Krin. *Jammin' at the Margins: Jazz and the American Cinema.* Chicago: University of Chicago, 1996.

Kassabian, Anahid. *Hearing Film: Tracking Identifications in Contemporary Hollywood Film Music.* New York: Routledge, 2000.

MacDonald, Lawrence E. *The Invisible Art of Film Music: A Comprehensive History.* New York: Ardsley House Publishers, 1998.

Smith, Jeff. *The Sounds of Commerce: Marketing Popular Film Music.* New York: Columbia, 1998.

Smith, Steven. *A Heart at Fire's Center: The Life and Music of Bernard Herrmann.* Berkeley: University of California, 1991.

PHILOSOPHY AND FILM

Allen, Richard. *Projecting Illusion: Film Spectatorship and the Impression of Reality.* Cambridge: Cambridge, 1995.

Allen, Richard and Murray Smith. *Film Theory and Philosophy.* Oxford: Clarendon, 1997.

Barnouw, Dagmar. *Critical Realism: History, Photography, and the Work of Siegfried Kracauer.* Baltimore: Johns Hopkins, 1994.

Burnett, Ron. *Explorations in Film Theory: Selected Essays from Cine-tracts.* Bloomington: Indiana University, 1991.

Carroll, Noel. *Theorizing the Moving Image.* Cambridge: Cambridge, 1996.

Casebier, Allan. *Film and Phenomenology: Toward a Realist Theory of Cinematic Representation.* Cambridge: Cambridge, 1991.

Charney, Leo. *Empty Moments: Cinema, Modernity, and Drift.* Durham: Duke, 1998.

Coates, Paul. *Film at the Intersection of High and Mass Culture.* Cambridge: Cambridge, 1994.

Currie, Gregory. *Image and Mind: Film, Philosophy, and Cognitive Science*. Cambridge: Cambridge, 1995.

Degli-Esposti, Christina, ed. *Postmodernism in the Cinema*. Providence, RI: Berghahn Books, 1998.

Denzin, Norman K. *Images of Postmodern Society: Social Theory and Contemporary Cinema*. London: Sage, 1991.

Easthope, Anthony. *Contemporary Film Theory*. London: Longman, 1993.

Flaxman, Gregory, ed. *The Brain Is the Screen: Deleuze and the Philosophy of Cinema*. Minneapolis: University of Minnesota, 2000.

Freeland, Cynthia A. and Thomas E. Wartenberg. *Philosophy and Film*. New York: Routledge, 1995.

Friedberg, Anne. *Window Shopping: Cinema and the Postmodern*. Berkeley: University of California, 1993.

Gaines, Jane. *Classical Hollywood Narrative: The Paradigm Wars*. Durham: Duke, 1992.

Hedges, Inez. *Breaking the Frame: Film Language and the Experience of Limits*. Bloomington: Indiana University, 1991.

Hietala, Veijo. *Situating the Subject in Film Theory: Meaning and Spectatorship in Cinema*. Turku: Akateeminen kirjakauppa, 1990.

Hollows, Joanne and Mark Jancovich. *Approaches to Popular Film*. Manchester: Manchester University, 1995.

Kupfer, Joseph H. *Visions of Virtue in Popular Film*. Boulder: Westview Press, 1999.

Lehman, Peter. *Defining Cinema*. New Brunswick: Rutgers, 1997.

McGee, Patrick. *Cinema, Theory and Political Responsibility in Contemporary Culture*. Cambridge: Cambridge, 1997.

Metz, Christian. *Film Language: A Semiotics of the Cinema*. Chicago: University of Chicago, 1991.

Nasta, Dominique. *Meaning in Film*. New York: Lang, 1991.

Natoli, Joseph P. *Postmodern Journeys: Film and Culture, 1996–1998*. Albany: State University of New York, 2001.

Perez, Gilberto. *The Material Ghost: Films and Their Medium*. Baltimore: Johns Hopkins, 1998.

Ray, Robert B. *The Avant-Garde Finds Andy Hardy*. Cambridge: Harvard, 1995.

Rodowick, David Norman. *The Crisis of Political Modernism: Criticism and Ideology in Contemporary Film Theory*. Berkeley: University of California, 1994.

Rothman, William and Marian Keane. *Reading Cavell's* The World Viewed*: A Philosophical Perspective on Film*. Detroit: Wayne State University, 2000.

Sihvonen, Jukka. *Exceeding the Limits: On the Poetics and Politics of Audiovisuality*. Turku: Finnish Society for Cinema Studies, 1991.

Snyder, Stephen. *The Transparent I: Self/Subject in European Cinema*. New York: P. Lang, 1994.

Sobchack, Vivian Carol. *The Address of the Eye: A Phenomenology of Film Experience*. Princeton: Princeton, 1992.

Stephens, Mitchell. *The Rise of the Image, The Fall of the Word*. New York: Oxford, 1998.

Trinh, T. Minh-Ha. *When the Moon Waxes Red: Representation, Gender, and Cultural Politics*. New York: Routledge, 1991.

Valenti, Miguel, comp. *More Than a Movie: Ethics in Entertainment*. Boulder: Westview Press, 2000.

Whittock, Trevor. *Metaphor and Film*. Cambridge: Cambridge, 1990.

Willemen, Paul. *Looks and Frictions: Essays in Cultural Studies and Film Theory*. Bloomington: Indiana University, 1994.

POLITICS AND FILM

Billingsley, Lloyd. *Hollywood Party: How Communism Seduced the American Film Industry in the 1930s and 1940s*. Rocklin, CA: Forum, 1998.

Booker, M. Keith. *Film and the American Left: A Research Guide*. Westport, CT: Greenwood Press, 1999.

Brownstein, Ronald. *The Power and the Glitter: The Hollywood-Washington Connection*. New York: Pantheon, 1990.

Christiansen, Terry. *Reel Politics: American Political Movies from Birth of a Nation to Platoon*. New York: Blackwell, 1987.

Clark, Michael. *Politics and Media: Film and Television for the Political Scientist and Historian*. Fairview Park: Pergamon, 1979.

Combs, James E. *Movies and Politics*. New York: Garland, 1993.

Combs, James E. and Sara T. Combs. *Film Propaganda and American Politics*. New York: Garland, 1994.

Corber, Robert J. *In the Name of National Security: Hitchcock, Homophobia, and the Political Construction of Gender in Postwar America*. Durham: Duke, 1993.

Cormack, Michael J. *Ideology and Cinematography in Hollywood, 1930–39.* Basingstoke: Macmillan, 1994.

Crowdus, Gary. *Political Companion to American Film.* Chicago: Lakeview, 1994.

Foster, Gwendolyn Audrey. *Captive Bodies: Postcolonial Subjectivity in Cinema.* Albany: SUNY, 1999.

Genovese, Michael A. *The Political Film: An Introduction.* 2nd ed. Needham Heights, MA: Simon & Schuster Custom Pub., 1998.

Gianos, Phillip L. *Politics and Politicians in American Film.* Westport, CT: Praeger, 1998.

Giglio, Ernest D. *Here's Looking at You: Hollywood, Film, and Politics.* New York: Peter Lang, 2000.

Greene, Eric. *Planet of the Apes as American Myth.* Jefferson, NC: McFarland, 1996.

Grenier, Richard. *Capturing the Culture: Film, Art and Politics.* Washington: Ethics and Public Policy Center, 1990.

Hooks, Bell. *Reel to Real: Race, Sex, and Class at the Movies.* New York: Routledge, 1996.

James, David E. and Rick Berg. *The Hidden Foundation: Cinema and the Question of Class.* Minneapolis: University of Minnesota, 1996.

Kelley, Beverly Merrill. *Reelpolitik: Political Ideologies in '30s and '40s Films.* Westport, CT: Praeger, 1998.

MacKinnon, Kenneth. *Politics of Popular Representation: Reagan, Thatcher, AIDS, and the Movies.* Rutherford: Fairleigh Dickinson, 1992.

May, Lary. *The Big Tomorrow: Hollywood and the Politics of the American Way.* Chicago: University of Chicago, 2000.

Murray, Timothy. *Like a Film: Ideological Fantasy on Screen, Camera, and Canvas.* London: Routledge, 1993.

Muscio, Giuliana. *Hollywood's New Deal.* Philadelphia: Temple, 1996.

Nadel, Alan. *Flatlining on the Field of Dreams: Cultural Narratives in the Films of President Reagan's America.* New Brunswick: Rutgers, 1997.

Naficy, Hamid, ed. *Home, Exile, Homeland: Film, Media, and the Politics of Place.* New York: Routledge, 1999.

Natoli, Joseph. *Hauntings: Popular Film and American Culture, 1990–1992.* Albany: SUNY, 1994.

———. *Speeding to the Millennium: Film and Culture, 1993–1995.* Albany: SUNY, 1998.

Neve, Brian. *Film and Politics in America.* London: Routledge, 1992.

Navasky, Victor. *Naming Names.* New York: Viking, 1980.

Orr, John. *The Art and Politics of Film.* Edinburgh: Edinburgh University, 2000.

Parenti, Michael. *Make-Believe Media: The Politics of Entertainment.* New York: St. Martin's, 1992.

Platt, David. *Celluloid Power: Social Film Criticism from the Birth of a Nation to Judgment at Nurenberg.* Metuchen: Scarecrow, 1992.

Powers, Stephen et al. *Hollywood's America: Social and Political Themes in Motion Pictures.* Boulder: Westview, 1996.

Prince, Stephen. *Visions of Empire: Political Imagery in Contemporary American Film.* New York: Praeger, 1992.

Rosenbaum, Jonathan. *Movies as Politics.* Berkeley: University of California, 1997.

Ross, Steven J. *Working-Class Hollywood: Silent Film and the Shaping of Class in America.* Princeton: Princeton, 1998.

Ryan, Michael and Douglas Kellner. *Camera Politica: The Politics and Ideology of Contemporary Hollywood.* Bloomington: Indiana University, 1988.

Scott, Ian. *American Politics in Hollywood Film.* Chicago: Fitzroy Dearborn, 2000.

Shapiro, Michael J. *Cinematic Political Thought: Narrating Race, Nation, and Gender.* New York: New York University, 1999.

Wood, Richard. *Film and Propaganda in America: A Documentary History.* 5 vols. New York: Greenwood, 1990–1994.

Zavarzadeh, Masud. *Seeing Films Politically.* Albany: SUNY, 1991.

PSYCHOLOGY AND FILM

Anderson, Joseph. *The Reality of Illusion: An Ecological Approach to Cognitive Film Theory.* Carbondale: Southern Illinois University, 1996.

Bergstrom, Janet. *Endless Night: Cinema and Psychoanalysis, Parallel Histories.* Berkeley: University of California, 1999.

Cowie, Elizabeth. *Representing the Woman: Cinema and Psychoanalysis.* Basingstoke: Macmillan, 1997.

Currie, Gregory. *Image and Mind: Film, Philosophy, and Cognitive Science.* Cambridge: Cambridge, 1995.

Dixon, Wheeler W. *The Transparency of Spectatorship: Meditations on the Moving Image.* Albany: SUNY,

1998.

Gabbard, Krin and Glen O. Gabbard. *Psychiatry and the Cinema*. 2nd ed. Washington: American Psychiatric Press, 1999.

Greenberg, Harvey R. *Screen Memories: Hollywood Cinema on the Psychoanalytic Couch*. New York: Columbia, 1993.

Grodal, Torben Kragh. *Moving Pictures: A New Theory of Film Genres, Feelings, and Cognition*. Oxford: Clarendon, 1997.

Harris, Kenneth Marc. *The Film Fetish*. New York: P. Lang, 1992.

Iaccino, James F. *Psychological Reflections on Cinematic Terror*. Westport, CT: Praeger, 1994.

Kenevan, Phyllis Berdt. *Paths of Individuation in Literature and Film*. Lanham: Lexington Books, 1999.

Lebeau, Vicky. *Lost Angels: Psychoanalysis and Cinema*. New York: Routledge, 1995.

Mitry, Jean. *The Aesthetics and Psychology of the Cinema*. Bloomington: Indiana University, 1997.

Moore, Rachel O. *Savage Theory: Cinema as Modern Magic*. Durham: Duke University, 2000.

Mulvey, Laura. *Fetishism and Curiosity*. Bloomington: Indiana University, 1996.

O'Brien, Geoffrey. *The Phantom Empire*. New York: Norton, 1993.

O'Donnell, Patrick. *Latent Destinies: Cultural Paranoia and Contemporary U.S. Narrative*. Durham: Duke University, 2000.

Paul, William. *Laughing, Screaming: Modern Hollywood Horror and Comedy*. New York: Columbia, 1994.

Plantinga, Carl and Greg M. Smith, eds. *Passionate Views: Film, Cognition, and Emotion*. Baltimore: Johns Hopkins University, 1999.

Smith, Murray. *Engaging Characters: Fiction, Emotion, and the Cinema*. Oxford: Clarendon, 1995.

Tan, Ed S. *Emotion and the Structure of Narrative Film*. Hillsdale: L. Erlbaum, 1996.

Valkola, Jarmo. *Perceiving the Visual in Cinema: Semantic Approaches to Film Form and Meaning*. Jyvaskyla: Jyvaskylan Yliopisto, 1993.

RELIGION AND FILM

Benne, Robert. *Seeing Is Believing: Visions of Life through Film*. Lanham, MD: University Press of America, 1998.

Bergesen, Albert and Andrew M. Greeley. *God in the Movies*. New Brunswick: Transaction Publishers, 2000.

Bliss, Michael. *The Word Made Flesh: Catholicism and Conflict in the Films of Martin Scorsese*. Metuchen: Scarecrow, 1995.

Fraser, Peter. *Images of the Passion: The Sacramental Mode in Film*. Westport, CT: Praeger, 1998.

Jewett, Robert. *St. Paul Returns to the Movies: Triumph Over Shame*. Grand Rapids, MI: William B. Eerdmans, 1999.

Johnston, Robert K. *Reel Spirituality: Theology and Film in Dialogue*. Grand Rapids, MI: Baker Books, 2000.

Keyser, Lester J. and Barbara. *Hollywood and the Catholic Church*. Chicago: Loyola, 1984.

Lee, C. J. P. *The Metaphysics of Mass Art: Cultural Ontology*. Lewiston: Edwin Mellen Press, 1999.

Marsh, Clive and Gaye Ortiz. *Explorations in Theology and Film*. Malden, MA: Blackwell, 1997.

Martin, Joel W. and Conrad E. Ostwalt, Jr. *Screening the Sacred: Religion, Myth, and Ideology in Popular American Film*. Boulder: Westview, 1995.

Martin, Thomas M. *Images and the Imageless: A Study of Religious Consciousness and Film*. 2nd ed. Lewisburg: Bucknell, 1991.

May, John R. *Image and Likeness: Religious Visions in American Film Classics*. New York: Paulist, 1991.

————. *New Image of Religious Film*. Kansas City: Sheed & Ward, 1997.

Miles, Margaret Ruth. *Seeing and Believing: Religion and Values in the Movies*. Boston: Beacon, 1996.

Parish, James Robert. *Ghosts and Angels in Hollywood Films*. Jefferson, NC: McFarland, 1994.

Scott, Bernard Brandon. *Hollywood Dreams and Biblical Stories*. Minneapolis: Fortress, 1994.

Vaux, Sara Anson. *Finding Meaning at the Movies*. Nashville: Abingdon Press, 1999.

SCANDALS IN THE MOTION PICTURE INDUSTRY

McLean, Adrienne L. and David A. Cook, eds. *Headline Hollywood: A Century of Film Scandal*. New Brunswick: Rutgers University, 2001.

SCREENWRITERS AND SCREENWRITING

Hamilton, Ian. *The Writer in Hollywood, 1915–1951*. New York: Harper & Row, 1990.

Maas, Frederica Sagor. *The Shocking Miss Pilgrim: A Writer in Early Hollywood*. Lexington: University Press of Kentucky, 1999.

Taylor, Thom. *The Big Deal: Hollywood's Million Dollar Spec Script Market*. New York: William Morrow, 1999.

Thompson, Kristin. *Storytelling in the New Hollywood: Understanding Classical Narrative Technique*.

Harvard: Harvard University, 1999.

SEMIOTICS AND FILM

Buckland, Warren. *The Cognitive Semiotics of Film.* Cambridge: Cambridge University, 2000.

Chatman, Seymour Benjamin. *Coming to Terms: The Rhetoric of Narrative in Fiction and Film.* Ithaca: Cornell, 1990.

Metz, Christian. *Film Language: A Semiotics of Cinema.* Chicago: University of Chicago, 1991.

Mitry, Jean. *Semiotics and the Analysis of Film.* London: Athlone, 1999.

Stam, Robert et al. *New Vocabularies in Film Semiotics.* London: Routledge, 1992.

Whittock, Trevor. *Metaphor and Film.* Cambridge: Cambridge, 1990.

SEXUALITY IN FILM

Bryant, Wayne M. *Bisexual Characters in Film.* Binghamton: Haworth, 1997.

McGillivray, David. *Doing Rude Things: The History of the British Sex Film.* London: Sun Tavern Fields, 1992.

Screen. *The Sexual Subject: A Screen Reading in Sexuality.* New York: Routledge, 1992.

Stoller, Robert J. *Porn: Myths for the Twentieth Century.* New Haven: Yale, 1991.

Straayer, Chris. *Deviant Eyes, Deviant Bodies: Sexual Re-Orientations in Film and Video.* New York: Columbia, 1996.

Tohill, Cathal and Pete Tombs. *Immoral Tales: Sex and Horror Cinema in Europe.* London: Primitive, 1994.

Tyler, Parker. *Sex in Film.* Secaucus: Carol, 1993.

Wilson, Wayne. *Sexuality in the Land of Oz: Searching for Safer Sex at the Movies.* Lanham: University Press of America, 1994.

Young, Lola. *Fear of the Dark: "Race," Gender and Sexuality in the Cinema.* London: Routledge, 1996.

SOCIAL ASPECTS OF FILM

Belton, John. *Movies and Mass Culture.* New Brunswick: Rutgers, 1996.

Charney, Leo and Vanessa R. Schwartz. *Cinema and the Invention of Modern Life.* Berkeley: University of California, 1995.

Davies, Jude and Carol R. Smith. *Gender, Ethnicity, and Sexuality in Contemporary American Film.* Chicago: Fitzroy Dearborn, 2000.

Denzin, Norman K. *The Cinematic Society: The Voyeur's Gaze.* Thousand Oaks: Sage, 1995.

Desser, David and Garth S. Jowett, eds. *Hollywood Goes Shopping.* Minneapolis: University of Minnesota, 2000.

Edgerton, Gary R. et al. *In the Eye of the Beholder: Critical Perspectives in Popular Film and Television.* Bowling Green: Bowling Green State University, 1997.

Gabler, Neal. *Life in the Movies.* New York: Alfred A. Knopf, 1998.

Gilmore, Michael T. *Differences in the Dark: American Movies and English Theater.* New York: Columbia University, 1998.

Ingram, David. *Green Screen: Environmentalism and Hollywood Cinema.* Exeter: Exeter University, 2000.

Lewis, John. *The New American Cinema.* Durham: Duke University, 1998.

Newbold, Chris. *Cinema, Film, and Mass Communication.* London: Arnold, 1999.

Sharrett, Christopher. *Crisis Cinema: The Apocalyptic Idea in Postmodern Narrative Film.* Washington: Maissonneuve, 1992.

Turner, Graeme. *Film as Social Practice.* 2nd ed. London: Routledge, 1993.

Uricchio, William. *Reframing Culture: The Case of Vitagraph Quality Films.* Princeton: Princeton, 1993.

THE SOUTH AND FILM

Campbell, Edward D.C., Jr. *Celluloid South: Hollywood and the Southern Myth.* Knoxville: University of Tennessee, 1981.

French, Warren. *South and Film.* Jackson: University Press of Mississippi, 1981.

Graham, Don. *Cowboys and Cadillacs: How Hollywood Looks at Texas.* Austin: Texas Monthly, 1983.

Williamson, Jerry Wayne. *Hillbillyland.* Chapel Hill: University of North Carolina, 1995.

———. *Southern Mountaineers in Silent Films.* Jefferson, NC: McFarland, 1994.

SPORTS AND FILM

Dickerson, Gary E. *The Cinema of Baseball.* Westport, CT: Meckler, 1991.

Tudor, Deborah V. *Hollywood's Vision of Team Sports: Heroes, Race, and Gender.* New York: Garland, 1997.

STEREOTYPES

Loukides, Paul and Linda K. Fuller. *Beyond the Stars: Stock Characters in American Popular Film.* Bowling Green: Bowling Green State University, 1990.

STILLS

Meadows, Daniel. *Set Pieces: Being About Film Stills Mostly.* London: BFI, 1993.

STUDIO SYSTEM

Davis, Ronald L. *The Glamour Factory.* Dallas: SMU, 1993.

Mordden, Ethan. *The Hollywood Studios: House Style in the Golden Age of the Movies.* New York: Knopf, 1987.

Schatz, Thomas. *The Genius of the System: Hollywood Filmmaking in the Studio Era.* New York: Henry Holt, 1996.

Staiger, Janet. *The Studio System.* New Brunswick: Rutgers, 1995.

SUSPENSE AND FILM

Howard, Tom. *Suspense in the Cinema.* Wyong, NSW: John Howard Reid, 1995.

Vorderer, Peter et al. *Suspense: Conceptualizations, Theoretical Analyses, and Empirical Explorations.* Mahwah: Erlbaum, 1996.

TEACHERS AND FILM

Joseph, Pamela Bolotin and Gail E. Burnaford. *Images of Schoolteachers in Twentieth-Century America.* New York: St. Martin's, 1994.

TELEVISION AND FILM

Anderson, Christopher. *Hollywood TV: The Studio System in the Fifties.* Austin: University of Texas, 1994.

Balio, Tino. *Hollywood in the Age of Telivison.* Boston: Unwin Hyman, 1990.

THEATERS AND MOVIEGOING

Fuller, Kathryn H. *At the Picture Show: Small-Town Audiences and the Creation of Movie Fan Culture.* Washington: Smithsonian, 1996.

Gomery, Douglas. *Shared Pleasures: A History of Movie Presentation in the United States.* Madison: University of Wisconsin, 1992.

Headley, Robert K. *Motion Picture Exhibition in Washington, D.C.* Jefferson, NC: McFarland, 1999.

Musser, Charles. *High-Class Moving Pictures: Lyman H. Howe and the Forgotten Era of Traveling Exhibition, 1880–1920.* Princeton: Princeton, 1991.

O'Brien, Margaret and Allen Eyles. *Enter the Dream House: Memories of Cinemas in South London from the Twenties to the Sixties.* London: BFI, 1993.

Stoddard, Richard. *Theatre and Cinema Architecture: A Guide to Information Sources.* Detroit: Gale, 1978.

Waller, Gregory A. *Main Street Amusements: Movies and Commercial Entertainment in a Southern City, 1896–1930.* Washington: Smithsonian, 1995.

VALUES AND FILM

Horsley, Jake. *The Blood Poets: A Cinema of Savagery, 1958–1999.* Lanham, MD: Scarecrow Press, 1999.

Medved, Michael. *Hollywood vs. America.* New York: HarperPerennial, 1993.

O'Brien, Tom. *The Screening of America: Movies and Values from Rocky to Rain Man.* New York: Continuum, 1990.

Williams, Oliver F. *The Moral Imagination: How Literature and Films Can Stimulate Ethical Reflection in the Business World.* Notre Dame: Notre Dame, 1997.

VILLAINS IN FILM

Turner, George E. and Michael H. Price. *Human Monsters: The Bizarre Psychology of Movie Villains.* Northampton: Kitchen Sink, 1995.

VIOLENCE AND FILM

French, Karl. *Screen Violence.* London: Bloomsbury, 1996.

Lovell, John P. *Insights from Film into Violence and Oppression.* Westport, CT: Praeger, 1998.

Prince, Stephen. *Savage Cinema: Sam Peckinpah and the Rise of Ultraviolent Movies.* Austin: University of Texas, 1998.

WOMEN AND FILM

    ENCYCLOPEDIAS

    Kuhn, Annette. *The Women's Companion to International Film.* Berkeley: University of California, 1994.

    GIRLS AND ADOLESCENTS IN FILM

    Bundy, Clare. *Girls on Film.* New York: HarperPerennial, 1999.

    HISTORY, GENRES, THEORY, AND INTERPRETATION

    Baker, Joynce M. *Images of Women in Film: The War Years, 1941–1945.* Ann Arbor: UMI, 1980.

    Basinger, Jeanine. *A Woman's View: How Hollywood Spoke to Women, 1930–1960.* New York: Knopf, 1993.

    Baty, S. Paige. *American Monroe: The Making of a Body Politic.* Berkeley: University of California, 1995.

Bell-Meterau, Rebecca. *Hollywood Androgyny*. 2nd ed. New York: Columbia, 1993.

Byers, Jackie. *All that Hollywood Allows: Re-Reading Gender in 1950s Melodrama*. Chapel Hill: University of North Carolina, 1991.

Cartmell, Deborah, ed. *Sisterhoods: Across the Literature/Media Divide*. London: Pluto Press, 1998.

Cavell, Stanley. *Contesting Tears: The Hollywood Melodrama of the Unknown Woman*. Chicago: University of Chicago, 1996.

Coolidge, Archibald Cary. *Hollywood Looks at Women*. Mt. Pleasant, SC: Maecenas Press, 2001.

De Lauretis, Teresa. *Alice Doesn't: Feminism, Semiotics, Cinema*. Bloomington: Indiana University, 1984.

Doane, Mary Ann. *The Desire to Desire: The Woman's Film of the 1940s*. Bloomington: Indiana University, 1987.

———. *Femmes Fatales: Feminism, Film Theory, Psychoanalysis*. New York: Routledge, 1991.

Erens, Patricia. *Issues in Feminist Film Criticism*. Bloomington: Indiana University, 1990.

Fenton, Jill Rubinson. *Women Writers, From Page to Screen*. New York: Garland, 1990.

Fischer, Lucy. *Cinematernity: Film, Motherhood, Genre*. Princeton: Princeton, 1996.

Green, Philip. *Cracks I: The Pedestal: Ideology and Gender in Hollywood*. Amherst: University of Massachusetts, 1998.

Haskell, Molly. *From Reverence to Rape: The Treatment of Women in the Movies*. 2nd ed. Chicago: University of Chicago, 1987.

Higashi, Sumiko. *Virgins, Vamps, and Flappers: The American Silent Movie Heroine*. Montreal: Eden, 1979.

Hollinger, Karen. *In the Company of Women: Contemporary Female Friendship Films*. Minneapolis: University of Minnesota, 1998.

Isaacs, Susan. *Brave Dames and Wimpettes: What Women Are Really Doing on Page and Screen*. New York: Ballantine, 1999.

Kaplan, E. Ann. *Motherhood and Representation: The Mother in Popular Culture and Melodrama*. New York: Routledge, 1992.

Kaplan, E. Ann, ed. *Feminism and Film*. Oxford: Oxford University Press, 2000.

———. *Women in Film Noir*. London: BFI, 1998.

Kirkham, Pat and Janet Thumim. *Me Jane: Masculinity, Movies, and Women*. London: Lawrence & Wishart, 1995.

LaSalle, Mick. *Complicated Women: Sex and Power in Pre-Code Hollywood*. New York: Thomas Dunne Books, 2000.

Lawrence, Amy. *Echo and Narcissus: Women's Voices in Classical Hollywood Cinema*. Berkeley: University of California, 1991.

Mank, Gregory W. *Women in Horror Films, 1930s*. Jefferson, NC: McFarland, 1999.

———. *Women in Horror Films, 1940s*. Jefferson, NC: McFarland, 1999.

Mayne, Judith. *Framed: Lesbians, Feminists, and Media Culture*. Minneapolis: University of Minnesota, 2000.

———. *The Woman at the Keyhole: Feminism and Women's Cinema*. Bloomington: Indiana University, 1990.

McHugh, Kathleen Anne. *American Domesticity: From How-To Manual to Hollywood Melodrama*. New York: Oxford University, 1999.

Meyers, Marian, ed. *Mediated Women: Representations in Popular Culture*. Cresskill, NJ: Hampton Press, 1999.

Modleski, Tania. *Feminism Without Women: Culture and Criticism in a "Postfeminist" Age*. New York: Routledge, 1991.

Moore, Suzanne. *Looking for Trouble: On Shopping, Gender, and the Cinema*. London: Serpent's Tail, 1991.

Morris, Bonnie J. *Girl Reel: A Lesbian Remembers Growing Up at the Movies*. Minneapolis: Coffee House Press, 2000.

Parish, James Robert. *Prostitution in Hollywood Films*. Jefferson, NC: McFarland, 1992.

Penley, Constance. *Feminism and Film Theory*. New York: Routledge, 1988.

Rabinovitz, Lauren. *For the Love of Pleasure: Women, Movies, and Culture in Turn-of-the-Century Chicago*. New Brunswick: Rutgers, 1998.

Rapping, Elayne. *Media-tions: Forays into the Culture and Gender Wars*. Boston: South End, 1994.

Read, Jacinda. *The New Avengers: Feminism, Femininity, and the Rape-Revenge Cycle.* Manchester: Manchester University, 2000.

Rich, B. Ruby. *Chick Flicks: Theories and Memories of the Feminist Film Movement.* Durham: Duke University, 1998.

Rowe, Kathleen. *The Unruly Woman: Gender and the Genres of Laughter.* Austin: University of Texas, 1995.

Smelik, Anneke. *And the Mirror Cracked: Feminist Cinema and Film Theory.* New York: St. Martin's, 1998.

Sochen, June. *From Mae to Madonna: Women Entertainers in Twentieth-Century America.* Lexington, KY: University Press of Kentucky, 1999.

Staiger, Janet. *Bad Women: Regulating Sexuality in Early American Cinema.* Minneapolis: University of Minnesota, 1995.

Stamp, Shelley. *Movie-Struck Girls: Women and Motion Picture Culture After the Nickelodeon.* Princeton: Princeton University, 2000.

Stoddard, Karen M. *Saints and Shrews: Women and Aging in American Popular Film.* Westport, CT: Greenwood Press, 1983.

Tasker, Yvonne. *Working Girls: Gender and Sexuality in Popular Cinema.* London: Routledge, 1998.

Thornham, Sue, ed. *Feminist Film Theory: A Reader.* New York: New York University, 1999.

Walker, Janet. *Couching Resistance: Women, Film, and Psychoanalytic Psychiatry.* Minneapolis: University of Minnesota, 1993.

Wexman, Virginia Wright. *Creating the Couple: Love, Marriage, and Hollywood Performance.* Princeton: Princeton, 1993.

Wood, Robin. *Sexual Politics and Narrative Film.* New York: Columbia, 1998.

Zalcock, Beverley. *Renegade Sisters.* London: Creation Books International, 1998.

INTERVIEWS

Lisanti, Tom. *Fantasy Femmes of Sixties Cinema: Interviews with 20 Actresses from Biker, Beach, and Elvis Movies.* Jefferson, NC: McFarland, 2001.

WOMEN IN EUROPEAN CINEMA

Harper, Sue. *Women in British Cinema.* London: Continuum, 2000.

Lant, Antonia. *Blackout: Reinventing Women for Wartime British Cinema.* Princeton: Princeton, 1991.

O'Sickey, Ingebourg Majer and Ingebourg von Zadow, eds. *Triangulated Visions: Women in Recent German Cinema.* Albany: State University of New York, 1998.

Sieglohr, Ulrike, ed. *Heroines without Heroes: Reconstructing Female and National Identities in European Cinema, 1945–51.* New York: Cassell, 2000.

WOMEN IN FILM IN DEVELOPING COUNTRIES

Robin, Diana and Ira Jaffe, eds. *Redirecting the Gaze: Women and New Cinema in the Third World.* Albany: SUNY, 1998.

WOMEN IN INDIAN CINEMA

Chatterji, Shoma A. *Subject Cinema, Object Women: A Study of the Portrayal of Women in Indian Cinema.* Calcutta: Parumita Publications, 1998.

WOMEN IN THE FILM INDUSTRY

Abramowitz, Rachel. *Is That a Gun in Your Pocket? Women's Experience of Power in Hollywood.* New York: Random House, 2000.

WORKING CLASS AND FILM

Ross, Steven J. *Working-Class Hollywood: Silent Film and the Shaping of Class in America.* Princeton: Princeton, 1998.

Zaniello, Tom. *Working Stiffs, Union Maids, Reds, and Riffraff: An Organized Guide to Films About Labor.* Ithaca: ILR, 1996.

YOUTH AND FILM

Bernstein, Jonathan. *Pretty in Pink: The Golden Age of Teenage Movies.* New York: St. Martin's, 1997.

Considine, David M. *The Cinema of Adolescence.* Jefferson, NC: McFarland, 1985.

Doherty, Thomas. *Teenagers and Teenpics.* Boston: Unwin Hyman, 1988.

Goldstein, Ruth M. *Screen Image of Youth.* Metuchen: Scarecrow, 1980.

Lewis, Jon. *The Road to Romance and Ruin: Teen Films and Youth Culture.* New York: Routledge, 1992.

Pettigrew, Terrence. *Raising Hell: The Rebel in the Movies.* New York: St. Martin's, 1986.

Pomerance, Murry and Jahn Sakeris. *Pictures of a Generation on Hold.* Toronto: Ryerson, 1996.

FILM HISTORY BY ERA

EARLY CINEMA

Abel, Richard. *The Red Rooster Scare: Making American Cinema, 1900–1910.* Berkeley: University of California, 1999.

Bengston, John. *Silent Echoes: Discovering Early Hollywood Through the Films of Buster Keaton.* Santa Monica: Santa Monica Press, 2000.

Bowser, Eileen. *The Transformation of Cinema, 1907–1915.* New York: Scribner, 1990.

Brownlow, Kevin. *Behind the Mask of Innocence.* New York: Knopf, 1990.

Butler, Ivan. *Silent Magic: Rediscovering the Silent Film Era.* New York: Ungar, 1988.

Corkin, Stanley. *Realism and the Birth of the Modern United States: Cinema, Literature, and Culture.* Athens: University of Georgia, 1996.

Elsaesser, Thomas. *Early Cinema: Space, Frame, Narrative.* London: BFI, 1990.

Everson, William K. *American Silent Film.* New York: Da Capo Press, 1998.

Fullerton, John, ed. *Celebrating 1895: The Centenary of Cinema.* Sydney: John Libbey & Co., 1998.

Gunning, Thomas. *D.W. Griffith and the Rise of the Narrative Film.* Urbana: University of Illinois, 1991.

Hansen, Miriam. *Babel and Babylon: Spectatorship in American Silent Film.* Cambridge: Harvard, 1991.

Koszarski, Richard. *An Evening's Entertainment: The Age of the Silent Feature Picture, 1915–1928.* New York: Scribner, 1990.

———. *The Rivals of D.W. Griffith.* New York: New York Zoetrope, 1980.

Leyda, Jay and Charles Musser. *Before Hollywood.* New York: American Federation of the Arts, 1986.

Maland, Charles J. *Chaplin and American Culture.* Princeton: Princeton, 1989.

Musser, Charles. *Before the Nickelodeon: Edwin S. Porter and the Edison Manufacturing Company.* Berkeley: University of California, 1991.

———. *The Emergence of Cinema: The American Screen to 1907.* New York: Scribner, 1990.

———. *Thomas A. Edison and His Kinetographic Motion Pictures.* New Brunswick: Rutgers, 1995.

Robinson, David. *From Peep Show to Palace: The Birth of American Film.* New York: Columbia, 1996.

Ross, Steven J. *Working-Class Hollywood: Silent Film and the Shaping of Class in America.* Princeton: Princeton University, 1998.

Slide, Anthony. *Early American Cinema.* Rev. ed. Metuchen: Scarecrow, 1994.

Sloan, Kay. *The Loud Silents: Origins of the Social Problem Film.* Urbana: University of Illinois, 1988.

Weiss, Ken. *To the Rescue: How Immigrants Saved the American Film Industry, 1896–1912.* San Francisco: Austin & Winfield, 1997.

THE DEPRESSION ERA

Balio, Tino. *Grand Design—Hollywood as a Modern Business Enterprise, 1930–1939.* New York: Scribner, 1993.

Bergman, Andrew. *We're in the Money: Depression America and Its Films.* New York: NYU, 1971.

Growder, Laura. *Rousing the Nation: Radical Culture in Depression America.* Amherst: University of Massachusetts, 1998.

Maland, Charles. *American Visions: The Films of Chaplin, Ford, Capra, and Welles, 1936–1941.* New York: Arno, 1977.

Shindler, Colin. *Hollywood in Crisis: Cinema and American Society, 1929–1939.* London: Routledge, 1996.

THE 1940s

Basinger, Jeanine. *The World War II Combat Film.* New York: Columbia, 1986.

Browder, Laura. *Rousing the Nation: Radical Culture in Depression America.* Amherst: University of Massachusetts, 1998.

Dick, Bernard F. *The Star-Spangled Screen: The American World War II Film.* Lexington: University Press of Kentucky, 1985.

Doherty, Thomas Patrick. *Projections of War: Hollywood, American Culture, and World War II.* New York: Columbia, 1993.

Friedrich, Ott. *City of Nets: A Portrait of Hollywood in the 1940's.* New York: Harper & Row, 1986.

Fyne, Robert. *Hollywood Propaganda of World War II.* Metuchen: Scarecrow, 1994.

Honey, Maureen. *Creating Rosie the Riveter: Class, Gender and Propaganda During World War II.* Amherst: University of Massachusetts, 1984.

Kane, Kathryn. *Visions of War: The Hollywood Combat Films of World War II.* Ann Arbor: UMI, 1982.

Koppes, Clayton R. and Gregory D. Black. *Hollywood Goes to War: How Politics, Profits and Propaganda*

    Shaped World War II Movies. New York: Free Press, 1987.

Myers, James M. *The Bureau of Motion Pictures and Its Influence on Film Content During World War II.* Lewiston: Edwin Mellen Press, 1998.

Schatz, Thomas. *Boom and Bust: The American Cinema in the 1940s.* New York: Charles Scribner's Sons, 1997.

Shindler, Colin. *Hollywood Goes to War: Films and American Society, 1939–1952.* Boston: Routledge & Kegan Paul, 1979.

THE 1950S

Biskind, Peter. *Seeing Is Believing: How Hollywood Movies Taught Us to Stop Worrying and Love the Fifties.* New York: Pantheon, 1983.

Brode, Douglas. *The Films of the Fifties.* New York: Carol, 1992.

Cochran, David. *American Noir: Underground Writers and Filmmakers of the Postwar Era.* Washington: Smithsonian Institution Press, 2000.

Monaco, Paul. *Ribbons in Time: Movies and Society Since 1945.* Bloomington: Indiana University, 1987.

Quart, Leonard and Albert Auster. *American Film and Society Since 1945.* 2nd ed. Bloomington: Indiana University, 1987.

Sayre, Nora. *Running Time.* New York: Dial, 1982.

Sikov, Ed. *Laughing Hysterically: American Screen Comedy of the 1950s.* New York: Columbia, 1994.

Sterritt, David. *Mad to Be Saved: The Beats, the '50s, and Film.* Carbondale: Southern Illinois University, 1998.

THE 1960S

Biskind, Peter. *Easy Riders, Raging Bulls: How the Sex-Drugs-and-Rock-'n'-Roll Generation Saved Hollywood.* New York: Simon & Schuster, 1998.

James, David E. *Allegories of Cinema: American Film in the Sixties.* Princeton: Princeton, 1989.

Man, Glenn. *Radical Visions: American Film Renaissance, 1967–1976.* Westport, CT: Greenwood Press, 1994.

Monaco, Paul. *The Sixties, 1960–1969.* New York: Charles Scribner's Sons, 2001.

Mordden, Ethan. *Medium Cool: The Movies of the 1960s.* New York: Knopf, 1990.

THE 1970S

Bernardoni, James. *The New Hollywood: What the Movies Did with the New Freedoms of the Seventies.* Jefferson, NC: McFarland, 1991.

Cagin, Seth and Philip Dray. *Hollywood Films of the Seventies.* New York: Harper & Row, 1984.

Cook, David A. *Lost Illusions: American Cinema in the Shadow of Watergate and Vietnam, 1970–1979.* New York: Charles Scribner's Sons, 2000.

Lev, Peter. *American Films of the '70s: Conflicting Visions.* Austin: University of Texas, 2000.

O'Brien, Tom. *The Screening of America: Movies and Values from Rocky to Rain Man.* New York: Continuum, 1990.

Wood, Robin. *Hollywood from Vietnam to Reagan.* New York: Columbia, 1986.

THE 1980S

Brode, Douglas. *The Films of the Eighties.* Secaucus: Carol, 1990.

Corrigan, Timothy. *A Cinema Without Walls: Movies and Culture After Vietnam.* New Brunswick, 1991.

Grunzweig, Walter et al. *Constructing the Eighties: Versions of an American Decade.* Tubingen: G. Narr, 1992.

Miller, Mark Crispin. *Seeing Through Movies.* New York: Pantheon, 1990.

Nowlan, Robert A. *The Films of the Eighties: A Complete, Qualitative Filmography.* Jefferson, NC: McFarland, 1991.

Palmer, William J. *Films of the Eighties: A Social History.* Carbondale: Southern Illinois University, 1993.

Ryan, Michael and Douglas Kellner. *Camera Politica: The Politics and Ideology of Contemporary Hollywood.* Bloomington: Indiana University, 1988.

Traube, Elizabeth G. *Dreaming Identities: Class, Gender, and Generation in 1980s Hollywood Movies.* Boulder: Westview, 1992.

Vineberg, Steve. *No Surprises, Please: Movies in the Reagan Decade.* New York: Schirmer Books, 1993.

CONTEMPORARY FILM

Bart, Peter. *Who Killed Hollywood?* Los Angeles: Renaissance Books, 1999.

Biskind, Peter. *Easy Riders, Raging Bulls: How the Sex-Drugs-and-Rock'n'Roll Generation Saved Hollywood.* New York: Simon & Schuster, 1998.

Farrell, Kirby. *Post-Traumatic Culture: Injury and Interpretation in the Nineties.* Baltimore: Johns Hopkins, 1998.

Jarvis, Brian. *Postmodern Cartographies: The Geographical Imagination in Contemporary American Culture.*

London: Pluto, 1998.

Lewis, Jon. *The New American Cinema*. Durham: Duke, 1998.

Neale, Steve and Murray Smith. *Contemporary Hollywood Cinema*. London: Routledge, 1998.

Stokes, Jane C. *On Screen Rivals: Cinema and Television in the United States and Britain*. Basingstoke: Macmillan, 1999.

Wyatt, Justin. *High Concept: Movies and Marketing in Hollywood*. Austin: University of Texas, 1994.

FILM GENRES

GENERAL WORKS

Altman, Rick. *Film/Genre*. London: BFI Publishing, 1999.

Browne, Nick, ed. *Refiguring American Film Genres: History and Theory*. Berkeley: University of California, 1998.

Cawelti, John G. *Adventure, Mystery, and Romance: Formula Stories as Art and Popular Culture*. Chicago: University of Chicago, 1976.

Coates, Paul. *Film at the Intersection of High and Mass Culture*. Cambridge: Cambridge University, 1994.

Dixon, Wheeler Winston. *Film Genre 2000: New Critical Essays*. Albany: SUNY, 2000.

Gehring, Wes D. *Handbook of American Film Genres*. New York: Greenwood Press, 1988.

Grant, Barry Keith. *Film Genre Reader*. Austin: University of Texas, 1986.

Grodal, Torben Kragh. *Moving Pictures: A New Theory of Film Genres, Feelings, and Cognition*. Oxford: Clarendon, 1997.

Landy, Marcia. *British Genres: Cinema and Society, 1930–1960*. Princeton: Princeton University, 1991.

Lopez, Daniel. *Films by Genre*. Jefferson, NC: McFarland, 1993.

Neale, Stephen. *Genre*. London: BFI, 1980.

Reed, Joseph W. *American Scenarios: The Uses of Film Genre*. Middletown, CT: Wesleyan University, 1989.

Schatz, Thomas. *Hollywood Genres*. New York: Random House, 1980.

ADVENTURE FILMS

Arroyo Jose, ed. *Action/Spectacle Cinema: A Sight and Sound Reader*. London: BFI, 2000.

Hofstede, David. *Hollywood's Heroes*. Lanham: Madison, 1994.

Tasker, Yvonne. *Spectacular Bodies: Gender, Genre, and the Action Cinema*. London: Routledge, 1993.

Taves, Brian. *The Romance of Adventure: The Genre of Historical Adventure Movies*. Jackson: University Press of Mississippi, 1993.

ANIMATION

Beck, Jerry. *Warner Bros. Animation Art*. London: Virgin, 1998.

Bendazzi, Giannalberto. *Cartoons: One Hundred Years of Cinema Animation*. London: Libbey, 1994.

Cholodenko. *The Illusion of Life: Essays on Animation*. Sydney: Power, 1991.

Cohen, Karl F. *Forbidden Animation: Censored Cartoons and Blacklisted Animators in America*. Jefferson, NC: McFarland, 1997.

Crafton, Donald. *Before Mickey: The Animated Film, 1898–1928*. Chicago: University of Chicago, 1993.

Furniss, Maureen. *Art in Motion: Animation Aesthetics*. London: John Libbey, 1998.

Gifford, Denis. *American Animated Films: The Silent Era, 1897–1929*. Jefferson, NC: McFarland, 1990.

Kanfer, Stefan. *Serious Business: The Art and Commerce of Animation in America*. New York: Scribner, 1997.

Klein, Norman M. *Seven Minutes: The Life and Death of the American Animated Cartoon*. London: Verso, 1993.

Levi, Antonia. *Samurai from Outer Space: Understanding Japanese Animation*. Chicago: Open Court, 1996.

Lotman, Jeff. *Animation Art: The Early Years, 1911–1953*. Atglen, Pa.: Schiffer, 1995.

McCarthy, Helen. *The Abnime! Movie Guide*. London: Titan, 1996.

Merritt, Russell. *Walt in Wonderland: The Silent Films of Walt Disney*. Baltimore: Johns Hopkins, 1993.

Sampson, Henry T. *That's Enough, Folks: Black Images in Animated Cartoons, 1900–1960*. Lanham: Scarecrow, 1998.

Smoodin, Eric Loren. *Animating Culture: Hollywood Cartoons from the Sound Era*. New Brunswick: Rutgers, 1993.

Thomas, Bob. *Disney's Art of Animation*. New York: Hyperion, 1991.

Thomas, Frank and Ollie Johnston. *The Illusion of Life: Disney Animation*. New York: Hyperion, 1995.

Wells, Paul. *Understanding Animation*. London: Routledge, 1998.

AVANT-GARDE AND EXPERIMENTAL FILM

Broadhurst, Susan. *Liminal Acts: A Critical Overview of Contemporary Performance and Theory*. London:

Cassell, 1999.

Dixon, Wheeler W. *The Exploding Eye: A Re-Visionary History of 1960s American Experimental Cinema.* Albany: SUNY, 1997.

Hawkins, Joan. *Cutting Edge: Art-Horror and the Horrific Avant-Garde.* Minneapolis: University of Minnesota, 2000.

Horak, Jan-Christopher. *Lovers of Cinema: The First American Film Avant-Garde, 1919–1945.* Madison: University of Wisconsin, 1995.

Levy, Emanuel. *Cinema of Outsiders: The Rise of American Independent Film.* New York: New York University, 1999.

MacDonald, Scott. *Avant-Garde Film: Motion Studies.* Cambridge: Cambridge, 1993.

Mellencamp, Patricia. *Indiscretions: Avant-Garde Film, Video and Feminism.* Bloomington: Indiana University, 1990.

Peterson, James. *Dreams of Chaos, Visions of Order: Understanding the American Avant-Garde Cinema.* Detroit: Wayne State, 1994.

Sidney, P. Adams. *Modernist Montage: The Obscurity of Vision in Cinema and Literature.* New York: Columbia, 1990.

Small, Edward S. *Direct Theory: Experimental Film/Video as Major Genre.* Carbondale: Southern Illinois University, 1994.

Sterritt, David. *Mad to Be Saved: The Beats, the '50s, and Film.* Carbondale: Southern Illinois University, 1998.

Suarez, Juan Antonio. *Bike Boys, Drag Queens and Superstars: Avant-Garde, Mass Culture, and Gay Identities in the 1960s Underground Cinema.* Bloomington: Indiana University, 1996.

Testa, Bart. *Back and Forth: Early Cinema and the Avant-Garde.* Toronto: Art Museum of Ontario, 1992.

Wees, William C. *Light Moving in Time: Studies in the Visual Aesthetics of Avant-Garde Film.* Berkeley: University of California, 1992.

Wilinsky, Barbara. *Sure Seaters: The Emergence of Art House Cinema.* Minneapolis: University of Minnesota, 2001.

BIBLICAL FILMS

Babington, Bruce and Peter William Evans. *Biblical Epics: Sacred Narrative in the Hollywood Cinema.* Manchester: Manchester, 1993.

Exum, J. Cheryl. *Plotted, Shot, and Painted: Cultural Representations of Biblical Women.* Sheffield: Sheffield, 1996.

Kreitzer, L. Joseph. *The New Testament in Fiction and Film.* Sheffield: JSOT, 1993.

———. *The Old Testament in Fiction and Film.* Sheffield: JSOT, 1994.

———. *Pauline Images in Fiction and Film.* Sheffield: Sheffield Academic Press, 1999.

BIOGRAPHICAL FILMS

Custen, George Frederick. *Bio/Pics: How Hollywood Constructed Public History.* New Brunswick: Rutgers University, 1992.

COLLEGE LIFE IN FILM

Hinton, David B. *Celluloid Ivy: Higher Education in the Movies.* Metuchen: Scarecrow, 1994.

COMEDIES

ENCYCLOPEDIAS

Miller, Blair. *American Silent Film Comedies.* Jefferson, NC: McFarland, 1995.

HISTORY, THEORY, AND INTERPRETATION

Burton, Alan and Laraine Porter, eds. *Pimple, Pranks and Pratfalls: British Comedy Before 1930.* Wiltshire: Flicks Books, 2000.

Gehring, Wes D. *American Dark Comedy: Beyond Satire.* Westport, CT: Greenwood Press, 1996.

———. *Parody as Film Genre: "Never Give a Saga An Even Break."* Westport, CT: Greenwood Press, 1999.

———. *Personality Comedians as Genre: Selected Players.* Westport, CT: Greenwood Press, 1997.

Horton, Andrew. *Comedy/Cinema/Theory.* Berkeley: University of California, 1991.

———. *Inside Soviet Film Satire.* Cambridge: Cambridge, 1993.

———. *Laughing Out Loud: Writing the Comedy-Centered Screenplay.* Berkeley: University of California, 2000.

Jenkins, Henry. *What Made Pistachio Nuts? Early Sound Comedy and the Vaudeville Aesthetic.* New York: Columbia, 1992.

Karnick, Kristine Brunovska and Henry Jenkins. *Classical Hollywood Comedy.* New York: Routledge,

1995.

MacCann, Richard Dyer. *The Silent Comedians*. Metuchen: Scarecrow, 1993.

McCaffrey, Donald W. *Assault on Society: Satirical Literature to Film*. Metuchen: Scarecrow, 1992.

Miller, Blair. *American Silent Film Comedies*. Jefferson, NC: McFarland, 1995.

Neale, Stephen and Frank Krutnik. *Popular Film and Television Comedy*. London: Routledge, 1990.

Rowe, Kathleen. *The Unruly Woman: Gender and the Genres of Laughter*. Austin: University of Texas, 1995.

Paul, William. *Laughing, Screaming: Modern Hollywood Horror and Comedy*. New York: Columbia, 1994.

Sanders, Jonathan. *Another Fine Dress: Role-Play in the Films of Laurel and Hardy*. London: Cassell, 1995.

Sennett, Ted. *Laughing in the Dark: Movie Comedy from Groucho to Woody*. New York: St. Martin's, 1992.

Sikov, Ed. *Laughing Historically: American Screen Comedy of the 1950s*. New York: Columbia, 1994.

Weales, Gerald. *Canned Goods as Caviar: American Film Comedy of the 1930s*. Chicago: University of Chicago, 1985.

Winokur, Mark. *American Laughter: Immigrants, Ethnicity and 1930s Hollywood Film Comedy*. Houndmills: Macmillan, 1996.

ROMANTIC COMEDY

Babington, Bruce and Peter William Evans. *Affairs to Remember: The Hollywood Comedy of the Sexes*. New York: St. Martin's, 1989.

Cavell, Stanley. *Pursuits of Happiness: The Hollywood Comedy of Remarriage*. Cambridge: Harvard, 1981.

Harvey, John. *Romantic Comedy in Hollywood from Lubitsch to Sturgis*. New York: Knopf, 1987.

Kendall, Elizabeth. *The Runaway Bride: Hollywood Romantic Comedy of the 1930's*. New York: Knopf, 1990.

Rubinfeld, Mark D. *Bound to Bond: Gender, Genre, and the Hollywood Romantic Comedy*. Westport, CT: Praeger, 2001.

SCREWBALL COMEDY

Byrge, Duane and Robert Milton Miller. *The Screwball Comedy Films: A History and Filmography*. Jefferson, NC: McFarland, 1991.

Gehring, Wes D. *Screwball Comedy*. Westport, CT: Greenwood Press, 1986.

QUOTATIONS

Langman, Larry and Paul Gold. *Comedy Quotes from the Movies*. Jefferson, NC: McFarland, 1993.

REVIEWS

Variety Comedy Movies: Illustrated Reviews of the Classic Films. London: Hamlyn, 1992.

CRIME FILMS

Chibnall, Steve and Robert Murphy, ed. *British Crime Cinema*. London: Routledge, 1999.

Hardy, Phil, ed. *Overlook Film Encyclopedia: The Gangster Film*. Woodstock, NY: Overlook Press, 1998.

Langman, Larry and Daniel Finn. *A Guide to American Crime Films of the Forties and Fifties*. Westport, CT: Greenwood Press, 1995.

———. *A Guide to American Crime Films of the Thirties*. Westport, CT: Greenwood Press, 1995.

———. *A Guide to American Silent Crime Films*. Westport, CT: Greenwood Press, 1994.

McCarty, John. *Hollywood Gangland*. New York: St. Martin's, 1993.

Munby, Jonathan. *Public Enemies, Public Heroes: Screening the Gangster from Little Caesar to Touch of Evil*. Chicago: University of Chicago, 1999.

Parish, James Robert. *Great Cop Pictures*. Metuchen: Scarecrow, 1990.

Rafter, Nicole Hahn. *Shots in the Mirror: Crime Films and Society*. Oxford: Oxford University, 2000.

Rosow, Eugene. *Born to Lose: The Gangster Film in America*. New York: Oxford, 1978.

Shadoian, Jack. *Dreams and Dead Ends: The American Gangster/Crime Film*. Cambridge: MIT, 1977.

Stempridge, Gerard. *Ordinary Decent Criminal*. London: Headline, 1999.

Stephens, Michael L. *Gangster Films*. Jefferson, NC: McFarland, 1996.

Vahimagi, Tise. *The Untouchables*. London: British Film Institute, 1998.

Yaquinto, Marilyn. *Pump 'Em Full of Lead: A Look at Gangsters on Film*. New York: Twayne, 1998.

CULT MOVIES

Mendik, Xavier and Graeme Harper. *Unruly Pleasures: The Cult Film and Its Critics*. Guildford: FAB, 2000.

Peary, Danny. *Cult Movies: The Classics, the Sleepers, the Weird, and the Wonderful*. New York: Gramercy

Books, 1998.

DETECTIVE STORIES

Reynolds, William and Elizabeth A. Trembley. *It's a Print!: Detective Fiction from Page to Screen*. Bowling Green: Bowling Green State University, 1994.

DOCUMENTARY FILM

Aitken, Ian, ed. *The Documentary Film Movement: An Anthology*. Edinburgh: Edinburgh University, 1998.

Bakker, Kees, ed. *Joris Ivens and the Documentary Context*. Amsterdam: Amsterdam University, 1999.

Barnouw, Erik. *Documentary: A History of the Non-Fiction Film*. 2nd ed. New York: Oxford, 1993.

Barsam, Richard Meran. *Nonfiction Film: A Critical History*. Bloomington: Indiana University, 1992.

Bruzzi, Stella. *New Documentary: A Critical Introduction*. London: Routledge, 2000.

Crusie, Jennifer. *Welcome to Temptation*. New York: St. Martin's Press, 2000.

Ellis, Jack C. *John Grierson: Life, Contributions, Influence*. Carbondale: Southern Illinois University, 2000.

Gaines, Jane M. and Michael Renov, eds. *Collecting Visible Evidence*. Minneapolis: University of Minnesota, 1999.

Grant, Barry Keith. *Voyages of Discovery: The Cinema of Frederick Wiseman*. Urbana: University of Illinois, 1991.

Grant, Barry Keith and Jeannette Sloniowski. *Documenting the Documentary: Close Readings of Documentary Film and Video*. Detroit: Wayne State, 1998.

Gwynn, William Howard. *A Cinema of Nonfiction*. Rutherford: Fairleigh Dickinson, 1990.

Klotman, Phyllis R. and Janet K. Cutler, eds. *Struggles for Representation: African American Documentary Film and Video*. Bloomington: Indiana University, 1999.

Leuthold, Steven. *Indigenous Aesthetics: Native Art, Media, and Identity*. Austin: University of Texas, 1998.

MacDonald, Kevin and Mark Cousins. *Imagining Reality: The Faber Book of the Documentary*. London: Faber and Faber, 1996.

MacDougall, David, ed. *Transcultural Cinema*. Princeton: Princeton University, 1998.

Moscovitch, Arlene. *Constructing Reality: Exploring Media Issues in Documentary*. Montreal: National Film Board of Canada, 1993.

Nichols, Bill. *Representing Reality: Issues and Concepts in Documentary*. Bloomington: Indiana University, 1991.

Plantinga, Carl R. *Rhetoric and Representation in Nonfiction Film*. Cambridge: Cambridge, 1997.

Ponech, Trevor. *What Is Non-Fiction Cinema?* Boulder: Westview Press, 1999.

Renov, Michael. *Theorizing Documentary*. New York: Routledge, 1993.

Roberts, Graham. *Forward Soviet! History and Non-Fiction Film in the USSR*. London: I.B. Tauris, 1999.

Rothman, William. *Documentary Film Classics*. Cambridge: Cambridge, 1997.

Russell, Catherine. *Experimental Ethnography: The Work of Film in the Age of Video*. Durham: Duke University, 1999.

Sherman, Sharon R. *Documenting Ourselves: Film, Video, and Culture*. Lexington: University Press of Kentucky, 1998.

Tobias, Michael, ed. *The Search for Reality: The Art of Documentary Filmmaking*. Studio City, CA: Michael Wiese Productions, 1998.

Vaughn, Dai. *For Documentary*. Berkeley: University of California, 1999.

Waldman, Diane and Janet Walker, eds. *Feminism and Documentary*. Minneapolis: University of Minnesota, 1999.

Warren, Charles. *Beyond Document: Essays on Nonfiction Film*. Middletown: Wesleyan, 1996.

Winston, Brian. *Claiming the Real: The Griersonian Documentary and Its Legitimations*. London: BFI, 1995.

———. *"Fires Were Started."* London: British Film Institute, 1999.

Zimmermann, Patricia Rodden. *States of Emergency: Documentaries, Wars, Democracies*. Minneapolis: University of Minnesota, 2000.

ETHNOGRAPHIC FILM

Barbash, Ilisa. *Cross-Cultural Filmmaking*. Berkeley: University of California, 1997.

Crawford, Peter Ian and David Turton. *Film as Ethnography*. Manchester: Manchester, 1992.

Devereaux, Leslie and Roger Hillman. *Fields of Vision: Essays in Film Studies, Visual Anthropology, and Photography*. Berkeley: University of California, 1995.

Heider, Karl G. *Seeing Anthropology: Cultural Anthropology Through Film*. Boston: Allyn and Bacon, 1997.

Husmann, Rolf et al. *Bibiliography of Ethnographic Films*. Gottingen: Lit, 1992.

Loizos, Peter. *Innovations in Ethnographic Film: From Innocence to Self-Consciousness*. Manchester: Manchester, 1993.

MacDougall, David. *Transcultural Cinema*. Princeton: Princeton, 1999.

Nichols, Bill. *Blurred Boundaries: Questions of Meaning in Contemporary Culture*. Bloomington: Indiana University, 1994.

Rollwagen, Jack R. *Anthropological Film and Video in the 1990s*. Brockport: Institute, 1993.

Rony, Fatimah Tobing. *The Third Eye: Race, Cinema, and Ethnographic Spectacle*. Durham: Duke, 1996.

FILM NOIR

CATALOGS

Meyer, David N. *A Girl and a Gun: The Complete Guide to Film Noir on Video*. New York: Avon Books, 1998.

HISTORY AND INTERPRETATION

Buss, Robin. *French Film Noir*. London: M. Boyars, 1994.

Cameron, Ian. *Book of Film Noir*. New York: Continuum, 1993.

———. *Movie Book of Film Noir*. London: Studio Vista, 1992.

Christopher, Nicholas. *Somewhere in the Night: Film Noir and the American City*. New York: Free Press, 1997.

Copjec, Joan. *Shades of Noir*. London: Verso, 1993.

Gifford, Barry. *Out of the Past: Adventures in Film Noir*. Jackson: University Press of Mississippi, 2000.

Hannsberry, Karen Burroughs. *Femme Noir: Bad Girls of Film*. Jefferson, NC: McFarland, 1998.

Kitses, Jim. *Gun Crazy*. London: BFI, 1996.

Krutnik, Frank. *In a Lonely Street: Film Noir, Genre, Masculinity*. London: Routledge, 1991.

Marling, William. *The American Roman Noir: Hammett, Cain, and Chandler*. Athens: University of Georgia, 1995.

Martin, Richard. *Mean Streets and Raging Bulls: The Legacy of Film Noir in Contemporary American Cinema*. Lanham: Scarecrow, 1997.

Maxfield, James F. *The Fatal Woman: Sources of Male Anxiety in American Film Noir, 1941–1991*. Madison: Fairleigh Dickinson, 1996.

Muller, Eddie. *Dark City: The Lost World of Film Noir*. London: Titan, 1998.

Naremore, James. *More than Night: Film Noir in Its Contexts*. Berkeley: University of California, 1998.

Palmer, R. Barton. *Hollywood's Dark Cinema: The American Film Noir*. New York: Twayne, 1994.

———. *Perspectives on Film Noir*. New York: G.K. Hall, 1996.

Richardson, Carl. *Autopsy: An Element of Realism in Film Noir*. Metuchen: Scarecrow, 1992.

Silver, Alain and Elizabeth Ward. *Film Noir*. 3rd ed. Woodstock, NY: Overlook, 1992.

Stephens, Michael L. *Film Noir*. Jefferson, NC: McFarland, 1995.

HISTORICAL FILMS

Barta, Tony. *Screening the Past: Film and the Representation of History*. Westport, CT: Praeger, 1998.

Burgoyne, Robert. *Film Nation: Hollywood Looks at U.S. History*. Minneapolis: University of Minnesota, 1997.

Cameron, Kenneth M. *America on Film: Hollywood and American History*. New York: Continuum, 1997.

Carnes, Marc C. *Past Imperfect: History According to the Movies*. New York: H. Holt. 1995.

Davis, Natalie Zemon. *Slaves on Screen: Film and Historical Vision*. Cambridge, MA: Harvard University, 2000.

Ellwood, David, ed. *The Movies as History: Visions of the Twentieth Century*. Stroud: Sutton, 2000.

Grindon, Leger. *Shadows on the Past: Studies in the Historical Fiction Film*. Philadelphia: Temple, 1994.

Landy, Marcia. *Cinematic Uses of the Past*. Minneapolis: University of Minnesota, 1996.

Landy, Marcia, ed. *Historical Film: History and Memory in Media*. New Brunswick: Rutgers University, 2001.

Marsden, Michael T. et al. *Movies as Artifacts*. Chicago: Nelson-Hall, 1982.

O'Connor, John E. *Image as Artifact: The Historical Analysis of Film and Television*. Malabar: R.E. Krieger, 1990.

O'Connor, John E. and Martin A. Jackson, eds. *American History/American Film: Interpreting the Hollywood Image*. New York: Ungar, 1979.

Osterberg, Bertil O. *Colonial America on Film and Television: A Filmography*. Jefferson, NC: McFarland, 2001.

Rollins, Peter. *Hollywood as Historian: American Film in a Cultural Context*. Lexington: University Press of Kentucky, 1983.

Roquemore, Joseph H. *History Goes to the Movies: A Viewer's Guide*. New York: Main Street Books, 1999.

Rosenstone, Robert A. *Revisioning History: Film and the Construction of a New Past*. Princeton: Princeton,

1995.

———. *Visions of the Past: The Challenge of Film to Our Idea of History.* Cambridge: Harvard, 1995.

Rosenthal, Alan. *Why Docudrama? Fact-Fiction on Film and TV.* Carbondale: Southern Illinois University, 1998.

Searles, Baird. *Epic: History on the Big Screen.* New York: Abrams, 1990.

Short, K. R. M. *Feature Films as History.* Knoxville: University of Tennessee, 1981.

Sklar, Robert and Charles Musser. *Resisting Images: Essays on Cinema and History.* Philadelphia: Temple, 1990.

Sobchack, Vivian. *The Persistence of History: Cinema, Television, and the Modern Event.* New York: Routledge, 1996.

Sturken, Marita. *Tangled Memories: The Vietnam War, the AIDS Epidemic, and the Politics of Remembering.* Berkeley: University of California, 1997.

Tashiro, C. S. *Pretty Pictures: Production Design and the History Film.* Austin: University of Texas, 1998.

Toplin, Robert Brent. *History by Hollywood: The Use and Abuse of the American Past.* Urbana: University of Illinois, 1996.

Wyke, Maria. *Projecting the Past: Ancient Rome, Cinema, and History.* New York: Routledge, 1997.

HORROR FILMS

Andriano, Joseph. *Immortal Monster: The Mythological Evolution of the Fantastic Beast in Modern Fiction and Film.* Westport, CT: Greenwood Press, 1999.

Badley, Linda. *Film, Horror, and the Body Fantastic.* Westport, CT: Greenwood Press, 1995.

Berenstein, Rhona J. *Attack of the Leading Ladies: Gender, Sexuality and Spectatorship in Classic Horror Cinema.* New York: Columbia, 1996.

Brunas, Michael et al. *Universal Horrors: The Studio's Classic Films.* Jefferson, NC: McFarland, 1990.

Carroll, Noel. *The Philosophy of Horror, or, Paradoxes of the Heart.* New York: Routledge, 1990.

Clarens, Carlos. *Illustrated History of Horror and Science-Fiction Films.* New York: Da Capo, 1997.

Clemens, Valdine. *The Return of the Repressed: Gothic Horror From the Castle of Otranto to Alien.* Albany: SUNY, 1999.

Clover, Carol J. *Men, Women and Chain Saws: Gender in Modern Horror Film.* Princeton: Princeton, 1992.

Crane, Jonathan Lake. *Terror and Everyday Life: Singular Moments in the History of the Horror Film.* Thousand Oaks: Sage, 1994.

Creed, Barbara. *The Monstrous-Feminine: Film, Feminism, Psychoanalysis.* London: Routledge, 1993.

Dyson, Jeremy. *Bright Darkness: The Lost Art of the Supernatural Horror Film.* London: Cassell, 1997.

Edmundson, Mark. *Nightmare on Main Street: Angels, Sadomasochism, and the Culture of Gothic.* Cambridge: Harvard, 1997.

Fischer, Dennis. *Horror Film Directors, 1931–1990.* Jefferson, NC: McFarland, 1991.

Flynn, John L. *Cinematic Vampires: The Living Dead on Film and Television.* Jefferson, NC: McFarland, 1992.

Fonseca, Anthony J. and June Michele Pulliam. *Hooked on Horror: A Guide to Reading Interests in Horror Fiction.* Englewood CO: Libraries Unlimited, 1999.

Freeland, Cynthia. *The Naked and the Undead: Evil and the Appeal of Horror.* Boulder: Westview Press, 2000.

Gelder, Ken. *Reading the Vampire.* London: Routledge, 1994.

Gordon, Joan and Veronica Hollinger. *Blood Read: The Vampire as Metaphor in Contemporary Culture.* Philadelphia: Pennsylvania, 1997.

Grant, Barry Keith. *The Dread of Difference: Gender and the Horror Film.* Austin: University of Texas, 1996.

Halberstam, Judith. *Skin Shows: Gothic Horror and the Technology of Monsters.* Durham: Duke, 1995.

Hanke, Ken. *A Critical Guide to Horror Film Series.* New York: Garland, 1991.

Hardy, Phil. *Horror.* Rev. ed. London: Aurum, 1993.

Hawkins, Joan. *Cutting Edge: Art-Horror and the Horrific Avant-Garde.* Minneapolis: University of Minnesota, 2000.

Hendershot, Cyndy. *The Animal Within: Masculinity and the Gothic.* Ann Arbor: University of Michigan, 1998.

Hutchings, Peter. *Hammer and Beyond: The British Horror Film.* Manchester: Manchester, 1993.

Iaccino, James F. *Psychological Reflections on Cinematic Terror.* Westport, CT: Praeger, 1994.

Jancovich, Mark. *American Horror from 1951 to the Present.* Staffordshire: Keele University, 1994.

———. *Rational Fears: American Horror in the 1950s.* Manchester: Manchester, 1996.

Jensen, Paul M. *The Men Who Made the Monsters.* New York: Twayne, 1996.

Jones, E. Michael. *Monsters from the Id: The Rise of Horror in Fiction and Film*. Dallas: Spence Pub. Co., 2000.

Kendrick, Walter M. *Thrill of Fear*. New York: Grove Weidenfeld, 1991.

Kinnard, Roy. *Horror in Silent Films: A Filmography*. Jefferson, NC: McFarland, 1995.

McCallum, Lawrence. *Italian Horror Films of the 1960s*. Jefferson, NC: McFarland, 1998.

Mank, Gregory W. *Women in Horror Films, 1930s*. Jefferson, NC: McFarland, 1998.

———. *Women in Horror Films, 1940s*. Jefferson, NC: McFarland, 1998.

Maxford, Howard. *The A–Z of Horror Films*. Bloomington: Indiana University, 1997.

Mayo, Mike. *VideoHound's Horror Show: 999 Hair-Raising, Hellish, and Humorous Movies*. Detroit: Visible Ink Press, 1998.

Meikle, Denis. *A History of Horrors: The Rise and Fall of the House of Hammer*. Lanham: Scarecrow, 1996.

Milne, Tom. *The Overlook Film Encyclopedia. Horror*. Woodstock: Overlook, 1994.

Newman, Kim. *BFI Companion to Horror*. London: Cassell, 1996.

Paul, William. *Laughing, Screaming: Modern Hollywood Horror and Comedy*. New York: Columbia, 1994.

Pindedo, Isabel Cristina. *Recreational Terror: Women and the Pleasures of Horror Film Viewing*. Albany: SUNY, 1997.

Rasmussen, Randy Loren. *Children of the Night: The Six Archetypal Characters of Classic Horror Films*. Jefferson, NC: McFarland, 1998.

Sachs, Bruce. *Greasepaint and Gore: The Hammer Monsters of Roy Ashton*. Sheffield: Tomahawk Press, 1998.

Senn, Bryan. *Golden Horrors: An Illustrated Critical Filmography of Terror Cinema, 1931–1939*. Jefferson, NC: McFarland, 1996.

Sevastakis, Michael. *Songs of Love and Death: The Classical American Horror Film of the 1930s*. Westport, CT: Greenwood Press, 1993.

Sherman, Frank. *Cyborgs, Santa Claus and Satan: Science Fiction, Fantasy and Horror Films Made for Television*. Jefferson NC: McFarland, 2000.

Skal, David J. *Hollywood Gothic: The Tangled Web of Dracula from Novel to Stage to Screen*. New York: Norton, 1990.

———. *Monster Show: A Cultural History of Horror*. New York: Norton, 1993.

———. *Screams of Reason: Mad Science and Modern Culture*. New York: Norton, 1998.

?????Don G. *The Poe Cinema: A Critical Filmography of Theatrical Releases Based on the Works of Edgar Allan Poe*. Jefferson, NC: McFarland, 1999.

Smith, Gary A. *Uneasy Dreams: The Golden Age of British Horror Films, 1956–1976*. Jefferson, NC: McFarland, 2000.

Soister, John T. *Of Gods and Monsters: A Critical Guide to Universal Studios' Science Fiction, Horror, and Mystery Films, 1929–1939*. Jefferson, NC: McFarland, 1999.

Stanley, John. *Creature Features: The Science Fiction, Fantasy, and Horror Movie Guide*. Updated ed. New York: Berkley Boulevard Books, 2000.

Stell, John. *Psychos! Sickos! Sequels! Horror Films of the 1980s*. Baltimore: Midnight Marquee Press, 1998.

Stine, Scott Aaron. *The Gorehound's Guide to Splatter Films of the 1960s and 1970s*. Jefferson, NC: McFarland, 2001.

Svehla, Gary J. and Susan, eds. *Son of Guilty Pleasures of the Horror Film*. Baltimore: Midnight Marquee Press, 1998.

Thrower, Stephen. *Beyond Terror: The Films of Lucio Fulci*. Guildford: FAB, 1999.

Tohill, Cathal. *Immoral Tales: Sex and Horror Cinema in Europe*. London: Primitive, 1994.

Watson, Elena M. *Television Horror Hosts: 68 Vampires, Mad Scientists, and Other Denizens of the Late-Night Airwaves Examined and Interviewed*. Jefferson, NC: McFarland, 2000.

Weaver, Tom. *Poverty Row Horrors: Monogram PRC, and Republic Horror Films of the Forties*. Jefferson, NC: McFarland, 1993.

———. *Return of the B Science Fiction and Horror Heroes*. Jefferson, NC: McFarland, 2000.

Weinberg, Robert E. *Horror of the 20th Century: An Illustrated History*. Portland: Collectors Press, 2000.

Williams, Tony. *Hearths of Darkness: The Family in the American Horror Film*. Madison: Fairleigh Dickinson, 1996.

MELODRAMA

Bratton, Jacky et al. *Melodrama: Stage, Picture, Screen*. London: BFI, 1994.

Byars, Jackie. *All that Hollywood Allows: Re-Reading Gender in 1950s Melodrama*. Chapel Hill: University of North Carolina, 1991.

Cavell, Stanley. *Contesting Tears: The Hollywood Melodrama of the Unknown Woman*. Chicago: University of Chicago, 1996.

Dissanayake, Wimal. *Melodrama and Asian Cinema.* Cambridge: Cambridge, 1993.

Klinger, Barbara. *Melodrama and Meaning: History, Culture, and the Films of Douglas Sirk.* Bloomington: Indiana University, 1994.

Landy, Marcia. *Imitations of Life.* Detroit: Wayne State, 1991.

Lang, Robert. *American Film Melodrama: Griffith, Vidor, Minnelli.* Princeton: Princeton, 1989.

MUSICALS

ENCYCLOPEDIAS AND REFERENCE GUIDES

Bradley, Edwin M. *The First Hollywood Musicals.* Jefferson, NC: McFarland, 1996.

Deutsch, Didier C. *MusicHound Soundtracks: The Essential Album Guide.* Detroit: Visible Ink Press, 1999.

Larkin, Colin. *Guinness Who's Who of Film Musicals and Musical Films.* Enfield: Guinness, 1994.

———. *Virgin Encyclopedia of Stage and Film Musicals.* London: Virgin, 1999.

HISTORY AND INTERPRETATION

Altman, Rick. *The American Film Musical.* Bloomington: Indiana University, 1987.

Barrios, Richard. *A Song in the Dark: The Birth of the Musical Film.* New York: Oxford, 1995.

Buhler, James, Caryl Flinn, and David Neumeyer, eds. *Music and Cinema.* Hanover: University Press of New England, 2000.

Citron, Marcia J. *Opera on Screen.* New Haven: Yale University, 2000.

Feuer, Jane. *Hollywood Musical.* 2nd ed. Basingstoke: Macmillan, 1993.

Green, Stanley. *Hollywood Musicals Year by Year.* Milwaukee: H. Leonard, 1990.

Henderson, Amy and Dwight Blocker Bowers. *Red, Hot and Blue: A Smithsonian Salute to the American Musical.* Washington: National Portrait Gallery, 1996.

Hirschhorn, Clive. *Hollywood Musical.* 2nd ed. London: Pyramid, 1991.

Marshall, Bill and Robynn Stilwell, eds. *Musicals: Hollywood and Beyond.* Exeter: Intellect, 2000.

Matthew-Walker, Robert. *From Broadway to Hollywood: The Musical and the Cinema.* London: Sanctuary, 1996.

Mundy, John. *Popular Music on Screen: From the Hollywood Musical to Music Video.* Manchester: Manchester University, 1999.

Parish, James Robert and Michael R. Pitts. *Great Hollywood Musical Pictures.* Metuchen: Scarecrow, 1992.

Rubin, Martin. *Showstoppers: Busby Berkeley and the Tradition of Spectacle.* New York: Columbia, 1993.

Wollen, Peter. *Singin' in the Rain.* London: BFI, 1992.

POLICE FILMS

King, Neal. *Heroes in Hard Times: Cop Action Movies in the U.S.* Philadelphia: Temple University, 1999.

Rafter, Nicole Hahn. *Shots in the Mirror: Crime Films and Society.* Oxford: Oxford University, 2000.

Rubin, Martin. *Thrillers.* Cambridge: Cambridge University, 1999.

RELIGIOUS FILMS

May, John R. *New Image of Religious Film.* Kansas City: Sheed & Ward, 1997.

Miles, Margaret Ruth. *Seeing and Believing: Religion and Values in the Movies.* Boston: Beacon, 1996.

ROAD MOVIES

Cohan, Steven and Ina Rae Hark. *The Road Movie Book.* London: Routledge, 1997.

SCIENCE FICTION

ENCYCLOPEDIAS AND REFERENCE GUIDES

Hardy, Phil. *The Overlook Film Encyclopedia. Science Fiction.* Woodstock: Overlook, 1994.

Holston, Kim R. *Science Fiction, Fantasy, and Horror Films Sequels, Series, and Remakes.* Jefferson, NC: McFarland, 1997.

Iaccino, James F. *Jungian Reflections Within the Cinema: A Psychological Analysis of Sci-Fi and Fantasy Archetypes.* Westport, CT: Praeger, 1998.

Kinnard, Roy. *Science Fiction Serials: A Critical Filmography.* Jefferson, NC: McFarland, 1998.

Lentz, Harris M. *Science Fiction, Horror and Fantasy Film and Television Credits.* Supplement 2. Jefferson, NC: McFarland, 1994.

Mitchell, Charles P. *A Guide to Apocalyptic Cinema.* Westport, CT: Greenwood Press, 2001.

Senn, Bryan and John Johnson. *Fantastic Cinema Subject Guide.* Jefferson, NC: McFarland, 1992.

Sherman, Fraser A. *Cyborgs, Santa Claus and Satan: Science Fiction, Fantasy, and Horror Films Made for Television.* Jefferson, NC: McFarland, 2000.

Soister, John T. *Of Gods and Monsters: A Critical Guide to Universal Studios' Science Fiction, Horror,* and Mystery Films, 1929–1939. Jefferson, NC: McFarland, 1999.

Stanley, John. Creature Features: The Science Fiction, Fantasy, and Horror Movie Guide. Updated ed. New York: Berkley Boulevard Books, 2000.

Young, R. G. Encyclopedia of Fantastic Film. New York: Applause, 1997.

HISTORY AND INTERPRETATION

Booker, M. Keith. Dystopian Literature: A Theory and Research Guide. Westport, CT: Greenwood Press, 1994.

Brosnan, John. The Primal Screen: A History of Science Fiction Film. London: Orbit, 1991.

Clarens, Carlos. Illustrated History of Horror and Science-Fiction Films. New York: Da Capo, 1997.

Fischer, Dennis. Science Fiction Film Directors, 1995–1998. Jefferson, NC: McFarland, 2000.

Galbraith, Stuart. Japanese Science Fiction, Fantasy, and Horror Films. Jefferson, NC: McFarland, 1994.

———. Monsters are Attacking Tokyo! The Incredible World of Japanese Fantasy Films. Venice, CA: Feral House, 1998.

Goldberg, Lee. Science Fiction Filmmaking in the 1980s. Jefferson, NC: McFarland, 1995.

Hardy, Phil. Science Fiction. 3rd ed. London: Aurum, 1995.

Hendershot, Cynthia. Paranoia, the Bomb, and 1950s Science Fiction Films. Bowling Green: Bowling Green State University, 1999.

Hunter, I. Q., ed. British Science Fiction Cinema. London: Routledge, 1999.

Kuhn, Annette. Alien Zone: Cultural Theory and Contemporary Science Fiction. New York: Verso, 1990.

Parish, James Robert and Michael R. Pitts. Great Science Fiction Pictures II. Metuchen: Scarecrow, 1990.

Penley, Constance. Close Encounters: Film, Feminism, and Science Fiction. Minneapolis: University of Minnesota, 1991.

Schelde, Per. Androids, Humanoids, and Other Science Fiction Monsters: Science and Soul in Science Fiction Films. New York: New York University, 1993.

Seed, David. American Science Fiction and the Cold War: Literature and Film. Chicago: Fitzroy Dearborn, 1999.

Sobchack, Vivian Carol. Screening Space: The American Science Fiction Film. 2nd ed. New Brunswick: Rutgers, 1997.

Stocker, Jack H., ed. Chemistry and Science Fiction. Washington, D.C.: American Chemical Society, 1998.

Telotte, J. P. Replications: A Robotic History of the Science Fiction Film. Urbana: University of Illinois, 1995.

Weaver, Tom. Return of the B Science Fiction and Horror Heroes. Jefferson, NC: McFarland Classics, 2000.

———. Science Fiction and Fantasy Film Flashbacks. Jefferson, NC: McFarland, 1998.

Westfahl, Gary, ed. Space and Beyond: The Frontier Theme in Science Fiction. Westport, CT: Greenwood Press, 2000.

Willis, Donald C. Horror and Science Fiction Films IV. Lanham: Scarecrow, 1997.

SOCIAL PROBLEM FILM

Aitkin, Ian. Film and Reform: John Grierson and the Documentary Film Movement. London: Routledge, 1990.

Braendlin, Bonnie and Hans. Authority and Transgression in Literature and Film. Gainesville: University Press of Florida, 1996.

Brownlow, Kevin. Behind the Mask of Innocence. New York: Knopf, 1990.

Roffman, Peter and Jim Purdy. The Hollywood Social Problem Film. Bloomington: Indiana University, 1981.

Sloan, Kay. The Loud Silents: Origins of the Social Problem Film. Urbana: University of Illinois, 1988.

SOUTH SEA ISLAND FILMS

Langman, Larry. Return to Paradise: A Guide to South Sea Island Films. Lanham, MD: Scarecrow Press, 1998.

SPORTS FILMS

Chandler, David. Boxer: An Anthology of Writings on Boxing and Visual Culture. Cambridge: MIT, 1996.

Tudor, Deborah V. Hollywood's Vision of Team Sports: Heroes, Race, and Gender. New York: Garland, 1997.

SPY FILMS

Black, Jeremy. The Politics of James Bond: From Fleming's Novels to the Big Screen. Westport, CT: Praeger, 2001.

Langman, Larry and David Ebner. *An Encyclopedia of American Spy Films*. New York: Garland, 1990.

Mavis, Paul. *The Espionage Filmography: A Complete Guide to Spy Movies*. Jefferson, NC: McFarland, 2000.

Rubin, Martin. *Thrillers*. Cambridge: Cambridge University, 1999.

WAR FILM

BIBLIOGRAPHIES

Wetta, Frank Joseph and Stephen J. Curley. *Celluloid Wars*. New York: Greenwood Press, 1992.

CATALOGS

Mayo, Mike. *VideoHound's War Movies: Classic Conflict on Film*. Detroit: Visible Ink, 1999.

GENERAL WORKS

Guttmacher, Peter. *Legendary War Movies*. New York: MetroBooks, 1996.

Paris, Michael. *From the Wright Brothers to Top Gun: Aviation, Nationalism and Popular Cinema*. Manchester: Manchester, 1995.

Parish, James Robert. *The Great Combat Pictures: Twentieth-Century Warfare on the Screen*. Metuchen: Scarecrow, 1990.

Quirk, Lawrence J. *The Great War Films*. Secaucus: Carol, 1994.

Suid, Lawrence H. *Guts and Glory: Great American War Movies*. Reading: Addison-Wesley, 1978.

————. *Sailing on the Silver Screen: Hollywood and the U.S. Navy*. Annapolis: Naval Institute, 1996.

CIVIL WAR

Kinnard, Roy. *The Blue and the Gray on the Silver Screen*. Secaucus: Carol, 1996.

VIETNAM WAR

Anderegg, Michael. *Inventing Vietnam: The War in Film and Television*. Philadelphia: Temple, 1991.

Auster, Albert and Leonard Quart. *How the War Was Remembered: Hollywood and Vietnam*. Westport, CT: Praeger, 1988.

Devine, Jeremy M. *Vietnam at 24 Frames a Second*. Jefferson: NC: McFarland, 1994.

Dittmar, Linda and Gene Michaud. *From Hanoi to Hollywood: The Vietnam War in American Film*. New Brunswick: Rutgers, 1990.

Gilman, Owen W., Jr. and Lorrie Smith. *America Rediscovered: Critical Essays on Literature and Film of the Vietnam War*. New York: Garland, 1990.

Hellmann, John. *American Myth and the Legacy of Vietnam*. New York: Columbia, 1986.

Hillstrom, Kevin. *The Vietnam Experience*. Westport, CT: Greenwood Press, 1998.

Muse, Eben J. *The Land of Nam: The Vietnam War in American Film*. Metuchen: Scarecrow, 1995.

Rowe, John Carlos and Rick Berg. *The Vietnam War and American Culture*. New York: Columbia, 1991.

Walker, Mark. *Vietnam Veteran Films*. Metuchen: Scarecrow, 1991.

WORLD WAR I

Campbell, Craig. *Reel American and World War I*. Jefferson, NC: McFarland, 1985.

DeBauche, Leslie Midkiff. *Reel Patriotism: The Movies and World War I*. Madison: University of Wisconsin, 1997.

Isenberg, Michael T. *War on Film: The American Cinema and World War I*. Rutherford: Fairleigh Dickinson, 1981.

Kelly, Andrew. *Cinema and the Great War*. London: Routledge, 1997.

Ward, Larry Wayne. *The Motion Picture Goes to War: The U.S. Government Film Effort During World War I*. Ann Arbor: UMI, 1985.

WORLD WAR II

Basinger, Jeanine. *The World War II Combat Film*. New York: Columbia, 1986.

Dick, Bernard F. *The Star-Spangled Screen: The American World War II Film*. Lexington: University Press of Kentucky, 1985.

Doherty, Thomas Patrick. *Projections of War: Hollywood, American Culture, and World War II*. New York: Columbia, 1993.

Fyne, Robert. *Hollywood Propaganda of World War II*. Metuchen: Scarecrow, 1994.

Kane, Kathryn. *Visions of War: The Hollywood Combat Films of World War II*. Ann Arbor: UMI, 1982.

WESTERNS

ACTORS

Nott, Robert. *Last of the Cowboy Heroes: The Westerns of Randolph Scott, Joel McCrea, and Audie Murphy*. Jefferson, NC: McFarland, 2000.

Koszarski, Diane Kaiser. *The Complete Films of William S. Hart: A Pictorial Record*. New York: Dover Publications, 1980.

JOHN WAYNE

Davis, Ronald L. *Duke: The Life and Image of John Wayne.* Norman: University of Oklahoma Press, 1998.

Fagen, Herb. *Duke, We're Glad We Knew You.* New York: Carol Pub. Group, 1996.

McGhee, Richard D. *John Wayne: Actor, Artist, Hero.* Jefferson, NC; London: McFarland, 2000.

Roberts, Randy and James S. Olson. *John Wayne: American.* New York: The Free Press, 1995.

Wills, Garry. *John Wayne's America: The Politics of Celebrity.* New York: Simon & Schuster, 1997.

BIBLIOGRAPHIES

Nachbar, John G. *Western Films: An Annotated Critical Bibiliography.* New York: Garland Pub., 1975.

Nachbar, John G., Jackie R. Donath, and Chris Foran. *Western Films 2: An Annotated Critical Bibliography from 1974 to 1987.* New York: Garland Pub., 1988.

BIOGRAPHICAL DIRECTORIES

Katchmer, George A. *A Biographical Dictionary of Silent Film Western Actors and Actresses.* Jefferson, NC: McFarland, 2000.

CREDITS

Lentz, Harris M., III. *Western and Frontier Film and Television Credits, 1903–1995.* Jefferson, NC: McFarland, 1996.

EUROPEAN HISTORIES AND INTERPRETATIONS OF WESTERNS

Bertelsen, Martin. *Roadmovies und Western: Ein Vergleich zur Genre-estimmung des Roadmovies.* Ammersbek bei Hamburg: Verlag an der Lottbek, 1991.

Brion, Patrick. *Le Western: Classiques, Chefs-D'Oeuvre et Decouvertes.* Paris: Editions de La Martiniere, 1992.

De Luca, Lorenzo. *C'era una Vlta il Western Italiano.* Roma: Istituto Bibliographico Napoleone, 1987.

Di Claudio, Gianni. *Il Cinema Western.* Chieti: Libreria Uniersitaria Editrice, 1986.

Gaberscel. Carlo. *Il West di John Ford.* Tavagnacco: Arti Grafiche Friulane, 1994.

Hanisch, Michael. *Western: Die Entwicklung Eines Filmgenres.* Berlin: Henschelverlag Kunst und Gesellschaft, 1984.

Hembus, Joe. *Western-Geschichte, 1540 bis 1894: Chronologie, Mythologie, Filmographie.* Munchen: C. Hanser, 1979.

———. *Western-Lexikon: 1272 Filme von 1894–1975.* Munchen: Hanser Verlag, 1976.

Jeier, Thomas. *Der Westernfilm.* Munchen: Wilhelm Heyne, 1987.

Kartseva, E. *Vestern: Evoliutsiia Zhanra.* Moskva: Iskusstvo, 1976.

Kezich, Tullio. *Il Mito del Far West.* 2nd ed. Milano: Il Formichiere, 1980.

Leguebe, Eric. *Histoire Universelle du Western.* Paris: Editions France-Empire, 1989.

Leutrat, Jean Louis. *L'Alliance Brisee: Le Western des Annees 1920.* Lyon: Presses Universitaires de Lyon: Institute Lumiere, 1985.

———. *Le Western: Archeologie d'un Genre.* Lyon: Presses Universitaires de Lyon, 1987.

Leutrat, Jean Louis and S. Liandrat-Guigues. *Les Cartes de l'Ouest: Un Genre Cinemaographique, Le Western.* Paris: A. Colin, 1990.

Mauduy, Jacques and Gerard Henriet. *Gographies du Western: Une Nation en Marche.* Paris: Nathan, 1989.

Morin, Georges Henry. *Le Cercle Brise: L'Image de L'Indien Dans Le Western.* Paris: Payot, 1977.

Moscati, Massimo. *Western All'Italiana.* Milano: Pan, 1978.

Seesslen, Georg. *Western: Geschichte und Mythologie des Westernfilms.* Marburg: Schuren, 1995.

———. *Western-Kino.* Reinbek bei Hamburg: Rowohlt, 1979.

FILMOGRAPHY

Blottner, Gene. *Universal-International Westerns, 1947–1963: The Complete Filmography.* Jefferson, NC: McFarland, 2000.

Eyles, Allen. *The Western.* South Brunswick: A.S. Barnes, 1975.

FILM ADAPTATIONS

Hitt, Jim. *The American West From Fiction (1823–1976) into Film (1909–1986).* Jefferson, NC: McFarland, 1990.

HISTORIES AND INTERPRETATIONS

Bull, Debby. *Hillbilly Hollywood: The Origins of Country and Western Style: Featuring the Vintage Costume Collection of Marty Stuart.* New York, NY: Rizzoli, 2000.

Calder, Jenni. *There Must Be a Lone Ranger.* London: Hamilton, 1974.

Cameron, Ian and Douglas Pye, ed. *The Movie Book of the Western.* London: Studio Vista, 1996.

Canfield, J. Douglas. *Mavericks on the Border: The Early Southwest in Historical Fiction and Film.* Lexington: University Press of Kentucky, 2001.

Cawelti, John G. *The Six-Gun Mystique.* Bowling Green, OH: Bowling Green University Popular Press, 1971.

———. *The Six-gun Mystique Sequel.* Bowling Green, OH: Bowling Green State University Popular Press, 1999.

Coyne, Michael. *The Crowded Prairie: American National Identity in the Hollywood Western.* London; New York: I.B. Tauris; [New York: distributed by St. Martin's Press], 1997.

Davis, Robert Murray. *Playing Cowboys: Low Culture and High Art in the Western.* Norman: University of Oklahoma Press, 1991.

Everson, William K. *The Hollywood Western.* Secuaucus, NJ: Carol Pub., 1992.

Fenin, George N. and William K. Everson. *The Western: From Silents to the Seventies.* Rev. ed. New York: Penguin Books, 1977.

French, Peter A. *Cowboy Metaphysics: Ethics and Death in Westerns.* Lanham: Rowman & Littlefield, 1997.

French, Philip. *Westerns: Aspects of a Movie Genre.* Rev. ed. New York: Oxford University Press, 1977.

Hamilton, John R. and John Calvin Batchelor. *Thunder in the Dust: Classic Images of Western Movies.* New York: Stewart, Tabori & Chang: Distributed by Workman Pub., 1987.

Hitt, Jim. *The American West from Fiction (1823–1976) into Film (1909–1986).* Jefferson, NC: McFarland, 1990.

Jacobs, Del. *Revisioning Film Traditions: The Pseudo-documentary and the Neo-Western.* Lewiston, NY: Mellen Press, 2000.

Lenihan, John H. *Showdown: Confronting Modern America in the Western Film.* Urbana: University of Illinois Press, 1980.

McDonald, Archie P., ed. *Shooting Stars: Heroes and Heroines of Western Film.* Bloomington: Indiana University Press, 1987.

Meyer, William R. *The Making of the Great Westerns.* New Rochelle, NY: Arlington House, 1979.

Mitchell, Lee Clark. *A Man Is Being Beaten: Constructing Masculinity in the American Western.* [Berlin: John-F. Kennedy-Institut fur Nordamerikastudien, 1993].

———. *Westerns: Making the Man in Fiction and Film.* Chicago: University of Chicago Press, 1996.

Nachbar, John G., comp. *Focus on the Western.* Englewood Cliffs, NJ: Prentice-Hall, 1974.

O'Neil, Paul and the editors of Time-Life Books. *The End and the Myth.* Alexandria, VA: Time-Life Books, 1979.

Parish, James Robert and Michael R. Pitts. *The Great Western Pictures.* Metuchen, NJ: Scarecrow Press, 1976.

———. *Great Western Pictures II.* Metuchen, NJ: Scarecrow Press, 1988.

Parks, Rita. *The Western Hero in film and Television: Mass Media Mythology.* Ann Arbor: UMI Research Press, 1982.

Pilkington, William T. and Don Graham, ed. *Western Movies.* Albuquerque: University of New Mexico Press, 1979.

Rainey, Buck. *The Reel Cowboy: Essays on the Myth in Movies and Literature.* Jefferson, NC: McFarland, 1996.

———. *Western Gunslingers in Fact and on Film: Hollywood's Famous Lawmen and Outlaws.* Jefferson, NC: McFarland & Company, 1998.

Rothel, David. *Those Great Cowboy Sidekicks.* Metuchen, NJ: Scarecrow Press, 1984.

Sarf, Wayne Michael. *God Bless You, Buffalo Bill: A Layman's Guide to History and the Western Film.* Rutherford, NJ: Fairleigh Dickinson, 1983.

Short, John R. *Imagined Country: Environment, Culture, and Society.* London: Routledge, Chapman and Hall, 1991.

Slotkin, Richard. *Gunfighter Nation: The Myth of the Frontier in Twentieth-Century America.* New York: Atheneum, 1992.

Sullivan, Tom R. *Cowboys and Caudillos: Frontier Ideology of the Americas.* Bowling Green, OH: Bowling Green State University Popular Press, 1990.

Thomas, Tony. *The West that Never Was.* New York: Carol Communications, 1989.

Tompkins, Jane P. *West of Everything: The Inner Life of Westerns.* New York: Oxford University Press, 1992.

Turner, Ralph Lamar and Robert J. Higgs. *The Cowboy Way: The Western Leader in Film, 1945–1995.* Westport, CT: Greenwood Press, 1999.

Tuska, Jon. *The American West in Film: Critical Approaches to the Western.* Westport, CT: Greenwood Press, 1985.

————. *The Filming of the West.* Garden City, NY: Doubleday, 1976.

Walle, Alf H. *The Cowboy Hero and Its Audience: Popular Culture as Market Derived Art.* Bowling Green: Bowling Green State University Popular Press, 2000.

Wallmann, Jeffrey M. *The Western: Parables of the American Dream.* Lubbock, Texas: Texas Tech University Press, 1999.

Wright, Will. *Six Guns and Society: A Structural Study of the Western.* Berkeley: University of California, 1975.

Yoggy, Gary A., ed. *Back in the Saddle: Essays on Western Film and Television Actors.* Jefferson, NC: McFarland & Co., 1998.

MASCULINITY IN WESTERNS

Mitchell, Lee Clark. *Westerns: Making the Man in Fiction and Film.* Chicago: University of Chicago Press, 1996.

MEMOIRS AND INTERVIEWS

Fagen, Herb. *White Hats and Silver Spurs: Interviews with 24 Stars of Film and Television Westerns of the Thirties Through the Sixties.* Jefferson, NC: McFarland, 1996.

Fraser, Harry. *I Went That-a-way: The Memoirs of a Western Film Director.* Edited by Wheeler W. Dixon and Audrey Brown Fraser. Metuchen, NJ: Scarecrow Press, 1990.

PRODUCERS AND DIRECTORS

Fraser, Harry. *I Went That-a-Way: The Memoirs of a Western Film Director.* Edited by Wheeler W. Dixon and Audrey Brown Fraser. Metuchen, NJ: Scarecrow Press, 1990.

Kites, Demetrius John. *Horizons West: Anthony Mann, Budd Boetticher, Sam Peckinpah, Studies of Authorship within the Western.* Bloomington: Indiana University, 1970.

Place, Janey Ann. *The Western Films of John Ford.* Secaucus: Citadel Press, 1974.

Seydor, Paul. *Peckinpah: The Western Films.* Urbana: University of Illinois Press, 1980.

REFERENCE GUIDES AND ENCYCLOPEDIAS

Adams, Les and Buck Rainey. *Shoot-Em Ups: The Complete Reference Guide to Westerns of the Sound Era.* New Rochelle, NY: Arlington House Pub., 1978.

Buscombe, Edward, ed. *The BFI Companion to the Western.* London: A. Deutsch, 1988.

Garfield, Brian. *Western Films: A Complete Guide.* New York: Da Capo Press, 1982.

Hardy, Phil, ed. *The Overlook Film Encyclopedia: The Western.* Woodstock, NY: Overlook Press, 1994.

Hardy, Phil. *The Western.* Rev. updated ed. London: Aurum, 1991.

Holland, Ted. *B Western Actors Encyclopedia: Facts, Photos, and Filmographies for More than 250 Familiar Faces.* Jefferson, NC: McFarland, 1989.

SILENT WESTERNS

Brownlow, Kevin. *The War, the West, and the Wilderness.* New York: Knopf, 1979.

Langman, Larry. *A Guide to Silent Westerns.* New York: Greenwood Press, 1992.

SINGING COWBOYS

Rothel, David. *The Singing Cowboys.* South Brunswick, NJ: A.S. Barnes, 1978.

SPAGHETTI WESTERNS

Frayling, Christopher. *Spaghetti Westerns: Cowboys and Europeans from Karl May to Sergio Leone.* Rev. Ed. London: I.B. Tauris, 1998.

Weisser, Thomas. *Spaghetti Westerns: The Good, the Bad, and the Violent: A Comprehensive, Illustrated Filmography of 558 Eurowesterns and their Personnel, 1961–1977.* Jefferson, NC: McFarland, 1992.

TELEVISION WESTERNERS

Jackson, Ronald. *Classic TV Westerns: A Pictorial History.* Secaucus, NJ: Carol Pub. Group, 1994.

TREATMENT OF INDIANS

Bataille, Gretchen M. and Charles L. P. Silet, eds. *The Pretend Indians: Images of Native Americans in the Movies.* Ames: Iowa State University Press, 1980.

——. *Images of Amerian Indians on Film: An Annotated Bibliography*. New York: Garland, 1985.

Churchill, Ward. *Fantasies of the Master Race: Literature, Cinema, and the Colonization of American Indians*. San Francisco: City Lights Books, 1998.

Friar, Ralph E. and Natasha A. Friar. *The Only Good Indian*. New York: Drama Book Specialists, 1972.

Deloria, Phil. *Playing Indian*. New Haven: 1998.

Hilger, Michael. *The American Indian in Film*. Metuchen, NJ: Scarecrow Press, 1986.

——. *From Savage to Nobleman: Images of Native Americans in Film*. Lanham, MD: Scarecrow Press, 1996.

Kilpatrick, Jacquelyn. *Celluloid Indians: Native Americans and Film*. Lincoln: University of Nebraska Press, 1999.

O'Connor, John E. *The Hollywood Indian*. Trenton, NJ: New Jersey State Museum, 1980.

Owens, Louis. *Mixedblood Messages: Literature, Film, Family, Place*. Norman: University of Oklahoma, 1998.

Peter C. Rollins and John E. O'Connor, eds. *Hollywood's Indian: The Portrayal of the Native American in Film*. Lexington: University Press of Kentucky, 1998.

WOMEN IN WESTERNS

Lackmann, Ronald W. *Women of the Western Frontier in Fact, Fiction, and Film*. Jefferson, NC: McFarland, 1997.

ETHNICITY IN AMERICAN FILM

GENERAL WORKS

Friedman, Lester D. *Unspeakable Images: Ethnicity and the American Cinema*. Urbana: University of Illinois, 1991.

Gevinson, Alan. *Within Our Gates: Ethnicity in American Feature Films, 1911–1960*. Berkeley: University of California, 1997.

Miller, Randall M. *The Kaleidoscopic Lens: How Hollywood Views Ethnic Groups*. Englewood: Ozer, 1980.

Pease, Donald E. *National Identities and Post-Americanist Narratives*. Durham: Duke, 1994.

Toplin, Robert Brent. *Hollywood as Mirror: Changing Views of "Outsiders" and "Enemies" in American Movies*. Westport, CT: Greenwood Press, 1993.

Woll, Allen L. and Randall M. Miller. *Ethnic and Racial Images in American Film and Television*. New York: Garland, 1988.

AFRICAN AMERICANS AND FILM

BIBLIOGRAPHY

Gray, John. *Blacks in Film and Television*. New York: Greenwood Press, 1990.

ENCYCLOPEDIAS

Bogle, Donald. *Blacks in American Films and Television*. New York: Garland.

FILMOGRAPHY

Klotman, Phyllis Rauch and Gloria J. Gibson. *Frame by Frame II: A Filmography of the African American Image*. Bloomington: Indiana University, 1997.

Richards, Larry. *African American Films Through 1959*. Jefferson, NC: McFarland, 1998.

AFRICAN AMERICAN FILMMAKING

Dash, Julie. *Daughters of the Dust: The Making of an African American Woman's Film*. New York: New Press, 1992.

Lee, Spike. *Five for Five: The Films of Spike Lee*. New York: Stewart, Tabori & Chang, 1991.

Walker, Alice. *The Same River Twice*. New York: Scribner, 1996.

HISTORY, CRITICISM, AND INTERPRETATION

Anderson, Lisa M. *Mammies No More: The Changing Image of Black Women on Stage and Screen*. Lanham: Rowman & Littlefield, 1997.

Berry, Venise T. and Carmen L. Manning-Miller. *Mediated Messages and African American Culture*. Thousand Oaks: Sage, 1996.

Bobo, Jacqueline. *Black Women as Cultural Readers*. New York: Columbia, 1995.

Bogle, Donald. *Toms, Coons, Mulattoes, Mammies and Bucks: An Interpretive History of Blacks in American Films*. 3rd ed. New York: Continuum, 1994.

Bourne, Stephen. *Blacks in the British Frame: Black People in British Film and Television, 1896–1996*.

London: Arts Council of England, 1998.

Cripps, Thomas R. *Black Film as Genre*. Bloomington: Indiana University, 1978.

———. *Making Movies Black: The Hollywood Message Movies from World War II to the Civil Rights Era*. New York: Oxford, 1992.

———. *Slow Fade to Black: The Negro in American Film, 1900–1942*. Oxford: Oxford University, 1993.

Diawara, Mathia. *Black American Cinema*. New York: Routledge, 1993.

Gaines, Jane M. *Fire and Desire: Mixed-Race Movies in the Silent Era*. Chicago: University of Chicago Press, 2001.

George, Nelson. *Blackface: Reflections on African Americans and the Movies*. New York: HarperCollins, 1994.

Grayson, Sandra M. *Symbolizing the Past: Reading Sankofa, Daughters of the Dust, and Eve's Bayou as Histories*. Lanham, MD: University Press of America, 2000.

Guerrero, Edward. *Framing Blackness: The African American Image in Film*. Philadelphia: Temple, 1993.

James, Darius. *That's Blaxploitation!* New York: St. Martin's, 1995.

Jones, G. William. *Black Cinema Treasures: Lost and Found*. Denton: North Texas, 1991.

Klotman, Phyllis R. and Janet K. Cutler, eds. *Struggles for Representation: African American Documentary Film and Video*. Bloomington: Indiana University, 1999.

Leab, Daniel J. *From Sambo to Superspade: The Black Experience in Motion Pictures*. Boston: Houghton, Mifflin, 1975.

Martin, Michael T. *Cinemas of the Black Diaspora*. Detroit: Wayne State, 1995.

Martinez, Gerald. *What It Is, What It Was! The Black Film Explosion of the '70s*. New York: Hyperion, 1998.

Null, Gary. *Black Hollywood: From 1970 to Today*. Secaucus: Carol, 1993.

Reid, Mark A. *Redefining Black Film*. Berkeley: University of California, 1993.

Rhines, Jesse Algernon. *Black Film, White Money*. New Brunswick: Rutgers, 1996.

Ross, Karen. *Black and White Media: Black Images in Popular Film and Television*. Cambridge: Polity, 1996.

Sampson, Henry T. *Blacks in Black and White*. 2nd ed. Metuchen: Scarecrow, 1995.

———. *That's Enough, Folks: Black Images in Animated Cartoons, 1900–1960*. Lanham: Scarecrow, 1998.

Smith, Valerie. *Not Just Race, Not Just Gender: Black Feminist Readings*. New York: Routledge, 1998.

———. *Representing Blackness: Issues in Film and Video*. New Brunswick: Rutgers, 1997.

Snead, James A. *White Screens, Black Images*. New York: Routledge, 1994.

Taylor, Clyde. *The Mask of "Art": Breaking the Aesthetic Contract—Film and Literature*. Bloomington: Indiana University, 1998.

Watkins, Samuel Craig. *Representing: Hip Hop Culture and the Production of Black Cinema*. Chicago: University of Chicago, 1998.

Willis, Sharon. *High Contrast: Race and Gender in Contemporary Hollywood Film*. Durham: Duke, 1997.

Yearwood, Gladstone Lloyd. *Black Film as a Signifying Practice: Cinema, Narration and the African American Aesthetic Tradition*. Trenton: Africa World Press, 2000.

Young, Lola. *Fear of the Dark: "Race," Gender and Sexuality in the Cinema*. London: Routledge, 1996.

FILM POSTERS

Kisch, John. *A Separate Cinema: Fifty Years of Black-Cast Posters*. New York: Farrar, Straus, and Giroux, 1992.

ASIAN AMERICANS AND ASIANS IN FILM

Hamamoto, Darrell Y. and Sandra Liu, eds. *Countervisions: Asian-American Film Criticism*. Philadelphia: Temple University, 2000.

Hsing, Chun. *Asian America Through the Lens: History, Representations, Identity*. Walnut Creek: AltaMira, 1998.

Marchetti, Gina. *Romance and the "Yellow Peril": Race, Sex and Discursive Strategies in Hollywood Fiction*. Berkeley: University of California, 1993.

Masavisut, Nitaya et al. *Gender and Culture in Literature and Film East and West*. Honolulu: East-West Center, 1994.

IRISH AMERICANS AND FILM

Curran, Joseph M. *Hibernian Green on the Silver Screen*. New York: Greenwood Press, 1989.

Gribben, Arthur. *Images of the Irish and Irish Americans in Commercial and Ethnographic Film*. Boston:

Northeastern, 1987.

Lourdeaux, Lee. *Italian and Irish Filmmakers in America*. Philadelphia: Temple, 1990.

Rockett, Kevin. *Irish Filmography: Fiction Films, 1896–1996*. Dublin: Red Mountain, 1996.

———. *Still Irish: A Century of the Irish in Film*. Dublin: Red Mountain, 1995.

ITALIAN AMERICANS AND FILM

Giordano, Paolo A. and Anthony Julian Tamburri. *Beyond the Margin: Readings in Italian Americana*. Madison: Fairleigh Dickinson, 1998.

Lourdeaux, Lee. *Italian and Irish Filmmakers in America*. Philadelphia: Temple, 1990.

JEWS AND FILM

GUIDES

Ankelwicz, Larry. *Guide to Jewish Films on Video*. Hoboken: Ktav Pub. House, 2000.

Bernheimer, Kathryn. *The 50 Greatest Jewish Movies*. Secaucus, NJ: Carol Publishing, 1998.

Plotkin, Janice et al., eds. *Independent Jewish Film: A Resource Guide*. 4th ed. San Francisco: San Francisco Jewish Film Festival, 2000.

HISTORY AND INTERPRETATION

Broderick, Peter. *Precious Images, Provocative Conversations: A Handbook for Film Groups*. New York: Jewish Media Fund, 1998.

Cohen, Sarah Blacher. *From Hester Street to Hollywood*. Bloomington: Indiana University, 1983.

Erens, Patricia. *The Jew in American Cinema*. Bloomington: Indiana University, 1984.

Friedman, Lester J. *The Jewish Image in American Film*. Secaucus: Citadel, 1987.

Rogin, Michael Paul. *Blackface, White Noise: Jewish Immigrants in the Hollywood Melting Pot*. Berkeley: University of California, 1996.

Samberg, Joel. *Reel Jewish*. Middle Village, NY: Jonathan David Pub., 2000.

Wright, Rochelle. *The Visible Wall: Jews and Other Ethnic Outsiders in Swedish Film*. Carbondale: Southern Illinois University Press, 1998.

JEWISH FILMMAKERS

Desser, David and Lester D. Friedman. *American-Jewish Filmmakers: Traditions and Trends*. Urbana: University of Illinois, 1993.

Gabler, Neal. *An Empire of Their Own: How the Jews Invented Hollywood*. New York: Crown, 1988.

LATINOS/LATINAS AND FILM

Baraarisse, Pamela. *Carnal Knowledge: Essays on the Flesh, Sex and Sexuality in Hispanic Letters and Film*. Pittsburgh: Ediciones Tres Rios, 1993.

Berumen, Frank Javier Garcia. *The Chicano/Hispanic Image in American Film*. New York: Vantage Press, 1995.

Fregoso, Rosa Linda. *The Bronze Screen: Chicana and Chicano Film Culture*. Minneapolis: University of Minnesota, 1993.

Hadley-Garcia, George. *Hispanic Hollywood*. New York: Carol, 1990.

Keller, Gary D. *Chicano Cinema: Research, Reviews, and Resources*. Binghamton: Bilingual Review/ Press, 1985.

———. *Hispanics and United States Film*. Tempe: Bilingual Press, 1994.

Limon, Jose Eduardo. *American Encounters: Greater Mexico, the United States, and the Erotics of Culture*. Boston: Beacon, 1998.

List, Christine. *Chicano Images: Refiguring Ethnicity in Mainstream Film*. New York: Garland, 1996.

Noriega, Chon A. *Chicanos and Film*. New York: Garland, 1992.

———. *Shot in America: Television, the State, and the Rise of Chicano Cinema*. Minneapolis: University of Minnesota, 2000.

Noriega, Chon A. and Ana M. Lopez. *The Ethnic Eye: Latino Media Arts*. Minneapolis: University of Minnesota, 1996.

Pettit, Arthur G. *Images of the Mexican American in Fiction and Film*. College Station: Texas A&M University, 1980.

Ranucci, Karen and Julie Feldman. *A Guide to Latin American, Caribbean, and U.S. Latino-Made Film and Video*. Lanham, MD: Scarecrow, 1998.

Reyes, Luis, and Peter Rubie. *Hispanics in Hollywood: An Encyclopedia of Film and Television*. New York: Garland, 1994.

Richard, Alfred Charles. *Contemporary Hollywood's Negative Hispanic Image*. Westport, CT: Greenwood Press, 1994.

———. *The Hispanic Image on the Silver Screen*. New York: Greenwood Press, 1992.

Rios-Bustamante, Antonio Jose. *Latinos in Hollywood.* Encino: Floricanto, 1991.

NATIVE AMERICANS AND FILM

Bataille, Gretchen M. and Charles L. P. Silet. *The Pretend Indian: Images of Native Americans in the Movies.* Ames: Iowa State, 1980.

Churchill, Ward. *Fantasies of the Master Race: Literature, Cinema, and the Colonization of American Indians.* San Francisco: City Lights, 1998.

Hilger, Michael. *From Savage to Nobleman: Images of Native Americans in Film.* Lanham: Scarecrow, 1995.

Kilpatrick, Jacqueline. *Celluloid Indians: Native Americans and Film.* Lincoln: University of Nebraska, 1999.

Morris, Rosalind Carmel. *New Worlds from Fragments: Film, Ethnography, and the Representation of Northwest Coast Cultures.* Boulder: Westview, 1994.

Owens, Louis. *Mixedblood Messages: Literature, Film, Family, Place.* Norman: University of Oklahoma, 1998.

Rollins, Peter C. and John E. O'Connor. *Hollywood's Indian.* Lexington: University Press of Kentucky, 1998.

WORLD CINEMA

BOOKS IN ENGLISH PUBLISHED SINCE 1989
GENERAL WORKS

Higson, Andrew and Richard Maltby. *"Film Europe" and "Film America": Cinema, Commerce, and Cultural Exchange, 1920–1939.* Exeter: Exeter University, 1999.

Hjort, Mette and Scott MacKenzie, eds. *Cinema and Nation.* London: Routledge, 2000.

Kindem, Gorham. *The International Movie Industry.* Carbondale: Southern Illinois University, 2000.

Nowell-Smith, Geoffrey and Steven Ricci. *Hollywood and Europe: Economics, Culture, and National Identity, 1945–95.* London: BFI Publishing, 1998.

Puttnam, David. *Movies and Money.* New York: Knopf, 1998.

AFRICAN FILM

Bakari, Imruh and Mbye B. Cham. *African Experiences of Cinema.* London: BFI, 1996.

Boughedir, Ferid. *African Cinema from A to Z.* Brussels: OCIC, 1992.

Davis, Peter. *In Darkest Hollywood: Exploring the Jungles of Cinema's South Africa.* Athens: Ohio University, 1996.

Diawara, Manthia. *African Cinema: Politics and Culture.* Bloomington: Indiana University, 1992.

Ekwuazi, Hyginus. *Film in Nigeria.* 2nd ed. Jos: Nigerian Film Corp., 1991.

Givanni, June, ed. *Symbolic Narrative/African Cinema: Audiences, Theory, and the Moving Image.* London: British Film Institute, 2000.

Gray, John. *Blacks in Film and Television: A Pan-African Bibliography.* New York: Greenwood Press, 1990.

Malkmus, Lizbeth and Roy Armes. *Arab and African Film Making.* London: Atlantic Highlands, 1991.

Martin, Michael T. *Cinemas of the Black Diaspora.* Detroit: Wayne State, 1995.

Russell, Sharon A. *Guide to African Cinema.* Westport, CT: Greenwood Press, 1990.

Schmidt, Nancy J. *Sub-Saharan African Films and Filmmakers, 1987–1992: An Annotated Bibliography.* London: Hans Zell, 1994.

Shiri, Keith. *Directory of African Film-makers and Films.* Trowbridge: Flicks, 1992.

Ukadike, Nwachukwu Frank. *Black African Cinema.* Berkeley: University of California, 1994.

Vieler-Porter, Chris. *Black and Third World Cinema: A Film and Television Bibliography.* London: BFI, 1991.

ARAB FILM

Arasoughly, Alia. *Screens of Life: Critical Film Writing from the Arab World.* St-Hyacinthe, Quebec: World Heritage Press, 1996.

Malkmus, Lizbeth and Roy Armes. *Arab and African Filmmaking.* London: Atlantic Highlands, 1991.

ASIAN FILM

Dissanayake, Wimal. *Colonialism and Nationalism in Asian Cinema.* Bloomington: Indiana University, 1994.

———. *Melodrama and Asian Cinema.* Cambridge: Cambridge, 1993.

Server, Lee. *Asian Pop Cinema: Bombay to Tokyo.* San Francisco: Chronicle, 1999.

AUSTRALIAN FILM

Craven, Ian, ed. *Australian Cinema in the 1990s.* London: Frank Cass, 2000.

Jennings, Karen. *Sites of Difference: Cinematic Representations of Aboriginality and Gender.* South Melbourne, Vic.: Australian Film Institute, 1993.

McFarlane, Brian and Geoff Mayer. *New Australian Cinema.* Cambridge: Cambridge, 1992.

Molloy, Bruce. *Before the Interval: Australian Mythology and Feature Films.* St. Lucia, Qld: Queensland, 1990.

Murray, Scott. *Australian Film*. St. Leonards, NSW: Allen & Unwin, 1994.

O'Regan, Tom. *Australian National Cinema*. London: Routledge, 1996.

Rattigan, Neil. *Images of Australia*. Dallas: SMU, 1991.

Sabine, James. *A Century of Australian Cinema*. Port Melborne, Vic.: Heinemann Australia, 1995.

Turner, Graeme. *National Fictions: Literature, Film, and the Construction of Australian Narrative*. 2nd ed. St. Leonards, NSW: Allen & Unwin, 1993.

BOLIVIAN FILM

Sanchez-H, Jose. *The Art and Politics of Bolivian Cinema*. Lanham, MD: Scarecrow Press, 1999.

BRITISH FILM

CATALOGS AND INDICES

Gifford, Denis, ed. *The British Film Catalog*. 3rd ed. London: Fitzroy Dearborn, 1999.

Goble, Alan, ed. *The Complete Index to British Sound Film Since 1928*. London: Bowker Saur, 1999.

DOCUMENT COLLECTIONS

Street, Sarah. *British Cinema in Documents*. London: Routledge, 2000.

HISTORY AND INTERPRETATIONS

Aldgate, Anthony and Jeffrey Richards. *Britain Can Take It: The British Cinema in the Second World War*. 2nd ed. Edinburgh: Edinburgh, 1994.

Ashby, Justine and Andrew Higson, eds. *British Cinema, Past and Present*. London: Routledge, 2000.

Barnes, John. *The Beginnings of the Cinema in England*. Rev. ed. Exeter: Exeter, 1998.

———. *Filming the Boer War*. London: Bishopsgate, 1990.

Barr, Charles. *Ealing Studios*. 3rd ed. London: Studio Vista, 1998.

Berry, David. *Wales and Cinema: The First Hundred Years*. Cardiff: Wales, 1994.

Bourne, Stephen. *Black in the British Frame: Black People in British Film and Television, 1896–1996*. London: Cassell, 1998.

———. *Brief Encounters: Lesbians and Gays in British Cinema*. London: Cassell, 1996.

Brooks, Xan. *Choose Life: Ewan McGregor and the British Film Revival*. London: Chameleon Books, 1998.

Burton, Alan, Tim O'Sullivan, and Paul Wells, eds. *The Family Way: The Boulting Brothers and Postwar British Film Culture*. Trowbridge: Flicks Books, 2000.

Caughie, John. *The Companion to British and Irish Cinema*. London: Cassell, 1996.

Chanan, Michael. *The Dream that Kicks: The Prehistory and Early Years of Cinema in Britain*. 2nd ed. London: Routledge, 1996.

Chapman, James. *The British at War: Cinema, State, and Propaganda, 1939–1945*. London: I.B. Tauris, 1998.

Cook, Pam. *Fashioning the Nation: Costume and Identity in British Cinema*. London: BFI, 1996.

Dickinson, Margaret, ed. *Rogue Reels: Oppositional Film in Britain, 1945–90*. London: British Film Institute, 1999.

Dixon, Wheeler Winston. *Re-Viewing British Cinema, 1900–1992: Essays and Interviews*. Albany: SUNY, 1994.

Drazin, Charles. *The Finest Years: British Cinema of the 1940s*. London: Andre Deutsch, 1998.

Eyles, Allen. *Gaumont British Cinemas*. Burgess Hill: Cinema Theatre Association, 1996.

Friedman, Lester. *British Cinema and Thatcherism*. London: UCL, 1993.

Geraghty, Christine. *British Cinema in the Fifties: Gender, Genre and the 'New Look.'* London: Routledge, 2000.

Gillliam, Terry and Bob McCabe. *Dark Knights and Holy Fools*. London: Orion Media, 1999.

Gilmore, Michael T. *Differences in the Dark: American Movies and English Theater*. New York: Columbia, 1998.

Glancy, H. Mark. *When Hollywood Loved Britain: The Hollywood "British" Film, 1939–45*. Manchester: Manchester University, 1999.

Gledhill, Christine and Gillian Swanson. *Nationalising Femininity: Culture, Sexuality, and the British Cinema in the Second World War*. Manchester: Manchester, 1996.

Harding, Colin. *In the Kingdom of Shadows: A Companion to Early Cinema*. Madison, NJ: Fairleigh Dickinson, 1996.

Harper, Sue. *Picturing the Past: The Rise and Fall of the British Costume Film*. London: BFI, 1994.

Higson, Andrew. *Dissolving Views: Key Writings on British Cinema*. London: Cassell, 1996.

———. *Waving the Flag: Constructing a National Cinema in Britain*. Oxford: Clarendon, 1995.

Hill, John. *British Cinema in the 1980's*. New York: Oxford, 1999.

Landy, Marcia. *British Genres: Cinema and Society, 1930–1960.* Princeton: Princeton, 1991.

Lant, Antonia. *Blackout: Reinventing Women for Wartime British Cinema.* Princeton: Princeton, 1991.

Low, Rachel. *Rachel Low's History of British Cinema.* New York: Routledge, 1997.

Macnab, Geoffrey. *Searching for Stars: Stardom and Screen Acting in British Cinema.* New York: Cassell, 2000.

Murphy, Robert. *British Cinema Book.* London: BFI, 1997.

———. *British Cinema of the 90s.* London: BFI, 2000.

———. *Sixties British Cinema.* London: BFI, 1992.

Park, James. *British Cinema: The Lights that Failed.* London: B.T. Batsford, 1990.

Petrie, Duncan J. *Creativity and Constraint in the British Film Industry.* London: Macmillan, 1991.

Rattigan, Neil. *This Is England: British Film and the People's War, 1939–1945.* Madison, NJ: Fairleigh Dickinson University, 2001.

Richards, Jeffrey, ed. *The Unknown 1930s: An Alternative History of the British Cinema, 1929–1939.* London: I.B. Tauris, 1998.

Ryall, Tom. *Alfred Hitchcock and the British Cinema.* 2nd ed. London: Atlantic Highlands, 1996.

Scrivens, Kevin. *The Travelling Cinematograph Show.* Tweedale: New Era, 1999.

Sedgwick, John. *Popular Filmgoing in 1930s Britain: A Choice of Pleasures.* Exeter: Exeter University, 2000.

Shafer, Stephen C. *British Popular Films, 1929–1939: The Cinema of Reassurance.* London: Routledge, 1997.

Street, Sarah. *British National Cinema.* London: Routledge, 1997.

Warren, Patricia. *British Cinema in Pictures.* London: Batsford, 1993.

———. *British Film Studios: An Illustrated History.* London: Batsford, 1995.

Williams, D. R. *Cinema in Leicester, 1896–1931.* Loughborough: Heart of Albion, 1993.

Williams, Tony. *Structures of Desire: British Cinema, 1939–1955.* Albany: SUNY, 2000.

CANADIAN FILM

Donohoe, Joseph I., Jr. *Essays on Quebec Cinema.* East Lansing: Michigan State, 1991.

Dorland, Michael. *So Close to the State/s: The Emergence of Canadian Feature Film Policy.* Toronto: University of Toronto, 1998.

Evans, Gary. *In the National Interest: A Chronicle of the National Film Board of Canada.* Toronto: Toronto, 1991.

Magder, Ted. *Canada's Hollywood: The Canadian State and Feature Films.* Toronto: Toronto, 1993.

Marshall, Bill. *Quebec National Cinema.* Montreal: McGill-Queen's University, 2001.

Pallister, Janis L. *Cinema of Quebec.* Madison: Fairleigh Dickinson, 1995.

CENTRAL EUROPEAN FILM

The Development of the Audiovisual Landscape in Central Europe Since 1989. Rev. ed. Luton: ULP/John Libby Media, 1998.

CHINESE FILM

Berry, Chris. *Perspectives on Chinese Cinema.* 2nd ed. London: BFI, 1991.

Browne, Nick. *New Chinese Cinemas.* Cambridge: Cambridge, 1994.

Chang, Hsu-tung. *Chinese Modernism in the Era of Reforms.* Durham: Duke, 1997.

Chow, Rey. *Primitive Passions: Visuality, Sexuality, Ethnography, and Contemporary Chinese Cinema.* New York: Columbia. 1995.

Donald, Stephanie. *Public Secrets, Public Spaces: Cinema and Civility in China.* Lanham, MD: Rowman & Littlefield, 2000.

Kuoshu, Harry H. *Lightness of Being in China: Adaptation and Discursive Figuration in Cinema and Theater.* New York: Peter Lang, 1999.

Lu, Sheldon Hsiao-peng. *Transitional Chinese Cinemas.* Honolulu: Hawaii, 1997.

Semsel, George S. et al. *Chinese Film Theory.* New York: Praeger, 1990.

———. *Film in Contemporary China.* Westport, CT: Praeger, 1993.

Silbertgeld, Jerome. *China into Film: Frames of Reference in Contemporary Chinese Cinema.* London: Reaktion Books, 1999.

Tam, Kwok-kan and Wimal Dissanayake. *New Chinese Cinema.* New York: Oxford, 1998.

Yeh, Wen-hsin, ed. *Cross Cultural Readings of Chineseness: Narratives, Images, and Interpretations of the 1990s.* Berkeley: Institute of East Asian Studies, 2000.

Zhang, Yingjin. *The City in Modern Chinese Literature and Film.* Stanford: Stanford, 1996.

Zhang, Yingjin and Zhiwei Xiao. *Encyclopidia of Chinese Film.* New York: Routledge, 1998.

DEVELOPING COUNTRIES

Marks, Laura U. *The Skin of the Film: Intercultural Cinema, Embodiment, and the Senses.* Durham, NC: Duke University Press, 2000.

EGYPTIAN FILM

Culhane, Hind Rassam. *East/West, An Ambiguous State of Being: The Construction and Representation of Egyptian Cultural Identity in Egyptian Film.* New York: P. Lang, 1995.

EUROPEAN FILM

Dyer, Richard and Ginette Vincendeau. *Popular European Cinema.* London: Routledge, 1992.

Ellwood, David W. and Rob Kroes. *Hollywood in Europe: Experiences of a Cultural Hegemony.* Amsterdam: VU University, 1994.

Everett, Wendy. *European Identity in Cinema.* Exeter: Intellect, 1996.

Finney, Angus. *Developing Feature Films in Europe.* London: Routledge, 1996.

———. *The State of European Cinema.* London: Cassell, 1996.

Hill, John et al. *Border Crossing: Film in Ireland, Britain and Europe.* Belfast: Institute of Irish Studies, 1994.

Ilott, Terry. *Budgets and Markets: A Study of the Budgeting of European Film.* London: Routledge, 1996.

Lev, Peter. *The Euro-American Cinema.* Austin: University of Texas, 1993.

Petrie, Duncan. *Screening Europe: Image and Identity in Contemporary European Cinema.* London: BFI, 1992.

Reeves, Nicholas. *The Power of Film Propaganda: Myth or Reality?* London: Cassell, 1999.

Segrave, Kerry. *The Continental Actress: European Film Stars of the Postwar Era.* Jefferson, NC: McFarland, 1990.

Sieglohr, Ulrike, ed. *Heroines Without Heroes: Reconstructing Female and National Identities in European Cinema, 1945–51.* New York: Cassell, 2000.

Snyder, Stephen. *The Transparent I: Self/Subject in European Cinema.* New York: P. Lang, 1994.

Stollery, Martin. *Alternative Empires: European Modernist Cinemas and the Cultures of Imperialism.* Exeter : University of Exeter Press, 2000.

Vincendeau, Ginette. *Encyclopedia of European Cinema.* London: Cassell, 1995.

Waldman, Harry. *Beyond Hollywood's Grasp: American Filmmakers Abroad, 1914–1945.* Metuchen: Scarecrow, 1994.

FRENCH FILM

Abel, Richard. *Cine Goes to Town: French Cinema, 1896–1914.* Updated and expanded ed. Berkeley: University of California, 1998.

Andrew, James Dudley. *Mists of Regret: Culture and Sensibility in Classic French Film.* Princeton: Princeton, 1995.

Austin, Guy. *Contemporary French Cinema.* Manchester: Manchester, 1996.

Biggs, Melissa E. *French Films, 1945–1993.* Jefferson, NC: McFarland, 1996.

Colombat, Andre Pierre. *The Holocaust in French Film.* Metuchen: Scarecrow, 1993.

Crisp, C. G. *The Classic French Cinema, 1930–1960.* Bloomington: Indiana University, 1993.

Dine, Philid D. *Images of the Algerian War.* Oxford: Clarendon, 1994.

Durham, Carolyn A. *Double Takes: Culture and Gender in French Films and Their American Remakes.* Hanover: University Press of New England, 1998.

Flitterman-Lewis, Sandy. *To Desire Differently: Feminism and the French Cinema.* Expanded ed. New York: Columbia, 1996.

Forbes, Jill. *The Cinema in France: After the New Wave.* Bloomington: Indiana University, 1993.

Greene, Naomi. *Landscapes of Loss: The National Past in Postwar French Cinema.* Princeton, NJ: Princeton University Press, c1999.

Hayward, Susan. *French National Cinema.* London: Routledge, 1993.

Hayward, Susan and Ginette Vincendeau, eds. *French Film: Texts and Contexts.* 2nd ed. London; New York: Routledge, 2000.

Higgins, Lynn A. *New Novel, New Wave, New Politics: Fiction and the Representation of History in Postwar France.* Lincoln: University of Nebraska, 1996.

Kline, T. Jefferson. *Screening the Text: Intertextuality in New Wave French Cinema.* Baltimore: Johns Hopkins, 1992.

Mazdon, Lucy. *Encore Hollywood: Remaking French Cinema.* London: British Film Institute, 2000.

Pauly, Rebecca M. *The Transparent Illusion: Image and Ideology in French Text and Film.* New York: P. Lang, 1993.

Powrie, Phil, ed. *French Cinema in the 1990s: Continuity and Difference.* New York: Oxford University Press,

1999.

Spaas, Lieve. *The Francophone Film: A Struggle for Identity.* Manchester: Manchester University Press, 2000.

Vincendeau, Ginette. *Companion to French Cinema.* London: Cassell, 1996.

Williams, Alan Larson. *Republic of Images: A History of French Filmmaking.* Cambridge: Harvard, 1992.

GERMAN FILM

Byg, Barton. *Landscapes of Resistance: The German Films of Daniele Huillet and Jean-Marie Straub.* Berkeley: University of California, 1995.

Corrigan, Timothy. *New German Film.* Rev. ed. Bloomington: Indiana University, 1994.

Davidson, John E. *Deterritorializing the New German Cinema.* Minneapolis: University of Minnesota, 1999.

Elsaesser, Thomas. *Fassbinder's Germany: History, Identity, Subject.* Amsterdam: Amsterdam, 1996.

Fehrenbach, Heide. *Cinema in Democratizing Germany: Reconstructing National Identity After Hitler.* Chapel Hill: University of North Carolina, 1995.

Fox, Jo. *Filming Women in the Third Reich.* Oxford: Berg, 2000.

Frieden, Sandra. *Gender and German Cinema.* Providence: Berg, 1993.

Ginsberg, Terri and Kirsten Thompson. *Perspectives on German Cinema.* New York: G.K. Hall, 1996.

Helt, Richard C. and Marie E. Helt. *West German Cinema: A Reference Handbook.* Metuchen: Scarecrow, 1992.

Hoffmann, Hilmar. *The Triumph of Propaganda: Film and National Socialism.* Providence: Berghahn, 1996.

Knight, Julia. *Women and the New German Cinema.* London: Verso, 1992.

Kreimeier, Klaus. *The UFA Story: A History of Germany's Greatest Film Company, 1918–1945.* Berkeley: University of California, 1999.

Kuzniar, Alice A. *The Queer German Cinema.* Stanford: Stanford University Press, 2000.

Linville, Susan E. *Feminism, Film, Fascism: Women's Auto/Biographical Film in Postwar German.* Austin: University of Texas, 1998.

Murray, Bruce Arthur. *Film and the German Left in the Weimar Republic.* Austin: University of Texas, 1990.

Murray, Bruce A. and Christopher J. Wickham. *Framing the Past: The Historiography of German Cinema and Television.* Carbondale: Southern Illinois University, 1992.

Pflaum, Hans Gunther. *Germany on Film.* Detroit: Wayne State, 1990.

Reimer, Robert C., ed. *Cultural History Through a Nazi Lens: Essays on the Cinema of the Third Reich.* Rochester, NY: Camden House, 2000.

Reimer, Robert C. and Carol J. Reimer. *Nazi-Retro Film: How German Narrative Cinema Remembers the Past.* New York: Twayne, 1992.

Rentschler, Eric. *The Ministry of Illusion: Nazi Cinema and Its Afterlife.* Cambridge: Harvard, 1996.

Romani, Cinzia. *Tainted Goddesses: Female Film Stars of the Third Reich.* New York: Sarpendon, 1992.

Santner, Eric L. *Stranded Objects: Mourning, Memory, and Film in Postwar Germany.* Ithaca: Cornell, 1990.

Saunders, Thomas J. *Hollywood in Berlin: American Cinema and Weimar Germany.* Berkeley: University of California, 1994.

Silberman, Marc. *German Cinema: Texts in Context.* Detroit: Wayne State, 1995.

Weinberger, Gabriele. *Nazi Germany and Its Aftermath in Women Directors' Autobiographical Films.* San Francisco: Mellen, 1992.

GREEK FILM

Koliodimos, Dimitris. *The Greek Filmography, 1914 through 1996.* Jefferson, NC: McFarland, 1999.

HONG KONG FILM

Hammond, Stefan and Mike Wilkins. *Sex and Zen and a Bullet in the Head.* New York: Simon & Schuster, 1996.

Logan, Bey. *Hong Kong Action Cinema.* London: Titan, 1995.

Teo, Stephen. *Hong Kong Cinema.* London: BFI, 1997.

INDIAN FILM

Agnihotri, Ram Awatar. *Film Stars in Indian Politics.* New Delhi: Commonwealth Publishers, 1998.

Chakravarty, Sumita S. *National Identity in Indian Popular Cinema, 1947–1989.* Austin: University of Texas, 1993.

Das, Santi, ed. *Satyajit Ray, An Intimate Master.* New Delhi: Allied, 1998.

Derne, Steve. *Movies, Masculinity, and Modernity: An Ethnography of Men's Filmgoing in India.* Westport, CT: Greenwood Press, 2000.

Dickey, Sara. *Cinema and the Urban Poor in South India.* Cambridge: Cambridge, 1993.

Indian Cinema: A Visual Voyage. New Delhi: Publication Division, Ministry of Information, 1998.

Kaul, Gautam. *Cinema and the Indian Freedom Struggle*. New Delhi: Sterling Publishers, 1998.

Kazmi, Fareed. *The Politics of India's Conventional Cinema: Imaging a Universe, Subverting a Multiverse*. New Delhi: Sage Publications, 1999.

Kazmi, Nikhat. *The Dream Merchants of Bollywood*. New Delhi: UBS Publishers' Distributors, 1998.

———. *Ire in the Soul: Bollywood's Angry Years*. New Delhi: HarperCollins, 1996.

Manto, Saadat Hasan. *Stars from Another Sky: The Bombay Film World in the 1940s*. New Delhi: Penguin Books, 1998.

Nandy, Ashis. *The Secret Politics of Our Desires: Nation, Culture, and Gender in Indian Popular Cinema*. New York: St. Martin's Press, 1998.

Prasad, M. Madhava. *Ideology of the Hindi Film: A Historical Construction*. Delhi: Oxford University Press, 1998.

Rajadhyaksha, Ashish and Paul Willemen. *Encyclopedia of Indian Cinema*. New revised edition. London: BFI, 1999.

Roberge, Gaston. *Communication, Cinema, Development: from Morosity to Hope*. New Delhi: Manohar, 1998.

INDONESIAN FILM

Heider, Karl G. *Indonesian Cinema: National Culture on Screen*. Honolulu: Hawaii, 1991.

Sen, Krishna. *Indonesian Cinema*. London: Zed, 1994.

IRANIAN FILM

Issa, Rose and Sheila Whitaker, eds. *Life and Art: The New Iranian Cinema*. London: National Film Theatre, 1999.

IRISH FILM

Burns-Bisogno, Louisa. *Censoring Irish Nationalism*. Jefferson, NC: McFarland, 1997.

Byrne, Terry. *Power in the Eye: An Introduction to Contemporary Irish Film*. Lanham: Scarecrow, 1997.

Caughie, John and Kevin Rockett. *The Companion to British and Irish Cinema*. London: Cassell, 1996.

Gray, Michael. *Stills, Reels, and Rushes: Ireland and the Irish in 20th Century Cinema*. Dublin: Ashfield, 1999.

Hill, John et al. *Border Crossing: Film in Ireland, Britain and Europe*. Belfast: Institute of Irish Studies, 1994.

MacKillop, ed. *Contemporary Irish Cinema: From The Quiet Man to Dancing at Lughnasa*. Syracuse: Syracuse University, 1999.

Monks, Robert. *Cinema Ireland: A Database of Irish Films and Filmmakers*. Dublin: National Library of Ireland, 1996.

Pettitt, Lance. *Screening Ireland: Film and Television Representation*. Manchester: Manchester University, 2000.

Rockett, Kevin. *The Irish Filmography*. Dublin: Red Mountain, 1996.

ISRAELI FILM

Ben-Shaul, Nitzan S. *Mythical Expressions of Siege in Israeli Films*. Lewiston: Edwin Mellen, 1997.

Kronish, Amy. *World Cinema: Israel*. Madison, NJ: Fairleigh Dickinson, 1996.

Tryster, Hillel. *Israel Before Israel: Silent Cinema in the Holy Land*. Jerusalem: Steven Spielberg Jewish Film Archive, 1995.

ITALIAN FILM

Bruno, Giuliana. *Streetwalking on a Ruined Map: Cultural Theory and the City Films of Elvira Notari*. Princeton: Princeton, 1993.

Cardullo, Bert. *What is Neorealism? A Critical English-Language Bibliography of Italian Cinematic Neorealism*. London: University Press of America, 1991.

Dalle Vacche, Angela. *The Body in the Mirror: Shapes of History in Italian Cinema*. Princeton: Princeton, 1991.

Gieri, Manuela. *Contemporary Italian Filmmaking*. Toronto: Toronto, 1995.

Landy, Marcia. *The Folklore of Consensus: Theatricality in the Italian Cinema, 1930–1943*. Albany: SUNY, 1998.

———. *Italian Film*. Cambridge: Cambridge University Press, 2000.

Marcus, Millicent Joy. *Filmmaking by the Book: Italian Cinema and Literary Adaptation*. Baltimore: Johns Hopkins, 1993.

Nowell-Smith, Geoffrey. *Companion to Italian Cinema*. London: Cassell, 1996.

Rocchio, Vincent F. *Cinema of Anxiety: A Psychoanalysis of Italian Realism*. Austin: University of Texas, 1999.

Sitney, P. Adams. *Vital Crises in Italian Cinema: Iconography, Stylistics, Politics*. Austin: University of Texas,

1995.

Sorlin, Pierre. *Italian National Cinema, 1896–1996*. New York: Routledge, 1996.

Vermilye, Jerry. *The Great Italian Films*. Secaucus: Carol, 1994.

JAPANESE FILM

Bennardi, Joanne. *Writing in Light: The Silent Scenario and the Japanese Pure Film Movement*. Detroit: Wayne State University, 2001.

Buehrer, Beverley Bare. *Japanese Films: A Filmography and Commentary*. Jefferson, NC: McFarland, 1990.

Davis, Darrell William. *Picturing Japaneseness: Monumental Style, National Identity, Japanese Film*. New York: Columbia, 1996.

Hirano, Kyoko. *Mr. Smith Goes to Tokyo: The Japanese Cinema Under the American Occupation*. Washington: Smithsonian, 1992.

Galbraith, Stuart. *Japanese Filmography*. Jefferson, NC: McFarland, 1996.

Kirihara, Donald. *Patterns of Time: Mizoguchi and the 1930s*. Madison: University of Wisconsin, 1992.

McDonald, Keiko I. *From Book to Screen: Modern Japanese Literature in Films*. Armonk, NY: M.E. Sharpe, 2000.

————. *Japanese Classical Theater in Film*. Rutherford: Fairleigh Dickinson, 1994.

Nolletti, Arthur, Jr. and David Desser. *Reframing Japanese Cinema: Authorship, Genre, History*. Bloomington: Indiana University, 1992.

Richie, Donald. *Japanese Cinema: An Introduction*. New York: Oxford, 1990.

Schilling, Mark. *Contemporary Japanese Film*. New York: Weatherhill, 1999.

Standish, Isolde. *Myth and Masculinity in the Japanese Cinema*. Richmond, Surry: Curzon, 2000.

Washburn, Dennis and Carole Cavanaugh, eds. *Word and Image in Japanese Cinema*. Cambridge: Cambridge University, 2001.

LATIN AMERICAN AND CARIBBEAN FILM

Balderston, Daniel and Donna J. Guy. *Sex and Sexuality in Latin America*. New York: NYU, 1997

Bernard, Timothy and Peter Rist. *South American Cinema: A Critical Filmography, 1915–1994*. New York: Garland, 1996.

Burton, Julianne. *Social Documentary in Latin America*. Pittsburgh: Pittsburgh, 1990.

Cham, Mbye B. *Ex-iles: Essays on Caribbean Cinema*. Trenton, NJ: Africa World Press, 1992.

Foster, David William. *Contemporary Argentine Cinema*. Columbia: University of Missouri, 1992.

Johnson, Randal and Robert Stam. *Brazilian Cinema*. Expanded ed. New York: Columbia, 1995.

King, John. *Magical Reels: A History of Cinema in Latin America*. London: Verso, 1990.

King, John et al. *Mediating Two Worlds: Cinematic Encounters in the Americas*. London: BFI, 1993.

Martin, Michael T. *New Latin American Cinema*. Detroit: Wayne State University, 1997.

Noriega, Chon A., ed. *Visible Nations: Latin American Cinema and Video*. Minneapolis: University of Minnesota, 2000.

Pick, Zuzana M. *The New Latin American Cinema*. Austin: University of Texas, 1993.

Ranucci, Karen and Julie Feldman. *A Guide to Latin American, Caribbean, and U.S. Latino-Made Film and Video*. Lanham, MD: Scarecrow, 1998.

Schwartz, Ronald. *Latin American Films, 1932–1994: A Critical Filmography*. Jefferson, NC: McFarland, 1997.

Stam, Robert. *Tropical Multiculturalism: A Comparative History of Race in Brazilian Cinema and Culture*. Durham: Duke, 1997.

Stevens, Donald F. *Based on a True Story: Latin American History at the Movies*. Wilmington: SR, 1997.

MEXICAN FILM

Berg, Charles Ramirez. *Cinema of Solitude: A Critical Study of Mexican Film, 1967–1983*. Austin: University of Texas, 1992.

Hershfield, Joanne. *Mexican Cinema/Mexican Women, 1940–1950*. Tucson: Arizona, 1996.

Maciel, David. *El Norte: The U.S.-Mexican Border in Contemporary Cinema*. San Diego: Institute for Regional Studies, 1990.

Noriega, Chon A. and Steven Ricci. *Mexican Cinema Project*. Los Angeles: UCLA Film and Television Archive, 1994.

Paranagua, Paulo Antonio. *Mexican Cinema*. London: BFI, 1995.

Rashkin, Elissa J. *Women Filmmakers in Mexico*. Austin: University of Texas, 2001.

NEW ZEALAND FILM

Churchman, Geoffrey B. *Celluloid Dreams: A* Century of Film in New Zealand. Wellington: IPL, 1997.

Martin, Helen. *New Zealand Film, 1912–1996*. New York: Oxford, 1997.

PAKISTANI FILM

Gazdar, Mushtaq. *Pakistan Cinema, 1947–1997*. New York: Oxford, 1997.

PHILIPPINE FILM

David, Joel. *Fields of Vision: Critical Applications in Recent Philippine Cinema*. Quezon City: Ateneo de Manila, 1995.

———. *The National Pastime: Contemporary Philippine Cinema*. Pasig: Anvil, 1990.

———. *Wages of Cinema: Film in Philippine Perspective*. Quezon City: [s.n.], 1998.

Del Mundo, Clodualdo. *Native Resistance: Philippine Cinema and Colonialism, 1898–1941*. Malate: De La Salle University, 1998.

Infante, J. Eddie. *Inside Philippine Movies, 1970–1990*. Manila: Ateneo de Manila, 1991.

RUSSIAN, SOVIET, AND EASTERN EUROPEAN FILM

Brashinsky, Michael and Andrew Horton. *Russian Critics on the Cinema of Glastnost*. Cambridge: Cambridge, 1994.

Faraday, George. *Revolt of the Filmmakers: The Struggle for Artistic Autonomy and the Fall of the Soviet Film Industry*. University Park: Pennsylvania State University, 2000.

Goodwin, James. *Eisenstein, Cinema, and History*. Urbana: University of Illinois, 1993.

Kenez, Peter. *Cinema and Soviet Society*. Cambridge: Cambridge, 1992.

Lawton, Anna. *Red Screen: Politics, Society, and Art in Soviet Cinema*. London: Routledge, 1992.

Petrie, Graham and Ruth Dwyer. *Before the Wall Came Down: Soviet and East European Filmmakers Working in the West*. Lanham: Univeristy Press of America, 1990.

Shlapentokh, Dmitry and Vladimir Shapentokh. *Soviet Cinematography, 1918–1991: Ideological Conflict and Social Reality*. New York: A. de Gruyter, 1993.

Slater, Thomas J. *Handbook of Soviet and Eastern European Films and Filmmakers*. New York: Greenwood Press, 1992.

Taylor, Richard, ed. *The BFI Companion to Eastern European and Russian Cinema*. London: BFI Publishing, 2000.

Taylor, Richard. *Film Propaganda: Soviet Russia and Nazi Germany*. 2nd rev. ed. London; New York: I.B. Tauris, 1998.

Taylor, Richard and Ian Christie. *Inside the Film Factory: New Approaches to Russian and Soviet Cinema*. New York: Routledge, 1991.

Taylor, Richard and Derek Spring. *Stalinism and Soviet Cinema*. London: Routledge, 1993.

Tsivian, Yuri. *Early Cinema in Russia and Its Cultural Reception*. London: Routledge, 1994.

Woll, Josephine. *Real Images: Soviet Cinema and the Thaw*. London: I.B. Tauris, 2000.

Youngblood, Denise J. *The Magic Mirror: Moviemaking in Russia, 1908–1918*. Madison: University of Wisconsin, 1999.

———. *Movies of the Masses: Popular Cinema and Soviet Society in the 1920s*. Cambridge: Cambridge, 1992.

SCANDINAVIAN FILM

Cowie, Peter. *Scandinavian Cinema*. London: Tantivy Press, 1992.

Qvist, Per Olov and Peter von Bagh. *Guide to the Cinema of Sweden and Finland*. Westport, CT: Greenwood Press, 2000.

SCOTTISH FILM

Bruce, David. *Scotland the Movie*. Edinburgh: Polygon, 1996.

Dick, Eddie. *From Limelight to Satellite: A Scottish Film Book*. London: BFI, 1990.

Petrie, Duncan J. *Screening Scotland*. London: BFI, 2000.

SPANISH FILM

Deveny, Thomas G. *Cain on Screen: Contemporary Spanish Cinema*. Metuchen: Scarecrow, 1993.

———. *Contemporary Spanish Film from Fiction*. Lanham, MD: Scarecrow Press, 1999.

D'Lugo, Marvin. *Guide to the Cinema of Spain*. Westport, CT: Greenwood Press, 1997.

Evans, Peter William, ed. *Spanish Cinema: The Auteurist Tradition*. Oxford: Oxford University, 1999.

Kinder, Marsha. *Refiguring Spain: Cinema, Media, Representation*. Durham: Duke, 1997.

Smith, Paul Julian. *Laws of Desire: Questions of Homosexuality in Spanish Writing and Film, 1960–1990*. Oxford: Clarendon, 1992.

———. *Vision Machines: Cinema, Literature, and Sexuality in Spain and Cuba, 1983–93*. London: Verso, 1996.

Talens, Jenaro, and Santos Zunzunegui, eds. *Modes of Representation in Spanish Cinema*. Minneapolis: University of Minnesota, 1998.

Vernon, Kathleen. *The Spanish Civil War and the Visual Arts*. Ithaca: Center for International Studies, Cornell,

1990.

SWEDISH FILM

Blackwell, Marilyn Johns. *Gender and Representation in the Films of Ingmar Bergman.* Columbia: Camden, 1997.

Qvist, Per Olov and Peter von Bagh. *Guide to the Cinema of Sweden and Finland.* Westport, CT: Greenwood Press, 2000.

Wright, Rochelle. *The Visible Wall: Jews and Other Ethnic Outsiders in Swedish Film.* Carbondale: Southern Illinois University, 1998.

FILM SITES ON THE WORLD WIDE WEB

CREDITS AND PLOT SUMMARIES

The All-Movie Guide: http://www.allmusic.com/amg_root.html

E! Online's Movie Finder: http://www.moviefinder.com/

Hollywood Online's MoviePeople Database: http://moviepeople.hollywood.com/

The Internet Movie Database: http://us.imdb.com

Microsoft Cinemania: http://cinemania.msn.com/movies/movies.asp

TV Guide's Movie Database: http://tvguide.com/movies/mopic/cgi-bin/page.c

DATABASE FOR CREDITS OF THE AMERICAN ANIMATED SHORT CARTOONS (1928–1972).

Animation Database: http://www.lib.shizuoka.ac.jp/betty.html

The Ultimate TV List: http://www.ultimatetv.com

FILM CRITICISM AND REVIEWS

Film.com: http://www.film.com/about/

Movie Review Query Engine: http://www.mrqe.com/lookup?

Rotten Tomatoes: http://www.rottentomatoes.com/

Women's Studies Film Reviews:
http://www.inform.umd.edu:8080/EdRes/Topic/WomensStudies/FilmReviews/

FILM LIBRARIES AND ARCHIVES

American Archives of the Factual Film: http://www.lib.iastate.edu/spcl/aaff.html

Bibliotheque nationale de France: http://www.bnf.fr/web-bnf/catalog/index.htm

Black Film Center/Archive, Indiana University: http://www.indiana.edu/~bfca/index.html

The British Library: http://www.bl.uk/

Haddon (Ethnographic films before 1945): http://www.rsl.ox.ac.uk/isca/haddon/HADD_home.html

Internet Moving Images Archives: http://www.archive.org/movies

Library of Congress Early Motion Picture Collections Site:
http://memory.loc.gov/ammem/papr/mpixhome.html

Library of Congress General Motion Picture Site:
gopher://marvel.loc.gov:70/11/research/reading.rooms/motion.picture

National Center for Jewish Film: http://www.brandeis.edu/jewishfilm/index.html

National Film Board of Canada: http://www.nfb.ca/E/index.html

Northeast Historic Film: http://www.acadia.net/oldfilm/

Pacific Film Archives: http://www.bampfa.berkeley.edu/search/

Public Motion Picture Research Centers and Film Archives: http://lcweb.loc.gov/film/arch.html

Repositories of Primary Sources: http://www.uidaho.edu/special-collections/Other.Repositories.html

UCLA Film and Television Archive: http://www.cinema.ucla.edu/default.html

WPA Library (British Pathe News etc.): http://www.mpimedia.com/wpa/

FLM SRIPTS ONLINE:

http://www.script-o-rama.com/index.shtml

GLOSSARY OF FILM AND VIDEO TERMS

On-Line Glossary: http://www.sunsetpost.com/glossary.htm

Academy of Motion Picture Arts and Sciences: http://www.oscars.org/ampas/

Academy of Television Arts and Sciences: http://www.emmys.org/

Directors' Guild of America: http://www.dga.org/dga-info/aboutdga.htm

JOURNALS

Film/TV/Media Journals listings: http://www.tcf.ua.edu/screensite/res/journals/index.htm

Actuacine (French film): http://www.imaginet.fr/~fcm/

American Cinematographe: http://www.cinematographer.com/magazine/index.htm

Animation Journal: http://www.chapman.edu/animation
basilisk (film, architecture, philosophy, literature, music, and perception):   http://www.basilisk.com
Bright Lights (analysis, history, and commentary):   http://www.brightlightsfilm.com
Camera Obscura (feminism and media theory):   http://www.indiana.edu/~iupress/journals/
Canadian Journal of Communication: http://www.cjc-online.ca/
Cinema Journal: http://www.cinemastudies.org/cj.htm
Classic Images: http://www.classicimages.com/
Cinema Technology: http://www.bksts.com
Continuum: http://kali.murdoch.edu.au/~cntinuum/
Critical Theory: http://www2.uchicago.edu/jrnl-crit-inq/
CTheory (reviews of books on theory, technology and culture):   http://www.ctheory.com/ctheory.html
DGA Magazine (Directors' Guild of America):   http://www.dga.org/magazine/index.htm
E! Online: http://www.eonline.com/
El Amante Cine (Argentina):   http://elamante.com.ar/
Film and History: http://h-net2.msu.edu/~filmhis/
Film and Philosophy: http://www.hanover.edu/philos/film/home.htm
Film Comment: http://www.filmlinc.com/fcm/fcm.htm
Film Culture: http://www.arthouseinc.com/filmculture/index.html
Film Feature Forum (essays and articles published in European film journals):
     http://gewi.kfunigraz.ac.at:80/~puntigam/FFF/index.html
Film-Historia: http://www.swcp.com/~cmora/historia.html
Film International: http://gpg.com/film/
Filmmaker: The Magazine of Independent Film: http://www.filmmag.com/
fps (animation):   http://www.cam.org/~pawn/fps.html
Film Quarterly: http://aaup.princeton.edu/cgi-bin/hfs.cgi/66/california/fq.ctl
Historical Journal of Film, Radio, and Television: http://www.carfax.co.uk/hjf-ad.htm
Hors Champ (film criticism and theory):   http://www.horschamp.qc.ca/
Indie Wire (independent filmmaking):   http://www.indiewire.com/index.html
Iris: A Journal of Image and Sound:
     http://www.uiowa.edu/~commstud/programs/filmstudies/iris/index.html
Journal of Criminal Justice and Popular Culture: http://www.albany.edu/scj/jcjpc/
Journal of Film Preservation: http://www.cinema.ucla.edu/fiaf/Journal/index.html
Journal of Popular Film and Television: http://www.heldref.org/html/body_jtf_t.html
Jump Cut (contemporary media):   http://www.tcf.ua.edu/JumpCut/
Kinema (film history, theory, and aesthetics):   http://arts.uwaterloo.ca/FINE/juhde/kinemahp.htm
Kulture Void Pictures (independent filmmaking):   http://www.kulture-void.com/
Lahikuva (audio-visual culture):   http://www.utu.fi/etvtiede/lahikuva/
L'Art du Cinema: http://www.imaginet.fr/secav/adc/
The MacGuffin (Alfred Hitchcock):   http://www.labyrinth.net.au/~muffin/
Micro-Film (independent and experimental film):
     http://www.artisticunderground.com/mf_unbound/micro_film.html
Millennium Film Journal (independent, experimental, and avant-garde cinema):
     http://www.sva.edu/MFJ/
Post Script (film as literature, language, and visual art):
     http://www.tamu.commerce.edu/coas/litlang/postscript.html
Premiere: http://www.premieremag.com/
Quarterly Review of Film and Video: http://www.gbhab-us.com/journals/304/304-top.htm
Screen (contemporary film and cultural theory):   http://www.oup.co.uk/jnls/list/screen/
Screening the Past (electronic journal of film history):
     http://www.latrobe.edu.au/www/screeningthepast/
The Silents Majority (silent film):   http://www.mdle.com/ClassicFilms/
Velvet Light Trap (film theory, criticism, and history):
     http://www.utexas.edu/utpress/journals/jvlt.html
Wide Angle (film theory, criticism, history, and aesthetics):   Vhttp://muse.jhu.edu/journals/wide_angle/
LINKS TO ON-LINE SCHOLARLY RESOURCES:
Cinemedia: http://afi.cinemedia.org/welcomes/you.html
Screensite: http://www.tcf.ua.edu/screensite/

LINKS TO ON-LINE POPULAR RESOURCES:
Cinema Sites: http://www.cinema-sites.com/
Movies on the Net: http://gen.com/ani/moviemks.htm
MUSEUMS:
American Museum of the Moving Image: http://nyctourist.com/ammi.htm
George Eastman House: http://www.eastman.org/
Museum of Modern Art: http://12.3.56.5/menu.html
Museum of the Moving Image: http://www.bfi.org.uk/museum/
National Museum of Photography, Film and Television: http://www.nmsi.ac.uk/nmpft/
SCHOLARLY DISCUSSION GROUPS:
H-Film@H-Net.MSU.Edu — Film History and the Uses of Media
Screen-L@ua1vm.ua.edu — Study of Film and Television
AMIA-L@ukcc.uky.edu — Association for Moving Image Archivists
Film-Philosophy@mailbase.ac.uk — Philosophy and Film
Film-Theory@lists.village.virginia.edu — Film Theory
SEARCHABLE FILM DATABASES:
All-Movie Guide: http://AllMovie.com/
Freeality Internet Search - Online Film Resources: http://www.freeality.com/film.htm
Internet Movie Database: http://us.imdb.com/
The Motion Picture Guide: http://www.tvgen.com/movies/mopic/cgi-bin/page.c
SCHOLARLY AND PROFESSIONAL ORGANIZATIONS AND ASSOCIATIONS
Academy of Motion Picture Arts and Sciences: http://www.ampas.org/body.html
Alliance for Canada's Audio-Visual Heritage: http://www.rcc.ryerson.ca/alliance/english/mission.html
American Film Institute: http://www.afionline.org/home.html
American Society of Cinematographers: http://www.cinematographer.com/
Artists' Rights Foundation: http://www.artistsrights.org/
Asian Cinema Studies Society: http://www.trentu.ca/academic/cultstudies/cinema97/
Association Française de Recherche sur l'Histoire du Cinéma (AFRHC):
    http://www.sosi.cnrs.fr/AFRHC/AFRHC.html
Association of Moving Image Archivists: http://www.amianet.org/
Association Québécoise des Études Cinématographiques (AQEC):
       http://leroy.cc.uregina.ca/~matherp/index.html
Canadian Communications Foundation: http://www.rcc.ryerson.ca/schools/rta/ccf/
Film Studies Association of Canada/Association canadienne des études cinématographiques
       (FSAC/ACEC): http://www.film.queensu.ca/FSAC/home.html
International Federation of Film Archives: http://www.cinema.ucla.edu/FIAF/default.html
International Federation of Television Archives: http://www.nbr.no/fiat/fiat.html
The Motion Picture Association of America: http://www.mpaa.org/home.htm
National Alliance for Media Arts and Culture: http://www.namac.org/
The Society for Cinema Studies: http://www.CinemaStudies.org/
Society of Motion Picture and Television Engineers: http://www.smpte.org/
Theatre Historical Society of America: http://www2.hawaii.edu/~angell/thsa/
University Film and Video Association: http://www.rtvf.nwu.edu/ufva/
SYLLABI
Course syllabi: http://www.tcf.ua.edu/screensite/teach/syl/
TRADE NEWSPAPERS
Hollywood Reporter: http://www.hollywoodreporter.com/
Variety: http://www.variety.com/
USEFUL ON-LINE FILM RESOURCES AND RESEARCH GUIDES
Alfred Hitchcock Scholars - MacGuffin Page: http://www.labyrinth.net.au/~muffin/news-home_c.html
American Mutoscope & Biograph Co. Inc.: http://www.altinet.net/biograph/
Association francaise de recherche sur l'histoire du cinema:
       http://www.sosi.cnrs.fr/AFRHC/AFRHC.html
Black Eye on Film: http://home.navisoft.com/bam/page2.htm
Early French film site: http://perso.magic.fr/concept/WELCOME2.HTM
Flicker (Alternative film site): http://www.sirius.com/~sstark/

The German-Hollywood connection: http://www.german-way.com/cinema/index.html
GRAFICS Early Cinema site: http://grafics.histart.umontreal.ca/default-eng.html
Historical Horror Site: http://www.drcasey.com/movie.html
History of the Moving Image from Antiquity to 1900:
    http://www.cinemedia.net/SFCV-RMIT-Annex/rnaughton/MAGIC_MACHINES.html
Internet Source book for Early German Film: http://alf.zfn.uni-bremen.de/~a14m/index.html
Patricia Aufderheide, Cross-Cultural Film Guide:
    http://www.library.american.edu/collects/media/aufderhe/aufderhe.html
The Serial Squadron (movie serials):   http://members.aol.com/serialhq/index.htm
Silent Film Bookshelf: http://www.cinemaweb.com/silentfilm/bookshelf/
Silent Movies: http://www.cs.monash.edu.au/~pringle/silent/
SOFIA (Study of Film as Internet Application):   http://www.unl.ac.uk/sofia/
Taylorology (on-line early film articles):   http://www.angelfire.com/az/Taylorology/
Women in Cinema: http://poe.acc.virginia.edu/~pm9k/libsci/womFilm.html
NATIONAL CINEMAS:
Arab Film Distribution: http://info@arabfilm.com/
Australia's National Sound and Image Archive Sales: http://www.aa.gov.au/nfsa/shop/pricem.htm#silent
California Newsreel (African Films):   http://www.newsreel.org/
Canada — Telefilm Canada: http://www.telefilm.gc.ca
Hong Kong — Hong Kong Cinema Database: http://egret0.stanford.edu/hk/
Hong Kong — Hong Kong Film Critics Society: http://filmcritics.org.hk/
India — Indian Movie Gallery: http://www.iit.edu/~kohlaga/indmov.html
Ireland — Irish Film Production Database: http://www.iol.ie/~standish/Data.html
Italy — Viaggio in Italia (in Italian only):   http://www.geocities.com/Hollywood/6841/
Japan — University of Iowa Japanese Film Studies Bibliography:
    http://www.lib.uiowa.edu/eac/japanfil.html
Mexico — Mexican Film Resource Site: http://www.wam.umd.edu/~dwilt/mfb.html
Poland — Polish Cinema Database: http://info.fuw.edu.pl/Filmy/
VIDEO/LASERDISC/DVD DISTRIBUTORS:
The Cinema Laser: http://www.thecinemalaser.com/
Criterion Collection - Voyager Company (laserdiscs/dvd):
    http://www.criterionco.com/criterion/whatsnew.html
Electronic Arts Intermix: http://www.eai.org/eaihome_dist.html
Facets Multimedia: http://www.facets.org/index.html
First Run Icarus Films (Latin American films):   http://www.echonyc.com/~frif/
Ken Crane's Laserdiscs and DVDs: http://www.kencranes.com/
Kino On-line: http://www.kino.com/index.html
The Latin American Video Archive: http://www.lavavideo.org/lava/
Silent Film Sources: http://www.cinemaweb.com/silentfilm/
Video France: http://www.francevision.com/vf/videofrance/index.htm
Video Oyster (rare and out of print videos):   http://secure.nyic.net/secure-s/videooyster/shop/index.cfm